DREAM ROUTES OF THE
WORLD

THE MOST BEAUTIFUL DESTINATIONS ON EARTH

The Erongo Mountains in Namibia were an ideal location for the hunters of the San: from the hills they oversaw the surrounding plains and were able to follow the migrations of the wildlife.

DREAM ROUTES OF THE
WORLD

THE MOST BEAUTIFUL DESTINATIONS ON EARTH

The cormorant fisherman are the symbol of the romantic landscape by the Li River in Guilin in southern China.

'Life is like a book, and those who do not travel just read a little about it,' wrote Augustine Aurelius (354-430), and a Far Eastern proverb says, 'If you do not you climb the mountains, you will not be able to experience the views.' Since ancient times people have been travelling for a variety of reasons, but they are always rewarded with experiencing a piece of the world and discovering something strange and new. Once upon a time there were traders, soldiers, pilgrims, explorers and scientists who overcame great distances. Today we often follow in their footsteps for fun along some of the legendary travel routes.

More than 28 carefully researched car tours lead us to the most fascinating destinations of our planet: DREAM ROUTES OF THE WORLD represents a whole variety of continents: Whether rural or cultural – this book leads through the innumerable facets of the earth – whether through deserts or rainforests to ancient cultures such as those of the Maya or Inca to vibrant modern cities such as New York or Singapore. With informative texts and interesting topics, brilliant colour photos, detailed touring maps and tips for trips, DREAM ROUTES OF THE WORLD offers a comprehensive overview of the diversity of our planet and makes us want to set out, travel the world and explore its indescribable diversity.

The trail to 'False Kiva' starts just before the trail to the Aztec Butte. This is not proven, but it is certainly one of the most beautiful viewpoints of Canyonlands National Park in Utah, USA for hikers.

EUROPE 12

Route 1: Scotland
Clansmen, whisky and the Highlands 14

Route 2: England
Magical locations in southern Britain 24

Route 3: Germany, Czech Republic, Austria, Slovakia and Hungary
The Route of the Emperors:
Berlin – Prague – Vienna – Budapest 36

Route 4: Switzerland, Italy and Austria
The Alps 52

Route 5: Netherlands and Belgium
Between Amsterdam and Bruges 62

Route 6: France
Via Turonensis: from Paris to Biarritz 74

Route 7: Spain
Andalusia – a Moorish legacy 88

Route 8: Portugal
The land of fado and peaceful matadors 98

Route 9: Italy
From fishing villages to Renaissance cities 108

Route 10: Italy, San Marino, Slovenia, Croatia, Bosnia and Herzegovina, Serbia, Montenegro and Albania
Around the Adriatic 118

Route 11: Greece
Classics of antiquity up close 130

AFRICA 142

Route 12: Morocco
Royal cities, kasbahs and oases 144
Route 13: Egypt
A journey through the Kingdom of the Pharaohs 160
Route 14: South Africa
Taking the Garden Route 174

ASIA 188

Route 15: China
From Beijing to Kunming 190
Route 16: Nepal and Tibet
On the Road of Friendship
across the Roof of the World 202
Route 17: India
Rajasthan and the 'Golden Triangle' 214
Route 18: Thailand and Malaysia
Pulsing cities and tropical natural paradises 226

The Harbor Bridge and the
Opera House (in the image on
the left in the background)
define the night skyline of
one of the most beautiful
cities in the world: Sydney.

AUSTRALIA AND NEW ZEALAND   240

Route 19: Australia
On Stuart Highway through the 'Red Centre'   242

Route 20: Australia
The Pacific Highway   258

Route 21: New Zealand
Glaciers, fiords and rainforests   270

USA AND CANADA   284

Route 22: Canada
On the Trans-Canada Highway
from Vancouver to the Great Lakes   286

Route 23: Canada and the USA
On the Pan-American Highway   298

Route 24: USA
The 'Wild West': cowboys, canyons and cactus   320

Route 25: USA
From Maine to Maryland   340

CENTRAL AND SOUTHERN AMERICA   356

Route 26: Mexico, Guatemala and Belize
Through the Kingdom of the Maya   358
Route 27: Peru and Bolivia
The Inca Trail   370
Route 28: Argentina and Chile
Through the Pampas and Patagonia   384

INDEX   394

PICTURE CREDITS/IMPRINT   399/400

In the main chapters, which are divided into the respective continents, a total of 28 routes are suggested, which lead through magnificent natural and cultural landscapes and to the most beautiful cities in the world. The overview map below shows the course of all tours at a glance. An introductory text to each tour gives an outline of the travel route and the respective countries and regions as well as their scenic, historical and cultural features. Supplemented by a multitude of brilliant colour photos, important places and sights are described, including the route and the roads. The numbers representing the places and sights can be found in the maps at the end of each route chapter. The main route is clearly

separated and is supplemented by suggestions for interesting detours. Pictograms (see adjacent list) indicate the location and nature of important sights along the routes. In addition, outstanding travel destinations are highlighted by colour images and short texts at the edge of the map. Important travel information about the time required and the length of the tour as well as the best travel time is provided by an information box for each route. Interesting aspects of culture and nature are explained in marginal columns. Worthwhile detours are additionally shown in coloured boxes in the margins.

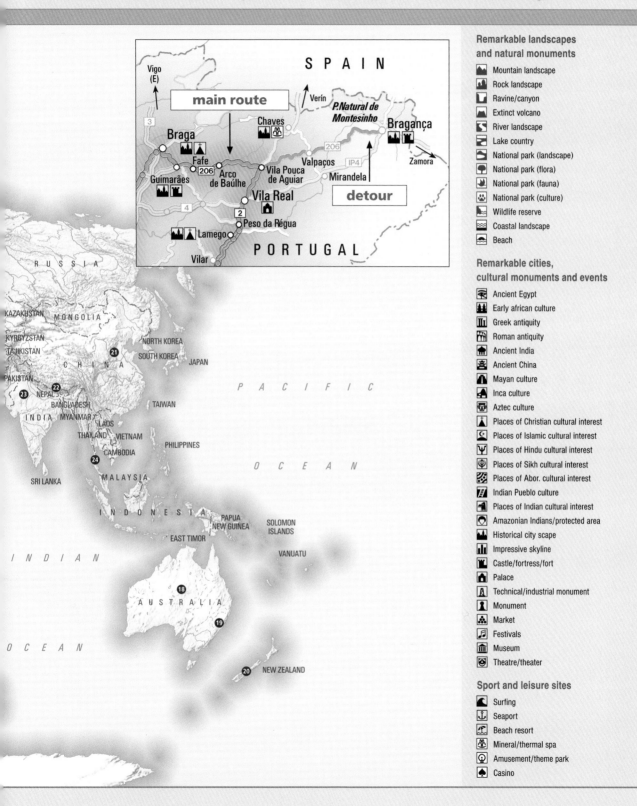

Remarkable landscapes and natural monuments

- Mountain landscape
- Rock landscape
- Ravine/canyon
- Extinct volcano
- River landscape
- Lake country
- National park (landscape)
- National park (flora)
- National park (fauna)
- National park (culture)
- Wildlife reserve
- Coastal landscape
- Beach

Remarkable cities, cultural monuments and events

- Ancient Egypt
- Early african culture
- Greek antiquity
- Roman antiquity
- Ancient India
- Ancient China
- Mayan culture
- Inca culture
- Aztec culture
- Places of Christian cultural interest
- Places of Islamic cultural interest
- Places of Hindu cultural interest
- Places of Sikh cultural interest
- Places of Abor. cultural interest
- Indian Pueblo culture
- Places of Indian cultural interest
- Amazonian Indians/protected area
- Historical city scape
- Impressive skyline
- Castle/fortress/fort
- Palace
- Technical/industrial monument
- Monument
- Market
- Festivals
- Museum
- Theatre/theater

Sport and leisure sites

- Surfing
- Seaport
- Beach resort
- Mineral/thermal spa
- Amusement/theme park
- Casino

Europe

Europe offers an endless abundance and variety of fascinating destinations: magnificent natural landscapes, beautiful churches and monasteries, castles and palaces, famous museums, charming medieval cityscapes and vibrant metropolises. 15 routes lead to the continent's most interesting destinations. Country by country, the most important regions and all worth seeing natural and cultural monuments, the most beautiful landscapes and cities are described in detail. Besides magnificent and at the same time such different landscapes as the Côte d'Azur and the Highlands, it is important to explore Europe's capitals such as London, Rome or Copenhagen.

This is where the jewels of Earth's history are buried: 185 million years ago the Jurassic Coast was created in the south of England, which is one of the most important fossil sites on Earth.

Route 1: Scotland

Clansmen, whisky and the Highlands

Whether you're a romantic, a lover of the outdoors or a culture connoisseur, Scotland's raw beauty rarely fails to move the souls of people who make the journey there. Those who choose to experience the rugged, often solitary landscape of the Highlands and the rich history and tradition of this country will be rewarded with unforgettable memories.

Route profile:

Length: approx. 1,200 km (745 miles), excluding detours
Time required: 2–3 weeks
When to go:
Between April and October is the best time.

Jagged escarpments covered in a lush carpet of green grass, deep lakes in misty moorlands, and torrential rivers tumbling down craggy valleys often typify our image of the Highlands and Scotland in general. But there is more to Scotland than the Highlands in the north, notably the interesting groups of islands to the west and a couple of lovely cities. Glasgow and the capital, Edinburgh, offer modern city living, with cultural events, attractive shopping possibilities and renowned festivals, while idyllic sandy beaches await discovery, for example on the Western Isles. On the mainland, Scotland's first national parks were recently opened around the Cairngorm Mountains and Loch Lomond. Poets such as Sir Walter Scott and the 'national poet of Scotland', Robert Burns, have written of this country's unique beauty. The modern revival of Gaelic music and language has long since spread beyond Scotland's borders, and Scottish customs like caber tossing and wearing kilts may seem peculiar to outsiders, but to the Scots they are part of their identity.

If you take one insider tip, make it this one: Scottish cooking. Once you have tried Angus steak, grouse or Highland lamb, you will no longer limit your praise of the country to single malt whisky. Having said that, there are about 110 whisky distilleries in Scotland, mainly spread around the

Left: The summit of Buchaille Etive Mor is a challenge for mountain climbers. Above: There is a wonderful view from the Stob Dubh summit.

Highlands and on the Western Isles. These world-famous single malt elixirs age for up to thirty years in old whisky and sherry barrels.

Scotland's territory covers a total of 78,000 sq km (30,014 sq mi), roughly the top third of the island of Great Britain. Most of its many islands are part of either the Hebrides (Inner and Outer), the Orkneys or the Shetlands. During the last ice age, glaciers formed deep valleys throughout the region. When they melted, they left behind lochs (lakes) and firths (fjords) along the country's 3,700 km (2,300 miles) of coastline. Among the characteristics of the Highlands, the most sparsely populated area of Scotland, are steep rock faces, heath-covered moors, deep lochs and rushing mountain streams. The Great Glen valley divides the Highlands into two parts. South of the Highlands are the Lowlands, a fertile

and densely populated area containing both Glasgow and Edinburgh. The Southern Uplands make up the border with England.

Despite what one might think, Scotland's oceanic climate rarely produces extreme weather conditions – but the weather really can change from sun to rain in a hurry. Wide areas of Scotland are renowned for their characteristic flora (heather, pine trees,

ferns) and a wide variety of wildlife.The Scots are the descendants of a mix of different peoples including the Picts, the Scots, who gave their name to the country, as well as the Scandinavians and the Anglo-Saxons. It was in the 9th century, under Kenneth MacAlpine, that Alba was founded, the first Celtic Scottish kingdom. From then on Scotland's history was plagued with struggles for independence and resistance against the evermightier forces of England. In 1707, the 'Acts of Union' created the Kingdom of Great Britain and with that came the end of Scotland's independence.

Things unfortunately went from bad to worse after that. The characteristic solitude of the Scottish landscape was a direct result of the Highland Clearances, a move by their own clan chiefs and aristocratic land owners in the 18th century to run small Highland

and island farmers off their plots to make room for more lucrative sheep breeding.After 300 years, Scotland now has its own parliament again, in Edinburgh, and about 5.1 million people. Although the official language is English, many Scots in the Highlands and on the Hebrides speak Scottish Gaelic, a Celtic language.

Left: Full, warm autumn colours at Loch Tulla and colourful fisherman's houses in Tobermory on Mull. Above: 'Clansmen' in Scottish national costume. Tobermory with its colourful houses lies on the northern end of the Isle of Mull.

The Scottish national sport of golf was already being played in the 15th century on the sandy beaches of St Andrews.

Detour

Blair Castle

At Arbroath the A933 makes its way west before you get to Forfar, where the pink-grey walls of Glamis Castle appear through the trees. It is a place steeped in history, from the murder of Duncan by Macbeth to numerous ghost apparitions and the childhood tales of the late Queen Mother, who grew up here.

The trip then continues north-west to Blair Atholl via the Killiecrankie Pass, scene in 1689 of a bloody battle between the English and the Scots. From there an alley lined with lime trees leads to Blair Castle, the residence of the Duke of Atholl. This fab-

A journey through Scotland: venerable buildings, mysterious stone circles and the occasional whisky distillery line your route, which begins in Edinburgh, takes you through the Highlands and ends in Glasgow. Detours to the Orkneys and Hebrides are highly recommended and can be easily organized from the various port towns.

1 Edinburgh (see page 17). Your route begins in the cultural metropolis of Edinburgh, travelling initially north-westward towards Stirling.

2 Stirling The charming city of Stirling, roughly 58 km (36 miles) west of Edinburgh, is built on the banks of the Forth at the point where it first becomes part of the tidal firth (fjord). It is often called the 'Gateway to the Highlands' and is dominated by a large castle. The oldest part of Stirling Castle dates back to the 14th century. The Church of the Holy Rood, which was built in the 13th century, is historically significant in that it is one of the very few churches from the Middle Ages to have survived the Reformation in Scotland.

3 Fife Peninsula The Fife Peninsula juts out between the Firth of Forth and the Firth of Tay. In the 4th century the region here made up one of the seven Scottish kingdoms. The northern coast of the Firth of Forth leads initially to Culross, a small town that blossomed as a

The origins of Blair Castle date back to the 13th century.

ulously equipped, brilliant white castle is among the most beautiful buildings in Scotland.

The Atholl Highlanders, as the Duke of Atholl's private army is called, are a curious band. Every year at the beginning of June an impressive parade is staged in front of the castle with a backing of bagpipe music.

trading center in the 16th century. Wealthy trade houses have remained intact and make for an enchanting atmosphere here. About 11 km (7 miles) to the east of Culross you'll come to Dunfermline, once a long-standing residence or 'burgh' of the Scottish kings. The ruins of the old castle, abbey and monastery can still be seen atop a hill to the south-west of the town.

A little further east, behind the Chapel Ness headland and between the coastal towns of Elie and Crail, is a series of picturesque fishing villages, castle ruins and old churches.

4 St Andrews Continuing on around the north-east side of the peninsula you will come to the proverbial golfing mecca of the world, St Andrews, about 10 km (6 miles) north of Crail. This, the first ever golf club, was founded here in 1754, and it is still possible to play on the famous Old Course.

The 16th-century ruins of Blackfriars Chapel, at one time Scot-

Large image: Edinburgh Castle towers mightily over the city.
Small image: Glamis Castle was the childhood home of the late Queen Mother.

The architectural contrast between the medieval old town of Edinburgh and the carefully planned late 18th century Georgian town is striking.

Edinburgh

Both the Old Town and New Town of Scotland's capital have been listed as UNESCO World Heritage Sites, and both are a fascinating display of architectural unity and its exceptional cultural activity. Summer is especially lively during the renowned Edinburgh Festival weeks.

The oldest core of the city, inhabited since the Bronze Age, is Castle Rock, a volcanic outcrop upon which King Edwin built the first castle in the 7th century – hence the name Edinburgh. The castle is still the city's eye-catcher but other higher buildings from the 17th century rise up around it like battlements. The attractions most worthy of a visit in the Old Town include Edinburgh Castle, a large edifice with buildings from numerous eras, of which St Margaret's Chapel (11th century) is the oldest; the Scottish royal insignia in the castle's Crown Room; the Palace of Holyroodhouse, the Queen's official residence in Scotland; and the Royal Mile between her residence and the castle with its many side streets.

The New Town, built at the end of the 18th century, is home to the National Gallery of Scotland with one of Europe's most important collections of paintings, the Museum of Antiques for early and art history, and the Scottish National Gallery of Modern Art (20th-century art), all of which are worth a visit.

Loch Morlich is a very romantic place to be at dusk. The lake is located in the Cairngorms National Park.

Detour

Balmoral Castle

This royal castle on the River Dee is in the Grampian Mountains, and thus within the limits of the Cairngorms National Park in Aberdeenshire. Prince Albert, Queen Victoria's consort, bought Balmoral Castle in 1846 and later had it replaced with a magnificent granite building in grand Scottish style. He personally oversaw the interior decoration, which was inspired by Scottish hunting lodges, with large check patterns and floral designs on upholstery that bear witness to the country style. The royal family came here to get away from court ceremonies in London.

Cairngorms National Park, established in 2003, is Great Britain's largest national park and stretches from Grantown on the Spey to Angus Glens near Glamis. Twenty five per cent of Great

Britain's endangered species live in the reserve and numerous rare plants grow only at the foot of the central Cairngorms range (Scottish Gaelic for 'Blue Mountain'). The various moorlands, heath and forests are typical of the area. Fields and pasture typify the lovely Spey and Dee valleys. Stone-Age monuments, medieval castles and towns steeped in tradition are testimony to the historical importance of the region.

land's largest church, are also worth a visit if golf isn't your cup of tea. There is a fabulous view of the grounds from the top of St Rule's Tower. The route then follows the coast through Dundee to Montrose, about 12 km (8 miles) north of Arbroath. A worthy detour here takes you to Blair Castle, roughly 65 km (40 miles) inland from Arbroath.

5 Montrose This port town and 'burgh' is built like a defensive wall on the peninsula of a natural bay. The House of Dun Mansion, built in 1730, stands on the bank of the Montrose Basin. The coastline north and south of Montrose impresses with long sandy beaches and steep cliffs.

6 Dunnottar Castle Following the A92 to the north you'll reach one of Scotland's most fascinating ruins just a few kilometers before Stonehaven – Dunnottar Castle. Built on a rock more than 50 m (60 yds) out to sea, the fortress is connected to the mainland only by a narrow spit of land. In the 17th century, the Scottish imperial insignia were stored here. Nowadays, only the ruins of the turret and the chapel remain of the once formidable construction.

7 Aberdeen This town is the capital of Europe's oil industry and one of the largest European ports. Despite its industrial leanings, however, there are a number of historic highlights to visit, including Kings College, St Andrew's Cathedral, St Machar's Cathedral and the Maritime Museum.

From Aberdeen the route leads inland to Ballater. (Here we recommend taking a detour to Balmoral Castle about 50 km (31 miles) away. The mountain road (A939) then goes from Ballater through Colnabaichin to Tomintoul, the starting point of the whisky trail, before heading to Dufftown and Keith.

You then go west through the Spey Valley to Aviemore where the A9 takes you to Inverness.

8 Inverness This modern-day industrial center at the northern tip of Loch Ness is the ideal starting point for trips to the home of 'Nessie', Urquhart Castle and into the wild and romantic Highland landscape.

Due to its exposed location, Inverness was regularly involved in military disputes, to the extent that few of its old buildings remain. Most of today's structures were erected in the 19th century.

9 East Coast of the Northwest Highlands From Inverness the A9 (and the A99) snake northwards along the striking east coast. Various sites like Dunrobin Castle, Helmsdale Castle or the mysterious Bronze-Age rock lines near Greg Cairns are

The Whisky Trail

The famous 110-km-long (68-mile) Speyside Malt Whisky Trail, which sets off from Tomintoul, is a well-signposted route leading past seven whisky distilleries. Among them are some well-known names such as Glenlivet, Glenfiddich and Glenfarclas.

Detour

The Orkney Islands

The Orkney Islands, of which only eighteen are inhabited, are around 30 km (19 miles) off the north-eastern coast of Scotland. They are best reached from the ferry ports of John o'Groats and Thurso. Mainland, Hoy and South Ronaldsay are the larger of the islands in the archipelago, with rolling hills formed by glaciers from the last ice age. Despite their northerly location, the islands benefit from a comparatively mild climate caused by the warm Gulf Stream.

The inhabitants of the Orkneys, descendants of Scots and Scandinavians, live mostly from farming, fishing and tourism these days. Rock

Marwick Head and Skara Brae on the Mainlan.

worth short visits on your way. One option is to take a long walk from the former fishing village of Wick out to the picturesque cliffs of Noss Head. Nearby are the ruins of Sinclair and Girnigoe Castles.

⑩ John o'Groats The village of John o'Groats is about 17 km (11 miles) north of Wick on the north-eastern tip of Caithness. Just before you get there, Warth Hill will offer an exceptional view of the area.

Ferries travel between John o'Groats, the Orkneys and the coastal seal colonies.

⑪ North Coast The A836 then takes you from John o'Groats along the north coast towards Bettyhill past deserted beaches that are often only accessible by short footpaths. Dunnet Head is the most northern point of the Scottish mainland. The popular holiday destination of Thurso, which is also the ferry port for travel to the Orkney Islands, was the scene of a memorable battle between the Scots and the Vikings in 1040. To the west of the village of Bettyhill, in the county of Sutherland, the A836 leads over the impressive Kyle of Tongue Fjord and on to Durness. Shortly before Durness is the Cave of Smoo, which was used as shelter by the Picts, then the Vikings, and later still by Scottish smugglers. Organized trips to Cape Wrath, the rocky outcrop on the north-westernmost point of Scotland, are offered from Durness.

⑫ North-west Coast up to Ullapool The wild north-west portion of Sutherland is not your typical holiday destination. Its steep mountains and fjords, deep blue lakes and glistening waterfalls are too secluded for the average traveller. The impassable valleys and deserted coastlines have thus become a paradise for hikers, hunters and fishermen.

Naturalists can observe seabirds, seals and dolphins and sometimes even whales from

The once strategic position of Dunnottar Castle is unmistakable: built on a rock promontory, a ravine separates the castle from the mainland. Above: Inverness. Left side: market cross in Aberdeen.

climbers and ornithologists are also fascinated by Britain's highest coastal cliffs (347 m/1,138 ft) on the island of Hoy, while the spectacular landscape and monuments, like the Stone-Age village of Skara Brae or the stone circle of Brodgar on Mainland, are popular with everyone who visits.

At Uig Bay, the twin islands of Isle of Harris and Isle of Lewis are reflected in the water.

Detour

The Outer Hebrides

The Atlantic islands to the west of Scotland are made up of the southern Inner Hebrides, near the Scottish mainland, and the Outer Hebrides (Western Isles) farther out towards the north-west. The main islands of the Outer Hebrides are, from north to south, the double islands of Lewis and Harris, North Uist and South Uist, joined by a dam, and Barra. You can reach the Western Isles by ferry from Ullapool or from Skye, the largest of the Inner Hebrides islands, which include Rum, Coll, Tiree, Mull, Jura and Islay.

The Hebrides have a long and varied past. In 563 the Irish minister Columban the Elder (who later became St Columba) established a Celtic monastery on the small island of Iona and began the process of Christianizing Scotland. In the 8th century the islands were invaded by the Norwegian Vikings, who kept their rule over much of the region for many hundreds of years. It was only in 1266, after the signing of the Treaty of Perth, that the Scots regained the upper hand and the islands were henceforth run by the clans MacDougall and MacDonald. Their rulers were thereafter

called 'Lord of the Isles'.Today's visitors are met by a world in which life is still greatly influenced by natural forces and the isolation of the Atlantic. History and time have left some clear traces in the partly undulating moor and heath landscape. In geological terms the islands consist of the oldest rocks in the entire British Isles. Stone-Age graves, Celtic Christian ruins, Viking settlements and Scottish forts can all be found around the various Hebrides islands.

The natural environment includes lakes and valleys, pristine white sand beaches, and rich animal and plant life that all help to attract a good number of adventurous tourists each year.

The Isle of Lewis and Harris

The two halves of the island of Lewis and Harris are connected by an isthmus and are not just the largest of the Western Isles, but the largest island around Great Britain after Ireland. Lewis and Harris have very differing landscapes: Lewis is littered with rocky hill ranges, fjords and bays, while Harris is covered with moors and heath. The A859 leads from the main town of Stornoway to south Harris, which is noteworthy for its fabulous sandy beaches. Don't miss the mysterious stone circles of Callanish on Lewis, which, like Stonehenge, were built thousands of years ago for cult rituals.

North Uist und South Uist

North and South Uist, and the island of Benbecula between them, are covered with countless lakes. Deep ocean bays line the east coast to such an extent that it resembles a series of islands that have grown together. The Stone-Age burial chambers on North Uist

and the low, reed-covered crofter houses, some of which have survived hundreds of years of wind and weather, are worth visiting. The A865 leads all the way around North Uist and down to the southern tip of South Uist, passing the prettiest areas of the island on the way. The east coast of South Uist has two 600-m (2,000-ft) peaks – Beinn Mhór and Hecla.

Barra

Ferries from Ludag on South Uist to the small island of Barra, the southernmost island of the Outer Hebrides, only take about 40 minutes. Barra's small neighbouring islands include Berneray with it tall lighthouse.The island, named after St Finbarr, is regarded as one of the prettiest islands of the Outer Hebrides due to the thousands of colourful flowers that grow there. Kisimuil Castle, the old residence of the MacNeils, dominates the port of the main town, Castlebay. The ring road, the A888, goes as far as Cille Barra in the north, with its ruins of a monastery built in the 12th century.

Isle of Lewis: the monumental 'Standing Stones of Callanish' form a 13 m by 11 m (40 ft by 35 ft) circle and were erected around 1800 BC.

Eilean Donan Castle was destroyed in 1719 by the English because it was a Jacobite stronghold.

these remote environs. Innumerable small alcoves are perfect for a relaxing break.

A narrow road, the A838, then leads from Durness towards the south-west. Just before Scourie you can take the A894, which branches off towards Handa Island, a seabird sanctuary with imposing cliffs where puffins and guillemots nest.

From Kylesku, which is further south, you can take boat trips to seal colonies and to Great Britain's highest waterfall along Loch Glencoul (200 m/656 ft). If you want to follow the tiny roads along the coast, turn off after Kylesku on to the B869. Otherwise follow the wider roads, A837 and A835, south to Ullapool. This beautiful stretch passes Loch Assynt and the ruins of Ardvreck Castle.

If you are interested, you can take the ferries that travel from Ullapool on Loch Broom to Lewis in the Outer Hebrides, and the steamers that travel to the nearby Summer Isles.

After Ullapool, stay on the A835 until shortly after Corrieshalloch Gorge (61 m/200 ft), a ravine with waterfall, where you will turn onto the A832.

13 Inverewe Gardens After Little Loch Broom and Gruinard Bay you come to Loch Ewe and the Inverewe Gardens. These gardens were planted in 1862 and exhibit a wonderful collection of rhododendron and hibiscus bushes.

Next you will come to Kinlochewe, in the Torridon Mountains, where the road to Shieldaig on the coast follows the Liathach Ridge out to a seabird sanctuary.

14 Eilean Donan Castle A bit further along the A87 is Eilean Donan Castle, a picturesque natural stone castle rising up from St Donan Island in Loch Duich. This edifice, which was badly damaged by the Jacobite Wars, was only rebuilt at the start of the 19th century.

Around 5 km (3 miles) from the castle, the A890 feeds into the A87, which leads to Kyle of Lochalsh. A toll bridge from there takes you over to the Isle of Skye. From Ardvasar in the south-west of Skye there is a ferry back to Mallaig on the mainland. Take the 'Road to the Isles' (A830) 40 km (25 miles) to the east to reach Fort William.

If you are short on time, travel directly from Eilean Donan Castle eastwards on the A87 and then turn south onto the A82 at Invergarry to reach Fort William.

15 Ben Nevis The highest mountain on the British Isles, at 1,344 m (4,409 ft), rises magnificently from the Grampian Mountains above Fort William. While the north-western face of the mountain is relatively easy to hike, the 460-m (1,509-ft) north-eastern rock face is reserved for experienced climbers. Before travelling on to Glencoe, take the A828 15 km (9 miles) to Castle Stalker near Portnacroish.

16 Loch Rannoch Fort William is the starting point for a small detour by train into the otherwise intractable Rannoch Moor. Rannoch Station, a tiny house in the wide landscape of the moor, is one of the most isolated stations in Great Britain. Small ponds and trout-rich streams cross the boulder-scattered moor and marshland. To the east of the moor lies the impressively calm Loch Rannoch.

17 Glencoe The Glencoe Valley begins roughly 16 km (10 miles) to the south of Fort William and is one of Scotland's must-see destinations. After the Jacobite Risings of the 17th century, the English attempted to take control over Scotland by exploiting clan rivalries and disputes. So it was

Detour

Isle of Skye

Skye, the largest island of the Inner Hebrides, is known for being one of the wildest, roughest and yet most beautiful islands in Scotland. Mountains like the 1,009-m-high (3,310-ft) Cuillin Hills, or the Quiraing Hills and bizarre geological formations like the Old Man of Storr give the island its unique character.

Fog, brief showers and plentiful rainbows make a trip around this island an unforgettable adventure. Dunvegan Castle, lounging seal herds, the Talisker whisky distillery, otter colonies and other fun sights invite the traveller to make pleasant stops along the way. Next to an open fire in a little restaurant offering local specialities like venison and raspberry dessert, you can imagine what may have come to pass on these remote islands while enjoying a glass of whisky and a Gaelic tune.

'The Old Man of Storr' is the needle-shaped rock on the Isle of Skye.

21

Once a symbol of the power of the clans, the castle ruins of Kilchurn Castle today leave you in Loch Awe.

Detour

Isle of Mull

Mull, one of the islands of the Inner Hebrides at the entrance to Loch Linnhe, has an unusual effect on visitors with its craggy, hilly landscape and castles. It is also one of the easier islands to reach by taking the quick ferry from Oban.

The west coast of Mull is particularly pretty. This is where you'll find The Burg nature reserve, among other things, and picturesque bays lining the northern side of the Ross of Mull Peninsula.

Just off the peninsula is the legendary Isle of Iona, the cradle of Christianity in Scotland, where the Celtic monk Columban the Elder founded the first monastery here in 563. For a long time Iona was even the final resting place of Scottish, Norwegian and Irish kings. The island has been in-

The coasts of the Isle of Mull are very rocky.

habited since the Stone Age, as archaeological digs have proven.

Also off the west coast of Mull is the Isle of Ulva, which was inhabited until the Highland Clearances in the middle of the 19th century before farmers were driven from their land in order to make way for more lucrative sheep farming.

that in 1692, soldiers led by the Clan Campbell of Glencoe and loyal to the new king, William of Orange, massacred the opposing Clan MacDonald almost in its entirety. Women and children were apparently left to perish in the elements. An impressive monument marks this gruesome event. Following the A82 you will soon cross the A85 at Tyndrum. If you are planning a trip to the Isle of Mull, follow the A85 west to Oban, a port on the Firth of Lorne. Ferries sail from here to Mull and the other islands of the Inner Hebrides.

18 Kilchurn Castle If you turn east from the A82 onto the A85, you will reach the northern tip of Loch Awe where you will find the ruins of the 15th-century Kilchurn Castle. The ruins were hit by lightning in the 18th century and completely abandoned. One of the turrets still lies upside down in the courtyard. Restored steamboats navigate Loch Awe, the longest freshwater loch in Scotland.

19 Inveraray The town of Inveraray, 15 km (9 miles) south of Loch Awe, was constructed

alongside Loch Fyne according to plans drawn up in the 18th century by the Duke of Argyll. He had his castle built in artistically arranged gardens. A prison museum in the old Inveraray Jail is also worth a visit. You can appear in court there, and even be locked up.

20 Loch Lomond The A83 leads further east to the holiday destination of Loch Lomond, Scotland's largest loch in surface area. The area is loved by hikers, water-sports enthusiasts and families looking to take a steamboat trip to the islands.

In 2002, Loch Lomond and the Trossachs National Park was opened to the east of the lake.

21 Glasgow For culture fans this city is one of Europe's hot destinations. Renowned museums and galleries as well as countless cultural programs vie for your attention. The million-strong city on the Clyde River is also an important industrial center. To get an overview of Glasgow's various highlights and attractions, take a double-decker bus tour. Only a few of the buildings in Scotland's

largest city date back to before the 18th century. Among them are the Gothic St Mungo's Cathedral and the classical Pollok House. The Hunterian Museum (with works by Charles Rennie Mackintosh, for example), the Burrell Collection (art and craftwork) and the Gallery of Modern Art are worth a visit.

A little way out of town is the New Lanark textile mill from the 18th century, which was recently listed as a UNESCO World Heritage Site – one of four in Scotland. This interesting museum town provides insight into factory life at the start of the 19th century.

Above: Busy Buchanan Street in Glasgow.

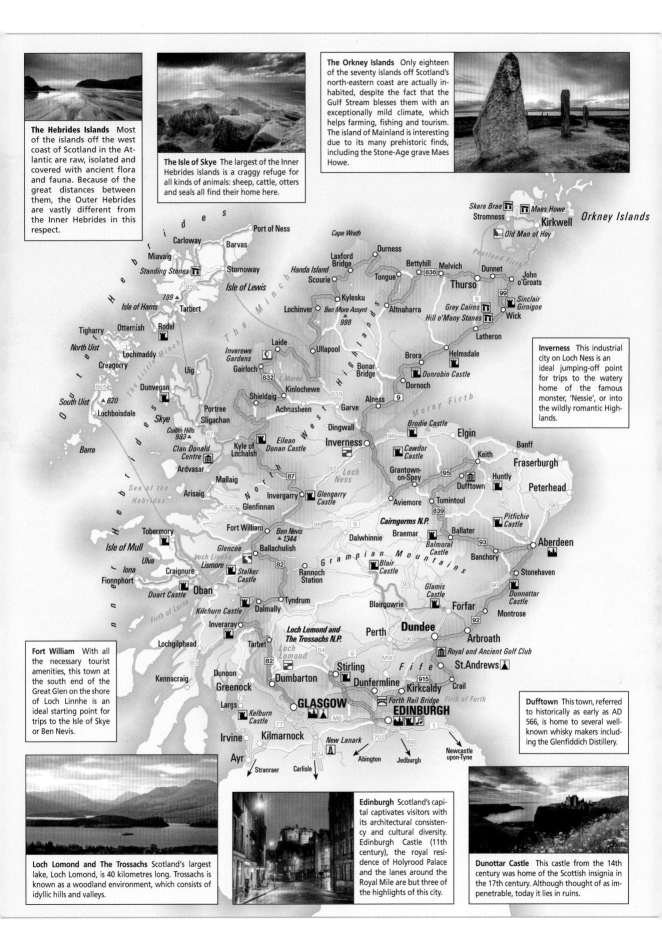

The Hebrides Islands Most of the islands off the west coast of Scotland in the Atlantic are raw, isolated and covered with ancient flora and fauna. Because of the great distances between them, the Outer Hebrides are vastly different from the Inner Hebrides in this respect.

The Isle of Skye The largest of the Inner Hebrides islands is a craggy refuge for all kinds of animals: sheep, cattle, otters and seals all find their home here.

The Orkney Islands Only eighteen of the seventy islands off Scotland's north-eastern coast are actually inhabited, despite the fact that the Gulf Stream blesses them with an exceptionally mild climate, which helps farming, fishing and tourism. The island of Mainland is interesting due to its many prehistoric finds, including the Stone-Age grave Maes Howe.

Inverness This industrial city on Loch Ness is an ideal jumping-off point for trips to the watery home of the famous monster, 'Nessie', or into the wildly romantic Highlands.

Fort William With all the necessary tourist amenities, this town at the south end of the Great Glen on the shore of Loch Linnhe is an ideal starting point for trips to the Isle of Skye or Ben Nevis.

Dufftown This town, referred to historically as early as AD 566, is home to several well-known whisky makers including the Glenfiddich Distillery.

Loch Lomond and The Trossachs Scotland's largest lake, Loch Lomond, is 40 kilometres long. Trossachs is known as a woodland environment, which consists of idyllic hills and valleys.

Edinburgh Scotland's capital captivates visitors with its architectural consistency and cultural diversity. Edinburgh Castle (11th century), the royal residence of Holyrood Palace and the lanes around the Royal Mile are but three of the highlights of this city.

Dunottar Castle This castle from the 14th century was home of the Scottish insignia in the 17th century. Although thought of as impenetrable, today it lies in ruins.

Magical locations in southern Britain

Ancient trading routes crisscross the south of England, and monumental stone circles bear witness to prehistoric settlements in the region. The Celts, the Romans, the Anglo-Saxons and the Normans came after the original inhabitants of the island and eventually transformed the magnificent natural environment here into a diverse cultural macrocosm.

Route profile:

Length: approx. 1,200 km (746 miles), excluding detours
Time required: 2–3 weeks
When to go: The weather in southern Britain is better than reputed. Recommended travel season: April to October.

Generally, the 'South of England' refers to the region along the south coast, extending northwards to Bristol in the west and London in the east. For some, however, the south only includes the coastal counties south of London like East and West Sussex, Hampshire and Dorset. Others think of just the south-east including London, while others of the south-west with Cornwall and Devon. In some references, the south even reaches up to the middle of England. Some areas, like

Greater London (with around eight million inhabitants) are densely populated, whereas others like Dartmoor in Devon appear at first glance to be deserted. In the end, the South of England is unspecific, but Britons look at it as an area 'steeped in history' and known for its contrasts: picturesque cliffs and small sailing villages, busy seaside resorts and modern port towns, green pastures and barren moorland.

Indeed, the bustling metropolis of London dominates the southeast, while the more relaxed south-west has a real holiday feel to it. The area has always attracted writers and artists: Shakespeare, Jane Austen, Turner and Constable all lived here, or at least gave the south a recognizable face in their various works. Numerous nature reserves and magical, manicured gardens invite you to take

peaceful walks. Geologically speaking, the British Isles 'separated' from the continent roughly 700,000 years ago. At the time, there had been a land bridge connecting what is now England to the mainland, with a river running through (now the English Channel). The water trapped in the ice at the end of the ice age about 10,000 years ago was then released, causing

sea levels to rise and gradually wash away the land bridge. The characteristic white limestone cliffs that we now see in places along the south coast like Dover and Eastbourne are the result of this 'river' flooding through the weakest point between the now divided land masses. The West Country consists mostly of granite, whereas the limestone is typical of the south-east. At the

The natural arch of Durdle Door on the Jurassic Coast of Dorset is the result of erosion by the pounding sea (above). Left: The most famous prehistoric construction in Europe – Stonehenge, erected around 3000 BC.

narrowest point in the channel, the Dover Strait, the distance between the United Kingdom and the European continent is only around 32 km (20 miles). Demographically, countless generations have created a rich landscape in Britain. Due to the geographical proximity to the continent, the south was always the arrival point for immigrants, invaders and traders. In about 3500 BC, farmers and livestock breeders migrated to the island. The fortuitously warm Gulf Stream provided them and their modern-day ancestors with a relatively mild climate. Natural resources like tin and copper also attracted invaders over the centuries. England has not been successfully subdued by an enemy power since 1066, when the Normans under William the Conqueror emerged victorious at the legendary Battle of Hastings. The vulnerability of the south coast is revealed by countless castles and fortresses, and also by installations from World War II. The varied history of settlements also features in the endless stories and myths that originate here. King Arthur and his Knights of the Round Table are among the prominent characters in these tales. Castles, cathedrals and grand old universities testify to the historical importance of the south while small fishing villages on the coast have developed into significant harbour towns that enabled the British Empire's rise to naval dominance. In return came exotic goods and peoples, changing yet again the cultural fabric of the traditional island inhabitants.

'High society' discovered the coast in the 19th century, and from then on vacationed in resort towns like Brighton and Eastbourne. Today the coastal economy relies primarily on services and tourism.

The roofed Pulteney Bridge in Bath (above) was built between 1769 and 1774 and is reminiscent of the Ponte Vecchio of Florence. Left side: Bodiam Castle.

Brighton

The well-known seaside resort of Brighton, which once attracted London's high society and even became a royal city of sorts, is still a wildly popular

The cathedrals of Salisbury, Exeter and Winchester

Salisbury Cathedral was built between 1220 and 1258 in what is known as 'Early English' style to the Britons, an English Gothic form that identifies with the early-Gothic architectural style. The cathedral has the tallest spine in England.

The silhouette of the diocesan city of Exeter is dominated by the Cathedral Church of St Peter, built between the 11th and 14th centuries in 'Decorated' style. England's largest surviving collection of 14th-century sculptures cover

Winchester and Exeter Cathedral (from the top)

the western facade and include angels, kings and apostles. The lusciously decorated interior contains an impressive carved arch.

The city of Winchester was England's capital until 1066, a pivotal year in the island's history when the Normans invaded and conquered it. The transepts and tower survive from the Norman cathedral (1079) while the Perpendicular nave and choir loft (with vertical framework on the windows) are from the 14th century.

This dream route through the South of England begins in London and heads down to the coast, which it then follows west until bending northwards at Land's End back towards Oxford and eventually back to the capital, London. Along the way you will experience everything from fashionable seaside resorts and Roman ruins to awe-inspiring cathedrals, desolate moors and craggy cliffs.

① London (see pp. 28–31 for a detailed description of the sights and sounds that await you in England's capital).

② Hastings Around 40 km (25 miles) south of London (A21) is possibly one of the most important battlefields in the long and distinguished history of the British Isles: Hastings, scene of the legendary battle in 1066 between Duke William of Normandy and the Saxon army under King Harold of England. The outcome of the Battle of Hastings was the coronation of the Duke of Normandy as the third king of England in Westminster following his victory. The first building he commissioned was the Battle Abbey on the site of the struggle. Nearby Bodiam Castle is also worthy of a visit. Purportedly intended as a fortress to protect against French attacks during the Hundred Years War, it has come to light that it was actually more for show, a purpose it fits well: the castle is guarded by eight mighty towers and is artistically placed in the middle spring-fed moat.

③ Eastbourne and the Seven Sisters The traditional sea resort of Eastbourne, about 17 km (11 miles) west of Hastings, is noteworthy for its wonderful sandy beaches and noble Victorian architecture. Just beyond Eastbourne is the fascinating Seven Sisters Country Park, named after seven bright limestone cliffs on the coast. A short walk leads to the South Downs Way, which meanders along the shore and over the remarkable limestone landscape.

From Beachy Head, the highest limestone cliff in Britain at 163 m (535 ft), you get a breathtaking view over the English Channel and the 100-year-old lighthouse out in the sea. The postcard panorama of the Seven Sisters, however, is only visible from the next cliff, South Hill.

④ Portsmouth and the Isle of Wight The narrow coastal road now travels past the elegant seaside resort of Brighton towards Portsmouth, an old harbour and trading port that is home to the Royal Navy. Some

of the attractions here include Lord Nelson's flagship from the Battle of Trafalgar (the most significant naval victory of the Napoleonic Wars), the Sea Life Centre and the house where Charles Dickens was born.

Ferries sail from Portsmouth to the Isle of Wight, the smallest county in England at 381 sq km (146 sq mi), once inhabited by the Romans. The island benefits from a varied landscape thanks to the warm Gulf Stream, which gives it a mild climate and allows colourful subtropical plants to blossom here between palm trees. Off the west coast are three limestone formations – The Needles. At the base of the last rock outcrop, a lighthouse defies the constant pounding of the waves. Back on the mainland, we continue inland to Winchester, which was the capital of England until 1066, and then on to Salisbury. About 16 km (10 miles) to the north of the town lies Stonehenge.

⑤ Stonehenge It should come as no surprise that the

getaway for city dwellers and beach lovers.

One of the attractions is the Royal Pavilion from the 19th century, a palace built in Indian Mughal style with minarets, columns and an ostentatious interior. It is still used for exhibitions and concerts. Before the advent of cheap package holidays, Brighton was famous for its West Pier, which was unfortunately destroyed by fire and storms in 2003.

most famous prehistoric site on the British Isles has been listed as a UNESCO World Heritage Site. Stonehenge is believed to have been erected in four stages between 3100 BC and 1500 BC by successors of the Bell-Beaker culture. The unbelievable 'engineering' and building capacity of these Stone-Age peoples inspires awe to this day: they transported eighty-two gigantic building blocks from the Welsh mountains, nearly 160 km (100 miles) away, presumably using rivers and rollers of some sort all the way to Stonehenge. Later, at the start of the Bronze Age, these blue stones were replaced by even larger sandstone blocks measuring 7-m (23-ft) high.

Indeed, the site was modified a number of times. Today two concentric stone circles make up the middle section. The outer circle, with a diameter of 30 m (98 ft), is made up of seventeen trilithons and two vertical monoliths with a horizontal stone. The inner circle is made up exclusively of monoliths. It is a source of discussion as to whether the site was used as a place of worship, an observatory or for monitoring the sun's behaviour. On the day of the summer solstice, the sun rises exactly over the Heel Stone, following the axis of the entrance, and throws its light through a stone window. Stonehenge has been a magical place for thousands of years. Celtic druids also used the site for their rites.

⑥ **Shaftesbury** About 20 km (12.5 miles) to the west of Salisbury, one of Britain's rare medieval hill towns continues to enchant visitors. Time seems to have stood still in Shaftesbury: ancient town walls and Gold Hill are reminiscent of a long forgotten time. The steep, cobbled lanes are lined with small, sometimes thatched houses and were at one time part of the pilgrimage route to the grave of Ed-

ward the Martyr, whose bones are now kept in Westminster Abbey. In the Middle Ages there was a prosperous Benedictine monastary here, but it was disbanded in 1539 and for the most part demolished.

The oft-photographed Gold Hill is classified today as Britain's prettiest street. From the top of it you get a view over green, hilly pastureland that is interrupted only by lush, dark-green hedges.

The A350 then leads south, back to the coast, past Blandford and on to the coastal town of Swanage on the lovely Purbeck Peninsula.

⑦ **Corfe Castle and Swanage** On your way to Swanage it is worth stopping at Corfe Castle, a wild and romantic set of ruins out on a high promontory. In 1646 the fort fell through a betrayal on the part of Oliver Cromwell's soldiers and was almost totally destroyed.

Swanage is a charming seaside town at the end of the narrow Purbeck Peninsula. The Old Harry Rocks are just a walk away from here. Like the Needles on the Isle of Wight, the limestone rocks in this formation were formed by the emergence of the Alps over thirty million years ago.

⑧ **Jurassic Coast** The coast between Swanage and Weymouth is not called the Jurassic Coast for nothing. The cliff formations here date from the period and because of their location are only partially accessible by car. In 2001 this stretch of coastline was classified a Natural World Heritage Site by UNESCO – the first site to be listed as such in the UK – because it documents nearly 185 million years of the earth's history.

The beaches and the cliffs here bear witness to periods within the Mesozoic Era, effectively the geological 'middle ages'. Ever since the spectacular find of an

Ichthyosaurus, an enormous fish dinosaur, in the 19th century, this area has also become world-famous among hobby fossil hunters.

Yet the region is also perfect for walks with breathtaking views. Shortly before Weymouth is the enchanting Lulworth Cove, a natural harbour with steep cliffs and golden sands. A footpath then leads you along the cliff edge to the impressive Durdle Door, a natural bridge that extends out into the ocean. St Oswalds Bay, with its fine sand beach, can also be reached from here by a steep path. Between Weymouth and Exeter there are many small coastal villages that

invite you for a break. In the dreamy village of Abbotsbury, the Swannery swan colony is home to about 1,000 swans, a sight to behold.

Chesil Bank is a gravel bank that is over 80,000 years old and stretches more than 29 km (18 miles). It resembles a pebble dune. Beyond the dune is a bird sanctuary in the brackish water of the lagoon.

Picture bar from above: Lighthouse at Beachy Head; Torquay Millennium Bridge; Gold Hill in Shaftesbury. Left side: Godrevy Lighthouse off the coast of St Ives.

Buckingham Palace is the official residence of the royal family, but only on weekdays. The magnificent castle dates back to 1705 and was originally owned by the Duke of Buckingham. In 1837, Queen Victoria moved from St. James's Palace to Buckingham Palace, which in the meantime had been converted and rebuilt into a veritable palace.

The Elizabeth Tower stands at the north end of Parliament House, Westminster Palace. The 96.30-metre-high tower houses five bells, the largest of which is Big Ben, which is usually used as a synonym for the entire tower. The bell tower itself was called the Clock Tower until 2012. Then it was renamed Elizabeth Tower to honour the Queen.

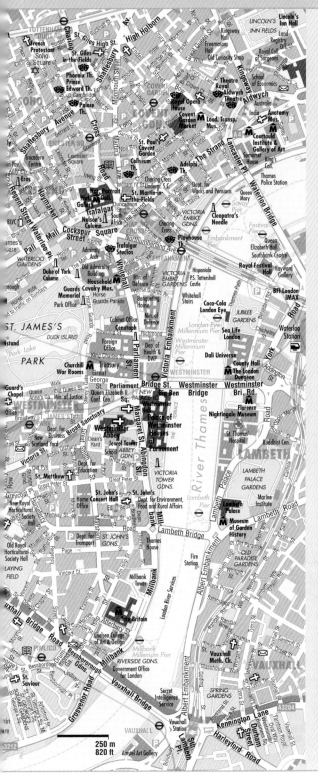

London

England's capital, London, is the seat of British government and an international financial centre of massive proportions, but above all it is a cosmopolitan city in the truest sense of the word. For a few centuries, London was the heart of the British Empire, and this is still very much perceptible in its dynamic atmosphere. Due to numerous restrictions for cars in the city centre, use of the excellent public transport network or a tour on a red sightseeing double-decker bus is highly recommended.

The western part of central London is typified by diversity – the administrative centre of Whitehall in the historic district of Westminster; posh residential and business districts like Knightsbridge and Belgravia; busy squares like Piccadilly Circus and Trafalgar Square; and the fabulous parks like St James's and the Kensington Gardens.

Starting with the district of Westminster, here is a handful of things to see, the first two being UNESCO World Heritage Sites: Westminster Abbey, the mighty Gothic church where English kings are crowned and buried (not to be confused with nearby Westminster Cathedral, a Catholic church from the 19th century), and the neo-Gothic Houses of Parliament on the Thames.

Then we have the only remaining part of the original medieval building, Westminster Hall, and next to that the clock tower housing Big Ben (1858). Westminster Bridge crosses the Thames. After that we have Buckingham Palace (early 18th century), the city residence of the Queen, Green Park and St James's Park, and the Tate Gallery with a first-class selection of English art.

In Whitehall you'll find 10 Downing Street, residence of the Prime Minister; the Palladian-style Banqueting House, opposite Horse Guards Parade for the Changing of the Guard; Trafalgar Square with Nelson's Column; the National Gallery with works from the 16th to 20th centuries, the National Portrait Gallery; Hyde Park, a public park from the 17th century with the famous Speaker's Corner; Madame Tussaud's Wax Museum.

In Knightsbridge are the Victoria and Albert Museum, the largest arts and crafts museum in the world; the Natural History Museum and the Science and Technology Museum; the legendary Harrods department store and the younger and less conventional Harvey Nichols department store.

Trafalgar Square with the National Gallery in the background.

Opened in 1894, Tower Bridge is not only London's iconic landmark, but also a significant testament to the engineering of the time. By the mid-19th century, the London East End was so densely populated that a bridge became necessary.

On the eastern edge of the city, the massive complex with the long name 'Her Majesty's Royal Palace and Fortress The Tower of London,' commonly known as the Tower, watches over the London. In the centre of the area lies the White Tower, a massive fortress built by William the Conqueror in 1078.

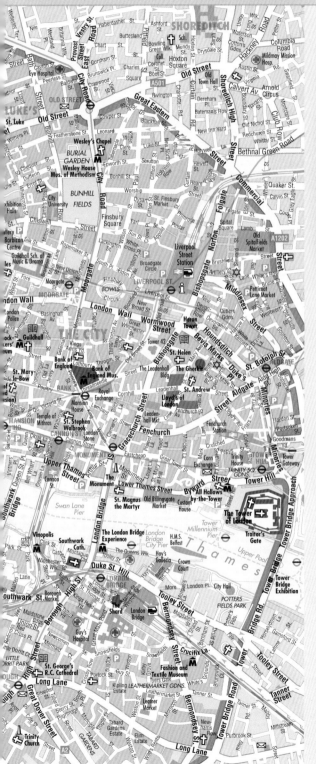

London

In 1851, when Great Britain was at the height of its imperial power and had just celebrated itself in a World Fair, London had around one million inhabitants. Today there are over twelve million people in Greater London and around eight within city limits – the latter makes it the largest city in Europe.

View from Millennium Bridge towards St. Paul's Cathedral

It began modestly almost 2,000 years ago, when the Romans conquered the island that is now England and founded Londinium on the Thames. Many peoples have come to the British Isles, but since William the Conqueror made London his capital in 1066, the city has remained the administrative centre of Britain, not least due to its strategic position – near the continent, yet protected in an estuary. The first block of the Tower of London, the city's most venerated building, was in fact laid by William the Conqueror in 1078.

A large fortress and medieval royal residence, the Tower of London complex is centred around the White Tower (11th century) and it is here that the Crown Jewels are on display. Another one of the most recognizable icons of London's cityscape is the Tower Bridge (1894) with its double towers and distinctive bascule bridge.

In the City district of London you should take time to go to St Paul's Cathedral (1674–1710), a Renaissance masterpiece with a walkway that goes all the way around its dome. North of St Paul's Cathedral are the futuristic Barbican towers – a culture and arts centre – and the famous London Stock Exchange from 1773.

In the West End you'll find countless theatres, cinemas, pubs and restaurants around Piccadilly Circus, London's most colourful square. Covent Garden, once a market, is now a pedestrian zone in the West End. The Royal Opera House and the British Museum, with a number of world-famous collections, are also here.

Interesting places in the Southwark area include the cathedral of the same name, which is the oldest Gothic church in London. It has a memorial for Shakespeare, whose Globe Theatre was rebuilt nearby almost in its original form. The Tate Modern is a striking art museum in a disused power station across the Thames on the Millennium Footbridge. The Docklands and Canary Wharf both feature modern architecture – Canada Tower and Canary Wharf Tower, respectively. The latter is the tallest building in the UK at 244 m (800 ft).

In Greenwich is the Royal Maritime Museum with sailing history, the historic Cutty Sark clipper ship, and the observatory, which crosses the prime meridian.

Through Dartmoor National Park

From Torquay, a route leads through Dartmoor National Park, a largely untouched area of moorland and forest on the south-west coast of England that covers approximately 945 sq km (363 sq mi) at an elevation of roughly 500 m (1,640 ft) above sea level. It is one of Europe's largest nature reserves. Dartmoor is not a primeval landscape, but rather an area that has been cultivated for thousands of years.

Numerous archaeological sites – remains of Stone Age villages, stone paths and circles, monuments such as burial sites, and

9 Torquay Torquay is around 40 km (25 miles) south of Exeter on what is commonly known as the English Riviera. This 30-km-long (19-mile) stretch of coast has been given this name because of its numerous idyllic bays, palm-littered beaches, mild climate and its urbane atmosphere. Three towns – Torquay, Paignton and Brixham – have become known as Torbay, though they have kept their own individual styles. Elegant hotels, Victorian villas and countless bars and restaurants around the little harbour give the area a holiday feel. After the impressive mountain road through Dartmoor National Park (with grades of up to twenty-five per cent), the A390 leads from Liskeard back down towards the coast and St Austell.

10 St Austell and the Eden Project Since the discovery of kaolin in the 18th century, the economic welfare of the town has been closely linked to the mining of this important base product used in the manufacture of porcelain. The story of china clay or 'white gold' is retold in St Austell's museum. The Eden Project was constructed over 14 ha (35 acres) on a disused kaolin quarry near Bodelva. In two gigantic greenhouses, gardeners have reproduced two climatic zones – tropical rainforest and Mediterranean.

The greenhouses are densely populated with plants from these respective regions in order to allow a natural ecosystem to develop. In another area, a cool zone was set up, in which indigenous plants from Britain and exotic plants from temperate Cornwall flourish. The larger of the greenhouses, the Humid Tropics Biome, is the largest greenhouse in the world covering an area of 1,559 ha (4 acres) at a height of 55 m (180 ft).

11 Mevagissey The Lost Gardens of Heligan north of Mevagissy are every bit as fascinating as the Eden Project – strange, prehistoric fallen tree trunks lie amid a subtropical landscape with giant bamboo, ancient tree ferns and mysterious ponds. The gardens were initially planted in the 18th and 19th centuries, but then fell into a long dormant phase. In 1990, the developer Tim Smit cut through the 5-m-thick (16-ft) thorn bushes and discovered a site that had been forgotten for nearly a hundred years.

After a painstaking reconstruction of the original gardens, the microenvironment was saved. The 32-ha (80-acre) site includes a ravine, an enchanting Italian garden, a grotto and ancient rhododendron bushes. Lost Valley, a jungle environment with a view over Mevagissey, is another highlight of the gardens.

12 Penzance The largest town in Cornwall lies 50 km (31 miles) to the west of here. A drive over the Penwith Peninsula to Land's End is definitely recommended. Due to its temperate climate, this striking region is also called the 'Cornish Riviera'.

Penzance was an important tin trading point for the Roman Empire and medieval Europe. The centre of town, between Chapel Street and Market Jew Street, is the oldest part of Penzance, where the long since vanished times of the seafarers can still be felt. The Barbican, which is an old storage house, and the Egyptian House (1830) are both worth visiting. Opposite the town stands the old castle of St Michael's Mount on top of a granite island in the bay of the same name. This former Benedictine monastery came into the Crown's possession in 1535 and was then converted into a fortress. Historians date the founding of the monastery back to the 8th century. At that time Celtic monks had built a monastery on Mont St-Michel in Normandy, which is remarkably, but not coincidentally, similar to its Cornish counterpart.

At low tide you can cross the bay on foot. At high tide there is a boat service. If you climb to the top of the 70-m-high (230-ft) outcrop, you'll get a fabulous view over Penwith Peninsula.

From Penzance, there is a 35-km (22-mile) road that leads round the peninsula to Land's End and on to St Ives.

13 Land's End The westernmost point of England is covered with an open moor and heath, and is absolutely riddled with archaeological treasures. Headstones from the ice age and Bronze Age, Celtic crosses and entire villages that date back to times before the birth of Christ all bear witness to thousands of years of settlement in the area. The continual breaking of the waves from the Atlantic over the mighty rocks led the Romans to

more – testify to the extensive human presence here.

An 800-km-long (500-mile) network of footpaths crisscrosses the countryside, and in some places the granite rises out of the earth in formations called tors, or craggy hills. Reddish-brown ferns, heather, windswept trees and shaggy Dartmoor ponies are among the park's simple selection of things to see, especially in the sparse western reaches. Tidy lanes and little villages are common on the more inhabited east side.

From Ashburton, a pretty town near idyllic Widecombe-in-the-Moor, your drive goes through the hilly landscape to Two Bridges, past Princetown with the infamous Dartmoor Prison. Tavistock, an earlier centre for tin and copper mining, was famous for hundreds of years because of its rich Benedictine monastery.

christen the place Belerion – Home of the Storms.

⑭ Scilly Isles About 40 km (25 miles) off the coast to the south-west lie the 140 Scilly Isles, which are reachable by ferry from Penzance. The 2,000 inhabitants, who live mostly from tourism and flower exports, are spread over only seven inhabited islands. With their rough granite rocks, white sandy beaches and turquoise bays, the Scilly Isles are best discovered on foot or by bicycle.

A collection of the exotic palms and plants that traditionally flourish in this mild climate can be seen in the Abbey Garden at Tresco.

Back on the mainland, the often steep coastal road then follows the Atlantic coast around to St Ives. Ornithologists come here to find rare visitors like thrushes, New World warblers and vireos that have come over from America accidental on the omnipresent Westerlies. Some of the best observation points are the lighthouses.

⑮ St Ives Grey granite houses populate this former fishing village, which also happens to have one of Cornwall's most beautiful beaches. Numerous artists and sculptors have been coming here since the last century, fascinated by the light and landscape. The Tate Gallery has even opened a 'branch' high above Porthmoor Beach where works by artists from St Ives are on display including paintings by Patrick Heron and Ben Nicholson, who lived here with his artist wife Barbara Hepworth.

The village of Gwithian just up the road is also worth a stop. The tiny fishing village of Port Isaac is near by, just off the A30. It has been spared a lot of the mass tourism that has become rampant in these parts, which makes it a refreshing alternative. The extremely steep streets probably put off a lot of visitors, so the best bet is to park the car above the village, and walk to Kellan Head on the coast.

⑯ Tintagel The legendary ruins on Tintagel Head are said to be the birthplace of King Arthur. Beyond the village of Tintagel a path leads over the cliffs to a green outcrop on the Atlantic that is crowned with crumbling ruin walls and can be reached via the steep staircase. As digs have proven, a Celtic monastery from the 5th century once stood here with a library, chapel, guest house, refectory and even a bath house. The castle, however, whose ruins are also still visible, only dates back to the 13th century, a fact that would cast a doubt over the speculation of it being the birthplace of the legendary king of England. And yet he who stands in the fog on the cliffs looking down at waves crashing by the dark entrance to Merlin's Cave can easily feel himself transported back to the times of King Arthur. The Norman church graveyard has a number of half-buried tombstones telling tales of dead seamen and grieving widows.

The A39 leads further north from Tintagel along the coast, passing between Blackmoor Gate and Dunster across Exmoor National Park. In order to fully appreciate the coast and the moorland here, you should walk a section of the Somerset and Devon Coastal Path, from Bossington for example.

⑰ Glastonbury and Wells At Bridgwater, the coastal road A39 finally turns inland and leads to Glastonbury, a mythical place that attracts countless esoteric types. There are many reasons for the concentration of mystical and

Left side: Birch Tor in Dartmoor National Park.
Picture bar from the top: Land's End; Ruins of Tintagel Castle; St. Michael's Tower at Glastonbury; Wells Cathedral.

33

The Romans in England

It's true, the Romans even ruled England, as Britannia, from around 55 BC to AD 410. After Julius Caesar's failed attempt, Emperor Claudius was the first to conquer the island all the way up to what is now Scotland, then called Caledonia, or 'Wooded Land'. Emperor Hadrian had built a wall there in around 122 BC to keep the fearsome Picts (Scottish predecessors) out of the Roman territories in England. The Romans remained on the island for a good 400 years. They selected Londinium as their capital and founded also other cities, with common suffixes like 'caster' or 'chester' being a throwback to

supernatural activity here: the remains of King Arthur are thought to be buried under the ruins of Glastonbury Abbey, and Glastonbury is often thought to be the legendary Avalon – a paradise to which Arthur was carried after his death. Historical facts date the foundation of the first monastery back to the 7th century while the construction of England's largest abbey came around the year 1000 and the dissolution of the monastery in 1539.

The small city of Wells, on the other hand, is known for its glorious cathedral, the first Gothic building in all of England. The main section was completed in 1240, but the western tower and chapel came much later. The western facade was at one time covered with 400 figures, testimony to the skill of the medieval masons here – one picture book carved into the stone relates biblical and world history. Adjacent to the cathedral is the Bishop's Palace, which is still used by the Bishop of Bath and Wells. Bath, your next stop, is the cultural centre of the county of Somerset and is around 30 km (19 miles) north of Wells on the A367.

⑱ Bath The Romans knew this hot-springs town as Aquae Sulis. They built magnificent swimming pools, Turkish baths and saunas, and turned the town into a meeting place for the Roman elite. Oddly, the unique baths were only discovered in the 18th century. Bath's rebirth as a health resort began in earnest in the 19th century when the city's grandiose Georgian architecture, concerts and balls enticed London's upper class to enjoy the recuperative benefits of its historic facilities. Visitors could also admire the dignified limestone buildings such as Queen Square, Royal Crescent and Pulteney Bridge. Today, you can taste the healing waters and take in the atmosphere in the Pump Room. A short detour of about 12 km (7.5 miles) via Chippenham leads

you to the archaeological site at Avebury in Wiltshire. Avebury is home to the remains of England's largest and most impressive stone circle, made up of over 100 stones erected around 3,500 years ago. Nearby, the 40-m-high (130-ft) Silbury Hill looks like a pyramid, but it was not used as a burial site.

⑲ The Cotswolds The A429 takes you through the deep, wooded valleys and gentle hills of the Cotswolds, an area that has been populated since prehistoric times. After the Romans, the Cotswolds bloomed through the Middle Ages thanks to wool production. The region then sank into a long period of dormancy before being reawakened

by tourism. The typical Cotswolds architectural style and fairy-tale charm can be best seen in places such as Bouton-on-the-Water where golden stone buildings stand side-by-side with little bridges crossing streams in quaint and colourful meadows. The town of Stow-on-the-Wold with its stone market hall sits atop a hill and was once a thriving sheep market. On the other side of the hill are the tiny villages of Upper Slaughter and Lower Slaughter, whose miniature appearance have made them into much-loved postcard images.

⑳ Stratford-upon-Avon The birthplace of William Shakespeare (1564) is the northern-

most point of your route. In 1594, the famous playwright left for London, where he was able to establish his legendary reputation as actor and writer in one of the leading theatre companies of the time. In 1610 he returned to his home town of Stratford, where he died in 1616. Despite thousands of tourists walking in the footsteps of the poet every year, Stratford has been able to retain some of its Shakespearian atmosphere. Visitors can tour the house where the playwright was born, learn about his life and work in the Shakespeare Centre, or watch one of his plays performed by the Royal Shakespeare Company in the Swan Theatre. A boat trip on the Avon

Stonehenge This world-famous prehistoric site was erected between 3100 and 1500 BC by a late Stone-Age people and given some detailed inscriptions in the Bronze Age. Some of the artistically sculpted stones originate from mountains in 'near-by' Wales.

Scilly Isles Fabulous bays and an exceptionally mild climate make the Scilly Isles a popular holiday destination. Roughly 45 km (28 miles) south-west of Land's End, only seven of the 140 islands are inhabited.

Wells This town was originally founded by the Romans. Its cathedral was begun in AD 700, and the Bishop's Palace is over 800 years old.

St Ives Two museums in St Ives show works by landscape-inspired artists who 'discovered' the fishing village at the end of the 1920s.

Land's End The stunning scenery from here, the westernmost point of England, has made it into a destination for visitors and artists alike.

St Michael's Mount Its resemblance to Mont St-Michel in Normandy was the inspiration for this isle's name.

the Roman word for fort. Some of their roads are still in use as well, for example the Fosse Way through the Cotswolds. When the Pict resistance grew too strong, the Romans retreated. Their ruins are now monuments.

The uncovered Roman baths of Bath (around 65-75 BC) are very close to the church abbey; it was rediscovered in 1870.

rounds off the visit. The A44 towards Oxford passes the impressive Blenheim Palace at Moreton-in-Marsh.

㉑ Blenheim Palace This impressive palace near Oxford was finished in 1722 and is Britain's largest private home. It was originally a gift from Queen Anne to John Churchill, the 1st Duke of Marlborough, after his defeat of Ludwig XIV in Blenheim, Bavaria (actually Blindheim near Höchstädt on the Danube). Blenheim Palace is recommended for a relaxing afternoon walk followed by tea. Many garden-lovers come here to visit the palace park, created by landscape gardener Capability Brown in typical English style.

㉒ Oxford The many spires of Oxford, especially Tom Tower of Christ Church and Magdalen Tower, are visible from the approach road. Oxford is known throughout the world as England's most prestigious university town. Its cathedral and the Picture Gallery, containing masterpieces from the Renaissance and baroque era, are worth a visit. Don't miss the Radcliffe Camera, Sheldonian Theatre and the Bodleian Library with its five million books. A coffee break with a book can be taken in the Blackwell Bookshop with a view over Radcliffe Camera.
The college tour is a classic, and leads around the buildings of Merton College, Corpus Christi and New College, among others.

Take a relaxing walk through the botanical gardens and its old greenhouses as well.

㉓ Windsor and Ascot Windsor Castle is in the Thames Valley west of London, and has been the primary residence of the English royal family since the Middle Ages. The fort, built in the 12th and 13th centuries, has been frequently remodelled over the years.
Many sections of Windsor Castle, one of the largest inhabited castles in the world, are open to the public. A trip to St George's Chapel and the Albert Memorial Chapel to view the burial sites of the monarchs is recommended. The Round Tower offers a wonderful view of the castle and

the Great Park. Opposite Windsor Castle is Eton College, founded in 1440–41. This exclusive private school favours a traditional English education with emphasis on the Classics and sport.
Windsor and Ascot, the famous racetrack, are separated only by a few kilometres. The Hippodrome, built in 1711 by Queen Anne, is among the most famous tracks in the world. From 1825 until 1945, the four-day Royal Meeting race was the only event staged there. Today twenty-five races take place each year.
The last stop now is London, with its historical monuments, impressive museums and world-famous churches.

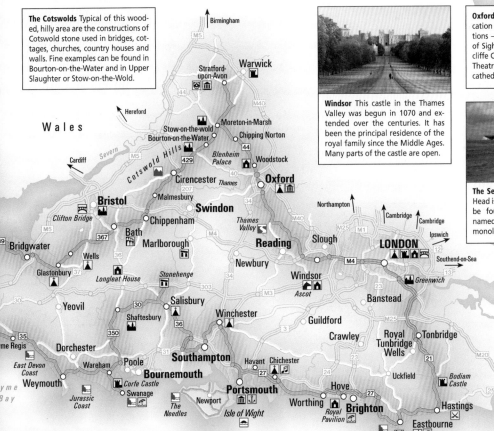

The Cotswolds Typical of this wooded, hilly area are the constructions of Cotswold stone used in bridges, cottages, churches, country houses and walls. Fine examples can be found in Bourton-on-the-Water and in Upper Slaughter or Stow-on-the-Wold.

Windsor This castle in the Thames Valley was begun in 1070 and extended over the centuries. It has been the principal residence of the royal family since the Middle Ages. Many parts of the castle are open.

Oxford This university town is England's education mecca and offers numerous attractions – the Ashmolean Museum, the Bridge of Sighs, the Bodleian Library with the Radcliffe Camera Reading Room, the Sheldonian Theatre, thirty-six colleges and the university cathedral of St Mary the Virgin.

The Seven Sisters At 163 m (535 ft), Beachy Head is Britain's highest limestone cliff. It is to be found in Seven Sisters Country Park, named after the seven distinctive limestone monoliths.

Bodiam Castle This moated castle from the 14th century is like a picture from a fairy tale in the heart of southeast England. The castle, though quite large, was built under the guise of protecting the area from French attacks.

The Route of the Emperors: Berlin – Prague – Vienna – Budapest

On this journey along the ancient European transport and trade arteries of the Elbe, Vltava and Danube rivers, Europe presents itself in all its historical and cultural diversity. On the various riverbanks, cities like Dresden, Prague, Vienna and Budapest show off their abundant monuments of art, and everywhere along the route are palaces, castles and urban gems surrounded by unique natural scenery.

Route profile:

Length: approx. 700 miles
Time required: at least 2 weeks.

No emperor could ever have imagined that at the beginning of the 21st century you would be able to travel all the way from the Spree River (Berlin) to the Danube without any complicated border checks, particularly after the centuries

of mini-states in the region and the tragic rift of the 20th century. What happened to the days when autocratic despots jealously erected border checkpoints and threw up 'iron curtains' to protect their territories? When the Viennese knew nothing of Budweis or Bratislava, and to the people of West Berlin, Dresden might as

well have been further away than the Dominican Republic? Gone inddeed are those days. These days, the road is free to explore what is so close and yet still quite unfamiliar, and there really is a lot to discover.

Berlin, Germany's old and new capital, is its very own unique tourist cosmos. It would take weeks to see even a fraction of its museum treasures, its continuously changing skyline with so much contemporary architecture, an art and restaurant scene that is just as dynamic as that of any other cosmopolitan city, and its large green parks. On this route, however, Berlin is but the starting point of a fascinating journey across Europe.

In Brandenburg and Saxony, both core regions of German intellectual history, one highlight seems

to follow the next. Potsdam, the royal residence of the Prussian kings, provides a magnificent overture to the Lutheran town of Wittenberg, to Weimar, the focal point of German classicism, and to the porcelain metropolis of Meissen, your next stops.

Dresden is simply irresistible as a tourist destination. The capital of Saxony, which rose like the

proverbial phoenix from the ashes (and from the floodwaters in 2002), enchants with its baroque and rococo buildings and its art galleries. Music lovers flock to highlights like the Semper Opera, the Staatskapelle orchestra and the famous Kreuzchor choir.

Attempting to describe in words the exquisite beauty of Prague is often an exercise in futility. The views across the Vltava River towards Hradčany Castle are some of the most unforgettable city sights anywhere on earth. And just like one of Mozart's melodies, the magic hovering above the picturesque alleyways in the Small Quarter and around the Old Town Square will leave no soul untouched.

From the splendidly restored spa towns of Karlovy Vary and Mariánské Láznû, to Litoměřice,

The Danube divides Hungary's capital into the mountainous Buda with the castle district on one side and the flat Pest with the cupola-crowned parliament building on the other side of the river (above). Left: Schönbrunn Palace in Vienna.

Hrad Karlštejn, České Budějovice and Český Krumlov – the number of five-star attractions in Bohemia is just incredible.

There are just as many amazing sights on the journey through Upper and Lower Austria – Freistadt, Linz, Enns, Grein and Krems, not to mention the Melk and Klosterneuburg monasteries. Away from urban attractions, na-ture will also spoil you along the route – the heathlands of lower Fläming and Lower Lausitz, the sandstone mountains on the Riv-er Elbe, the Vltava Valley, the Bo-hemian Forest, the Mühl Quarter, Wachau and the Viennese Forest. Between city tours and museums you can tank up on oxygen every-where on this trip. On top of that, you can always sample the tasty

delicacies that the local cuisine has to offer.

An almost exotic piece of scenery awaits you at the end of your tour, east of Budapest across the River Tisza – the Hortobágy Na-tional Park, a real piece of the idyllic Hungarian Puszta.

Left: Proud baroque splendour in Berlin: Charlottenburg Palace. Above: The Charles Bridge leads over the Vltava river in Prague. The baroque sculptures on the railings represent the saints.

Moritzburg Castle was used by the Elector Friedrich August II of Saxony as a hunting lodge.

Detour

Following in Luther's footsteps

Wittenberg, the town of Luther and one of the focal points of German intellectual history, is located 30 km (18 miles) west of the impressive medieval town of Jüterbog. To get there, take the B187. As a university town, the cradle of the Reformation and the 'workshop' of seminal humanists, Wittenberg was one of the intellectual centres not only of Germany in the 16th century, but of Central Europe. It was here that the influential scholar Martin Luther came in 1508 to hang his famous ninety-five Theses fulminating against the clerics on the Castle Church door, thereby kicking off the Reformation. Memories of him and of the theologian Philipp Melanchthon are still alive. In the house where Luther lived from 1508 to 1546, there is a museum on the history of the Reformation. The house where Melanchthon lived, studied and died is also open to the public, and is also the only private home remaining from the 16th century. The town church of St Mary where Luther used to give his sermons is also worth seeing. Despite it being off your route, a visit to Wartburg castle is highly recommended. About 250 km (160 miles) from Dresden you'll find Eisenach, where Luther went to school. South-west of Eisenach, in the middle of the Thuringian Forest, is the medieval Wartburg Castle, built in 1150. It was here that Luther translated the New Testament from Greek into what was then the first-ever German version of the bible in 1521–22.

From the Spree in Berlin to the Danube in Budapest – a journey through the European heartland of old empires is now possible without border checks, through five countries from the German capital to the Hungarian capital. It will give you a comprehensive overview of its cultural depth and scenic beauty.

1 **Berlin** (see pp. 40-41).

2 **Potsdam** Our first stop outside the city limits of Berlin is Potsdam, the state capital of Brandenburg. It is famous mainly for the beautiful baroque and neoclassical buildings and its magnificent parks dating from the era of the Prussian kings. The best-known attraction of this town, which is 1,000 years old and has been partially declared a UNESCO World Heritage Site, is Frederick III's pompously decorated summer palace. Its park covers 300 ha (740 acres) and was designed by Lenné.
It is an architectural gem in itself, full of statues and monuments such as the neighbouring park of Charlottenhof. In Potsdam's Old Town, the Old Market with the St Nicholas Church and the former town hall, the Marstall stables, the Dutch Quarter and the old Russian colony of Alexandrowka are all worth a visit.
Another must-see is the New Garden with its Marble Palace and Cecilienhof Castle. From Potsdam, drive to the old town of Beelitz, and from there east to the B101 south towards Luckenwalde.

3 **Luckenwalde** At first glance, this medieval market town may seem dull and industrial, but its interesting historical centre has been well preserved. Its landmark is the steeple of St Johannskirche with its Gothic frescoes and important altar statues. A former hat factory, built at the beginning of the 1920s by Erich Mendelsohn, is also remarkable.

4 **Jüterbog** This town, located 15 km (9 miles) further south at the edge of the lower Fläming heathlands, still has most of its original fortifications, including three beautiful gates. Sites here include the Liebfrauenkirche, the Nikolaikirche and the town hall, but the main attraction is really 5 km (3 miles) to the north: the ruins of the Cistercian monastery of Zinna, with important Gothic wall paintings. Driving along the edge of the Lower Lausitz heathlands for about 100 km (62 miles) on the B101, you will pass Elsterwerda and Großenhain before you reach the Elbe River and the porcelain centre of Meissen.

5 **Meissen** In the 12th century, this 'Cradle of Saxony', where the German emperors founded the first settlement on Slavic soil, was a royal residence of the House of Wettin. Until the devastations of World War II it was able to preserve its medieval imprint, with the Gothic cathedral and Albrecht Castle representing both religious and worldly power. These are still visible from the historic Old Town with its market square and half-timbered buildings.
Today the town is more famous for its 'white gold' than for its 1,000 years of history. Home of Europe's first hard porcelain, Meissen has produced this valuable product since Augustus the Strong founded the factory in 1710. It continues to be exported all over the world.
Past Radebeul, the route along the B26 takes us to Dresden, the Saxon state capital 25 km (16 miles) away.

The oldest castle in Germany: Albrechtsburg castle in Meissen on the banks of the Elbe was built between 1471 and 1524 in a late gothic style.

Detour

Weimar

This Thuringian city attracts visitors from far and wide. You reach Weimar from Dresden via the A4 Autobahn. In 1990 it was the European Capital of Culture and it certainly dressed itself for the occasion. Luther, Bach and Cranach all worked here; Goethe, Schiller, Wieland and Herder took German classicism to its peak. Attractions are the Goethe House and Schiller House, the Bauhaus Museum, the Duchess Anna Amalia Library, the historic

6 Dresden This former elector's residence, which has also been praised as the 'Florence of Germany' or the 'Baroque Pearl', is doubtless one of Europe's major cultural centres. In 1485 it became the seat of the Albertinian government, and during the

17th and 18th centuries, Augustus the Strong and his successors turned it into one of the most magnificent baroque residence cities in all of Germany. The devastating bomb raids in February 1945 were unfortunately fatal for the city, destroying the Old Town almost beyond recognition. However, many of the famous buildings have either already been restored or are still works in progress, chief among them being the Zwinger, housing the 'Old Masters' art gallery; the Semper Opera; the castle;

the Frauenkirche; the Japanese Palace; the Albertinum, housing the 'New Masters' art gallery; the Green Vault; and the Brühl Terraces high above the riverbank. You should definitely visit the important attractions in the surrounding area, above all Pillnitz Castle, Moritzburg Castle and the so-called Elbe Castles. If you are not intending to do the detour to Weimar and Wartburg Castle, you now follow the B172 upriver from Dresden. You'll pass Pirna, with its picturesque centre and the interesting Großsedlitz baroque gardens, and enter the spectacular Elbe Sandstone Mountains.

7 Elbe Sandstone Mountains In order to get the best possible views of these bizarre sandstone rock formations, you

would really have to do a boat trip on the meandering river. Barring that, you can get some magnificent views from the road. Most of the area is now included in the 'Saxon Switzerland' National Park, with its monumental plateaus. Königstein Castle and the bastion in the spa town of Rathen are quite popular. Bad Schandau is the starting point for hiking and climbing tours to the Schrammsteine rocks and through Kirnitz Valley up to the Lichtenhain waterfalls.

8 Děčín The rocky sandstone scenery continues in all its grandeur here on the Czech side of the border. From the town of Hřensko, for example, there is a beautiful 4-km (2.5-mile) walk to the spectacular Pravčická Gate stone formation. An ideal starting point for trips into the park area is Děčín, where the famous 'Shepherd's Wall' towers 150 m (492 ft) over the river.

On the way to the Ústí nad Labem region you'll find another magnificent rock formation, crowned by

Top: Dresden owes its nickname, the 'Florence of Germany', to its baroque cityscape. **Above:** New Palace in the parc of Sanssouci.

cemetery and the castle with its collection of art.

From the top: Weimar Market; Goethe and Schiller in front of the National Theatre in Weimar; inside the Anna-Amalia-Library.

In the Nikolai quarter, where after the Second World War almost nothing was left standing, you will find a real old Berlin environment with many quaint restaurants, arts and crafts and souvenir shops.

Brandenburg Gate, built in the late 18th century, is considered the most important landmark of Berlin and of the German Reunification.

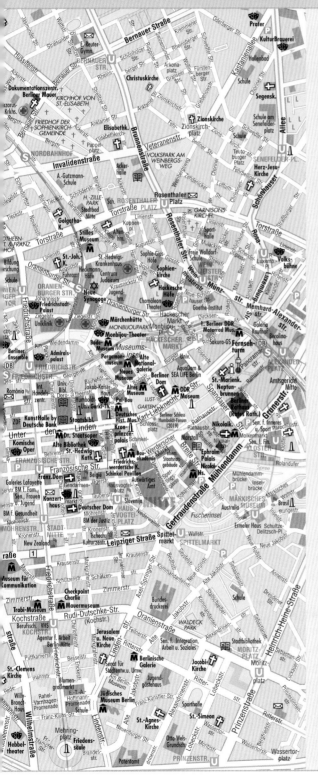

Berlin

Things have been changing rapidly in Berlin since the Berlin Wall came down in 1989. Now it seems the whole world knows that the lively German capital is a cosmopolitan city on a par with the likes of New York, Tokyo and London.

Berlin, whose history began in the 13th century, is not one of Germany's older cities. It was Prussia's rise to a great European power in the 18th century that made the capital significant. Berlin then became larger and more beautiful, finally being named the capital of the German Empire in 1871.

Under the National Socialists, terror and annihilation spread from the capital, but in 1945 it was reduced to rubble. After being divided in 1961, it went on to inspire the reunification of East and West Germany in 1989 with the opening of the Berlin Wall. Since then it has changed dramatically. Today, Berlin is still not one entity but rather a grouping of districts. In a way, however, this is a blessing – for it is the city's variety and its contrasts that define this metropolis.

In the Charlottenburg district visit: Kurfürstendamm, the city's principal shopping boulevard, the ruins of the Emperor William Memorial Church and the Zoological Gardens.

Outside the city centre visit the Charlottenburg Castle and Park, the 'German Versailles', palace of the Prussian kings (built 1695–1746); the Egyptian Museum with Nefertiti; and the Museum Berggruen with great modern art.

In the Tiergarten district check out Berlin's largest city park with Bellevue Castle and Park, the residence of the German president; the Cultural Forum with the Philharmonic, the Museum of Musical Instruments, the Arts and Crafts Museum, a gallery with European paintings to the 19th century, the New National Gallery with 20th century art, the memorial to the German Resistance in the former Wehrmacht headquarters; the Road of 17 June with Victory Col-

umn (67 m/220 ft) between Brandenburg Gate and Ernst-Reuter-Square.

West of city centre go to Grunewald, Berlin's forest, the Wannsee, and the Dahlem Museum with an outstanding collection of ethnological exhibits.

In Kreuzberg see the ruins of Anhalt Station, the Martin Gropius Building, the Jewish Museum by Daniel Liebeskind, the German Technology Museum, and Victoria Park with Kreuzberg Memorial.

Berlin 'Mitte' (centre): the Brandenburg Gate (1791); 'Unter den Linden' historic boulevard with a memorial of Frederick the Great; the New Guard by Schinkel; St Hedwig's Cathedral from the 18th century; the neoclassical public opera house, the baroque Zeughaus with the German Historical Museum; the Crown Prince's Palace (18th century); Humboldt University; the Gendarmes Market; the French and German Cathedral (18th century); the Schinkel Theatre (1821); the Reichstag (Parliament) with glass dome by Sir Norman Foster; Potsdam Square's modern architecture, Museum Island with Pergamon Museum, the Old Museum (antiquities), the New Museum, the Old National Gallery, the Bode Museum and Lustgarten. Beyond that is the Berlin Cathedral (late 19th century), 'Alex' TV tower (365 m/1,198 ft), old Checkpoint Charlie with the Berlin Wall museum; St Mary's Church (13th century); historic Nikolai Quarter; Märkisches Museum of the city.

In the Scheunenviertel go to the Hamburger Bahnhof Gallery (modern art), the New Synagogue with its centre on the history of Berlin's Jewish community, and the Hackesche Höfe from 1906, once the largest working and living compound in Europe.

View over Prague's Charles Bridge with the Old Town bridge tower and the church of St Franciscus in the background.

Detour

Karlovy Vary and Mariánské Lázně

Just over 40 km (25 miles) south of the German-Czech border, near Ústí nad Labem, follow the N13 west via Most and Chomutov to the Karlovy Vary, formerly the German Karlsbad ('Charles Bath'). Legend has it that it was actually Emperor Charles IV himself who found the hot salty springs in the area when he was out hunting deer in the 14th century. Over the next 500 years, Bohemia's most famous and most glamorous spa town developed around these springs, with European elites from politics, art and society all making their way here to see and be seen. After fifty years of drabness during the Communist era, a glittering rebirth followed in 1989. Most of the Wilhelminian buildings, including the Mühlbrunn Colonnades, the town theatre and the Grandhotel

Cast iron colonnade in Mariánské Lázn.

Pupp, now radiate again with all their former glory. From the densely settled banks of the Tepla River, take the turnoff onto the N21 just outside Cheb and drive just 60 km (37 miles) to the second legendary spa town of Mariánské Lázně ('Mary's Bath'), where Goethe wrote his 'Marienbad Elegies' in 1823. Its stucco facades were completely restored. Especially magnificent are the 120 m (131 yds) of cast-iron colonnades.

the ruins of Strekov castle. From here you can take a detour heading west on the N13 via Most and Chomutov to the renowned spa towns of Karlovy Vary and Mariánské Lázně.

⑨ Litoměřice At the confluence of the Eger and the Elbe (Labe), where the Bohemian hills flatten out towards the plains, is the ancient town of Litoműfiice surrounded by vineyards and orchards. Its Old Town is among the most beautiful in Bohemia. At its centre is the market square, which is around 2 ha (5 acres) in size. Don't miss the 'Kelchhaus', the town hall and St Stephen's Cathedral on Cathedral Hill.

About 4 km (2.5 miles) to the south, Terezín invokes memories of darker times. In World War II, the German occupation was not good to this town, which was originally built by Joseph II as a fortification against Prussia. There was a large concentration camp here.

⑩ Mělník High above the junction of the Vltava and Elbe Rivers is the much-visited town of Mělník, with its market square surrounded by beautiful stately houses. The town's most

eye-catching sight, however, is its castle, a cherished possession of the local nobility for more than 1,100 years. The terrace of the castle restaurant has some fantastic views over the idyllic river valley. From Mělník it is 40 km (25 miles) to Prague, the fairy-tale city on the Vltava River, and only 30 km (18 miles) to what is considered Bohemia's most famous castle.

⑪ Prague For detailed information see p. 43.

⑫ Karlštejn After 16 km (10 miles) on the R4, you head westbound at Dobřichovice for around 40 km (25 miles) until you get to this monumental castle perched majestically on a limestone rock 72 m (236 ft) above the Berounka Valley. It was built in the mid 14th century by Emperor Charles IV as his royal residence and a depository for the treasures. Its highlight in terms of art history is the Chapel of the Cross in the Great Tower with its gold-plated arches.

Back on the R4, you go to Příbram, which is located 50 km (31 miles) south-west of Prague, just off the main road.

⑬ Příbram This industrial and mining town, where silver has

been mined since the 14th century and uranium since 1945, would not be worth mentioning if it were not for one of the Czech Republic's most visited pilgrimage destinations at its south-eastern edge – the Church of Our Lady of Svatá Hora with its baroque additions.

South-east of Příbram, not far from the B4, are two imposing castles on the bank of the Vltava River, which actually forms a reservoir more than 100 km (62 miles) long in this area. One of them is Zvíkov Castle, built in the 13th century on a towering rock outcrop; this former royal residence is worth a visit for its Chapel of St Wenceslas and the late-Gothic frescoes in its Great Hall. Orlík Castle, owned by the Schwarzenberg family for more than 700 years and reconstructed in neo-Gothic style in the 19th century, captivates with its richly decorated interior.

⑭ Písek On your way south on Road 20 you'll cross the Otava River after 50 km (31 miles). The well-manicured centre of this lit-

Above: The buildings of Karlštejn Castle are built at different heights - a symbol of power.

In the Old Town Square, in the heart of Prague's Old Town, there are numerous Renaissance and Baroque – style buildings, the foundations of which date back to the Middle Ages.

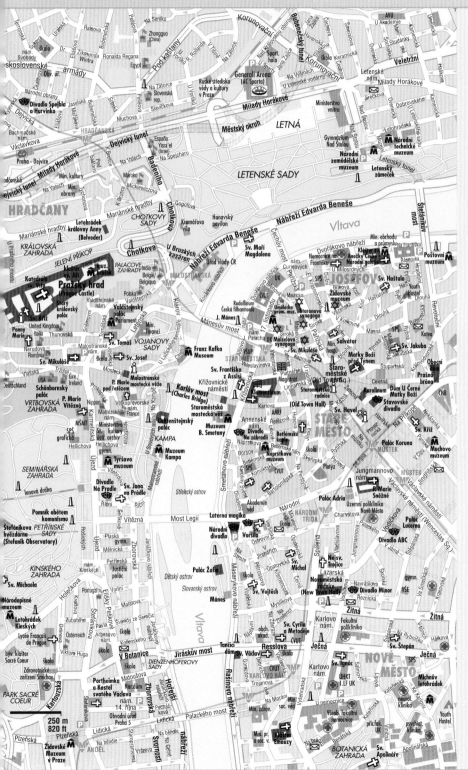

Prague

For centuries, the 'Golden City' has been an important intellectual and cultural centre, characterized by unique and beautiful architecture throughout the entire city.

Although Prague escaped destruction in World War II, time has still taken its toll on the city's buildings over the centuries. Thanks to an expertly managed restoration, however, Prague can once again show off the magnificence of more than 1,000 years of history. The Czech people can be proud of their capital, which is the former residence of Bohemian kings and Habsburg Emperors. Hradčany Castle, where they used to reside, provides you with the best views of this masterpiece of historical urban architecture – the entire city is designated a UNESCO World Heritage Site.

In the Old Town go see the Altstädter Ring with rows of historic houses; the baroque Týn Church and Jan Hus Memorial; the art-nouveau Representation House; St Wenceslas Square with buildings from the 19th and 20th centuries; the Gothic town hall with its astronomical clock; and the late-Gothic gunpowder tower.

In the Castle Quarter on the Hradčany visit the castle (royal residence since the 10th century); the Golden Alleyway; the King's Palace with Renaissance Hall; the St Veit's Cathedral, with relics from St Wenceslas, the national saint; St George's Basilica (12th century).

In the Josefov district see the Old Jewish cemetery, the Old New Synagogue, and the Pinkas Synagogue.

In the Lesser Quarter visit the Charles Bridge (14th century); St Nicholas Church, Prague's most important baroque church and the Waldstein Palace of the commander Wallenstein.

The oldest stone bridge in Bohemia crosses the river Otava in the town of Písek.

The Castle of Český Krumlov

There are many good reasons why the castle of Český Krumlov, located high above the Vltava River, is a UNESCO World Heritage Site – it comprises forty buildings and palaces with a total of 320 rooms and halls, as well as five courtyards and castle gardens measuring 7 ha (17 acres), with some very interesting detailing.

The castle buildings, erected on different rock formations, are connected by a three-storey viaduct with a canopied three-level walkway. The entrance is dominated by the tower, painted in 1590. The rococo castle theatre dating from 1767 still has its original, and still functional, stage engineering. This open-air stage in the castle park is unique because it is the audience – not the stage – that turns when there is a

The gigantic castle of Český Krumlov rises up high above the city.

change of scene.

The Masque Hall is also worth seeing. It is painted with figures from polite society and the Commedia dell'Arte (completed by J. Lederer in 1748). Also worth mentioning are the four bears guarding the entrance to the compound.

tle town used to be an important stopping point on the so-called Golden Path, the trade route between Prague and Passau. Deer Bridge recalls the town's importance as an ancient traffic hub. The bridge, which was built in the second half of the 13th century, is Bohemia's oldest stone bridge.

15 České Budějovice Another 50 km (31 miles) on, you come to České Budějovice, which is world-famous for its breweries. Since Ottokar II founded the town in 1265, its centre has been the market square. The most dramatic sight on this huge square, which covers an area of 133 by 133 m (145 by 145 yds) and is surrounded by arcades on all sides, is the Samson Fountain.

From the viewing platform of the steeple (72 m/236 ft), you can easily spot the other sights of the town – the baroque ca-

thedral of St Nicholas, the town hall, the Dominican Monastery and the Church of Our Lady, as well as the Salt House.

Around 10 km (6 miles) to the north, the battlements of Hluboká Castle appear on the horizon. Considered 'Bohemia's Neuschwanstein', this lavishly furnished castle was also owned by the Schwarzenberg family until 1939.

16 Český Krumlov Upriver from České Budějovice, it is another fifteen minutes by car along the Vltava River to the famous town of Český Krumlov. UNESCO certainly had its reasons for declaring this gem of more than 700 years as a World Heritage Site. Its location on both sides of a narrow hook in the river is incredibly scenic, and the labyrinthine alleyways of the Old Town and the Latrán with its shingled roofs are almost unsurpassably quaint.

Highlights of every city tour are the Gothic St Vitus Church and the Schiele Centre. The painter Egon Schiele worked and lived in Český Krumlov in 1911.

The defining attraction of the town, however, is its castle. It is Bohemia's second-largest, and is surpassed only by the Hradčany in Prague. It was originally owned by the Rosenberg family for 300 years, then by Emperor Rudolph II before landing in the hands of the counts of Schwarzenberg in the early 18th century.

A guided tour of the castle shows you the living quarters, gallery, chapel, the Masque Hall with frescoes and a fine rococo open-air theatre. It has been a designated UNESCO World Heritage Site since 1992.

17 Freistadt Right across the border in Austria you'll come to the next delightful example of medieval town planning.

Market square in Budweis with the Samson fountain and the town hall, both are gems dating back to the Baroque period.

Linz

In the last couple of decades, Linz, which had long endured a bad reputation as an unattractive industrial town, has radically polished up its image. Contemporary art, using the most modern media and technology available, now defines Linz's cultural identity.

The Lentos Museum of Modern Art, the Ars Electronica Festival and the Design Centre all pay their tribute to modern times. Every year, the bigwigs of computer art turn up for the Ars Electronica Festival, and a multimedia wave of sound and light descends on the city. Beyond all this modernism is also the neatly restored historic centre around the town square, which includes the Renaissance Landhaus (house of the provincial government), the castle, the Church of St Martin, the parish church and the

The centre of the northern Mühl District, developed under the Babenberg Dynasty, quickly became the most important trading post between Bohemia and the Danube. To this day it has kept its 14th-century fortifications.

Take a stroll through the narrow alleyways between the Linz Gate and the Bohemia Gate, past the town's handsome mansions and the huge town square to the church. Make sure not to miss the Mühl District House in the castle, which has a superb collection of reverse glass painting.

Your next stop is Linz, the capital of Upper Austria, and from there our route follows the northern banks of the Danube (B3) towards Vienna.

18 **Linz** (see sidebar on the right).

19 **Enns** This attractive town near the Danube dates back to a Roman fort called Lauriacum and is one of the most ancient towns

in Austria. Its landmark is the city's free-standing tower, which measures 60 m (197 ft). Antiquity is brought to life in the Museum Lauriacum, which is located on the town square. On the left bank of the Danube, some miles north of Enns, lies the market town of Mauthausen.

A monument in the local granite quarries commemorates the fact that the Germans ran a concentration camp here, where around 100,000 people lost their lives.

Around 30 km (18 miles) downriver, at the start of the 'Strudengau', a stretch of river that is feared for its strong currents and dangerous sandbanks, is the little town of Grein.

It originally became wealthy because local mariners would guide travellers through the dangerous waters.

It also has a very delightful rococo theatre. Close by, the castle ruins of Klam are also very worth seeing.

20 **Ybbs** This traditional market and toll location marks the beginning of the next section of the valley, the so-called 'Nibelungengau'. North of the power station (1958), the historic castle of Persenbeug keeps vigil over the valley. The castle remains the property of the Habsburg family and can only be viewed from outside.

A little further east, there are two reasons for a short excursion up to Maria Taferl, a Lower Austrian market town with no more than a thousand inhabitants. In addition to the baroque pilgrimage church, whose exuberant colours and shapes are truly beguiling, it is mainly the view from the terrace that is so captivating – the entire Nibelungengau of Burgundian legend

Below the huge castle complex of Ceský Krumlov, the Vltava winds its way through the city.

Linz skyline with the Danube and the Brucknerhaus in the foreground.

old and new cathedrals, as well as a number of interesting galleries and museums.

An integral part of any sightseeing trip should also be a boat ride on the Danube with the Linz City Express, or a journey up the Pöstlingberg mountain on the ancient mountain railway.

The Melk Abbey – a spiritual centre on the Danube

As far back as AD 976, Margrave Leopold I had established Melk Castle as his residence. Over the years, his successors equipped it with treasures and relics. Then, in 1089, Margrave Leopold II handed the castle over to the Benedictine monks of the nearby Lambach Abbey. To this day, the monks continue to live at the abbey according to the Rule of St Benedict. Over the course of centuries, the monks collected and also produced valuable manuscripts for the abbey's library. In many areas of the natural and social

Wachau

The transverse valley of the Danube, between Melk and Mautern and Emmersdorf and Krems, is the very image of a central European cultural landscape. No surprise, then, that it has been listed as a UNESCO World Heritage Site. Blessed with a sunny climate and surrounded by picturesque, painstakingly terraced vineyards, it is just as famous for its good wines and fruit, especially its apricots, as for its history and stone memorials.

In addition to the historic treasures of Krems, Stein, the old Kuenringer town of Dürnstein and the monasteries at Göttweig and Melk, the many small towns with their Gothic churches, covered arcades on the vineyards and medieval castles are among the highlights of a drive through this region 'wrapped in the silver band of the Danube'.

Must-sees along the northern river bank are Spitz with the Museum of Navigation, St

The icon of Wachau – the baroque monastery at Dürnstein.

Michael with its bizarrely decorated filial church, Aggsbach, the wine-growing towns of Weißenkirchen, Joching and Wösendorf, and last but not least, Dürnstein with its monastery and legendary castle.

sprawled out at your feet. In good weather, you can even see large parts of the Eastern Alps.

㉑ Melk A real baroque icon salutes us from a rock outcrop 60 m (197 ft) above the south bank across the river, around 10 km (6 miles) east of the pilgrimage church. It's the Benedictine abbey of Melk with a church, two steeples and a facade of more than 360 m (393 yds) – undoubtedly one of the most magnificent of its kind in the world. This religious fortification, which was built in the early 18th century, impressively symbolizes the euphoria among the clerics and the nobility after their dual triumph – over the Reformation and over the Turks. There is exuberant splendour everywhere in the edifice: in the Emperor's Wing with the Emperor's Gallery, which is nearly 200 m (219 yds) long; in the marble hall with its frescoes by Paul Troger; in the vast library with approximately 100,000 volumes; and also in the church, with ceiling frescoes by Johann Michael Rottmayr.

Back on the northern riverbank, the B3 takes us past the Jauerling Nature Park via Aggsbach, Spitz, Weißenkirchen and Dürnstein to the spectacular transverse valley of the Wachau River. Many of these places have an interesting history, like the Aggstein Castle on a rock outcrop high above the Danube. It is said that a series of unscrupulous men abused the castle's position on the river to rob passing Danube boats and charge exorbitant tolls. The ruin of Dürnstein tells the tale of the capture of Richard the Lionheart and Blondel, the singer, who recognized him.

㉒ Wachau (see sidebar left).

㉓ Krems This town is located on the exact spot where the Danube trade route meets one of the main routes between the Alpine foothills and the Bohemian Forest, and where traders and mariners as far back as the early Middle Ages came to exchange their goods. This mercantile centre at the eastern entrance to the Wachau is not only one of the oldest, but also one of the most beautiful towns in the whole area. As a way into its restored alleyways, take the Steiner Tor ('Stone Gate'). From here, there is a circular walk across Corn Market to

sciences, as well as in music, the members of the Melk Abbey have chalked up some outstanding achievements. To this day, the monks continue to be active in counselling, economy, culture and tourism. Ever since it was founded, Melk Abbey has been an important spiritual and religious centre in Austria.

The Melk Abbey stands impressively above the Danube.

the Dominican Church, which houses the wine museum, and on to Gozzoburg on the High Market. From the gunpowder tower you have a beautiful view onto the more modern districts, the harbour and the Danube over to Göttweig Monastery. On the way back you go along the road, past such architectural gems as the Bürgerspitalkirche, Gögl House and the town hall.

At the western end of Krems is the town of Stein. Must-sees here are the Minorite and St Nicholas Churches and a number of magnificent buildings as well as a former monastery which now houses the 'House of Lower Austrian Wines'.

Driving along the Wagram, a steep slope where lovely vineyards drop colourfully and abruptly down towards the Dan-

ube, it takes just under thirty minutes to get to Tulln.

24 Tulln This town on the Danube, which started out as a Roman fort called Comagenis, has an impressive architectural ensemble of parish churches and a former charnel house. A visit to the mighty salt tower with its Roman core is also worth doing, and can easily be combined with a stroll along the riverside promenade. A museum with around ninety original paintings commemorates Egon Schiele, the town's favourite son and ground-breaking expressionist.

25 Klosterneuburg This small town right outside Vienna on the southern bank of the Danube is world-famous thanks to its Augustinian monastery. The

monumental building was built in the early 12th century by the Babenberg Duke Leopold III and soon after donated to the order. For centuries, it was the scientific centre of the country. The dazzling emperor's rooms, the emperor's staircase and the marble hall are the primary attractions. Don't miss the enamel Verdun Altar by Nicholas of Verdun in Leopold's Chapel. The monastery also houses the largest religious library in the country, a museum and a treasury.

26 Vienna (see p. 49). After ample time in Vienna, the capital of Austria, you can take an interesting excursion to Lake Neusiedl. Your best option is the A4 to Neusiedl on the lake's northern shore. Alternatively, carry on along the Danube.

27 Carnuntum Around 35 km (22 miles) east of Vienna, where the 'Amber Road' (between the Baltic Sea and the Mediterranean) and the East-West Route along the Danube meet, are the Roman remains of Carnuntum, south of the river. Nowhere else in Austria have archaeologists found such rich ancient heritage. The excavation site, officially made into an 'archaeological park' in 1996, comprises the whole of the civilian town with its network of ancient walls and streets, a reconstructed Diana

Large image: The Wachau spreads smoothly below the Vogelberg. Small images from the left: Melk Abbey staircase and library, Church of Stift Klosterneuburg, Carnuntum Museum.

The mighty Bratislava Castle towers high above the Danube with the New Bridge and the magnificent St. Martin's Cathedral.

Detour

Lake Neusiedl

This steppe lake in the northern Burgenland region, which is 30 km (18 miles) long and a maximum of 2 m (6.5 ft) deep, is not called the 'Sea of the Viennese' for nothing.

In summer, it is a paradise for water sports. For the rest of the year. It is a Mecca for amateur ornithologists who can observe a large number of rare birds in the reed belt around the lake that is 1–3-km wide (0.6–2-miles). From Illmitz, you can take regular guided tours through the national park by bike, horse-drawn carriage or on horseback.

The areas in the west, north and south of Lake Neusiedl (its south-eastern corner is part of Hungary) are among Austria's most famous wine-growing regions. Villages in the area like Rust, Mörbisch, Donnerskirchen, Breitenbrunn or Podersdorf are worth seeing because of their picturesque town centres

and neat farmhouses with stork's nests crowning their chimneys. From mid July to late August, operettas are regularly performed on the open-air stage in Mörbisch as part of the Lake Festival.

You definitely should not miss the 'excursion within the excursion' here to Eisenstadt, where you can visit the palace of the Esterházy princes and the mausoleum of Joseph Haydn in the Bergkirche church.

Temple and a long piece of the original Roman Limes Road (Border Road). A little further away are the ruins of a palace, baths, an amphitheatre and the Heathen's Gate. Many of the rich findings are on display in the Museum Carnuntinum in Bad Deutsch-Altenburg.

㉘ Bratislava When the Turks conquered Budapest in the middle of the 16th century and kept it for nearly 150 years, Bratislava, now the capital of Slovakia, was called Pozsony and was the capital of free Hungary until 1848. In modern times it was behind the Iron Curtain until 1989. Since then, it has not only forged closer ties to the Western world, but also undergone a radical beautification and rejuvenation.

The sins of socialist town planning cannot be undone, and the prefabricated tower blocks in Petržalka on the southern bank of the Danube, for example, will continue to be an eyesore for quite some time. Staré Mesto, by contrast, the largely car-free Old Town, has done itself up rather nicely. Its most important sights are St Martin's Cathedral, the archbishop's palace, the Slovak National Gallery, the National Theatre and Museum and the

castle residing above the river. East of Bratislava, Road 63 (E575) takes you down into the Danube Plains (Podunajsko), which are completely flat and extremely fertile. During the summer months fresh fruit and vegetable stands are everywhere. During World War II, this region was particularly hard hit. Reconstruction led to local towns looking very much alike.

This route, however, now takes us away from the Danube to the south – back through Austria to Fertőd in Hungary.

㉙ Fertőd/Esterházy-Palast Around 5 km (3 miles) east of Fertő-tó (the Hungarian name of Lake Neusiedl), we come to Fertöd and Esterházy Palace. The Esterházys are an old Hungarian dynasty from which many politicians and military men have come.

㉚ Győr This large city has an important harbour on the Danube and is worth seeing for its 12th-century cathedral which was given a baroque makeover in the 17th century.

㉛ Komárno/Komárom Located where the River Váh meets the Danube, the town has always

been of the utmost strategic importance. The Romans even had a fort here called Brigetio. In the course of the 19th century, the Habsburg Dynasty turned the town into a 'city of fortifications' like no other in the monarchy. After Ferenc I, King of Hungary, had found shelter from Napoleon's army in Komárno in 1809, it was made the central defence post of the Habsburg Empire.

Ever since the Treaty of Trianon (1920) marking the Danube as the border of the realm, the city has been divided into two parts. The former Old Town on the northern shore is now part of the Slovakian town of Komárno. On the Hungarian side, three fortifications are an interesting attraction for military history enthusiasts.

Monostor, the largest of the forts with 640 rooms and 4 km (2.5 miles) of underground shelters, is sometimes nicknamed 'Gibraltar of the Danube' and there are guided tours around it. The Igmánd fort, which is significantly smaller, houses a museum with findings from Roman times.

Viennese cathedrals: St. Peter's Church and St. Stephen's Cathedral.

Esterházy Palace was built by Prince Nicholas (1765–1833) in a Rococo style, with impressively large dimensions.

Vienna

Located on the 'beautiful blue Danube', the Austrian capital has a uniquely charming atmosphere and seems still to radiate the Old World feel of the Dual Monarchy.

Vienna, the old royal city and former centre of the 'multicultural' Habsburg Empire, has architecture and art treasures from all eras of its long history. As a result, you will need some time to explore this city, especially if you want to catch a bit of its famous atmosphere. Your best bet is in the 'Heurigen' wine taverns, in the coffee houses or on the traditional 'Naschmarkt' (literally 'Nibbles Market'). Definitely visit the Stephansdom with Romanesque, Gothic and late-Gothic sections, richly ornate facade and precious interior; the Hofburg, until 1918 the imperial residence with treasure chamber, emperor's rooms and palace chapel; the Art History Museum with its collection of European paintings; and the baroque Josefsplatz with Na-

Old Imperial Palace in Michaelerplatz

tional Library; the Gothic Augustinerkirche with its Capuchin crypt of the Habsburg emperors; the Spanish Riding School; the Karlskirche, the most beautiful baroque building in Vienna; the Museum of Applied Art; Belvedere Castle with Lower Belvedere (baroque museum) and Upper Belvedere (19th- and 20th-century paintings); Schönbrunn, a baroque Versailles imitation with park, Gloriette classical arcades with a beautiful view of the castle and town.

Detour

Puszta - the central European steppe

Driving east from Budapest on the M3 motorway and then from Füzesabony on the N33, you reach Hortobágy, Hungary's oldest national park. Here, ancient prairie lands stretch out between the Tisza and Debrecen Rivers, the last vestige of the puszta landscape that once covered the entire steppe. Crossing this grassland by car (it was designated a UNESCO World Heritage Site in 1999), you can hardly see anything but flat countryside. In order to see it in all its beauty you need to go ex-

32 Tata This spa town at the bottom of Gerecse Hill gives off an atmosphere of cosiness and charm with its lakes and complex labyrinth of rivers and canals. But its location and its history have not been kind to the 'City of Water' – for 150 years it was situated on the border between the territories of the Habsburgs and the Ottoman Empire, which resulted in consistent large-scale devastation of its buildings

But every cloud has a silver lining. In around 1730, the Esterházy princes, then rulers of the town, initiated the reconstruction of the Tata, whose myriad baroque architectural ensembles shape the town to this day. Be sure to visit the ruins of the castle, built in the 14th century and later expanded into a magnificent Renaissance Palace by Matthias Corvinus. Don't miss Esterházy Castle and the former synagogue, which houses about 100 plaster-of-Paris copies of famous antique sculptures.

Halfway between Tata and Budapest – you can see it from the M1 motorway – is an apogee of Hungary's Romance architecture reaching high up into the sky. The Zsámbék Church itself actually collapsed in the middle of the 18th century, along with the adjacent Premonstratensian priory.

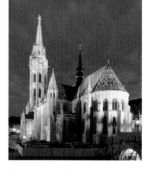

Even as ruins, though, the colossal dimensions of the building are truly spectacular.

33 Budapest The Magyar metropolis has around two million inhabitants on a location where the Romans had already founded a town called Aquincum. Like many others, the two medieval communities of Ofen and Pest were devastated by the Mongols in 1241.

After the reconstruction, Ofen became Hungary's most important city, but was overtaken in the early 19th century by its sister town of Pest. The two cities were finally united in 1872. In the early 20th century, Budapest was considered the 'Paris of the East', a reputation it is still hoping to regain despite the devastation of World War II and more than four decades of Soviet rule. The first thing on a long list of things to do just has to be the castle mountain. It is here on this limestone rock, nearly 1.5 km (0.9 miles) long, above the right bank of the Danube that the country's historical heart has been beating ever since the first king's castle was constructed upon it by Béla IV. Combining the Matthias Church, the Fisherman's Bastion and the castle, which houses several first-rate museums, this quarter has some of the most important sights in the city. And there are also some unforgettable panoramic views down to the city and to the river. The view from the neighbouring Gellért Mountain is just as scenic.

The majority of the city's sights are located on the left bank of the Danube, in the Pest district. Once you leave behind the narrow Old Town centre, the cityscape is typified by extensive Wilhelminian ring and radial roads.

You can visit St Stephen's Basilica, the National Opera, the National Museum, the Grand Synagogue and, directly by the river, the large market hall and the even larger houses of parliament. Out in the city forest are Vajdahunyad Castle, the Széchenyi Baths and the Museum of Fine Arts.

A must-see is, of course, the baroque palace in Gödöllő 30 km (18 miles) north-east of the city centre, where Emperor Franz Joseph I and his wife Elizabeth ('Sisi') lived.

Impressions from Budapest: Fisherman's Bastion (above), Heroes' Square and St. Matthias Church.

ploring on foot, by bike, by boat or by horse-drawn carriage. Right next to the famous Bridge of Nine Arches in Hortobágy Village, a museum takes you back to the everyday life of the Puszta herdsmen, a lifestyle that has all but disappeared. You can encounter animal breeds such as grey cattle, woolly boars and Raczka sheep. Riding performances, bird watching and a meal of the local savoury pancakes round off your visit.

Sanssouci The rococo ensemble, whose name means 'Carefree', is the most visited attraction in Potsdam, capital of Brandenburg. You can take a stroll through the summer residence of Friedrich II.

Wartburg Legend has it that the castle was founded in 1067. Located at the edge of the Thuringian Forest it was probably the site of the German minstrels' contest. Luther translated the bible into German here.

Karlovy Vary This spa town on the Eger River has some healing springs as well as historical and modern spa facilities.

Wachau The forest and wine-growing area of Wachau extends from Melk to Krems – a transverse valley of the Danube that is 18 miles long.

Melk The Benedictine abbey high above the Danube is baroque architecture in all its perfection.

Vienna The Austrian capital is always worth a visit. The sights in this metropolis on the Danube are simply overwhelming. Pictured here is the Austrian Parliament Building.

Berlin The old and new German capital has become even more attractive since the Berlin Wall came down. Located on the Spree and Havel rivers, it has a lot of greenery, vibrant nightlife and myriad cultural highlights. Pictured is the Charlottenburg Palace.

Meißen The centre of this porcelain town and 'Cradle of Saxony' has a medieval atmosphere. Above it is the towering cathedral and the Albrecht Castle.

Saxon Switzerland Whether you prefer hiking or a boat trip on the Elbe River, the bizarre plateaus, rock outcrops and gorges of the Elbe Sandstone Mountains near Dresden are fascinating. Most of the area has been made into a national park.

Prague The Czech capital is located on the Vltava River and has an unusual skyline. Hradčany Castle, Charles Bridge and the art-nouveau buildings of this 'Golden City' are unique. This photograph is of Týn Church.

České Budějovice The centre of this world-famous city of breweries and beer is the market square with Samson Fountain.

Český Krumlov Its location on a curve in the Vltava River, its dreamy Old Town, and the huge castle on the hill make the Bohemian town of Krumlov a real gem.

Budapest One of the landmarks of the Hungarian capital is the mighty suspension bridge (1839–49). The list of further sights in the metropolis on the Danube is a long one – from Fisherman's Bastion and the crown of St Stephen in the National Museum to the neo-Gothic Houses of Parliament and the terrific art-nouveau bath houses.

Map labels

GERMANY

Neubrandenburg · Szczecin · Hamburg · Magdeburg · **BERLIN** · **Potsdam** · Beelitz · Trebbin · Frankfurt (O.) · Luckenwalde · Kloster Zinna · Lutherstadt Wittenberg · Jüterbog · Frankfurt (O.) · Herzberg · Cottbus · Leipzig · Elsterwerda · Torgau · Großenhain · Görlitz · Nordhausen · Weimar · Leipzig · Moritzburg · **Erfurt** · Jena · **Meißen** · **Dresden** · N.P. Hainich · **Eisenach** · Altenburg · Bad Schandau · Pirna · Wartburg · Gotha · **Gera** · N.P. Sächs. Schweiz · Suhl · **Chemnitz** · Ústí n.L. · Děčín · Liberec · Nürnberg · Hof · Most · Mladá Boleslav · Chomutov · Litoměřice · Hradec Králové · Mělník · Loket · Karlovy Vary · Bayreuth · Hořovičky · Mariánské Lázně · Karlštejn · **PRAGUE** · Brno

CZECH REPUBLIC

Příbram · Milín · Plzeň · Zvíkov · Nepomuk · N.P. Šumava · Písek · Tábor · Vodňany · CHKO Třeboňsko · Holašovice · Hluboká · **České Budějovice** · Český Krumlov · CHKO Novohradské hory · Vyšší Brod · Freistadt · Znojmo · Brno · CHKO Malé Karpaty · Trenčín · Krems · Tulln · Wachau · Klosterneuburg · **Bratislava** · Danube · Maria Taferl · **Linz** · **VIENNA** · Zvolen · Hollókő · Bükki N.P. · **Miscolc** · Passau · Grein · Ybbs · Melk · Carnuntum · **SLOVAKIA** · Duna-Ipoly N.P. · Eger · Polgár · Enns · Salzburg · Eisenstadt · **Győr** · Komárno · Füzesabony · Hortobágy · Graz · N.P. Neusiedler See · Komárom · Tata · Aszód · Tiszafüred · **AUSTRIA** · Sopron · Csorna · Öreg-tó · Bicske · Gödöllő · Alföld · Hortobágyi N.P. · Fertőd · Pannonhalma · Székesfehérvár · **BUDAPEST** · Szombathely · **HUNGARY** · Szekszárd · Kecskemét

---

The Alps

Looking at any map, it is immediately clear that the Alps form a sort of backbone for the European landmass. This route will take you on a journey of exploration through every facet of this complex terrain, from the shores of Lake Geneva to a world of rock and ice around Zermatt and Grindelwald, from glamorous winter resorts to the fairy-tale scenery of the Dolomites, and from the Grossglockner High Alpine Road to the Salzburg region and the birthplace of Mozart.

Route profile:

Length: approx. 715 miles
Time required: at least 12–14 days

For many, the Alps are the 'most beautiful mountains in the world'. All told, this high Central European range covers an area of 200,000 sq km (77,200 sq mi). The western section alone is home to about fifty peaks rising over 4,000 m (13,124 ft). There are many more in the 3,000 and 2,000 m (9,843 and 6,562 ft) range – nearly 2,000 in Austria alone. The range features the jagged limestone spikes of the Dolomites, bulky gneiss and granite massif, and lower layers made of sandstone, slate and flysch. It stretches from mighty Mont Blanc, at 4,810-m (15,782-ft) the tallest peak in the Alps, to the gentle knolls of the Wienerwald (Vienna Woods).

Famous rivers such as the Rhine and the Rhône, the Po and the Save, the Drava and the Inn originate in the Alps, and vast lakes such as Lake Constance, Lake Geneva and Lake Lucerne are all nestled in their valleys. Immense waterfalls like the ones in Krimml, Lauterbrunnen, Gastein or on the Tosa thunder down granite faces, while glistening glaciers continue to hold their own in the highest and more remote areas – though the effects of climate change can be seen.

The main charm of the area lies in the juxtaposition of contrasts; the Côte d'Azur is just a stone's throw from the foothills of the Maritime Alps, and the glaciers of the Bernese Oberland are not far from the Wallis (Valais) wine region. An hour's drive will take you from the rocky peaks of the Dolomites to the cypress-lined lanes of Lago di Garda, and it wouldn't take much longer to get from the icy cold cirque lakes of the Hohe Tauern to the warm swimming lakes of Carinthia.

The mightiest mountain ranges in the world, such as the Himalayas or the Andes, might have more exalted reputations and are more sparsely populated, but what sets the Alps apart is indeed their human dimension. Extreme mountaineers do not need permits, visas or porters to indulge in their passion.

When it comes to infrastructure, accommodation and dining, people seeking a more comfortable experience will be delighted by the ease of travel and the pletho-

ra of options. Even the desire for a more urban environment can be satisfied in cities such as Grenoble, Bolzano and Innsbruck. And yet those seeking temporary refuge from civilization will also find more than enough solitude on hikes, climbs or just relaxing in a meadow all day long – all without bumping into another single person.However, what makes the journey along the backbone of Europe so fascinating is not just the spectacular scenery, but rather the distinctive and diverse cultural traditions that seem to change as often as the landscape, and the undeniable natural charm of the Alps. Rural architecture, customs and handicrafts form an 'alpine heritage' that is once again being enthusiastically promoted in many places – without necessarily being motivated by tourism.

Aside from the dominant peaks like the Matterhorn, the Jungfrau, the Eiger, the Mönch, Bernina, Marmolada, the Tre Cime di Lavaredo and the Grossglockner, mention should certainly be made of the fruit and wine growers along the Rhône or Adige, the anonymous architects of the Engadine or East Tyrolean manors, the thousands and thousands of alpine dairy farmers and dairy-maids, and the creators of all the frescos, sgraffiti, shingle roofs, and carved altars in the village churches, castles and manors.

Located near Montreux on an island in Lake Geneva, Château de Chillon consists of 25 fascinating interlocking buildings.

Lake Geneva

Lake Geneva is the largest lake in the Alps, its elongated crescent shape covering roughly 584 sq km (225 sq mi) between the Savoy and Waadtland (Vaud) Alps and the Jura Mountains. Sixty percent of it is in Switzerland and forty percent to France. The lake is 372 m (1,221 ft) above sea level, 72 km (45 mi) long, 14 km (9 mi) across at its widest point, and 310 m (1,017 ft) deep. It is fed by the Rhône River, which rises at a glacier. On northern shore are the La Côte and Lavaux territories, known for their particular beauty. Picturesque fortresses, vineyard towns and quaint old villages abound in this very popular holiday region, set against the backdrop of gently rolling hills and steep mountains scattered with grapevine terraces.

The most famous towns on the lake, apart from the big cities of Geneva and Lausanne, are Coppet, Nyon – a garrison town going back to the time of Julius Caesar, Rolle, Morges, Cully, the upscale resort towns of Vevey and Montreux, and Villeneuve near the Rhône Delta.

The most famous towns along the French southern banks of the lake include Thonon-les-Bains, the ritzy thermal spa resort of Evian-les-Bains, and the home of Evian water.

Recommended vista points enjoy the panoramic views of the lake and landscape include Signal de Bougy (above Rolle), Signal de Sauvabelin (above Lausanne), the Grand Roc at Meillerie and, east of Lausanne, the Corniche de Lavaux, which connects a series of reputable wine-growing towns amidst the vineyards high above the lake. A ride onboard one of the eight old paddle boats is a great way to see the lake.

Those exploring the Alps will quickly discover the charms of this historically significant and culturally diverse region: from elegant resort towns to quaint hamlets, and from the Mediterranean-like shores of Lake Geneva to remote mountain stations among the high glaciers and peaks.

① Geneva Your journey begins at the south-westernmost point of Switzerland at the end of Lake Geneva, known by French-speaking locals as Lac Léman. Geneva is nestled among the Jura and Savoy Alps and sits on one of the lake's many bays. The city's most famous landmark is the Fontaine du Jet d'Eau, which shoots its water up to 145 m (476 ft) into the air. The 'Protestant Rome', where Jean Calvin preached his rigorous reform ideas some 450 years ago, and Henri Dunant founded the Red Cross in 1864, is today a truly international city. One-third of its residents are foreigners, and 200 international organizations, including the United Nations (UN) and the World Health Organization (WHO), are based here.

But apart from the diplomats, the expensive clocks and fancy cigars, there are also a number of other attractions: St Peter's Cathedral with its archaeological burial site, the adjacent Place du Bourg-de-Four, the ornate Museum of Art and History, the Palais des Nations – today UN headquarters – and the monument to native son, Jean-Jacques Rousseau.

Follow the A1 along the northern shores of Lake Geneva toward the next Swiss city on the lake, Lausanne.

② Lausanne The metropolis of Vaud is a reputable university and trade fair city as well as the home of the International Olympic Committee. Tucked in among exclusive residential neighborhoods and spanning several hills, the Cité, or Old Town, is best accessed by the funicular railway from the port district of Ouchy. The main at-

traction there is the early-Gothic cathedral with its rose window, while the most interesting of the many museums are the Art Brut Collection and the Pipe Museum.

③ Vevey and Montreux These two resort towns form the center of the wine-indulged 'Vaud Riviera' and have enjoyed international prominence since the early 19th century.

Vevey, where the first Swiss chocolate was made at the start of the 19th century, is also the home of Nestlé, the largest foodstuffs corporation in the world. Montreux is known primarily for the annual TV awards show, the 'Golden Rose', its worldfamous jazz festival and the Château de Chillon, located on the shores of the lake just 3 km (2 mi) to the south-east of town. Heading away from the lake, your route follows the Rhône

The Cathedral of St. Peter rises from the centre of the old town of Geneva, where John Calvin preached and where his chair can still be visited.

Detour

Bern

Just 150 years after it was founded in the late 12th century, Bern had already become the mightiest city-state north of the Alps. It has been the national capital since the

Schützenbrunnen fountain and clock tower in Old Town Bern.

Federal State of Switzerland was created in 1848. The Old Town, situated neatly on a bend in the Aar River, a tributary of the Rhine, continues to radiate the comfortable aura of entrenched middle-class wealth. Its cobblestone lanes reflect the grid-like pattern of many medieval settlements and are lined by tightly packed, shingled guild and burgher houses. The center is a UNESCO World Heritage Site characterized by eleven historic fountains and the 4 miles of covered arcades that invite you to take a stroll even on rainy days.

Bern's most famous landmark is the Zytglogge, clock tower from the 13th century, and the lategothic St Vincent's Cathedral. The Protestant Church of the Holy Spirit provides a stunning example of Baroque architecture, and the Bundeshaus, or Federal Assembly Building symbolizes Bern's function as the political center of Switzerland.

The so-called Bärengraben, or Bear Pit, is inhabited by some of Bern's furry animal mascots and is a curious place indeed.

Valley through Martigny and Sion to Visp, where the road turns right into the Matter Valley. Park the car in Täsch about 30 km (19 mi) further on, as the most famous Swiss mountain town can only be reached by railway, bus or taxi.

ing mountaineers from the British Isles in the mid-19th century who became the first to conquer the imposing four-sided pyramid in 1865, led by locals.

Today, 3,000 people flood the 'summit of all European summits'

way on the continent, is unforgettable. In forty minutes, it climbs up to 3,089 m (10,135 ft) over a stretch of 10 km (6 mi) before you continue another 400 m (1,312 ft) by cable car.

The mountain station provides a 360-degree panoramic view of twenty-nine peaks in the 4,000 m (13,124 ft) range.

❹ **Zermatt and Matterhorn** The most renowned village in the Wallis region owes its fame to the 4,478-m-high (14,692-ft) Matterhorn, the primary icon of the Swiss Alps. The region's popularity was developed predominantly by dar-

every summer. In the town itself, a number of old houses attest to the pioneer days. Particularly worth seeing are the Alpine Museum, and the 150-year-old Hotel Monte Rosa. A ride on the Gornergrat Railway, the highest cog rail-

❺ **Brig** Back in the Rhône Valley, follow the river upstream to the capital of the Oberwallis region. Once an important trading hub for goods being transported over the Simplon, Furka and Grimsel passes, Brig experienced its heyday in the 17th and 18th centuries.

The main attraction in Brig is Stockalper Castle, an extensive late-Renaissance complex whose imposing towers and golden onion domes can be seen from afar. In the suburb of Glis,

Large image: Twilight over the Stellisee with a view of the Matterhorn. Small image: Rue du Lac in Vevey.

Furka-Oberalp Railway

Whether you take the St Gotthard, Grimsel, Furka or Oberalp Pass, the 2,000-m-high (6,562-ft) passes are generally closed off for four to six months during the

winter in every region of the Alps, which forms part of the watershed between the Rhine and Rhône. During this time, if you want to avoid masses of snow and the risk of avalanches, you can load your car onto the car-

riages of the Furka-Oberalp Railway. While you let the breathtaking mountain scenery pass by from your compartment, the narrow-gauge locomotive handles the transport. Loading ramps are located in Oberwald-Realp for

Detour

Lower Engadine

The charm of this valley landscape lies in its originality, sprawling as it does at the feet of the Silvretta cluster. Zernez, at the confluence of the Inn and Spöl rivers, was almost completely destroyed by fire in 1872 and has barely any of its historic buildings left, but it is the starting point for many wonderful hikes into the Swiss National Park (172 sq km/66 sq mi) – the first of its kind in Europe (established in 1909) and the only one in Switzerland. Guarda and Ardez are the most beautiful towns of the Lower Engadine. Both come under strict protection as listed historic monuments and consist of irresistibly quaint Engadine houses. Often, they are

hundred-year-old estates with artistic sgraffiti gazebos, carefully paneled parlors and sleeping quarters behind walls more than a yard thick. The valley widens after Ardez, which is also the site of a tourist center, Scuol, which is dominated by Tarasp Castle. The town was called the 'Queen of the Alps Bathing Towns' until 1915 because of its twenty healing wells, but it fell into a bit of a slumber, only to be brought back to life in the 1990s by the opening of an ultra-modern spa and wellness resort. Further east, the valley narrows again, and becomes wilder and more remote. A few small villages, such as Sent, Ramosch and Tschlin, nestle into the narrow terraces before the road and river cross over the Austrian border beyond Martina, near the ravine at the Finstermünz Pass.

Chamois live in the Swiss National Park.

it is worth paying a visit to the lavish St Mary's pilgrimage church. From here, head west again along the Rhône as far as Höge Steg, then take the car on the train through the 14.6-km-long (9-mi) Lötschberg tunnel. From Kandersteg you will go through Thun, along the northern shore of Lake Thun, past Oberhofen Castle and into the town of Interlaken. It is especially worthwhile making a detour beforehand to the Swiss capital of Bern, roughly 25 km (16 mi) from Thun. You can easily explore the perfectly preserved Old Town on foot.

6 Interlaken Situated between Lake Thun and Lake Brienz on the 'Bödeli', the Aar River floodplain, Interlaken was named after the inter lacus monastery, founded in the 12th century. It has long been one of the cornerstones of Swiss alpine tourism as the starting point for excursions into the Jungfrau region. The Höhenweg, lined with hotel mansions from the turn of the 20th century, affords breathtaking panoramic views of the snow-capped peaks to the south.

7 Grindelwald A 20-km (12 mi) detour will take you to Grin-

delwald, even closer to the Jungfrau region, the first alpine landscape to become a UNESCO World Natural Heritage Site, in 2001, as home to forty-seven peaks over 4,000 m (13,124 ft) and the Great Aletsch Glacier. The Grindelwald climatic spa resort is encircled by the three mighty peaks of the Eiger at 3,970 m (13,026 ft), the Wetterhorn at 3,701 m (12,143 ft) and the Schreckhorn at 4,078 m (13,380 ft). It has been the greatest tourist draw in the Bernese Oberland for over 150 years. Don't miss a ride on the Jungfrau railway from the Kleine Scheidegg pass through Eigerwand and Mönch to Europe's highest train station – the Jungfraujoch at 3,454 m (11,333 ft). From Grindelwald, it's back to Interlaken and then south along Lake Brienz over the Grimsel Pass (2,165 m/7,103 ft) and the Furka Pass (2,431 m/7976 ft) to Andermatt.

8 Andermatt The highland resort town of Andermatt is at the junction of the north-south route between Lake Lucerne and St Gotthard, where Wallis (Valais) turns into the Upper Rhine Valley region. It has a lovely rococo church and a carefully designed valley museum, and is an

the Base Tunnel beneath the 2,431-m-high (7,976 ft) Furka Pass. To conquer the Oberalp Pass (2,044 m/6,706 ft), you will have to wheel your vehicle onto the tracks in Andermatt or Sedrun/Camischolas.

With the Schöllenenbahn you cross the impressive Schöllenen Gorge on the Teufelsbrücke (Devil's Bridge) on the way over the Gotthard Pass.

ideal starting point for hikes and mountain tours. For travelers, however, it is primarily a traffic hub. Continuing east, you have to cross the Oberalp Pass (2,044 m/6,706 ft), before skirting the Upper Rhine tributary to Flims. The Furka-Oberalp railway is a nice alternative to the passes.

9 Flims This spa resort, where Rhaeto-Romanic dialects are still spoken, is situated on a ledge in a sunny high valley that owes its existence to a massive landslide during prehistoric times.
It comprises the old Flims-Dorf center and the new Flims-Waldhaus hotel complex. The town and its romantic surroundings offer a variety of sporting activities in summer, and in winter it joins Laax and Falera to form a vast ski area known as the 'White Arena'.Before heading to the mountains of Graubünden (Grisons) take the 10-km (6-mi) detour at Reichenau to Chur.

10 Chur This cantonal capital, which obtained its Roman town charter in the 3rd century and was the first diocesan town north of the Alps in the 4th century, puts off many newcomers with its unsightly strip of highrise buildings. But a charming Old Town with a number of his-

toric treasures lies hidden behind this unfortunate blemish. The most important of these are the St Mary's Cathedral and museum, the Winegrowing and Rhaetian museums, the Bündner Art Museum with works by Chur painter, Angelika Kauffmann.

11 Via Mala Back in Reichenau, you route initially heads upstream along the Lower Rhine. Over the millennia, this tributary cut a 6-km-long (4 mile) and up to 600-m-deep (1,969 ft) gorge into the rock. The romantic Via Mala is best experienced from the old road built in the early 19th century (a branch off the A13 about 1 km/0.6 mi beyond Rongellen). At the south end, in Zillis, pay a visit to St Martin's Church for its painted wooden ceiling.
Back in Thusis, the route now heads to Tiefencastel, in the Albula Valley, and then through parts of the very steep Albula Pass (2,321 m/7,615 ft) into the Upper Engadine region.

12 St Moritz This glamorous resort town in the heart of the Upper Engadine is considered

Aletsch Glacier (above) and the wild ravine of the Via Mala (right) are just two of the highlights of the route.

Merano: Tyrol Castle

Perched high above Merano and the Vinschgau is a castle that is a detailed reflection of Tyrol's eventful history and gives the en-

Müstair Benedictine Monastery

Where the B38 from Stilfser Joch reaches the Adige Valley, a detour heads along the B40 towards the Resia Pass as far as Schluderns. From there, it climbs over the Ofen Pass back to Zernez in the Lower Engadine region.
Müstair, located just 1 km (0.6 mi) over the border at an altitude of 1,240 m (4,068 ft), welcomes its guests with a monument known throughout Europe: the St John's Benedictine Monastery. The building, which gave the town its name (Müstair means minster and is derived from the Latin monasterium), was founded by the bishop in Chur at the end of the 8th century and was subsequently expanded on several occasions. The complex's main attraction is the nearly 1,200-year-old minster.
Not very imposing on the outside, the monastery houses a treasure that prompted UNESCO to declare it a World Heritage Site back in 1983: around ninety frescoes from the 8th to the 12th centuries, which two art historians unearthed rather accidentally under a new painted surface at the start of the 20th century. The oldest of these date back to the time of Charlemagne and depict scenes from the life and passion of Christ, as well as the Last Judgement. They are considered the world's most extensive cluster of frescos preserved from Carolingian times. Roughly 400 years newer, but just as impressive, are the Romanesque paintings depicting the martyrdom of St Stephen and other religious themes.

the cradle of winter tourism and, along with Davos, the most upscale address in Graubünden. It hit the world stage as the two-time host of the Winter Olympics (1928 and 1948).
Located at the gateway to unique lake scenery (Lake St Moritz, Lake Silvaplana, and Lake Sils), it offers a wide range of outdoor sporting options in both winter and summer. The Cresta Run, or 'skeleton sled run', and the bob run to Celerina are legendary.
A varied programme of nightly entertainment meets the needs of the guests, who are as famous as they are wealthy.
From St Moritz, the B27 takes you down the Inn River through Samedan and Zuoz to the Lower Engadine region – a worthwhile detour for those who appreciate the old-world charm of Graubünden villages.
The main route now heads from St Moritz over the Pontresina and Bernina Pass at 2,323 m (7,622 ft), past the dream-like panorama of the glaciated Bernina Group, into the valley of the upper Adda, the Veltlin, and into Italy.
From here, the spectacular Stilfser Joch pass rises to 2,578 m (8,458 ft) at the foot of the Ortler (Ortles) peak and heads to

Bormio before taking you through the Trafoi Valley down to the Etsch (Adige), where it is worth making a detour through Schludern (Sluderno) to St John's Monastery in the Val Müstair. Continue east to Merano.

⑬ Merano This city on the Passer River blossomed under

the rule of the counts of Tyrol until the mid-14th century. After the Habsburgs took over co-rule in South Tyrol and moved the residence to Innsbruck, Merano's significance waned. It did not return to the spotlight until the 19th century, when word spread about the healing effect of the local springs and mild cli-

tire region its name. Tyrol Castle, built by local counts in 1140–60, experienced its golden age in the 14th century under Margarethe Maultasch, when it resisted the siege by King Charles of Bohemia. Once the royal residence had been moved to Innsbruck, the castle began to fall into a state of disrepair. After extensive restorations, the castle, which can be reached on foot in just twenty minutes, is now home to a regional museum. The Romanesque entrances at the forecourt of the great hall and the chapel entrance are gems of art history.

The cute Tyrol Castle above Merano.

mate. Reputable figures began coming in droves from all over Europe to seek rest and recuperation.The main sites in the Old Town, with its narrow lanes, quaint arcades and old burgher houses, include the Gothic St Nicholas Church (with the St Barbara Chapel), the Hospital Church and the sovereigns' castle with 15th-century frescos in the chapel. It is also worth taking a walk through the elegant residential area of Obermais.

⑭ Bolzano The capital of South Tyrol is located at the confluence of the Isarco and the Adige rivers and is not only the economic center of the region, but also a hub of alpine art and culture. A stroll through the narrow lanes between Lauben, the Kornplatz and the Obstmarkt re-

veals a charming Old Town that dates back to the Middle Ages. Highlights include the Dominican and Franciscan monasteries, Maretsch Castle, Runkelstein Fort, the City Museum, and the old parish church in the Gries district, with part of an altar by Michael Pacher.South-east of Bolzano, the SS241 takes you into the dreamy landscape of the Dolomites, littered with breathtaking limestone towers and peaks. The Karer Pass (with a view of the Rose Garden), the Fassa Valley and Passo Sella are the next stops, and the jagged rock formations here never fail to impress.

The road heads along the twisting SS242 with a view of Sassolungo toward the Val Gardena through Ortisei until you reach the vast Val d'Isarco. Continuing

north, you will arrive in Klausen. From there you can take a short detour to get a stunning view of the Funes Valley.

On the way back through the Isarco and Gardena valleys, turn off on SS243 after the town of Plan and head towards the Passo Gardena. A breathtaking backdrop of giant rock walls unfolds as you pass the Sella Group via Colfosco and Corvara. As you cross the Passo di Campolongo you will be further delighted by the geological wonders here before reaching the 'Great Dolomite Road' which leads to Cortina d'Ampezzo.

⑮ Cortina d'Ampezzo This famous spa and winter sports resort is surrounded by some of the most beautiful 3,000-m-high (9,843 ft) peaks in the region. Indeed, they contain the very epitome of Dolomite magnificence, the Tre Cime de Lavaredo, which come into view as you make your way toward Misurina. The next stops are Schluderbach and Toblach. You are in the Drava Valley here, but will soon cross into Austria and arrive in Lienz just under 40 km (25 mi) away.

⑯ Lienz The capital of East Tyrol is surrounded by splendid mountains and is home to a

number of charming buildings including St Andreas Parish Church, with the tomb of the last count of Görz, and the baroque St Michael's subsidiary church. Bruck Castle has Tyrol's largest homeland museum, and the city's Roman roots are evidenced by the graveyards of its predecessor, Aguntum.

⑰ Heiligenblut Over the Iselsberg at 1,204 m (3,950 ft) and through the Upper Möll Valley (B107), you arrive in the ever popular pilgrimage and mountaineering town of Heiligenblut. The church here, with its pointed tower standing against the stunning backdrop of the Grossglockner, Austria's highest peak at 3,798 m (12,461 ft), is a longtime favorite among photographers.

From here, you follow one of the most impressive mountain roads in the world, the Grossglockner High Alpine Road, which has run from Carinthia through the main alpine ridge to the Fusch Valley

Above: The small chapel at the Dreizinnenhütte seems tiny against the background of the mighty Drei Zinnen. Left side: View over St. Moritz and the lake; Laubengasse in Merano. Left: Stilfser Joch.

The Grossglockner High Alpine Road

With twenty-seven hairpin turns, this 48-km (30 mi) panoramic road runs above the Hohe Tauern National Park between Heiligenblut and Fusch. Access roads lead to Edelweiss Peak and the Kaiser-Franz Joseph's Heights, with a unique view over the Grossglockner and the 10-km (6 mi) Pasterze Glacier. Brochures at the toll booths provide information on the exact route. The road is open from the end of April until roughly early November.

near Salzburg since 1935. It is also in the Hohe Tauern National Park.

⑱ Werfen From the end of the valley at Bruck-Fusch (Lake Zeller is just a few miles away), follow the Salzach upstream through Lend and the Pongau to Bischofshofen and Werfen. The picturesque Hohenwerfen Fort is perched above the quaint 12th-century market place here. The fort was erected by Archbishop Gebhard around 1077, to ensure control over the Lueg Pass. Those who climb the steep path from the parking lot into the inner ward will get a good feeling for how daunting this fortress must have once been for would-be attackers.
Another must-see here is the Eisriesenwelt or 'World of the Ice Giants', the largest ice caves in the world.

⑲ Hallein The 'small Hall', about 25 km (16 mi) down the Salzach, was a center for salt production from the 13th century to 1989. The precious substance has been mined from the Dürrnberg for 4,500 now. The Celts were specialists at this, and their culture is today documented at an open-air museum, the Celts Museum, down in the valley on the edge of this lively city with its charming Old Town.
The mine has been converted into an ornate display that is open year-round.

⑳ Salzburg Finale furioso on the Salzach: You actually get the impression that the Creator and his earthly helpers wanted to demonstrate clearly to the people here that it is possible to create a beautiful harmony between the European spirit and a benevolent natural environment. The cathe-

Geneva Numerous international companies and organizations are based here. The city's attractions include St Peter's Cathedral, the Museum of Art and History, the Palais des Nations and the 145-m-high (476-ft) Fontaine du Jet d'Eau.

Lake Thun Mediterranean-like vegetation characterizes the Lake Thun area, at an altitude of roughly 560 m (1,837 ft). Oberhofen Castle on the north shore is worth a visit.

Bernese Alps Eiger, Mönch and Jungfrau are the best-known mountains in the western Alps. Many peaks of the 'Bernese Alps' reach heights of over 4,000 m (13,124 ft) and have impressive glaciers.

Stilfser Joch This alpine pass at 2,757 m (9,046 ft) runs along the border of Lombardy, Trentino and South Tyrol and affords fantastic views. The passage was opened in 1826.

Aletsch Glacier The largest glacier in mainland Europe: 170 sq km (66 sq mi) and 25 km (16 mi) long.

Detour

The Berchtesgaden Region

This German national park is also referred to as the 'Yellowstone of the German Alps', a name coined in the 19th century that is no ex-aggeration. The dominant feature is the 2,713-m (8,901-ft) Watz-mann, a truly breathtaking peak, but the number one tourist mag-net is the 8-km-long (5-mi) Königssee lake. A hike to a fa-mous painters' enclave or a boat ride to the St Batholomä Penin-sula are also worthwhile.

In Berchtesgaden, be sure to vis-it the salt mines and the associ-ated museum.

---

dral, residence, collegiate church, St Peter's Abbey, Nonnberg Mon-astery, the Getreidegasse and, above all, mighty Hohensalzburg Fortress certainly speak for it. Salzburg, on the left bank of the Salzach, with its large squares and narrow lanes, myriad foun-tains and statues, and the vivid marble and stucco work, all form a unique combination of urban design that continues to inspire artists from all over the world and attract admirers in their droves.

Long in the shadow of the prince-bishop center on the left bank, however, is the district lo-cated on the east bank, with Mi-rabell Park and Castle, Mozart's home, the Marionette Theater, the St Sebastian Cemetery and the tiny alleyways at the foot of the Kapuzinerberg mountain. It offers a multitude of first-class tourist attractions, and you should not miss a visit to Hell-brunn Castle and Anif Water Castle.

Those wanting to experience an-other alpine gem should head along the B305 from Salzburg to Berchtesgaden and the national park of the same name, located just 20 km (12 mi) away.

Mozart

The ' Master of all Masters' was born January 27, 1756, at Getreidegasse 9 in Salz-burg. Today, the house is one of the most important memorials to the composer. Wolfgang Amadeus Mozart received his basic musical education from his father. At the age of six, he traveled far and wide for auditions, but despite a three-year trip around Europe and journeys to Italy, Munich and Vienna, the city on the Salzach re-mained the center of his per-sonal and professional life until 1781.

Left side: The glacier path Pasterze at the foot of the Grossglockner leads past moraines and lakes, which created the melted ice. Left: Celtic Museum in Hallein.

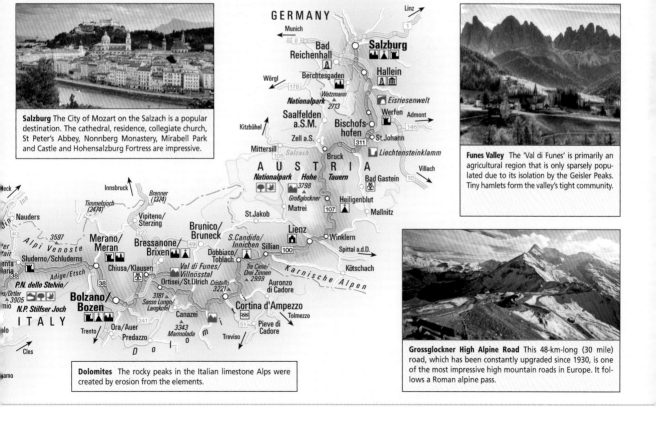

Salzburg The City of Mozart on the Salzach is a popular destination. The cathedral, residence, collegiate church, St Peter's Abbey, Nonnberg Monastery, Mirabell Park and Castle and Hohensalzburg Fortress are impressive.

Funes Valley The 'Val di Funes' is primarily an agricultural region that is only sparsely popu-lated due to its isolation by the Geisler Peaks. Tiny hamlets form the valley's tight community.

Dolomites The rocky peaks in the Italian limestone Alps were created by erosion from the elements.

Grossglockner High Alpine Road This 48-km-long (30 mile) road, which has been constantly upgraded since 1930, is one of the most impressive high mountain roads in Europe. It fol-lows a Roman alpine pass.

Route 5: Netherlands and Belgium
Between Amsterdam and Bruges

Flatlands, canals, dykes, windmills, clogs, and medieval houses reflected in the canals and waterways – these are all the things we associate with the Netherlands and Belgium, along with charming landscapes covered in vibrant fields of tulips, famous sea ports and bustling cities with old markets, squares and town halls.

Route profile:

Length: approx. 400 km (249 mi)
Time required: at least 8–10 days
When to go: Generally from May to October. Holland is at its most beautiful inspring when everything is in bloom. From June to late August, southerly winds bring sunny days. At that time, the average maximum temperature is around 20°C (68°F). Only in high summer is swimming really an option.

When we think of the Netherlands, there are certain pictures that come to everyone's mind: world-famous Dutch cheeses; the stately old windmills that were once used to drain the countryside and now dot the landscape like beautiful gems; or the countless dykes that have become an essential element in protecting the country against ocean tides. For centuries, the Dutch have been trying to conquer new land from the North Sea: they build levies and embankments, pump it dry, and then settle and farm it. In fact, two-thirds of all Dutch people today live in the 'lower' lands, which are up to 7 m (23 ft) below sea level. This is made possible by canals and drainage ditches that are often located higher than the roads, fields or villages.

In contrast to 'life on the seafloor', the sprawling metropolitan areas are home to six million people – 40 percent of the total population. However, the cities at the edge of the 'Randstad' chain, which includes Amsterdam, Leiden, Haarlem, The Hague and Rotterdam, only make up a mere tenth of the country's area and are surrounded by a wonderfully green landscape of croplands, marshes and moors. In many cities, it is still easy to get a sense of how successful the Netherlands was over the centuries as a world trading power whose colonies brought great wealth to the country. That wealth is reflected in the ornate buildings of the Old Towns,

which line the quaint canals. Today, more than 55,000 houses in the Netherlands are listed buildings.

The wealth of earlier times has also naturally also benefited the arts. Painters like Rembrandt, Franz Hals, Jan Vermeer and Piet Mondrian are synonymous with the Netherlands. Ultimately, this historically seafaring nation's experiences with distant lands and foreign cultures has created an atmosphere of open-mindedness that has been preserved until the present day.

There is also an extra special ambience in the land of the Flemings and Walloons, who united to form the kingdom of Belgium some 160 years ago. Although Belgium has some first-class references in men like George Simenon and Jacques Brel, and is loved for its Brussels lace, Ardennes ham and a highway that is lit up at night, it is not a classic holiday destination – but that is short-sighted.

The coastal resorts along the North Sea, the wide sandy beaches and the spectacular dune landscapes alone are worth making the trip. And it's not just roman-

The Keizersgracht canal in
Amsterdam is spanned by
fourteen bridges.
Left: UNESCO World Heritage
Site: Windmills of Kinderdijk.

tics who go into rapture over the ornate façades and wonderful buildings that reflect off the canals and waterways, or the church spires that soar high above the historic Old Towns of Bruges and Ghent. Brussels, which proudly calls itself the Heart of Europe, is home to one of the most beautiful market squares in the world – the Grand' Place – and the stunning Museum of Fine Art displays works by masters from Rubens to Magritte. On an unusual note: no other country has a higher population of comics illustrators per square mile – which means that comic strips, along with Brussels lace, Antwerp diamonds and Belgian pralines, are among the most commonly exported Belgian products. At every turn, it is apparent that Belgians know how to live. Surprising as it may seem, no other country in Europe has as many award-winning restaurants.

The most popular drink in Belgium is beer, and there are almost five hundred types produced in over hundred breweries. And as far as snacks go, well, pommes frites (french fries or chips) are said to have been invented here.

Rembrandt (1606–1669)
immortalized himself in
numerous self-portraits; this
one dates from 1660 (left
side). Left: Gothic town hall at
the Grand Place in Brussels.

The tulip fields seem to extend endlessly towards the horizon. Flowers are cultivated in the southern Dutch region around the Keukenhof.

Detour

Zaandam and Alkmaar

Zaandam was once the center of the Dutch shipbuilding industry and is located just 15 km (7 mi) from the city of Amsterdam. Czar Peter I (1672–1725) studied the latest in shipbuilding technologies at the time, and his house has been made into a museum. Further to the north-west, the old mills, pretty houses and exhibits of the Zaanse Schans open-air museum display everyday village life from different eras.

From April to mid-September, the town of Alkmaar comes under the influence of its cheese culture. In the picturesque Old Town quarter farmers sell their delicious cheese balls and cheese wheels on the open-air market.

Cheese market in Alkmaar.

Along the Dutch and Belgian coast: In Holland, the route heads through the 'nether lands', with their seemingly endless fields of flowers, and then to the bustling metropolises. In Belgium you visit cities with charming, medieval Old Towns and priceless works of art.

1 Amsterdam (see pp. 66–67) Your journey begins in Amsterdam. From there, you can initially take a day trip to Zaandam just 15 km (9 mi) north to the Zaanse Schans open-air museum and the cheese town of Alkmaar a bit further north.

2 Haarlem This city is about 20 km (12 mi) west of Amsterdam and was officially mentioned in the 10th century. It has a picturesque Old Town quarter whose Grote Markt was once a sports arena.

The beautifully decorated 17th-century gabled houses are evidence of the wealth the city once achieved as the stronghold of the drapery and fabric bleaching guild.

At the south end of the square is the Grote or St Bavokerk, a late-Gothic cruciform basilica. The nursing home where painter Frans Hals spent his final years was converted into a museum in 1912, with important works by the great artist.

3 Keukenhof The Bollenstreek between Haarlem and Leiden takes you through a sea of flowers. It is home to the fields of around 8,000 nurseries that specialize in wholesale flowers. The Tulip Route leads to the most important of these nurseries; the

mecca among them for all flower lovers is the world-famous Keukenhof.

The information center was jointly founded by a community of flower growers in 1949.

4 Noordwijk aan Zee In the height of summer, this seaside resort after the turnoff at Sassenheim attracts tens of thousands of beachgoers with 13 km (8 mi) of strand and vast sandy dunes. Just like Katwijk ann Zee a few

miles further south, Noordwijk has a style that is reminiscent of English seaside resorts. From here it's another 20 km (12 mi) to Leiden.

5 Leiden The oldest university town in the Netherlands was already home to 11,000 students back in the mid-17th century. The most beautiful view over the town and its canals can be seen from the Burcht or fort, a mound fortified with brick curtain walls over 1,000 years ago that was built to protect against Holland's most persistent enemy: flooding. The Pieterskerk, a Gothic cruciform basilica with five naves, is

The magnificent spa hotel in Scheveningen – a luxury hotel since 2014 – is reminiscent of a baroque splendour with its three-winged complex.

worth seeing and, of course, the city's most famous native son is Rembrandt Harmensz van Rijn, born here in 1606. A few of his works are on display in the Stedelijk Museum de Lakenhal.

6 Scheveningen The center of this North Sea coastal resort is the magnificent old Art Nouveau health spa establishment that is

today a luxury hotel. The 3-km-long (2-mi) beach boardwalk and the Scheveningen Pier, which extends 400 m (437 yds) out into the North Sea, are also well-known features of the town. The International Sand Sculptures Festival is held here every year in May.

7 The Hague The third-largest city in the Netherlands is the seat of government as well as the headquarters of the International Court of Justice with the UN War

Crimes Tribunal. The city's history goes back roughly 750 years and began with a few houses built around the hunting grounds of the Count of Holland. One of these houses, the Binnenhof or 'Inner Court', was built in the 13th century and is still home to the nation's politics – it is the seat of government and the Parliament. The city's most important tourist attraction is the Maurits-shuis, a neoclassical building with an art gallery featuring priceless works by famous Dutch painters from the 'Golden Age' as well as Flemish Masters.

The Mesdag Panorama, a cylindrical painting created by Hendrik Willem Mesdag in 1881, is 120 m (131 yds) long and 14 m (46 ft) high and hangs in a building at Zeestraat 65. It gives visitors the impression of standing in the middle of the Scheveningen dune

landscape. The nearby Mesdag Museum has additional paintings from the Hague School of the late 19th century. Another building that constantly makes headlines is the Vredespalais in the Carnegieplein. This half neo-Gothic, half neoclassical Peace Palace is the venue for the controversial meetings of the International Court of Justice.

8 Delft Halfway between The Hague and Rotterdam is Delft, with its historic Old Town and charming canals. It is particularly famous for its pottery.

9 Rotterdam Container terminals, trans-shipment centers, warehouses and silos all line up beside one another over 20 km (12 mi) along the Nieuwe Waterweg at the world's largest port. All kinds of goods are moved through this port at the mouth of the Maas and Rhine rivers.

It is not difficult to see that emphasis is placed on modern high-rise architecture in 'Maashattan'. One of the most amazing sights is the Erasmusbrug,

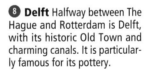

Modern architecture icons in Rotterdam: Erasmusbrücke and Markthalle (left side). At the top: Windmill in Haarlem; left: Amsterdam.

Detour

Lake IJssel

The cities around Lake IJssel still evoke the time of the explorers.

It was from Hoorn, for example, that Captain Willem Schouten set off for the southern tip of South America in 1616, now Cape Horn. Abel Tasman, the first European to discover New Zealand and Tasmania in 1642, also set sail from here.

The West Frisian Museum has exhibits on other colonial adventures that originated from Hoorn. Enkhuizen was the spice-trading center of the East India Company. The Zuiderzee Museum, in a former warehouse in the historic center, has interesting exhibits on shipping and fishery, while an open-air complex with farmhouses and handicrafts gives you an idea of life in the old days.

The tall, narrow canal houses on the Amstel are closely built together. Together with the Prinsengracht and the Herengracht, the Keizersgracht forms the historic Amsterdam canal belt.

Over time, many small side waterways emerged, so that at the end of the 'golden' 17th century the city had many miles of navigable waterways. That made the construction of bridges necessary for pedestrians, of which there are 1280 in Amsterdam today!

Amsterdam

The capital of the Netherlands is one of the smallest and most manageable metropolises in Europe. It is tolerant and cosmopolitan, but also characterized by a rich history, so it is no coincidence that Amsterdam, the headstrong city at the mouth of the Amstel, is a popular tourist destination.

Amsterdam is the world's largest pile-dwelling settlement. The foundations for the buildings in the entire Old Town district are formed by countless logs beaten up to 30 m (98 ft) into the ground, creating some seventy man-made islands – and the romantic flair of a city on water. Amsterdam's Golden Century, which roughly equates to the 17th century, marked the beginning of construction on the crescent-shaped Three Canals Belt. In the historic center alone, four hundred bridges span the canals. Water levels are maintained at a constant height using a system of locks and pumps, and some goods are still transported through the city by water even today.

Hundreds of houseboats are moored at the docks of the 160 canals in the Canal Belt and are just as much part of the townscape as the numerous cyclists, flower stands with 'tulips from Amsterdam', and the beautiful barrel organs that play the world-famous popular song. Amsterdam's cityscape resembles a bustling open-air museum, and its open-mindedness, cultural diversity, international cuisine, and the countless options for all types of accommodation suit every budget and every standard. All of this makes the capital of the Netherlands one of the most popular destinations in Europe.

Amsterdam is also a very youthful and tolerant city, often leading the way in areas such as fashion and design. It is also easy to get to from just about anywhere.

The tourist attractions in the Old Town include: the oldest church, the Oude Kerk (14th century, rebuilt in the 16th); the late-Gothic Nieuwe Kerk where Queen Beatrix was crowned; Dam, once a market place with the Nationaal Monument; the 17th-century town hall, Koninklijk Paleis, whose façade frieze is dedicated to sea trade; Museum Amstelkring, an original canal house used by ostracized Catholics as a secret church in the 17th century; Beurs van Berlage, the 19th-century merchants' stock exchange; Montelbaanstoren, the former city tower (1512); the seven-towered Waag, formerly a city gate and part of the mighty fort; and the Rembrandt House, the master's home with a modern museum wing.

In the former Jewish quarter: the Portuguese synagogue (1675) and Joods Historisch Museum; a museum complex housed in four former synagogues; the neo-Gothic Central Station (19th century); Amsterdam's historic museum in the complex of the former orphanage; and the Begijnhof, a former Beguine convent.

In the Canal Belt: Westerkerk (17th century); the Anne Frank House, preserved in its original state; and the historic working quarter of Jordaan with the beautifully renovated Hofjes, historic residential complexes.

In the museum quarter: The Rijks-museum, the world's most famous collection of Dutch Masters; the Van Gogh Museum; Stedelijk Museum for Modern Art; and the Vondelpark landscaped gardens.

The Schelde Estuary (Walcheren, Beveland)

North of Antwerp, the Schelde opens out into a wide delta. Al-though the estuary is a natural landscape, it has been politically divided between the Netherlands and Belgium since 1585. The former North Sea islands of Walcheren and Beveland provide holidaymakers with sand, surf and sea, charming villages and historic towns. Middelburg is one of the oldest cities in Holland, with a beautifully restored historic center that earned it the title of European Heritage City in 1975. Af-

Gouda

Gouda – this city is virtually synonymous with cheese. In actual fact, the nourishing, golden-yellow delicacy is one of the most popular varieties in the world. It comes on the market in either 'natural' flavor or refined with herbs, mustard, pepper or caraway, and is brought to you by Frau Antje, a prim and proper blond woman wearing a traditional Dutch bonnet – an invention of savvy marketing specialists over forty years ago. Since then she has advertised 'authentic cheese from Holland' from 700,000 tonnes (770,000 tons) of milk and seventy million cows.

After a short tour of the city, it becomes clear that Gouda has more to offer than just the cheese market, which is held every Thursday morning from mid-June until the end of August on the square between the town hall and the Renaissance building of the Waag. The first thing you notice at the market place is the Gothic Stadhuis (town hall) made from grey blocks of stone. It is adorned with merlons, turrets and red-and-white shutters, and has musical figurines on its eastern façade that every half hour commemorate the granting of the town charter in 1272. The Grote or St Janskerk at the southern end of the market is home to one of the treasures of the Old Town quarter, which is surrounded by canals. The church, built at the end of the 16th century and measuring 123 m (135 yds), is the longest church in the Netherlands. Its greatest attraction are its seventy stained glass windows from the 16th century – the most beautiful church windows in the country.

a suspension bridge over the Nieuwe Maas constructed by Ben van Berkel in 1996.

The city museum, which has an interesting display of the history of Rotterdam, is in the Het Schielandshuis, a former administrative building that managed the 17th-century dyke systems. The Boijmans van Beuningen Museum at the Museumspark is home to a sizeable collection of Old and New Masters. A variety of artwork is also exhibited at the Rotterdamer Kunsthal.

From Rotterdam it's roughly 20 km (12 mi) north-east to the country's most famous 'cheese town', Gouda. Just a few miles south of Rotterdam, the route leads to one of the country's iconic landmarks – the windmills of Kinderdijk.

⑩ Kinderdijk It really is an impressive sight: nineteen old polder mills lined up in a tidy row along the town's drainage canals. The ingenious constructions at the confluence of the Noord and Lek rivers once drove pumping stations that regulated water levels. These days, the blades, which are covered in canvas and have a span of up to 28 m (92 ft), only rotate on Saturday afternoons. The mills were declared a UNESCO World Heritage Site in

1997, and are particularly impressive in the second week of September when they are illuminated at night by floodlights.

⑪ Breda With its numerous barracks and military facilities, this garrison city at the confluence of the Mark and Aa rivers has a lot to offer visitors. Beautiful burgher houses on the Old Town market square, for example, date back to the 18th and 19th centuries and include the Stadhuis. And, as is often the case, the Old Town is surrounded by charming canals. The Kasteel van Breda is encircled by moats and features four corner towers. It is considered the ancestral castle of the House of Orange, the Dutch royal family. Breda is also home to another moated castle, Kasteel Bouvigne, and the city's most important building is the Gothic Onze Lieve Vrouwe Kerk (Church of Our Lady) with a spire 97 m (318 ft) tall.

Those looking to head back to the North Sea before continuing on to Belgium are advised to visit the islands of Walcheren and Beveland. They are connected to the mainland by a series of dams and bridges. From Breda, the N263 takes you through green, flat and sparsely settled landscapes towards Antwerp, the first real metropolis on this journey.

⑫ Antwerp The port here in Belgium's second-largest metropolitan area is the lifeblood of

ter the dreadful storm surge of 1953, the barrier of the Oosterschelde Dam was built north of Middelburg.

Kasteel Westhove near Domburg now houses a youth hostel.

the city and home to a number of automotive and chemical industry companies. The port is the second-largest in Europe after Rotterdam, a fact that has created an open-minded attitude and contributed greatly to Antwerp's rise as the center of the diamond trade. The 1993 European Capital of Culture is home to historic monuments and a vibrant cultural scene. Most of its tourist attractions are in the inner city, which forms a semicircle on the right bank of the Schelde. The most striking part of Antwerp is the Steen, the former fort complex whose oldest section dates back to the 9th century. It now houses the National Shipping Museum, with a 15th-century Flemish warship as its centerpiece. The fort's lookout platform provides an amazing view over the Schelde – which is 500 m (547 yds) wide at this point – the bridges, the old wharf, and the sea of countless cargo derricks along the horizon at the modern port. The Museum of Municipal History is housed in the late-Gothic meat market, while the Diamond Museum on Lange Herentalsestraat in the Jewish Quarter lets you watch diamond polishers at work. The Rubens House, a symbolic city palace reminiscent of an Italian palazzo,

was home to Peter Paul Rubens from 1610 to 1640. The master's lavish quarters, studio and art cabinet as well as some works by the painter and his students are on display.

⑬ Mechelen This city south of Antwerp has a rich history. It experienced its heyday when Margarethe of Austria ruled the country from here and her statue at the Grote Markt, which marks the city center, commemorates this time. The square is encircled by the town hall, a Gothic palace and the former cloth hall from the 14th century.

In the second century, the 97-m-tall (318-ft) spire of the Romboutskathedraal was designed as the highest symbol of

Christianity, and its carillon of forty-nine bells still charms listeners today. From Mechelen, it's just a half-hour drive to the Belgian capital. Those wanting to head towards the North Sea after that will initially pass through Aalst, the 'Gateway to Flanders', on the way to Bruges.

⑭ Brussels (see pp. 70–71).

⑮ Aalst This city is heavily influenced by industry and, well, flowers. Every morning there is a flower market at the Grote Markt, and beautiful Gothic row houses line the square.

⑯ Gent A center of the textile industry since the Middle Ages, Ghent has continued to remain

true to this tradition even today. Fruits, vegetables and even flowers play only a supporting role. The most important attractions are found in the well-preserved historic city center between the Count's Castle and the St Bavo Cathedral (14th century). The cathedral is on a rise and is visible from afar. Its most valuable treasure is the Ghent Altarpiece, also known as the Adoration of the Mystic Lamb, completed by the van Eyck brothers, Hubert and Jan, in the 15th century. The cathedral tower once housed thirty-nine bells, but only seven remain now. The others were sold or destroyed. The Belfort bell tower, opposite the cathedral, is 91 m (312 ft) high and was considered the symbol of the aspiring middle classes in the 14th century. The Belfort is 88 m high (289 ft) and has forty-seven bells. It has also served as a municipal treasure chamber and a watchtower. The cloth hall, the Great Meat Market, the Count's Castle, and the town hall are also worth visiting while downtown.

Left side: Grote Markt and station hall in Antwerp; above: Windmills of Kinderdijk; left: St. Niklas Church and the Belfry in Ghent.

The Grand Market or Grand Place in Brussels is one of the most beautiful places in the world with its unique ensemble of public and private buildings. Victor Hugo called the place 'a true miracle'.

The Square measures only 110 metres in length and 68 metres in width, but the dense buildings with guild houses around the town hall makes it one of the most beautiful architectural complexes in Europe. When the rich Brussels guilds replaced the aristocratic city regiment in the 15th century, they created themselves a memorial to this square and its precious guild-halls.

Brussels

Belgium's confident metropolis awaits visitors with grandiose cultural monuments and special culinary treats. It calls itself the Capital of Europe, which is true at least as far as the institutions of the European Union.

Brussels has been a wealthy city for centuries. Between the Middle Ages and the baroque period, it was primarily the middle classes who adorned their city with majestic row houses. The 19th century saw some wonderful additions to the unique townscape, which then suffered during the construction boom of the 20th century. The EU's ambitious buildings claimed many architectural victims, for instance in the Quartier Léopold, which was razed. Luckily, numerous Art Nouveau works remained intact. At the turn of the 20th century, Brussels was one of the focal points of this architectural style, and artists such as Victor Horta, Henry van de Velde and Philippe Wolfers enriched the city with a series of unique edifices. Brussels is Belgium's most important cultural city and scientific center, with a university, the polytechnic, the Royal Academy and numerous technical colleges and art schools. The city is at the crossroads of major transport routes and it is home to Belgium's national bank. Furthermore, Brussels is the second largest industrial city in the country after Antwerp. 'Fine goods' such as the famous Brussels lace, woolen, cotton and silk goods, carpets and even porcelain are all produced here. And of course, world-famous culinary products such as exquisite chocolates, delectable pralines, and even beer – virtually a given in the hometown of fabled King Gambrinus – keep visitors coming back for more. Although Brussels has a number of tourist attractions and gets a lot of attention as the 'Capital of Europe' and the headquarters of NATO, the Belgian capital is overshadowed by metropolises like Paris, London and Amsterdam. This actually

makes it a very interesting destination: slightly chaotic, not always pleasant, easy to access and never overrun. It's still an insiders' tip! Particularly worth seeing are: the Manneken Pis, the famous peeing boy statue and icon of the city from 1619; Grand' Place, one of the most beautiful squares in Europe and a World Heritage Site with the Hôtel de Ville and the Gothic town hall with its ornate façade; the Cathédrale St Michel; the Center Belge de la Bande dessinée, a comics museum in an Art Nouveau building; the 'Old England' Grand Magasin, a fanciful building; Musées Royaux des Beaux Arts with an outstanding collection of old and new masters from Brueghel to Magritte; Hôtel van Eetvelde, a magnificent building from the late 19th century; Hôtel Hannon, Maison Cauchie and Maison St Cyr, three examples of Brussels Art Nouveau residential architecture; Musée Charlier, 20th-century art in an Art Nouveau building; Musée du Cinquantenaire (works from the Middle Ages to the 19th century); Place du Grand Sablon with galleries and antique stores, and an antiques market on weekends; and Place du Jeu de Balle in the multicultural Marolles (Dutch: Marollen) district.

A journey back in time to the Middle Ages is possible when visiting historic Bruges. The town hall dates from 1376.

Knokke

Knokke-Heist, the most elegant town on the Belgian coast along with Ostend, is located amidst a spectacular dune landscape near the Dutch border. The sandy beach is 12 km (7 mi) long. The rise of Knokke began in 1880, when it rapidly grew from a small fishing village to one of the most glamorous coastal resorts in Europe. The walking trails are particularly lovely: 'Bloemenwandeling' in the Het Zoute villa district, and the 'Landelijke Knokke' and 'Polderwandeling' through the beautiful dune landscape. In Heist, the Polder- en Visserijmuseum Sincfala, with its exhibits on fishing and everyday life on the coast, is also worth a visit.

Promenade of Knokke.

About 15 km (9 mi) from Ghent, between Deinze and Ghent, is the 17th-century Ooidonk castle complex. The moated castle's name means 'high location in a swampland', which can be traced back to an older Low Franconian word 'hodonk'. Both Flemish and Dutch are creations of a linguistic root dating back to the Franconian empire.

On the way to Bruges, you will pass through Eeklo, where jenever (gin) is made in the historic van Hoorebeke distillery. The jenever is spicier than its English counterpart and the oude genever, or old-style jenever, is yellower in hue.

⑰ Brugges With its semi-circular Old Town full of canals, the capital of Western Flanders is a perfect example of medieval city architecture and, in those days, was considered the richest and most magnificent city in the known world after Venice. All major trading houses were based in Bruges, the dukes of Burgundy held court here, and art was of the utmost importance. Artists such as Jan van Eyck and Hans Memling were dedicated city painters.

The best way to discover Bruges is on a circle tour. The Grote Markt, once the scene of lively jousting competitions, continues to form the city center, which is also home to the 83-m-high (272-ft) Belfort tower.

From the Grote Markt, Vlamingstraat heads to the 'Hanseatic Bruges' with its beautiful patrician homes and trading houses from the 14th and 15th century; the Old Customs House; and then the Burgplein before continuing on to the Groeninge Museum with Belgian contemporaries; and finally the

15th-century Gruuthusepalais, a lavish palace that was home to patricians who earned their money by taxing the brewery for their ingredients, the 'Gruute'. The Gothic Onze Lieve Vrouwekerk, or Church of Our Lady, has a spire 122 m high (400 ft) that is in an atypical position on the left side of the church. It is home to the city's greatest artistic gem: the Bruges Madonna from 1503, the first of Michaelangelo's works to make it across the Alps during his lifetime.

The sluice-house at the southern end of Wijngaardplaats is also interesting. It is used to regulate the water levels of the canals. The Minnewater, behind the house in a park, was the city's main dock in the Middle Ages. After all of this journeying back in time to the Middle Ages, the charming coastal resorts on the North Sea may be calling: Knokke, Zeebruges, Blankenberge and Ostend are all just a few miles away from Bruges.

Above: The historic town of Bruges takes you on a journey through time. Here: the Belfort tower reflected in the waters of the Dijver.

The town hall of Bruges with its Gothic hall is worth visiting with its colourful vault, whose murals date back to the 19th century.

Haarlem The Old Town quarter of this bulb-growing city features gabled houses and the mighty Grote Kerk church.

Alkmaar The traditional cheese market includes weighing and tasting at the quaint market square. It is held every Friday in summer.

Hoorn Cape Horn owes its name to a sailor from Hoorn, but this cute town on Lake IJssel is significantly less rugged than the South American headland.

The Hauge The Dutch government, the International Court of Justice and the UN War Crimes Tribunal hold meetings in famous historic buildings while the museums exhibit some fine art.

Delft The Grote Markt, the Nieuwe Kerk, and the Stadhuis make the city of blue-and-white porcelain tiles one of the prettiest in the Netherlands.

Edam The cheese trade has been booming in Edam since the 17th century, and a lovely cheese market is held every Wednesday from July to August. Before this small town on Lake IJssel was made famous by its cheese balls encased in red or yellow packaging, it was well known as a shipbuilding town.

Kinderdijk A picture-perfect panorama unfolds at the confluence of the Lek and Noord rivers: a row of nineteen polder mills that once drove a pumping station to drain the fields for agriculture.

Map labels

Leeuwarden
Afsluitdijk
Heerenveen
Westfriesland
IJsselmeer
Alkmaar
Enkhuizen
Droogmakerij de Beemster
Hoorn
Markermeer
IJmuiden
Zaandam
Edam
Lelystad
Haarlem
AMSTERDAM
Zandvoort
Noordwijk aan Zee
De Keukenhof
Almere
Katwijk aan Zee
Loosdrechtse Plassen
Scheveningen
Leiden
Utrecht
The Hague
Apeldoorn
Delft
Gouda
Hoek van Holland
Lek
Rotterdam
Arnhem
Ridderkerk
Hellevoetsluis
Kinderdijk
Nijmegen
Spijkenisse
Dordrecht
Oosterscheldedam
Zierikzee
NETHERLANDS
Waal
Domburg
Walcheren
's-Hertogenbosch
Efteling
Middelburg
Goes Bergen op Zoom
Roosendaal
Breda
N.P.Loonse en Drunense Duinen
Beveland
Eindhoven
Zeebrugge
Knokke-Heist
Tilburg
Blankenberge
Westerschelde
Oostende
Brugge
Eindhoven
Dunkerque
Terneuzen
Turnhout
Eindhoven
Calais
Eeklo
Zelzate
Aalter
Antwerp
Lier
Liège
Lokeren
Kortrijk
Gent
Mechelen
Maastricht
BELGIUM
Aalst
Leuven
Oudenaarde
Ninove
BRUSSELS
Liège
Tournai
Waterloo
Namur
Ste-Gertrude
Six Flags
Charleroi

Bruges The Old Town in Bruges has numerous canals, grand squares and patrician houses from the 14th and 15th centuries, as well as churches and museums that cannot be matched anywhere in Europe.

Mechelen The treasures of the Romboutskathedraal include a van Dyck painting and the glockenspiel. The spire is 97 m high (318 ft) and was originally supposed to reach a height of 167 m (548 ft).

Antwerp The port on the Scheldt is one of the largest in the world and has made the city the centre of the diamond trade. Especially worth seeing are the Rubens House and the Grote Markt.

Brusels The Belgian capital (and Capital of Europe) is known around the world for its excellent cuisine. World-famous symbols of Brussels also include the vast Grand' Place and the Atomium, the 60-cm-tall (2-ft) Manneken Pis (peeing boy), the city's Art Nouveau buildings, museums, palaces and, of course, fine Brussels lace.

Route 6: France

Via Turonensis: from Paris to Biarritz

The Via Turonensis was mainly travelled by pilgrims from the Netherlands and northern France on their way to Santiago de Compostela in Galicia, the far north-west corner of Spain. They mostly went on foot to their imminent salvation. Today, there are still pilgrims who follow the Camino de Santiago (St James' Way) and its various 'side streets' for religious purposes, but most people these days are simply interested in seeing the wonderful sights along the way.

Route profile:

Length: approx. 1,100 km (684 miles), excluding detours
Time required: 10–14 days
When to go: The best seasons to visit the Île-de-France and the Loire Valley are spring and autumn, when the Loire Valley is ablaze with all shades of yellow and red.

Four different trails originally led pilgrims through France to the tomb of St James in Santiago de Compostela – the Via Tolosana from Arles through Montpellier and Toulouse to Spain; the Via Podensis from Le Puy through Conques, Cahors and Moissac to the border; the Via Lemovicensis from Vézelay through Avallon, Nevers and Limoges; and finally, the fourth route, the Via Turonensis, known as the 'magnum iter Sancti Jacobi' (the Great Route of St James).

The route's name comes from the city of Tours, through which it passed. The pilgrims started at the tomb of St Dionysius in St-Denis before heading through Paris, down the Rue St-Jacques to the church of the same name, where only the tower still stands on the right bank of the Seine. The tomb of St Evurtius was the destination in Orléans, while the tomb of St Martin, who was often compared to St James, awaited pilgrims in Tours. In Poitiers, there were three churches on the intinerary: St-Hilaire, Notre Dame la Grande and Ste-Radegonde. The head of John the Baptist was the object of worship in St-Jean-d'Angély, and pilgrims would pray at the tomb of St Eutropius in Saintes. Bordeaux was also the custodian of important relics like the bones of St Severin and the Horn of Roland.
The pilgrims of the Middle Ages would most certainly have been

Château de Chambord, in the middle of a large forest, is a structure of fairy-tale proportions. Left: The old harbour of La Rochelle and the watchtowers of St-Nicolas and Tour de la Chaîne.

amazed and would have shaken their heads at the buildings that the modern pilgrims along the Via Turonensis today find so fascinating. While the largest and most beautiful buildings in the Middle Ages were erected to honour and praise God, modern man seems obsessed with himself and his comforts. 'Pilgrims' nowadays are most interested in visiting the castles along the Via Turonensis, drawn to the extravagance as if by magic.

Perfect examples of this absolutism are just outside Paris in the Île-de-France – the enormous palace complex of Versailles and the castle of Rambouillet which, as the summer residence of French presidents, continues to be a centre of power. Many other magnificent buildings are scattered along the Loire River and its tributaries, the Indre, Cher and Vienne, including the colossal Château de Chambord, a dream

realized by King Francis I, the Château de Chenonceaux, and others like Beauregard, Chaumont, Valençay, Loches, Le Lude and Langeais.

The area around Bordeaux is home to a completely different kind of château. Médoc, Bordeaux and Entre-Deux-Mers are names that make the wine-lover's heart skip a beat. This region is the home of myriad great wines, in particular red wine. The

wineries around Bordeaux, most of which look like real castles in the middle of vast vineyards, are referred to as châteaus and include internationally renowned names such as Mouton-Rothschild, Lafitte-Rothschild and Latour.

Last but not least, today's 'car pilgrims' are attracted to destinations that are far off the beaten track and would have seemed rather absurd as a detour to the

pilgrims of the Middle Ages – namely, those on the Atlantic coast. The sandy beaches and coves of the Arcachon Basin and the sections of coast further south on the Bay of Biscay provide wind and waves for windsurfers and surfers. The elegant life of the 19th century is celebrated in the charming seaside resort of Biarritz and, from here, it's not much further to the Aragonian section of the Camino de Santiago, which stretches along the northern coast of Spain.

Left above: The modern glass pyramid by I.M. Pei in front of the magnificent Louvre building has been the museum's main entrance since 1989. Left: Jeanne d'Arc Arriving at Orléans, a painting by Jean Jacques Scherrer. Above: The Château Cos d'Estournel winery.

The beautiful Chombard Castle is surrounded by extensive forests.

Detour

Chartres

Even from a great distance, Chartres Cathedral is an impressive edifice, soaring like a mirage above the vast expanse of cornfields in the Beauce region. Up close, any doubts of its stature vanish immediately. This masterpiece of Gothic architecture, a large portion of which was built in the second half of the 12th century, simply overwhelms with its dimensions and design. The facade and, in particular, the entrance area are a dazzling sight full of lavish ornamentation, but the cathedral's greatest treasure is inside: glass paintings unsurpassed in their number and beauty anywhere else in the world. The stained-glass windows depict both biblical and historical scenes, and thus provided literate and illiterate believers alike with

The choir banister in the cathedral.

their wealth of information. The rose windows are also stunning, and their engraved tracery contains an extensive range of images. The southern and western rose windows illustrate the Last Judgement, while the eastern rose window is dedicated to the Virgin Mary. Chartres Cathedral, a UNESCO World Heritage Site since 1979, should not be missed.

The Via Turonensis follows one of the four major French routes of the St James' pilgrimage trail. Starting in the Île-de-France, you'll head to Orléans on the Loire, continue downstream past some of the most beautiful and famous Loire châteaus and then, from Saumur onwards, make your way south into the Gironde to Bordeaux. Prior to arriving in Biarritz, you stop in St-Jean-Pied-de-Port, the former last stop for pilgrims before crossing the Pyrenees.

1 Saint-Denis The actual pilgrim route begins in Saint-Denis, north of Paris. During the heyday of the Camino de Santiago (St James' Way) pilgrimages, this town was located north of the former city border and was the meeting place for the pilgrims coming from Paris. The French national saint, Dionysius, is buried in the city's cathedral. The basilica, where almost all of France's kings are entombed, is considered the first masterpiece of Gothic architecture.

2 Paris (see pp. 78-81). South-west of Paris is Versailles. The name of the palace is intrinsically tied to the Sun King, Louis XIV, and is a symbol of his display of absolutist power.

3 The Palace of Versailles Louis XIII first had a small hunting lodge built on the site where this magnificent building now stands. Under Louis XIV, the lodge was gradually expanded to the immense dimensions we know today, followed by some 'insignificant' extensions like the opera,

built under Louis XV. During the reign of the Sun King, Versailles was the place where anyone who wanted to have any sort of influence in the State had to stay. Apart from the large, opulent reception rooms such as the Hall of Mirrors, the Venus Room, the Hercules Room or the Abundance Salon, there were also the king and queen's lavishly furnished private chambers. The opera is a real gem, completed in 1770.

Beyond the water features of the Bassin d'Apollon is the vast park complex, which is home to the Grand Trianon, Petit Trianon and Le Hameau. The Grand Trianon was built under the orders of Louis XIV – one wing for him and the other for his beloved, Madame de Maintenon. The Petit Trianon was built for Louis XV's mistresses. Le Hameau is almost an absurdity – a small village with a homestead, dairy farm, mill and pigeon loft, where Marie Antoinette played 'peasant', a game that did not win her any fans among supporters of the revolution – she wound up under the guillotine on the Place de la Concorde.

4 Rambouillet Although the palace is the summer residence of the French president, it can be visited most of the time. The building consists of wings designed in different architectural styles including Gothic, Renaissance and baroque.

This castle only became royal property in 1783, when Louis XVI acquired it as a hunting lodge. The park and the adjacent Rambouillet forest are ideal places to take a relaxing stroll. On the way to Orléans to the south of Paris, it's worth making a detour to Chartres, whose name is automatically associated with its Gothic cathedral, the largest in Europe.

5 Orléans This city's cathedral, Ste-Croix, is built in Gothic style, though only very small parts of it date back to the Gothic period. The original building, destroyed during the French Wars of Religion, was rebuilt under Henry VI, and the architects of the 18th and 19th centuries continued to use the Gothic style.

The city's liberator lived in the

The Salle des Etats Generaux is the oldest part of the Chateau Blois on the Loire.

house named after her – the Maison de Jeanne d'Arc. The half-timbered house, which was destroyed in World War II, was reconstructed identically to the original. Only very few of the beautiful old houses and noble palaces were spared from the severe attacks of the war, but the

Hôtel Toutin, with its gorgeous Renaissance interior courtyard, is one that was. Of course, Orléans wouldn't be complete without the statue of Jeanne d'Arc, erected on the Place du Martroi in 1855.

Before heading on to Blois, it's well worth making a detour to the beautiful moated castle of Sully-sur-Loire, some 40 km (25 miles) south-east of Orléans. From Orléans, you have two options for reaching Chambord, which is somewhat outside of the Loire Valley – either along the right bank of the Loire to Merand and across a bridge, or along the left bank of the Loire on small rural roads.

6 Chambord King Francis I had this château built on the site of an older hunting lodge. Lost among the vast forests, the result was a vast dream castle with an incredible 440 rooms, seventy staircases, corner towers, a parapet and a moat. Leonardo da Vinci was apparently involved in its construction as well, designing the elaborate double-helix staircase whose two spirals are so intertwined that the people going up cannot see the people going down, and vice versa.

One of the château's real charms is its unique roof silhouette with its numerous turrets and chimneys. Francis I did not live to see the completion of his château, and work was not continued on it until the reign of Louis XIV. Louis XV gave it as a gift to the Elector of Saxony, who had it gloriously renovated. The château fell into temporary neglect after his death.

7 Blois In the first half of the 17th century, Blois was the centre of France's political world.

The town revolves around its castle, where the individual building phases are very easily recognized. The oldest section is Louis XII's wing, constructed in red brick with white limestone decorations. The Francis I wing is far more lavish, built in Renaissance style with traces of French Gothic in parts. The king would often have his heraldic animal, the salamander, displayed in certain areas. What really catches your eye is the Renaissance-style staircase tower in the interior courtyard, where the royal family could attend events.

Noble palaces such as the Hôtel Sardini, the Hôtel d'Alluye and the Hôtel de Guise are proof that, apart from royalty, numerous other aristocrats also had their residences along the Loire. The St-Louis Cathedral is not Gothic and only dates back to the 17th century, the previous building having been extensively destroyed by a hurricane. An especially lovely half-timbered house, the Maison des Acrobates, is located on the cathedral square. If you are interested in Gothic

Above: The famous Palace of Versailles is a UNESCO World Heritage Site. Above left: The Sainte-Croix Cathedral in Orléans.

Louis XIV and the Absolutism

L'état c'est moi – I am the State. This statement by Louis XIV aptly characterizes his understanding of power. The 'Sun King' was born in 1638 and, following the death of his

father in 1643, proclaimed king at the tender age of five. His reign was subsequently defined by his love of all things opulent and gaudy, and the Palace of Versailles is the most impressive and repeatedly copied example of this. After the death of Cardinal Mazarin, Louis XIV limited the rights of parliament and the aristocracy and strengthened the army. He ruled with absolute power until his death in 1715.

The Arc de Triomphe in the Place de l'Étoile marks the end of the Champs-Elysées. Napoléon ordered it to be built after his victory in Austerlitz. Visitors have a great view over the city from its viewing platform.

The Place de la Concorde was built in the second half of the 18th century. Particularly noteworthy is the obelisk of Luxor (left side of the image), donated by the Egyptian viceroy Muhammad Ali Pasha of France in 1835.

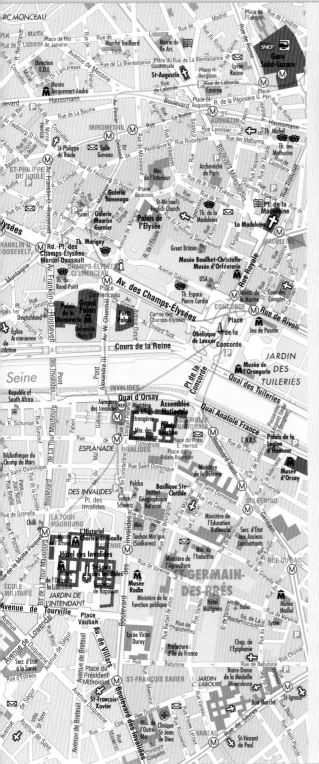

Drolerism on the facade of Notre Dame Cathedral.

Paris

The French capital is a city of thrilling contrasts – rich in tradition and at the same time avant-garde, enormous in size and yet captivatingly charming. Paris is also a university city and the place of government, a global centre for fashion and art, incredibly multicultural and yet still very much the epitome of all things French.

Throughout its long history, Paris has continually been in a state of expansion. The city always appeared to be bursting at the seams. Today, greater Paris covers an area of about 105 sq km (40 sq miles) and is home to some twelve million people – more than twenty per cent of the entire population of France. This city's non-stop growth is not least due to the fact that Paris does not accept any rivals. The nation's capital has always been unchallenged in its political, economic and cultural significance.

On the south side of the Seine you won't be able to miss the Eiffel Tower, the symbol of Paris built for the World Fair in 1889. The iron construction, towering 300 m (984 ft) over the city, took engineer Gustav Eiffel just sixteen months to completed.

The viewing platform, accessed by elevator, is one of the city's major attractions. The Hôtel des Invalides, a complex crowned by the Dôme des Invalides, was built by Louis XIV for the victims of his numerous wars. North of the Seine is probably the most magnificent boulevard in the world, the Champs-Elysées, with the Arc de Triomphe providing a great view of the streets emanating from its centre. Be sure to see the

Place de la Concorde, an excellent example of wide boulevards and geometric plazas that gave the French capital its 'big city' look during its renovation in the 18th century. Also visit the park complex Jardin des Tuileries, which leads up to the Louvre; the Place Vendôme with its upmarket shopping; the Palais Garnier, an opulent 19th-century opera house; and the 17th-century Palais Royal. Montmartre, on the north side of town, is great for exploring both day and night. Things to see include the historic Moulin de la Galette with its outdoor garden restaurant; the Sacre Coeur basilica up on the hill, with fantastic views of the city; the Père Lachaise Cemetery (east, outside city centre), one of three large cemeteries built around 1800 with the graves of numerous celebrities (Oscar Wilde, Jim Morrison, Edith Piaf, Eugène Delacroix and Frédéric Chopin, for example). All the cemeteries have detailed maps available at the main entrance.

In the northern suburb of St-Denis you will find the early-Gothic church of St-Denis, the burial place of the French kings, and the Stade de France, a football stadium with capacity for 80,000, built for the 1998 World Cup.

One of the most beautiful things to do in Paris is probably a night stroll along the Seine as the lights of the city flood the shore in a romantic light. In the image you can see St. Michel's bridge, which leads across the river.

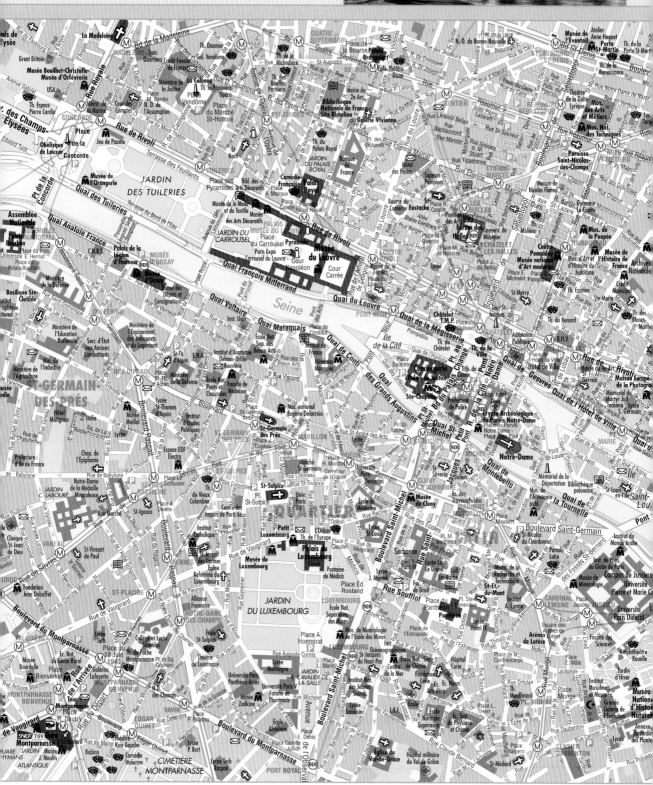

The Louvre is probably the most famous museum in the city. Here you will find the world famous Mona Lisa, who is said to follow viewers with her gaze. Besides Leonardo da Vinci, other significant artists such as Hieronymus Bosch and Albrecht Dürer are also represented here.

Paris

The historic centre of the 'City of Light' is easy to navigate, and many sights can be reached on foot. However, you should allow yourself copious amounts of time – after all, if you fancied it, you could spend days just wandering around the Louvre.

The interior of Notre-Dame overlooking the choir.

During the Middle Ages, when Paris was arguably the most important city in Europe, three factors determined the city's development and status – the church, its royalty and the university, all of which have left their mark on the historic city centre.

Out on the Île de la Cité – the city's oldest core settlement where the Romans, Merovingians and Carolingians based their dominions – stands one of France's most splendid cathedrals: Notre Dame.

As of 1400, medieval royalty focused their power on the northern banks of the Seine at the Louvre, which was begun in 1200 as part of a first ring of fortifications and developed into a magnificent residence over the centuries. On the other side of the river, in the Latin Quarter, professors and students united to establish the Sorbonne at the end of the 12th century. The riverbank, with its grand buildings, is a UNESCO World Heritage Site.

On the Île de la Cité, don't miss the early-Gothic Cathédrale Notre Dame (12th/13th centuries), where you can climb both 68-m-high (223-ft) towers; the former palace chapel of Ste-Chapelle, a high-Gothic masterpiece; the Conciergerie, part of the medieval royal palace; Pont Neuf, one of the most beautiful bridges on the Seine; and the idyllic Île St-Louis, south-east of the Île de la Cité, with its Renaissance buildings.

North of the Seine visit the Louvre, first a medieval castle, then the royal residence until the 17th century, then rebuilt and made into one of the largest art museums in the world; the Centre Pompidou, a cultural centre with exemplary modern architecture; the Hôtel de Ville, the 19th-century town hall at the Place de Grève; the Marais quarter with the romantic Place des Vosges, the avant-garde Opéra National de Paris, the Gothic church of St-Gervais-et-St-Protais, the Picasso museum, and the Hôtel Carnavalet's museum on the city's history.

South of the Seine go to the famous Latin Quarter; the St-Germain-des-Prés and Montparnasse Quarters and the Jardin du Luxembourg park.

Romanesque church art in Poitiers and Parthenay-le-vieux

The Romanesque style of the Poitou region is typified, for the most part, by rich sculptural decorations. The facade of the former collegiate church of Notre Dame la Grande in Poitiers, completed in the mid 12th century, is a particularly good example of this. Above the three portals, as well as to the left and right of the large second-storey window, is an ornately sculptured series of images depicting themes from the Old and New Testament such as Adam and Eve, the prophet Moses, Jeremiah, Josiah and Daniel, the Tree of Jesse, the Annunciation, the birth of Christ, the twelve apostles and, in the gables, Christ in the Mandorla with two angels. The church of St-Pierre in nearby Parthenay-le-Vieux was built in the late 11th century. The

Jeanne d'Arc (Joan of Arc)

Jeanne d'Arc was born in 1412, the daughter of a rich farmer in Domrémy in the Lorraine region. At the time, France had been heavily involved in the Hundred Years War with England since 1337, and the English had advanced as far as the Loire. At the age of thirteen, Jeanne began hearing voices in her head telling her to join forces with the French heir apparent, Charles VII, and expel the English from France. After she recognized him in Chinon, despite his disguise, people started believing in her divine mission. She was then given his support and went with the French army to Orléans, which was occupied by the English. With her help, the city was liberated on 8 May 1429.

Jeanne was also able to persuade Charles VII to follow the dangerous road to Reims to be crowned. The ceremony took place in July 1420 in the Reims cathedral. However, the farmer's daughter from Lorraine, who was now France's heroine, had enemies too. In 1430, the Burgundians, who were allied with England, succeeded in imprisoning and handing Jeanne over to the English. She was accused of heresy and witchery in Rouen in 1431 and, as Charles VII thought it to be politically incorrect to help her, condemned to be burned at the stake on 30 May 1431. The conviction was overturned in 1456 and in 1920 Jeanne d'Arc was granted sainthood.

churches, pay a visit to the 12th-century St-Nicolas.

8 Cheverny This castle, built between 1620 and 1634, is still owned by the family of the builder, Henri Hurault. It is also probably thanks to this fact that the castle still contains a large part of the original, opulent interior decor. The ceiling frescoes in the dining hall and bedroom are particularly worth inspecting.

9 Chenonceau Powerful women played a large role in the history of this romantic pleasure palace. For example, Cathérine Briçonnet supervised its construction in the early 16th century while her husband was in Italy. After Thomas Bohier's death, the building fell into the hands of the king and Henry II gave it as a gift to his beloved, Diane de Poitiers, who extended it to include a bridge over the Cher. Following Henry's death, his wife, Catherine de Medici, kept the castle for herself, and it is thanks to her idea that the Florentine-style bridge was built, including its own gallery.

After Catherine de Medici, the widow of the assasinated Henry III, Louise de Lorraine, proceeded to live a life of mourning in what was actually a very bright and cheerful-looking castle. This spirit returned in the 18th century with the arrival of middle-class Louise Dupin, who saved the castle from the destruction of the revolution. Only very little remains of the original decor, but Renaissance furnishings have been used to give an impression of what the interior may have been like. Located on the bridge pier is the gorgeous kitchen, where copper pots and pans still hang in an orderly fashion.

10 Amboise Perched on a hill sloping steeply into the Loire is France's first major Renaissance château. Although only parts of the construction have been preserved, they are still very impressive in their size and grandeur. Following an expedition to Italy in 1496, Charles VIII brought back with him Italian artists, craftsmen and works of art to decorate the palace. The interiors of the mighty towers were constructed in such

a way that a rider on a horse could reach up into the storey above. The Chapelle-St-Hubert is a good example of Gothic architecture. Not far from the château is the Le Clos-Lucé mansion, where Leonardo da Vinci spent the final years of his life. Francis I had originally arranged for the Italian universal genius to come to France, and a small museum displaying models of Leonardo's inventions pays homage to this influential man. The small town located below the château, a row of houses, and the clock tower all date back to the time of this region's heyday. From Amboise, a small road leads through the middle of the Loire Valley to Tours.

11 Tours This is the town that gave the Via Turonensis its name, and the tomb of St Martin here was an extremely important stop for St James pilgrims. Revolutionaries demolished the old St-Martin Basilica at the end of the 18th century. The new St-Martin Basilica, in neo-Byzantine style, contains the tomb of the saint, consecrated in 1890. It is an example of the monumental church archi-

most striking part of this building is the eightcornered transept tower, but the most beautiful features are the decorative figures on the facade. Samson's battle with the lion is depicted here, as well as the horseman, which is typical for the Romanesque style in Poitiers. The image of the Melusine fairy, which appears more than thirty times, is an original element.

The western facade of the Notre Dame Cathedral in Poitiers.

tecture of the time, one that made use of many different styles.

The St-Gatien Cathedral is the city's most important historic church. The two-storey cloister provides a great view of the towers' tracery and the finely carved flying buttresses.

In some parts of the Old Town, like the Place Plumereau, you could be forgiven for thinking you were back in the Middle Ages. Charming half-timbered houses with pointed gables and often ornately carved balconies are proof of the wealth of the traders at the time. A waxworks cabinet is located in the historic rooms of the Château Royal (13th century).

12 Villandry The last of the great castles to be built in the Loire during the Renaissance (1536) fell into ruin in the 19th century and its Renaissance gardens were then made into an English-style park. The Spanish Carvallo family eventually bought it in 1906 and it is thanks to them that the castle has been renovated. More importantly, the gardens were remodelled in the original Renaissance style. This explains why a lot of the people who visit the castle today are lovers of historic landscaping. Whether it be beds of flowers or vegetables, everything is laid out artistically and trees and hedges are perfectly trimmed into geometric shapes.

13 Azay-le-Rideau This castle on the Indre, built between 1519 and 1524, captivates visitors with the harmony of its proportions and its romantic location on an island in the river. However, it did not bring its builder, the mayor of Tours, Gilles Berthelot, much luck. Like other French kings, Francis I could not tolerate his subjects openly displaying their wealth. Without further ado, he accused the mayor of infidelity and embezzlement, and seized the castle.

14 Ussé The Château d'Ussé was built on the walls of a fortified castle in the second half of the 15th century. With its turrets and merlons, as well as its location at the edge of the forest, it's easy to see how it was the inspiration for authors of fairy tales. The Gothic chapel houses an important work of art from the Italian Renaissance, a terracotta Madonna by the Florentine sculptor Luca della Robbia.

15 Saumur Horse lovers around the world should be very familiar with the name Saumur. The cavalry school, founded in 1763, is still France's national riding school. The castle was built in the second half of the 14th century and is located on a hillside above the city.

Today, it houses two museums, an art museum and the Musée du Cheval. In the Old Town, half-timbered houses like the town hall on the Place St-Pierre, which was created in 1508 as a patrician palace, and the numerous 17th-century villas are all worth a look. In the Gothic church of Notre Dame de Nantilly, the side aisle, which Louis XI had built in a flamboyant style, is home to a prayer chapel that an inscription identifies as being the royal oratorio. On rainy days there are two interesting museums worth visiting: a mask museum (Saumur produces a large quantity of carnival masks) and a mushroom museum. These precious fungi are grown in the surrounding area in numerous limestone caves.

From Saumur, the westernmost point of the journey through the Loire, the road heads 11 km (7 miles) back towards Fontevraud-l'Abbey.

16 Fontevraud-l'Abbaye This abbey was founded in 1101 and existed as such until the 19th century. In the tall, bright church (consecrated in 1119) is the tomb of Eleonore of Aquitania. South-west France 'wedded' England when she married Henry Plantagenet, later Henry II of England. Eleonore's husband and their son, Richard the Lionheart, are also buried in Fontevraud.

Above left: Castle in Saumur above the city. Above right: Chenonceau Castle on the River Cher. Below right: Chaumont Castle from the 15th century.

Chinon on the Vienne is best known for the ruin of its historic castle towering over the city.

Detour

La Rochelle and Île de Ré

A detour to Île de Ré first takes you to La Rochelle, an important harbour town since the 11th century In 1628, Cardinal Richelieu seized the town, which had for too long taken the wrong side in the political debate of the day – over 23,000 people died during the brutal occupation. Today, its main attraction is the Atlantic harbour, where yachts bob up and down in a picture-perfect scene. The city's best-known tourist sites are down by the Old Harbour – the Tour St-Nicolas and the Tour de la Chaîne. In times of war, an iron chain was stretched between the two towers to

The harbour of Île de Ré.

protect the harbour from enemy ships. The town hall (1595–1606) is built in Renaissance style with an arcaded interior courtyard. The Île de Ré – also known as the 'White Island' – is connected to the mainland by a 4-km-long (2.5-mile) bridge. Vineyards and salt marshes dominate the scene and are surrounded by pretty villages. The main town on the island is St-Martin-de-Ré, with a citadel that was constructed by the famous fort builder, Vauban. St-Clément-des-Baleines is also interesting – it has two lighthouses worth seeing.

The 16th-century cloister is the largest in all of France. However, the abbey's most original building is the monastery kitchen, which almost looks like a chapel with six arches.

⑰ **Chinon** This castle-like château high above the banks of the Vienne played an important role in French history. This is where Jeanne d'Arc first met Charles VII and recognized him despite his costume, his courtiers, who were hiding him, and the fact that she had never seen him before. It is for this reason that the large tower, the Tour de l'Horloge, houses a small museum dedicated to her. Other parts of the castle, originating from the 10th to 15th centuries, are only ruins now. A highlight of any visit to the castle is the view over the Vienne valley.

⑱ **Châtellerault** This town, no longer of much significance, was once an important stop for pilgrims on the Camino de Santiago. Pilgrims would enter the town, as did Jeanne d'Arc, through Porte Ste-Cathérine. The church of St-Jacques, the destination of all pilgrims on the

Camino de Santiago, was furnished with an ornate set of chimes. Some of the houses, such as the Logis Cognet, enable you to imagine what life was like in the 15th century.

⑲ **Poitiers** This old city, which was an important stop for pilgrims on the Camino de Santiago, found an important patron in Duke Jean de Berry. In the second half of the 16th century, it became a centre of spiritualism and science and its churches still show evidence of this today.

⑳ **Marais Poitevin** The marshland located west of Poitiers and stretching all the way to the coast seems to have remained stuck in time. The most important and often the only means of transport in the 'Venise Verte' (Green Venice) is one of the flat-bottomed boats. The Romanesque churches of Parthenay-le-Vieux, some 50 km (31 miles) west of Poitiers, are well worth a visit. You have to return to Poitiers before continuing on to St-Jean-d'Angély.

㉑ **Saint-Jean d'Angély** Although it has now paled into insignificance, this town was once

an important destination for St James pilgrims as it was here that they had the opportunity to pay their respects to John the Baptist. Only ruins remain of the Gothic church, but a row of beautiful half-timbered houses, the Tour de la Grosse Horloge (clock tower) dating from 1406, an artistic fountain (1546), and the 17th-century abbey enable modern visitors to take a trip back in time.

From here, it's worth making a detour to the harbour town of La Rochelle on the Atlantic, where you can make an excursion out to the Île de Ré.

㉒ **Saintes** The capital of the Saintonge looks back on a long history, traces of which can still be seen today.

The Arc de Germanicus, which was originally the gateway to a bridge, dates back to Roman times. When the bridge eroded, it was saved and rebuilt on the right bank. The ruins of the amphitheatre, dating back to the 1st century and today overgrown with grass, once seated 20,000 people. There are also some impressive remains from the Middle Ages.

The Abbey Fontevraud was a mixed monastery. Its Romanesque church has been restored again and again.

Detour

Château Mouton-Rothschild

In the Bordelais wine region, château does not mean castle, but rather a large vineyard. One of this region's world-famous vineyard abodes is the Château Mouton-Rothschild in Pauillac on the Gironde. Predominantly upmarket Cabernet-Sauvignon grapes are grown here, on a piece of land covering about 80 ha (198 acres).

Baron Philippe de Rothschild came up with the idea to make his wine bottles into small works of art.

As a result, for over half a century artists have been creating labels for the property's top red wines. The list of contributing painters

Top: Vineyards as far as the eye can see. Bottom: The château's wine cellar.

reads like a 'Who's Who' of modern art – Jean Cocteau (1947), Georges Braque (1955), Salvador Dalí (1958), Juan Miro (1969), Marc Chagall (1970), Pablo Picasso (1973), Andy Warhol (1975), Keith Haring (1988). You can admire these artworks, as well as many other exhibits, in the château's wine museum.

The Abbaye aux Dames, for example, was founded in 1047, and the Romanesque church was built in the 11th and 12th centuries. The Gothic St-Pierre Cathedral was constructed in the 13th and 14th centuries and the tower was added in the 17th century. The church of St-Eutrope, dating from the late 11th century, was one of the destinations of the St James pilgrims. They prayed here in the spacious crypt at the tomb of the city's saint, Eutropius.

From Saintes you head southeast towards Cognac.

23 Cognac This town, on the banks of the Charente, today very much revolves around the drink of the same name, which expert noses will be able to catch whiffs of as they stroll through the town. The Valois Castle, from the 15th and 16th centuries, has a cognac distillery.

An exhibition at the town hall allows you to get a better understanding of the history and production of the precious brandy, which takes between five and forty years to mature. Some of the distilleries offer interesting tours of their facilities.

You head south-west from here to Pons before continuing on to Libourne.

24 Libourne This small town is a typical bastide, a fortified town, built at the time when South-West France was an apple of discord between England and France (1150–1450).

Every bastide is surrounded by a wall and has a grid-like layout and a large market square. Libourne was founded in 1270 and was for a long time a very important harbour for shipping wine out of the region. Today, it's worth taking a stroll around the Place Abel Surchamp.

25 Saint-Émilion Soaring out of the sea of vineyards that belong to the Saint-Émilion appellation, which produce very high-quality wines, is the small town whose beginnings trace back to a monastery. The sizeable rock-hewn church here (9th–12th centuries), whose understated facade faces towards the pretty market place, is a special attraction. The collegiate church was built in the 12th century and its main aisle is Romanesque. By no means should you

miss having a look at the very well-preserved cloister.

The donjon, a relic from the royal fort, towers high above Saint-Émilion where the 'Jurade' wine confrèrie meets to test the new wines. Every year, from the tower platform, the members ceremoniously declare the grape harvest open.

26 Bordeaux This old city on the Garonne has long been dominated by trade – predominantly the wine trade.

An historic event had a profound effect on the city – in 1154, Bordeaux fell under English rule and, thanks to their huge interest in the region's wines, trade boomed. Even when Bordeaux was again part of France, it still maintained a close relationship with the British Isles.

The Place de la Comédie, with the classical columned facade of the Grand Théâtre, is an ideal place to start a stroll through the city. The Esplanade des

Top left and right: With its medieval houses, squares and streets, St-Émilion is a charming little town in the middle of the lovely wine region.

A bridge leads across the Nive to the church of Notre-Dame in Saint-Jean-Pied-de-Port.

Detour

Côte d'Argent and Côte des Basques

The Côte d'Argent refers to the stretch of coast between the Bassin d'Arcachon and Biarritz, where it turns into the Côte Basque, straddling the French-Spanish border. Apart from excellent swimming, the Côte d'Argent also hosts a unique natural landscape.

The Dune de Pilat is Europe's highest dune, fluctuating between 105 m and 120 m (345 ft and 394 ft), with a width of 500 m (1,640 ft), and a length of 2.7 km (2 miles). The Parc Ornithologique du Teich is also worth a visit. The Côte Basque is home to one of few swanky seaside resorts in the region – Biarritz. It experienced its heyday during the Belle Époque, when Napoleon III and his wife, Eugénie, spent their holidays here. The Rocher de la Vierge (Rock of the Virgin) and its statue of the Madonna have a charming location out in the sea. A footbridge leads you out to the isolated formation.

The casino and many of the hotel palaces are evidence of the glitz and glamour of Biarritz' golden age. St-Jean-de-Luz is a picturesque old town with the typically Basque half-timber style. The Sun King met his bride, the Spanish Infanta Maria Theresa, for the first time here in the Maison Louis XIV. Her house, the Maison de l'Infante, is located just a little further on.

The romantic coast of Biarritz.

Quinconces here is considered the largest square in Europe. You shouldn't miss seeing the city's churches. The St-André Cathedral was built between the 13th and 15th centuries and fascinates visitors with its Porte Royale, a magnificent door lavishly decorated with sculptures. Apart from the church, there is the Tour Pey-Berland, a free-standing tower. St-Michel was constructed somewhat later, in the 14th/16th centuries, and is furnished in 17th-century baroque style.

Those following in the foot-steps of Camino de Santiago pilgrims should pay a visit to St-Seurin. Worshipping St-Severin (St-Seurin) was an important part of the route. The early-Romanesque crypt dates back to this time.

Bordeaux has a lot more to offer than just St James relics – the city gates of Porte de Cailhau, Porte d'Aquitaine, Porte de la Monnaie and Porte Dijeaux, for example.

The Pont de Pierre (a stone bridge) and the tall, modern bridge, Pont d'Aquitaine, datingfrom 1967, are also worth a look.

Those interested in seeing the region's world-famous vineyards should make the 50-km (31-mile) journey along the Gironde to the Château Mouton-Rothschild in Pauillac.

27 Les Landes This is the name given to the landscape typical of the area south of Bordeaux – flat, sandy earth with sparse pine forests. The forests are planted by hand and are still used for their lumber by-products, predominantly for the extraction of resin. The region's capital is Mont-de-Marsan, located somewhat off the beaten track in the southeast and home to some interesting Romanesque houses, the 15th-century Lacataye donjon and some very pretty parks.

28 Dax This small town on the Adour is one of France's most frequently visited thermal baths. Water at a temperature of 64°C (147°F) bubbles out of the Fontaine de la Néhé. The 17th-century cathedral here is also worth seeing. The apostle gate from the earlier Gothic building is significant in an art-history context. A visit to the Musée Borda in a beautiful city palace and a stroll along the banks of the Adour round off the visit.

If you want to go to the seaside, you can can drive 40 km (25 miles) from Dax to the southern end of the Côte d'Argent and then further on to the Côte des Basques around Biarritz.

On the other hand, those wanting to get a whiff of the mountain air in the Pyrenees should continue south-east along the spectacular route to Orthez.

29 Saint-Jean-Pied-de-Port In the Middle Ages, this mountain town was already an important stop for pilgrims – and the last before the strenuous crossing of the Pyrenees over the Roncesvalles Pass and across the Spanish border. 'Saint John at the Foot of the Pass' manages to preserve its medieval character even today. The banks of the Nive River are lined with houses from the 16th and 17th centuries and the Gothic church of Notre Dame du Bout du Pont.

30 Bayonne The capital of the Pays Basque is a densely settled area but it has managed to retain much of its charm in its centre with bridges on two rivers, large squares and rows of houses packed closely together around the Gothic cathedral of Ste Marie. Its city festival is famous, held every year on the second weekend in August.

Above: The buildings of Bordeaux are reflected in the Garon.

View over the Nive on a typical Basque half-timbered house line in Bayonne.

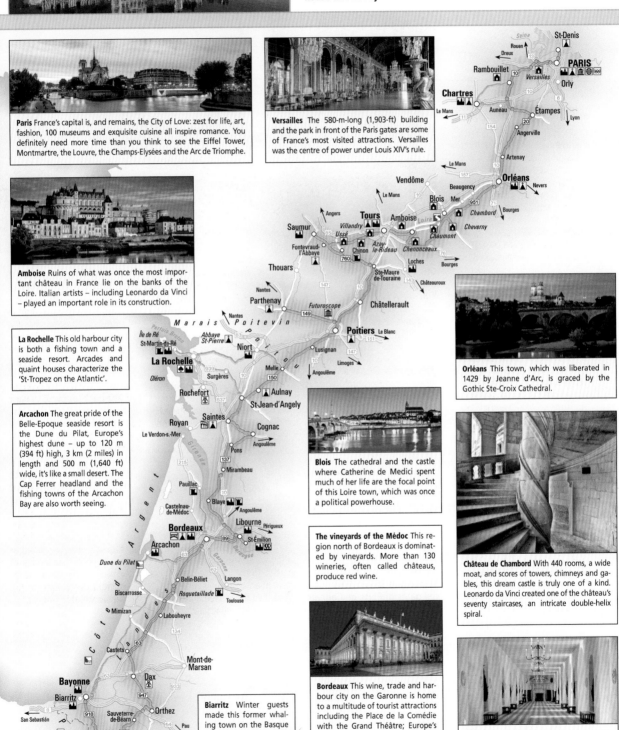

Paris France's capital is, and remains, the City of Love: zest for life, art, fashion, 100 museums and exquisite cuisine all inspire romance. You definitely need more time than you think to see the Eiffel Tower, Montmartre, the Louvre, the Champs-Elysées and the Arc de Triomphe.

Versailles The 580-m-long (1,903-ft) building and the park in front of the Paris gates are some of France's most visited attractions. Versailles was the centre of power under Louis XIV's rule.

Amboise Ruins of what was once the most important château in France lie on the banks of the Loire. Italian artists – including Leonardo da Vinci – played an important role in its construction.

La Rochelle This old harbour city is both a fishing town and a seaside resort. Arcades and quaint houses characterize the 'St-Tropez on the Atlantic'.

Arcachon The great pride of the Belle-Epoque seaside resort is the Dune du Pilat, Europe's highest dune – up to 120 m (394 ft) high, 3 km (2 miles) in length and 500 m (1,640 ft) wide, it's like a small desert. The Cap Ferrer headland and the fishing towns of the Arcachon Bay are also worth seeing.

Orléans This town, which was liberated in 1429 by Jeanne d'Arc, is graced by the Gothic Ste-Croix Cathedral.

Blois The cathedral and the castle where Catherine de Medici spent much of her life are the focal point of this Loire town, which was once a political powerhouse.

The vineyards of the Médoc This region north of Bordeaux is dominated by vineyards. More than 130 wineries, often called châteaux, produce red wine.

Château de Chambord With 440 rooms, a wide moat, and scores of towers, chimneys and gables, this dream castle is truly one of a kind. Leonardo da Vinci created one of the château's seventy staircases, an intricate double-helix spiral.

Bordeaux This wine, trade and harbour city on the Garonne is home to a multitude of tourist attractions including the Place de la Comédie with the Grand Théâtre; Europe's largest square, the Esplanade des Quin-conces; the ornate St-An-dré Cathedral (13th–15th centuries).

Biarritz Winter guests made this former whaling town on the Basque coast popular in the 19th century. Its beaches and promenades still enjoy huge popularity.

Château de Chenonceau It was mainly women who influenced the tone of this Renaissance building on the banks of the Cher in the Loire Valley.

Andalusia – a Moorish legacy

Andalusia is a region filled with passion and culture. The fertile agricultural land here is blessed with plentiful sun where olives trees grow against a backdrop of snow-covered mountains and the tidy whitewashed houses recall Moorish architectural styles. This natural setting coupled with the local aromas of leather and sherry and the rhythms of the castanets and flamenco all combine to create a truly unforgettable experience.

Route profile:

Length: approx. 1,600 km (994 miles), excluding detours
Time required: at least 8–10 days
When to go: The best times to travel are spring and autumn. Summer can be brutally hot.

'Al Andaluz' – the 'Land of Light' – is what the Arabs called this sunny southern part of Spain. Interestingly, it was not meant as a metaphor. This region, where two continents and two seas meet, actually possesses a unique light that seems not to exist anywhere else in the world, and whose clarity never ceases to amaze its inspired visitors.

Andalusia covers an area of more than 87,000 sq km (33,582 sq mi). Its landscape is defined by the Sierra Morena Mountains and the Betic Cordillera Range, whose 3,481-m-high (11,421-ft) Sierra Nevada Mountains are covered in snow almost all year long.

The area is home to ancient settlements that pre-date the Romans, including Cadiz, which was first settled by the Phoenicians in around 1100 BC. Since then, Greeks, Romans, Vandals and Visigoths have taken turns settling and farming the sun-drenched land in the south of Iberia. It wasn't until the 8th century that the Arabs ended the reign of the Visigoths and took control of the area.

It turns out to have been an easy campaign for the Arabs to gain their foothold in Andalusia. When they secretly crossed the Strait of Gibraltar under Tariq ibn Ziyad, and later Musa ibn Nusair in 711, they only needed gradually to seize the already deteriorating kingdom of Roderic, the Visigoth ruler. After that,

Above: Picturesque view of Zahara de la Sierra behind a reservoir. Left: The expensive yachts are lined up in the port of Marbella and are a real eye-catcher.

virtually no one else stood in their way and their expansion reached as far as Galicia and the Pyrenees. They were only halted by Charles Martell in 732 at the Battle of Tours in France.

In Spain, however, the Arabs reigned supreme for over half a century. Abd ar-Rahman I made Córdoba the capital of his Caliphate and adorned the city with an exquisite mosque. In Granada, Islamic culture developed with consummate splendour. Over the centuries, the Moors erected some truly magnificent buildings all throughout this region, in architectural styles that remain the defining element of Andalusia even to this day.

In the 13th century, the Christian 'Reconquista' of the Iberian Peninsula began in earnest and a huge victory was won for the Catholic monarchs Ferdinand and Isabella when Seville fell in 1248. When Granada was taken

as well in 1492, the last Muslim minorities were expelled, marking the start of a new Andalusia that would not just ride the tide of good fortune that came with the discovery and conquest of the 'New World', but even dictate its development. Following the conquests of Mexico and Peru, the city of Seville became the most important trading centre in all of Spain.

Today, the autonomous region of Andalusia, which enjoys 3,000 hours of sun a year and where oranges, olives, wine and almonds all flourish, is home to some seven million people and has around 760 towns and communities. Traditional festivals and religious life are of extreme importance to Andalusians, and these are celebrated with full fervour and devotion especially

during the Semana Santa, or Holy Week, when numerous pilgrimages and processions take place.

Community culture is reflected in the local festival weeks, the ferias, as well as in the bullfights and diverse flamenco styles. These events show the true Andalusia, the land of bold caballeros, beautiful señoritas, formidable black bulls – the land that gets your blood pumping like no other place. And the natural landscape is breathtaking and diverse, from the glorious beaches of the Costa del Sol to the magnificent snow-covered peaks of the Sierra Nevada.

Left side: A city could not be as dramatically built as this one: Ronda occupies the platform of a 750 meter high mountain. Above: Moorish architecture in the patio of the Generalife in Granada.

Legends surround the once imposing palace city of Medina Azahara, whose construction began in 940.

Flamenco

Flamenco is 'the' dance of Spain, but it was actually a mix of non-spanish minorities who were responsible for its survival. The gitanos (gypsies) who travelled the area around Cádiz and Seville in the 15th century are said to have invented the 'cante andaluz' (Andalusian canto) or 'cante jondo' (deep canto). Flamenco was later used as background music in brothels until it became acceptable in the 1920s.

The musical form has been internationally renowned since Carlos Sauras' sensational film Carmen. Flamenco is not just a dance to an exciting rhythm or a simple form of entertainment with catchy tunes, it is also a way of opening up the soul. For many, it is also the impressive reflection of a way of life – pride and passion under the torrid Andalusian sun.

Your Andalusian excursion takes you 1,600 km (994 miles) through the mountains of the Sierra Nevada Range, across the fertile plains of the Guadalquivir River and on down towards the Costa del Sol and the Costa del Luz. You'll visit the charming 'white villages' and the magnificent cities that are home to Moorish architectural masterpieces.

1 Seville For detailed information see p. 91.

2 Vega del Guadalquivir After leaving Seville on the C431 towards Córdoba you will emerge onto the flat, green and fertile plains known as the Vega del Guadalquivir. It is one of Andalusia's primary agricultural regions, with orange plantations, cornfields and sunflower fields sprawling across a wide valley formed by the river that made Seville a world power in the days of the explorers.

Small villages pop up along the route, with tidy white houses perched on top of lush hills. Most of the people in the area live off the rich agricultural bounty.

3 Palma del Río Its prime location at the confluence of the Guadalquivir and Genil is romantic enough. Add to that the verdant green surroundings and you've got two good reasons why this area is called 'Andalusia's Garden'.

The impressive 12th-century city walls have been well preserved in parts and recall the town's

rich history, which goes back to the Romans who founded it. Palma del Río then played a special role in Spain's history from the 16th to 18th centuries when the Convento de San Francisco regularly sent missionaries to the New World. One of them was Brother Junípero Serra, who was responsible in large for the fabulous mission churches that can still be seen in California. But those times have long passed and the monastery has been given a new purpose now – beautifully renovated, today it is used as a hotel.

4 Medina Azahara Just before reaching Córdoba, a road turns off towards the ruins of Medina Azahara, the old palace city built on three terraces where the caliphs lived together with their royal suite between the mid 10th and early 11th centuries. Parts of the complex have been renovated and give you a pretty good idea of the former beauty of the 'Flower City', a masterpiece of Islamic architecture.

5 Córdoba This city was an important political and cultural

centre as early as Roman times – one of its most famous sons is the philosopher, Seneca, from the 3rd century BC. By AD 929, Córdoba had risen to become one of the Caliphate's most resplendent metropolises on Spanish soil, competing even with the likes of the former cosmopolitan city of Baghdad. Jews, Arabs and Christians lived in harmony with each other. Science and philosophy flourished like never before.

In the old city centre, traces remain of this heyday when the mighty Caliphate city had over a million inhabitants. It has now become a provincial capital with a population of just 300,000, but Córdoba remains a gem indeed: the Old City's narrow little alleyways, whitewashed houses and inner courtyards decorated with flowers all create an idyllic scene.

At the centre of it all is the Mezquita – previously a mosque and now a cathedral – standing

In 1911 began the excavations and reconstructions of the palace city of Medina Azahara.

Santa Maria de la Sede, the cathedral of Seville, is the largest gothic church in the world.

Seville

To experience Spain you simply have to visit Seville, the capital of Andalusia.

Seville is one of the country's most charming cities, competing directly with Granada, Andalusia's second Moorish treasure, for the position. After America was discovered, Seville had its heyday as a river port on the Guadalquivir and as an important trading centre where goods from Spanish colonies overseas were unloaded and transported to the inte-rior. This brought extreme wealth and a breath of fresh air from the New World to this old city!

Particularly worth seeing here are the 15th-century Santa María Cathedral, a complex with lavishly designed porticos, the Patio de los Naranjos, the former mosque courtyard with early medieval marble bowls, and the Giralda bell tower, built as a minaret in the 12th century; the Reales Alcázares, built in the 12th century by the Almohadas, used as a Christian royal palace from 1248 and continually expanded until the 16th century.

Highlights of any visit also include the exquisitely decorated interior courtyards around which the palace buildings are grouped, as well as the gardens there (the cathedral and the Alcázares are UNESCO World Heritage Sites); the Barrio de Santa Cruz, the Jewish quarter with its narrow alleys, tiled inner courtyards and wrought-iron balconies; the Casa de Pilatos, a rambling private palace combining a fascinating mix of styles; the Hospital de la Caridad (17th century), the most important piece of Sevillian baroque architecture; the Museo de Bellas Artes with collections focusing on Spanish baroque art; the Plaza de España, a dazzling structure with ceramic paintings in the city park, Parque de María Luisa. Outside the city are the ruins of the Roman Itálica.

The churches of Iglesia de la Villa (16th century) and Iglesia de la Encarnación (18th century) tower over Montefrío.

Moorish art

Andalusia owes its most magnificent buildings to the Arabs who once ruled the area – the Mezquita in Córdoba, the Alhambra in Granada, and the Alcázar and the Giralda in Seville.

One of the outstanding features of Moorish style is its ornate attention to detail. Because Islam prohibits the depiction of any of Allah's creatures, exquisite wall patterns were created in inscriptions and by combining geometric, floral and calligraphy motifs. The grandiose ornamentation often incorporated mosaics, ceramics, Koranic proverbs sculptured in marble and glass compounds adorned with Byzantine patterns imported from the eastern end of the Mediterranean. Mosques usually contained extravagant domes and entire halls of columns.

The style of arch most frequently used are the rounded, spiked or the Moorish horse-

Mezquita in Córdoba

shoe arch. The most popular building material during the time of the caliphs was ashlar rock. The Almohadas used natural stone for foundations and pedestals, and fired bricks and stamped clay for other parts of the structures. Apart from the religious buildings and the palaces, Moorish architecture is still visible in the maze of streets in many of the Old City quarters in Andalusia.

strong like an old fortification. The enormous building, with the magnificent prayer hall supported by 856 ornate columns, was declared a UNESCO 'Legacy of Mankind'. Nineteen naves and thirty-eight transepts, exquisite Oriental decorations and light casting mysterious shadows on the pillars make the Mezquita a truly unforgettable sight.

Just next to the Mezquita is the Judería, the former Jewish quarter with narrow streets adorned with flowers. One of the most beautiful of these is the aptly named Calleja de las Flores. The former synagogue and the bullfighting museum, which incidentally is one of the most interesting in all of Spain, are also worth a visit.

The Alcázar de los Reyes Cristianos, a royal residence built as a fort in the 14th century, has really lovely gardens. The Museo Arqueológico Provincial, located in a Renaissance palace, has a number of Roman, Visigoth and Arabic exhibits. In the quarter around the Christian churches, Córdoba has another tourist attraction in store – the Palacio de Viana, a mansion with twelve inner courtyards and spectacular gardens. The two most important centres during Spain's Moorish period, Córdoba and Granada,

are connected by the Caliphate Route. Today it is known as the N432, a slightly less romantic name, but it still passes through a hilly region with relatively little settlement, some small homesteads and a handful of wellfortified castles and towers. At the town of Alcalá la Real, nestled in the shadow of the Moorish Castillo de la Mota, you leave the N432 for a leisurely drive through the villages of the fertile highlands of the Vega.

6 Montefrío This town lies in a unique mountain landscape and is known for its castle, Castillo de la Villa, which was built around 1500 on the walls of an old Moorish fort.

After some 20 km (12 miles) you come to the A9 heading towards Granada.

7 Granada The geographic location of this city is fascinating in itself – bordered in the west by a high plateau, in the south by the northern bank of the river Genil, and with the snowcapped peaks of the Sierra Nevada as a background set-ting. However, what really gives Granada its 'One-Thousand-and-One-Nights' feel is the extensive Moorish legacy that has defined this city for more than seven hundred years now.

Granada experienced its heyday between the 13th and 15th centuries, before the Moors were pushed south by the gathering armies of the Christian 'Reconquista'. At that point the city had been the capital of the independent Kingdom of the Nasrids for 250 years, and it was during this time that its most magnificent edifice was built – the Alhambra.

A total of twenty-three sultans from the Nasrid Dynasty contributed to this tour de force of

Detour

Carretera Granada–Veleta

Europe's highest mountain road runs for 46 km (29 miles) from Granada to Pico Veleta, the sec-ond-highest peak in the Sierra Nevada at 3,392 m (2,108 ft). The mountain is normally only free of snow from August to September, snow fields are quite common along the road, which has an average incline of 5.1 per cent from Granada and 6.5 per cent from the start of the slope. The view from the top is sensational, spanning from the mountains of the Sierra Nevada over Granada, the Mediterranean and to the North African coast.

Spanish-Arabic constructions. Now the castle, at once fortress-like and elegant, is the pearl of the city of Granada.

The Alhambra, whose name 'The Red One' derives from the reddish ochre of its walls, is an enormous complex of fortifications, towers, royal residential palaces, mosques and gardens. It comprises four main sections – the defences, or Alcazaba, on the western tip of the hill; the Palacio Árabe (Alhambra Palace); the Palacio de Carlos V, a Renaissance palace with the Museum of Fine Arts in the centre of the hill; and the gardens of the Generalife in the east. Apart from the gardens, which were part of a summer residence, all other buildings are surrounded by fortified walls with towers. The Palacio de los Leones, with its arcade passage adorned with filigree work, and the lion fountain are two of the most impressive parts of the Alhambra, along with the water features in the gardens, which have a real oasis feel. But the Alhambra is not all that this splendid city has to offer.

The Albaicin is also something to behold – the whitewashed Moorish quarter is an architectural gem in its own right, with tiny alleyways and the mirador, the San Nicolás lookout. In addition, there is the area around the 16th/17th-century cathedral, the Capilla Real, the late-Gothic royal chapel and the Carthusian monastery, founded in the early 16th century – each and every one of them worth a visit. A must for poetry-lovers after all this is the small detour from Granada to Fuente Vaqueros, the birthplace of García Lorca, 17 km (11 miles) away on the plains. From there it is up into the mountains for a detour into the Sierra Nevada over Europe's highest pass. As you leave Granada heading east on a small road parallel to the A92, the landscape becomes sparser and wilder. This effect is enhanced when you see the first cave dwellings dug into the rocky hillsides.

8 Guadix This truly ancient city with grand Moorish ruins and a history that dates back to Roman times also has a section with cave dwellings – some five thousand gitanos (gypsies) live here underground in the Barrio de Santiago. Their homes, painstakingly carved into the steep loess slopes and actually comprising multiple rooms, are even connected to the city water supply and electricity network.

The landscape remains sparse for a while now. After Guadix, the castle of La Calahorra is worth a detour. The Gulf of Almería soon comes into view.

9 Almería This fine city has always benefited from its special geographic location. Protected from the mainland by mountain ranges, the vast Gulf of Almería

Left side: Puente Romano and Torre de la Calahorra in Córdoba. Above: Views of the Alhambra of Granada.

Detour

Sierra Nevada

The Sierra Nevada, whose name literally means 'Snowy Range', is Spain's highest mountain range. Its name obviously says a lot about these mountains – they are often snow-capped, even in sum-

Snowy Sierra Nevada

mer. There are fourteen peaks here over 3,000 m (9,843 ft), in front of which are mountain ranges also reaching up to 2,000 m (6,562 ft) in height. The highest point is the Cerro de Mulhacén at 3,481 m (11,421 ft). Between the second-highest peak, the Pico Veleta, and the town of Pradollano, located at an elevation of 1,300 m (4,265 ft), is an excellent region for skiing with nineteen lifts and a total of 61 km (38 miles) of trails.

The small town of Olvera has a lot of pomp: The La Encarnación church is fighting for supremacy over the Moorish castle.

Costa del Sol

'Costa del Sol' – the Sunshine Coast – refers to a roughly 150-km-long (93-mile) stretch of the southeastern coast of Spain. And rightly so, because this lovely area of Andalusia enjoys a pleasant, sunny climate, with mild temperatures even in winter. It is certainly one of the reasons that the Costa del Sol has become one of the most popular holiday destinations in the world. Many of the small, once poor, fishing towns like Fuengirola and Torremolinos have now become tourist hot spots with enormous hotel and apartment complexes, holiday villas, golf courses and yacht harbours.

Some of the former villages have kept their Andalusian charm, including Estepona. Even Marbella, the luxurious and glamorous city favoured by the international jetset, has preserved traditional houses, lanes, squares and gardens in its historic centre.

fulfills all the right conditions for a nice harbour and a good centre for trade. The Phoenicians even recognized this and built a harbour that became the foundation for the Roman Portus Magnus. Pirates later found it to be an ideal hideout, too.During the time of the caliphs, Almería experienced yet another rise as an important trading centre, becoming the capital of a kingdom to which the likes of Córdoba, Murcia, Jaén and even parts of Granada temporarily paid allegiance. In 1489, the city was reconquered by the Christians and from then on only played a secondary role.Today, Almería is very much an agricultural town. The surrounding area is home to rows of enormous greenhouses where fruit and vegetables are grown for export. The nearby Andarax Valley is home to the region's orchards and vineyards. Almería is a predominantly modern town with wide, palm-lined streets dominated by the massive alcazaba (fort), which sits on top of a hill as if on its own throne. Construction began on the alcazaba in the 10th century and it is one of the most powerful and best-preserved fort complexes in all of Andalusia. The Old Town, with its picturesque fishing and gitano quarter

on the castle hill, La Chanca, still has an undeniable Moorish feel to it. The colourful cubic houses and the cave dwellings look like relics from distant times. For the next part of the journey there is an alternative route to the highway – the very picturesque 332/348, which take you inland through the mountains of the Sierra Nevada and then back down the coast. Passing through Motril, the road continues towards the Costa del Sol through the fertile plains where tropical fruits are a speciality. Along the way, a good place to stop is Nerja, about 50 km (31 miles) before reaching Málaga. Perched on a ridge, this town is home to the amazing Cueva de Nerja dripstone cave.

⑩ Málaga Málaga is a very important economic centre, Andalusia's second-largest city with over half a million inhabitants, and the second-largest Spanish port on the Mediterranean after that of Barcelona. It is the main trading centre for the agricultural products from the nearby plains, in particular wine and raisins.

In terms of tourist attractions, Málaga does not have a lot to offer. However, it is well worth climbing up to the Gibralfaro, the Moorish citadel and lighthouse that gives you a beautiful view of the semicircular expanse of land.

Today, next to nothing remains of the splendour of the alcazaba – often compared to the Alhambra in Granada – and the cathedral, whose construction started in the 16th century but was not completed: the middle section of the tower, 'La Manquita', (the missing one) is still open for all to see. From Málaga, the Costa

The waterfront of Cádiz is breathtaking with the neo-classical monumental building built in 1722. The new Cathedral with a mighty yellow cupola sits in the background.

Detour

Gibraltar

The first impression is imposing: the 425-m-high (1,394-ft) limestone rock of Gibraltar suddenly soars out of the sea, connected to the mainland only by a flat alluvial plain. This is where the airfield was built, and where every visitor must pass upon presenting their passport or personal ID. The British enclave, just 6 sq km (2.3 sq mi) in size and with a population of 30,000, controls the strait between Europe and Africa. Its name derives from Djebal al-Tarik, – Tarik's Mountain – the name of its Arab conqueror from 711.

The British originally seized the strategically important southern tip of Spain in 1713 during the War of the Spanish Succession, and at the start of the 19th century they built the Anglican Church here. Today, the British governor resides in a former Franciscan monastery dating back to the 16th century. The official language on the island is English and the most interesting tourist attraction is the cable car to the top of the rock. From the top there is an amazing view of the Bay of Algeciras, the Gibraltar harbour and the North African coast.

The darlings of all visitors to Gibraltar, however, are the frisky Barbary apes, which can be fed without any problem. Legend has it that Britain's rule of Gibraltar will be protected as long as the apes continue to inhabit the rock.

del Sol continues along coastal road 340 with its large holiday resorts. After Marbella, the main road turns off into San Pedro de Alcántara. For those who want to enjoy some beautiful scenery, however, drive another 30 km (19 miles) west and take the route at Manilva that heads up into the Serranía de Ronda. If you wish to to visit Gibraltar you can do so by continuing another 40 km (25 miles) from Manilva along the coastal road.

11 Ronda If for nothing else, this town is worth seeing for its adventuresome location. It lies at the edge of a high plateau divided by the Río Guadalevín, which flows by in a gorge that is up to 200 m (656 ft) deep. Its houses and numerous mansions are built right up to the edge of the cliff.

The 98-m-high (322-ft) Puente Nuovo, built in the 18th century, spans the gorge. Ernest Hemingway was as fascinated with the city, the deep gorge, the houses and the cliffs as was the poet Rainer Maria Rilke, who once wrote: 'I have searched everywhere for my dream city and I have found it in Ronda.'

Ronda is divided into three sections. The oldest, La Ciudad, lies in the middle of the limestone plateau and is bordered on one side by a Moorish wall and on the other by steep terrain; sprawled at its feet is the San Francisco Quarter, with a street network lined with farms; and on the other side of the 'Tajo' gorge is the modern area El Mercadillo, where most of Ronda's 35,000 inhabitants live.

One of the most important attractions here is the Casa del Rey Moro in the La Ciudad. Inside the rock, a staircase with 365 steps leads down from this Moorish palace into the gorge. The cathedral, the Palacio de Mondragón and the Casa del Gigante with their Arabic ornamentation and decorative elements are worth seeing.

Then there is the bullfighting arena. Built in 1785, it is one of the oldest in Spain. Ronda was also the place where bullfights were given a sort of 'constitution' in the 18th century.

It is absolutely essential to do day trips around Ronda where the 'white villages' are charmingly tucked into the rugged mountains and valleys – Prado del Rey, with its neatly planned streets; Ubrique, capital of the Sierra de Cádiz, known for its leather products; Zahara or Setenil, which look like large eyries with their houses clinging to the rock; and of course Olvera, a town whose architecture is still entirely Moorish and whose walled upper city is dominated by a 12th-century castle.

12 Arcos de la Frontera The route now continues towards the Atlantic coast, passing by Embalse de Zahara. This town has a population of 30,000 and sits on a rocky ridge basically in the middle of the Guadelete River. Its whitewashed houses still create a Moorish atmosphere, while the church of San Pedro is most definitely worth a look, perched directly on a cliff with an impressive view of the gorge and the plains with their seemingly endless olive groves. The route now follows Highway 328 towards the Atlantic coast, although it is worth making a detour to Cádiz beforehand.

13 Cádiz This city is considered the oldest in Spain; the Phoenicians were already making good use of its narrow, 10-km-long (6-mile) peninsula as a storage yard. Much later, after America was discovered, the city became

Left side: Ronda and the fortress-like Cathedral of Almería; Above: Port of Málaga with a bullring.

95

Sherry

It stood prominently on the crest of a hill, stood out in deep black and looked almost threatening against the bright blue sky, his horns appearing sharp and pointy in the silhouette. For a long time, the bull was an advertisement for a type of sherry, but it has long been the unofficial symbol of Spain. Thanks to Sir Francis Drake the sherry bull is now a recognised symbol that goes beyond its hometown of Jerez. In a raid in 1587, a pirate took 3000 hoses to England. The British royal court wanted more of the fine drink. In the region boasts the ideal requirements: The vines grow in Jerez on very

Detour

Coto de Doñana

This region covering 757 sq km (292 sq mi) of the Guadalquivir delta area has been a national park since 1969. Formerly a royal hunting ground, a sand dune separates the marsh from the sea. This allowed numerous biotopes to develop where rare and endangered animal species live and migratory birds make temporary stops.

Visiting the dunes in summer: bee-eaters.

extremely wealthy. Cádiz is still the second most important shipyard in Spain after El Ferrol. Fish is also an important source of revenue, as is salt, which is obtained from enormous salt refineries in the south-east of the city. The best way to discover Cádiz is to take a taxi ride around the Old Town, which is especially picturesque with the golden cupola of the Catedral Nueva towering over the tiny square houses. The treasures of its church include the largest and most precious processional monstrance in the world. The Church of San Felipe Neri downtown is also worth a visit as the location where the Cádiz Cortes government in exile declared Spain's liberal Constitution in 1812. The Museo de Bellas Artes has some beautiful works by Spanish masters such as Francisco de Zurbarán and Murillo. North of Cádiz on the Atlantic coast is a series of lovely resort towns – Puerto Real, Puerto de Santa Maria, Rota and Chipiona all have long, wide, fine sandy beaches.

⑭ Sanlúcar de Barrameda This dignified city, located at the mouth of the Guadalquivir, is the export hub for the famous Manzanilla sherry. The Fino variety is only produced here in Sanlúcar. The city is divided into

two sections, the upper and lower city. Be sure to pay a visit to the palace of the once influential dukes of Medina-Sidonia and the superb Mudejar portico of the Church of Santa Maria. Another attraction is the royal equestrian school, the Real Escuela Andaluza de Arte Ecuestre, where you can witness Spanish dressage riding styles. This famous port saw Columbus begin his third voyage to America, and Magellan also set off from here on the trip on which his ship became the first to circumnavigate the globe. Long before that, the Holy Virgin is said to have appeared here, hence the name Coto de Doñana (Coast of the Mistress). Today, you can take a boat to the Parque Nacional de Coto de Doñana from the quay. From Sanlúcar the C440 'Ruta del Vino', or Wine Road, leads into the home of jerez (sherry).

⑮ Jerez de la Frontera A visit to one of the most wonderful bodegas – wine cellars – is a must in this charming city so rich in tradition. Many of these bodegas also have something special to offer apart from sherry. The Bodega Domecq in Calle Ildefonso, for example, enchants visitors with its Moorish interior, while the ironwork in the Bodega González Byass was done by none other than Gustave Eiffel. Those still keen on seeing more sights after the enticing bodegas should head to the Old Town and have a look at the 17th/18th-century Church of San Salvador, the 11th-century Alcázar and the 'Cartuja', somewhat outside the city, whose Gothic church is particularly ornate.
From Jerez, highway E05 then heads back to your starting point, Seville.

At the top: The Cathedral of San Salvador of Jerez de la Frontera. Above: Every year a traditional horse race takes place on the beach of Sanlúcar de Barrameda.

calcareous soil; the grapes are dried before being pressing on the mild, salty air. This gives them the typical sweet taste.

Seville The capital of Andalusia and host of the 1992 EXPO lies on the banks of the Guadalquivir. It was an important trading centre after the discovery of the Americas. The 15th-century cathedral, with Moorish elements from the 12th century, the former royal palaces, the museums, the Plaza de España and the former Jewish quarter all make this city an absolute must.

Córdoba The hometown of the philosopher, Seneca, was already of importance during Roman times and in 929 became the centre point of the Spanish Caliphate. There are still traces of this around the great Mezquita – once a mosque, now a cathedral.

Granada Surrounded by the Sierra Nevada and the Río Genil, Granada's greatest treasure is the Alhambra, a sultan's residence with fortress walls, towers, residential palaces, mosques and gardens, inhabited by twenty-three Nasrid rulers over the centuries.

Montefrío A lovely view of Montefrío from the south with its white houses, quaint churches and Moorish ruins all clinging to the jagged slopes.

The Sierra Nevada National Park The country's highest mountain range is home to excellent ski slopes and is often covered in snow until well into summer.

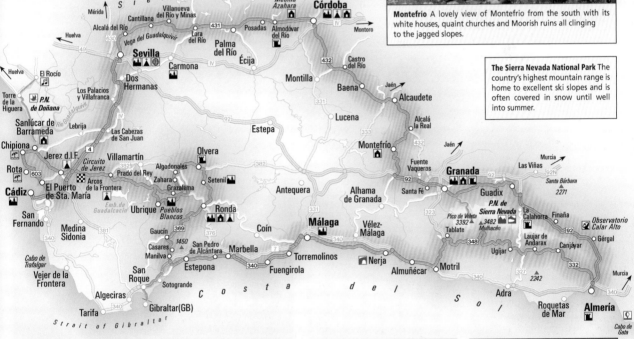

Ronda Hemingway was one of many famous artists and writers to have spent long periods of time in this fascinating town.

Gibraltar A trip up the 425-m-high (1,394-ft) rock inhabited by the famous Barbary apes is worth it: the view of the British outpost and North Africa is spectacular.

Arcos de la Frontera Whitewashed houses give the town a slightly Arabic feel. The views from the village over the area and the gorge are fantastic.

Almería This coastal city has a picturesque Old Town and a mighty cathedral, towered over by the Alcazaba (10th century), the largest Moorish fort in Spain.

Route 8: Portugal

The land of fado and peaceful matadors

When it was still a province of the Roman empire, what is now Portugal was once called Lusitania. In the sixth century it was part of the Visigothic empire. In the 8th century the Moors took over, but as a result of the 'Reconquista' to take back Iberia, it became a kingdom separate from Galicia and León. Portugal finally gained independence in around 1267, and takes its name from the port city of Porto (Latin: porto cale).

Route profile:

Length: approx. 1,250 km (775 mi)
Time required: 14–16 days
When to go: The best times to visit Portugal are spring and autumn. Summer can be gruellingly hot.

Portugal was known in Antiquity and in the Middle Ages as the 'edge of the world' and, even in the 20th century, its location on the edge of the continent had both advantages and disadvantages. It is a relatively narrow country, roughly 150 km (93 mi) wide and 550 km (342 mi) in length, but it has 832 km (517 mi) of coastline characterized by steep cliffs and miles of glorious beaches.

The mighty Tagus River (Tejo) divides the mountainous north, the Montanhas, from the rolling south known as Planícies, or plains. In the north you journey through what is still largely an untouched forest and mountain landscape with abundant water resources, the Costa Verde with its pine groves, the fertile Minho region with the vineyards of the Douro Valley, and the remote 'land behind the mountains', Trás-os-Montes.

Central Portugal has a very different character, with the Serra da Estrela range rising to an altitude of almost 2,000 m (6,562 ft), with vineyards dotting the river valleys and the flood plains of the Tagus. Southern Portugal is dominated by Alentejo, Portugal's 'breadbasket', with its vast landed estates that were dissolved after the 'Carnation Revolution' of 1974. It is a flat, open region extending as far as the Serra de Monchique. Portugal's best-known region, of course, is Algarve, with its rocky cliffs and sandy beaches.

The population distribution is

uneven throughout the country. While the sparse mountain regions are largely empty, there are almost three million people in Lisbon and almost one million in the greater Porto region. Cork is one of Portugal's best-known agricultural products: the country has more than eighty-six million cork oaks and they have to be twenty years old before the bark can be peeled for the first time. Today one in three of the world's wine corks still comes from Portugal.

As with most European countries, Portugal, too, has a diverse historical and cultural heritage to look back on. Unique throughout all of Europe, however, is the Manueline architectural style, which enjoyed its heyday during the reign of King Manuel I (1495–1521), arguably

Above: The view from the opposite bank of the Douro in Porto's Ribeira district and the towering cathedral is unparalleled.
Left: City centre of Braga with the impressive cathedral.

Portugal's 'golden age'. The Manueline is a mixture of Gothic and Renaissance elements, supplemented with frenzied decoration inspired by exploration. The cultural influence of the Portuguese voyages of discovery saw the development of exotic, maritime ornaments that were utilized in abundance everywhere. The azulejos, the usually blue and white tiles that can be found almost everywhere in Portugal, are a Moorish legacy and, in addition to their aesthetic function, they protect against heat, provide sound insulation, reflect light and liven up surfaces. Those hoping to immerse themselves in the world of the Portuguese will not be able to avoid saudade, a word that somehow defies translation because it denotes a sentiment that seems to exist only in Portugal and that is also intricately linked to the language's long development. The word derives from the Latin 'solus', meaning loneliness, and therefore also expresses feelings such as solitude, yearning, melancholy, mourning, pain, and a restrained joy of life. Saudade is best expressed in fado, the traditional Portuguese folk song alleged to originate from Lisbon's Alfama district and from Coimbra. They are tristful songs mostly concerned with unfulfilled longing, lost love or despair. In Lisbon, fado is primarily performed by female singers accompanied by two guitarists, while in Coimbra it is typically young men who convey this sense of 'fatum' (fate) deriving from social and political circumstances, like Jose Afonso with his fado number 'Grandola', which accompanied the 1974 Carnation Revolution leading to the overthrow of the Salazar dictatorship.

It is a telling reflection of Portugal – a beautiful country with a hint of sadness.

Left side: Waves breaking on the rocks at Praia da Marina near Carvoeiro in the Algarve.
Above: Lisbon is also called the 'white city on the Tagus'.

You can walk around the town wall in Óbidos in around 45 minutes.

Sintra and the Palácio Nacional da Pena

This former Moorish town and later summer residence of the Portuguese kings and aristocracy lies at the base of a rocky outcrop with dense vegetation. It is characterized by winding alleyways, picturesque street corners and charming quintas. In the town center is the Paço Real, the Manueline city palace (15th/16th century) that offers a mixture of diverse architectural styles. Its oversized chimneys are the landmark of the town. The Palácio is visible from a distance and dominates the town of Sintra from atop the highest of its rocky promontories.

This Portuguese fairy-tale creation is a pseudo-medieval fortified castle with a truly bewildering mix of styles, from Gothic doors, Manueline windows, Byzantine ceilings and minaret-like towers to Moorish azulejos and other Romanesque and Renaissance ele-

ments. The whole thing is fascinatingly bizarre.

It was built between 1840 and 1850 by the Baron of Eschwege on behalf of Prince Ferdinand of Saxe-Coburg.

This circuit of Portugal begins in Lisbon and takes you west from the capital as far as Cabo da Roca before heading north to the culturally exciting cities of Porto and Braga. After a detour to the ancient town of Bragança, it then turns to the south passing through the Ribatejo and Alentejo regions on the way to Faro in the Algarve before returning to Lisbon along the coast.

1 Lisbon (see p. 101)

2 Cascais The long beaches here have transformed this fishing village into a popular destination with plenty of cafés and boutiques.

The daily fish auction provides something of a contrast to the main sightseeing attractions, which include the Parque da Gandarinha as well as the ornate azulejos in the old town hall and in the Nossa Senhora de Nazaré chapel.

A scenic coastal road takes you to Europe's western-most point north of Cascais. Cabo da Roca rises up 160 m (525 ft) out of the pounding Atlantic.

3 Sintra (see sidebar left)

4 Mafra North of Sintra is Mafra, home to a colossal palace completed in 1750, with which King João V once aimed to overshadow the Spanish El Escorial. Behind the 220-m-long (241-yd) façade are 880 rooms,

a chapel the size of a cathedral and a sizable basilica.

5 Óbidos From Mafra, you continue north along the coast as far as Peniche, one of Portugal's largest fishing ports. Situated on a prominent headland jutting out into the sea, Peniche has an 18th-century maritime fort that is worth visiting before heading inland toward Óbidos. Óbidos, also known as the Queen's Village, is a must-see in Portugal. The fortified hilltop village boasts charming alleys with tidy white houses decorated with flowers, all contained within a picturesque medieval town wall that is up to 15 m (49 ft) high in places.

6 Alcobaça It is hard to believe that one of Christianity's largest sacral buildings – the former Cistercian Mosteiro de Santa Maria de Alcobaça – was built in this town of just under 6,000 inhabitants north of Caldas da Reinha. Founded in the

late 12th century and completed in about 1250, it was the first Gothic edifice in Portugal.

The three-storey baroque façade (18th century) is 220 m (241 yds) wide and 42 m (138 ft) high. The three naves of the Gothic interior are also impressive due to their unusual dimensions: 106 m (16 yds) long, 20 m (66 ft) high, but just 17 m (19 yds) wide. Many of the visitors here are pilgrims visiting the tombs of King Pedro I and his murdered mistress Ines de Castro, who is buried directly opposite him so that, 'at the resurrection, each of them should see the other first of all'. The complex is a UNESCO World Heritage Site.

7 Batalha This simple country town is on the way to Leiria and is also a UNESCO World Heritage Site for the world-famous

Above: Exceptional rock formations on the beach in front of Cabo da Roca.

Left: Lisbon by night: Praça do Restauradores in the bustling Baixa district; Below: Equestrian statue on the Praça do Comércio.

Lisbon

The sea of buildings in the 'white city' extends from the wide mouth of the Tagus River up the steep hills of the Barrio Alto. Lisbon's wonderful location attracts visitors from all over the world who, like the locals, navigate the hilly city in eléctricos, creeky old trams.

Sights particularly worth seeing in Lisbon include: Alfama, the oldest and most picturesque district with labyrinthine streets on a fortified hill, dominated by the ruins of the Castelo de São Jorge; the two (of many) lovely miradouros, or viewing terraces, that make Lisbon so enjoyable, are tucked between the ruined fortress and the medieval Sé Cathedral; the Avenida da Liberdade, a 90-m-wide (98-yd) boulevard from the 19th century; the Barrio Alto (upper town), an entertainment district with bars and fado taverns; Baixa, the lower town rebuilt in a regimented fashion following the devastating earthquake of 1755, today a banking and shopping district; Chiado, the former intellectuals' district in Belle Époque style; the Elevador de Santa Justa (1901) between the upper and lower town; the Museu do Azulejo in the Madre de Deus monastery; the Museu Calouste Gulbenkian, an oil magnate's foundation with top-ranking European art; the Museu de Arte Antiga, the largest museum of Portuguese art; the Oceanário, a magnificent aquarium; and the Palácio dos Marqueses da Fronteira with its magnificent baroque garden.

The 'royal cloister' in the Santa Maria da Vitória Monastery, Batalha.

Detour

Fátima and Tomar

Fátima is an unassuming place on the Cova da Iria plateau north of the Tagus, but it has also been one of the most important Catholic pilgrimage destinations since 1917. The Virgin Mary appeared before three shepherd's children on a total of six occasions. At the last appearance, 70,000 people witnessed the 'Milagre do Sol', when the sky is said to have darkened and the sun, blood red, circled around itself. Following an eight-year period of research, the Vatican ultimately recognized the apparition of the Virgin and had the Rosary Basilica built at the site in 1928, which attracts hundreds of thousands of pilgrims every year.

Not far from Fátima is the small town of Tomar, which is dominated by the fortress-like former convent belonging to the Order of Christ, an order of medieval knights founded in 1314, following the suppression of the Knights Templar (founded in 1119) and

Convent in Tomar

which was subject to the will of the king and not of the Pope. The order's red cross was long resplendent on the sails of Portuguese caravels. The former Templar fort was later converted to a monastic castle in the Manueline style and is now a UNESCO World Heritage Site.

Santa Maria da Vitória monastery. Construction began in 1388, following João I's historical victory at Aljabarrota (1385), but it was not completed until 1533. The complex has become a kind of national shrine for the Portuguese as a symbol of the country's independence from Spain. A 15-m-high (49-ft), elaborately decorated Manueline portal invites you to enter the cathedral, which is nearly as long as a football field and 32 m (105 ft) high. It is adjoined by the 'royal' cloister and contains the tomb of King João I.

⑧ Leiria Portugal's coat of arms contains the images of seven castles. One of these is in Leiria and it is one of Portugal's most beautiful. The history of its construction begins with the Romans, is influenced by the Moors, and continues through

to the crusaders. The complex is now a mix of Gothic and Renaissance styles and affords a magnificent view of Portugal's largest pine forest.

From Leiria it is worth taking a detour to the south-east, first to Fátima, a pilgrimage site about 30 km (19 mi) away, and then to the Templar castle in Tomar.

⑨ Coimbra This town on the steep banks of the Rio Mondego is one of Europe's oldest university towns (12th century) and in fact was the only one in Portugal until 1910. The center boasts a fortress-like cathedral (Sé Velha, the largest Romanesque church in Portugal), also dating from the 12th century. Behind the cathedral you then continue up to the old university, which is the former royal palace. The highlight here is the library (1716–1728), Portugal's loveliest ba-

roque construction featuring gilded wood and fresco ceilings by Portuguese artists. Not far from the library, in the former bishop's palace, is the Museu Machado de Castro, with the Sé Nova (new cathedral), a former Jesuit church (1600) high on the slope above it.

A short walk takes you through a maze of alleys to the Mosteiro de Santa Cruz, a former Augustinian monastery. Take a break in the Parque de Santa Cruz, part of the monastery grounds. The Quinta das Lágrimas estate was the setting for the love story between Spanish Crown Prince Pedro and his mistress Ines that ended in such tragedy. The Fonte las Lágrimas (Fountain of Tears) supposedly originated with Ines' tears after her death. Life in Coimbra is heavily influenced by the 20,000 students who still wear the tradi-

The monumental baroque stairway up the Bom Jesus do Monte pilgrimage church in Braga.

tional capa gown, and not just for special occasions like the Queima das Fitas festival.

⑩ Porto It was no coincidence that Portugal's second-largest town on the Costa Verde was the European Capital of Culture in 2001. The port at the mouth of the Rio Douro has a great deal to offer visitors. Five bridges now link Porto with Vila Nova de Gaia, where a majority of the port wineries are based.
The streets and rows of houses in Porto's Old Town seem to cling precariously to the steep granite cliffs. At the lower end of the Avenida dos Aliados is the Praça Liberdade with the Torre dos Clerigos, the highest church tower in Portugal at 75 m (246 ft). At the other end is the town hall with its 70-m-high (230-ft) bell tower. The huge azulejo scenes on the wall of the São

Bento railway station are especially worth seeing as well.
En route to the Ponte de Dom Luis I you come to the cathedral with its sacrament altar made from 800 kg (1,764 lbs) of silver. From here you can go down into the Bairro da Sé district, the oldest part of Porto, or to the Largo do Colegio. The Praça da Ribeiro and the Praça Infante Dom Henriques make up the heart of the Ribeira district, where wealth and poverty collide – the stock exchange is juxtaposed with narrow, dingy alleyways.

⑪ Braga This old episcopal city is inland and to the northeast of Porto and is home to twenty churches closely packed together. The originally Romanesque cathedral was frequently remodeled over the centuries and has two massive towers. Other sites include the 18th-cen-

tury Palácio dos Biscainhos, surrounded by a magnificent garden; the Oratorio São Frutuoso (7th century) is located 4 km (2.5 mi) outside town; the baroque pilgrimage church of Bom Jesus do Monte, 7 km (4 mi) away, is also famous for its elaborate staircase designed to match the Stations of the Cross (18th century). It is Portugal's second-most important pilgrimage destination after Fátima.

⑫ Guimarães This town 22 km (14 mi) south-west of Braga proudly claims to be the 'Cradle of Portugal'. It was here that the founder of the Kingdom of Portugal, Afonso Henriques, was born in 1111.
His Romanesque castle with its mighty 27-m (89-ft) tower stands high on the 'holy hill' above town, and the palace of the dukes of Bragança (15th century) is in the charming Old Town. Nossa Senhora da Oliveira Church is also worth seeing. From Guimarães, the scenic N206 heads to Bragança in the north-east of Portugal. It is a

Large Image: Alley in the old quarter of Porto; Left side: Mosteiro de Santa Cruz in Coimbra; Above: Castle of Guimarães.

Detour

Bragança

This town in the somewhat spare, north-eastern reaches of Portugal was once the ancestral seat of the last Portuguese royal family. The castle, which dominates the town, was built in 1187, has eighteen towers and a mighty keep, the 15th-century Torre de Menagem.

Torre de Menagem

In front is a 6.4 m (21 ft) pillory (pelourinho) on a granite wild boar.
In the town itself is the Domus Municipalis, a type of Romanesque style town hall. The cathedral was originally Romanesque, but later converted to the Renaissance style in the 16th century.

103

Detour

Elvas

This town close to the Spanish border is situated among olive groves and plum orchards. The former border town has maintained a Moorish medieval character with its ramparts, fortified towers, terraces and the old aqueduct from the 17th century. Part of this ensemble is the fortress-like Gothic Nossa Senhora da Assunção church with its pyramid-shaped, tapered bell tower, built between 1515 and 1520 on the black and white paved Praça de República. The famous Pelourinho de Elvas, an octagonal marble column with

worthy detour despite the distance (230 km/143 mi).

If you are wanting to head south, the road branches off to the south at Vila Pouca de Aguiar and brings you to Vila Real and the Palácio de Mateus.

⑬ **Vila Real** This 'royal town' on the Rio Corgo has a number of palaces and is famous for its black pottery. The baroque wine estate belonging to the Mateus family is located 4 km (2.5 mi) to the east. Not far from Vila Real is also the magnificent Solar de Mateus country estate.

⑭ **Viseu** This town's history goes back to the Romans and the Visigoths, whose last king, Roderich, was defeated here by the Moors. A stroll through the picturesque Old Town will bring you to the cubic proportions of the cathedral with its two-storey 13th-century cloister. The Manueline vaults are remarkable. The Museu Grão Vasco documents the history of the famous 'Viseu' school of painting.

The scenic N10 now brings you to Guarda 100 km (60 mi) away.

⑮ **Guarda** Portugal's highest town is situated on a cliff 1,056 m (3,465 ft) up in the Serra de Estrela range and was one of Portugal's most important border fortresses for a long time. The older forts and the cathedral in particular are testimony to this history. It is well worth taking a stroll through the picturesque Old Town.

⑯ **Castelo Branco** The next stop is the capital of the Beira Baixa, a town which was a political bone of contention for centuries due to its proximity to Spain. Only the ruins of the 13th-century fortress remain. The somewhat bizarre Jardim Episcopal, which belongs to the bishop's palace, is considered to be one of the loveliest baroque gardens in Portugal. Taking the N18 now to the south, you then turn off at Alpalhão and head for the mountains in the east.

⑰ **Marvão** This mountain village dating back to the Moors perches like an eagle's nest on the 870-m-high (2,854-ft) cliff. Its mighty fortress once played an important role in the border wars with Spain. You get a magnificent view of the small town ringed by the old town walls, the Serra de São Mamede, the Serra de Estrela and you can even see Spain. With its palaces, townhouses, monasteries, castle, cathedral and medieval town

walls, the small town 16 km (10 mi) to the south, Estremoz, is like a open-air museum.

⑱ **Estremoz** In the Middle Ages this town was home to one of the most important fortresses in Alentejo, of which only the massive keep (13th century) survives today. It is known for its pottery, which is sold on the large marble-paved marketplace on Saturdays and Sundays.

From Estremoz, we highly recommend an excursion to Elvas, situated around 30 km (19 mi) east of Estremoz close to the Spanish border.

⑲ **Évora** The largest and most scenic town in Alentejo has been declared a UNESCO World Heritage Site because of its historical Old Town, its plazas, 16th- and 17th-century townhouses, palaces, churches and its medieval town wall. From the Praça do Giraldo, with its lovely Renaissance fountains and Santo Antão Church (1557), you will come to the cathedral, a Gothic church building completed in the 14th century. This fortress-like edifice combines both Romanesque and Gothic elements along with having a Renaissance portal and a baroque altar. Today it adjoins the Museu de Arte Sacra and the Museu Regional. North of the cathedral is the Templo Romano (2nd century) with fourteen Corinthian pillars. Their reliefs are in surprisingly good condition despite centuries of misappropriation.

The Casa dos Ossos in São Francisco Church is a somewhat macabre attraction: the walls are 'adorned' with skulls.

⑳ **Monsaraz and Mourão** The medieval village of Monsaraz about 50 km (31 mi) east of Evora features an intact town

a pyramid-shaped top, is located on the Largo de Santa Clara. The town is enclosed by old fortified walls that also include the Fortaleza Nossa Senhora da Graça (1763–1792). To the south of the town lies the Fortaleza de Santa Lucia (1640–1687), today a pousada, or state-run guest house accommodation. The 7.5-km-long (4.7-mi) Aqueduto da Amoreira, which is still in use, ends at the Fonte da Vila (1498–1622) and its 843 superimposed arches measure up to 31 m (102 ft) in height.

Street cafes on the beautifully designed Praça da Republica in Elvas is very inviting during the twilight hours.

The Mateus Wine Estate in Vila Real

The splendid Casa de Mateus is featured on the label when you buy a bottle of the famous Mateus Rosé. Situated about 4 km (2.5 mi) east of Vila Real, this country estate from the mid-18th century belongs to the old aristocratic wine-making family Mourão. The grounds have a palace-like character and the building is considered a gem of Portuguese baroque architecture.

The façade itself is indeed impressive enough, with whitewashed walls and granite balustrades, minaret-like towers reflected in the water of the grand pond built in front of it in the 1930s. The gable wall is flanked by classical statues and is crowned by the family's coat of arms, which you again encounter under the chestnut-wood paneled ceiling of the foyet. The different rooms, including the Four Seasons Room, the Blue

wall, a Castelo (14th century), a Gothic parish church and a pelourinho, or pillory, from the 17th century. On the opposite side of the Rio Guardiana, the road takes you to Mourão, situated on Europe's largest reservoir lakes, the Barragem do Alqueva. It serves as a catchment for the Rio Guadiana. Small country roads lead to the next stop, Moura.

㉑ Moura The name of this thermal hot springs resort alone (with its well-maintained spa gardens and music pavilion) is indicative of its Moorish origins. A castle (13th century) is also testimony to that fact. The old Moorish district with its simple white houses and curious chimneys is worth a stroll.

㉒ Beja Passing through Vidigueira you then reach Beja, the second-largest town in Alentejo and one of the hottest towns in Portugal. Originally a Roman settlement, it was then declared a diocesan town under the Visigoths before being ruled by the Moors for 400 years.
It is worth visiting the Old Town for its maze of alleyways, the Convento Nossa Senhora da Conceição with a cloister decorated with lovely old azulejos, and Santo Amaro Church, which dates back to the Visigoth era. The Castelo (1300) is dominated by the highest keep in Portugal.

㉓ Mértola The terraces of this scenic little town on the right bank of the Rio Guadiana nestle up against the slope beneath the Castelo dos Mouros. The snow-white Igreja Matriz was a mosque up until 1238.

㉔ Faro Today the 'Gateway to the Algarve' is a rather unappealing fishing and industrial town situated on a large lagoon, but it has an attractive Old Town around the cathedral at Largo da Sé and is enclosed by a medieval town wall. The Carmo Church (18th century) with the Capela dos Ossos (skulls) is also worth seeing. You have the option of taking an excursion from Faro to the fishing port of Olhão with its market halls. The Ria Formosa nature reserve extends between Olhão and Faro, with the Cabo de Santa Maria, the southernmost point in Portugal, at its southern tip.

㉕ Albufeira This former fishing village west of Faro does not have many sightseeing attractions to offer but its favorable Algarve location makes it a tourist stronghold nonetheless. To some extent it is the Saint-Tropez of the Algarve, boasting countless beaches and bizarre cliffs combined with bars and nightlife to suit all tastes. The

Top left: A wonderful view from the Castello de Vide in Marvão of the Serra de São Mamede. Botton left: The World Heritage Site of Evora: Diana Temple. Top right: Mansaraz is dominated by a 13th-century castle. Above: Inside the Convento of Beja.

Casa de Mateus country estate in Vila Real.

Room, the Dining Room and the Four Cornered Room, house magnificent furnishings and valuable porcelain, with impressive paintings adorning the walls.
The family chapel and the family museum are also worth a visit.
Afterwards, take a stroll through the surrounding gardens with their boxwood hedges, and down the cedar-lined lane.

The Alentejo Coast

Alentejo means 'beyond the Tejo' (Tagus) and today the term refers to the entire area south of the Tagus up to the Upper Algarve. It comprises nearly one-third of Portugal's total surface area and extends from the western Atlantic coast across the country to the Spanish border. It can be extremely hot in the interior in summer as none of the cool sea breezes make it this far. Nevertheless, Alentejo has its own character and its own beauty that have been shaped by its climate and rugged location. The expansive ochre-colored plains are dotted with olive trees and cork oak plantations as well as scattered wheat and rice fields of remarkable size, vegetable plantations and wine estates. Alentejo is known as Portugal's 'breadbasket' and was therefore also a region traditionally controlled by the landed gentry both

buildings in the attractive Old Town sprawl up the steep, scenic coastal slopes.

26 Portimão The second-largest tourist stronghold on the Algarve is primarily known for its 1.5-km-long (1-mi) Praia da Rocha beach, which features beautiful and bizarre cliffs. If you have time, it is possible to take an excursion from here to Silves, a town in the interior that has a striking castle complex and a lovely Gothic cathedral (13th century). In addition to a cork museum, it also boasts the only museum dedicated to Portugal's Moorish era. At that time Xelb, the present-day Silves, served as the capital city.

27 Lagos This was the port from which the droves of Portuguese seafarers used to put to set sail in their caravels. In fact, Lagos has been a shipbuilding center since the time of Henry the Navigator (1394–1460). The slave trade forms part of the darker side of the town's history: Lagos was a market and trans-shipment center for the trade in African slaves, the first of whom were auctioned on the Praça da Republica in 1443.
The town is dominated by the Ponta da Bandeira fortress, which dates back to the 17th century. The sandy and rocky

beaches around Lagos are a very popular destination for water sports enthusiasts. The fortified walls and the baroque Santo Antonio Church (17th century) are worth seeing, as are the magnificent cliffs on the Ponta Piedade around 2 km (1.2 mi) to the south.

28 Sagres This port played a significant role in the 15th and 16th centuries as it is alleged to have been the location of Henry the Navigator's legendary navigation school, a fact that is documented by the giant stone compass on the rocky ledge of the Ponta de Sagres, close to the Fortaleza de Sagres. The rose-shaped compass has a diameter of 43 m (47 yds). The Cabo de São Vicente is close by and has 24-m-high (79-ft) lighthouse that protrudes out of the sea, marking the south-westernmost point in Europe. Before Columbus, the 60-m-high (197-ft) cliffs were considered to be 'World's End'.

29 The west coast of the Algarve From Sagres, the road back to Lisbon largely follows the Atlantic coast. The first stop is the village of Vila do Bispo, where the Ermida de Nossa Senhora de Guadelupe chapel is worth a visit.
From there, the journey continues to Aljezur where the ruins of the Castelo afford a magnificent view. Nearby Carrapateira is to be recommended for anyone wanting to make a short detour to the beach.
From Aljezur, the road leads to Odemira, a small country town on the Rio Mira, which is controlled by the 44-km (27-mi) lake above the Barragem de Santa Clara dam 30 km (19 mi) to the south-east.
The next stop is Vila Nova de Milfontes, with sandy beaches and water sport options. The road initially heads inland after Sines, before turning back toward the coast after the fortress-liked town of Alcácer do Sol with its Moorish castle, towards Setúbal.

30 Setúbal Portugal's third-largest port was already an important fishing port during Roman times and the bay formed by the mouth of the Rio Sádo is dominated by the port facilities, sardine factories and dockyards. The lively fishing port is an attractive setting as is the still picturesque Old Town with its winding alleys.
Setúbal is often referred to as a 'Manueline jewel', and the Igreja de Jesús (1491) with its elaborate columns is undoubtedly a jewel of this architectural style. The cathedral (16th century) boasts magnificent 18th-century azulejos.
You can get a wonderful view over the town from the Castelo São Filipe to the west. Anyone then wanting to head for the beach should take the ferry over to the Tróia Peninsula. Otherwise, the journey now takes you directly back to Lisbon.

Large image: Lagos on the banks of Bensafrim; Small image: Praia da Falésia near Vilamoura.

before and after the Carnation Revolution of 1974. Whitewashed villages and small towns pop up in the wide open landscape. The road network is relatively good, and occasionally lead you past herds of cattle and sheep on your left and right. The mostly low, one-storey houses often have blue trim, which represents the color that consistent blesses the country's skies. The large chimneys are an indication that it can also be very cold here in the winter. The larger towns in Alentejo are Portalegre, Evora, Beja and Setúbal, while the most attractive coastal towns include Vila Nova de Milfontes, Sines, Carrapateira and Costa de Santo André.

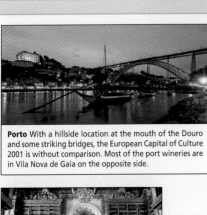

Porto With a hillside location at the mouth of the Douro and some striking bridges, the European Capital of Culture 2001 is without comparison. Most of the port wineries are in Vila Nova de Gaia on the opposite side.

Coimbra Fado bars, the largest Romanesque church in Portugal and a former royal palace are what make this university town special.

Batalha The Santa Maria da Vitoria monastery was built between the 14th and 16th centuries. It is a symbol of independence from Spain.

Lisbon Portugal's capital enjoys a unique location on top of several hills around the mouth of the Tagus and is easily explored by means of the trams (eléctricos). The host of the 1998 EXPO has both modern sights and old attractions such as Lisbon's landmark, the Torre de Belém (16th century).

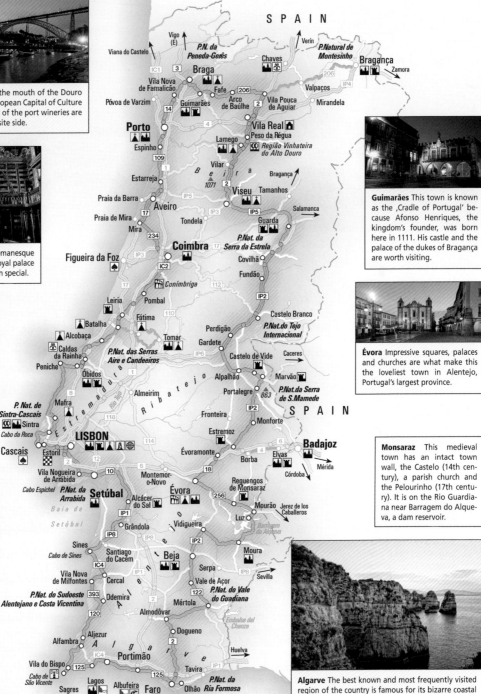

Guimarães This town is known as the ‚Cradle of Portugal' because Afonso Henriques, the kingdom's founder, was born here in 1111. His castle and the palace of the dukes of Bragança are worth visiting.

Évora Impressive squares, palaces and churches are what make this the loveliest town in Alentejo, Portugal's largest province.

Monsaraz This medieval town has an intact town wall, the Castelo (14th century), a parish church and the Pelourinho (17th century). It is on the Rio Guardiana near Barragem do Alqueva, a dam reservoir.

Algarve The best known and most frequently visited region of the country is famous for its bizarre coastal cliffs, magnificent sandy bays and pleasant climate all year round. The water quality is also excellent.

From fishing villages to Renaissance cities

From golden rolling hills, aromatic pine forests and stylish cypress boulevards to extraordinary art treasures and mouthwatering cuisine – Tuscany is a perfect holiday destination for nature lovers, art connoisseurs and gourmets. With rustic villages, a rich history and unique landscapes, this attractive region presents itself as one of Europe's 'complete artworks'.

Route profile:

Length: approx. 1,200 km (745 miles), excluding detours
Time required: 2 weeks
When to go: Italy is dry and hot in the summer, mild in the winter. The rain falls in autumn, October and November mainly, and July and August can be oppressively hot. The recommended travel season for Tuscany is therefore spring.

Travelling in Tuscany is simply an intoxicating experience for the senses. Your eyes feast on the magnificently cultivated landscape, the delicate hints of rosemary and lavender please the nose, and your palate is spoilt for choice with world-famous Chianti wines and a cuisine that, with great help from the Medici family, had already begun conquering the world during the Renaissance. If that were not enough, nearly all Tuscany's charming ancient towns offer abundant art treasures as well. Historically, central Italy is a region that has been inhabited for thousands of years, and proof of that fact is not hard to find. The ubiquitous remains of Etruscan necropolises, ruins from Roman settlements or the medieval town of San Gimignano make the point clear enough. Tuscany reached its zenith primarily during the medieval and Renaissance periods, and rightly regards itself as the 'Cradle of European culture'. Modern art, including painting, sculpture and architecture, can be traced back to this region.

The most important role in the region's rise to glory was played by the Medici, a Florentine family of vast wealth and influence that decisively dictated politics and the arts in that city for almost three hundred years, be-

tween 1434 and 1743. The pronounced cultural interest of the Medici drew the renowned artists of the time into their fold and, as patron of the arts, the family commissioned some of the most important works of the Renaissance period.

The cultural bounty of Tuscany attracts a great number of tourists every year. But a visit to Tuscany should include not only the well-known towns but also the countryside, as Tuscany is as fa-

mous for its ancient rural aesthetic as it is for its urban culture. This extraordinary countryside was planned in incredible detail and cultivated for centuries, with the landed gentry as well as the farmers playing a part in the development. The farms, with a geometrical layout unchanged over the years, were placed on hilltops and all boasted a cypress-lined drive to their entrances. These splendid, centuries-old cypress lanes indicate

Above: Depicted in one of the first landscape depictions, Ambrogio Lorenzetti's fresco cycle of the good and bad regiment (1337–1343) in the town hall of Siena, the Val d'Orcia served as a model of an ideal landscape. Left: The Cathedral of Santa Maria Assunta towers over Siena.

their penchant for precise planning here.

Geographically, Tuscany stretches from the Apennine Mountains in the north to the Monte Amiata in the south, offering a varied landscape with rugged mountains, gentle rolling hills, the fertile coastal area of the Maremma and the green valleys of the Arno river. Southern Tuscany differs considerably from other Tuscan regions, being much hotter and having a less lush vegetation,

dominated by maquis – dense, evergreen shrubs.

Industry and tourism are the economic backbones of Tuscany. Agriculture's main product is olive oil, but agriculture nowadays only supports a small part of the population. As a holiday destination, Tuscany is almost perfect all year round – between May and June an abundance of plants blossom in an extraordinary range of colours, while summer is dominated by the radiant red

of the poppies and the glowing yellow of sunflower fields. Autumn is the time of the grape harvest, when the chestnut trees and the beeches change colour in late October and transform the landscape into a sea of mellow golden and red.

Your tour also enters the Emilia, a region between the river Po and the Apennine Mountains where Bologna is the city of note. On the west coast you reach Liguria with the Riviera di

Levante and the tourist mecca, La Spezia. And from the hills of eastern Tuscany you finally reach Umbria.

Top: Built in 1463, the Palazzo Comunale in Piazza Pio II houses the town hall of Pienza. Above left: The castle on the Vernazza promontory dates back to the 11th century. Left: Michelangelo's David in Florence.

109

The Romanesque church of San Sepolcro houses the tomb of Saint Petronius and is one of Bologna's many artistically and historically significant ecclesiastical buildings.

The Medici

Almost no other Italian family managed to attain as much power and influence in politics and the arts as the Medici. A Florentine family of wealthy bankers, the Medici began their rise under Cosimo 'the Elder' (1389–1464) and reached their peak under the tutelage of Lorenzo 'the Magnificent' (1449–92). Cosimo was basically able to rule his home town without ever holding any political office. He and his grandson Lorenzo were generous patrons of the arts and sciences and, under their auspices, geniuses such as Brunelleschi and Donatello eventually made Florence their home. In the 16th century the family rose to princely status, but its decline began soon thereafter, continuing until the Medici line died out in 1737.

Tuscany – your tour through this magnificent region is also a journey through the Middle Ages and the Renaissance, starting in the lovely city of Florence. A highly recommended day trip leads to three towns on to the Ligurian coast, and the romantic country roads offer you a unique chance to get to know the varied Tuscan landscape in all its glory.

❶ Florence (see p. 111). Your circular tour through Tuscany begins in beautiful Florence. Only 8 km (5 miles) north of there is the village of Fiésole.

❷ Fiesole Founded in the 6th century BC by the Etruscans, this hilltop village is a far cry from the hustle and bustle of the big city and offers a fantastic panoramic view of Florence. In centuries past it was an ideal summer retreat for Florence's aristocracy, who were looking for respite from the city's heat and dust. The wide Piazza Mino da Fiesole with the San Romolo Cathedral (begun in 1028) is the centre of the village. North-east of the cathedral, remains of some partially well-preserved Roman settlements were discovered, including the ruins of a theatre that seated up to three thousand people. Continuing via Florence you come to lively Prato, Tuscany's third-largest town.

❸ Prato With its daring mixture of medieval buildings and modern architecture, Prato is a city of stark contrasts. As it was the metropolis of textile manufacture, wool-weavers began settling here in the Middle Ages. Medieval ramparts enclose the historic town centre, which has a cathedral modelled on the cathedrals of Pisa and Lucca. The imposing Castello dell' Imperatore, built by Emperor Frederick II between 1237 and 1248, is a remarkable sight.

❹ Pistoia Following the SS64, an often very winding road that negotiates considerable differences in altitude, you reach Pistoia, a lively town steeped in tradition that is surrounded by nurseries and colourful flora. The picturesque markets and the beautiful 9th-century church of Sant'Andrea is worth a visit with its legendary pulpit by Pisano (1298).

❺ Bologna Tuscany is not alone in the area as a custodian of Italy's art treasures. The SS64 leads you to the neighbouring province of Emilia-Romagna and three cities that are as richly steeped in history as any Tuscan locations. Like so many of the cities in this area, Bologna, the capital of Emilia-Romagna, was founded by the Etruscans. It lies in a fertile plain in the foothills of the Apennines and is home to one of Europe's oldest universities, dating back to 1119. Important churches, arcaded lanes, towers and palaces bear witness to Bologna's period of prominence back in the Middle Ages. Among other sights, the Church of San Petronio is worth visiting. Its interior ranks up there with the most exemplary of Gothic architectural works. The two 'leaning towers', built in brick for defence purposes, are the hallmark of the city. The SS9 now leads you on to Modena, about 40 km (25 miles) to the north-west.

❻ Modena Located in the Po river valley, Modena is worth a visit for its magnificent cathedral and celebrated art treasures.

'And why go to Florence?' Goethe once asked his Torquato Tasso. The view over the city answers his question.

The Ponte Vecchio was built in 1345 and is the oldest bridge in Florence. Since 1593, goldsmiths and jewellers have been working in the bridge's workshops.

Florence

Florence's influence on the history of Western civilization is unequalled – it is considered the birthplace of the Renaissance. The city boasts a long list of famous sights, and attracts a phenomenal number of tourists each year. If you want to see the city from above, go to the Piazzale Michelangelo, situated 104 m (341 ft) above the historic town centre – the view of Florence stretching picturesquely over both sides of the Arno river is breathtaking.

Almost all the sights in the old part of town are within walking distance of one another. Florence's architectural jewel, the 'Duomo' (Santa Maria del Fiore, built 1296–1436), dominates the Old Town with its magnificent octagonal dome by Brunelleschi. Opposite that is the Baptistry of San Giovanni (11th–13th centuries) with its three sets of bronze doors by Pisano and Ghiberti, and the famous 'Gates of Paradise' doors. The Uffizi Gallery houses one of the oldest and most important art collections in the world, including masterpieces by Giotto and Botticelli. Nearby, the Ponte Vecchio, Florence's oldest bridge, is famous for the goldsmiths' and jewellers' shops built on it in the 16th century. Back on the Piazza del Duomo, be sure to take a stroll along the Via Calzaiuoli to the Piazza della Signoria, Florence's most beautiful square and home to the 14th-century Palazzo Vecchio, the city's massive town hall with a slim, crenellated tower. A visit to the Giardino di Boboli is then a lovely finish to your leisurely stroll through town.

On the site of today's Dome of Parma was once a pre-Christian sanctuary. The nearby baptistry ist one of the most important baptisteries in the world.

Detour

Portofino

An excursion to the picturesque village of Portofino is highly rec-ommended – but leave your car behind! This swanky seaside resort is among the most beautiful on the Italian Riviera coast, and as such the traffic on the one small road to get there is generally horrendous. It's better to take the ferry over from Santa Margherita Ligure. The charming fishing village of Portofino and its cute little harbour is surrounded by olive groves, vineyards and cypresses. In the 19th century, rich industrialists started to come to the village with its tidy red- and ochre-coloured houses and left their imprint by constructing luxurious villas.

After strolling through the narrow alleys and hilly streets, you come to the medieval church of San Giorgio on the esplanade. The loca-

Luxury yachts anchored in Portofino's harbour.

tion offers a spectacular panoramic view. The Castello di San Giorgio (16th century) is your next stop. Towards the end of the 19th century, Baron von Mumm converted this former military hospital into a luxury villa.

If you follow the picturesque path up to its southern peak, you reach the lighthouse of Punto Capo, which affords magnificent views across the Tigullian Gulf.

The centre of town boasts extensive squares and leafy arcades. The Cathedral San Geminiano (1184), with its impressive 88-m (288-ft) bell tower, and the Piazza Grande have been given joint status as a UNESCO World Heritage Site.

7 Reggio nell'Emilia Like Modena, Reggio nell'Emilia was founded by the Romans and mainly belonged to the House of Este. The town is situated on the edge of Italy's northern plain, a fertile area with great agricultural yields. The cathedral, whose construction began in the 9th century, the 16th-century San Prospero Church and the Church of the Madonna della Ghiaira, a baro-que edifice featuring stucco and frescoes (1597–1619), are all well worth visiting.

8 Parma The city of Parma, near the Apennine Mountains, was founded by the Etruscans, but now has a modern layout due to reconstruction after devastating bombings in World War II. The Piazza Garibaldi, with the Palazzo del Governatore, marks the centre of town. On the Piazza del Duomo stands the 12th-century Romanesque cathedral with its famous frescoes,

while further west you'll find the Palazzo della Pilotta. Inside this unfinished brick edifice is a beautiful inner courtyard and some museums, such as the Galeria Nazionale.The journey continues now across the 1,055-m (3,460-ft) Cento Croci Pass (SS62 and SS523), a very curvy road with breathtaking scenery that runs from Varese Ligure via Rapallo along the Riviera di Levante.

9 Cinque Terre These five legendary coastal villages built on the cliffs of the Riviera di Levante have become one of the most popular tourist areas in all of Italy. Ever since the steeply terraced landscape in the area was made accessible to automobiles, the villages – Monterosso, Vernazza, Corniglia, Manarola and Riomaggiore – are practi-

cally household names.

However, visitors are strongly recommended to leave their cars in Levanto and take the train instead. The roads leading to the villages are very steep and winding – and often full of traffic.

To be able to enjoy the natural beauty of this place to the full, you need to take the five-hour walk on the footpath that links the five villages. Italy's most beautiful walking trail offers absolutely awe-inspiring views of the Mediterranean and the magnificent cliffs. After a short excursion to Portofino, another elegant former fishing village, the journey continues south to La Spézia.

10 La Spezia One of Italy's most beautiful bays is located at the southernmost point on the Gulf of Genoa, with the

Piazza dell'Anfiteatro, in the heart of Lucca, is a large open-air café during the summer, where entertainers and street musicians entertain.

spectacular Apennine Mountains as a backdrop. La Spezia, Liguria's second-largest town, is one of Italy's most important military and commercial ports, a fact that has rendered the town less attractive over the years. However, its charming shopping streets date back to the 19th century and the museum of archaeology and the shipping museum make a visit worthwhile. A short trip south leads to Lerici.

⓫ Carrara Here in the north-west of Tuscany, Carrara marks the beginning of the Versilia Coast, a beautiful stretch scattered with white sandy beaches and the Apuan Alps providing the film-set backdrop.
The road takes you through a unique marble region where exhausted marble quarries have

left rather bizarre formations that now seem to dominate the landscape. Even in Roman times, Carrara was famous for its fine-grained white and grey marble. Today, Carrara is home to an academy for sculptors, where artists have the luxury of learning to work with the rock directly at its source. In the workshops of the Old Town of Pietrasanta, you can see stonemasons at work, happy to let tourists watch while they create. It is also well worth taking a stroll through the historic town centre to admire the 13th-century Cathedral San Martino with its charming brick campanile.

⓬ Viareggio Even in the coastal resort town of Viaréggio, people's livelihood depends to an extent on the marble industry. Other options, however, in-

clude shipbuilding and, of course, tourism. Europe's high society discovered this picturesque fishing village in the 19th century, as the art deco villas and audacious rococo-style cafés will illustrate.
From Viareggio it is only 25 km (15 miles) to Lucca, which is not to be missed on your trip. The road now leaves the coast and runs parallel to the regional nature reserve, Parco Naturale Migliarino-Massaciuccoli, which stretches all the way down to Livorno.

⓭ Pisa About 21 km (13 miles) south of Viareggio is Pisa, well-known for its unique buildings around the Campo dei Miracoli, the 'Field of Miracles'. Among the masterpieces here are the Duomo (the cathedral) and the Baptistry – and most important of all, the Leaning Tower of Pisa, which began leaning to the south-east almost immediately

Above: A picturesque view over the harbor and houses of the former fishing village Portovenere in the very south of the Riviera di Levante. Left side: Piazza Grande in Modena. Above: Ensemble on the Campo dei Miracoli in Pisa.

Detour

Lucca

Lucca, situated in a fertile plain near the Appuan Mountains, is rightly regarded as the archetypal Tuscan city. It boasts a number of palaces and towers and fully intact Old Town walls. This erstwhile Roman settlement retained its independence for a very long time and only fell under the rule of nearby Pisa for a brief period. The traditional trading city today has an important silk, paper and textile industry. You enter the historic centre through one of the seven old gates and are immediately enthralled by the ambience of its tiny streets and alleyways. The Duomo San Martino (c. 11th century) is Lucca's most prominent religious structure. Its nave and transepts were rebuilt in the Gothic style in the 13th and 15th centuries. The Church of San Michele in Foro has a spectacular Romanesque arcaded facade and is named after the Roman forum that once stood here. For centuries the Piazza San Michele was regarded as the centre of town. Nearby is the villa of the Guinigi family, with an unusual tower that has trees sprouting from it. After a climb to the top, you are rewarded with a wonderful view across the red roofs of the Old Town. Afterwards you should consider taking a walk on the 4-km (2.5-mile) wall around the Old Town, which offers magnificent views of the surrounding countryside. On the way out of town to the resort of Bagni di Lucca you come to the famous Ponte del Diavolo – the 'Devil's Bridge' – from the 11th century, which dramatically spans the River Serchio.

When visiting Livorno, a walk along the Terrazza Mascagni by the sea is a must.

Detour

Elba

Even the ancient Etruscans and Romans recognized the unique beauty of this mountainous island. Its iron resources were already well-known in Roman times when mines were established. Due to its mild climate, Italy's third-largest island offers a diverse natural landscape that includes not only chestnut trees, vineyards and olive groves, but also Mediterranean scrub brush. Hills, mountains and low plains are all wonderfully mixed together. Taking the ferry from Piombino, you reach the island's capital of Portoferraio on the north coast in one hour. Napoleon's former summer residence, Villa Napoleonica, is in San Martino just 6 km (3.7 miles) from the dock. On a round trip of the island, you first arrive in Procchio, with a beautiful bay that is ideal for swimming. Continuing along the

Bay of Elba

picturesque winding road, you come to the island's favourite seaside resort, Marciana Marina. Shady pine forests stretch from here to the sea. Marina di Campo on the south coast has a broad sandy beach and is the island's main tourist resort. Porto Azzurro is sheltered from the constant wind. Above the town rises the star-shaped Fort Longone, which has served as a prison for the last 150 years.

after construction began in 1775. Although these structures were built at different times, they were all erected with white Carrara marble and therefore have the effect of being one harmonious entity.

Pisa's role as an important commercial and naval port earned the city the epithet of 'Queen of the Sea', and its influence was considerable. Its decline came when Pisa was defeated by powerful rivals from Genoa and Venice, and the port silted up. The only leading institution remaining in Pisa is its university, proof of a deep-rooted educational tradition. If you wish to relax, visit the romantic botanic gardens, established in 1543.

⑭ Livorno One can hardly believe that Livorno is part of Tuscany, its ambience is so different. But this is probably due to the late construction of the town. It was not until 1571 that this small fishing village was expanded into a port by Cosimo I (see the Medici sidebar p. 128) because Pisa's port was in danger of silting up. The dyke protecting the port here was built between 1607 and 1621. Today, Livorno is Tuscany's most important port. At the seaside visitors can admire the 'Old Fortress' (1521–23) and the 'New

Fortress' (1590) and enjoy a visit to the aquarium. South of Livorno the route continues along the cliffs to San Pietro in Palazzi, past some sandy bays. From here you take the exit onto the SS68 heading east and continue for another 33 km (20 miles) inland until you get to Volterra, high above the road on a hillside.

⑮ Volterra Medieval ramparts surround Volterra's historic town centre with its narrow and dark little alleyways and tall rows of houses. The town's livelihood comes mainly from the alabaster industry. The Etruscan Museum, containing thousands of funerary urns and sarcophagi, is a must for anyone interested in this ancient culture.

The view from the top of the city hall's tower is breathtaking – on clear days you can even see the sea. The old town has been left intact for a rather dramatic reason – Volterra is in danger of subsiding because the steep hill it is built on frequently suffers landslides, making the town unattractive to developers. A turn-off from the SS68 leads onto a small road of outstanding natural beauty – this is the heart of Tuscany, with its typical landscape of vineyards and olive groves.

⑯ San Gimignano For a time, the merchant families of San Gimignano built tall towers to display their wealth – the taller the tower, the richer the family.

Volterra's atmosphere makes its story almost tangible. Many medieval buildings are still well preserved.

Seventy-two of them guarded the dreamy Piazza della Cisterna in the historic centre of town. Only fifteen are standing now, but these perfectly preserved 14th-century towers, the iconic skyline of San Gimignano, make you feel as if transported back to the Middle Ages. Returning along the same route, you reach the coast again about 72 km (45 miles) further along. Follow the old Via Aurelia south to San Vincenzo, and continue on a small coastal road until you get to a series of beaches that look inviting for a dip.

17 Piombino The ferries for Elba leave from Piombino, a port town with an interesting harbour promenade and charming views of the old anchorage and the island of Elba. Populonia, an ancient Etruscan port town with the impressive necropolis of San Cerbone, is nearby and worth a visit. Getting back on the S1 at San Vincenzo, continue to Follónica, where the SS439 turns inland.

18 Massa Marittima Roughly 26 km (16 miles) from the sea, the small town of Massa Marittima lies on the edge of the Maremma, a former marshland that was drained in the 19th century. From the upper part of town – in particular the Torre del Candeliere – you can get a magnificent view of the Old Town's red roofs and the surrounding Tuscan countryside. A diocesan town in the 12th and 13th centuries, Massa Marittima boasts magnificent medieval buildings such as the Duomo San Cerbone (1228–1304). Stay on the SS441 and SS73 for 75 km (46 miles) to Siena.

19 Siena Siena's red-brick palaces and extraordinary flair often give this town a more authentic ambience than its great rival Florence. The 'Gothic City' stretches over three hillsides in the heart of the rolling Tuscan countryside. Its historic centre has long been designated a UNESCO World Heritage Site. Siena is also home to what is arguably Italy's most beautiful square, the shell-shaped Piazza del Campo, surrounded by Gothic palaces. Twice a year it hosts the legendary Palio horse race, which attracts up to fifty thousand spectators and causes total chaos throughout the city. The Duomo (12th century) is Siena's cathedral and one of the jewels of the Gothic period. It should not be missed. Other architectural

Large image: 'Manhattan of the Middle Ages': San Gimignano. Small image: The heart of Siena is the Piazza del Campo, where the Palio is held every year.

Dynastic towers

In the medieval towns of yore, noble families who had made it rich in the wool, wine or spice trade competed with one another by erecting fortified towers that also served as dwellings. These rivalries between families were focused mainly on the height of the towers – the height being an indication of power. But apart from being symbols of power, the towers actually served the very real purpose of providing shelter from enemies. They were also the sites of family feuds. The 'skyline' of San Gimignano is unique – fifteen towers of varying height are still intact and have earned the city the rather fanciful name of the 'Manhattan of the Middle Ages'.

Route 10: Italy, San Marino, Slovenia, Croatia, Bosnia and Herzegovina, Serbia, Montenegro and Albania

Around the Adriatic

Sometimes rather sparse, sometimes lush Mediterranean vegetation – but always a view of the sea. Journeying along the Adriatic through Slovenia, Croatia and Italy you will encounter medieval towns, art and culture in spades, as well as tiny rocky coves and beaches stretching for miles.

Route profile:

Length: approx. 1,320 miles
Time required: at least 3 weeks

The northern reaches of the Mediterranean were originally named after the ancient Etruscan town of Adria on the Po Delta, which today is a good 40 km (25 mi) inland to the south-west of Chioggia and is now only linked to the sea by a man-made canal. The town was taken over by the Greeks after the Etruscans, and since that time the mouth of the Po has moved eastwards at a rate of up to 150 m (164 yds) per year. The Adriatic is actually a shallow arm of the Mediterranean, reaching depths of no more than 1,645 m (5,397 ft) between Bari and the Albanian coast. Venice,

the first stop on your journey around the Adriatic, is a trip in itself. The gondolas, palaces and unique cultural monuments of the lagoon city are the result of its rise to power in the 13th century, when influential patrons attracted the greatest artists of the age. It was the Renaissance in particular that shaped not only the city but also the entire look of coast's culture. For it is not only at the start of the journey through the autonomous region of Friuli-Venezia Giulia that you will encounter Venetian towns. Venetian architectural jewels are also scattered along the adjoining coastline of the Istrian Peninsula as well as along the entire Croatian coast. Many foreign cultures have laid claim to Istria over the centuries due to its fortuitous geographical position. With 242 km (150 mi) of coastline and idyllic medieval

towns, the peninsula has now developed into a popular holiday destination, with tourism providing the coastal residents with a lucrative livelihood. Between Istria and the mainland is the Kvarner Gulf, which includes the islands of Cres, Lošinj, Krk, Pag and Rab, but the lively port city of Rijeka is the starting point for our journey along the Croatian coast. The coastal road is lined by relatively barren landscape, an intense mix of light, sea and

limestone. All the more surprising, then, that the valleys behind the ridge are so fertile, protected from the infamous bora, an icy autumn wind. Vineyards and lush Mediterranean vegetation are pleasing to the eye and provide a refreshing contrast to the lunar landscape of the limestone cliffs. With its steep coastline, the Adria Magistrale is considered one of the most dangerous stretches of road in Europe. On the other hand, there are many

When photography had not yet been invented, artists captured St. Mark's Square in Venice (above) from a variety of perspectives in their paintings. Its spell is still unbroken today. Left: The blue hour cloaks the city in a very special light and the view over Split is even more beautiful.

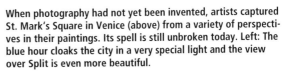

interesting destinations and worthwhile attractions that can only be reached via this route. And, with the Serbo-Croatian War having left very few scars along the coast, tourism has undergone a revival in recent years. As a result, the service sector has also become the most important economic engine for the whole coastal region.

The ferry from Dubrovnik to Bari links the Croatian and Italian coastlines, which are at once similar and different. The section along the Italian side of the Adriatic covers a total of five regions: Apulia, Abruzzi, the Marches, Emilia-Romagna and Veneto, each with an individual culture and landscape. The settlement of the area goes back a long way. The Etruscans, the Greeks, the Venetians and the Romans all established towns throughout this coastal region. And the coast itself is as diverse as the region: the cliffs of the Gargano Peninsula rise dramatically from the water while south of Ancona the foothills of the Apennines protrude into the ocean. The tourist centers beyond Rímini are very different again. There, sandy beaches stretch for miles and have mutated into centers of mass recreation.

Veneto, on the other hand, paints a very different picture with canals, lagoons and tidy little islands off the coast at about the same latitude as the university town of Padua.

Left side: In autumn, the forests around the Plitvice Lakes are bathed in bright colours. Top left: The small, colourful houses of Poreč give the town a special charm. Above: The Basilica of San Vitale in Ravenna features impressive mosaics.

The frescoes in the Basilica of Santa Maria Assunta in Aquiléia are reminiscent of St Mark's Basilica in Venice.

Murano and Burano

For centuries, Murano glass was considered the best in the world and the small island has served as the headquarters of the Venetian glass industry since the 13th century.

A museum provides interesting insights into the art of glass blowing. In addition to the quality glass products, the triple-nave Maria e Donato Basilica from the 12th century is also worth visiting. The building with its wonderful apse design is a mixture of Venetian-Byzantine and Early Romanesque elements and boasts a fine mosaic floor dating back to 1140. Venetian nobility discovered the island in the

Strong contrast: above Murano, below Burano.

16th century and made it their their summer holiday location of choise, the elegant villas and parks bearing witness to this golden era. Burano paints a different picture. This lively little fishing island has wonderfully vibrant cottages and is the center of the Venetian lace industry. A small museum displays a collection of the finest lacework covering two centuries and includes veils, dresses and fans.

An incomparable landscape combined with cultural diversity are what characterize this tour around the Adriatic, but a number of things remain constant as you pass through Italy, Slovenia and Croatia: the idyllic nature of the coastlines and clear seas, dramatic rock formations and cliffs, the gentle valleys and the tantalizing coves with magnificent beaches.

1 Venice (see page 121) Following one of the undisputed highlights of this tour right at the outset, namely a visit to Venice, you continue along the B14 as far as the intersection with the B352.

2 Aquileia Aquileia was one of the largest towns in the ancient empire of Augustus, but today it is home to just 3,400 inhabitants. The remains of the Roman town as well as the Romanesque Basilica of Our Lady, with its magnificent 4th-century mosaic floor, have both been declared a UNESCO World Heritage Site.

3 Udine Erst im Hochmittelalter entwi It was only in the late Middle Ages that this former Roman settlement developed into the region's main city. The influence of Venice can be seen throughout the town, as well as on the Piazza Libertà, whose loggias and the splendid clock tower (1527) truly make it one of the loveliest squares in the world. The Renaissance Castello di Udine towers over the

Old Town and the Santa Maria Annunziata Cathedral (14th century) features masterful altar pieces and frescos by Giambattista Tiepolo. With its high limestone cliffs dropping sharply to the ocean, the Riviera Triestina has very little in common with the rest of the Italian Adriatic. Continuing from Udine via Monfalcone to Trieste along the B14 you get a taste of the craggy, bizarre landscape that awaits in Dalmatia.

4 Trieste This Mediterranean port was part of Austria for over five hundred years, from 1382 until 1918, when the city was annexed by Italy after World War I. Open squares and cozy cafes are testimony to the former presence and influence of the Austro-Hungarian monarchy, before it lost influence as a center of trade and culture. The atmosphere of the Grand Canal with its small boats is dominated by the imposing Sant' Antonio Church (1849).

5 Koper and Piran The Slovenian coast is only 40 km (25

mi) long and yet three towns here offer you virtually all of the aspects of the sea and seafaring you could want: Koper, the country's trading port, Izola the fishing port and Piran, where the beachgoers sun themselves. Formerly an island, Koper is now linked to the mainland by a causeway. The center of the historic Old Town has a Venetian flair and is dominated by the Titov trg and the Praetorian Palace, the cathedral and the bell tower. One palace loggia on the square has been converted into a relaxed coffee house. Izola was also built on an island and before being later linked to the mainland. There are ample signs of a Venetian past here too, but Izola is primarily a fishing village and port. Piran, on the other hand, is one of the loveliest towns along the Adriatic, and lives primarily from tourism. The town's focal point is Tartini Square, lined by

Venice's flair is unique. The gondoliers, who gently push their boats through the water, can only be found here.

The Doge's Palace in Venice was the residence of the Doge from the ninth century as well as the seat of the Venetian government.

250 m
820 ft

Venice

A visit to the magnificent lagoon city is simply unforgettable, regardless of the time of year.

If you can somehow avoid the high season when thousands of tourists jam the narrow alleys around Piazza San Marco, you are lucky. But Venice (a UNESCO World Heritage Site) is so extraordinarily beautiful that it is a treat all year round.

As a maritime power, Venice was once the queen of the eastern Mediterranean. The city is unique, and not least because of its medieval architectural design that is an amalgamation of Byzantine, Arab and Gothic elements. This capital of the northern Italian province of Venezia includes over one hundred islands in a sandy lagoon in the Adriatic. The city is linked to the mainland via causeways and bridges, and was built on piles. There are over 150 bridges and 400 canals. Originally, Venice was a refuge built after the invasion of the Huns, and its inhabitants actually remained independent for centuries in what was then a remote location. They even managed to take over the legacy of Ravenna in the eighth century, but by the 15th century, the flow of world trade had shifted, leaving the former queen without its foundation. Venice stagnated thereafter, stuck in the early stages of becoming a metropolis. Sights here include: the Piazza San Marco; the Basilica di San Marco with its priceless décor (11th century); the Doge's Palace, a masterpiece of the Venetian Gothic; the Grand Canal with the Rialto Bridge; the Church of Santa Maria Gloriosa dei Frari; the Scuola Grande di San Rocco, the Galleria del L'Accademia with collections of Venetian paintings from the 14th to 18th centuries; and the other islands of Murano, Burano and Torcello.

121

The basic grid of the old town of Poreč is still largely preserved from Roman times.

Detour

Rab and Cres

Whether you are a fan of culture or the sea, Rab island will not disappoint. Revealing all of its magic behind a protective row of cliffs, Rab is an oasis with forests and a wealth of agriculture. A former Roman colony, the island has been under Croatian, Venetian, and even Austrian rule. The picturesque Old Town of Rab, with the unmistakable silhouette of its four bell towers, is tiny, its waterfront and the medieval alleyways inviting visitors for an easy stroll. For swimmers, the road continues to Suha Punta with its oak and pine forests and numerous small coves.

The neighboring island of Cres has a more rugged charm of

The Coastal landscape on Cres with city Beli.

its own. Journeying along the main road you get the impression that you are in the mountains but then every now and again you get a breathtaking view of the ocean. Cres is also linked by a small spit of land to the nearby island of Lošinj. The port of Mali Lošinj, with its vibrant late baroque buildings, is a popular stop with magnificent yachts from all over the world anchoring here.

a semi-circular row of old buildings on the one side and with views of the small fishing port on the opposite side. In Piran, the best thing to do is go for a stroll and let yourself be enchanted by the delightful details of the loggias, fountains and wells.

The onward journey now takes you onto Croatian soil.

6 Umag The craggy west coast of Istria, from Savudrija to Rovinj, has lively coastal resorts, fishing villages and small Venetian towns on the seaside that feature a varied landscape. The road initially travels through reddish, open countryside where you arrive in the 'breadbasket' of Istria, the focal point of which is the lovely town of Umag. This former Venetian port on a spit of land has a historic Old Town that is surrounded almost completely by the sea. In the Middle Ages, Umag – then still an island separated from the mainland – belonged o the Bishop of Trieste. The route then continues along small, scenic roads along the coast to Poreč.

7 Poreč Headlands covered in pine forests, lagoons with crystal-clear water and craggy cliffs of marble are the hallmarks of the 70-k-long (43-mi) riviera between Poreč and Vrsar, and it is no surprise that the little town of Poreč, originally settled by the Romans, has developed into Istria's tourism center. The main attractions include the towers of the former town walls, the 15th-century bell tower and the Euphrasian Basilica with its elaborate décor and fine mosaics – the most significant monument to Byzantine sacral architecture from the 3rd to 6th centuries. In order to reach the medieval coastal town of Rovinj by car you will need to round the Limski zaljev bay on the E751 and, after a very short drive through the interior, turn off to the west of the peninsula.

8 Rovinj Insiders know that this coastal village, with its Venetian bell tower, numerous brightly painted houses, charming alleyways, and myriad swimming options is one of the country's loveliest. The rocky island has been settled since antiquity and was a prosperous fishing and trading center under the Venetians.

A stroll through the Old Town should begin at the waterfront promenade with its lovely views. The unique flair of Rovinj's center is formed by the Trg Tita Square, which opens out onto the waterfront with welcoming cafés, a town museum and a splendid late-Renaissance clock tower. The imposing St Eufemija baroque church (1736) with its bell tower is also worth visiting.

The route now returns to the E751 in order to reach the next stop.

After passing through the very impressive limestone landscape you ultimately reach the southern part of Istria in a winegrowing area interspersed with stone walls.

9 Pula This port and industrial town with its imposing Roman arena is located at the southern end of the peninsula. Pula had developed into a prosperous provincial capital even during the era of Emperor Augustus. With its 62,400 residents, it is today still the peninsula's cultural and economic center.

Visitors are drawn by the museums and the ring-shaped Old Town laid out around the castle hill, but the most impressive sight remains the amphitheater, a huge structure with arcade arches up to 33 m (108 ft) in height. Pula's undisputed landmark is of course also a UNESCO World Heritage Site.

10 Labin The journey now takes you along the east coast of Istria to the north-east.

The E751 crosses the Raša Valley, which is a steep canyon in places, and then climbs rapidly up to the delightful medieval town of Labin, high above the sea. The stretch along the winding east coast is now dominated by Ucka, Istria's highest moun-

The 'Girl with the Seagull' welcomes arriving guests to the Kvarner Bay.

Detour

The Plitvice Lakes

An unforgettable natural spectacle awaits visitors to the Plitvička jezera National Park in the north Dalmatian hinterland. The waters of the Korana River plunge down a total of 156 m (512 ft) into a series of stepped lakes and waterfalls over dolomite and limestone terraces. There is a total of sixteen lakes in the park, each one as beautiful as the last, glistening in shades of deep blue and green. The unmistakable hues come from the limestone, which is the dominant type of stone in the region. The ninety waterfalls and cascades are located in what is largely still pristine mixed forest, The national park's most impressive waterfalls are the Plitvice Falls where the waters of the Plitvice River plunge 72 m (236 ft) down into the canyon. One of the park entrances is located conveniently close to the falls while another gate opens at the largest of the Plitvice lakes, the Kozjak jezero. The idyllic landscape is easily accessible on the many miles of boardwalks and the 40 km (25 mi) of hiking trails. Electric boats and a mini tourist railway help to ensure that the longer distances can be negotiated comfortably. Caution: brown bears, wolves and wildcats roam through the forests and canyons. The lake landscape has countless whitewater sections and crashing waterfalls. They have been used in a number of films. The wild landscape around the Plitvička jezera covers an area of 295 sq km (114 sq mi) and was made into a national park in 1928. It was then declared a UNESCO World Heritage Site in 1979.

tain at 1,400 m (4,593 ft). This is the beginning of the Opatijska Riviera, with the charming 19th-century seaside resorts of Lovran and Opatija. Brestova marks the end of the Istria region, which is now Kvarner Bay.

11 Opatija BBelle Époque styles, blossoming gardens and elegant coffee houses are all traces of the Austro-Hungarian monarchy here in Opatija. After being designated as a spa in 1889, this seaside resort developed into an urban work of art. In addition to the obvious beach pursuits, Opatija offers splendid walks along the 8-km (5-mi) waterfront promenade. European high society used to meet in An-giolina Park (1885) in the town center, and the glamour of those days can still be relived with a walk under the acacia, cedar and lemon trees.

12 Rijeka The port and industry town of Rijeka often serves only as the starting point for a drive along the coastal road. But that would not do the city justice. One of its attractions is the 33-m-high (108-ft) bell tower of the St Marija Cathedral (13th century, façade from the 19th-century), known as the 'Leaning Tower of Rijeka' due to its angle. There are also a number of museums and the pedestrian zone lined with boutiques and shops. Be sure to visit the

Trsat fortress (13th century), which towers above the town affording a fantastic panoramic view of the mountains and the sea.

The journey continues along the Croatian coast on the E65, also known as Adria-Magistrale, a 600-km (373-mi) stretch between Rijeka and Dubrovnik that follows the coastline almost the whole way, passing through a unique landscape comprising limestone mountains, shimmering, crystal blue water and – typically – bright sunshine. Anyone with time for a longer detour should turn off at Kraljevica towards Krk and cross over at Valbiska to the island of Cres with its impressive, barren lunar landscape.

13 Crikvenica T his seaside resort is situated about 30 km (19 mi) away from Rijeka. In the summer it attracts tourists with a wide sandy beach and the

Left page and large image:
Plitvice Lakes National Park.
Above: The Roman amphitheater in Pula.

Detour

Korčula

There are only a few places along the Adriatic coast where an island is this close to the mainland, in this case Korčula and the Pelješac Peninsula. Korčula, a mountainous island with comparatively lush vegetation, covers 276 sq km (107 sq mi) and has a good variety of activities to offer visitors. Legend has it that the famous Moreška sword dances, performed only on specific feast days, derive from the threat posed by the Ottoman Empire. The island's capital has Venetian-style architectural gems

Detour

Kotor, Budva and Sveti Stefan

You can make a very interesting detour now from Dubrovnik into Montenegro. Awaiting you in the quaint coastal town of Kotor are narrow, labyrinthine alleyways, charming little squares and a number of well-preserved medieval buildings. The fortress, intended to protect against attacks from the sea, has a wall around it measuring 4.5 km (2.7 mi) at a height of 20 m (66 ft). Of the three city gates still standing, the ninth-century south gate is the oldest. The Cathedral of St. Tiphun, (1166), has magnificent 14th-century frescoes and is an important example of Romanesque architecture. In fact, Kotor is one of the best-preserved medieval towns in the region. In Budva, situated on a small island linked to the mainland by a causeway, visitors are also immersed in the Middle

Bay of Kotor.

Ages. The historic Old Town with its narrow alleys and cultural monuments such as St Ivan's Church (17th century) and St Sava's Church (14th century), is surrounded by a fortress boasting gates and towers. The medieval fishing village of Sveti Stefan lies in the middle section of the Budvanska Riviera. The 15th-century town, originally built on an island, has today become a seaside resort.

8-km-long (5-mi) waterfront promenade, which extends as far as Selce. A visit to the aquarium is also worthwhile and provides an insight into the wealth of Mediterranean fish and plant life. About 30 km (19 mi) further on is the town of Senj. From there it is worth taking the detour to the Plitvice lakes, roughly 90 km (56 mi) away. Back on the coastal road this stretch is lined with small towns inviting you to stop over. The ferry port of Jablanac is located halfway between Rijeka and Šibenik and from here it is worth taking a detour to the scenic island of Rab – the crossing only takes ten minutes.

14 Zadar The Dalmatian capital boasts some historic buildings from the Venetian era such as the circular St Donatus Church and the campanile of St Anastasia's Cathedral dating from the 12th and 13th centuries. The ruins of the medieval town fortress and the Roman forum are also worth visiting.

15 Šibenik This charming port is dominated by the glistening white cathedral by Jura Dalmatinác (1441). The talented builder spent most of his life working on his masterpiece, which is a unique embodiment of the transition from the Gothic to the Renaissance style. The apses contain a row of seventy-four heads, each of which displays an individual vitality and are especially intriguing.

The surrounding landscape is a bit more hospitable here than the northern section of the coastal road. The vegetation also becomes more Mediterranean. Close to Šibenik is the start of the Krka National Park, a singular landscape of natural springs, babbling brooks and tumbling waterfalls – the realm of Croatian fairies and water sprites.

The route continues via Primošten. Wine has been produced in this area for centuries, with elaborate walls of white stone built to protect the vines from the cold winds of the bora.

16 Trogir The charming Old Town of Trogir is situated on a small island.

The winding alleys and a cathedral by the famous master builder Radoan transport visitors back to the Middle Ages. The town, which only has 7,000 residents, was once a Greek and then a Roman colony before becoming Croatia's political and cultural center from the 9th to 11th centuries, as is evidenced not only by the very impressive cathedral (13th–16th century), but also by the many splendid churches and palaces.

The magnificent Old Town has since been declared a UNESCO World Heritage Site.

17 Split The stunning port of Split, with 188,700 residents, is the cultural and economic center of Dalmatia and has numerous museums and theaters. It is out on a peninsula dominated by Marjan hill. The Old Town has a curious mixture of Roman, medieval and modern buildings, with the impressive Diocletian Palace (built at the turn of the 4th century) and the 13th-century cathedral – the entire Old Town was declared a UNESCO World Heritage Site. Unfortunately, it suffered significant damage during the Serbo-Croatian War, but that is slowly being repaired.

18 Makarska-Riviera This stretch of the Croatian coast becomes narrower and narrower as the journey progresses, until there is only the Biokovo moun-

combined with a walled medieval Old Town, a triumphal arch, St Mark' Cathedral and the bishop's palace.

The city of Korčula gives off a romantic image.

tain range separating the coast from Bosnia-Herzegovina. This is home to the once popular seaside resort area known as the Makarska Riviera, which was a passenger liner stop back in the 19th century. Sadly, a great many of the historic buildings from that era were destroyed by an earthquake in 1962. The high mountain ridge results in a mild climate that has inspired wine grape and olive cultivation. The picturesque fishing villages, pleasant pebble beaches and pine forests invite visitors to stop in. A few miles before Donta Deli there is a turnoff leading to the Pelješac Peninsula. You can catch ferries from here to the island of Kor ula.

In order to provide Bosnia-Herzegovina with access to the sea, Croatia had to surrender a tiny piece of its coast. The road to

Dubrovnik therefore passes through another border crossing.

⑲ Dubrovnik Viewed from the air, this town looks as if it is clinging to the rocks like a mussel. In the Middle Ages, Dubrovnik was known as the seafaring republic of Ragusa. The Old Town, which features a mix of Renaissance and baroque buildings, winding alleys and a wide main street lined with cafés, is surrounded by mighty walls that open up toward the sea in only a few places.

Basically impregnable for centuries, the town nevertheless faced near complete destruction on two occasions: from a strong earthquake in 1667, and from shelling by the Yugoslavian army in 1991. Fortunately, the bombed-out roofs of the public

buildings were rebuilt with a great deal of effort, such that the townscape has largely been restored.

Other attractions include testimonies to the golden 15th century when Ragusa vied with Venice for power. The Rector's Palace with its arcades, harmoniously round arch windows and baroque staircase dates from this era, as does the completely intact town wall with a total length of 1,940 m (2,122 ft). Kotor, Montenegro, is roughly 90 km (56 mi) from Dubrovnik, but the small medieval town is worth the detour. Bari, on the east coast of southern Italy, can be reached from Dubrovnik on a 16-hour ferry crossing.

⑳ Bari The capital of Apulia (331,600 residents) was initially founded by the Romans and was long subject to changing rulers. Foreign trade with Venice and the Orient brought wealth to the city, which still has a historic Old Town of Byzantine origin. Large parts of the region surrounding Bari are used for agriculture, in particular olive cultivation. The onward route takes you along the Autostrada 98 for a few miles before turning off at Ruvo di Púglia onto a smaller road towards Castel del Monte.

㉑ Castel del Monte This hunting castle from 1240, also known as the 'Crown of Apulia', towers up from the plain and can be seen from quite a distance. The castle was built according to the laws of numerical mysticism by the German Staufer Emperor Frederick II (1194–1250) who had a passion for science and magic. The symmetrical, octagonal castle has a ring of octagonal towers, so that the only variations are those brought about by the changing daylight, an impressively active design element within the building. The route continues along an equally small road to Barletta and from there 39 km (24 mi) along the coast to Manfredónia. A few miles further on it continues up to Monte S. Angelo. The journey now takes you past two lagoons: Verano and Lesina. At Térmoli the route joins the N16. Térmoli itself holds little appeal, but the road now twists through the hilly, coastal landscape, revealing consistently good views. Inviting coves and picturesque villages like Vasto or Ortona

Large image: View of Dubrovnik. Left side: Picturesque old town of Trogir. Above: The octagonal Castel del Monte.

Many locals go on holiday and enjoy the beaches, mountains or the good food in the numerous fish restaurants on the beautiful peninsula of Gargano.

Detour

Urbino

Urbino, the cradle of humanism and the birthplace of Rafael, lies amid a graceful landscape of rolling hills, fields and forests. It was here that Duke Federico di Montefeltro lived, a patron of the arts and sciences in the mid-15th century who turned the town into the center of humanist philosophy. The magnificent brickwork buildings of the Old Town are protected by a medieval wall and are entirely dominated by the gigantic Palazzo Ducale. This imposing building is a UNESCO World Heritage Site. All of the main streets lead to the Piazza della Repubblica. From there the Via Vittorio

View of Urbino (above) with the Palazzo Ducale (below one of his chapels).

Veneto leads up the hill to the Palazzo Ducale. The ducal palace is considered one of the most important Italian Renaissance buildings and, with its elegant courtyard lined with round arched arcades, it is an absolute highlight in the history of architecture.

perched on the cliffs tempt a stopover.

22 Vieste and Gargano Peninsula The spur of the Italian boot consists of a wild limestone massif (1,000 m/3,281 ft) that is mostly uninhabited. Monte San Angelo is the highest town on the Gargano Peninsula at 850 m (2,789 ft). You have a wonderful view of the plateau and the Gulf of Manfredónia from the town, which has been an important southern Italian pilgrimage destination ever since the apparition of the Archangel Michael in a nearby grotto at the end of the 5th century. A 12th-century bishop's throne and other valuables adorn the grotto, which is shielded by bronze gates from Constantinople (1076).
Vieste is on the eastern tip of the peninsula. It has splendid beaches and a lovely medieval Old Town where the traditional outdoor mignali (staircases) are linked by narrow archways.

23 Pescara The largest town in the Abruzzi region always seems to be bustling. Large sections of the town were sadly destroyed in World War II but they have been rebuilt with generous, open architecture. Only a very small historical Old Town still

exists now around the Piazza Unione. The town's attractions include its fine sandy beaches and the annual jazz festival in July, where legendary musicians like Louis Armstrong have performed. Pescara is at the mouth of the river of the same name.

24 S. Benedetto del Tronto Italy's largest fishing port is a lively and vibrant place. The town's icons include the splendid, palm-lined promenades, the elegant villas and a long sandy beach. The fishing museum and the fish market are also worth a brief visit.
The steep Riviera del Conero, with the Monte Conero promontory, features stunning limestone cliffs, forests and narrow pebble beaches. It is worth taking some detours inland from here, for example to Loreto, perched like a fortress on a hill above Porto Recanati.

25 Ancona
g Ancona The foothills of the imposing Monte Conero drop down to the sea in steps while Ancona, the attractive regional capital of the Marches, sits down at sea level on the natural port. Although the port and industry town with 98,400 residents was originally founded by

the Greeks and boasts a rich history as a seafaring republic, its historical monuments unfortunately tend to be second rate. In Ancona you should immerse yourself in the port atmosphere, which actually might be a welcome change from all the beach time and medieval towns. The San Ciriaco Cathedral (dating from the 11th–14th centuries) is perched high above the town. The Byzantine-influenced building is one of the most impressive Romanesque churches in Italy. En route to Pésaro there are a number of historical villages inviting you to stop a while, including Senigallia, the first Roman colony on the Adriatic coast. The Old Town there features the imposing Rocca Roveresca fortress.

26 Pesaro At the exit from the Foglia Valley is the industrial town and port of Pesaro. The Old Town, with its Palazzo Ducale (15th–16th centuries) on the Piazza del Popolo is worth visiting. Continuing now toward Rimini the, coastal strip becomes noticeably narrower and the hinterland more mountainous. From Pesaro it is worth taking an excursion to the Old Town of Urbino 35 km (22 mi) to the south-west.

The Conero Natural Park features an impessive combination of green cliffs and the deep blue sea.

27 From Cattolica to Rimini
This is where you will find the tourist strongholds of the Adriatic, coastal resorts which, with their sandy beaches stretching for miles, a diverse range of sporting opportunities and vibrant nightlife are focused on entertaining the masses. Rímini's history goes back a long way, however, so make sure you enjoy that aspect too.
Having first gained major significance as an Etruscan port, Rimini is divided into two districts that could hardly be more dif-

ferent. While the site of the Roman town is still recognizable in the Old Town, the coastal section is one of the liveliest seaside resorts on the Adriatic. After San Marino there is a tiny scenic road for about 20 km (12 mi) that leads past Rímini. You can also take the SS72.

28 Ravenna Art metropolis as well as an industrial city, Ravenna is a multifaceted place surrounded by the nature reserves of the Po Delta region. Indeed, as port in Roman times, imperi-

al Ravenna was once directly on the coast. But the port silted up and the location's importance dwindled. Only when the marshlands were drained in the 19th century did the economic recovery begin. Further impetus came in 1952 with the discovery of natural gas. Ravenna draws visitors with its early Christian churches and the charming Old Town. The numerous cultural monuments include the San Vitale and Sant' Apollinaire Nuovo churches; the mosaics in the Sant' Apollinaire Basilica in Classe; the Orthodox baptistery; the Arian baptistery; Galla Placidia's mausoleum; and the tomb of Ostrogothic King Theoderich. Santa Maria in Porto fuori, the Sant' Orso Cathedral and Dante's tomb date from later eras. From Ravenna the route then takes you to Chióggia, where the unique coastal landscape south of the main Po Delta has been made into a lovely nature reserve. The lagoons and hidden channels as well as the vast fields of the open plain are

Ravenna's churches are definitely worth a visit. Sant'Apollonare Nuovo (above) as well as San Vitale (below) are best known for their mosaics.

Detour

San Marino

On the eastern edge of the Apennine Mountains, which form the spine of Italy, is Monte Titano with its towering fortresses built to protect the world's smallest republic, San Marino, from potential harm. The republic comprises the capital of the same name and eight other villages. The stonemason Marinus, thought to be from the island of Rab in what is now Croatia, originally sought refuge here in around AD 301 after fleeing persecution as a Christian in Diocletian times. The inhabitants drew up their own constitution in the 13th century and declared themselves an independent commune. San Marino's liveli-

The Palazzo Pubblico is the Government headquarters of the small State.

hood is based on stamps and coins, on handicrafts and agriculture. Parking is available in the lower town of Borgo Maggiore. From here you continue either by foot or via the Funivia, a cable car. The historic Old Town has tiny alleys and is surrounded by a wall. There is a fantastic panoramic view from the Piazza della Libertà and the Palazzo del Governo. It is also worth visiting the San Francesco Church (1361). The three fortresses of Monte Titano are also worth seeing and are reached via the Salita alla Rocca steps.

Early Christian-Byzantine Churches in Ravenna

The Roman imperial star was already sinking when Ravenna experienced its golden age: Honorius made Ravenna the capital in 395. He and his sister Galla Placidia had Ravenna built up into an imperial city; the Germanic military leader Odoaker took over power after 476 and ruled his empire from Ravenna.

Numerous early Christian churches survive from this glittering era. The mosaic cycles here were created by unknown artists and display a remarkable degree of technical perfection. The stylistic similarities seem to indicate that the mosaics were created by Roman craftsmen or by artists from Ravenna who had at least learnt their craft from the Roman masters. The luminosity of the mosaics derives from their material: the in-

quite beautiful. Along the river causeways anglers can try their luck with the legendary Po catfish.

㉙ Chioggia Gracious palaces with their 'feet in the water', three canals with boats and a number of charming bridges, those are the things that justify this baroque lagoon town's nickname of 'Little Venice'.
Initially founded by the Romans, Chiógga was once very powerful but was ultimately overshadowed by La Serenissima for many centuries. In addition to enjoying the charming Venetian ambiance, it is also worth visiting the baroque St Maria Assunta Cathedral. Lovely beaches are to be found at Sottomarina and Isola Verde.

㉚ Padua This ancient university town on the edge of the Euganean Hills is the last stop on our tour around the Adriatic. The long arcade corridors and historic buildings characterize the town's appearance and Padua is one of the loveliest of the Italian towns from antiquity.
The main attractions are the Cappella degli Scrovegni, where Giotto painted his most important series of frescos in 1305, in a simple chapel; and the magnificent Basilica di Sant' Antonio from the 15th/16th centuries, which is still one of the country's most important pilgrimage destinations to this day.
Other buildings that are significant for their art history and ought to be visited are the 12th century-Palazzo della Ragione, the former Augustinian Eremitani Church (13th century) with frescoes by Mantegna, the Santa Giustina Church (16th century) and the monument to the military leader Gattamelata, an equestrian statue by Donatello, most of whose works are otherwise to be seen in Florence.
It is worth taking a detour to the Abano Terme and Montegrotto Terme hot springs to the southwest of town.

When looking at the Canale della Vena (large image), Chioggias is very closely located to Venice. The Botanical Garden of Padua (small image) is a UNESCO World Heritage Site.

dividual pieces (tesserae) were made from glass and carefully positioned so as to reflect the light to tremendous effect. San Vitale Church (526) is well worth seeing: it is based on the Hagia Sophia in Istanbul and its greatest treasures are the elaborate Byzantine mosaics. Behind this is Galla Placidia's mausoleum, an unassuming brick building from the outside but the interior is also decorated with exceptionally grand mosaics. The mosaics cover the cupola and the barrel vaults and are even older than those of San Vitale.

Padua This ancient university town is one of Italy's loveliest. Its particular attractions include the Cappella degli Scrovegni with Giotto's cycle of frescos, and the Basilica di Sant'Antonio, which is visited by millions of pilgrims every year.

Venice The 'Queen of the Eastern Mediterranean' is a combination of splendor and disrepair, land and water, Gothic, baroque and Renaissance. Attractions: Canal Grande, Piazza San Marco, Bridge of Sighs, Accademia, Palazzo Ducale.

Split This port is the cultural and economic center of Dalmatia. The center boasts Roman sites such as the Palace of Diocletian (c. AD 300) and severla other medieval buildings such as the cathedral.

Rovinji The best view of this Istrian port is from the water. The Venetian influence is easily recognizable in buildings such as the Church of St Euphemia.

Trogir Winding alleyways and a cathedral (13th–16th centuries) characterize the old heritage-protected town situated on an island.

Murano and Burano Two islands in the Venice lagoon are especially noteworthy: Burano, a fishing island with bright buildings and small lace-making workshops, and Murano, the embodiment of quality glasswork since the 13th century, and home to a remarkable early Romanesque and Byzantine basilica.

Ravenna Once the capital of the Ostrogothic King Theoderich the Great's empire, this town is primarily known for its early Christian-Byzantine churches.

Castel del Monte The hunting castle of the Staufer Emperor Frederick II (1194–1250) is visible from a distance and is enchanting with its perfect octagonal symmetry and strict simplicity.

Gargano The spur of the Italian boot is made of limestone mountains reaching an altitude of up to 1,000 m (3,281 ft). Monte Sant' Angelo is the highest.

Dubrovnik Only a few years after the severe damage caused by the Balkan war, this city is again intact and an idyllic location in many respects: Renaissance and baroque buildings and the splendid fortified walls are what give 'Venice's competitor' its unique magic.

Route 11: Greece
Classics of antiquity up close

Greece is the cradle of western civilization, and it is no surprise that the legacy of the ancient Greeks and its classic antiquities have inspired waves of fascination in the country. But a trip to Hellas is more than just a journey back through time: Greece is also a place of great natural beauty, with impressive mountainous landscapes, idyllic islands, wild coasts and pristine white-sand beaches.

Route profile:

Length: approx. 1500 km (932 mi)
Time required: 3 weeks
When to go: The best seasons in Greece are spring between March and May, or autumn from October to November. Summers are extremely hot and dry.

One-fifth of Greece's total area comprises islands. No place in the entire country is farther than 140 km (87 mi) from the sea, and the 14,000 km (8,700 mi) of coastline offer endless possibilities for spectacular hiking, swimming, sailing or just relaxing on the beach.

On the mainland and the Peloponnese, less than one-third of the land is suitable for farming. Agriculture is therefore concentrated on the plains of the country's north-east. The national tree of Greece, for example, the

olive tree, can thrive up to elevations of around 800 m (2,625 ft), and does so on the mainland as well as on the islands.

Greece's mountainous landscape and its proximity to the sea have obviously shaped civilization here for millennia. The most significant evidence of this is that, throughout the country's long history, the combination of mainland and archipelago prevented the formation of a central power. Instead, small city-states were the natural entities created here since ancient times, despite the fact that these were more easily conquered and ruled by foreign powers than a centralized structure might have been.

When the Roman Empire broke up in AD 395, Greece was part of the Eastern Roman Empire (Byzantium). It became Christian very early on. After the Crusades (11th–13th centuries), and in

some cases well into the 16th century, large parts of the country fell under the rule of the Venetians, whose legacy can still be seen in various place names and architecture. In 1453, the Ottomans seized Constantinople and later large parts of Greece. When it came to beliefs, the Turks were tolerant, and their Greek subjects enjoyed religious freedom. The Orthodox Church thus became a unifying and protective force for all Greeks during the Ottoman era. Isolated from the important cultural and intellectual developments in the rest of Europe, Greece remained untouched by the Renaissance, Reformation and Enlightenment. National pride, which emerged in the late 18th century, finally led to revolution in 1821, but it was quashed by the Turks.

It was not until 1827 that the Greeks, with help from the British, French and Russians, were

Above: Where today only ruins can be found, ancient people saw the centre of the world. Delphi, with its sanctuaries and famous oracle, was of almost unimaginable importance. Left: The Varlaám Monastery, dramatically positioned on a rock, is one of the famous Metéora monasteries.

sea, with whitewashed houses on a hillside above a quaint port – and not incorrectly. Regardless of whether you are hopping around the more than 2,000 islands or exploring the mainland, Greek hospitality is an exceptional national quality here.

A word of warning, however: their driving can be rather 'adventurous' at times. Some think the middle of the road belongs to them, even on curves, so make sure you drive with caution!

able to shake off Turkish rule and proclaim a sovereign state. After independence in 1830, the Greeks made Bavarian Prince Otto von Wittelsbach the king of their nation as Otto I, after which a number of German architects worked in Athens to en-

sure the nation was transformed into worthy capital of the new Greece after centuries of decline.

At the time, however, some areas of Greece were still under Turkish rule, which again led to wars with the Turks – with var-

ying success – and it was not until the early 20th century that Crete and a number of other Aegean islands were returned to Greece.

As a travel destination, Greece is often presented with deep blue skies above a turquoise

Left side: In Kalambaka, the gateway to Metéora, a weekly market takes place where tourists can buy colourful iconostases. Above: The Lion Gate with a striking relief is the main gate of the ancient Mycenae.

Oracle of Delphí

The Oracle of Delphí began having a significant effect on the fates of many Greek city-states in the 8th century BC. Rulers would address their questions to Apollo, for whom priestess Pythia then communicated his replies. She sat perched over a crevice, out of which hot steam rose, presumably sending her into a trance. The wisdom of the oracles was often ambiguous

Detour

Euboea

A bridge connects the mainland with Greece's second-largest island, which has still somehow remained largely untouched by mass tourism. Long stretches of the two main roads in the north and south head alternately along rugged cliffs and sandy beaches, passing picturesque fishing villages and small seaside resorts. The mountain roads and between remote villages provide spectacular views of the island. Halkida is the capital of Euboea, and its main attractions include the Turkish-Venetian Kastro quarter with an imposing mosque, an aqueduct and a fortress.

Heading north, Route 77 initially skirts the west coast. After Psahná, however, it becomes more mountainous, and the scenery is characterized by olive groves and pine forests before you are taken into the narrow Kleisoura Gorge. The mountain village of Prokópí lies at the foot of Kandillo, the highest peak in the northern half of the island at 1,246 m (4,088 ft).

Anyone not wanting to miss out on seeing the sandy beaches on Euboea should continue on to Agriovótano on the northern tip. The interior of Euboea is similarly rugged, and from Sténi Dírfios you can climb Dírfis, the highest mountain on the island at 1,745 m (5,725 ft) in about four hours.

Expressway 44 connects you with the south of the island along the west coast to Erétria. The few ruins of the ancient city include the theater, the acropolis and a temple of Apollo. Following the Gulf of Euboea you reach Alivéri, with its interesting Venetian tower. The nearby mountain village of Stíra is known for its 'dragon houses'. The journey ends in Káristos, which is dominated by the mighty Venetian fort Castello Rosso.

This journey through the Greece of antiquity will take you through majestic mountains and glorious coastal landscapes to the most important remnants of this ancient civilization, as well as to the legacies of Roman, Byzantine and Venetian eras on the southern mainland, Attica and the Peloponnese peninsula.

❶ Athens (see pp. 134–135)

❷ Cape Sounion From Athens, you initially head about 70 km (43 mi) south along Highway 91 to the outermost point of the peninsula. The lovely beaches at Voúla and Vouliagméni are worthwhile spots to stop along the Attic Coast between Piréas (Piraeus) and Soúnio. At the bottom of the cape is an amazing temple dedicated to Poseidon, god of the sea, from 444 BC. It provides stunning views down to the Saronic Gulf.

From Cape Sounion, the route continues north along the eastern side of the peninsula. Then, east of Athens, you take Highway 54 toward Marathón. The Marathón Plain was where the Greeks defeated an army of Persians in 490 BC. On the day of the battle, a messenger in a full suit of armour brought news of the victory to Athens and the 42-km (26-mi) stretch became the reference distance for the modern marathon.

❸ Thebes From Halkída, Highway 44 heads to Thíva, the new name of ancient Thebes, which is today an insignificant provincial town. The few historic remnants from what was once the mightiest city in Greece, in the 4th century BC, are on display in the Archaeological Museum. Continuing north-west you will pass the tower of a 13th-century fort built by Franconian crusaders.

Heading towards Delphi, you initially take Highway 3 and then turn onto Route 48. The city of Livádia lies in the middle of vast cotton fields. After Livádia you will get some spectacular views over Mount Parnassus to the north-west.

❹ Ósios Loukás After about 13 km (8 mi), a road turns off southward toward Distomo, and

and therefore required interpretation by a priest of some ranking. Roman emperors tried to resurrect the cult in the 2nd century, but the oracle fell silent in AD 393 and the sanctuary was eventually shut down.

In ancient times, rulers travelled the temples to ask for a divine intervention or an oracle.

a 13-km-long (8-mi) street leads to the Ósios Loukás Monastery, considered one of the most beautiful Greek Orthodox monasteries from the Byzantine era (10th century). It houses some magnificent mosaics from the 11th century.

Another 24 km (15 mi) down the often steep and winding Highway 48 and you arrive in Delphí.

5 Delphí Evidence of Delphí's magic can be seen in both its mythology and in its beautiful natural setting. Located amid a picturesque mountain landscape on the steep slopes of Mount Parnassus, the town was considered by the ancient Greeks to be the center of the world. The Oracle of Delphí in the Sanctuary of Apollo was a regular center of consultation between the 8th century BC and AD 393.

The most famous sites of ancient Delphí include the amphitheater from the 2nd century BC, with a stunning view of the Temple of Apollo from 200 years earlier; the Holy Road; and the Sanctuary of Athena Pronaia with the Tholos, a famous circular temple. The Archaeological Museum's many sculptures and a re-construction of the sanctuary is also worth a visit. The highlight is the life-size bronze charioteer, which had been dedicated to Apollo as a reward for a victorious chariot race in 478 BC.

From Delphí, it is worth making a 220-km-long (137-mi) detour to the Metéora monasteries (see pp 326–327) in the mountainous heart of northern Greece.

Anyone wanting to omit the detour north will initially follow the same route back to Thíva, then continue along Highway 3 toward Athens as far as Asprópirgos before finally turning off west onto a small road that runs parallel to the coast. The route follows Salamis Bay, where the Greeks defeated the Persian fleet in 480 BC. Past Mégara, you will get some spectacular views of the Gulf of Aegina.

The icon of Athens: a view of the Acropolis, with the imposing Parthenon in the center of the complex and Mount Lycabettos (large picture). Above left: Temple of Poseidon at Cape Sounion; left below: Monastery of Ósios Loukás.

The Acropolis of Athens once required the ancient taxpayers to make a great sacrifice. Today you can admire the remains of the huge building

The ceiling of the Caryatid Porch at the Erechtheion on the Acropolis is supported by columns in the shape of young women, so-called caryatids.

Athens

The Greek capital is a pulsating, modern metropolis with three million inhabitants, approximately one third of whom live in the greater Athens area. The city's most recognizable icon is visible from afar and is the epitome of ancient Greece: the Acropolis.

Athens is a city of contrasts: chaos on the roads, traffic jams, complicated environmental problems and oppressive smog polluting the entire valley, while the greatest ruins from antiquity, especially the Acropolis, still stand tall on the south side of city center.

Athens' most famous site is the mighty Acropolis – a UNESCO World Heritage Site –, the castle hill of the ancient city that was converted into a holy district around 800 BC and mainly used to worship the goddess Athena, the city's patron saint. The Acropolis sits atop a steep, rugged, 156-m-high (512 ft) pale limestone plateau and was an important place of refuge for the population in times of need. The early beginnings of a castle wall already existed in the 13th century BC. After the old temple was destroyed by the Persians in 480 BC, the complex of monumental marble buildings with the Propylae gate construction, the small Temple of Nike, the imposing Doric Parthenon (447–432 BC), and the Ionic Erechtheum with its Caryatid Porch were all created in the first half of the 5th century BC, the time of Pericles.

The most extensive damage to the Parthenon dates back to the 17th century when a Venetian grenade hit the Turkish powder warehouse in the Parthenon and sent the roof flying into the air. Important sculptures and reliefs are also on display in the Acropolis Museum.

The main attractions below the Acropolis are the Theater of Dionysus, where the dramas of Aeschylus, Euripides and Sophocles premiered in front of an audience of 17,000; and the Roman Odeion (AD 160), a construction commissioned by the wealthy Athenian, Herodes Atticus.

The Acropolis project ultimately required a huge sacrifice from the Athenian taxpayers: the total costs were more than 2,000 ancient gold talents, an enormous sum of money for a city-state the size of Athens.

Clustered around the Agora, the ancient market place from 600 BC and the center of public life for centuries, you will find the Doric Temple of Hephaistos, or Theseion (449–440 BC); the Attalos Stoa portico, once an artisans' center with discoveries from the ancient Agora, now reconstructed as a museum; the octagonal Tower of the Winds (1st century BC), formerly a clepsydra and sundial with a weather vane; the Roman Agora, from around the birth of Christ; and the adjacent Fethiye Mosque (15th century).

In the Plaka, the picturesque Old Town quarter with narrow alleyways, small shops, cafés and taverns, are several Byzantine churches, such as the beautiful Little Mitropolis (12th century) and Athens' oldest Christian church, the 11th-century cross-in-square Kapnikarea church on the fashionable Ermou shopping street. Also worth seeing is the Panagía Geogoepíkoös cross-in-square church (12th century) at the Plateía Mitropóleos, as well as a small bazaar mosque and the ruins of the Roman Library of Hadrian at Monastiraki Square.

Around the bustling Syntagma Square in modern Athens, you should see the Parliament building (Voulí), built by the architect Friedrich von Gärtner in 1842; the national garden created in 1836 with exotic plants; the Numismatic Museum in the home of Heinrich Schliemann; the ruins of Hadrian's Gate and the Temple of Zeus (Olympieion) dating back to Roman times; the ancient Kallimármaro Stadium, reconstructed for the first modern Olympic Games in 1896; the National Archaeological Museum with a unique collection of ancient Greek art; the Museum of Cycladic Art; the Byzantine Museum; and the Benáki Museum (Byzantine works, Coptic textiles).

The surrounding area features: the Kaisariani Byzantine monasteries with the St Mary's Church, built around 1000, and 11th-century Dafni, which has some ornate gold leaf mosaics in the main church, UNESCO World Heritage Site.

It is worth taking a day trip out to Piraeus, Athens' port since ancient times, with the Mikrolimano fishing port, Hellenic Marine Museum and the Archaeological Museum. Also visit the Poseidon Temple on Cape Sounion, 67 km (42 mi) away, and the islands in the Saronic Gulf, home to Aegina with the Temple of Apollo and the Temple of Aphaia, the island of Poros with its charming scenery, and the artists' island of Hydra.

The Metéora monastery frescos

Even in ancient times, painting the walls was a common form of artistic and spiritual expression. Indeed, these colorful murals ful-filled an important role in the Byzantine Empire (Eastern Roman Empire) and the form even experienced a sort of heyday in the 9th century. Frescos (from the Italian 'fresco', meaning fresh) were created by applying fresh water-colors to wet lime surfaces. The mineral dyestuffs penetrated the fresh rock and bonded chemically with the lime and sand to form a hard surface. Built by Eastern Orthodox monks hoping to escape the imminent conquest of the Turks, some of the Metéora monasteries are still home to rich murals from the 14th to 16th centuries. Due to their natural inaccessibility perched on top of dramatic limestone towers, many of the frescos have in fact been

Detour

Metéora Monasteries

The name Metéora means 'floating rocks' – and the literal sense of the term becomes apparent to any visitor as soon as they arrive at this vast monastery complex. The Metéora monasteries are some of the most beautiful and impressive attractions in all of Greece.

From Delphí, the road initially heads west as far as Ámfissa, where you turn onto Highway 48 towards Brálos. From there, Highway 3 passes through Lamía to Néo Monastíri, and continues along Highway 30 through Tríkala to Kalambáka. The first sandstone towers can be seen on the horizon from quite a distance. The monastery buildings sit atop high cliffs, which soar up vertically out of the Thessalia Plain to heights of 300 m (984 ft). The roughly 1,000 sandstone formations are deposits from a large lake whose waters eroded out the pillars before the sea level dropped.

After the 9th century, when foreign invaders began their conquest of the region, some hermits sought refuge in this remote world of rock towers. One of them was a recluse named Barnabas, who settled here at the end of the 10th century. Many others soon followed suit on the nearby towers. The monasteries themselves were not built until the 14th and 15th centuries, when the Serbs threatened with invasion. In 1336, the monk Athanásios from Athos established the first monastery, which was followed by twenty-three others. The buildings on the cliffs were used by the recluses as both places of refuge in the face of foreign invaders, as well as places of worship. The foundations were financed by wealthy private individuals looking to secure themselves a place in heaven;

some monasteries still even bear the names of their founders. The monks lived according to strict monastic rules that prohibited women from entering the monasteries. Even in times of need, they were not allowed to accept food from women.

The monasteries were built in places out of the military's reach and could only be accessed in a very circuitous route using rope-ladders or other climbing aids. If a situation appeared unsafe, the monks could retract their ladders; or they could receive welcome guests, drop down a basket or net and pull the visitors up. Everyone visiting Metéora for the first time will automatically ask themselves, when looking at the steep cliffs, how the first hermits climbed these tall, sharp rocks, which can today only be mastered by sport climbers.

One supposes they beat pegs into narrow crevices and worked their way up. The paths quarried into the rock were only created in more recent times. The architectural construction of the individual monasteries is largely a function of their varying positions on a crag or over an abyss. The internal structure of the monasteries is relatively uniform, and they have all the essential facilities required by occidental monasticism: a prayer chapel, a kitchen, a refectory (dining hall), a cistern, monk cells, a library and a treasure chamber. From 1490, all monasteries were subordinate to the

very well preserved, for example the ones in the small Stéfanos Chapel, which date back to the early 16th century. The Ágios Nikólaos Monastery, built in the late 14th century and expanded in 1628, also houses a vast collection of frescos. A monk named Theophanes painted some of the most beautiful frescos here around 1527. The nuns of the Ágios Stéfanos Convent continue to operate an icons workshop even today.

abbot of the Metamórfosis Monastery, built between 1356 and 1372, and one of the oldest monasteries in Metéora. The monks stayed in their monasteries even after the Turkish conquest of northern Greece and new monasteries were still being founded in Metéora in the late 15th century. Some of the monasteries were large properties and were thus subject to tribute to the Turkish rulers.

The 16th century was the heyday of monastic life in Metéora, but also a time of fierce conflicts between the various monasteries. Towards the end of the 18th century, the first monastery complexes had already fallen into ruin because of difficulty in maintaining their basic structures. Today, there are still thirteen monasteries that are in parts completely impoverished and have largely fallen into disrepair, but some of them still have valuable libraries. In total, six monasteries can still be visited. The most spectacular of these is undoubtedly the little Moní Rousánou Monastery, perched atop a crag and founded by two brothers from Epirus in 1545. For a long time the location was only accessible using rope-ladders and was often used by the people from the surrounding area as a place of refuge. The oldest preserved monastery in Metéora bears the name Moní Hypapante. Three monasteries are particularly worth seeing: Várlaam was founded in 1518 and its church (Katholikón) is home to beautiful frescos. Perched 623 m (2,044 ft) up, Megálo Metéoro is the highest and largest monastery, and the hermit caves of its founder can still be visited today. Ágios Stéfanos is a convent and was founded by Byzantine Emperor Andronikos III in 1332.

The spectacular location gave the monasteries their name.

The church of Agios Dionysios is where the saint, after whom it was named, is buried. Every year on the day of his death in December, a procession takes place in his honor.

The Corinth Canal

Corinth was Greece's most important trading city in ancient times thanks to its various points of access to the Aegean and the Ionic seas. To avoid sailing around the stormy southern cape of the Peloponnese, people began early on searching for ways to cross the narrow isthmus. In some places, ships were hauled over a 6-km-long (4-mi) cobblestone road. Work on a navigable channel started at the narrowest point even in ancient times, but the canal was eventually only completed in 1893. The resulting waterway is 23 m (75 ft) wide, 8 m (26 ft) deep and is cut through walls that are 52 m (171 ft) high.

sporting competitions took place outside the Altis, and the sites include a stadium for runners, the hippodrome (for chariot races) and the training sites of Gymnasion and Palaestra.

Other attractions are the Pryentaion, where the Olympic torch was lit and the Heraion, a temple dedicated to the goddess Hera. The Olympic torch is still lit in front of this temple before all Olympic Games.

The Echo Hall, a foyer with two naves, was famous for its sevenfold echo. Columns at the ruins of the Temple of Zeus from 450 BC testify to the vast size of the former building. Olympia's Archaeological Museum is one of the best in Greece.

North of Pírgos you will drive along a road lined with olive trees, vineyards and sugar cane plantations.

15 Zákinthos Ferries to this, the southernmost of the Ionic Islands, operate from the port town of Kilíni on the north-west coast of the Peloponnese. you can easily drive around the island in one day. Almost all of

the Venetian buildings in the main town were destroyed in an earthquake in 1953, but the Agios Dionísos Church (1925) and the traditional Arcadian houses are worth seeing.

The Blue Caves on the North Cape can be accessed by boat from Agios Nikólaos. Another of the island's attractions is the beach shipwreck on the northwest coast, while Laganás Bay in the south is a breeding ground for loggerhead turtles.

16 Patras From Lehená, take Highway 9 to Patras. It is worth making a detour here to the lagoons along the coast. Stretching through this area is one of Europe's largest wetlands where swamps, stone pines and dunes are used by migratory birds as a stopover point. There is a visitors' center at Lápas.

The naval Battle of Lepanto took place in the strait north-east of Patras, the third-largest city in Greece with no notable attractions. This was where Don Juan d'Austria defeated the Ottoman fleet in 1571.

17 Diakoftó Rather than taking Highway 8, we recommend you follow a small rural road along the coast. For a little diversity along the way, it is worth taking a ride on the cog railway from Diakoftó some 40 km (25 mi) east of Patras to Kalávrita at a height of 700 m (2,297 ft). The journey over this 22-km-long (14-mi) stretch with fourteen tunnels and a number of bridges takes approximately one hour and travels through some picturesque mountains. If you choose to drive between these two towns, you will see the Méga Spíleo Monastery perched up in the mountains as if clinging to a rock face.

The monastery, which is said to be the oldest in the country, was where the Greeks began their revolution against the occupation of the Ottomans. From Diakoftó, the road that runs parallel to the Gulf of Corinth will take you back toward Corinth and eventually back to the capital, Athens.

The Blue Caves are one of Zákinthos' main attractions.

The lighthouse of Patras is the landmark of the city. It is no longer used, but its light can still be ignited.

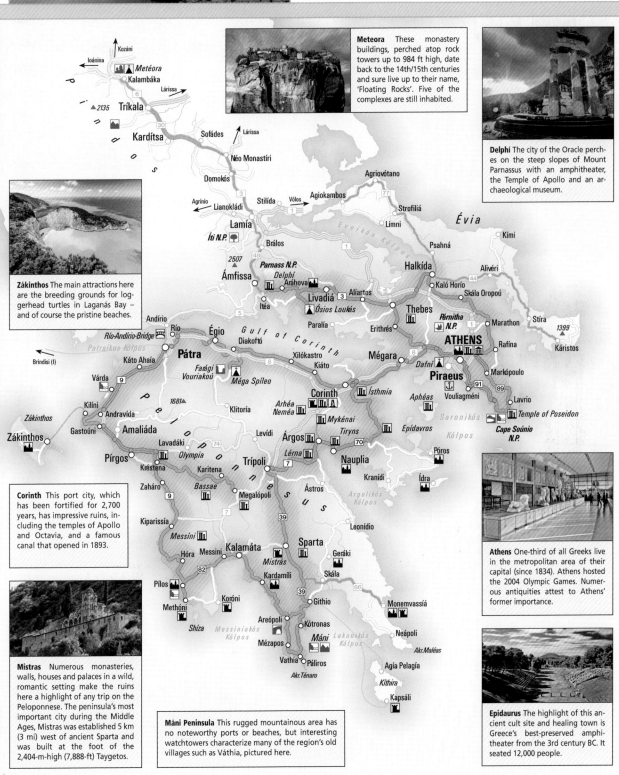

Meteora These monastery buildings, perched atop rock towers up to 984 ft high, date back to the 14th/15th centuries and sure live up to their name, 'Floating Rocks'. Five of the complexes are still inhabited.

Delphi The city of the Oracle perches on the steep slopes of Mount Parnassus with an amphitheater, the Temple of Apollo and an archaeological museum.

Zákinthos The main attractions here are the breeding grounds for loggerhead turtles in Laganás Bay – and of course the pristine beaches.

Corinth This port city, which has been fortified for 2,700 years, has impressive ruins, including the temples of Apollo and Octavia, and a famous canal that opened in 1893.

Mistras Numerous monasteries, walls, houses and palaces in a wild, romantic setting make the ruins here a highlight of any trip on the Peloponnese. The peninsula's most important city during the Middle Ages, Mistras was established 5 km (3 mi) west of ancient Sparta and was built at the foot of the 2,404-m-high (7,888-ft) Taygetos.

Máni Peninsula This rugged mountainous area has no noteworthy ports or beaches, but interesting watchtowers characterize many of the region's old villages such as Váthia, pictured here.

Athens One-third of all Greeks live in the metropolitan area of their capital (since 1834). Athens hosted the 2004 Olympic Games. Numerous antiquities attest to Athens' former importance.

Epidaurus The highlight of this ancient cult site and healing town is Greece's best-preserved amphitheater from the 3rd century BC. It seated 12,000 people.

Africa

The African continent is so difficult to comprehend in all its unique-
ness, not only because of its sheer size – the seemingly countless
and multifaceted cultures and differing natural landscapes, ranging from dust-dry deserts to all flooding bodies of water, make
this part of the earth as surprising as it is exciting. The silence of
the sand deserts of the Sahara, the palaces of Morocco and the
pyramids of Egypt in the north of Africa, the red flame of the Namib desert in the southwest, the raging waters of Victoria Falls
and the majesty of Kilimanjaro in the southeast and the roaming
magnificent wildlife represent the breathtaking diversity of the
continent.

Impression of the Namib Desert: The desert begins on the outskirts of Swakopmund. It is the oldest desert in the world – where at the same time the highest star dunes in the world can be found, with a height of up to 350 m. The red sand sea of the Namib is one of the most impressive landscapes in Namibia.

Royal cities, kasbahs and oases

The magic of Oriental medinas and palaces, the austere beauty of the Atlas Mountains, the bright white of the harbour cities, the green of the Saharan palm oases, and the colours and aromas of 'a thousand and one nights' in the souks of the royal cities make this tour an experience for the senses.

Route profile:

Length: approx. 3,100 km (1,926 miles), excluding detours
Time required: 21–25 days

Tangiers is the starting point on the Strait of Gibraltar. Strolling through the maze-like medina (old Arab quarters with tiny streets), you get a sense of the special Arabic-Spanish atmosphere that made Tangiers a jet-setters' haunt in the 1960s. East of the city, the rugged mountains of the Rif slope gently back towards the Mediterranean coast. Tétouan, with its well-preserved medina, and the small, picturesque mountain town of Chefchaouen are two fascinating stops on your way south. To the south of the Rif mountains, the columns and gates of the ruined Roman city of Volubilis soar above golden

cornfields. Not far away, the holy city of Moulay Idriss clings to the hillside as if painted on with watercolours. Moulay Idriss I brought Islam to Morocco in the 8th century and founded the first dynasty here. His mausoleum in the city's holy quarter is the most important pilgrimage site in the country. Nearby is the royal city of Meknès with its sturdy walls, storehouses and palaces.Fez was the first royal city under Moulay Idriss II and his Idriss Dynasty. Above the labyrinth of alleys, squares, markets and palaces, the minarets of countless mosques rise up towards the heavens.

The architectural treasure of Fez, its colourful, aromatic souks (marketplaces) around the mausoleum of Idriss II, the palace area of the Dar el-Makhzen, and the dignified Kairaouine Mosque make this city of trade and science over a thousand years old,

an Oriental gem.

Heading south through the densely forested areas of the Middle Atlas, you pass Ifrane and Azrou and the Col du Zad. Vegetation in this area now becomes more scarce and the nearby desert begins to expand. From Ar-Rachidia onwards, the route follows the palm-filled valley of Oued Ziz on its way to Erfoud, a garrison city that is the jumping-off point for tours into

the majestic Erg Chebbi Desert, a dream landscape of extraordinary golden sand dunes.

From Erfoud, you now follow the famous Route of the Kasbahs where mud fortresses tower above the palm tree oases of Tinerhir and Boumalne Dadès. Both towns lie at the mouth of wildly romantic gorges that lead deep into the mountainous realm of the High Atlas. A day trip south through the Drâa Val-

Above: Ksar Aït-Ben-Haddou, located in southeastern Morocco, makes an overwhelming impression. Villages are known as ksar in Morocco. It is probably the most beautiful and best-preserved facility of its kind in the country. It consists of a total of six nested Kasbahs and was nominated of the UNESCO in 1987 as a World Heritage Site. Left: The city market, which takes place on Place el Hedim in Meknes, is full of activity.

ley passes Ouarzazate to the old oases of Agdz, Zagora and Tamegroute. Ksar Aït Ben Haddou is probably the most frequently photographed movie set in Morocco. The mud city was abandoned by its inhabitants and is to be restored under the UNESCO protectorate. Over the Tizi-n' Tichka pass, the route continues north through the 3,000-m (9,843-ft) High Atlas to the royal city of Marrakech.

Here, the minaret of the Koutoubia Mosque soars high above this ancient city, and goods from every land fill the souk.
From Marrakech, our dream route heads towards the Atlantic, but before reaching Agadir it briefly breaks south into a landscape where erosion has created some amazing formations. Tafraoute and the Valley of Ammeln in the Anti-Atlas display the ancient world of the

Berbers. The route now passes through the silver city of Tiznit and the resort of Agadir, and follows the Atlantic coast towards Essaouira. The harbour town protected by many forts has a beautiful medina. Further north, the modern metropolis of Casablanca is home to the largest, most magnificent mosque in the Maghreb, while the foundation and base of the Hassan Tower minaret tell of a similarly ambi-

tious mosque project in nearby Rabat that was started in 1150 and never completed. Passing through Larache and Asilah you arrive back in Tangiers.

Left: The magnificent interior of the mausoleum of Moulay Ismail in Meknes. Top left: Old town of Tétouan. Above right: Characteristic of the old town of Fez is the tanners' quarter.

Volubilis

Volubilis, near Meknès, is one of the most beautiful ruins in North Africa. In its day, the city had over 15,000 residents, many living in luxurious villas

Our tour through Morocco uniquely combines culture with nature. In addition to royal cities, the journey includes oldstyle earthen fortresses against the backdrop of the Atlas Mountains as well as resorts on the stunning Atlantic coast.

① Tangiers Founded in Roman times, the first impression made by this harbour city on the Strait of Gibraltar is one of a hectic Oriental marketplace. High over the city, the former royal palace is enthroned in the kasbah, which also houses the Archaeological Museum with exhibits from Volubilis. From Tangiers, the N2 winds its way south-east through the foothills of the Rif mountains.

② Tétouan The largest city in the Rif is a UNESCO World Heritage Site for its architecture, which is heavily influenced by Andalusian styles and indeed was part of Spain until Moroc-

can independence in 1956. Within the walled medina you will see numerous vaulted arch alleyways, and many houses with windows covered in wrought-iron bars. Tétouan's souk is the fourth largest in Morocco. On market days, country-women from the Rif bring their products into the city.

The fully restored N2 heads south through the cedar- and holm-oak-covered Rif mountains.

③ Chefchaouen The white houses of the medina here clutter the mountainside like building blocks, with the high peaks of the central Rif mountains in

the background. In 1492, many Jews and Muslims settled here following their expulsion from Spain during the Reconquista. Even today you cannot help but notice the Spanish influence in the architecture of the picturesque labyrinthine alleys in the medina.

After crossing the Rif you reach Ouezzane and follow Highway 417 to the N3 intersection, then head first north-west travelling from Sidi-Kacem, and then south to Volubilis (180 km/112 miles).

④ Volubilis The ruins of this former Roman settlement lie at the foot of the Djebel Zerhoun. Founded in the first century BC,

Volubilis was the capital of the Roman province Mauretania Tingitana until AD 285. The city became prosperous through the olive oil trade as well as by selling wild animals for Roman arena events. A mere 2.5 km (1.5 miles) away from Volubis is the pilgrimage site of Moulay Idriss.

⑤ Moulay-Idriss Your first stop here should be the 'Terrace', a vista point with fantastic views over the maze of the

At the top: View over Tetouan. Above: Volubilis: Triumphal Arch of Caracalla (left) and floor mosaic in the 'House of Orpheus' (right).

with artistic mosaic floors. These have been wonderfully preserved, for example in the 'House of the Nymphs', the 'House of the Twelve Labours of Hercules' or the 'House of Venus', where a beauty emerging from the bath adorns the floor mosaic.

The triumphal arch of Caracalla towers imposingly over the Decumanus Maximus. The main axis crosses the ancient city from the south-west to the north-east. In the southern part of the ruins, the basilica, with its elegant porticos, was the place where markets were held and the law administered. Just alongside is the Capitol Temple of Jupiter, Juno and Minerva.

When Rome's shining star began to fade in North Africa, Volubilis was surrendered. Today, Roman history is vividly presented at these UNESCO World Heritage ruins and in the associated museum.

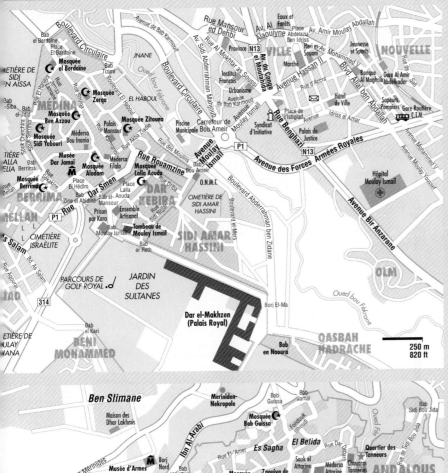

Meknès

Moulay Ismail, who chose Meknès as his royal city at the end of the 17th century, was a megalomaniac ruler and his monumental buildings are testimony to this.

The Ville Impériale, surrounded by mighty walls, the magnificent city gate Bab el-Mansour, the Heri es-Souani storehouse used as a stable and granary, and finally the lavishly decorated mausoleum of the ruler are all part of the city's UNESCO World Heritage offering. The medina, with its colourful souks, is labyrinthine and intimate in comparison. Among the Old City's maze of alleys, the Medersa Bou Inania conceals a special gem of neo-Moorish architecture.

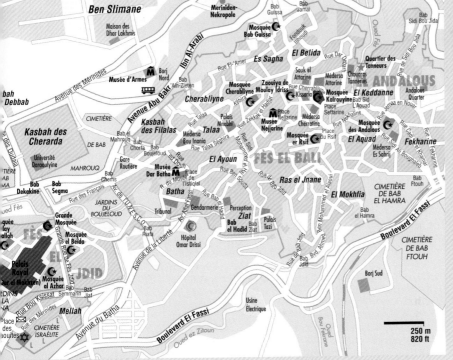

Fez

Fez el-Bali, the old Fez, sprawls like a labyrinth in the basin beneath the Marinid fortress. In AD 809, Idriss II deemed the town a royal city. Since then, Fez has become a modern metropolis.

Madrasahs and palaces, the mausoleum of the city's founder and the venerated Kairaouine Mosque are adorned with a real fusion of Arabic-Berber decorative art, with carvings, mosaics and gypsum stucco work. In the souks, spice merchants, cobblers, carpet sellers and goldsmiths vie for customers' business while sheep and goat skins are made into leather in the tanners' quarter.

Detour

Erg Chebbi – in Morocco's 'Sea of Sand'

The adventurous trip to Erg Chebbi can also be done with a suitable off-road vehicle and goes from Rissani (41 km/25 miles, a few sandy sections) or Erfoud (46 km/28.5 miles, uneven road) on the marked track to the hamlet of Merzouga and further on into Morocco's largest sand dune region, the Erg Chebbi. This sand sea is part of the eastern foothills of the Great Western Erg. There are several simple restaurants at the base of the dunes and camel herders offer rides. At dawn and dusk,

medina with its mosques surrounding the central sanctuary mausoleum of Idriss I.

A direct descendant of the prophet Mohammed, Idriss I, founded this town around AD 788, succeeded in converting the Berber people to Islam and subsequently formed the first Moroccan dynasty. Passing now through an idyllic hill landscape, you will come to the royal city of Meknès just 28 km (17 miles) away.

6 Meknès (see p. 147). Just 70 km (43 miles) down the N6 is Fez.

7 Fez (see p. 147). From Fez, the N13 continues south into the foothills of the Middle Atlas.

8 Ifrane After roughly 60 km (37 miles) you will be pleasantly surprised by picturesque mountain scenery that many say is quaintly reminiscent of Switzerland. The health resort of Ifrane could just as easily be in

the sand dunes are bathed in a fire-red light. About 26 km (16 miles) further south, near Taouz, you'll find desert rock drawings (only with police authorization and a guide). From here, the same road leads back to Erfoud.

Erg Chebbi is like a huge ocean with gentle waves of sand..

N13 wind lazily through the impressive cedar forests. With a bit of luck, you will encounter some Barbary Apes. Once you've passed the 2,178-m (7,146-ft) Col du Zad, the landscape becomes more sparse and after the mining city of Midelt, the route winds its way through the enchanting eastern foothills of the High Atlas. North of Ar-Rachidia, the road continues up along the spectacular Gorges du Ziz.

⑨ Ar-Rachidia This town at 1,060 m (3,477 ft) is an important traffic and trade junction in southern Morocco. Surrounded by oasis gardens, it is the epitome of a typical oasis, but with the added backdrop of the majestic High Atlas. The town itself is rather modern and functional, with very few traces of traditional architecture. This is where the Tafilalt oases begin, fed by the Oued Ziz originating in the Atlas, and where the current royal family resides, the Alouites. The N13 follows the river past oasis gardens and small settlements until it reaches Erfoud 74 km (46 miles) away.

⑩ Erfoud Founded by the French only in 1917, Erfoud still looks like a desert garrison city with barracks, modern head-

quarters and wide, dusty streets. It is the centre of the Tafilalt, the largest valley oasis in Morocco. Many souvenir dealers have specialized in selling fossils from the Sahara.

From here you travel another 22 km (13.5 miles) south through the fascinating desert landscape.

⑪ Rissani Some 3,000 inhabitants populate the narrow, often vaulted-arch alleyways of the medina beyond the town gate. If a market is held on a Sunday, oasis farmers and cattle breeders from the surrounding villages fill the main town square. It is interesting to do a day trip to the oasis of Rissani, the mausoleum of Moulay Ali Cherif, the founder of the Alouite dynasty, and to Ksar Abbar, whose mud walls are decorated with Islamic geometric patterns. In contrast, the ruins of the once most important trading city in southern Morocco, the legendary Sijilmassa, are disappointing. 100,000 people lived and traded goods here from the 11th to 15th centuries, acquiring caravans from the sub-Saharan African kingdoms of the south. Only a few mud walls have been preserved underneath the desert sand.

the European Alps. Gabled houses, cool, fresh mountain air, a few nearby ski lifts – this is what Morocco's alpine holiday destinations look like. Morocco's most prestigious university is in Ifrane, and the royal family also

owns a magnificent palace here. Enjoy a typically Moroccan pastry, the Cornes de Gazelle, before the upcoming 300-km-long (186-mile) stretch through the Middle and High Atlas. The N8 and, from Azrou onwards, the

Large picture: Traditional craftsmanship determines a whole district in Fès. Left side: Morocco has a share in the Sahara, the largest dry desert in the world.

Top left: The Bab el-Mansour is the main city gate of Meknes. Above: The Madrasa Bou Inania teaches both the Koran and other disciplines such as mathematics.

Detour

Gorges du Dadès and Gorges du Todra

Turning off the N10 for about 1 km (0.6 miles) before Tinerhir

brings you approximately 15 km (9 miles) up the winding S6902 to the narrowest point of the Gorges du Todra. Numerous villages and campsites line the road, and there are always amazing panoramic views of the Todra

River valley, which originates in the High Atlas. After 15 km (9 miles) you can only continue by foot. The Todra must be repeatedly crossed on artificial fords. The nearly vertical rock faces stretch to the sky on your

The Valley of the Roses

Damascene roses are the most important industry for oasis farmers in El Kelaa M'Gouna. They are the source of extremely valuable rose oil, which is used to make perfume and exported predominantly to Paris. A separate process extracts rose water, which plays a vital role in Moroccan cuisine and cosmetics. Following the annual rose harvest in May, a big party is held in El Kelaa M'Gouna.

From El Kelaa M'Gouna, an easily navigated track follows the Assif M'Goun river valley into the mountains. Pass-ing a fascinating series of abandoned kasbahs, you eventually arrive at Tourbist after 18 km (11 miles), an oasis consisting of several abandoned tighremt situated picturesquely on a bend in the river.

From Rissani, you can also make a detour to the sand dunes of Erg Chebbi near Merzouga. Otherwise, return to Ar-Rachidia on the same route through Erfoud and travel west on the N10.

12 Tinerhir The majestic range of the High Atlas accompanies the route in the north, while a grey-brown plain sprawls out to the south. You will then see what looks like an oversized molehill. These are the entry craters of the ancient 'foggaras' un-

derground irrigation system. In the canals, water from the High Atlas is channelled into the arid foreland to irrigate the fields. The system must be serviced regularly and cleared of stones and refuse – a dangerous task that is usually carried out by the unlucky descendants of former slaves.

At the mouth of the Gorges du Todra, at 1,342 m (4,403 ft), Tinerhir, the 19th-century kasbah, keeps watch over the town with its old mud houses around the

rosé-coloured minaret of the mosque. The deep-green oasis gardens sprawl around the town, pomegranates, tomatoes, carrots and clover growing in the shade of the palm trees to feed the livestock.

Following the southern edge of the High Atlas, the route continues west to Boumalne Dadès, 53 km (33 miles) away. In the south, the Djebel Sarhro mountain range now draws near. You'll begin to see more and more mud kasbahs, constructed

left and right. Not quite so dramatic is the Gorges du Dadès, which you approach from Boumalne Dadès (S6901 turn-off from the N10 approximately 1 km/0.6 miles after Boumalne Dadès). The access road passes eroded granite sculptures and wide open rock formations. After approximately 10 km (6 miles), the route passes the two impressive kasbahs of Aït Yul and Aït Arbi. Passing by other Kasbahs and villages, it continues on to Aït Oudimar (28 km). This is where the narrowest part of the gorge with steep rock faces starts. The asphalt road ends here after 30 km (18 miles), and you can explore the gorge on foot, returning on the same road.

A narrow mountain stream meanders through the Todra Canyon with its steep cliffs.

for the safety of the trade routes and to guard the oases. At the turn of the 20th century, the infamous Pasha of Marrakech, El-Glaoui, built these kasbahs to safeguard his domain and station his loyal troops.

⑬ Boumalne Dadès This oasis at 1,586 m (5,203 ft) is also tucked into the opening of a deep mountain gorge formed by the Dadès. It accompanies the road from Boumalne to Ouarzazate. The Dadès Valley is also called the Route of the Kasbahs because of its many mud castles. The small market town is made up of several tighremt, Berber family castles built from mud and guarded by four towers, over which the well-fortified kasbah kept watch from high on the plateau. Some tighremt are still inhabited. Fruit and olive trees as well as vegetables grow in the oasis gardens but palm trees are rarely seen at these heights. Boumalne Dadès is the starting point for day trips to the Gorges du Dadès and the Djebel Sarhro. This high desert mountain range is home to Bedouin folk who roam between the mountains and river oases of the Dadès and the Drâa with goats and camels. Kasbahs and ksars (villages) line the road west to El Kelaa M'Gouna just 24 km (15 miles) away.

⑭ El-Kelaâ M'Gouna Just 10,000 people live in this settlement at an altitude of 1,467 m (4,813 ft). They farm the oasis gardens whose most valuable asset is the Damascene Rose (see sidebar at right). El Kelaa M'Gouna is also under the watchful eye of an old kasbah originally built by El-Glaoui to control trade routes.

Like other towns along this route, there is also a river here, the Assif M'Goun, that comes down from the High Atlas Mountains and flows into the Dadès River.

On the 94-km (58-mile) stretch heading toward Ouarzazate, the road is bordered by the High At-las in the north and the Djebel Sarhro in the south. A series of kasbahs, sometimes in the midst of green palms and other times on stark mountain ledges, once again provides photo opportunities. Of particular interest is the oasis of Skoura with its reddish-brown mud castles.

⑮ Ouarzazate Shortly before reaching Ouarzazate, 'The Door of the Desert' (1,160 m/3,806 ft), the waters of the Barrage El Mansour Eddahbi glimmer like a mirage in the otherwise bleak landscape. The golf course, with its deep-green lawn alongside the dam, is an equally unusual sight.

You then reach the Taourirt kasbah, one of Morocco's largest mud settlements and a small city in itself. The mud walls conceal

In the High Atlas (large image) lies the Dadès gorge.
The river created a canyon-like landscape here (small images).

Souks

Most Europeans associate the Persian word 'bazaar' with the market area of an Arabian city. In Morocco, this area is called a souk, the Arabic word for mar-ket. Morocco's largest souk is found in the royal city of Mar-rakech. The alleyways are pro-tected from the sun by straw mats or brick arches. In some of the souks, or sellers' alleys, deal-ers and artisans offer their goods separately according to their trade. Here you find the realm of the goldsmiths and the alleyways of the ceramic sellers gleaming in all the colours of the rainbow. The tailors' souk is filled with the sound of sewing

Detour

Drâa Valley

At Ouarzazate, the well-built N9 turns towards the south-east, first crossing a stark pre-desert landscape and fi-nally meandering up the slopes of the Djebel Sarhro to the Tizi-n-Tinififft pass at 1,680 m (5,512 ft). Here you can catch your first glimpse of the verdant Drâa Valley. The road then winds its way back down through the wild craggy highlands.

About 70 km (43 miles) fur-ther on, you reach Agdz at the foot of the 1,531-m-high (5,023-ft) Djebel Kissane. This lively market town is the beginning of the river oasis along the Oued Drâa before you reach Mhamid 200 km (124 miles) away. Fields, palm groves, and fruit and olive tree plantations line the river. Even here, the well-for-tified kasbahs oversee the villages.

Roughly 4 km (2.5 miles) fur-ther on from Agdz, a detour takes you over the river to the Tamnougalt kasbah and the village below it with its mud castles. Back on the N9, you follow the river until reaching Agdz Zagora 96 km (60 miles) away.

Surrounded by the desert mountains of the Djebel Zag-ora, Zagora is a historically significant stop – It takes fif-ty-two days for a caravan to reach Timbuktu from here, as a road sign proudly points out. Zagora was an impor-tant trading and caravan town for goods from that once legendary city. About 18 km (11 miles) south-east on the N9 takes you to Zaouya Tamegroute, the re-ligious centre of an Islamic brotherhood founded in the 16th century.

numerous dwellings as well as the palace of Pasha El-Glaoui, where two rooms are open to the public.

Ouarzazate itself is a modern city without any charm as such, but it is an important stopping point thanks to its excellent of-fering of hotels and restaurants. It owes its nickname of the 'Hol-lywood of Morocco' to the local film studios that have produced numerous international films in the south of this picturesque country.

The N9 leaves the city to the north-west towards Marrakech. Some 26 km (16 miles) out of Ouarzazate a sign points you to the ksar Aït Ben Haddou.

⑯ Aït Ben Haddou The 9-km (5.5-mile) access road here ends at one of Morocco's most beau-tiful vista points looking out over a rocky plateau – the silvery gleaming Asif Mellah Riv-er snakes through the valley be-low while mud castles and store-houses of the ksar on the other side of the valley are piled on top of each other like honey-comb on the hillside. Above it all are the ruins of the kasbah. Cinema-goers will recognize the landscape here. In addition to David Lean's Lawrence of Arabia and Orson Welles' Sodom and Gomorra, a good many other movies have been filmed here. At high tide, mule herders guide tourists over the river, while at low tide it is possible to cross on foot. Strolling through the nar-row alleys of the ksar, in parts lined with palm trunks, you'll see facades decorated with de-lightful geometric patterns and artistic palaces at the entrance towers, but also clear traces of decay. Restoration of the castles and granaries is progressing only very slowly due to compli-cated land tenures.

From Aït Ben Haddou, a rugged track that is only navigable with off-road vehicles leads through spectacular scenery to Telouèt, parts of the road following the Asif Mellah River and traversing dramatic mountain passes along the way. You reach the town more easily by going back down

machines. The Rahba Khedima souk whisks you into the magical world of herbs and esoteric remedies, and carpets are auctioned in the area known as Criée Berbère. It is virtually impossible to navigate your way with any purpose through the labyrinth of busy alleys. It is better just to let yourself be led by them.

Sheltered market alleys invite you to wander around.

the N9 and following it into the mountainous region of the High Atlas. The slopes are stony and stark, but in the valleys green terraced fields line the mountain streams and dark-brown mud houses cling to the hillside. In contrast to the tighremt in the Dadès Valley, the houses here are basic and almost bare.

After 65 km (40 miles) of sometimes narrow serpentine roads, you climb 2,280 m (7,480 ft) to the Tizi-n'Tichka pass. Just 2 km (1 mile) further on, the route branches off towards Telouèt.

17 Telouèt The journey now leads to one of Morocco's most unique kasbahs 20 km (12 miles) down the road. Telouèt was the headquarters of the Glaoua, a powerful subgroup of the Atlas Berbers that controlled much of the southern part of Morocco. Their most famous patriarch, El-Glaoui, also the Pasha of Marrakech, had the former family home converted into a magnificent mud castle but it has been falling to ruin since his death in 1956. Inside, valuable wooden inlays on doors and ceilings, as well as stucco ornaments on the walls, are exposed to the elements without any form of protection. Storks nest in the spires. El-Glaoui was opposed to King Mohammed V and had made an agreement with the French. As a result, his property was abandoned by the state.

Back on the main route N9 it's another 20 km (12 miles) to the market town of Taddert.

18 Taddert You must drive very carefully here, as children selling minerals and fossils often jump out into the road suddenly to stop passing cars. Taddert is famous for its grill restaurants and takeaway food stores, where you can take a break and still enjoy the panoramic views of the High Atlas. Around this striking valley, the peaks of the High Atlas reach 4,000 m (13,124 ft) and even in summer the weather is pleasant and cool. The N9 then winds its way down again, passing pine plantations that are an attempt by the state to reforest the eroded hillsides.

After just 40 km (25 miles) you will arrive at the Haouz plain, one of the most fertile areas of Morocco. The fields have abundant crops, and early vegetables are grown in the many greenhouses. It becomes clear now that Marrakech is approaching as greater signs of settlement appear and traffic becomes increasingly chaotic.

The clay walls of the 'Red City' can be seen from afar. The N9 opens out into the multi-lane Route des Remparts, which forms a ring road that almost completely encircles Marrakech.

19 Marrakech (see p. 155) The N10 heads south through Asni over a pass in the High Atlas that initially leads through green promontory landscape before finally entering an increasingly sparse mountain region.

20 Tizi-n'Test After approximately 100 km (62 miles) it is worth stopping at the 12th-century Almohada mosque, Tin Mal. The almost square building, with four corner towers and a crenellation, is more reminiscent of a fortress than a place of worship. Shortly after that begins the steepest and most winding part of the route to the 2,093-m (6,867-ft) Tizi-n'Test Pass, which you have completed after 35 km

Large image: Atlas Mountains. Left side: Ksar of Aït-Ben-Haddou. Right side: Market on the Djemaa el-Fna in Marrakech.

Detour

A camel ride through the desert

Tour operators in southern Morocco offer an extraordinary adventure – camel treks with the Tuareg.

The 'Blue Men', as they are also known because of their indigo-blue robes, lead their guests through the amazing landscape of the north-western Sahara on their classic mode of desert transport. They explain the magnificent flora and fauna and the old customs and practices of the Tuareg people. In the evening, tents are pitched and food cooked over a bonfire.

(22 miles) before arching back towards the valley. The views of the mountains are amazing. You reach Taroudannt after a total of 230 km (143 miles).

㉑ Taroudannt 'Marrakech's younger sister' is completely surrounded by a mud wall with storks nesting on the pinnacles. In the medina it is worth visiting the Place Assarag where Berbers from the surrounding region hold a market on Thursdays and Sundays. This is the start of the maze of souks, which all still have a very original feel. In Taroudannt you'll have the opportunity to stay in one of the most beautiful hotels in Morocco, the 'Salam'.

Leaving the city heading west on the N10, the route now crosses Morocco's most important agricultural region, the Souss plain. In Aït Melloui, just before reaching the spa resort of Agadir, you turn off onto the P509 and head south-east towards Biougra.

In a steady climb, the route crosses the quilt-like mountain landscape of the Anti-Atlas where prickly pears and argania spinosa are the main vegetation, along with the odd almond tree. Storage chambers of the Chleuh Berbers, so-called Agadire, sit on top of table plateaus above the villages.

After 160 km (99 miles), the pinkish houses of Tafraoute come into view, sprawled out in a gorgeous mountain valley.

㉒ Tafraoute Some 1,000 m (3,300 ft) up, and surrounded by a palm oasis, Tafraoute is the main hub of the Ammeln, a subgroup of the Chleuh.

From here, it is possible to make detours on foot or by car to villages such as Oumesnat (get back on the P509 heading north, then turn left after 6 km/4 miles), where one of the region's traditional stone houses is open to interested visitors as a museum. Approximately 3 km (2 miles) south on the S7146 gravel road you then come to a valley full of strangely eroded granite with an array of rock

drawings. From Tafraoute the asphalt S7074 heads up and over the 1,200-m-high (3,936-ft) Col du Kerdous into another valley to Tiznit about 114 km (72 miles) away.

㉓ Tiznit This city of silversmiths initially disappoints with its modern outskirts, but a lively souk atmosphere reigns around the Place Mechouar. The Tiznit silversmiths are famous for the quality of their work.

Large image: Koutoubia minaret. Above left: Taroudannt city wall; Top right: The houses of Tafraoute are pink like the granite rocks of the valley.

The Menara Gardens, which belong to the UNESCO World Heritage Sites, were built in 1156–1157 under the Almohad ruler Abd al-Mu'min.

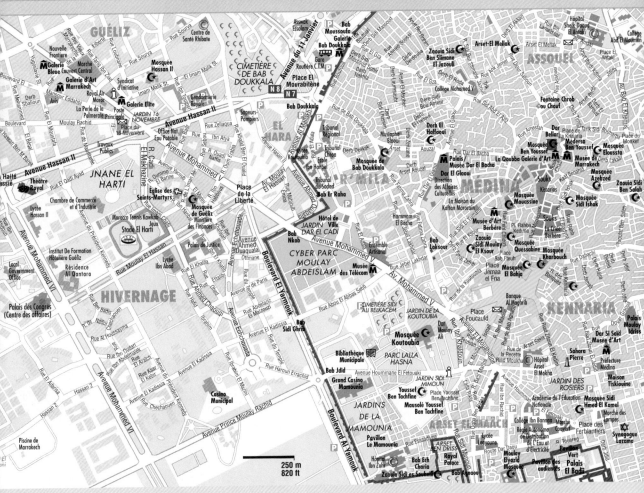

Marrakech

Some 750,000 people live in Marrakech, 'Pearl of the South'. This vibrant city is surrounded by palm groves and gardens and bordered by the often snow-capped peaks of the High Atlas mountains. With its colourful souks, time-honoured mosques, ornate mausoleums, magnificent palaces and lively nighttime bustle on the Djemma el Fna, the almost 1,000-year-old city attracts tourists and locals alike.

Marrakech was founded in 1062 by the Almoravids, a strictly orthodox dynasty with a strong connection to the origins of Islam. In 1126–27, it became the capital of the Almoravid Kingdom. In the centuries that followed, Marrakech was constantly competing with Fez for the seat of the Sultan. Ultimately, trans-Saharan trade restored Marrakech to its former prosperity and French colonization in the 20th century further shaped the city.

Architectural highlights include the 12th-century Koutoubia Mosque and the magnificent 16th-century mausoleum of the Saadier, with its marble floors and numerous gravestones decorated with calligraphy. Similar in opulence is the 14th-century Medersa Ben Youssef in the medina. The city wall, built of clay bricks, is another unique monument interspersed with lavishly decorated gates.

You can take a worthwhile and relaxing excursion around the 'Remparts' and a detour to the Jardins Majorelle by calèche, or carriage. The villa and garden of the artist Majorelle form a perfect scene of varying blue and green hues. Apart from wandering your way through Morocco's largest souks, the undisputed highlight of Marrakech is a visit to the Djemma el Fna, the city's main square and one that is used by both tourists and locals alike. Amid the bustling food and drinks stalls, the square transforms into a street performers' stage when the sun sets. The nightly shows include acrobats, story-tellers, Chleuh dancing boys, magicians, snake charmers and even traditional medicine peddlers.

Here the Alavid sultan Moulay el-Yazid is buried.

The evening sun casts its golden rays on the Medina of Essaouira.

They make jewellery as well as traditional dagger accessories. Your route now heads north, and another 90 km (56 miles) on the N1 takes you through flat, stark terrain until you reach the town of Agadir.

24 Agadir This spa resort was rebuilt after a devastating earthquake in 1960. The modern city, located on a wide sandy beach lined with hotels, is a pleasant place to stop before taking the N1 coastal road and heading north to Essaouira.
It winds its way along a dramatic, steeply sloping coastline and is bordered with argania groves with a particular attraction – goats climbing to the tops of the trees to nibble at the leaves.

25 Essaouira This harbour city, with its stout walls and the Scala Fortress, has a slightly Portuguese flavour to it, but it was founded in 1760 by the Sultan Mohammed Ben Abdallah and is a UNESCO World Heritage Site. Fishmongers at the harbour, the souk where beautiful thuja-wood furniture is sold, and the many art galleries with their dreamy images of the Gnaoua make the city an extremely popular desti-nation for individual travellers. The N8 heads inland for a while through argania groves before branching off on the N1 to the intersection with Highway 204, which then continues west and ends in Safi (148 km/92 miles).

26 Safi This harbour city is famous for pottery. North-east of the old city, factories and shops are grouped opposite the Bab Chaaba on 'potters' hill'. Safi's blue-glazed ceramics are in high demand.
Heading further north on the narrow but spectacular P121 coastal road you will pass Oua-lidia, where the Atlantic forms a peaceful lagoon behind a sand bar that is ideal for bathing. About 144 km (89 miles) on, the brilliant white walls of El-Jadida come into view.

Essaouira, the 'White City' on the sea, was previously an artist colony and is today a popular tourist destination on the Atlantic coast. Above: Rabat – mausoleum Mohammed V. (left), gate Bab al Had (right).

The old town of Essaouira, completely surrounded by a fortified wall, reflects the influence of European military architecture.

Rabat

Along with the twin city of Salé, Morocco's capital has more than 1.5 million inhabitants, yet it is a pleasant experience thanks to the elegant villa neighbourhoods.

In the 12th century, Rabat became the Ribat el Ftah Fortress under the Almohada rule. Buccaneers later settled there and the pirate 'republic' of Rabat-Salé spread terror on the high seas between the 17th and 19th centuries.

In 1956, Rabat became the capital of independent Morocco. The historic heart of the city is the Oudaïa, a kasbah on a bank above the Bou Regreg River. The 12th-century Bab des Oudaï, decorated with magnificent stone masonry, leads to a maze of partly vaulted alleys ending at the 'platform', with a view over neighbouring Salé. East of the kasbah are the 200 pillar bases and the minaret of the Hassan Mosque designed by Yacoub el-Mansour, which was ultimately left incomplete after the death of the sultan in 1199. The charming minaret is often compared to the Giralda in Seville.

Opposite this is the neo-Moorish mausoleum of Kings Mohammed V and Hassan II built, in 1967. The royal quarter around the Dar el Makhzen palace is not accessible to tourists. The archaeological museum with the most beautiful finds from the Moroccan excavation sites is well worth a visit. The Marinid necropolis of Chellah south-east of Rabat also makes for an interesting detour. The ruins of a Zaouya (Koran school) and several sultans' graves are a picturesque sight indeed.

Hassan II Mosque

In 1993, King Hassan II dedicated the country's largest mosque in Casablanca to himself. It was built on an artificial platform over the sea and appears to float on the water. More than 3,000 builders from all over the country decorated the mosque in traditional style with majolica mosaics, stucco, the finest inlays and dark cedar-wood carvings. The prayer room holds 25,000 worshippers, and another

㉗ El-Jadida Behind the fully preserved city wall with numerous bastions lies a lovely medina, whose main attraction is the Portuguese cistern, a water reservoir covered by groined vaults. Only 16 km (10 miles) north is another harbour town of particular charm, Azemmour.
Here it's worth visiting the Tuesday market. From there it's another 100 m (62 miles) along the coastal road to Casablanca.

㉘ Casablanca This metropolis of 3 million people is particularly worth a stop to take a look at the Hassan II Mosque and the neo-Moorish centre, which originates from the French colonial era. It is not advisable to visit the ruins of the medina.
The route continues for 95 km (59 miles) along a lovely coastline through the popular resorts of Mohammedia and Skhirat Plage, ending at the nation's capital, Rabat.

㉙ Rabat (see page 157). From Rabat, the N1 heads north through Ksar-el-Kebir on its way to Larache.

㉚ Larache The French poet, Jean Genet, is buried in the cemetery of this small, picturesque harbour town.
The excavation site of the Roman Lixus with an amphitheatre and the ruins of the ancient fish-processing factory lies 4 km (2.5 miles) further north.
Tangiers is another 87 km (54 miles) on the N1 along the Atlantic coast, beyond the small town of Asilah founded in the 15th century.
After 84 km (52 miles), it's worth taking a detour of about 9 km (5.5 miles) to Cap Spartel, where the Atlantic meets the Mediterranean Sea, and to the Hercules Grottoes where you get an exceptional view of the sea from a natural crevice shaped like the African continent.

Large image: The cistern in El-Jadida belonged to a castle. Above left: The minaret is an imposing part of the Hassan II mosque. Above right: the Portuguese fort of El-Jadida.

80,000 can pray on the forecourt in the shadow of the minaret. A laser beam from the top of this minaret points to Mecca for correct worship. The Mosque is the only one in Morocco which non-Muslims are allowed to visit.

Left side: The old town of Casablanca with the Hassan II Mosque. Left: The splendor of the mosque proves that the complex construction was worthwhile.

Agadir After a devastating earthquake in 1960 destroyed this Atlantic Berber settlement, only the kasbah on the hill remained unscathed. After this, the city was rebuilt. Today, Agadir is primarily known as a holiday resort. Countless hotels, restaurants and a kilometre-long (0.6-mile) sandy beach provide ideal conditions for rest and relaxation.

Safi At the edge of the medina, potters manufacture ceramics typical of the region in their traditional workshops. The old harbour city of Safi has so far barely been touched by tourists.

Rabat The Moroccan capital, with 1.7 million inhabitants, has a picturesque location at the mouth of the Bou Regreg River. The Ouadaï kasbah forms the foundation of the royal city.

Essaouira This fishing town appears rather Portuguese but was in fact founded by Arab peoples. Its atmosphere is adored by alternative lifestyle enthusiasts and artists.

Marrakech The 'red' royal city is surrounded by lush gardens. Every evening in the Djemma el Fna, people watch acrobats and snake charmers.

El-Jadida The white city walls were built in the 19th century. The medina houses a Portuguese cistern where Orson Welles once filmed scenes from his film version of Othello.

Aït Ben Haddou This UNESCO-protected ksar is at risk of falling into ruin. The former inhabitants abandoned the old mud castle and live in a modern village opposite. The walled city has been a set for films.

Gorges du Dadès In the deep gorges not far from the 'Route of the Kasbahs', farmers make use of every square metre of fertile land. Tomatoes, alfalfa and sorghum are grown on plots of all sizes.

Tinerhir Numerous kasbahs watch over the oasis gardens of Tinerhir at the mouth of the Gorges du Todra in the Dadès Valley. An old trade route passes through here.

High Atlas These mountains form the border between fertile Morocco and the desert.

Volubilis Between AD 42 and 285, Volubilis was the capital of the Roman province of Mauretania Tingitana. The ruins of the basilica, Capitol Temple, the triumphal arch and the villas with their mosaic floors tower over the fertile landscape.

Fez The royal city's medina is a unique work of art, with plenty of Moorish architecture and lively souks. The finest leather is dyed by hand in the tannery pools shown here.

Tangier
Cap Spartel
Ceuta (E)
Asilah
Tétouan
Lixus
Et-Tleta-de-Oued-Laou
Bou-Ahmed
Souk-el-Arba-des-Beni-Hassan
Larache
Chefchaouen
Ksar-el-Kebir
Bab-Taza
Al Hoceima
Moulay-Bousselham
Ketama
Ouezzane
Ourtzarh
Souk-el-Arba-du-Rharb
Taounate
Sidi-Allal-Tazi
417
Mahdija-Plage
Kénitra
Sidi-Kacem
Sidi-Abdallah-des-Rhiata
Salé
RABAT
Sidi-Allal-el-Bahraoui
Volubilis
Moulay-Idriss
Fès
Taza
Mohammedia
Meknès
Bir-Tam-Tam
CASABLANCA
Skhirat
Khemisset
Sefrou
Ribat-el-Kheir
Azemmour
Ben-Slimane
Rommani
El-Hajeb
Imouzzèr-Kandar
El-Jadida
Bir-Jdid
Berrechid
Cascade de Vierges
Sidi-Moussa
Ben-Ahmed
Ito
Ifrane
Sidi-Smaïl
Settat
Oued-Zem
Azrou
Boulemane
Mrirt
Timahdite
Oualidia
Chaouïa
Cap Beddouza
Sidi-Bennour
Barrage Al-Massira
Kasba Tadla
Col du Zad (2178)
Gorges d'Aouli
Zaïda
Safi
Dukkâla
Bougouedra
Chemaïa
Beni-Mellal
Middle
Boumia
Midelt
Tizi-n-Taïrhemt (1907)
Sebt-des-Gzoula
Cirque de Jaffar
Dar-Caïd-Hadji
Sidi-Bou-Othmane
Amouguèr
Rich
Gourrama
Talmest
Tamelelt
Agoudal
Gorges du Ziz
Essaouira
Ounara
Sidi Moktar
MARRAKESH
Aït-Ourir
Oued Tessaout
Ar-Rachidia
Bouânane
Et-Tnine
Chichaoua
Vallée de l'Ourika
Taddert
Gorges du Dadès
Gorges du Todra
Source Bleu de Meski
Boudnib
Imi-n-Tanoute
Asni
Tizi-n-Tichka (2280)
Telouèt
Tinerhir
Vallée du Ziz
Tamanar
Oukaimeden
El-Kelaâ M'Gouna
Goulmina
Dar-Caïd-Ilal-bou-Fenzi
Djebel Aoulime 3555
Aït Ben Haddou
Skoura
Boumalne Dadès
Tafilalt
Erfoud
Tamri
Imouzzer-des-Ida-Outanane
El-Jemaa
Tizi-n'Test (2093)
4167
P.N. du Toubkal
Vallée du Dadès
Réserve de Biosphère
Erg Chebbi
Cap Rhir
Taroudannt
Ouarzazate
Djebel Sarhro
Alnif
Rissani
Merzouga
Agadir
Aoulouz
Barrage El-Mansour-Eddahbi
des Oasis du Sud Marocain
Inezgane
Oulad-Teïma
Tazenakht
Nekob
Taouz
Inchadèn
Biougra
Ouarzazate
Agdz
Tazzarine
P.N. Sous-Massa
Aït-Baha
Taroudannt
Chorée
Rés. de Biosphère Arganeraie
Tinzouline
Djebel Lekst 2359
Zagora
Tiznit
Assaka
Tamegroute
Mirleft
Tagounite
Tafraoute
Tagmegroute
Sidi Ifni
Chapeau napoléon
Mhamid
Guelmim
Tleta-Akhssass

Route 13: Egypt

A journey through the Kingdom of the Pharaohs

The pyramids of Giza are the most powerful emblem of ancient Egypt. The pharaohs who built them instilled the fabulous structures with dreams of immortality. Egypt's cultural legacy was also influenced by Christianity and Islam. In the desert, time-honoured monasteries are evidence of the religious zeal of the Copts, who are still very much alive today. The various Muslim dynasties gave Cairo its numerous mosques.

Route profile:

Length: approx. 1,400 km
(870 miles), excluding detours
Time required: 14–20 days
When to go: October to May

Egypt gives visitors an insight into an exotic realm situated at the crossroads of African, Asian and European civilizations, and which is indeed an intersection of myriad cultures. Obviously the monumental tombs and temples are still a subject of fascination today, but their mysterious hieroglyphics and ancients scripts also captivate our curiosities. The ancient societies of Egypt and the pharaohs began over 5,000 years ago. Most of the monuments from the time of the pharaohs run along the Nile. Along with the pulsating metropolis of Cairo, the 300-km (186-mile) stretch between Lux-

or and Aswan offers history buffs a multitude of impressive sights. Luxor's attractions include the Valley of the Kings, the tremendous temple complex of Karnak and the funerary temple of the female pharaoh Hatshepsut.
Further south, the temples of Edfu and Kôm Ombo are evidence of the fact that even the Greek and Roman conquerors of Egypt succumbed to a fascina-

tion with the Pharaonic culture. Near Aswan, history and the modern world collide. The construction of the Aswan Dam meant the old temples were at risk of being submerged. It was only at great expense that they were relocated in the 1960s. The most famous example of this act of international preservation is the two rock temples of Abu Simbel. Over 95 per cent of Egypt's total surface area is de-

sert that covers more than one million sq km (386,000 sq mi). Only very few of the 75 million inhabitants earn their living in the oases of the western deserts, on the shores of the Red Sea or on Mount Sinai. The vast majority of the population live close together in the Nile valley. As early as the 5th century BC the Greek historian Herodotus wrote that 'Egypt is a gift of the Nile'. The hot climate and the Nile's

The four colossal figures of Pharaoh Ramses II tower 20 m (65.5 ft) before the facade of the rock temple of Abu Simbel.

tion's capital dazzles visitors with the most diverse of sights. The pyramids in Giza in the west tower above the modern city. In the city centre minarets, church towers and high-rise buildings vie for the attention of worshippers as Christians and Muslims make their way to prayers. Meanwhile, people of all backgrounds and nationalities stroll along the Nile in this, the 'Mother of the World' as locals have come to call their rich city.

summer floods, which are nowadays controlled by the Aswan Dam, mean that farmers harvest two to four times a year depending on the crop being cultivated. This enables production of the country's basic food supply despite a rapidly increasing population.

In ancient times the Nile delta in the north of Egypt consisted of five branches bringing fertile alluvial soil with the ever plentiful waters. However, over the course of thousands of years the landscape has changed drastically.

Today there are only two remaining branches that stretch from the north of Cairo through Lower Egypt to the Mediterranean Sea and water traffic on the river is now divided up with the help of an extensive canal network. The Nile delta, which covers an area of 24,000 sq km (9,264 sq mi), is Egypt's most important agricultural region producing everything from corn, vegetables and fruit to the famous Egyptian long-fibre cotton. In the 19th century, Alexandria benefited enormously from this 'white gold' and developed into a modern, Mediterranean port city.

Cairo is located at the southern tip of the delta and connects Upper and Lower Egypt. The na-

Left side: The Pyramids of Giza are the only surviving of the seven wonders of the ancient world. Above left: Cairo Islamic sciences are taught in the Madrasa. Above right: Giant columns stand out in the Karnak temple complex.

Detour

The Suez Canal

It was a long-time dream of the Egyptians to connect the Mediterranean Sea with the Red Sea.

The dream finally became a reality in the mid 19th century after attempts had already been made as far back as ancient times to integrate the Nile Valley into the trade route. The first measurements made by Austrian engineer

Alois von Negrelli confirmed that a direct waterway without locks between Port Said in the north and Suez in the south would be possible. It was Ferdinand de Lesseps who finally convinced Pasha Ismail to build the canal,

which would shorten the trade routes between Europe and Asia by up to 85 per cent. The Compagnie Universelle du Canal de Suez was then founded in 1858. Egypt wanted to secure the funds for the construction by selling

The Copts

Egypt's Christians have been known as Copts since the 7th century. This term originally applied to all people living in Egypt. Following Islamic expansion, it was restricted to just the Christians living in the Nile Valley. Christianity gained ground in Alexandria as early as the 1st century, from where it quickly spread throughout the country over the following decades. Heavy persecution by the Roman Emperor in the 3rd century led to thousands of people being tortured and killed because of their belief. The calendar

The Coptic monastery in the Wadi el-Natrun.

of the Coptic Church reflects the particularly cruel persecution of Christians under Diocletian – his accession to power in AD 284 corresponds to the year 0, the Anno Martyrii.

Not more than 200 years later there were conflicts between Christians that led to the persecution of Egyptian Christians and finally, in AD 451, the separation of the Coptic Church. Even today, Copts do not recognize Rome's pope as their figurehead, but rather follow their own patriarch, who is the successor of the apostle, Mark. The Copts make up 8 to 14 per cent of Egypt's population, which is itself a hotly disputed number – Copts are also entitled to jobs in the public sector.

From the Mediterranean to the 'Nubian Sea', Egypt is home to a plethora of sites that are loaded with history. You'll experience both ancient and modern worlds through-out the approximately 1,400-km (870-mile) journey and the route follows large stretches of the country's oldest traffic route, the Nile. The trip only branches off into the desert between Alexandria and Cairo.

① Alexandria Alexander the Great, after whom this town was named, founded Alexandria in 332 BC. Home to the Ptolemaic Dynasty (323–330 BC), it became the capital of Egypt and gained a great reputation as a centre of scholarship and the sciences. The Temple of Serapi, the famous library and the lighthouse were the icons of the city.

However, after being conquered by the Romans its monuments fell into decay and Alexandria only prospered again under the leadership of Mohammed Ali (1805–49). Fundamental city sanitation measures were introduced at the end of the 20th century and have restored the attractiveness of this important port city. Discoveries dating back to

the time of Egypt's last ruler, Cleopatra, were recovered from the eastern port basin and made worldwide headlines.

With a population of close to five million, Alexandria is the country's second-largest city. Its beaches are very popular. Alexandria's eastern sprawl almost reaches the city of Rashid (Rosetta), where French esearchers discovered the famous trilingual Rosetta Stone (now in the British Museum in London) at the end of the 19th century. This stone helped to decipher hieroglyphic scripts that had proved impossible to understand. South-west of Alexandria you turn off coastal road 55 towards one of the most important early Christian pilgrim sites on the Mediterranean.

② Abu Mena The martyr Mena was murdered in AD 296 under orders from the Roman emperor, Diocletian, and was buried here, some 50 km (31 miles) from Alexandria. Soon after that the well near his grave was said to possess healing powers. In the 5th century a large public bath was built that attracted tens of thousands of faithful to its magical waters. The ruins of churches, monastery complexes and pilgrim quarters that were rediscovered in 1905 are now UNESCO World Heritage Sites, though they are severely threatened by rising ground-water levels. In 1959, the new monastery of Abu Mena was built. The highway-like desert road 11 takes you further south.

shares. But due to a lack of interest in Europe, Egypt kept most of its shares and thus fell into enormous national debt. Nevertheless, after eleven years of construction Khedive Ismail held a lavish party to celebrate the opening of the canal in 1869. 1875 Great Britain took over Egypt's shares.

By 1878 it controlled the canal together with France who was still the principal owner of the canal project. In 1956 President Nasser nationalized the Canal and paid a catastrophic price in the Suez Crisis. Only in 1975 did the canal start bringing profit to Egypt.

Port Said is a port city on the Suez Canal.

3 Wadi el-Natrun About 110 km (68 miles) south of Alexandria you'll come to a valley that is 22 m (72 ft) below sea level in the desert area west of the delta. Nitrate (sodium bicarbonate) extracted during the time of the pharaohs gave the valley its name, which means Nitrate Valley. Surrounded by olive and date palm groves, four of the once more than fifty monasteries are still standing.

In the 4th century, hermits would gather around spiritual leaders like the holy Makarios forming what would be the first monasterial communities. The oldest of these monasteries, built in the 4th century, is the Deir el-Baramus in the north of the valley. The monks of the Deir Amba Bschoi and the Dei res-Suryan also accept non-Coptic guests.

Back on the desert road you'll pass Medînet es-Sadat, one of the planned cities built under the rule of President Anwar Sadat (1970–81). These satellite cities were built in circles in the desert around Cairo. Industrial plants created jobs and kindergartens, schools, parks and leisure activities topped off the activities.

Taking the northern section of the ring road that circumvents most of Cairo's traffic will bring you to the Nile relatively quickly.

4 Cairo (see pp. 164-165). In Arabic, Egypt's capital is called Al-Qahira, 'The Victorious One'. It is home to some 20 million people and counting. Throughout its long history, the Egyptian metropolis has had many different looks, the city centre having shifted from the Nile to the citadel in the foothills of the Moqattam mountains and then back to the Nile.

Nowadays, the glass facades of hotels, government offices and shopping malls distinguish the modern heart of Cairo. Residential and office buildings twenty to thirty floors high loom large along the river where the property is most expensive.

Further on from the centre are the old quarters such as Heliopolis or Maadi, filled with elegent villas and green parks. Then there are the concrete jungles of closely packed residential areas for the rest of Cairo's locals. And at the base of the citadel sprawls the Islamic Old Town with its hundreds of mosques.

5 Giza The provincial capital of Giza is a close relative of Cairo located on the western bank of the Nile.

The three great pyramids of the pharaohs Cheops, Chephren and Mykerinos stand regally on a limestone plateau over the city. The rulers had them constructed in the 3rd millennium BC as tombs to withstand the ages.

The blocks piled on top of each other to create the tremendous mountain that is Cheops' pyramid weigh an average of 2 tonnes (2.2 tons) a piece. Even without the finely sanded coating they originally had, the pyramids are a majestic and awe-inspiring sight. They used to stand almost 147 m (482 ft) high, but they have shrunk over time by 10 m (33 ft).

In the Middle Ages, Cairo's master builders helped themselves to the almost endless quarry. Part of the coating has been preserved on the neighbouring pyramid of Chephren. Significantly smaller in size at just 65.5 m

Large image: Pyramids of Giza. At the top: Abu Mena is one of the most important early Christian pilgrimage sites. Above: Different Islamic style epochs characterise the Kairos cityscape.

The Kairo's mosques are all impressive. Their interiors are magnificently designed as in the Mosque of Muhammad Ali.

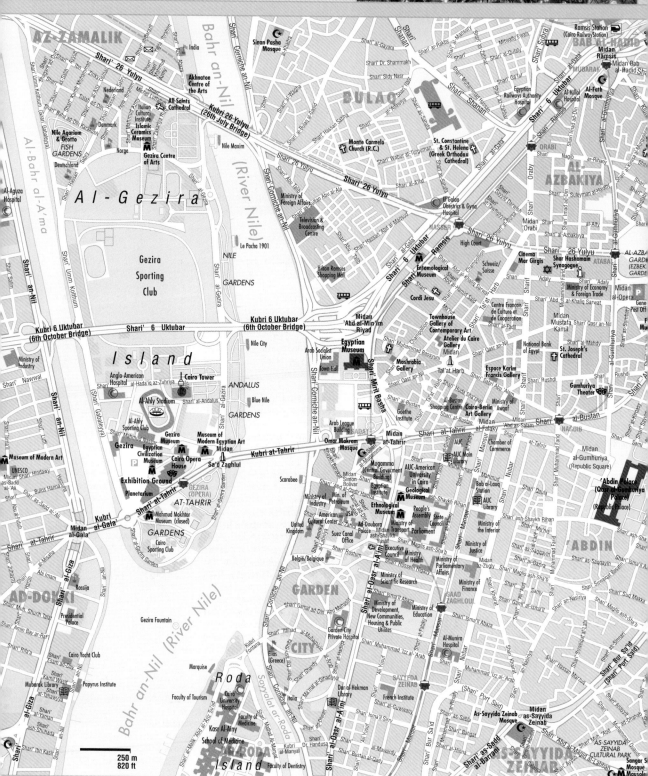

Its builder is buried in the mausoleum of the magnificent Sultan Hasan Mosque.

Cairo

The view from the citadel sweeps west over the minarets and the Nile to the silhouettes of the pyramids of Giza – if you're lucky. The Nile city is often hidden from view by the heavy, opaque cloud that floats above it. Humidity from the river, sandstorms from the encroaching desert and pollution from the congested traffic in the inner city are all part of the problem.

A Nilometer at the southern tip of Roda Island is testimony to the Egyptian capital's dignified age. Long before it was given the name of Cairo in the 10th century BC, priests serving ancient Egyptian gods set up wells all over the country to measure the level of the yearly Nile flood and then calculated taxes. Opposite the island on the eastern bank was one of the country's most important inland ports, Per Hapi en Junu. When the Romans fortified the harbour, the early Christians made use of the well-protected area to build their first churches here. In the 'Candles Quarter' directly next to the Mari Girgis metro station, the Moallka Church, dedicated to the Virgin Mary, rises high upon the foundations of the Roman fortress. In the next neighbourhood is the Ben-Ezra Synagogue where the famous scholar Moses Maimonides presided in the 12th century. It is famed as the location where the pharaoh's daughter rescued the baby Moses from the Nile. Just a few hundred metres north of the synagogue, Africa's oldest mosque gleams after extensive renovations. Amr Ibn el-As had it built in the centre of the new capital, Fustat, in AD 642. Almost 235 years later, Governor Ibn Tulun, appointed by the Abbasids, created an independent entity here on the Nile. His residence must have been magnificent. The enormous courtyard mosque (AD 876–879) is the only structure to have been preserved from this time and is still one of the largest mosques in the world,

covering 2.5 ha (6.2 acres). New rulers arrived in Egypt ninety years later – the Fatimid shi'ites, who also needed their own new residence, of course. Surrounded by well-fortified walls they ensconced themselves in the palaces of Al-Qahira. Their Friday Mosque, el-Azhar, was built in AD 969 and is to this day one of the most important institutions in the Islamic world. Bejewelled Islamic architecture was created between the city gates Bab el-Futuh and Bab en-Nasr in the north and Bab es-Suweila in the south. Over a period of 600 years, Fatimids, Ajjubids, Mamlucks and Osmans had elegant mosques, palaces, commercial establishments, wells and schools built in Cairo. Salah ed-Din, who came to power in AD 1171, had his residence moved to the citadel, but Al-Qahira remained the lively centre of the city. Even today, visitors are still fascinated by the bustling bazaars of the Khan el-Khalili. City planners were again kept busy under Mohammed Ali's reign, who used Paris as a model to transform Cairo into a modern metropolis in the 19th century. Art-nouveau facades between the Midan el-Opera and the Midan Talaat Harb are evocative of these times. From here, it's just a stone's throw into modernity at the Midan et-Tahrir, where the first metro station was built, the Arab League has its headquarters and, at the northern end of the square, the treasures of the national museum take you back to the times of the pharaohs.

The al-Azhar mosque was built as the third mosque in Egypt (construction began in 970).

The reliefs in the tomb of
Ti often depict everyday
situations, such as the milking
of a cow.

(215 ft) is the tomb of Mykerinos, which appears to have missed out on this detail and is humbled by the presence of its formidable neighbours.

The Sphinx lies to the east of these three monuments. Carved out of existing rocks at its location, the Sphinx embodies the divine rising sun. A shrine built of blocks of rock soars before its paws.

Directly next to it, Chephren had his valley temple constructed out of pink granite and alabaster.

6 Memphis The first capital of Egypt, its administrative headquarters, the largest garrison city, and the sacred place of the god Ptah – Memphis covered a lot of bases throughout the course of its long history. Today not much is left of this former cosmopolitan city.

Its palaces and residences of clay bricks have long been reclaimed by the earth and transformed into fertile farmland. The monumental figure of Ramses II and the alabaster sphinx are the only legacy of the city's former glory. They are housed in the open-air museum among palm groves near the small village of Mitrahina on the south-western edge of Giza.

7 Sakkara One of Egypt's largest cemeteries sprawls in the desert approximately 20 km (12 miles) south of Giza. Great tombs of kings were already being constructed here in the early civilizations of the pharaohs. But this cemetery only gained in significance when the first pyramid was built under Djoser's reign (around 2750 BC). Its architect, Imhotep, invented the idea of using stone as a building material and laid the foundations for a tradition that now goes back three thousand years. The step pyramid subsequently attracted many other rulers and dignitaries who had their tombs erected here. The tomb of Ti, with its illustration of the entombed man hunting in the papyrus coppice, is one of the largest and most beautiful private tombs from the Ancient Kingdom (2750–2195 BC).

The Mastaba is the final resting place of Officer Ti and his wife.

Almost a thousand years later, General Haremhab had his 'Eternal House' constructed here before becoming pharaoh in 1320 BC and acquiring an even more magnificent tomb in the Valley of the Kings.

Another 10 km (6 miles) further south the lane turns off toward the next field of pyramids.

8 **Dahshûr** Snofru was the father of the pharaoh Cheops who set up the 'Pyramid Experimentation Field'. In fact, two of these mighty constructions originate from his reign. The Red Pyramid gets its name from its red-coloured limestone. Compared to Cheops' majestic edifice, it crouches much lower in the desert landscape.

Snofru's master builders had become cautious following serious problems at the preceding building some 2 km (1 mile) further south – fissures had formed inside the so-called bent pyramid, meaning it had to be completed with a softened, sloping angle. Further to the south-east are the 'Black Pyramids'. Amenemhet III had them built around 1800 BC using a completely different method. The frame was a cross-shaped limestone shell on top of which a mighty mountain of mud bricks was piled.

After 45 km (28 miles), road 2 runs parallel to the Nile to the turn-off for Meidum.

9 **Meidum** Snofru also carried out work here at the edge of the fertile valley of Faijûm. The ruins of the shell-design pyramids look like gigantic sand cakes. There are some famous murals from the graves of the neighbouring royal suite – the Meidum Geese can be admired in Cairo's National Museum.

Back on road 2 the route heads further south through smaller settlements before reaching the provincial capital of Beni Suêf after 42 km (26 miles). Here we recommend you drive over the bridge to the eastern bank of the Nile where a quicker desert road makes the rest of the journey to El-Minia a lot easier.

10 **El-Minia** With some 250,000 inhabitants, El-Minia is one of the busiest cities in Middle Egypt. As an administrative headquarters, a university town and an industrial centre it provides employment for people from the surrounding areas while also acting as a popular starting point for interesting sightseeing tours. The large number of churches is a noticeable feature of the city's skyline. Minia is home to a great many Copts.

11 **Beni Hassan** From the western bank of the Nile approximately 25 km (15.5 miles) south of El-Minia you can take a boat to the graves of the princes of Beni Hassan. These structures were hewn into the precipice during the 11th and 12th dynasties between 2000 and 1755 BC. The murals on the walls depict interesting scenes: children dancing and playing with balls, craftsmen, mythical creatures in the desert and the famous wrestling scenes of Egyptian soldiers practising martial arts. The choice of themes is an indication of the independence and creativity of the provincial rulers.

12 **Ashmunein/Hermopolis** On the western bank 8 km (5 miles) north of Mallawî are the ruins of Ashmunein. This is where Thot was worshipped, the god of wisdom. Statues of baboons are still testimony to his cult where they were one of the sacred animals. In Christian times a St Mary's basilica was built over the ruins of a Ptolemaic temple.

13 **Tuna el-Gebel** This graveyard of Ashmunein is located in the adjacent desert area west of town. The large, underground burial complex for the sacred animals of Thot is rather unusual and includes a wide array of mummified animals in addition to ibises and baboons. Even crocodiles and fish were found in the maze of crypts. Priests at the temple of Thot were also laid to rest here. The tomb of the high priest Petosiris from early Ptolemaic times displays ancient Egyptian and Greek art side by side.

The journey continues south through Mallawî and over a narrow lane near the village of Deir Mawas towards the banks of the Nile. A boat can take you to the other side of the river where off-road vehicles are ready to take visitors to the very widely scattered tourist sites.

14 **Tell el-Amârna** In around 1350 BC, Akhenaten founded the new capital of Akhetaten, meaning the 'Horizon of Aten', in an expansive valley. Palace complexes and residences for the new elite were built along with new temples for the only god, Aten. Luckily for archaeologists, the city was abandoned after the heretic king's death and despite heavy destruction the excavations at the start of the 20th century revealed that many of the unique artworks from this time were still intact. The famous bust of Queen Nefertiti (today in the Egyptian Museum in Berlin) was discovered on 6 December 1912.

15 **Assiût** After travelling approximately 75 km (46.5 miles) through the many villages and towns along the Nile you will eventually reach the next provincial capital on the trip, Assiût. Here, the long desert road turns off towards the oases of Kharga and Dakhla where a 19th-century dam regulates the Nile floods. We recommend you go back over the bridge to the less developed eastern bank before continuing on.

Large image: Ruins of Giza. Above left: Step pyramid in the necropolis Sakkara. Above right: The colossal statue of Ramses II is 3200 years old and was found in 1820.

Ramses II, whom this statue depicts at the Luxor Temple, was one of the greatest rulers of ancient Egypt.

16 Sohâg/Akhmîm These two sister cities 120 km (74.5 miles) south of Assiût are connected by one of the few Nile bridges. Outside Sohâg on the western bank are the ruins of Deir el-Abjad, the 'White Monastery', evidence of Egypt's early Christian history. Many of the blocks used to build the Deir el-Abjad and the accompanying church originate from pharaoh-era constructions.

The monastery, which housed up to 4,000 monks in its heyday, became famous under its abbot Schenute (AD 348–466), the father of Coptic literature, who fought fiercely against the still existing ancient Egyptian cults and traditions.

On the western bank it's another 50 km (31 miles) on the main road until a sign at Balyana points to the turn-off to Abydos.

17 Abydos In ancient Egypt's early days, Abydos was already of paramount significance as a burial site for kings and princes. It was the main cult town for the god of life, death and fertility, Osiris, and one of the country's most important pilgrimage destinations. The belief in life after death is illustrated in tomb complexes, funerary temples and memorial stones.

Greatly worshiped as the rightful judge and ruler of the afterlife, Osiris also symbolized the hope for resurrection. The funerary temple of Sethos I (1290–79 BC) is an impressive sight with a series of very elegant reliefs. After Nag Hammâdi, another 35 km (22 miles) south, the main road 2 continues along the eastern bank. The stretch on the western bank leads through rural areas and a number of villages.

Following a bend in the Nile that sweeps around to the east, you will reach the turn-off to the temple of the ancient goddess Hathor in Dendera after approximately 60 km (37 miles).

18 Dendera Hathor was celestial goddess of a great many things including love, music and debauchery. She was very popular among the Egyptians. Her temple, which was fitted with proper public baths, was visited by pilgrims in their droves even until Roman times. The 'caring mother' aspect of the great goddess was embodied through her sacred animal, the cow – the reason Hathor was often depicted as a woman with cow ears.

The astronomical images on the ceilings of the entrance hall and the so-called animal circle in an oratory on the roof are some of the interesting details of this Ptolemaic-Roman temple. Crypts embedded in the masonry were used as secret storage places for valuable cult devices.

From Dendera the journey continues over the bridge to the eastern bank towards Qena, one of the country's best-tended provincial capitals. A 160-km (99-mile) route through the eastern desert to Safâga on the Red Sea begins here. Luxor is just 60 km (37 miles) away to the south.

19 Luxor The city of Luxor is one of the main destinations for tourists visiting Egypt. It has had its own international airport for many years with commercial as well as chartered traffic. There is a wide selection of hotels to suit all budgets here. Tourism is the region's main source of in-

The temples were traditionally decorated with reliefs. The columns of Medînet Hâbu – part of the necropolis of Thebes-West - was designed with a variety of hieroglyphics and figures.

come and employment. Right in the centre of the city the columns of the Temple of Amun loom large. Built during the Amenhotep III (1390–53 BC) and Ramses II (1279–13 BC) eras, this extremely important temple in the history of Egyptian priest- king worship is particularly spectacular at dusk when its reliefs are accentuated. It is connected to the second temple for Amun by a 3-km (1.8-mile) avenue lined with sphinxes. This

impressive complex, Al-Karnak, spreads over an area of approximately 30 ha (74 acres) and is the largest ancient religious site in the world, second only to Giza in terms of visitors.

The Al-Karnak complex includes the secondary temples of the lion-headed Mut, the mother goddess, Montu the god of war and Maat the goddess of truth as well as a holy forum. The temple complex was under construction for nearly 2,000 years. The great

columned hall is an impressive site with a total of 134 gigantic papyrus columns towering over a vast area of 5,000 sq m (5,980 sq yds). Numerous discoveries from both temples and other surrounding sites are displayed in the interesting Luxor Museum and include the blocks from a Temple of Aten dating back to the reign of the later ostracized pharaoh Amenhotep IV. The museum's treasures include statues from the time of Amenhotep III

and Haremhab discovered in 1989 in the Luxor Temple.

A small mummification museum below the road along the Nile gives an overview of the preservation process.

20 Thebes West The area on the opposite side of the river is home to one of the most famous cemeteries in the world. In a remote basin of crumbling limestone mountains, pharaohs of the New Kingdom (1540–1075 BC) had their tombs built in what became known as the Valley of the Kings.

The world public got its first glimpse of this in 1922 when Howard Carter discovered the still unlooted tomb of the young King Tutankhamun. The small tomb's opulent adornments are today exhibited in the National Museum of Cairo. In the valley itself, people continue to marvel at the incredible murals whose bright colours are still preserved in some areas. Painted on the walls of the long passages and in the coffin chambers, these murals describe Ra the Sun god's journey through the night to the sunrise. The pharaohs hoped to take part in this journey and the daily rejuvenation that went with it.

The funerary temples built at the edges of the fertile land here were used for the cultish care of the pharaohs in the afterlife. The most unique of these was constructed for the female pharaoh Hatshepsut (1479–58 BC). Divided into three monumental terraces, the perfectly symmetrical modern-looking building is nestled in the valley of Deir el-Bahri.

Officers, priests and other dignitaries built their own magnificent tombs on the path leading to the Temple of the Pharaohs

Luxor: Sphinx alley (large image), temple (right side). Both images above: Reliefs in the structure of Medînet Hâbu.

The Little Temple – the Hathor Temple of Abu Simbel – was dedicated to Ramses' wife Nefertari and the goddess Hathor. Here six colossal still images rule the facade.

as well as on the northern and southern mountainsides. The reliefs and murals in these cave tombs, ranging from very small to imposingly large depending on their wealth, often depict scenes from everyday life.

Believing in eternal life, the tomb owners are shown having frivolous parties with their family and friends. Important stages of their careers are also illustrated. The artisan colony of Deir el-Medina is quite famous for its colourful tombs, where religious themes are shown on the walls. The Valley of the Queens is home to the tombs not only of the great pharaohs' wives, but also of the young princes of the kingdoms. The tomb of Nefertari, the royal wife of Ramses II (also known as Ramses the Great), was restored at great expense here. Only very few parts of this funerary temple have been preserved, mainly because his successor, Ramses III, used blocks from the older construction to build his temple in Medînet Habu.

㉑ Esna Just 60 km (37 miles) south of Luxor down the main road on the eastern bank is Esna. Cross the bridge to the western bank. Keep in mind that the bridge is closed twice a day to let the cruise ships pass.

Deep under the bustling bazaar are the remains of a Roman temple to the god of creation, Khnum. You can only see the atrium with its columns of plants. Other parts of the temple are possibly still underneath the modern buildings above.

㉒ El Kab The journey continues back over to the eastern bank, where rock tombs on the eastern side of the mountains draw you to a halt after some 35 km (22 miles). El Kab was a significant place early on, being the cult site of the goddess of Upper Egypt, Nechbet. Two of these tombs are of historic interest – that of Ahmose Son of

Ibana who was a naval commander during the reign of Ahmose I (roughly 1550–25 BC) and helped expel the Hyksos who had occupied Lower and Middle Egypt for more than 100 years. He even documented the event in an inscription due to its far-reaching effects for the whole of Egypt.

His grandson, Paheri, earned the respect of the royals by educating the prince under the reign of Thutmosis III. On his tomb he is depicted with the king's son on his lap. South of the graves the Wadi Hilal opens up and its entrance is marked with small temple buildings.

㉓ Edfu It is just another 30 km (18.5 miles) to the country's best-preserved ancient Egyptian temple. On the outskirts of the vibrant city of Edfu on the west bank of the Nile is a massive Ptolemaic temple that is still surrounded by a mighty clay brick wall. Horus, with his human

body and falcon head and one of the longest surviving cult gods in Egypt, was worshipped here. As the son of Osiris, who was murdered by his brother Set, it was his job to get revenge on his father's death. Horus thus came to represent new beginnings and was the guarantor for law and justice. The pictures in the temple's tower gallery make reference to the mystery theatre performances that took place every year depicting the battle between Horus and his father's murderer. The temple's inscriptions contain very precise instructions for the priests in their important task of reconstructing the ancient Egyptian cults.

㉔ Gebel el-Silsila A good 40 km (25 miles) south of Edfu are the sandstone formations of Gebel el-Silsila close to the banks of the Nile. In the time of the pharaohs, sandstone was quarried on both the banks for their many construction projects. To-

day the mountains further south give way to fertile land where sugar cane is the predominant crop processed in local refineries. After the Aswan Dam was built, this region became the home for resettled Nubians.

㉕ Kôm Ombo The picturesque remains of the mighty double temple of Kôm Ombo rise up next to the banks of the river. Built in Ptolemaic-Roman times for the falcon-headed Horus and the crocodile-shaped Sobek, the extraordinary details on this temple include the depiction of the Roman Emperor Trajan who dedicated medical devices to the deity, Imhotep.

Crocodiles, kept by the priests as the sacred animals of Sobek, were carefully mummified after their deaths and buried near the temple. A few examples of these can be seen today in a small chapel dating back to the time of Hadrian.

The Nubian monuments on Agilkia originally stood on the now flooded island of Philae.

㉖ Aswan Aswan is considered one of the most beautiful cities in Egypt because of its location at the first Nile cataract. Numerous small islands made from granite blocks worn smooth by the water rise up out of the river. A sailing trip in a traditional felucca should be part of a visit to the Nubian capital.

Elephantine Island, the actual birthplace of the city, lies in the centre of Aswan. Taking a walk through the excavations around its southern tip transport you back to the early times of the ancient Egyptian settlement of Abu, which means 'ivory'. German and Swiss archaeologists discovered Egypt's earliest cult site here – one of the recesses between the granite blocks dedicated to the goddess Satet.

Over the centuries these humble beginnings were developed into an impressive temple. From the end of the Old Kingdom, rulers of this border town had their tombs constructed in the moun-

tainside on the western bank. Steep slopes lead to the burial sites. The ruins of the Simeon Monastery, home to a great many monks between the 7th and 13th centuries, are also located on the western bank. Looming large on a nearby hill is the Fatimid mosque-style mausoleum of the 48th imam of the Shia Ismaili Muslims, Aga Khan III (1877–1957).

South of the city two dams seal off the Nile Valley. The older dam was built as a water-regulating mechanism between 1898 and 1902, while the second is known as the High Dam (Sadd Ali). It holds back the waters of the Nile to Lake Nasser, which is 500 km (311 miles) long. Its construction (1960–71) had economic, developmental and political consequences. After the US and Britain backed out of the financing of the project, President Nasser decided to nationalize the Suez Canal to pay for the dam. This led to the Suez

Crisis and tensions between Egypt and the West. Egypt subsequently accepted an offer from the Soviets to finance the dam. As part of the construction of the Aswan High Dam, the flood-threatened area of Nubia was explored and a number of monuments moved to other locations.

New areas of settlement were developed for Nubia's population in Egypt and Sudan. The Nubian Museum was opened in 1997 and has a memorial to their history.

㉗ Philae The temple complex of the goddess Isis is sitated on an island between the two dams that is only accessible by boat. This was one of the monuments moved to higher ground before the dam was built. Isis' followers continued to render homage to their goddess in the Ptolemaic temple until the 6th century AD. The first hall of columns was transformed into a church of St

Stephen under the reign of Emperor Justinian to replace old Egyptian beliefs.

㉘ Kalabscha Directly south of the High Dam on the western bank is the new location of four ancient temples. A boat ride takes you to the Temple of Kalabsha.

During its relocation by German archaeologists, blocks from an older temple were discovered inside the walls. These blocks have been put back together and are today displayed as the Kalabsha Gate in the Egyptian Museum in Berlin. The temple, which was built in Roman times, was built for the god Mandulis, a Nubian version of the falcon god, Horus. At its southern edge

Large image: Cruise on the Nile. At the top: Murals in Hathor Temple. Above: Interior of a temple of Philae, which today is on Agilkia island.

Detour

Lake Nasser

Roughly two-thirds of Lake Nasser's 5,000 sq km (1,930 sq mi) belong to Egypt while one-third is in Sudan. The lake is of utmost importance to Egypt as a water reservoir to control the fluctuations of the Nile flood. It has helped to increase agricultural revenues and provide Upper Egypt with electricity. The hydro-

are blocks containing prehistoric petroglyphs depicting giraffes and elephants, thus providing information on the essentially humid climate of the times 5,000 years before Christ.

The columns and statues of the temple of Gerf Hussein are a stout reminder of the time of Ramses II. Reliefs in the rock temple of Beit el-Wali, which were relocated just 100 m (328 yds) west of the Kalabsha Temple and created in the same era, are much more elegant in comparison.

The graceful kiosk with Hathor column capitals was originally located at the Kertassi quarry and promised divine protection for the men working there.

29 Neu-Sebua The asphalt road now stretches through the desert west of Lake Nasser. Abu Simbel is about 300 km (186 miles) from Aswan. Halfway down, an access road leads to the shores of the lake near New

Sebua, where you can see three temples at their new locations. The largest of the three was named for the sphinx figures in front of it – Wadi es-Sebua means 'Valley of the Lions'. Ramses II appears arrogantly on the temple walls; inside, he sits on an equal level with the gods. The Temple of Ad Dakkah was dedicated to Thot, the god of wisdom. Thot had travelled to Nubia as a messenger from the gods to entice Tefnut to Egypt, the daughter of the Sun god Ra. The scene of an ape dancing in front of a lioness plays on this divine myth.

The Chapel of el-Maharraka is still small and incomplete. In Roman times its location marked the border between the Roman Empire and the Kingdom of Meroë whose capital was unearthed north of Khartoum.

Finally, it's back on the main road for another 40 km (25 miles) to the south until the next road turns east.

30 New Amada When Thutmosis III (1479–26 BC) was pharaoh, Egypt had expanded its empire to the south.

The temple for Amun-Ra and Ra-Harakhte symbolizes the power of the Egyptian gods. In the 20th century archaeologists put the temple on a track and pulled it to this higher, drier bank.

The neighbouring temple of ed-Derr was also built by Ramses II. The scenes in the hall of columns are stunning.

The third monument in New Amada is the small rock tomb of Pennut, a reputable administrator in the conquered province.

31 Toschka Canal This canal goes straight through the desert for 50 km (31 miles) to Abu Simbel.

It is the most recent land reclamation project. The hope is to create a new Nile Valley. Green open spaces seem to indicate success.

32 Abu Simbel The relocation of this rock temple in the 1960s made worldwide headlines. Four colossal figures of Ramses II were cut out of the rock and rebuilt at a site 64 m (210 ft) higher. Inside, the walls display images of historic battles and ritual scenes. Ramses dedicated this smaller temple to his wife Nefertari and the goddess Hathor.

The four mighty statues of Pharaoh Ramses II were relocated with the support of UNESCO when Egypt's President Gamal Abdel Nasser built the Aswan High Dam and Lake Nasser in the 1950s that would have flooded the ancient ruins.

electric power station can generate up to 10 billion kWh a year. Loss of agriculturally viable territory on the Mediterranean coast, soil salinity and the usage of artificial fertilizers are the negative aspects of the project.

Both pictures: The Abu Simbel Temples are a monument to Pharao Ramses II.

Alexandria This city was founded by Alexander the Great in 332 BC and was once home to one of the most important libraries in the world, which was replaced in 2002 with a worthy successor.

Cairo In just a few decades the population of Egypt's capital grew from 3 million to over 20 million people – a real melting pot. In 1979, UNESCO declared the Islamic Old City a World Heritage Site.

The pyramids of Giza Built over 4,500 years ago (around 2700–500 BC), Egypt's largest and most famous pyramids are found in the Cairo suburb of Giza. The Sphinx next to the pyramids has the body of a lion and a human face. Nobody knows who destroyed its nose.

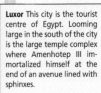

Luxor This city is the tourist centre of Egypt. Looming large in the south of the city is the large temple complex where Amenhotep III immortalized himself at the end of an avenue lined with sphinxes.

Valley of the Kings Starting with the 11th dynasty, the pharaohs built their tombs on the western bank of the Nile near Thebes. It is still an enormous necropolis.

Temple of Queen Hatshepsut This temple near Deir el-Bahri is a spectacular sight below the 300-m (984-ft) rock face.

Sakkara The step pyramid of the pharaoh Djoser lies in the middle of a large temple area west of Memphis.

Esna Far below today's ground level is the Temple of Esna, a significant monument from Ptolemaic times (332–30 BC). The Nile Perch was worshipped here.

Edfu The Temple of Horus is an example of Ptolemaic architecture located at the site of an older temple. Horus and Set, who killed his father Osiris, were important Egyptian deities worshipped here.

Dendera This temple complex was the most important cult site of the goddess Hathor. Her divine husband Thoh was also worshipped here.

Philae The main temple in the complex on this island in the Nile near Aswan is dedicated to the goddess Isis and her son Horus.

Aswan Egypt is dominated by the desert, but the Nile enabled civilization to prosper. A highlight is a cruise on the Nile to Aswan in a felucca, a traditional Arab sailing boat.

Al-Karnak This vast temple city near Luxor was built over 2,000 years ago and is one of the ancient wonders of the world.

Abu Simbel At night, the facades of the two temples of Abu Simbel are bathed in a light that makes them seem even more mystical.

Kôm Ombo This double temple is dedicated to the deities Sobek and Horus. Its magical location is captivating.

Map labels: Rosetta, ALEXANDRIA, Kafr el-Sheikh, Port Said, Damietta, Tanis, Medînet el'Ameriya el Guedida, Damanhûr, Tanta, Ismâ'ilîya, Suez Canal, El-Alamein, Abu Mena, Sâdât City, Tûkh, CAIRO, Palace of Abbâsi, El Agrud, Wadi el-Natrun, Giza, El Agrud, Suez, Memphis, Sakkara, Dahshûr, Ain Sukhnah, Baharîja Oasis, Pyramid of Meidum, El Ghurdaqah, Pyramid of El Lâhûn, El Burumbul, Medînet el-Faijûm, Beni Suêf, Deir Samû'il, El Fashn, Beni Mazâr, Samâlût, Djebel at Tayr, El-Minia, El Fikriya, Beni Hassan, Hermopolis, Mallawî, Tuna el-Gebel, Tell el-Amârna, Deir Mawas, Dairût, Manfalût, Assiût, El Badârî, Tima, Dâw el Kabîr (Antaeopolis), Kôm Ishqaw (Aphroditopolis), Akhmîm, Kharga Oasis, Sohâg, Safâga, Deir el-Abyad, Girgâ, Balyana, Dendera, Qena, El Quseir, Abydos, Nag Hammâdi, Valley of the Kings, Western Thebes, Qûs, Karnak, Temple of Hatshepsut, Luxor, Kharga Oasis, Esna, El Kab (Nekheb), Marsa Alam, Temple of Khnum, Kom el Ahmar (Nekhen), Edfu, El Ridisiya Bahari, Temple of Horus, Silwa Bahari, Gebel el-Silsila, Kagug, Kôm Ombo, Daraw, Aswân, Tombs of the Nobles, Monastery of St.Simeon, Temple of Philae, Medînet Sahara (Sahara City), Aswân High Dam, Kalabsha, Kharga Oasis, Lake Nasser, New Sebua, Toshka project, New Amada, Abu Simbel, Wadi Halfa, SUDAN

173

Route 14: South Africa
Taking the Garden Route

Our drive along the African continent's evergreen southern tip offers a series of enchanting natural spectacles. Animal lovers and amateur botanists will get their money's worth, as will wine-lovers, water-sports enthusiasts and fans of Cape Dutch architecture. Cape Town, a truly cosmopolitan city below the famous Table Mountain, is an experience of itself, while the drive back through the colourful Little Karoo Valley makes a fascinating contrast to urban life.

Route profile:

Length: approx. 1,120 miles
Time required: at least 7–10 days
When to go: The best months for visiting are February, March and April when the long school holidays are over and the air and waters are still pleasantly warm.

In many respects, the southern tip of Africa is really a world of its own. Well-groomed parklands, orchards, vineyards and forest jungles are all set against a backdrop of striking mountain ranges and breathtaking coastline. Beautiful beaches vie for attention with rugged rock promontories, seaside resorts and fishing villages on the oceanside. What's more, the region is blessed with a mild climate throughout the year and it rains regularly, so that the veg-

etation is abundant and colourful. It is no coincidence that the area is often called an 'earthly paradise' or that the English explorer
Sir Francis Drake called it the 'earth's finest cape' when he first came here in the late 16th century. The drive along the N2 coastal road (the Garden Route)

from Cape Town to Port Elizabeth and returning through the stunning backcountry is one of the main highlights of any trip to South Africa. If at any time you want to leave your car behind, you can take a ride on the luxurious Blue Train, a rail line that runs parallel to the coastal road here as part of its route

from Pretoria to Cape Town. Without doubt, however, the chief attraction of this 'Garden of Eden' is its nature, which is at its most spectacular on the Garden Route between Mossel Bay and the mouth of the Storm River. Nature-lovers can make good use of a well-organized and expansive network of hiking

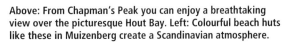

Above: From Chapman's Peak you can enjoy a breathtaking view over the picturesque Hout Bay. Left: Colourful beach huts like these in Muizenberg create a Scandinavian atmosphere.

east, there are some magnificent vineyards where wine-lovers can taste some of the classier local wines. Culture and history buffs will enjoy the beautifully maintained villages from the pioneer days of European settlement, where Cape Dutch-style buildings and a few interesting museums recount a not-so-distant past when the Dutch East India Company established its first stations here, and both Amsterdam and London vied for this profitable new colony.

In the far west, against the commanding backdrop of Table Mountain, the lively metropolis of Cape Town provides a charming contrast to the pristine natural landscapes. Every year millions of visitors from around the globe are attracted by its lively markets, noble Wilhelminian architecture, elegant mansions set away from the coast, sandy bays and hip quarters like the 'Wa-

terfront' with its trendy cafés, restaurants and boutiques. To get away from it all, you can take a spin along the scenic Chapman's Peak Drive towards the Cape of Good Hope on Africa's southern tip. The heather-clad countryside and colourful fishing villages in the area evoke scenes of Scandinavia.

The beauty of South Africa is unrelenting as you move away from the coast to the starkly contrasting desert interior, where the arid steppe of Little Karoo is world-famous for its ostrich farms and stalactite caves.

Exciting rock formations can be found in the arid area of the Little Karoo (left side). The contrast is the sea, over whose surf the lighthouse towers in Mossel Bay (right side).

trails that run along the coast and through the forests.

The area also offers plenty of opportunities to watch elephants, whales and a host of other exotic animals in their natural habitats. The Addo Elephant National Park is a good example of a wildlife experience. And for those who want nothing more

than to sit on the beach and enjoy the consistently sunny weather, the entire south coast is a virtual paradise. Water sports are also fantastic in the dynamic surf of the Indian Ocean.

Up country from Cape Town, in the hills around Paarl, Franschhoek and Stellenbosch to the

Chapman`s Peak Drive

It may only be a drive of 10 km (6 miles), but you will never forget this scenic road cut directly into the steep coastal rock faces south of Hout Bay by Italian pris-

Cape fauna

On the Garden Route you usually have to visit game reserves if you want to see some of the stars of the safari world up close: giraffes, lions, cheetahs, hippos, rhinos and elephants. Yet the wildlife specific to the southern cape is also incredibly varied. In many places along the coast you can see mongoose, baboons, chivet cats and even porcupines. Some species of antelope are also common, among them springbok gazelles, the national animals of South Africa. The most famous animals

Cape gannets and seal colonies live here.

of the Little Karoo, however, are its ostriches. Marine life is even more varied. Antarctic plankton is the base of a long food chain comprising rich stocks of fish, seal colonies and sea birds including penguins, cape gannets and cormorants. Even the 'kings of the sea', blue whales and sperm whales, breach off the Cape coast.

A drive from Cape Town to Port Elizabeth is definitely the crown jewel of a trip to South Africa. Starting in the metropolis at the foot of Table Mountain, this round trip takes you across the Cape Peninsula on the famous Garden Route along the south coast to Port Elizabeth, and from there back to Cape Town via the Little Karoo and the vineyards around Stellenbosch.

❶ **Cape Town** (see pp. 178–179.) Before heading out immediately from Cape Town on the N2, you should definitely take a day trip out to the famous Cape of Good Hope.

❷ **Cape Peninsula** 'The fairest cape in the whole circumference of the earth.' These enthusiastic words about Africa's rocky southern tip were uttered by none other than Sir Francis Drake, the second captain to circumnavigate the globe. Later generations of seafarers surely felt the words were nothing but mockery, as the Cape came to be feared for its storms and high waves, and dozens of ships have run aground on its reefs. Shipwrecks testify to the perils of the passage. In fact, you should check the weather before setting off in a rental car, and remember to take a windcheater.
There are two ways to get out to the Cape – the route west of Table Mountain and the Twelve Apostles along the idyllic beaches past decadent mansions such as Sea Point, Clifton, Camps Bay and Llandudno, or the route fur-

ther south-east via Kirstenbosch and Groot Constantia. They both reconnect at Hout Bay, a charming fishing town.
Now take Chapman's Peak Drive to Noordhoek and carry on to Kommetjie and Scarborough, a pair of idyllic fishing villages on the small road to Smitswinkelbay. On the last 13 km (8 miles) you cross the southern part of the 'Cape of Good Hope Nature Reserve'. The low scrub and heathers of this reserve are distinctly reminiscent of Scotland. You're likely to see antelope, ostrich, wildebeest and zebras and almost certainly some baboons. The last few hundred yards are

covered by shuttle bus. Then it's 133 steps to Cape Point 200 m (650 ft) above the waves where you get an absolutely magnificent view over the peninsula and False Bay – you'll know what Drake meant. The Cape of Good Hope is actually a few kilometres to the west, but the view is much less spectacular from there.
Your return journey goes along a wild, rocky coastline via Simon's Town with its pretty Victorian centre and the fishing ports of Fish Hoek and Kalk Bay. In the surfers' paradise of Muizenberg beach, the colourful huts recall times gone by.

oners-of-war during World War II. Starting in an idyllic fishing port, the road winds its way around the colourful cliffs up to Noordhoek. From its highest point at 600 m (1,970 ft) above Chapman's Bay there is a breathtaking view across to Hout Bay, a rocky outcrop called 'The Sentinel' and the hills around Constantia.

The Hout Bay offers an incredible view.

Cape flora

Botanists have divided the earth's plants into seven floral kingdoms. The smallest but by far the most varied of these is the Cape floristic region.

On roughly 70,000 sq km (27,000 sq mi) of space there are approximately 8,600 species of flowering plants.

A third of these are native to just the Cape Peninsula, an area measuring only 518 sq km (200 sq mi).

The most characteristic element of the local flora is the so-called fynbos vegetation, which primarily consists of

After 20 km (12 miles) eastbound on Baden Powell Drive, which runs in a large arc along the flat beaches of False Bay, you get back to the N2. But at Somerset West you leave it behind again. For 60 km (40 miles) you then drive along the so-called Whale Route at the base of the Koeeberg mountains where lovely coastal scenery,

and possibly some majestic marine mammals, will accompany you via Kleinmond to Hermanus.

3 Hermanus This picturesque town, founded by fishermen in 1855, is located on the northern shore of Walker Bay between Kleinrivierberge and the sea. It is famous not only for its many wild flowers, magnificent beach-es and outstanding water-sports options, but also for its deep-sea fishing. Many people from Cape Town come to spend their weekends in this holiday village where fishing boats, dreamy cottages and the old harbour give it the feel of an open-air museum.

During the winter, from July to November, Hermanus is a hot spot for whale-watchers from all around the world. They even have a bellman employed at the beach to ring when humpbacks, right whales or even orcas are sighted. Harold Porter National Botanic Gardens in the Kogelberg Nature Reserve west of the town have a good exhibition of Cape flora.

Before returning to the N2 take the scenic detour via Cape Agulhas. Passing through Bredasdorp, the R318 will take you back to the N2 and on to Swellendam.

4 Swellendam The country's third-oldest town was founded by the Dutch East India Compa-

Top: View over Capetown. Left: African Penguins on the Cape Peninsula. Above left: Cape of Good Hope Left: a humpback whale near Hermanus.

The variety of wildflowers is astounding.

heather and protea plants. The coastal regions receive high levels of rain during the colder months. By contrast, the inland Karoo steppe is semi-arid with vegetation mostly made up of succulents – herbs and shrubs with fleshy leaves and magnificent flowers. Large forests like the ones near George are relatively rare in South Africa.

The Cape Town Convention Center hosts important international meetings.

The mighty Table Mountain towers above the night-illuminated Cape Town.

Cape Town

To many globetrotters, the 'Mother City', as South Africans fondly call the oldest city in their country, is the world's most beautiful port city. It is mainly Cape Town's unique location against the imposing backdrop of Table Mountain that makes it special – on the cape where the Atlantic and Indian Oceans meet.

When the Dutchman Jan van Riebeeck moored in Table Bay for the Dutch East India Company on 7 April 1652, he and his handful of pioneers were the first white peo-

ships and sailing vessels ply the busy waters.

The climate here is Mediterranean, with none of the drastic temperature changes that are so typical of the inland areas. A constant sea breeze seems even to blow away most germs and smog, inspiring the locals to gratefully call it the 'cape doctor'. Beyond its natural setting, the city's population is also far more cosmopolitan than any other in sub-Saharan Africa. Blacks, whites, Cape Coloureds, Chinese, Malays, Indians, Jews and countless immigrants from around the globe all contribute to the fascinating mix of colours, cultures and cuisine.

Both victorian and modern houses are typical of Cape Town's different quarters.

ple ever to land here. They were met by Khoikhoi ('Men of men' in their language) and San ('Bushmen'). 'Hottentots' is a term given to the Khoikhoi by the Dutch to mean 'stutterer'. San in turn is Khoikhoi for 'outsider'.

The fortifications on the cape quickly became a kind of 'tavern of the seas', a refuge and supply station for seafarers on the way between Europe and Asia. Many lives were saved here.

The city's backdrop is second to none. The entire 3 km (2 miles) of the mountain plateau are often draped in clouds and the city is sprawled out at its feet. Outside, in the port of Table Bay, cargo

A handful of must-sees while you are there are the Castle of Good Hope, which is more than 300 years old, the Bo Kaap Malay Quarter, the Houses of Parliament, Kirstenbosch Gardens, the South African Museum, the National Gallery, Signal Hill, a view from Table Mountain by cable car, and the busy waterfront by the port with its choice of stylish restaurants, boutiques and galleries. And last but by no means least, do not forget Robben Island, home to the prison where Nelson Mandela was forced to wait half his life for Apartheid finally to come to an end.

Great White Sharks

Long before the young Steven Spielberg directed his classic film in 1974, these sharks were infamous throughout the world. They were and still are considered bloodthirsty beasts.

In reality, however, sharks are in great need of protection from human predators, not the other way round. Their huge jaws and long rows of razor-sharp teeth may instill fear in many a water-sports enthusiast, and attacks do happen. But attacks on humans are actually much rarer than myths would lead us to believe, and they are usually caused by curiosity, not sheer lust to kill. 'Carcharodon carcharias', as this predator is also known, habitually tests out unknown objects simply by taking a bite. White sharks live all around the globe, which makes it surprising that so little conclusive research has been carried out on them. But their mys-

ny in 1745. It is located against the impressive backdrop of the Langeberg Mountain Range, whose ridge is called the '12 O'Clock Rock' by locals because at noon the sun is vertically above it. Long alleyways of ancient oak trees are the town's landmark and in many places you can still feel a bit of atmosphere from the pioneer days. The town's biggest attraction is 'The Drostdy', the erstwhile residence of the bailiff (landdrost), which was built in 1747. This thatched mansion, which was renovated and enlarged between 1812 and 1825, now houses a stylish museum with furniture and common household objects dating from the 18th and 19th centuries. An old post office and a vivid documentation of old arts and crafts complete the museum compound.

About 6 km (4 miles) south of Swellendam is Bontebok National Park, home to numerous very rare species of bird and various antelopes. The park is 18 sq km (7 sq mi). One of these birds is the pied buck (Bontebok), which gave the park its name. It is nearly extinct in the wild. If the weather is good, take a swim in the wonderful Breede River.

Just after the bridge across Kafferkuils River, exit the N2 once again and take a detour (about 20 km/13 miles) to Stilbaai at the coast.

5 Stilbaai Even prehistoric fishermen who settled in this area valued 'Still Bay' as a plentiful fishing ground. Its remarkably long beaches have turned it into a classic holiday resort. For nine months of the year the holiday cottages along its flat sandy shores remain closed up. Many of them are built on stilts. At the end of the school year, however, they come back to life almost overnight.

6 Mossel Bay Mossel Bay marks the beginning of the real Garden Route, where the N2 drops right down to the coast. It is also the location where explorers Bartholomeu Diaz and Vasco da Gama landed before 1500. Offshore oil and gas discoveries have added an industrial feel to this much-visited holiday village, but around the turn of the last century it was briefly famous for the export of ostrich plumes.

During the holiday season local beaches, which are separated by rocky outcrops, are crowded. Sun worshippers and swimmers go to Munro's Bay, Santos Beach and Diaz Beach, whereas surfers prefer The Point and De Bakke.

In the historic town centre, the Bartholomeu Diaz Museum Complex is well worth a visit. It houses a reconstruction of the vessel used by Diaz in 1488 when he was the first European to navigate the Cape. This reconstructed caravel is only 23 m (75 ft) long. The neighbouring Shell Museum displays a large collection of seashells. A local curiosity is a 500-year-old milkwood tree that seafarers used as a 'post office'. They deposit-

terious patterns and elusive behaviour make that difficult. What we do know is that their numbers are declining dramatically. The reason is that collectors on the black market pay up to 50,000 dollars for a set of shark teeth, and in Asia their fins are considered a delicacy for soup. There are probably no more than 10,000 of these sharks left in the world's oceans. The World Conservation Union placed them on its 'red list' of endangered species, and in some countries, like South Africa, they are strictly protected.

White sharks are a constant presence in the coastal waters around the South African cape.

ed their letters in a boot hung in the branches of the tree, where they would then be picked up by vessels bound for home.

7 George The Garden Route's 'unofficial' capital is about 50 km (31 miles) further on, just away from the coast at the base of the Outeniqua Mountain Range. The range peaks at just under 1,600 m (5,250 ft). The name means something like 'they who bear honey'.
Moist sea air causes plenty of rainfall here, ensuring an abundance of verdant green vegetation. George is surrounded by forests and towards the sea there are some park-like landscapes. In the town centre Cape Dutch and classical-style buildings stand alongside the oldest

Catholic church in the country, 'Moederkerk', which is adorned with beautiful wood carvings. Next to it stands an almost 200-year-old oak. Slaves were once chained to it before being sold.
A ride on the Outeniqua Choo-Tjoe Train across to Knysna goes through some striking coastal scenery and is a unique experience. The train crosses a long bridge (2 km/1.5 miles) over the Knysna Lagoon before entering the town of Knysna.

8 Wilderness National Park These days the resort town of Wilderness on the N2 does not really do justice to its name. About 12 m (7.5 miles) east of the Kaaiman River's deep gorge you are confronted with an excessive number of holiday cot-

tages and hotels. But the town's fine sandy beach and the luscious forests in the surrounding countryside do make it a sight to behold.
The neighbouring Wilderness National Park is a stretch of coast around 20 km (13 miles) long interspersed with a number of lagoons and lakes surrounded by dense forests. It's a picture-book natural paradise that is most famous for its seabirds, but you can also go fishing, surfing, canoeing and boating. A hike on Kingfisher Trail along the mouth of the Touw river is perfect for a day trip.
Just outside Knysna you pass the Goukamma Nature Reserve, a strip of rocky coastline that stretches 14 km (9 miles) and can only be explored on foot.

9 Knysna A hundred years ago this holiday resort located at the northern shore of a huge lagoon was the centrepoint of a tempestuous gold rush. These days it is mainly known for its oysters and the substantial forests nearby that have provided generations of local people with the economic base for a thriving timber industry. The forests are also home to a small herd of free-roaming elephants. A regional speciality is handcrafted hardwood furniture made from yellow wood, iron wood and stink wood.
The town's landmarks are two giant sandstone cliffs called 'The Heads', which tower above the small canal connecting the lagoon to the open ocean. West of Knysna is the Featherbed Nature Reserve, home to the rare blue duikers and a host of other rare bird species.

Large Image: Coast at Noordhoek. Left side: Bay to bay on steam power: the Outeniqua Choo-Tjoe Train at Dolphin Point ; 'The drostdy' in Swellendam (bottom). Right Side: Jubilee Creek in Knysna Forest.

Detour

Cape Agulhas

The bearing is 34° 52' south of the equator – Africa's southernmost point! This headland is located 160 km (100 miles) south-east of Cape Town and was christened Agulhas ('needle cape') by Portuguese sailors, supposedly because of the sharp-edged reefs just off the coast. The local countryside is full of sheep pastures and corn fields and is not very spectacular by South African standards. The more sensational aspect is the sea just off the rocky shore. Why? It is where the Atlantic

The Cape Agulhas Lighthouse.

meets the Indian Ocean. Two powerful ocean currents meet here – the Agulhas current and the Benguelas current. The former carries water at temperatures of around 20°C (68°F) from equatorial regions, which evaporates easily and thus provides the Eastern Cape with plenty of rainfall and luscious vegetation. The latter carries nutrient-rich but colder water from the Antarctic in the south-west, creating next to no clouds but only fog. This ocean current is the reason that the coastline in South Africa's western regions and Namibia is so bare. The constant temperature differences at the Cape cause pretty severe weather conditions including winds and high waves.

181

Detour

Addo Elephant National Park

The addo elephants that live here are only a small relic of the giant herds that once roamed freely across the Eastern Cape. However, an encounter with one of them is still a very impressive experience. About 200 of these reddish and slightly smaller variants of the true African elephants live in this national park, which is located just 70 km (43 miles) north of Port Elizabeth. When the first settlers arrived in the area near the Sunday River in the 1820s, a peaceful coexistence of humans and elephants proved to be impossible. The giant animals continuously devastated local harvests. In 1919, the farmers hired a game hunter to put an end to the problem. The man did a very thorough job. Only around a dozen addo elephants survived.

The most magnificent beaches in the area are called Brenton and Noetzie. The Elephant Nature Walk in Diepwalle State Forest offers some truly outstanding hiking. You get to it along the N9, which branches off inland a few miles after Knysna heading towards Prince Alfred's Pass and Avontour.

10 Plettenberg Bay There are some ideal opportunities for hiking in the forests of Kranshoek and Harkerville, approximately 30 km (18 miles) east of Knysna. A few minutes after that in the car take a look to your right off the N2 to see some truly fantastic scenery.
Plettenberg Bay, with its almost 10 km (6 miles) of immaculate sandy beaches and crystal blue waters, really is the essence of the 'South African Riviera'. From July to September there are whales calving within sight of numerous exclusive hotels.

11 Tsitsikamma National Park This national park, covering 5,000 ha (12,350 acres) of land, has everything that nature-lovers may desire — bizarre cliffs, lonely beaches, steep gorges and luscious vegetation if you make it further up country. Founded in 1962, the area also includes the rich coastal waters. The Otter Trail, which starts in Nature's Valley and runs along the rocky shore for 42 km (26 miles) right up to the mouth of the Storms River, is one of the country's most attractive long-distance hiking trails. To do it you first have to acquire a permit — only the first 3 km (2 miles) from the eastern entrance are open to those without one. However, even within that distance you are fortunate enough to be able to visit the huge waterfalls and a spectacular hanging bridge that stretches 190 m (623 ft) over the chasm at a height of 130 m (427 ft). If you are into snorkelling, there is an underwater nature trail where you can go exploring the large variety of marine plants and animals.

12 Cape St Francis Near Humansdorp a road turns off to Cape St Francis on your right. This jaunt towards the coast is about 60 km (40 miles) and is well worth doing for a few reasons. First is that the village at the end of the cape really does have a charm of its own with its whitewashed houses and black rooftops. Second is that the long beaches towards Oyster Bay and Jeffrey's Bay to the east are among the most beautiful in South Africa. The third reason has to do with the waves that break here.
In the 1960s Jeffrey's Bay was made legend in the movie The Endless Summer, and the waves still break perfectly here, sometimes for hundreds of yards from the point into the bay. Watching the surfers on this world-famous wave is an enjoyable way to spend a day at the lovely beach.

Above: Plettenberg Bay. Small pictures: Spectacular stretches of coastlines in Tsitsikamma National Park. Right side: Elephants in the Addo Elephant National Park.

In 1931, in order to protect the remaining specimens, some farmers established a reserve measuring 86 sq km (33 sq mi) and providing the herbivorous animals with ideal conditions for their survival. Today, a total of

45 km (28 miles) of roads and tracks criss-cross the national park.

Today nearly 200 elephant giants live on 9,000 ha (22,000 acres) of reserve land.

The area around the tranquil town of Piketberg is a scenic jewel.

Back on the N2 it is only 70 km (43 miles) to Port Elizabeth.

⑬ Port Elizabeth The Port Elizabeth P.E., as the locals call this important port city, has the gold and diamond trade to thank for its rise. These days the heart of the South African car industry beats a little upriver in Port Elizabeth's 'twin city' of Uitenhage on the banks of the sizeable Swartkops River. Although 'Cape Detroit' is definitely not known for its scenic beauty, this port metropolis with its one million inhabitants still exudes its own personal brand of Victorian charm.

Its lively centre and the starting point for guided tours is called Market Square, where the town hall is magnificent and the 'campanile' tower (52 m/170 ft) even has a viewing platform. From Park Donkin Reserve, you have a magnificent view over Algoa Bay and there are some beautifully restored houses from the Victorian era as well as an old lighthouse.

The Museum Complex includes a snake park, dolphin shows in the Oceanium and a regional museum that promise a good variety of entertainment. Close by there are some exquisite beaches such as Kings Beach and Humewood Beach.

Instead of taking the same coastal route back towards Cape Town, we recommend driving the N62/60, which takes you further into the heartland of South Africa.

This inland route branches off about 20 km (13 miles) west of Humansdorp, winding its way westwards past Joubertina, Avontour, Uniondale and De Rust – all of which are smart and tidy but otherwise unremarkable agricultural towns. The landscape of the Little Karoo, as this interior plateau is called, extends over 250 km (155 miles) over a swathe of land about 60 km (40 miles) wide and is strikingly different to the coastal ar-

eas. This area, sandwiched between the Kouga and Swart Ranges to the north and the Outeniqua and Langeberg Ranges to the south, gets very little rain. There are colourful rock formations on either side of the road and large areas of the abundant fertile soil are irrigated. Over the years, ostrich farms have developed into a hugely important impetus for the local economy.

⑭ Oudtshoorn This provincial town with 50,000 inhabitants is the 'urban centre' of the Little Karoo. You can hardly imagine it these days, but in the late 19th century it was even a fashion hub and, at one point, a group of inventive farmers decided on a new tack for the fashion scene.

They started large-scale ostrich breeding operations in this dry valley and subsequently managed to convince the haute couture of Vienna, Paris and New York that feather boas, capes or fans made from ostrich plumes were indispensable accessories for the fashionably up-to-date. At the height of the resulting boom around 750,000 birds were delivering 500 tonnes of feathers a year. Having become rich overnight, these ostrich 'barons', as they now called themselves, erected decadent mansions of stone and cast iron, the so-called 'feather palaces'. After a downturn lasting several decades, the ostrich business has recently regained some momentum in the wake of the low-cholesterol craze. Ostrich meat is now exported on a large scale, as is their leather. On some farms, you can try out specialities such as ostrich steaks and omelettes made from the birds' giant eggs, watch ostrich races or even risk a ride on one. Located 30 km (18 miles) north of the town is an absolute five-star attraction – the Cango Caves. These are some of the world's most terrific stalactite caves and you get to see all their beauty during the course of a two-hour guided tour.

Ostrich farms and other plantations, neat towns with names such as Calitzdorp, Ladismith or Barrydale, and an imposing backdrop of mountain ranges accompany you through this charming region.

After passing Montagu, a charming centre for growing fruit and wine at the western end of Little Karoo Valley with numerous historic buildings, the road winds its way up more than 6 km (4 miles) to Cogmanskloof Pass. It then goes through a tunnel under a jagged barrier called 'Turkey Rock' and carries on down into the wide and fertile Bree Valley.

⑮ Robertson This small town is blessed with a wonderfully mild climate and extremely fertile soil. High-quality apples, apricots and above all grapes

The Paarl vineyards grow some renowned high-quality wines.

grow here in luscious abundance. Wild roses, old oak trees and jacaranda trees grow by the roadside. A long sandy beach along the riverbank is reminiscent of the French Riviera.

The area also has a plethora of accommodation in the form of holiday apartments or campsites. Sheilam Cactus Garden is a must for hobby botanists. It is located 8 km (5 miles) outside the town and has one of the most comprehensive cactus collections anywhere in the world. The next main town on the N60 is Worcester, which has few attractions apart from its botanic gardens and Kleinplasie Farm Museum, which invites you to

take a touching journey back in time to the daily routine of an 18th-century farm. There is a worthwhile detour here via Wolseley to the small town of Tulbagh, which is 70 km (43 miles) north of our route.

⓯ **Tulbagh** Also surrounded by extensive orchards and vineyards, Tulbagh was devastated by an earthquake in 1969 but has since been fully restored. The town centre around Church Street is considered to be the most complete collection of Cape Dutch architecture in the country. The town's oldest building is Oude Kerk (Old Church), which was built in 1743.

⓱ **Paarl** To reach this small town on the Berg River from Tulbagh follow the narrow, winding R44 via the jagged Bain's Pass. It is the industrial centre of the wine-growing region and the seat of the wine-growers' co-operative KWV, which was founded in 1918 and now looks after more than 5,000 individual vintners.

It stores more than 300 million litres (66 million gal) of wine, and more than three times this amount is processed here every year. There are guided tours that take you to five wine barrels alleged to be the largest in the world. Each of them holds more than 200,000 litres (909,000

gal), was made without nails and weighs 25 tonnes (27.5 tons). The town was named after 'The Pears' ('De Paarl'), giant granite summits that sparkle in the sunlight after it rains. On one slope of Paarl Mountain, 600 m (1,970 ft) high, the Tall Monument, an imposing granite needle, commemorates the development and spread of Afrikaans, the Boer language. Local vineyards such as Nederburg, Rhebokshof, Fairview, Backsberg or Kanonkop are consid-

Left side: Town hall in Port Elizabeth (above), Afrikaans Language Monument (below). Above: Cango Caves.

The Qinghai-Tibet Plateau – the official name – covers not only Tibet, but also mountains like the Himalayas and the Karakorum. Formed 50 million years ago, the Tibetan Plateau is the highest plateau in the world.

Asia

The Asian continent is as big as it is diverse. Sandy deserts dominate the Arabian peninsula in southwest Asia, through which camels pass. Here, in extreme contrast, there are also modern metropolises, in which skyscrapers zealously compete in height. In seemingly endless China, the paths through subtropical areas and deep gorges continue in the footsteps of the world's oldest civilized people to vibrant megacities - and over one of the highest mountain systems in the world, the Himalayas in Nepal and Tibet. In Southeast Asia Thailand, Malaysia and Indonesia attract visitors with their endless sandy beaches, tropical rainforests and fascinating cultures.

Route 15: China

From Beijing to Kunming

If you travel by train from the capital to the southwest, you will travel through the continental north as well as the subtropical south, journeying through wide loess plains and through deep mountain ravines. You will experience the rich testimonies of the oldest cultural people on earth as well as the colourful diversity of national minorities.

Route profile:

Length: approx. 3600 km (2,237 mi), excluding detour, approx. 4400 km (2,734 mi) with detours
Time required: approx. 5 weeks

China is almost the size of a continent in terms of its surface area. Over half of China's territory is made up of highlands, high mountains and plateaus. There are also the great rivers that flow through China from west to east: the Huang He in the north and the Chang Jiang (Yangtzekiang) in the center. These waterways are the ancient centers of Chinese culture.

The great contrasts of the country are also reflected in stark climatic differences: The north of China experiences a winter that lasts for almost half a year and in the south the summer lasts longer than six months. While it hardly rains more than 100 mm a year in the northern deserts, the extreme south receives around 6000 mm of rainfall annually. Especially in winter dry, dust-laden northwest winds sweep over northern China, sometimes blocking out the sun in Beijing. In contrast Kunming esperiences spring weather all year round. This is partly due to the strong sunlight - Kunming is not far from the northern tropic - on the other hand, it is located at about 1900 m above sea level. The vegetation is just as diverse: the palette ranges from the lush dark green subtropical forests in the south to the light green pastures in inner Mongolia, from the colourful larch and pine forests of the high mountains in the northwest to the barren highlands in the west and the mosaic of fields in the Red Basin.

Since ancient times, the fertile plateau of the central reaces of Huang He and its tributary Wei He has been considered the cradle of Chinese civilisation and the area where many of the modern world techniques were

Above: The 40 kilometre Wu Xia, the 'witches' canyon', is considered the most beautiful of the three canyons of the Yangtze River. The Wu Gorge is bordered by twelve high mountains. Left: The Qianmen Street in Beijing is very inviting, particularly in the evening, when spotlights stylishly illuminate the beautifully restored shops and gates.

first developed. From here, the Chinese principalities were united as a central state - 221 BC under the rule of the Qin Dynasty. The route leads right through this historic core landscape. After many days of river travel up the Yangtze river, you reach another core area of recent Chinese history: the Red Basin in the Sichuan Province. The colour of the fertile soil is what gives the basin its name. It was made arable early on and today is one of the most densely populated areas in China.

The farther the train travels southwards, the deeper it penetrates into the territory of national minorities, be it the Miao, the Dong, the Shui, the Bai, the Li or the Naxi. These and other small nations have, over the centuries, withdrawn to the hard-to-reach mountains of the '10,000 chasms and torrents' where they have preserved their traditional cultures.

Left side: Section of the Great Wall near Beijing; Top from left: sculptures on the Dazu Grottoes and actress of Peking Opera.

191

The Forbidden City

Emperor Yong Le had the imperial palace built between 1407 and 1420. His successors expanded the facility without changing the structure. The general population was strictly forbidden to enter the 'Purple City' until 1911, hence the name. Three axes run north to south through the Forbidden City: The central axis leads through the main buildings and the emper-

The extremely spectacular railway line not only crosses wide plains and valleys, but also overcomes high mountain ranges. The train travels in galleries along steep slopes, through long tunnels and over deep gorges. If you would rather travel by water, you can take a several day trip up the Yangtze River by boat. Two worthwhile excursions lead from Kunming to the southern Chinese mountains near Dali and Lijiang.

1 Beijing (see pp. 194–195): After visiting Beijing, the journey begins at the new central station. It's worth making a detour to the Great Wall, the Ming Tombs, and Chengde (see page 285).

2 Datong It is worth stopping off at the industrial city not only to visit the Nine Dragon Wall and the cities monasteries, but also the 16 km long western caves of Yungang. The caves with their 51,000 statues and reliefs are UNESCO World Heritage Sites. Also the worth visiting are the wooden pagoda of the Ying-Xian Fo-Gong Monastery and the Hanging Shan Monastery on the sacred Mount Heng Shan.

3 Taiyuan The capital of the Shanxi Province is a modern business metropolis with a bustling business district. From here, it is you can take a trip

by bus to the northern Wutai Shan, one of the four sacred places of Buddhism. The walk to the summet, taking several hours to reach, is lined with many temples and monasteries.

4 Pingyao The small, approximately 2,700 year old city of Pingyao is located 90 km south of Taiyuan and today looks almost exactly like most Chinese cities 300 years ago. A 6.4 km long wall with six gates and a series of towers surround the city. Their course is similar to the outline of a turtle. On the 12 m high and 5 m wide structure you can circle Pingyao on foot or in a rickshaw. Pingyao gained its former wealth thanks to trade and banking. The first

**Above: Hanging monastery;
Top left: Buddha figures in the
Yungang Grottoes; Bottom
left: Pingyao.**

or's apartments, the eastern axis runs through the palaces of the imperial family and the western axis runs through the buildings housing the concubines and the eunuchs guarding them. The Imperial Palace was the centre of the empire and the navel of the world: its palaces are painted purple, the colour of the polar star around which all other stars circle. Its position on earth corresponds to that of the Emperor, the son of heaven. A 10 metre high wall with towers and four gates surrounds the approximately 100 hectare Forbidden City.

On a three-level marble pedestal stand the palace's highest ranking buildings, the Hall of Supreme Harmony, the Hall of Perfect Harmony and the Hall of Conservation of Harmony. This is where the emperors were enthroned, received official delegatons and held ceremonies.

Detour

Great Wall, Ming Tombs and Chengde

Three major attractions are located in the north of the capital, all three have been declared a World Heritage Site by UNESCO.

The Great Wall at Badaling
50 km of the Great Wall runs along the northwest of Beijing - the massive fortress extends over 6700 km from Shanhaiguan in the east to Jiayuguan in the western province of Gansu.
Badaling is one part of the Great Wall that is worth seeing, which has been restored. In the 3rd century BC Emperor Qin Shi Huangdi had the stone walls of the northern principalities form a continuous barrier.
At a distance of 180 m each, two-storey watchtowers, approx. 12 m high, tower over the wall, so that messages could be transmitted at lightning speed. About 500 years ago, the wall gained its present appearance under the Ming emperors. Visitors can hike on the approximately 7 metre high, 7 metre deep and 6 m wide wall and experience the steepness of the terrain up close.

Ming Tombs
In a valley about 50 km north of Beijing lie the graves of 13 rulers of the Ming Dynasty (1368-1644) spread over a 40 km wide area. Geomancers once selected this burial ground; it is protected from the influences of evil spirits by mountains in the north.
Today, as a tourist, you are no longer able to cover the 6.4 km long 'Path of souls' with its marble gate, but are only allowed to walk the last stretch on foot. Here there are 24 animal sculptures to protect the souls - twelve on each side of the road, each animal includes one lying and one standing - and another twelve human figures. Among them is the fearsome mythical creature Qi Lin, which features deer hooves, a bovine tail, a horn on its head, and a scaly body. All figures are from the 15th century. The three-arched Dragon and Phoenix Gate leads to the palatial underground tombs, two of which have been restored and can be visited. The modern living harmony of the Fengshui was created from the search for a place that the soul of a deceased could be put to rest. The graves are located in a picturesque setting.

Chengde
The summer resort of Chengde is located 250 km northeast of Beijing in the Hebei province.
In the 18th century, the Qing emperors built an extensive summer residence with several palaces and impressive gardens in the mountainous north of the city. They spent five to six months of the year here.
At the foot of the mountains stand the eight outer temples, which were designed according to the architectural styles of various Chinese nationalities.

From above: Wall near Badaling; Chengde; Ming grave.

193

Looking from the north, from the Tiananmen Gate, over the gigantic dimensions of Tiananmen Square, you can not only see the National Museum building and, on the right, the Great Hall of the People, but also the moat which surrounds the Forbidden City.

Although the central business district is thought to be located in the heart of Beijing, it is actually located just outside the centre on the third ring road. Nevertheless, it is not just a worthwhile trip for business people; Lovers of modern architecture will also be impressed by the rather idiosyncratic skyscraper constructions.

Beijing

The structure of the modern capital of China is the result of nearly 1000 years of development. It is reflected to this day in the layout of the city, because according to the rules of geomancy the cardinal directions began as an essential guideline for the city.

The first structure of the 'Northern Capital' - the translation of Beijing - comes from the Jin Dynasty (1115-1234). After its destruction, Beijing was rebuilt under the Ming emperors between 1368 and 1420 based on its predecessor. The city was an image of the cosmos, whose laws were reflected in the construction of the settlement.

The old city centre forms the Forbidden City, which was created on both sides of a central north-south axis. The huge Tiananmen Square lies south of the modern centre of Beijing. It was named after the Tiananmen Gate, from which Mao Zedong proclaimed the founding of the People's Republic of China in 1949. With the installation of the square, from 1958 the capital has acted as a socialist heart with its 'state cathedral'. The Changan east-west highway is located perpendicular to the traditional north-south axis, outside the Forbidden City. Mao Zedong also built this 40 km long and 120km wide road near Tian'anmen Square from 1956. Today, the Changan Avenue is lined with government representative buildings and large companies as well as new hotel buildings.

The inner city districts correspond in their extent essentially to the historic city. The old quarters were formerly characterised by courtyard houses and narrow streets (hutong). Only small Hutongs have been preserved

and restored, such as in the area of the drum tower. Most were demolished, however, to make way for new streets and multi-storey residential buildings. At the beginning of the socialist era, the inner city districts were also interspersed with iron and steel works, car and machine factories, locomotive and wagon manufacturing plants, and the production of electrical appliances and agricultural machinery. These measures were intended to turn the middle-class consumer city of the imperial era into a modern-day producing city. Beijing thus became the largest industrial city in China. The historic wall ring was sacrificed to the city expansion. Its course is characterised by the main axes of the road network and thus reflect the former expansion of the imperial city. Bei-

Hall of Harvest Prayer in the district of the Heaven Temple

jing has a number of spacious recreational areas in the old parks. One of the most famous and largest is the 270-acre park that surrounds the Temple of Heaven (Tian Tan) with the Hall of Prayer for Good Harvest and the Altar of Heaven. Both were built at the beginning of the 15th century.

The Yellow River

IIn the wake of numerous dam failures and the resulting floods, the Huang He, the still unregulated 'Yellow River', once again changed its lower course on its way to the Yellow Sea. From the source in the Kunlun Mountains in the highlands of Tibet, the river flows through numerous canyons to Lanzhou, meets the Great Wall of China several times, passes through a loess plateau and reaches a wide plain before flowing into a wide delta into the sea. The Huang He is one of China's two rivers of fortune next to the Yangtze River. Its course was followed by the ancestors of the Chinese, who made the land arable and its valley was the historical ground of the development of ancient China.

After the terrible flood of 1855, the Yellow River was squeezed between 10m high dikes, which were unable to prevent flooding.

bank in China was founded here, paper money was issued for the first time and checks were introduced.

5 Xi'an The railway line follows the 500 km journey from Pingyao to Xi'an the Fen He Valley. In the densely populated loess area, fertile wheat and cotton fields are spread across both sides of the rails. The train crosses the dammed area of Huang He and travels through the fertile valley of Wei He to Xi'an, the capital of the Shaanxi Province. In recent decades the city has become the archaeological centre of China. No place is as connected to China's culture as old Chang'an ('Eternal Peace'), as Xi'an was known as the centre of eleven dynasties until the 10th century.

The historical evidence dates back to the Neolithic period. The old town is completely enclosed by a Ming city wall. In the historical core of the city, only the Muslim Hui section with its small-scale layout, the course of the streets and one or two story courtyard houses serve as a reminder of how the old town once stood. Xi'an's attractions include a number of temples, notably the Great and Small Wild Goose Pagoda, and the Provincial Museum.

A visit to the Terracotta Army of the first emperor of China, Qin Shi Huangdi is definitely worthwhile. It can be visited between Xi'an and Weinan (see pahe 289). His grave still remains unopened to this day – a huge mound of earth covers it.

6 Sanmenxia The train ride from Xi'an to the east passes many small towns and villages. In Sanmenxia the railwayline is very closely located to Huang He, where a trip up the river by boat is definitely worth doing. The journey to the nearby dam requires a little more time; It leads through an intensively used mountainous loess country.

7 Luoyang In the west of Henan province lies the ancient capital Luoyang, where it is most likely that paper was invented in the 1st century AD.10 km east of the city lies the oldest Buddhist temple in China from the year 66 BC - it was named after the white horse, which transported the scriptures on his back to the temples. 14 km south of the city, the Yi River breaks through the Longmen Mountains. This is where the 'caves of the 1000 Buddhas' were created in the 5th century: the 1352 caves hold more than 90,000 statues and 3600 inscriptions.

8 Yichang After travelling over 500 kilometers by train you will finally reach the city of Yichang. From here you can take the bus to the 185 metre high and over 2 km long Yangtze dam, which dammed the stream, creating the approximately 600 km long Three Gorges Dam. Right at the start of the three-day voyage up the river, the ship glides through the Three Gorges, Xi Ling Xia (73km), Wu Xia (40km) and Qutang Xia (8km). Hundreds of villages and towns have been flooded by the Yangtze River.

9 Chongqing The final stop of the cruise is in Chongqing. Due to its location it is also called 'the city of the mountains' (Schancheng). 30 million people live in the agglomeration. 110 km to the west lie the caves of Dazu, which are hailed as a treasure trove of the stonemasons because of their rich sculptural decoration. The journey then continues northwest by train to Chengdu.

10 Red Basin and Chengdu Sichuan, the 'land of the four streams,' is encircled on all sides by mountain ranges and is thereby protected from cold

north winds. In the subtropical climate, two to three harvests a year can be gathered. It is no wonder that the Red Basin, the 'heart of China,' is one of the most densely populated areas in the country.

After a more than 300 km journey, Chengdu, the capital and the industrial and economic center of Sichuan province, is reached. The city is still considered a 'green city', even though much has changed. There is a good 55 km between Chengdu and Dujiangyan (see page 290–921).

The journey by train will take you along the foothills of the meridonal mountain ranges of Qionglai towards Emei Shan.

11 Emei Shan and Leshan The bus takes you to the 3099 m high holy mountain Emei Shan, the destination of Buddhist pilgrims and Daoists. The ascent takes two days by foot. The path is lined with more than 60 temples and monasteries where you can spend the night. The journey continues by bus to Leshan which can be reached in less than an hour, where the rivers Minjiang and Dadu He merge.

The biggest attraction is the 71 metre tall Giant Buddha, which is best viewed as part of a boat trip on the Minjiang. The most adventurous section of the train journey begins in Emei Shan. Although the distance to Kunming is only about 500 km as the crow flies, by train the route is much longer. Large investments were needed for the construction of this elaborate railway line in the 1980s. Initially, the railway line follows a narrow,

China is a country where history and modernity lie close together: large cities like Chongqing, Chengdu (above) and Xi'an (above right), Buddhas in Leshan and Longmen (below right).

Today, only a third of its body of water reaches the estuary, because the withdrawals for drinking water supply, industry and agricultural irrigation lead in summer to the partial dehydration of the riverbed.

It gets its nickname from the masses of loess dust which gives it its yellow colour.

Detour

Emperor Qin Shi Huangdi's Terracotta Army

In 1974, when a farmer drilled a well some 40 km from Xi'an and found parts of a life-sized terracotta figure, the archaeological sensation was perfect: A clay army of almost 8,000 helmeted and armed warriors and horses from the 3rd cen-tury BC was found. At that time, Qin Shi Huangdi was the first emperor in China. He was buried near Xi'an, the former Chang'an and then capital of the country.

The excavations are still not complete as hundreds of archaeologists continue to dig there successfully for more treasures.

Originally, the terracotta warriors were colourfully painted.

Detour

Dujiangyan

Northwest of Chengdu, at the northern tip of a small river island, lies the Dragon Taming Taoist Temple. Legend has it that a wicked dragon lived on this exact point, causing the Minjiang River to overflow its banks again and again. The Governor of Sichuan Province, Li Bing, and his son Erlong succeeded in taming

deeply cut river valley with wide meanders. The train then overcomes several mountain ranges in numerous turns and a multitude of long tunnels and bridges. The line also crossed the Yangtse-king, which is called Hinsha Jiang ('gold sand river'). Finally, the train reaches an 1,800 to 2,000 metre high plateau with shallow pools and lakes and individual ridges. Here lies Kunming, the capital of Yunnan province.

⑫ Kunming 24 ethnic minorities that shape the streetscape of the 'City of Eternal Spring' live in the southwesternmost province of China. Above all,

they are encountered outside the city at the touristic focal points. In the south of the city, for example, this includes Dian Chi, the 'shimmering lake' which is about 2,040 m high, and is bordered by the western mountains. Those who take the trouble to climb to the Taoist temple of San Qing Ge at the summit can enjoy a great view.

The famous limestone forest of Shilin lies 120 km southast of Kunming. The pinnacles raised out of the limestone can be up to 35 metres high and are reminiscent of swords, lotus flowers, old men or graceful ladies.

The 220 km northwestern city of Yuanmoun can be reached by

the dragon in the 3rd century BC. Li Bing had an artificial island built in the river as a watershed and a dyke. He also built a weir. Thanks to this ingenious system, the Minjiang has not overflowed in the last 2200 years.

The old irrigation system is still used today.

train. From there, there is another 20 km to the bizarre natural landscape of the Earth Forest, whose colours and shapes are quite magical.

Two other popular destinations in Kunming are Dali and Lijiang. It is about 300 km to Dali, which can be reached by train, bus or plane.

⑬ Dali Once you have reached the 2,000 metre high city of Dali with its traditional houses, you will meet the members of the Bai tribe.

On the outskirts of the city lie the Three Pagodas (San Ta Si), whose highest measures 69 metres. They formed the centre of

a temple in the 9th century. A boat trip on the lake He Hai is usually connected with a visit to a Bai village.

Lijang lies another 200 km from Dali. The road runs parallel to the He Hai river and then through a mountain landscape.

⑭ Lijiang In Lijiang, the Naxi people still cultivate their traditions today. Due to the well-preserved beautiful old town of Dayan with its narrow streets and countless canals Lijiang was made a World Heritage Site by UNESCO in 1998.

The visit to the Dongba music performance in the evening should be on your itinery as well

as a hike to the 'pond of the Black Dragon'.

A trip the the 5,596 metre high 'Jade Dragon' snowy mountains, as well as a trip to the famous 'Tiger Leaping' gorge (Hutiao) are very worthwhile. deepest and longest gorges on earth.

**Large image: The Wuhua Tower of Dali towers over the city gates.
Above: The old town of Lijiang with its alleys and houses is considered one of the best preserved in China, especially the Black Drake pond park with the Shuocui Bridge is particularly beautiful. Left side: The Kunming Biji gate.**

270 million years ago, a karst mountain, the Shilin-Karst ('Stone Forest'), was created near a flat lake near Kunming.

Bottom left: The three pagodas of the Chongshen Monastery are located near the old town of Dali. They were built in between 822 to 859 AD. Left: The Xilang Gorge on the Yangtze River.

The Great Wall The 6700 km long structure is said to have been created in just 10 years. 300 000 workers built the world-famous fortress. Tourists can visit a restored section near Beijing.

Ying Xian The impressive pagoda of the Datong Monastery is one of China's most famous pagodas: a masterpiece of traditional carpentry.

Yangtze River China's richest river, the Yangtze Rive is about 6300 km long. Its source is in Tibet and it then flows through the northwest of Shanghai into the East China Sea.

The Terracotta Army in Xi'an The life-sized terracotta army consisting of 8,000 warriors and horses is one of the largest archaeological finds in the world.

Longmen Shiku The caves of 1,000 Buddhas (image) are located near Luoyang along with one of the oldest Buddhist temples in China.

Lijiang Parts of the well-preserved old town and its canals have been UNESCO World Heritage Sites since 1998. Here you can find numerous cosy restaurants and craft shops. Not far from the city, the Yangtze River has created one of the deepest and longest canyons on earth.

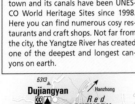

Leshan The 71 metre high and 24 metre wide statue is the second largest Buddha figure in the world.

Beijing China's capital is an exciting mix of tradition and modernity. Here is the view of the CCTV headquarters, the landmark of the business district.

Red Basin The subtropical climate in Sichuan allows for several annual harvests. The region is therefore one of the most densely populated in the country with the city of Chengdu as its centre.

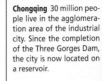

Chongqing 30 million people live in the agglomeration area of the industrial city. Since the completion of the Three Gorges Dam, the city is now located on a reservoir.

Yichang The main attraction near the village is the approximately 2 km long and more than 185 m high dam of the Yangtze River. It is a main element of the 600 km long Three Gorges Reservoir.

Dali (Xiaguan) The well-known Three Pagodas survived several earthquakes despite their height of up to 69 m. Also, the local houses of the people of the Bai are definitely worth seeing.

Shilin South of Kunming, visitors will find a natural wonder, Shilin, a karst rock forest. The bizarre rock formations reach heights of up to 35 metres.

Route 16: Nepal and Tibet

On the Road of Friendship across the Roof of the World

The path over the main crescent of the Himalayas easily makes it into our list of dream routes. After all, you cross part of the highest mountain range in the world, passing turquoise-coloured lakes and endless high steppe regions that are still traversed by nomads with yak, goat and sheep herds. Add monasteries perched on impossible bluffs and you've got an unforgettable journey. Our route begins in Kathmandu, meanders through central Nepal and ends in Lhasa on the Kodari Highway.

Route profile:

Length: approx. 900 km
(559 miles), excluding detours
Time required: 2–3 weeks

Foreigners have only been allowed to visit the previously sealed-off country of Nepal since 1950. Much has changed culturally since then, but fortunately the fascination that the country inspires has not. About a third of the country is taken up by the Himalayas, the highest point of which lies on the border to Tibet – Mount Everest, at 8,850 m (29,037 ft). Between the protective Mahabharat Range in the south and the mighty main crest of the Himalayas in the north lies the valley of Kathmandu, which contains the three ancient and royal cities of Kathmandu, Patan and Bhaktapur. Even in the age of the automobile the

spirit of times past is palpable in the capital, and Kathmandu continues to impress visitors with its royal palace and the hundreds of temples, statues and beautiful woodcarvings on the facades and monuments.
The second of the ancient royal cities, Patan, lies on the opposite shore of the Bagmati. Once again, a former royal palace and over fifty temples remind us of Nepal's glorious past. South-

east of Kathmandu lies Bhaktapur, where the alleys and streets are dominated by Newari wood-carvings. Before you start off from Bhaktapur towards Lhasa, it is worth undertaking a journey to Pokhara in the northwest, on the shore of the Phewasees at the bottom of the Annapurna Massif. Via Lumbini, the birthplace of Buddha, and Butwal the round trip leads you to Bharatpur, the gate to the

Royal Chitwan National Park, and eventually back to Bhaktapur.The Kodari Highway then brings you over the main ridge of the Himalayas into Tibet. Along this panoramic route you are constantly under the spell of 7,000 to 8,000-m-high (22,967 to 26,248-ft) mountains. In Tingri, for example, you finally experience Everest as an impressive single entity. The journey here can become arduous at

Top: The Tibetan plateau is the world's highest plateau. It exists more than over 50 millions of years. In the summer months lots of Tibetans, which still live as nomads, benefit from the lush high valley for their cattle.
Left: Up to the escape of the Dalai Lama the Potala Palace was domicile of the Tibetan government.

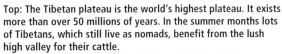

ples with pagodas, stupas and palaces. Lhasa, the 'Place of the Gods', lies at an elevation of 3,700 m (12,140 ft) and was chosen by Songsten Ganpo (620–49), the first Tibetan king, as his royal residence. Where today the famous red and white Potala Palace looks down on the city, Ganpo had built a fortification that later became Tibet's theocratic centre of power, including all pictorial works and national treasures – the icon of Tibetan religiosity.

times, as the highway leads over passes where the air is rather thin – over 5,000 m (16,405 ft) above sealevel on the Lalung-La Pass, for instance.

Tibet, 'The Land of Snow', has been closely linked to China since the 13th century. The current Tibet Autonomous Region (TAR) of China has an extremely low population density – roughly 2.5 million Tibetans, and 350,000 Chinese live on 1.2 million sq km (463,000 sq mil) of land. The Chinese dominate the economy, politics and government. Since the 9th century, Tibetans have followed Lamaism, a Tibetan variant of Buddhism whose religious and political head is the Dalai Lama.

The route through Gutsuo, Tingri, Lhaze, Yigaze, Gyangze and Nagarze into the city of Lhasa, which was once forbidden to foreigners, is lined by Lamaist monasteries – at least, the ones that weren't destroyed by the Chinese cultural revolution. Sakya is one of the oldest monasteries in Tibet and the 15th-century Buddhist monastery of Tashilhunpo has also been preserved – the latter contains a 26-m-high (85-ft) bronze Buddha. It is unlikely that anybody wouldn't be fascinated by the Kubum monastery in Gyangze, a monumental complex of tem-

Left side: The Shishapangma is the lowest of the Himalayan eight-thousanders (8027 meters) – ten of the 14 highest mountains in the world are located here. Left: The stupa in Boudhanath is 40 m (131 ft) high, the tallest in all of Nepal. Right: Mural painting in the Potala Palace in Lhasa.

The Tamang ethnic group living in a mountain village lost their home in the Langtang Valley during a landslide and had to be resettled.

The royal cities of Nepal

In the 3rd century, Indian Emperor Ashoka brought Buddhism to the Kathmandu Valley and had five stupas erected in what today is Patan.

From about 300 to 879 Lichchavi rulers from India dominated the Kathmandu Valley and for their part furthered the proliferation of Hinduism. The small principalities that developed between 879 and 1200, including Kathmandu, became centres of Buddhism.

The year 1220 marked the beginning of the Malla Dynasty, which reigned until 1768. Yaksha Malla (1428–82) bequeathed his kingdom to his

The Road of Friendship was built only twenty years ago, stretches 950 km (590 miles) and connects Nepal and Tibet. Apart from beautiful villages and monasteries that represent hundreds of years of history, it is the grandiose mountain scenery that so impresses travellers.

Durbar Square in Bhaktapur has a great variety of pagoda and shikhara-style temples.

three children who ended up falling out and founding their own royal cities: Kathmandu, Patan und Bhaktapur. For three hundred years they competed with each other by erecting increasingly elaborate buildings.

① Kathmandu (see sidebar right).

② Patan Over the years Patan (or Lalitpur), which has been famous for its metalworks for centuries, has almost completely melded with Kathmandu and is only separated from it by the Bagmati River. The Old Town here is particular worth visiting due to its royal palace. The more than fifty temples in Patan that are at least three storeys high were erected using either traditional wood or stone. The most important Shiva shrine is the five-storey Kumbeshvra Temple, not far from the 'Golden Temple'.

③ Bhaktapur Situated about 15 km (9.3 miles) from Kath-

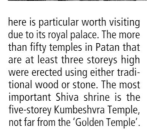

mandu, Bhaktapur was founded in the 12th century and life here still seems to flow at a mostly rural pace. The potters' market is full of locally produced goods and there are wood-carvers all around town. The main sights are at Durbar Square around the royal palace. The magnificently gilded Sundhoka Gate connects the two wings of the palace and simultaneously marks the entrance to the Taleju Temple, the main shrine within the palace.

④ Langtang National Park North of Kathmandu and Patan is Langtang National Park. The southern entrance near Dhunche is about six or seven hours away. The park, which covers an area of 1,710 sq km (660 sq mi), gets its name from the 7,245-m-high (23,771-ft) Langtang Lirung peak and runs from Dhunche to the Tibetan border. Luxurious pine, birch and rhododendron forests are home to musk deer, collar bears, small pandas, snow leopards, tahrs, and rhesus and langur monkeys. Starting from Kathmandu, a four-day trek leads you to the sacred lakes of Gosainkund via the monastery of Sing Gompa, which lies at an elevation of more than 4,400 m (14,436 ft).

Nepal's capital and its surroundings (above) were badly affected by an earthquake in May 2015. Large image: Langtang National Park.

With almost one million inhabitants, Kathmandu is Nepal's largest city. While national agencies and aid organizations are located in its newer part, the old town is characterised by numerous temples and traditional small shops.

Kathmandu

This ancient royal city at an elevation of 1,300 m (4,265 ft) is the centrepiece of the Kathmandu Valley. Its many palaces, temples and monasteries mirror the centuries-old traditions and history of the Nepalese kingdom. Even back in the 10th century this city, which is located at the confluence of the Bagmati and Vishnumati rivers, was an important marketplace that eventually developed into a religious, cultural and political centre competing with Patan and Bhaktapur ultimately to become the sole royal city. The Old Town presents the visitor with a plethora of streets and alleys where people, carts, bicycles, rickshaws and cars struggle to negotiate their way through the traffic. In the centre of the city is Durbar Square, which the Nepali call Hanuman Dhoka. Here there are Buddhist and Hindu temples and shrines as well as the old royal palace where Malla and Shah kings resided. The oldest parts developed in the 16th century include the great inner courtyard Nasal Chowk, or coronation court. In the centre of the Hanuman Dhoka is the Jagannath Temple, one of the most beautiful examples of Nepalese temple architecture. The Shiva Temple was built in 1690 and is flanked by two Vishnu temples and the Vishnu Parvati Temple. After the Hanuman Dhoka is the Basantapur, which has been taken over by souvenir sellers.

Some of the most startling buildings on the square are the nine-storey Basanthapur Pagoda, with beautiful wood-carvings, and the richly decorated palace of Kumari, a living goddess. Surrounding the old town are more UNESCO World Heritage Sites – about 5 km (3 miles) from the centre is the Boudhanath Stupa, the largest shrine of Tibetan Nepalese people; west of Kathmandu is the Swayambunath Stupa; and on the eastern edge of the city is the temple of Pashupatinath.

Annapurna Massif

The mountain massif north of Pokhara is one of the most popular walking and trekking areas of Nepal. The surrounding countryside is full of glorious variety and is easily accessible. In just three weeks you can circle the entire massif and get impressively near to most of the sixteen peaks of the range. The Annapurna stretches over 50 km (31 miles) between the rivers Kali Gandak and Marsyandi. Its main peaks include Annapurna I at 8,091 m (26,547 ft), Annapurna II at 7,937 m (26,041 ft), Annapurna III at 7,555 m (24,788 ft) and Annapurna IV at 7,525 m (24,690 ft). The first ascent of Annapurna I

Back in Kathmandu the serpentine drive takes you through mountain landscapes on a road of varying quality into Pokhara.

❺ Gorkha On your way back, you can make detour to the Gorkha valley just before you reach the town of Mugling. The drive passes through green rice plantations set in a fascinating mountain landscape on its way to the village of Gorkha at 1,000 m (3,300 ft), which is overlooked by a fortification from the 17th century. The giant mountains Dhaulagiri, Ganesh Himal and Manaslu present an overwhelming panorama. Ghorka has an important place

in Nepalese history. In 1768, King Prithvi Narayan Shah conquered Kathmandu from Gorkha, then proceeded to Patan and Bhaktapur, thereby laying the foundations for his royal dynasty.

❻ Pokhara Only on the last few kilometres to Pokhara does the road flatten out into a broad valley. Nepal's third-largest city lies at an elevation of 800 m (3,150 ft) on the shores of Lake Phewa. In stark contrast to the surrounding mountainscape, the subtropical climate here has produced ample vegetation. For many trekkers the city is the 'Gateway to the Himalaya'. From Pokhara you get a magnificent view of the central Himalayas, which are now only 30 km (18 miles) away. Peaks that you can see from here include Dhaulagiri at 8,167 m (26,796 ft), the Annapurna Massif and the sacred mountain of Machapuchare at 6,977 m (22,892 ft). The sights nearby include the dripstone cave at Batulechaur, the ravine of Seti and Devin's fall. The seven-storey fortification of Nuwakot arguably offers the most beautiful view of

was made in 1950 by a French expedition – three years before the first climbing of Everest. Three well-signposted routes make their way through the Annapurna region, partly overlapping as they go: the Muktinath Trail, the Mustang Trail (a continuation of the Muktinath) and the Annapurna Circle Trail. A shorter trail leads you to the Annapurna Shrine of the Gurung people who also live in these parts. It's an enormous moraine surrounded by peaks between 6,000 and 8,000 m (19,686 and 26,248 ft) where the Annapurna Base Camp is located.

The nature around the massif is protected by the Annapurna Conservation Area.

Dhaulagiri, Annapurna and Manaslu. The winding road to Lumbini leads down through a richly forested mountain landscape. After Butwal the scenery flattens out, giving way to rice fields and willows that come right up to the street.

7 Lumbini The birthplace of Siddharta Gautama, Buddha's birthname, is surprisingly off the beaten track. Excavations have been taking place in this previously forgotten place since the 1970s. Finds include Emperor Ashoka's column from the 3rd century, which was only discovered in the jungle in 1896, and the Maya Devi Temple, both grouped around a sacred pool of water in which Buddha's mother (Maya Devi) allegedly bathed shortly before his birth. To head for the Royal Chitwan National Park from here, drive back to Butwal and from there to Bharatpur.

8 Royal Chitwan National Park This large national park covers 932 sq km (360 sq mi) and is bordered by the Rapti, Reu and Narayanif rivers. The park is dominated by jungle and grasslands that are home to elephants, rhinos, Bengal tigers, leopards, gaurs, sloth bears, gavial crocodiles, freshwater dolphins and more than 400 types of birds. A variety of options for enjoying the park are available to visitors here – elephant safaris, rafting boat rides or guided tours.
The road back to Kathmandu leads through Bharatpur and Hetauda to Kathmandu.

9 Dolalghat The Chinese gave the beautiful Kodari Highway its nickname – 'The Friendship Road' – when they built it in 1967. The route connects Nepal with Tibet and travels 114 km (71 miles) from Bhaktapur via Dolalghat to the border town of Kodari. After a three-hour drive from Bhaktapur you arrive

at the village of Dolalghat by the Sun Kosi at a modest elevation of 643 m (2,110 ft). The village is situated at the junction where the Bhote Kosi and the Indrawati rivers form the Sun Kosi (Golden River), which flows to the west along the Mahabharat. Dolalghat is primarily known as a jumping-off point for white-water rafting trips on the Sun Kosi. Near Dolalghat a road leads to the Sagarmatha Nature Reserve. Once you have arrived in Kodari at 1,660 m (5,446 ft), the 'Friendship Bridge' takes you over the Bhote Kosi to Zhangmu. The route now follows Highway 318 all the way to Lhasa.

10 Nyalam On a clear day you get a magnificent view from Nyalam (4,100 m/13,452 ft) of the Xixabangma Feng at 8,012 m (26,287 ft) rising up to the west. All around the old town are typical flat-roof clay houses, makeshift shacks of the Chinese inhabitants.
The drive continues past snow-capped mountains 6,000–8,000 m (19,686–26,248 ft) high until you finally reach the Lalung-La Pass at 5,200 m (17,061 ft), which leads to the Tibetan plateau. Here you'll find the village of Gutsuo, which has accommodation and provisions as well as a small hospital.
Tingri is known for its fantastic view of Cho Oyu at 8,153 m (26,750 ft), Mount Everest at 8,850 m (29,037 ft), Lhotse I at 8,516 m (27,941 ft) and Makalu I at 8,463 m (27,767 ft). We recommend you head south from here towards Rongbuk Monastery.

11 Lhaze Beyond Tingri the road winds down to Lhaze at 4,030 m (13,222 ft), which has a hotel, restaurants, a gas station and a monastery. This village is right on the road that leads west of the sacred mountain of Kailash and is located in

Left side above: Dhaulagiri mountain peak at sunrise from Poon Hill view point.
Left side below: At Phewasee the inhabitants of the surrounding villages still practice traditional fishing.
Images from above: The Royal Chitwan National Park is an animal and plant paradise. Here live rhinos and tigers and yaks roam the valleys at Nyalam.

Edmund Hillary and Tenzing Norgay were the first to climb Mount Everest in 1953.

Detour

Sagarmatha National Park

Chomolungma, the 'Goddess Mother of the Earth', is what the Tibetans respectfully call the highest mountain on earth. Mount Everest, as the rest of the world knows it, peaks at 8,850 m (29,037 ft) above sea level on the border between Nepal and Tibet. The Nepalese refer to the mountain as Sagarmatha, 'King of the Heavens', and in 1976 a national park of the same name was established in the Khumbu Himal region.

From the northern edge of the national park, Sagarmatha leisurely watches over the neighbouring monoliths of Lhotse I (8,516 m/27,941 ft), Makalu I (8,463 m/27,767 ft), Cho Oyu (8,201 m/ 26,907 ft) and Nuptse

(7,879 m/25,851 ft), all surrounded by the 'Royal Court' of six-thousanders. This royal court is worshipped by locals as the residence of the gods. Enormous glaciers flow into deep valleys, the largest of which reside on the Lhotse, Khumbu, Imja, Ngozumba and Nangpa mountains. The entire national park covers an area of 1,243 sq km (770 sq mi) and the entrance is between the villages of Monjo at 2,845 m (9,334 ft) and Jorsale. From bottom to top the park spans an elevation difference of 6,000 m (19,680 ft). In October and November the park can get bitterly cold at night. Between December and February the temperatures reach a maximum of 5°C (41°F). From June to September you can expect daily monsoon rains and correspondingly bad views of the central ridge of the Himalaya. Flora and

fauna are extremely diverse due to the differences in altitude – below 3,500 m (11,484 ft) there are still pines or blue spruce trees, but above that, to the tree line at 4,500 m (14,765 ft), you find silver spruce, birch, junipers and rhododendron (in flower in April and May).

With a bit of luck you will run across not only the omnipresent yaks in the lower zones of the national park but also Himalaya

black bears, Himalaya tahrs, musk ox and the yellow-tailed pheasant, which is the Nepalese national bird. Further up are the very rare snow leopards.

The easiest way to reach the national park is by plane. Flights from Kathmandu to Lukla at 2,840 m (9,318 ft) last just 40 minutes and the two-day trek to Namche Bazar, the park offices, starts in Lukla and leads through the Dudh Kosi Valley, famous for

All 14 over 8000 m high mountains on Earth are located in Asia: ten of them in the Himalayas, four in the adjacent Karakorum.

its forests and rhododendrons. On the way you pass Nepalese villages like Phadking, inhabited by the indigenous Sherpas who originally immigrated in the 16th century from Eastern Tibet and have been cultivating barley, potatoes, spinach, radishes and onions ever since, in addition to working as porters for climbers. Since the first ascent of Everest by Edmund Hillary and legendary Sherpa Tenzing Norgay in 1953, trekking has almost become a national sport in the park. On the way into the Mount Everest Base Camp, Namche Bazar, at 3,446 m (11,306 ft) you'll notice that the air is already getting thinner. But it is from here that visitors can gaze upon Everest and Lhotse for the first time. The busy village is the starting point for all trekkers on their way to the Mount Everest Base Camp, and provides everything needed for the trip. An hour north of Namche Bazar the famous Mount Everest View Hotel boasts the highest landing strip in the world. The journey then continues through the Sherpa villages of Khumjung and Kunde. Definitely worth seeing on the way is the Tengpoche Monastery at 3,867 m (12,688 ft), where the famous Mani Rimdu dances take place every year in autumn.North of the Pangpoche Monastery trekkers cross the vegetation limit and the air gets unpleasantly thin. Many take an extended break in Periche (4,270 m/14,010 ft) to acclimatize before the trail continues with yak caravans up to Dhuka at 4,620 m (15,158 ft). The last stop before Base Camp is Gorakshep at 5,140 m (16,864 ft). Then comes Everest Base Camp at an elevation of 5,364 m (17,599 ft) after crossing the bizarre Khumbu Glacier.

Large image: View of Everest from Mount Makaku. Left side: A Dzo train transports firewood to the Everest region. Above left: Prayer flags all around Mount Everest. Above right: A Sherpa woman carries the luggage of a trekking group.

The Kumbum Stupa of the Pelkhor Monastery is the only surviving Tibetan relics shrine...

Detour

Rongbuk Monastery

Shortly before Shergar a road leads over the Pang-La Pass at 5,150 m (16,897 ft) toward the main ridge of the Himalaya.

It is a good 65 km (40 miles) from Tingri to the monastery, which is at the end of some pretty adventurous roads. At 5,151 m (16,900 ft) it is reputed to be the highest monastery in the world.

After more than 400 years of meditating in makeshift shelters, a proper monastery was finally built here in 1899. Rongbuk Lama, its founder, looked at the first climbers as heretics, but

Chorten at Rongbuk Monastery, Mount Everest.

provided them with food and drink. During the Chinese Cultural Revolution the monastery was largely destroyed, but starting in the 1990s it has been partly rebuilt and reinhabited by monks.

Whoever starts out for the Mount Everest Base Camp about 10 km (6 miles) away will be irresistably drawn to the magnificent view of the bizarre Rombuk Glacier and the north wall of Everest. Due to the 'passing trade' to the base camp, the monastery now offers a hostelry and a shop.

a fertile valley whose green fields provide colourful contrast to the arid Tibetan plateau.

12 Sa'gya The fortified monastery of Sakya was founded in 1073 and was the original monastery of the Sakya Order. Of the original 108 chapels in the north wing, only one is left today. A white stupa stands nearby on the mountain's edge. The southern monastery is enclosed by mighty walls with four watchtowers, as the Sakya dynasty had to defend itself against many enemies.

Heading to Xigaze you cross the Tso-La Pass at 4,500 m (14,765 ft) where you have a good view of Everest on a clear day.

13 Xigazê After the devastation of the Cultural Revolution, only the foundations of the once impressive fortifications of the Tsang Dynasty kings (16th/17th century) are left. Today the main sight in Xigaze, former capital of Tibet, is the Tashilhunpo Monastery, home of the Panchen Lama that once housed 6,000 monks. Founded by the first Dalai Lama in 1447, the complex at the bottom of the Drölma consists of red and ochre-coloured buildings whose gilded roofs glimmer from afar.

14 Gyangzê This small town at 4,070 m (13,354 ft) on the north shore of Nyangchu still gives a traditional Tibet impression with its white facades and colourful eaves, windows and door frames. Towering over the city is an impressive Dzhong (fortification) from 1268, which offers a splendid view of the walled monastery city of Pälkhor Chode (15th century). The extensive grounds are dominated by octagonal Kumbum Chorten and the Nepalese-influenced stupa is a magnificent example of Tibetan architecture.

From Gyangzee to Lhasa the road leads past little villages through fertile valleys where yaks graze at leisure. Then you must traverse the Karo-La Pass at 5,045 m (29,906 ft). The landscape is of overwhelming beauty here. On the way you'll see

... It contains 108 small chapels and 27529 depictions of deities in its interior.

Detour

The Gonggar and Samye monasteries

About 70 km (43.5 miles) south of Lhasa is the Gonggar Monastery, which was founded in 1464 and was one of the centres of the Sakyapa school. There used to be about 160 monks living here. Today there are about thirty. During the Chinese Cultural Revolution large parts of the monastery were destroyed. Only the main temple remained untouched. Especially worth seeing are the murals of Khyentse Chenmo, which depict scenes from the life of Buddha, tantric deities and personalities from the Sakyapa School. The Samye Monastery is 30 km

Der Utse-Tempel im Kloster Samye

(20 miles) north-west of Zetang on the northern shore of Yarlung Zangbo Jiang and is reachable by ferry and bus from Zetang. Situated on a steppe landscape, it is the oldest monastery in the whole of Tibet (c. 770). The architect's concept of the monastery was an image of the universe – the three-storey gilded main temple was a symbol of the cosmic world mountain, Meru; around it are twelve temples that picture four continents with their subcontinents; and two smaller shrines to the north and south of it represent the sun and the moon.

along the shore for several kilometres passing grazing horses, yaks and goats.

A visit to castle ruins and the 13th-century Samding Monastery is worthwhile. The way to Quxu leads over the Kampa-La Pass at 4,898 m (16,070 ft), then it is just 20 km (12 miles) into the valley.

16 Quxu The bridge over the Yarlung was opened in the mid 1970s and provides a connection between western and eastern Tibet. The place itself is a good starting point for trips to the monasteries of Gonggar and Samye to the east. North of Quxu is the region of Nethang, which houses the monastery of the same name founded by Atisha (982–1054), an Indian Bud-

the Karo-La glacier, stunning waterfalls and mountain streams. You then descend the serpentine pass via Lungmar to Ralung with its monastery dating from 1180 and continue on to Nagarze.

15 Nagarzê The village of Nagarze at 4,200 m (13,780 ft) sits between the snow-covered Noijin Kangsang at 7,100 m (23,295 ft) and the sacred lake of Yandrok Tso, one of the biggest and most beautiful lakes in central Tibet. The street runs

When Buddhism spread in Tibet in the 7th century, the monasteries (large image: Pelkhor, right side top: Tashilhunpo, including: Sakya) first emerged as abodes for monks in the rainy season. Left side: The fortress overlooks the city of Gyangzê.

Detour

Sera and Ganden

The Sera Monastery is situated in a rocky environment about 4 km (2.5 miles) north of Lhasa.

As early as around 1770 there were roughly 2,850 monks living here and at the beginning of the 20th century there were 6,600. Today, after the trials of the Chinese Cultural Revolution, about 300 have returned – a success

in itself. Sera has always been a centre of monastic education in Tibet along with Drepung and Ganden. The Ganden Monastery is about 45 km (28 miles) east of Lhasa on the road to Sichuan. It was founded three years be-

dhist. Now we head back to the Tibetan capital through the Lhasa Valley.

⑰ Drepung About 10 km (6 miles) north of Lhasa is a monastery dating from 1416 that used to be the biggest in Tibet with 10,000 monks. As the religious and political centre of the Gelugpa School (yellow-cap sect) its abbots were decision-makers in religious as well as political matters.
Before the Potala became their residence it even housed the first five Dalai Lamas. Despite the destruction by the Chinese Red Guards, the main buildings of the monastery have remained unharmed, including Ganden Palace, the four theological faculties and the great congregation hall. Today some 600 monks are living here again.

⑱ Lhasa The capital of the Tibet Autonomous Region lies on the Lhasa River (Kyichu) at an elevation of 3,658 m (12,002 ft) and was founded in the 7th century. Originally the residence of the Tibetan kings (7th–9th centuries) it became the seat of government of Lamaistic theocracy under Dalai Lama rule. For centuries Lhasa was a 'forbidden city' to foreigners. It even closed its doors to Sven Hedin, the famous explorer of Asia.
In the heart of the old town you'll find the two-storey Jokhang Temple from the 7th century, the oldest Buddhist monastery in Tibet and akin to a national shrine. All roads in Lhasa therefore lead to the Jokhang temple, which is also once again home to monks.
Nearly as old as the Jokhang is the Ramoche Temple with fortified walls, which goes back to the times of the Chinese princess

Wencheng. Unfortunately, the Red Guards destroyed or stole many of the statues here during the Cultural Revolution.
Many associate Lhasa with the Potala Palace towering impressively over the city with its thirteen storeys (110 m/361 ft). Its facade alone is 360 m (1,181 ft) long and it reputedly houses 999 rooms with 130,000 sq m (1,399,308 sq ft) of living quarters. The part of the palace painted white houses administration and storage space while the red part was the residence of the Dalai Lama up to his flight in 1959. Since then the palace is only has been used as a museum.
Opposite the Potala is the cave temple Drolha Lubuk with depictions of Buddhist deities that reputedly created themselves. The summer palace of the Dalai Lama, Norbulingka, is also in the west of the city and was built on

an even larger scale. On the northern edge of the city is the monastery of Sera, and on the road to Sichuan (a good 45 km/30 miles east of Lhasa) is the monastery of Ganden.

Large image: Potala Palace. Above left: In Jokhang Monastery there is a walkway with prayer wheels. Above: Bodhisattva figures in Drepung Monastery.

fore Sera by Tsonkhapa and later became the centre of the Galupa School, which asserted itself in the whole of Tibet from the 17th century. Of the original 200 buildings, only fifty have been restored. In the centre of the monastery is the tomb of the founder and his relics are kept in a chorten.

The red Ganden monastery stands out clearly.

Lake Phewa Fishing, rowing, and swimming – this lake leaves no wishes unfulfilled, and you have a view of Annapurna.

Kathmandu In the 'City of the Gods' it is mainly Durbar Square, a colorful bazaar surounded by wood and brick buildings, that is well worth a visit.

Patan Patan The Bagmati River separates this mainly Buddhist-inhabited city from its neighbour, Kathmandu. Patan's old town has countless workshops to visit, as well as the Mahabuddha Bahal temple and Jawalakhel, a part of town that is inhabited by Tibetan refugees.

Lhasa The 'Red Palace' of the Potala was commissioned by the fifth Dalai Lama in the 17th century. The white buildings were added in the 19th century. The palace has some 999 rooms and thirteen storeys. Since the occupation of Tibet by China and the flight of the Dalai Lama, the palace is used only as a museum.

Royal Chitwan National Park This park can be explored on the back of an elephant or in a rafting boat. It is known for its 400 rhinoceroses as well as tigers, gavial crocodiles, leopards and buffalo.

Annapurna Massif The tenth highest peak in the world was first ascended in 1950. It is surrounded by mountains that often seem higher than the peak that gives the region its name. Especially outstanding is the sacred, and thus unconquered, Machapuchare.

Bhaktapur Time seems to have stood still in this beautifully restored town situated at the east end of the Kathmandu Valley. Highlights include the Dattatraya Square and the temple pagodas on Taumadhi Square.

Sera Elaborate religious ceremonies are still held in this former monastery and university village on the edge of Lhasa.

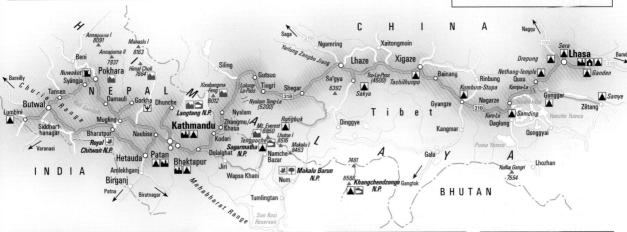

Mount Everest At 8,850 m (29,037 ft) this is the highest mountain in the world, and is locally known as Chomolungma or Sagarmatha. The first successful ascent was in 1953 by Edmund Hillary and Sherpa Tenzing Norgay.

Sakya-Kloster 'Grey Earth' – such is the name of a monastery near Xigaze in South Tibet of the red-cap sect, a branch of Tibetan Buddhism founded in 1073. Until 1354 its leaders were the landlords of Tibet.

Xigazè Tibet's second-largest city is home to a the 15th-century monastery. The Panchen Lama residence survived the Cultural Revolution.

Gyangze Gyangze This village south-west of Lhasa has a monastery worth visiting (Pälkhör Chode). The Kumbum Stupa is considered Tibet's most beautiful sanctum.

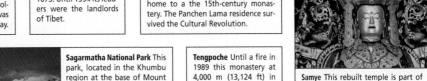

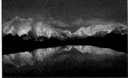

Lumbini Siddharta Gautama – aka Buddha – was born here in southern Nepal in the 6th century BC. Visit the sacred garden and the Maya Devi Temple.

Sagarmatha National Park This park, located in the Khumbu region at the base of Mount Everest, is home to a variety of rare animals like the black bear, snow leopard and musk deer.

Tengpoche Until a fire in 1989 this monastery at 4,000 m (13,124 ft) in the Khumbu Valley was the largest in the region. It is still well worth seeing.

Samye This rebuilt temple is part of the oldest Tibetan monastery. It was built around 770 and is situated in the mountains on the north shore of Yarlung Zangbo Jiang.

Rajasthan and the 'Golden Triangle'

Rajasthan means 'Land of the Kings', yet many villages in this region of India live in extreme poverty. Exploring the land of the Rajputs, you very quickly realize one irony about this 'desert state' – there is a lot more green than you might think. And where else does India dazzle with such vivid colours and magnificent palaces as in Rajasthan?

Route profile:

Length: approx. 3,200 km
(1,988 miles), excluding detours
Time required: 4–6 weeks
When to go: The best time to visit
Rajasthan is from October to March
when the weather is milder and
many festivals take place.

Due to Rajasthan's size and diversity, it can be difficult to decide what to do first after arriving in Delhi. Despite being the capital of the state, the glorious Maharaja city of Jaipur is not always the first stop. Instead, many visitors are initially, and naturally, drawn to the Mughal city of Agra in the state of Uttar Pradesh, which makes up the other corner of India's 'Golden Triangle' (Delhi-Agra-Jaipur). After all, it is the home of the immediately recognizable Taj Mahal, the white marble mausoleum built by

Mughal Emperor Shah Jahan for his favourite wife Mumtaz Mahal. The Islamic building has ironically become the most visible icon of India despite Hinduism being the dominant religious and ethnic identity factor in this culturally multifarious country. About eighty-two per cent of the people living in India are Hindus – the rest are a mix of Muslims, Christians, Sikhs, Buddhists and Jains. Continuing westwards to Jaipur, now the capital of the whole of Rajasthan and barely four hours away from Delhi on the new motorway, you pass through Mathura, the legendary birthplace of the god Krishna and a holy pilgrimage destination for Hindus. Again, though, one is struck by the number of large mosques here. You will see this type of religious coexistence almost everywhere in Raj-asthan, not just in the so-called 'Golden Triangle'. The mighty walls of the

Maharaja's fort bear witness to the centuries of power struggles between the Rajput dynasties and the Mughal emperors.
Part of the legacy of the Rajputs are their former hunting grounds, which are now some of India's most beautiful national parks and reserves. East of the long Aravalli Range near Bharatpur, for example, are three fabulous ones

– Keoladeo Ghana, Sariska and Ranthambore. In the latter two it is possible to witness tigers in the wild, especially in the 400-sq-km (154-sq-mi) Ranthambore National Park.
West of the Aravalli is the semi-arid Thar Desert, which extends far into Pakistan. Former caravan routes through the Thar have become tourist tracks in re-

Top: The Taj Mahal: a monumental marble grave built by Shah Jahan on the Yamuna River in Agra not far from the 'Red Fort'. The mausoleum took twenty-two years to complete and houses the sarcophagus of the Mughal emperor's favourite wife, Mumtaz Mahal, who died giving birth to their fourteenth child in 1631. His own sarcophagus followed in 1666. Left: The Ganesh Pol in Fort Amber feature elaborate paintings.

cent decades. The camel safaris to the sand dunes around Jaisalmer and Bikaner are a whole new riding experience and visits to desert villages, carpet weavers and potters are interesting. The indigenous population of this region, the Bishnoi, have been carefully cultivating native flora and fauna for 600 years. Rajasthan is not all rustic – the engineering feat of the century, the Indira Ghandi Canal, brings water from the Himalayas and the Punjab into the Thar. Stony desert soil becomes farmland and the desert shrinks. Modernity has also changed transportation – instead of running on a narrow gauge, trains are now rolling into the desert on standard Indian gauge. Looking for remnants of the magic of 'a thousand and one nights'? You'll find it in more than a few places – Rajasthan tempts visitors with bazaars, temples and palaces

from Alwar to Jaipur, from Udaipur to Jodhpur, from Bikaner into the Shekhawati land of 'painted cities'.Rajasthan also provided the model for Heritage Hotels, which are now all over India but nowhere as prevalent as in Rajasthan. Heritage Hotels are opulent palaces, glamorous merchants' houses (havelis) or

relaxing country houses that have been turned into hotels by their owners. In some of them, royal personages stay under the same roof as normal hotel guests. From a comfortable bed to extreme luxury, every taste is catered for at Heritage Hotels – again a piece of 'a thousand and one nights' in Rajasthan.

Left side: In rickshaws Delhi can be explored in a comfortable way (at least for the passenger). Above: The tomb of Salem Chisthi is an architectural jewel.

215

Keoladeo Ghana National Park

About 100 years ago, Maharajas irrigated the bushland south of Bharatpur using dams and canals in order to attract birds, which

Detour

Gwalior

Gwalior is situated on the northern edge of the Vindhya Mountains in the state of Madhya Pradesh.
Its fame comes mostly from two things – the truly enormous fort that dominates the city from a high plateau and the colossal Jain sculptures that reach 17 m (56 ft) and are hewn into the fortified mountain. Embattled for centuries, this city with over a million inhabitants is proud of its heroes, singers and po-

The mighty walls of Man Singh's Gwalior Fort.

The Jain sculptures represent teachers and saviors.

ets. Hunting trophies and curiosities are shown in the Jaivilas Palace of the Scindia Maharajas, but parks and temples are also worth a visit. During the uprising against colonial rule in 1857 the Maharaja sided with the British, but his troops rebelled and fought against them, led by the much admired Rani (princess) Lakshmi Bai of Jhansi, who died weapon in hand.

Opulent columned halls, defiant fortifications, tombs of Muslim saints and Indian Maharajas – the first stops on your journey to India offer some of the greatest architectural sights this ancient land has to offer. The state of Rajasthan, which is roughly the size of Germany, awaits you with magnificent fortresses, decadent palaces and the unique landscape of the Thar Desert.

❶ Delhi (see pp. 218–219). From Delhi our journey leads us in two or three hours on mainly good roads to Agra, the former capital of the Mughal emperors. Roughly 150 km (93 miles) south of Agra, a town called Mathura is a worthy stop on our route.

❷ Mathura East of Mathura's town centre you'll see the broad Yamuna River lined with ghats (steps) and cobblestone streets. It is a pilgrimage destination for hundreds of thousands of Hindus. The reason for this ist that Mathura is the birthplace of Krishna, and therefore one of the holiest cities in India. Apart from Ganesha, the son of Shiva who provides success and wealth, Hindus worship virtually no other god more than the flute-playing Krishna. Mathura's many temples were destroyed by Muslim conquerors, in particular Mahmud of Ghazni in 1018. Sculptures from the school of Mathura dating back to around 100 AD are of remarkable quality and depict gods and 'Yakshis' – semi-divine beings. They are on display in the Archaeological Museum of Mathura.

❸ Agra For quite a long time this city was chosen by the Mughal emperors as their capital, which makes the number of extravagant buildings hardly surprising. The Taj Mahal, which Shah Jahan built as a tomb for his favourite wife, Mumtaz Mahal, is known as one of the most

beautiful buildings on earth. Also well worth a visit here is of course the Red Fort, the two tombs Chinika Rauza and the slightly older Itmad-du-Daulah (a finance minister had them erected during his lifetime). The miniature example of the latter may have inspired the architect of the Taj Mahal.

Only 37 km (23 miles) to the south-west of Agra we find the ruins of another Mughal capital, albeit a shorter-lived one.

❹ Fatehpur Sikri Akbar the Great was one of the most successful among a succession of very successful Mughal rulers.

His reign lasted from 1556–1605 and his influence helped extend the empire throughout most of India.
For years Akbar waited in vain for the birth of an heir, and it was only after a pilgrimage to the Muslim saint Shaik Salim Chisti that his wife bore him a son. Out of gratitude for this gift and due

were subsequently shot in their thousands by Anglo-Indian hunting parties. In 1983 the area was declared a national park covering 29 sq km (18 sq mi). It is home to more than 370 bird species, among them the Siberian Crane.

The best time to visit the park is during the months of October to March.

In addition to storks (far left) monkeys (left) also live in the national park..

to his victories over the Rajputs, Akbar had a new residence built on the spot where Shaik Salim Chisti had prophesied him a son – Fatehpur Sikri, the 'City of Victory'.

Built on a waterless plateau above the plains west of Agra, this city was abandoned soon after it was built. It remains nearly fully intact and is a place of particular fascination to this day.

An hour from Agra you suddenly find yourself behind an enormous gate in the halls of an abandoned palace and in courts surrounded by columns. Individual marble structures are embedded like jewels into the sumptuous red sandstone architecture.

Pilgrims stream to the domed tomb of Shaik Salim Chisti, decorated with exquisite stone carvings. Children squat in the shadow of the mosque with their books and their teachers. Tourists admire the reception hall where Akbar discussed the possibility of a common religion ('Din-I-Ilahi') with the representatives of different faiths within his empire.

A trip to the Keoladeo Ghana National Park is well worth it for nature lovers and it is not too far from Bharatpur. In Bharatpur a street turns off in the direction of Dig to the north and from there it is 80km (50 miles) to Alwar via the town of Nagar.

⑤ Alwar Set into the rocky Aravalli Mountains, Alwar is an old trading centre with a royal palace and relatively few foreign visitors. Agra, Jaipur and the nearby national parks provide more of a draw for tourists than the ancient royal residence of Alwar, a town that received mention in India's great Mahabharata Epic from the 2nd century BC. All of this makes the city and the Rajput palace and gardens even more authentic.

Oddly, many of the palace's rooms serve the banal purpose of storing government files, which are stacked to the ceiling in places.

Only the fifth floor has a museum with some of the hunting trophies, silver tables, metre-long scrolls and works of the Bundi school of painting.

⑥ Sariska National Park This reserve covers an area of about 800 sq km (308 sq mi) roughly 37 km (23 miles) south of Alwar, and was made a national park in 1979 with a focus on conserving the tiger. There is plenty of space for the tigers to live peacefully in the jungle here – they are actually rather afraid of people.

Failing a tiger sighting, you may catch a glimpse of beautifully spotted Chital deer, Chowsingha antelope, hyenas, a pack of wild boar or very likely a pack of rhesus monkeys.

There are also Mughal forts and temples both within and around the park.

Take Highway 8 via Shahpura 100 km (62 miles) to Jaipur where you will be greeted first by magnificent Fort Amber.

⑦ Jaipur This old town, also known as the 'Pink City' for the colour of its facades, was planned on a nine-part rectangular grid in 1727 – very rational and geometric town planning. At the same time, the nine old-town quarters of Jaipur symbolize the Brahmin Hindu cosmos. The open-air observatory Jantar Mantar at the palace also fits in well with this cosmic association and is one of the main attractions here. You can even walk on some of its 'instruments', which are made of brick. Jaipur, which is the western point of the 'Golden Triangle' (Delhi-Agra-Jaipur), is home to over two million people and is thus the only town with over a million inhabitants in Rajasthan. To this day the city is full of palaces. The first Maharaja of Rajasthan to convert Rambagh, his summer palace, into a hotel was Sawai Man Singh II in 1957. Since then his aristocratic brethren all over India seem to have adopted the 'Palace and Heritage Tourism' concept. Jaipur is also a centre for jewellery, jewels, precious inlaid marble and all sorts of other arts and crafts.

Large image: Jami Masjid Mosque. Left side: Akshardham Temple in Delhi, the world's largest Hindu temple. Above: Taj Mahal.

The gate of the Red Fort. The fortification is surrounded by a sandstone wall and is almost a kilometre long and over 500 m (1,640 ft) wide.

A UNESCO World Heritage Site – Mughal Emperor Humayun's tomb from around 1570.

Delhi

Delhi has always been an important strategic town on the north Indian plain. Approximately as old as Rome, over the centuries this city was made the capital of many an empire. Since the end of British colonial rule in 1947, Delhi is the political centre of the Republic of India.

With its crowded bazaars, countless rickshaws and rumbling overcrowded buses, no traveller to Delhi would ever doubt that the population here has increased dramatically over the last century to its present 14 million. Indeed, Delhi has many faces. One leftover from colonial rule is the expansive capital of India, New Delhi. Its broad avenues are home to ministries, the parliament, the presidential palace and magnificent muse-

The Jama Masjid Mosque.

ums, all of which form the centre of power for the apparatus of government. Edwin Lutyens and Herbert Baker designed the circle of arcades that is Connaught Place in the heart of New Delhi in the first part of the 20th century. The circles and 'spokes' around it form Connaught Circus. High-rise buildings from the last two decades tower over this attractive shopping and commercial area. Lutyens and Baker created New Delhi in a style that mixed neo classicism with Indian Palatial. Old Delhi, the old town, with its bazaars, temples and many mosques, is focused between the Yamuna River and the rail lines and has grown massively over centuries. Even if you have little time to spend in Delhi, we highly recommend a wander through the street bazaars of Chandni Chowk to experience the hustle and bustle of sellers, carts, cows and children – it certainly eclipses any department store adventure. The two main

monuments of Old Delhi are quite close to one another. The first is the Jama Masjid (Friday Mosque), India's largest, with a minaret that you can climb. The 'Mosque with a View of the World' – its original name – was commissioned by Shah Jahan, grandson of the great Akbar. By no coincidence, he was also responsible for Old Delhi's other feature attraction, a fortification and palace for the great Mughal rulers, the Red Fort. The Persians

The Red Fort.

stole the legendary 'Peacock Throne' from its imperial halls and other conquerors removed the inlaid jewels from the columns and walls. Despite these thefts, a wide variety of art works from all the great epochs of Indian art can be found in Delhi. The National Museum displays great sculptures and miniatures, and nowhere else can you find as much contemporary Indian art and traditional arts and crafts as in Delhi. The Craft Museum is a good example, located in a village complex near the ruins of Purana Quila – said to be the location of Delhi's oldest city, Indraprashta. Basically, it's all here – numerous museums and parks, fine dining, luxurious shopping, theatres and cinemas.

Almost three million people a year also visit another temple, this one designed in the shape of a lotus flower with twenty-seven marble leaves: the Bahai House of Worship.

The Jains

Much like the Hindus, the faith of the Jains theoretically leads them through a series of reincarnations to 'Moksha', which is a sort of liberation from earthly existence. The Jains worship the 'Tirthankaras', the twenty-four forerunners, as their teachers, the last of which was Mahavira who lived in the 6th century BC. Apart from 'Ahimsa' (peacefulness), Jains also preach 'Asteya' (not taking from others), 'Brahmacharya' (moderation as far as food, drink and sexuality are concerned) and 'Aparigraha' (inner distance from worldly possessions).

8 Ajmer A defiant fortress built upon a stark rocky plateau overlooking a walled city, the model for many cities in this area where for centuries it was necessary to defend against the repeated attacks of ambitious conquerors. At Fort Taragarh in Ajmer, there is not much left of the often 4-m-thick (13-ft) walls built by a Hindu ruler some 900 years ago. But Ajmer presents itself as a lively, pulsating city in many respects. It is home to many schools and universities and a pilgrimage destination for pious Muslims and Jains. In fact, about a quarter of the more than 400,000 inhabitants are Jains. Following the example of British public schools, the still highly regarded Mayo College in Ajmer was founded in 1873 for the sons of the Rajputs.

The Dargah Sharif Mosque Centre is even older and was developed around the tomb of Khwaja Moinuddin Chisti, who was a friend of the poor. In memory of his works, two enormous iron vats of food are still provided for the needy at the entrance to the holy district. Even Emperor Akbar made a pilgrimage to Ajmer.

A more recent building that is worth a visit is the Nasiyan Temple from 1864, built by the Jains. A two-storey hall fantastically depicts the heavenly cosmos of the Jains, including golden temples and the airships of the gods. About 11 km (7 miles) from Ajmer you'll come to Pushkar.

9 Pushkar The name Pushkar means 'lotus blossom'. But in this case we are not talking about just any lotus blossom. It is the one that Brahma allegedly dropped to the floor to create Pushkar Lake. That is why the little town of Pushkar with its 15,000 inhabitants is one of the holiest sites in India. Half surrounded by mountains, this little town with tidy white houses and the fresh green fauna of a nearby oasis possesses a majestic beauty. Unfortunately, it has been so overrun by tourism in the last few years that Pushkar's priests, beggars and numerous self-appointed Sadhus ('holy men') have developed a business sense to accompany their piety. They constantly invite travellers to the 'Puja', the washing ceremony, which takes place at the fifty-two ghats, the steps down to the lake. Then without delay they demand payment with rupees or, even better, dollars. The 'Little Varansi' at Pushkar Lake is therefore best visited in the morning – the temples open early. The view from the hill with the Savitri Temple, dedicated to Brahma's wife, is especially beautiful. It can be reached after a good half-hour hike. From Pushkar you'll need a day of driving through winding mountain landscapes to get to Ranakpur. On the way, you'll be tempted to take a detour to one of the biggest forts in Rajasthan – the 15th-century Fort Kumbhalgarh. The 36-km (22-mile) wall around the perimeter of this fort is said to be second only to the Great Wall of China in length and protects a total of 360 temples – 300 Jains and the rest Buddhist. You get a splendid view of the Aravalli Mountains from atop the wall.

10 Ranakpur Completely different from Pushkar, this holy temple town of the Jains typically allows you to enjoy its treas-

Each one of the 1444 columns in the Jain Temple of Ranakpur has been decorated differently.

low is a city of 75,000 inhabitants founded in the 8th century and once the capital of Mewar. The steep walls of the rocky plateau rise to 150 m (492 ft), but despite its formidable gates and walls it was still conquered three times by Mughal armies. Each of these invasions culminated in a 'Jauhar' by the women and children – the heroic ritual of collective suicide by throwing themselves onto burning pyres. The men then committed 'Saka': battling to their last breath. Dozens of sprawling palace and temple ruins, a narrow 15th-century 'victory' tower, which you can climb, and some pavilions and ponds are all that is left of the glory and decline of this medieval residence. Back in Udaipur the journey continues via Som straight through the Aravalli Mountains to the north-west in

ures in peace and quiet. It is set back from any larger neighbours in a forested valley with family farms, two reservoirs and a handful of hotels. One of these is the Maharani Bagh Orchard Retreat, a former fruit garden and picknicking spot of the Maharaja of Jodhpur. It is just an hour's walk from the Jain temples and the pilgrim hostels. Before climbing the steps to the temples you will be required to remove anything you have that is made of leather or other animal products. The four temples here date from the 15th and 16th centuries. Three of them are dedicated to the 'forerunners' Adinath, Parsvanatha and Neminath, and the fourth is dedicated to the Sun god Surya. Take a look at the unique stonework on the hundreds of columns and domed prayer halls. Flowers are placed before the pictures of Jain saints and music echoes through the rooms.

It is now a good 80 km (50 miles) to Udaipur, the biggest city in the south of Rajasthan.

⓫ **Udaipur** Also known as the 'Queen of the Lakes', Udaipur is considered by many to be the

most beautiful city in Rajasthan. Today it has 400,000 inhabitants, and from its founding in the year 1568 it was constantly under the rule of the Sisodia Maharanas until Indian independence in 1947. The title Maharana ('Great King') is equivalent to Maharajah. In the old realm of Mewar, the Sisodias took the top position in the royal hierarchy of India, and their influence is still felt today. Nearly 500 years ago they were responsible for many of the reservoirs and artificial lakes that were built in the area. In the midst of the most beautiful of these, Lake Pichola, summer palaces were built on two islands opposite the mighty towering complex of the city palace. The bigger of the two island palaces became world famous as the Lake Palace Hotel. The list of celebrated guests is endless. The nightly spectacle of the lake bathed in lights is best enjoyed from one of the roof terrace restaurants in the old town.

Parks like the 'Garden of the Ladies of Honour' (Saheliyon ki Bari) contribute not only to the charm of Udaipur when the lotus ponds and roses are in bloom, but also reveal the artistic sense and

craftsmanship present here. Behind the city palace and in the small side streets are countless studios and shops where you can witness hundreds of indigenous artists and craftsmen that still specialize in the miniature paintings of the old academies and the skilled carpet weaving of the region.

⓬ **Chittaurgarh** even mighty gates once secured the ascent to the plateau over the Berach River 100 km (60 miles) to the east of Udaipur. On the plain be-

the direction of Abu Road. When the heat begins to hit the plains in April, the hotels in Rajasthan's 'hill station' Mount Abu begin to fill up. Close to the border to Gujarat, Abu Road winds its way to 1,200 m (3,937 ft) where you can live comfortably in this mountain village (20,000 inhabitants) even in the summer.

Large image: Udaipur.
Left side: Antiques can be purchased in small shops in Udaipur. Above: Pushkar.

Desert fortresses

There is hardly a city in the Thar Desert that doesn't have an accompanying fort. Peaceful times were rare in this wild region all the way up until the 19th centu-ry, and protective walls were a necessity. Some fans of Rajasthan travel exclusively from fort to fort, inspecting the wooden gates crowned by iron spikes and reinforced with iron bands, climbing steep steps and marvel-ling at the collections of weapons and opulent chambers.

Khimsar, one of the most romantic forts, lies by the side of a small road between Jodhpur and Nagaur south of Bikaner. It was restored by its owners and not

The Thar Desert

The only great desert on the subcontinent stretches from the foothills of the Aravalli Mountains to the Indian-Pakistani border to the Indu Valley, and occupies nearly half of Rajasthan, an area of 250,000 sq km (155,000 sq mi). But the Thar Desert is not like the Sahara desert. Sand dunes without vegetation are only found in small areas to the west and south of Jaisalmer. Geologists consider it a semi-arid region. The journey from Jodhpur to Jaisalmer and from Jaisalmer to Bikaner takes hours. You'll see sand swirling in the hot wind, green, withered, thorny acacia bushes on the horizon, and maybe a tree, but only few villages.But the Thar is not devoid of human life. Women by the side of the road balance all manner of supplies on their heads as they walk along the road – water jugs, or sand and stones for a building site. And they wear brightly coloured dresses threaded with silver. Adolescents herd their goats and men drive colourfully painted trucks over the sandy road or journey on camels with turbans of yellow or red. If you take the time for a detour from Highway 15, ideally with a guide, you'll come to a few farms and villages in the middle of the stony landscape where the stone or mud buildings are surrounded by thorny bushes to protect the sheep and goats from dogs and hyenas. West of the Thar the landscape of the desert changes to green fields thanks to the Indira Ghandi Canal. Though it is not without its environmentally damaging effects, this 'engineering feat of the century' in India pumps water from the Punjab into Rajasthan and gives many farmers a chance to cultivate crops in an otherwise wasteland area.

⑬ Mount Abu The hilly forest and hiking areas, Nakki Lake, the splendid view from 'Sunset Point' and a protected wildlife area for leopards, bears and red deer, all quite close to the centre of town, make Mount Abu an enjoyable diversion for tourists, particularly if you've come in hotter months. The Dilwara temples outside of Mount Abu are well-known among art lovers.

On a par with the Jain temples of Ranakpur, the skilful stone carvings and sculpture in the five main temples here (11th–18th centuries) are even considered by some to be the best Jain work ever done. To the left and right of Abu Road heading towards Jodhpur there are a number of Rajput residences, small country palaces with gardens usually near a village, and some former 'havelis' in their modern guise as 'Heritage Hotels'. Among the 'havelis' are the Ghanerao Royal Castle, Karni Kot Sodawas, Bera, Bhenswara, Sardasamand, Fort Chanwar Luni and Rohet Garh.

⑭ Jodhpur In stark contrast to the rural landscape along the road, Jodhpur is Rajasthan's second-largest city and has more than 800,000 inhabitants. It is also the south-eastern point in the great 'Desert Triangle'.

Once you are in town, the streets of Jodhpur are dominated by hectic traffic and lively trade in the bazaar. But high above it all stands the mighty Meherangarh Fort, built by the Rathore rulers, more than 120 m (393 ft) above the Old Town alleys in the northwest of the city. The fort's palaces are known for their superb filigree stone patterns and spacious courtyards.

Across the city on Chittar Hill is the magnificent Umaid Bhawan Palace, the last of the monumental residences built by the Rajput (1929–43). Museums, markets,

only has an attractive dining room and a refreshing pool, but also a cosy private cinema.

To protect the inhabitants massive walls were built around the Jaisalmer Fort.

arts and crafts and antiques await you here.

⑮ Jaisalmer For many people, the most lasting impression of their desert travels in Rajasthan is the moment the honey-gold walls of Jaisalmer appear above the sandy plains. Since the 12th century the ninety-nine bastions of these fortifications have dominated the hills of the city of Jaisalmer. Even until far into the 19th century, the caravans of the spice and silk traders travelled in and out of the city. Ironically, it was the faraway Suez Canal that made the difference. By boosting sea trade with Europe it more or less put an end to the overland business. As a result, Jaisalmer's wealthy traders and their fairy-tale mansions with opulent facades, bay windows and balconies became a thing of the past virtually overnight. After the tumultuous division of India and Pakistan in 1947, Jaisalmer's strategic location on the western border gave

it renewed significance and India soon invested in streets and railways. Yet the conversion from the narrow-gauge railways to the Indian wide-gauge system is actually a recent development, and one that greatly benefited tourism. Since the 1990s the industry has grown dramatically, and the population of Jaisalmer has doubled to 40,000 in the last decade. Jaisalmer is now the centre of desert tourism in India and a main gathering point for camel drivers and thousands of souvenir sellers. The adventure is not all lost, however, on a trip to Desert National Park west of the city, which includes oases and deserted medieval cities like Kuldhara and Kabha. The Akal Wood Fossil Park, located 17 km (11 miles) south of Jaisalmer on the road to Barmer, has fascinating fossilized tree trunks 180 million years old. In just two hours from here you can also reach Pokaran, a small desert town with only 20,000 inhabitants.

⑯ Pokaran The name of Pokaran went through the international press in 1998 when the Indian government demonstrated its status as a nuclear power by carrying out several test detonations near the neighbouring town of Khetolai. But what is also worth seeing in Pokaran is the fort built in the 14th century, whose imposing walls are an example of a private restoration initiative.
The family of the Thakur Rajputs has been living in this fort for thirteen generations and has installed not only a Heritage Hotel but also a small museum, which specializes in archaeology and folklore.
When the owner can spare the time, he willingly explains to his guests how the neglected rooms of the palace are being restored to former glory.

⑰ Gajner Wildlife Sanctuary This well-preserved old palace on the lake is surrounded by old trees and almost seems

haunted. The grounds, which are only 30 km (18 miles) west of the large city of Bikaner, were once used by their owner as hunting territory until India's conservationists and biologists pressed for the creation of a nature reserve under the auspices of 'Project Tiger'.
The primary objective of the reserve was obviously to protect and increase the number of species living here.
The secondary objective was to increase tourism in the area. The Gajner Wildlife Sanctuary is now a paradise for birds and wild animals, and the Gajner Palace itself was turned into a Heritage Hotel. The rooms are decorated with antiques and enjoy a view of the bird-lake activities including boating, golf, cycling and

Above left: View over Jaisalmer and its fort. Above: The red saris contrast nicely with the ,blue city' Jodhpur. Left: Thar Desert.

223

The many camels that live in Rajasthan are used for safaris.

hiking. However, during longer stretches of drought or a non-existent monsoon, there is nothing to be done – the lake dries out and the birds move on.

18 Bikaner The main roads to Bikaner, an old city of the Maharajas with a current population of about 500,000, have improved over the years as more and more palaces have recently converted to hotels. But the contrast between the present and the past, between bazaar alleys and shanty towns is more stark than in Jaipur or Udaipur.

The forward-planning Maharaja Dungar Singh had an electricity network installed comparatively early, in 1886. His successor then had schools, hospitals and canals built. A mighty ring of walls surrounds Junagarh Fort, which was

Shekhawati

As long as their caravans crossed the country, the merchants in Shekhawati in the north-east of Rajasthan were rich. Well, they are still wealthy but have long since moved their houses and businesses to Kol-

The havelis are decorated with wonderful colours.

kata or Mumbai. The 'havelis', their opulently decorated town houses, are mostly deserted now. But it is with amazement that you behold the colourful facades of these mansions, which depict stories of gods, dancers, railways and the first motor cars, all with a seemingly naive delight.

built towards the end of the 16th century. Its mirrored cabinets, delicately decorated chambers and its opulent coronation hall make it one of the highlights of Indian palatial architecture in the region.

Away from the city on a visit to India's only state camel-breeding farm you get to see first-hand why 750,000 of the five million camels worldwide live right here in Rajasthan.

A slightly unusual facet of Hindu culture presents itself to visitors about 30 km (18 miles) south in Deshnok at the Karni Mata Mandir, a temple with silver doors and marble reliefs. Rats are worshipped here as holy animals and run around uninhibited.

According to legend, they are the souls of dead poets and singers.

19 Mandawa There are no big cities in the Shekhawati region east of Bikaner and north of Jaipur. Mandawa, founded in 1790 and now the tourist centre of the area, is accordingly modest in size. Comfortable accommodation is limited here. The best option is the former Rajput palaces where the owner often lives in a separate wing. The Roop Niwa Palace in Nawalgarh is an option, or try the 18th-century Castle Mandawa.

Desert sands blow around the walls of the former fort of Mandawa (begun in 1760), behind which the Rajput Rangir Singh continues to restore the decaying splendour of palace halls and boudoirs to provide space for more visitors. No room here is the same as another. Exploring Mandawa you can find several large

'havelis' (Gulab Rai and Saraf, for example), a deep well with steps leading down to it, or a few antiques and arts and craft shops. Mandawa is a convenient starting point for excursions into the partly green, partly desert landscape around the city and to a dozen other typical Shekhawati villages. The neighbouring village of Nawalgarh about 25 km (15 miles) away has more 'havelis' than any other town in the Shekhawati region. Several open their doors to visitors.

The Poddar Haveli Museum from the 1920s has around 750 images on its facade, not counting the painted passages in the inner courtyard, as well as collections of musical instruments and historical photographs.

The drive to our last destination, Neemrana, takes around six hours (225 km/140 miles). Take the turn-off about 15 km (9 miles) north of Behror on Highway 8 between Jaipur and Delhi.

20 Neemrana For those who enjoy castles and exotic living, Neemrana is a very desirable destination. Some years ago a Frenchman and an Indian turned medieval Fort Neemrana above the village into a Heritage Hotel. With a sure sense of style and every detail of attention to the needs of their guests, they created an array of terraces, balconies, rooms and suites that spoil you without overdoing the decadence.

From the city of Neemrana it is another 120 km (74 miles) via the Delhi-Jaipur Highway back to the starting point, Delhi.

Above: Neemrana Fort is now home to a hotel. Below: A golden throne can be seen in Junagarh Fort.

Jaisalmer With ninety-nine bastions, Jaisalmer towers 80 m (263 ft) above the Thar Desert. It was the residence of the Bhati Rajputs, a contested headquarters for caravan trade. The fort dates back to the 17th century.

Fort Amber This Palace (17th/18th century) in the fort of the same name is adorned with mirrors, marble halls, imposing gates and grand views of the stark mountains outside. The Mata Temple has a black marble depiction of Kali.

Delhi Mughal Emperor Shah Jahan had the Red Fort (Lal Quila) built between 1639 and 1648. The most beautiful of its buildings is the reception halls. Also worth seeing are the Jama Masjid Mosque, the tomb of Mughal Emperor Humayun, the Lodi graves and the minaret.

Jodhpur In front of the steep rock of Meherangarh Fort sits the 'Jhaswant Thada', a white marble palace built in memory of Maharaja Jhaswant Singh II to honour his progressive policies.

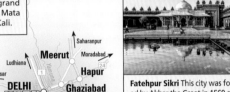

Fatehpur Sikri This city was founded by Akbar the Great in 1569 at the zenith of Mughal power in India. The Jama Masjid (Friday Mosque) is the centre of the city's holy district.

Desert National Park This national park in the Thar Desert is a superb example of the ecosystems here and the rich variety of species (Dorkas gazelles, desert lynx, giant Indian bustards).

Sariska National Park Formerly the hunting ground of the Maharaja of Alwar, this region is alive with tigers and dense forest. Located in the Aravalli Range, it became a national park in 1979. The Maharaja's summer palace nearby is now a hotel.

Agra The Red Fort (1565–73), built as a fortification with deep and broad trenches, soon became an example of imperial luxury and prestigious architecture. It is accentuated with large courtyards, palaces, and opulent columned halls.

Ranakpur The 15th/16th-century temples built by the Jains are considered among the most important masterpieces in all of India.

Udaipur The city palace of the Maharanas of Mewar, the oldest dynasty in Rajasthan, has been continuously expanded since it was built in the 16th century.

Jaipur The 'Palace of the Winds' was built with stone lattice windows to allow the ladies of the court to see without being seen.

Gwalior Fort The enormous walls of this mighty fortress rise high above the town. It contains the Man Singh Palace, built around 1500, and four other palaces.

Taj Mahal Tomb and monument of a great love: the great Mughal Emperor Shah Jahan had this mausoleum built for his wife, who died at the age of 37.

Route 18: Thailand and Malaysia
Pulsing cities and tropical natural paradises

South-East Asia – teeming urban centres and quiet villages, tropical rainforests and idyllic white sand beaches, historic sites and modern daily life. A trip along the region's North-South Highway will show you the many diverse faces of the region and immerse you in local life with all of glorious scenery and culture.

Route profile:

Length: approx. 2,020 miles
Time required: at least 3 weeks
When to go: North: November–February; East coast: Avoid the rainy season from October to February; West coast: April–October

Starting in Thailand's mountainous north, this route first takes us down to the fertile plain of the Mae Nam Chao Phraya River and its many tributaries in Central Thailand. The Menam Basin, also nicknamed Thailand's 'rice bowl', has been the country's most densely settled economic region since the time of the first Thai kingdoms.
South of the Thai capital of Bangkok, the highway then takes us onto the Malay Peninsula, which stretches 1,500 km (930 miles) between the Indian Ocean (Andaman Sea) and the

Pacific Ocean (Gulf of Thailand and South China Sea).
At its narrowest point, the Isthmus of Kra, the peninsula is a mere 50 km (31 miles) wide. Its backbone is formed by a mountain range that reaches its highest elevations in Malaysia at more than 2,000 m (6,500 ft).
The tropical plants and animals of Thailand and Malaysia are almost unbeatably varied and abundant. Nevertheless, in recent years the once so prevalent tropical rainforests have had to give way to large-scale plantations, rice paddies and urban sprawl. Only in mountainous regions and individual national parks can you still find real virgin rainforests with their wealth of plants and animals. You'll find giant trees, wild orchids and epiphytes, and these South-East Asian rainforests are also home to several species of apes as well as snakes and tigers.

As the climate of the area is very favourable, large areas of both countries have been devoted to agriculture. In some places in

Thailand there are rice paddies as far as the eye can see, and in Malaysia there are massive oil palm and rubber tree plantations. Being one of South-East Asia's most ancient kingdoms, Thailand has a large number of historic sites dating from differ-

ent periods in its history. Many of these monumental buildings, such as those of Sukhothai and Ayutthaya, are very well-maintained. Their size and the skill employed in their construction are truly impressive.
Malaysia and Singapore, by contrast, claim much shorter histories. Their oldest historic sites date from the colonial period. These days places like George-

226

Top: The courtyard at the Ayutthaya temple is lined with innumerable statues of the sitting Buddha. It is an open-air museum of Buddhist high culture. Left: James Bond Rock in Phang Nga Bay.

town, Melaka and Singapore have numerous preserved and restored colonial buildings that provide visitors with a lively impression of this bygone era.

All three states have ethnically diverse populations, and this variety makes the region all the more attractive. In Thailand a majority of around 80 per cent of the population is Thai, in Malaysia 50 per cent are Malay, and in Singapore 70 per cent are Chinese. The remainder of the Thai population is made up of mountain tribes and Chinese descendants. Malaysia and Singapore also have large Indian populations. The Chinese, who account for a very small percentage of the population of Thailand, for example, exercise significant influence on the regional economy and local trade. In fact, they make up the vast majority of South-East Asia's economically powerful.

Yet despite the region's ethnic diversity and the corresponding cultural and traditional differences, people mostly live together in harmony and welcome foreign visitors with all the legendary Asian friendliness.

A journey from northern Thailand to Singapore via Malaysia thus becomes a journey through a very diverse region in terms of scenery, ethnicity and culture. You will be both surprised and enchanted by the ever-changing human and natural landscape.

Singapore (left) and Bangkok (above) are undoubtedly the most fascinating and contrasting metropolises in South Asia.

Padaung neck rings

From Chiang Mai you can take an interesting excursion 100 km (62 miles) along Highway 108 to the west into the scenic region of Mae Hong Son.

Here at the border to Myanmar you will find a few villages of the Padaung people, whose women are probably among the most photographed in all of Thailand. From early childhood, girls wear heavy bronze rings around their necks. Each year one more is added.

Long necks are a thing of beauty to the Padaung and the rings also represent status and wealth. X-ray photographs have shown that the weight of these

Rice cultivation

Around 70 km (45 miles) west of Bangkok on Highway 4 is the little town of Nakhon Pathom, which was the capital of the Dvaravati kingdom from the 6th to the 11th centuries. Buddhist monks who had come from India founded this kingdom in the early 6th century directly in the heart of modern Thailand.

during the Mon Period (6th century) in the same place. This means that it was probably the first Buddhist building ever erected on Thai soil. It was repeatedly destroyed and expanded and only achieved its current height in 1860.

In the middle of the 19th century King Mongut had tried in vain to restore the old chedi and finally ordered a new one

At Chiang Mai rice terraces dominate the image.

Nowadays the town is a much-visited pilgrimage destination with two absolute highlights of Buddhist culture – Phra Pathom Chedi at 127 m (417 ft) is the highest Buddhist monument anywhere and the Buddha inside is the world's largest at 40 m (131 ft) high.
At the heart of this giant, bell-shaped chedi covered in orange bricks are the remains of another chedi, which was built

to be built on top of the old. The National Museum at Phra Pathom chedi houses some precious findings from the heyday of this early kingdom, among them some impressive wheels of law and beautifully made stone carvings.
The gardens around the Sanam-Chan palace to the west of the temple compound are a fantastic oasis of peace and quiet.

❶ Chiang Mai The Thais call Chiang Mai the 'Rose of the North'. Thailand's second city is the tourist centre of northern Thailand. Using Chiang Mai as a base, you can take trekking tours into the mountains and visit the hill tribes who live in them. Under King Mengrai this settlement, founded in 1292, became the capital of the Lanna Kingdom and an important centre for Theravada Buddhism. The king and his successors built the majority of the numerous temples (wats) in the so-called Lanna style. The most important among them are Wat Phra Sing (1345), Wat Chedi Luang (c. 15th century) and Wat Chiang Man. The quadratic centre of the Old Town, with its picturesque alleyways and traditional houses, is surrounded by well-preserved trenches that today separate the historic city centre from modern Chiang Mai.
Outside the Old Town you'll find the National Museum with its large and beautiful terracotta collection, a small ethnological museum and numerous other temples. Nature and art lovers should make sure to pay a visit to the densely forested national park Doi Suthep Doi Pui, 16 km (10 miles) north-west of Chiang

Mai. The park is the home of Doi Suthep, the most important Buddhist temple in northern Thailand, situated at an elevation of 1,600 m (5,250 ft) above sea level. Precisely 304 steep steps lead up to it. Taking Highway 11 south you now drive through some lush green hills and mountains and pass some steep valleys with carefully maintained fields and rice paddies.

❷ Chae Son National Park This is a mountainous national park around 50 km (31 miles) further south-east. Its forests are home to black bears, wild boar and monkeys as well as some rarely seen tigers. The main trail through the national park starts in Khuntan and after an 8-km (5-mile) hike it takes you up to the summit of Yot Se (1,373 m/4,505 ft). From there you have some wonderful views of the surrounding mountain scenery.

❸ Mae Ping National Park Rafting tours and boat trips are the main reason that so many people come to visit Mae Ping National Park, located west of Highway 1. By car you get to it via Lamphum (30 km/19 miles south of Chiang Mai) on High-

does not stretch the neck but that, instead, the women's collarbones and shoulders are pushed down. The muscles normally supporting the head lose their function and with time, they wither. These women have problems drinking – they have to bend over forwards and use straws to drink. In recent years, this idiosyncratic attire has come back into fashion after almost disappearing from Padaung culture.

ways 106 and 1087. The park is roughly 100 km (62 miles) away. Most visitors take a two-hour boat ride on the Ping River from Doi Tao Lake, which takes them into the park. From there they carry on to the village of Ko. In addition to a white-water ride and some impressive limestone cliffs and caves, this national park offers a good insight into the different plants and animals living in the rainforests.

4 Lampang What is fascinating about this 7th-century town are its temples, traditional houses and an old market with a variety of different architectural styles represented in the surrounding buildings. In the 19th century Lampang became a centre for teak produc-

tion. The town's brightly painted horse-drawn carriages date from this era and they are still Lampang's standard form of public transport. The town's most important temple is Wat Phra Kaew Don Tao. In the south-west you'll find one of northern Thailand's most beautiful temples – Wat Phra That Lampang Luang, dating from the 15th century. Leaving Lampang, you take Highway 1 to the south. The mountains soon give way to more gentle hills that eventually flatten out towards the plains of the upper Menam Basin. Rice is cultivated in expansive paddies here for as far as the eye can see. From Tak you can take a worthwhile excursion on Highway 12 to Sukhothai, the former capital of

Thailand, which is 80 km (49 miles) away.

5 Sukhothai UNESCO declared the ruined city of Old Sukhothai a World Heritage Site in 1991. With more than forty temples, this city recalls the heydey of the Sukhothai kingdom, the most powerful in the Menam Basin between 1240 and 1320. Founded in 1238, the city was the capital of the first Thai nation for more than 120 years. The large compound stretches over 70 sq km (27 sq mi) and includes an historic park and so many other attractions that you can easily spend several days here.

At the heart of the historic park is the Old Town, which is surrounded by a wall 1.6 km (1 mile) by 2 km (1.3 miles) long. The royal palace and the Wat Mahathat (13th century) temple alone encompass an area of more than 16 ha (40 acres). The complex is completely surrounded by a trench.

6 Kamphaeng Phet Founded in 1347, Kamphaeng Phet used to be a royal garrison town. In the north are the town's historic quarters, and in the south you will find the modern town. Surrounded as they are by a moat, the historic quar-

Left: Wat Mahathat in Sukhothai; Top: Wat Phra Singh in Chiang Mai; right: Wat Si Chum in Sukhothai.

The 'Bridge Over the River Kwai'

Not far from Kanchanaburi is the 'Bridge Over the River Kwai', which was made famous by the novel by Pierre Boulle. During World War II the Japanese constructed a railway line here. Its construction cost the lives of 16,000 allied prisoners of war and around 100,000 local labourers, most of whom died of starvation, malaria and cholera.

The current bridge over the river Kwai is a reconstruction of the building by the Japanese.

Detour

Nakhon Pathom

Around 70 km (45 miles) west of Bangkok on Highway 4 is the little town of Nakhon Pathom, which was the capital of the Dvaravati kingdom from the 6th to the 11th centuries. Buddhist monks who had come from India founded this kingdom in the early 6th century directly in the heart of modern Thailand.

Nowadays the town is a much-visited pilgrimage destination with two absolute highlights of Buddhist culture – Phra Pathom Chedi at 127 m (417 ft) is the highest Buddhist monument anywhere and the Buddha inside is the world's largest at 40 m (131 ft) high.

At the heart of this giant, bell-shaped chedi covered in orange bricks are the remains of another chedi, which was built during the Mon Period (6th century) in the same place.

This means that it was probably the first Buddhist building ever erected on Thai soil. It was repeatedly destroyed and expanded and only achieved its current height in 1860. In the middle of the 19th century King Mongut had tried in vain to restore the old chedi and finally ordered a new one to be built on top of the old. The National Museum at Phra Pathom chedi houses some precious findings from the heyday of this early kingdom, among them some impressive wheels of law and beautifully made stone carvings. The gardens around the Sanam-Chan palace to the west of the temple compound are an oasis of peace and quiet.

ters give you an idea of what Old Sukhothai might have been like. The National Museum and the temple compound with Wat Phra Kaeo and Wat Phra That are also worth seeing.

⑦ Nakhon Sawan The most interesting thing here is not the provincial capital itself but the confluence of the Mae Nam Ping

and Mae Nam Yom rivers. They come together in this region to form the Menam Chao Phraya, whose flood plains are the most fertile and densely populated region in Thailand. All you can see for miles are the thousands of rice paddies, dotted here and there with hills and mountains. From Nakhon Sawan take Highway 32 through the fields and hills towards Ayutthaya.

⑧ Ayutthaya From 1350 to 1767 Ayutthaya was the capital of Siam (Thailand). Historical sources claim that it was Asia's most impressive city at the time. Visitors from Europe back then were overwhelmed by its splendour and many said that they had never seen anything to equal it. The kings of thirty-three different dynasties ruled the country from

here until the city was razed to the ground by the Burmese in 1767. The historic Old Town is located at the confluence of three rivers and completely surrounded by water. The most impressive sights are located on the island in the middle of these three rivers. Among them are the temples of Wat Na Phra Men, which was not destroyed in 1767, and Wat Phra Si Sanphet with its three chedis.

From Ayutthaya, it is only around 40 km (25 miles) to Bangkok.

⑨ Bangkok (see pp. 232–233). From Taksin Bridge the highway sweeps west along the bay onto the Malay Peninsula. West of Bangkok you can visit Nakhon Prathom with its giant temple compound and Kanchanaburi with the famous 'Bridge Over the River Kwai'. Both sights are relatively close to Highway 4.

Carry on southbound along the east coast (west side of the bay). Around 20 km (13 miles) after Ratchaburi, a road turns off to Thailand's largest national park, Kaeng Krachan National Park, which is well worth visiting.

⑩ Kaen Krachan National Park Thailand's largest park is surprisingly unknown among travellers despite the fact that its dense, evergreen tropical rainforests cover mountains that rise to 1,200 m (4,000 ft). The park is home to tigers, Malaysian bears, leopards, tapirs and elephants as well as gibbons and langurs. The next 370 km (230 miles) south of Ratchaburi run along the east coast before you get to Chumphon where Highway 4 changes to two lanes and you switch to the west

A rescue station for working elephants has been set up near the ruins of Ayutthaya. Here, the animals are lovingly cared for.

Detour

Similan Islands

The Similan Islands are located around 100 km (62 miles) north-west of Phuket and it takes three hours to get there by boat from Thap Lamu. The archipelago with its nine islands really is a diving paradise.

In 1984 the islands were declared a marine national park because of their unique sea life. They have been attracting divers from all around the world for years. The species-rich underwater landscape is probably unbeatable in Thailand. Just off the islands there are some granite rocks with many grottoes and tunnels. From turtles to doctor fish to whale sharks, many different marine animals call this home.

But even swimming or snorkelling will be a thrill. The most beautiful island is called Ko Miang. The months with the best underwater views are from December to

coast for another 350 km (217 miles). At Kra, the Malay Peninsula narrows to only 50 km (31 miles) wide. Soon after that you will arrive in Khuraburi and the next national park in the midst of a tropical mountain landscape.

⑪ Khao Sok National Park
This hilly national park with luscious rainforests is regarded

as Thailand's most beautiful forest. It has some very good hiking among the impressive limestone cliffs and the numerous waterfalls, which are the park's principal attractions. Among them are Nam Tok Sip Et Chan, where the water cascades down eleven glorious levels. With a bit of luck you might even find a specimen of the world's largest flower, a species of Rafflesia with a diam-

eter of around 1 m (3.5 ft). After Thap Lamu (see sidebar right for a worthwhile excursion to the diving paradise of the Similan Islands) the road runs along the Khao Lak coast riddled with lonely beaches against the backdrop of the extensive tropical monsoon forests of Khao Lak National Park. Past the turn-off for the incredibly touristy island of Phuket you can carry on to Phang Nga, the starting point for trips into the Phang Nga Bay.

⑫ Phang-Nga-Bucht This bay's dense mangrove forests make it one of Thailand's most impressive regions. It is protected as a national park and has some bizarre, partly overgrown limestone rocks that rise up to 350 m (1,150 ft) out of the clear

azure waters. Many of the rock faces have karst caves and tunnels. The most important stations on a boat trip in this bay are Panyi, a village on stilts, the Suwan-Kuha caves with a reclining Buddha, and some other stalactite caves. To the east, the karst landscape continues on the mainland and into the Khao Phanom Bencha National Park north of Krabi.

⑬ Krabi Most visitors come here because of the dream beaches and limestone cliffs in the area to the south and west of town. These are the 'beach images' that most people have come to associate with Thailand nowadays and some are truly spectacular.

Krabi, which is surrounded by karst cliff formations, has 21,000 inhabitants and is a good jumping-off point for boat trips into Phang Nga Bay; the famous Phi Phi Islands 40 km (25 miles) south with their magnificent

Large image: Tropical island paradise Ko Tub in front of Krabi. Above: Phang-Nga Bay. Wat Arun is visible from afar, Bangkok's Temple of the Dawn (left side).

The crystal clear water is ideal for snorkeling.

April, just before the rainy season. The islands, which are not well developed for tourism, are partly covered in tropical rainforests.

On the left and right side of Chao Phraya the skyscrapers shoot up in downtown Bangkok.

'Place of Love', Bang Rak, is the name of one of the downtown areas of Bangkok, where Thanon Silom, a popular street in the banking district, can be found.

Bangkok

With its roughly twelve million inhabitants, Bangkok is Thailand's largest city and its cultural, political and social centre. The city's most important sight, the Grand Palace with the temple of Wat Phra Kaeo, is located on the eastern shore of the Chao Phraya River. These two form the centre of spiritual and worldly power in the kingdom.

As many as ten per cent of the Thai population lives in and around the capital, which as a result suffers from high levels of pollution, heavy traffic and incessant noise.

These days Bangkok is certainly one of the most lively and exciting metropolises in South-East Asia, but with its unspeakably chaotic traffic it can be quite stressful as well. Every day three million cars, trucks, motorcycles and bicycles fight their way through a city whose road network is simply not up to the task. In order to forestall a total collapse, some through roads have been constructed on stilts, but expensive road tolls are charged for their use and they do nothing to enhance the city's beauty. The numerous palm-lined Khlongs that once gave Bangkok the nickname 'Venice of the East' are only visible in some of the outer districts like Thon Buri or around Wat Arun. Most of them have been paved over in recent years. To visitors the city can seem extremely confusing. Many of the principal sights are far away from each other and it can be quite an adventure to get from one to the next. The Old City's main sights include the King's Palace (construction started in 1782) with the Dusit Throne Hall, Amarinn Winichai Hall, Inner Palace and Sivalai Gardens; a city wall 1,900 m (2,078 yds) long that surrounds the 'city within the city' housing Wat Phra Kaeo, Thailand's most sacred temple with its golden chedi and Emerald Buddha; Wat Po with its reclining golden Buddha, Bangkok's oldest temple and a centre for traditional medicine; and Wat

Saket on the Golden Hill with a good view over the city.

The most important museums are the National Museum with exhibits on the history, arts and crafts of Thailand and the National Gallery, the largest gallery for contemporary Asian art.

Worth seeing in Chinatown, the 200-year-old Chinese trade centre of Bangkok, are Songwat Road, which still exudes a 19th-century atmosphere; the Buddhist shrine of Leng Noi Yee; different markets (Kao-Market, Pak-Khlong-Market, Pha-

The Grand Palace of Bangkok was once a royal residence.

hurat-Market); Yaowarat Road, the main traffic artery of Chinatown and Wat Traimit with a golden image of Buddha. Sights in the Dusit governmental centre are Dusit Park with its several museums; Wat Banchamabophit temple; Phitsanulok Road and the government buildings. Worth seeing in the town centre are the old foreigns' quarter with the Assumption Cathedral (1910), the Oriental Hotel, and the Jim Thomson House, a traditional Thai living quarter with museum. Thon Buri has a number of other attractions as well – Wat Arun with its chedi covered in thousands of porcelain fragments, and the old Khlongs with their floating markets and traditional buildings.

In 1897, Church Street Pier was built in George Town, Penang. After a few decades of neglecting the construction, it now shines again.

the largest and most beautiful in Malaysia. With its very slender minarets and onion domes it embodies beautifully everyone's mental image of an oriental mosque.

16 **Insel Penang** The tropical island of Penang, which is up to 700 m (2,300 ft) high in places, is located in the Gulf of Bengal and connected to the mainland by a bridge. Visitors from around the globe are attracted to the beaches at its northern end and to Georgetown, its lively capital. With Chinese shopping streets, narrow alleyways, numerous temples, magnificent clan houses (such as Khoo Kongsi) and colonial buildings such as Fort Cornwallis (18th century) it always makes for a pleasant stroll.

17 **Kuala Kangsar** For more than 150 years Kuala Kangsar, located 110 km (68 miles) further south, has been the residence of the Sultans of Perak. This pleasant town on the wide Perak River has two cultural monuments worth seeing – the former sultan's palace of Istana Kenangan built in 1926, and Masjid Ubudiah, which was built 1913–17 and whose golden domes and minarets make it one of the country's finest mosques.

18 **Ipoh** The state capital of Perak has 500,000 inhabitants and owes its economic rise to the profitable tin deposits in the area. These were exploited well into the 1980s. Ipoh seems quite provincial for a city its size. The Kinta Valley to the north and south of the town is dominated by steep, partly forested limestone cliffs. There are some caves with Buddhist sanctuaries

Detour

Batu Caves

The Batu Caves are among the most visited attractions in the Kuala Lumpur area. They are located 15 km (9 miles) north of the city on Highway 68 to Kuntan.
These giant limestone caves are part of a huge labyrinth of rock openings and tunnels. Because of a shrine inaugurated in the main cave in 1892, this is one of the most important pilgrimage destinations for Malay Hindus.
Every year in January and February thousands of Hindu faithful come to the Batu Caves during the festival of Thaipusam, celebrated here for two days. Its highlight is a procession of penitents with metal hooks poked into their backs and chests.

beaches, steep karst rock faces and good diving; and a host of other white sand beaches and islands. The temple compound of Wat Tham Sua with its beautiful view of the bay and the surrounding countryside is located on a rock outcrop 8 km (5 miles) north of Krabi. From here we carry on across the southern Thai plains, which are among the most fertile in the country.

14 **Hat Yai** For many Thais this city is a shopping paradise because there are a lot of goods smuggled from Malaysia in the shops and markets. West of the town centre at Wat Hat Yai Nai is the world's third-largest reclining Buddha at 35 m (115 ft) long

and 15 m (50 ft) tall. From Hat Yai you can do a little detour to Songkhla about 25 km (16 miles) and the lakes on the east coast north of town.A short drive south to Sadao takes you to the Malay border where the road turns into Malaysia's Highway 1. As an alternative to the North-South Highway, which is a dual carriageway, you can take the old road, which mostly runs parallel to the new one.

15 **Alor Setar** The state capital of Kedah is located in the middle of a wide, fertile plain with picturesque rice paddies. The region is known as 'Malaysia's rice bowl'. The town landmark, the Zahir Mosque (1912), is one of

**Top left: The Zahir Mosque in Alor Setar was built in 1912.
Left: Hat Yai is so popular thanks to its numerous shops.
Right: Petronas Towers in Kuala Lumpur.**

Ayutthaya At its zenith, this former capital of Siam was one of the most magnificent cities in Asia as the ruins of its palaces, halls, fortifications and temples and its stupas and Buddhas show.

Phuket This island used to be an important trading post for European merchants. Its magnificent bays and palm-lined beaches now make it a first-class tourist destination.

Phi Phi Islands This archipelago located about 50 km (31 miles) south of Phuket has some excellent diving and some bizarre rock formations in the Ko Phi Phi Marine National Park.

Penang Its dream beaches have turned this tropical island into Malaysia's best-known tourist destination, but it also has some interesting colonial buildings and temples. The picture shows the Buddhist temple Kek Lok Si.

Singapur Founded as recently as 1819 as a trading post, Singapore has quickly become one of the most important traffic hubs and financial and commercial centres in South-East Asia.

Chiang Mai Thailand's second-largest city has some famous temple compounds built in the Lanna style: Wat Phra Sing, Wat Chedi Luang, Wat Chiang Man, and Wat Phra That Doi Suthep a little further out. It is also a centre for outstanding arts and crafts.

Sukhothai The extensive palaces and temples of the Sukhothai Kingdom (13th–14th centuries) extend over an area of 70 sq km (27 sq mi). In 1991 the compound was declared a UNESCO World Heritage Site. The picture shows a Buddha at Wat Mahathat.

Bangkok This city of twelve million inhabitants is the political, cultural and social heart of Thailand. One of its main sights is the Old King's Palace and Wat Phra Kaeo, the most important temple in Thailand.

Kuala Lumpur A testimony to the dynamic nature of Malaysia's capital are the Petronas Towers, until recently the highest buildings in the world.

Tioman This tropical island, accessible by plane or express boat from Singapore, has every ingredient of a dream holiday: white sandy beaches, reefs and coral gardens, mountains and forests that are home to monkeys and reptiles.

Melaka Under the name of Malacca, this town was an important transportation centre for trade with China. This can still be seen today in its numerous colonial buildings and Chinatown. The Portuguese built here the fortress A Famosa.

Taunggyi
Si Lanna N.P.
Chiang Mai
Doi Suthep Doi Pui N.P.
Lamphun
Chae Son N.P.
Lampang
Mae Pok
Sung Men
Doi Tao Lake
Uttaradit
Mae Ping N.P.
Sukhothai
Nam Tok Chattrakan N.P.
Lom Sak
Tak
Nam Nao N.P. Khon Kaen
Phitsanulok
Kamphaeng Phet
Phetchabun
Maulamyaing (MYA)
Sai Thong N.P.
Nakhon Sawan
Si Thep
T H A I L A N D
Singburi
Lop Buri
Nakhon Ratchasima
Ayutthaya
Saraburi
Khao Yai N.P.
Nakhon Pathom
Phnom Penh (KH)
BANGKOK
Kanchanaburi
Ratchaburi
Chon Buri
Petchaburi
Tham Khao Luang
Trat
Kaeng Krachan N.P.
Cha-am
Pattaya
Hua Hin
Khao Sam Roi Yot N.P.
Tham Praya Nakhon Cave
Prachuap Khirikhan
Huai Yang N.P. 1292
Thap Sakae
Bang Saphan
Chumphon
Kra Buri
Isthmus of Kra
Ranong
Lang Suan
Kapoe
Tab Khon Falls
Koh Samui
Khuraburi
Khao Sok N.P.
Sri Phang-Nga N.P.
Surat Thani
Tai Rom Yen N.P.
Ko Similan N.P.
Takua Pa
Thap Lamu
Khao Phanom Bencha N.P.
Nakhon Si Thammarat
Phang Nga
Krabi
Thung Song
Ron Phibun
Ko Phuket
Phuket
Phang Nga Bay
Phatthalung
Thale Luang
Mo Ko Phi Phi N.P.
Trang
Ton Tae Falls
Songkhla
Tone Nga Chang Falls
Hat Yai
Ko Tarutao
Satun
Narathiwat
Langkawi
Sadao
Kuah
Jitra
Kota Bharu
Alor Setar
Betong
Georgetown
Sungai Petani
Tasik Temenggur
Lenggong Valley
Penang
Kuala Kangsar
Taman Negara N.P.
Tasik Kenyir
Taiping
Ipoh
Cameron Highlands Hill Resort
Kellie's Castle
Kampar
M A L A Y S I A
Kuantan
Batu Caves
KUALA LUMPUR
Kelang
Tioman
Morib
Seremban
Mersing
Endau Rompin N.P.
Melaka (Malacca)
Muar
Kluang
Batu Pahat
Pontian Kechil
Johor Bahru
SINGAPORE
SINGAPORE
Berakit
Bintan

A mountain island in the middle of nowhere: This is the well-known Ayers Rock, a symbol of Australia, which the Aborigines call Uluru, which means 'shade giving place'.

Australia and New Zealand

Australia is extreme compared to the other continents. No other is as dusty, has as many poisonous animals, and the loneliness of the Outback is incomprehensible. The magic of this country is that it has so much to offer. New Zealand is completely different: 'Kia ora!' or 'Welcome!' is what the whole country calls out to visitors. New Zealand, a huge adventure playground on the other side of the world, offers travellers a warm hospitality in an overwhelming natural environment.

Route 19: Australia

On Stuart Highway through the 'Red Centre'

The Stuart Highway stretches 3,200 km (1,987 miles) from Adelaide on the south coast all the way across the legendary outback, the 'Red Centre' of the continent, to Darwin in the north on the Timor Sea. Along this dream route you pass some of Australia's most impressive natural sights. Indeed, long portions of the journey are devoid of any signs of life, much less human settlements, but it is precisely this emptiness and solitude that make this journey so fascinating.

Route profile:

Length: approx. 3,200 km (1,987 miles), excluding detours
Time required: 3 weeks
Traffic information: Drive on the left in Australia. If you want to explore the outback, a four-wheel drive vehicle is recommended.

The starting point for the adventure across the entire Australian continent is Adelaide, known as the 'greenest town' in the country. Today, tree-lined streets in this tidy city have replaced the rugged seaport where, in 1836, about 550 German settlers arrived bearing grape vines and a vision for the future. The heart of Australian wine production is now concentrated in a handful of picturesque regions including the Adelaide Hills, the Barossa Valley and the Clare Valley.
Port Augusta, 317 km (197

miles) further north, is the real starting point of the Stuart Highway. It is named after John Mc-Douall Stuart, an explorer who in 1862 became the first white man to cross the continent from north to south. At one time known for being one of the country's most hazardous roads, the highway, which has been surfaced now since 1987, has become a fully developed traffic route. Parts of the road can become impassable after unusually heavy rainfall.
The first stretch of your route, from Port Augusta to Glendambo, is marked by dried-out salt lakes that are visible from the road. The first real town to the north after Port Augusta is Coober Pedy in the Stuart Range, a relatively inhospitable area where dramatic sandstorms are commonplace. It was here, in the 'opal capital of the world', that the first opal was discov-

ered by chance during the gold rush of 1915.
In general, between Port Augusta and Darwin what may look like a town along the highway on the map is often nothing more than a roadhouse where you can buy fuel, spend the night and stock up on basic food supplies. One of these is the

Kulgera Roadhouse, just 'across the border' in the Northern Territory. There are only 185,000 people living in this massive state (six times the size of Great Britain), and half of them live in Darwin. Coarse, rocky terrain and the endless spinifex grass steppe cover the land as far as the eye can see. The land is rusty

242

Top: The Kakadu National Park covers almost the entire catchment area of the South Alligator River, which crashes over the cliffs of Twin Falls and Jim Jim Falls. The Twin Falls are only accessible to visitors during the dry season. Left: Signs warning motorists of kangaroos are not a rare sight on Australia's roads.

At Renner Spring one finally leaves the inhospitable arid plains of the 'Red Centre' behind and the coastal savannah comes into view.

From the town of Katherine you can reach the Cutta Cutta Caves Nature Park as well as the Nitmiluk National Park with the spectacular canyons of Katherine Gorge. At Pine Creek, you have a choice between taking the road to Darwin or the drive through Kakadu National Park towards Jabiru.

Either way, after 3,200 km (1,987 miles) of hard going, you have finally reached the 'Top End'.

Kakadu National Park is one of the most beautiful in the country. There you will find the birds that bear the same name (left side) and a charming landscape (top).

red for hundreds of kilometres, with termite hills shimmering dark red in the hot sun. It is a unique symphony of shifting shades of red earth in which you will only rarely see anything other than natural landscapes. Roughly 80 km (50 miles) over the border at Erlunda, the Lasseter Highway turns off towards Uluru National Park where two of Australia's most famous landmarks are located – Uluru (Ayers Rock) and Kata Tjuta (The Olgas). The most important city in the area is Alice Springs in the Macdonnell Ranges, a town that is also the geographical centre of the country and a comfortable starting point for trips to many well-known national parks – Finke Gorge, Watarrka and the West Macdonnell Ranges. The next tourist highlight on the way to 'Top End' are the bizarre spheres of the Devils Marbles. Tennant Creek has been known as 'Gold Town' ever since the short gold rush that took place there in 1932.

On the Adelaide Hills, different varieties of grape are cultivated including Chardonnay, Sauvignon Blanc and Pinot Noir.

Giant kangaroos

If you follow the Stuart Highway north towards Darwin you will regulary come across signs warning you of kangaroos crossing the road. These marsupials are the continent's national animal with an estimated population of about twenty-five million. Despite their cuddly popularity with tourists, these vegetarian creatures are viewed by local farmers as pests because they graze uncontrollably on valuable sheep pastures. In Australia there are fifty-six kangaroo species, divided into two families. Some are as small as large rabbits while others, like the giant red kangaroo, can reach 2 m (6.5 ft) standing on their hind legs. Kangaroo offspring are actually born during a late phase of embryonic development, the rest of which is completed from within the mother's pouch. Females

Giant red kangaroos.

have only one baby per year, which then feed for seven to ten months in her pouch while she feeds another offspring with milk outside the pouch.

Kangaroos' long and powerful tails are used as counterweights for hopping and jumping, but their soft leathery feet do not damage the ground below them. In the open grasslands of the dry centre, you regularly come across giant red kangaroos which, like all kangaroos, live in herds.

Shortly after starting out from Adelaide, the Stuart Highway leads straight into the outback. Ayers Rock and Alice Springs lie at the halfway point of the route. The landscape turns into savannah in the far northern sections, and numerous national parks give travellers an idea of the Northern Territory's flora and fauna.

①　Adelaide (see page 246) With more than a million inhabitants, Adelaide lies on the north and south sides of the Torrens River. The city's many parks, gardens, historic arcades and churches give it a very European flair. Yet despite all this, Adelaide is often considered a bit of a backwater by people from other Australian cities, or is even called 'wowserville', but this seems off the mark. Every two years one of the world's most important cultural festivals takes place here – the Festival of Arts, held in the Adelaide Festival Centre. It is a tolerant and multicultural city with several museums along the 'Cultural Mile', including the Art Gallery of South Australia, the Ayers House Historical Museum (one of the most attractive colonial buildings in Australia), the Migration Museum on the history of immigration, and the South Australia Museum, with a good collection of Aboriginal tools, weapons and everyday items. For a great view of the city go up to Montefiori Hill. Then take a break in the enchanting Botanic

Gardens. If you feel like a swim, take one of the nostalgic trams down to Glenelg or Henley Beach. A worthwhile day trip is the drive into the Adelaide Hills or to the Barossa Valley. The first vineyards were planted here in 1847 by a German immigrant, Johann Cramp. Today in the Barossa Valley, 40 km (25 miles) long and 10 km (6 miles) wide, there are over 400 vineyards producing wines that have slowly but surely gained recognition around the world. One of the year's cultural highlights is the Vintage Festival with music, sauerkraut, brown bread, apple strudel, and of course wine. Another interesting detour takes you to Kangaroo Island, 113 km (70 miles) southwest of Adelaide, which can be reached via the Fleurieu peninsula with its inviting sandy beaches. Australia's third-largest island is 155 km (96 miles) long and 55 km (34 miles) wide. You will come face to face here with the kangaroos that gave the island its name. In the Seal Bay Conservation Park, thousands of sea lions bask on rocks in the

sun. In Flinders Chase National Park, koalas lounge in the eucalyptus trees.

The real trip to the far north begins on Highway 1 from Adelaide. On the northern banks of Spencer Gulf is the industrial harbour town of Port Pirie, 250 km (155 miles) from Adelaide. Enormous grain silos bear witness to the extensive wheat farming in this region. Zinc and silver ore are processed here too, as is lead. About 65 km (40 miles) further north, on the way to Port Augusta, it is worth taking the scenic detour into Mount Remarkable National Park at the south end of the Flinders Range. From the 959-m-high (3,146-ft) Mount Remarkable you can get a fabulous panoramic view of the entire region. After another 70 km (43 miles) along Spencer Gulf, the industrial port town of Augusta awaits you and marks the actual starting point of Stuart Highway (Highway 87).

②　Port Augusta This town is often called the 'Gateway to the outback'. In preparation for the

The opal deposits in the area around Coober Pedy is enormous.

Detour

Flinders Ranges National Park

From Port Augusta take scenic Highway 47 through Quorn and Hawker to the mighty wall of the Wilpena Pound. Gravel roads then lead to the most important sights of the 950-sq-km (370-sq-mi) Flinders National Park, one of the most beautiful in South Australia. It protects the 400-km-long (240-mile) Flinders Range, which extends like a wedge between the salt lakes of Lake Torrens, Lake Eyre and Lake Frome and continues far into the outback, providing life support to many of the animal and plant species in this arid region.

The often bizarre rock formations come in red and violet hues, especially at sunrise and sunset. Bright, colourful flowers also grow in the val-

Wildflowers make the national park shine.

trip, a visit to the Wadlata Outback Centre is highly recommended. A few historically important buildings including the Town Hall (1887), the Court House (1884) and St Augustine's Church, with lovely stained-glass windows, are worth seeing. The Australian Arid Lands Botanic Gardens north of town familiarize you with the flora and fauna of the outback.

A short detour to the nearby Flinders Ranges National Park is an absolute must.

3 Pimba This little town is right next to the enormous Woomera military base. Interestingly, the 'restricted area' on the base contains the largest uranium source in the world.

Australia's largest natural lakes can also be found outside of Pimba. These salt lakes are only pe-

riodically filled with water and are the remnants of what was once a huge inland sea. In the dry season they transform into salt marshes or salt pans.

To the east of Stuart Highway is Lake Torrens, in the national park of the same name, which covers an area of 5,800 sq km (2,240 sq mi). Frome Lake and Eyre Lake are also in the park. Further west is Lake Gairdner, another salt lake that is part of a separate national park.

4 Coober Pedy In 1915, fourteen-year-old Willie Hutchinson and his father discovered Australia's first opal completely by chance, about 270 km (168 miles) north of Pimba. The name Coober Pedy originates from the Aborigine 'kupa piti' (white man in a hole). Since then it has been overrun with pits up to 30 m

(98 ft) deep and giant slag heaps that, due to consistent demand for opals, are constantly being expanded. In fact, 70 per cent of the world's opal mining takes place in the Coober Pedy area. The raging sandstorms and intense heat in the area have compelled nearly half of the 3,000 inhabitants to live in 'dugouts', underground homes built in decommissioned opal mines. The often well-furnished apartments maintain consistent temperatures between 23°C and 25°C (73°F and 77°F) and can be up to 400 sq m (4,305 sq ft) in size. There is even an underground church in Coober, as well as underground bed and breakfast accommodation. Be sure to pay a visit to the lovingly restored Old Timers Mine while you are here. Eventually, the Lasseter Highway makes its way west at Erlunda towards the Yulara Resort and the Visitor Centre of the Uluru and Kata Tjuta National Parks (1,325 sq km/511 sq mi).

If you are looking for outdoor adventure, turn left off the highway onto a track towards Chambers

Large image: Sunrise over Lake Eyre. Above: In summer, Lake Gairdner National Park is mostly dry.

leys and gorges of the mountains in springtime. Giant red kangaroos live here, as do yellow-footed rock wallabies and other smaller species of rock wallabies. Broad-tailed eagles and brown falcons circle in the sky above.

The highlight of a trip into the national park is the Wilpena Pound, one of Australia's greatest natural wonders: a 17-km (10.5-mile) by 7-km (4.3-mile) crater-like 'cauldron' that resembles a natural amphitheatre.

The cultural centre of Adelaide is located on the River Torrens.

Adelaide

Although some 70% of the state's population now live in the capital of South Australia, it has remained an English-style idyll to this day.

Adelaide is the only big city in Australia built without recourse to convict labour.
Perfectionist planner William Light worked on his design for four years before the cornerstone was finally laid in 1836: parks alternate in the grid layout with boulevards and streets. The model for Light's urban planning vision was Catania in

Adelaide's Train Station.

Sicily. Adelaide was named after Amelia Theresa Carolina Adelheid of Saxony-Coburg-Meiningen, German consort of King William IV.
Adelaide is known as the city of churches or even, as ,the Holy Land' because, besides St Peter's Anglican Cathedral, it boasts Roman Catholic St Fran- cis Xavier Cathedral and 430 other places of worship of vari- ous denominations. The main Post Office across from the Town Hall is a relic of colonial times: during the day it used to fly a red flag and at night a red lantern indicated that post had come from England.

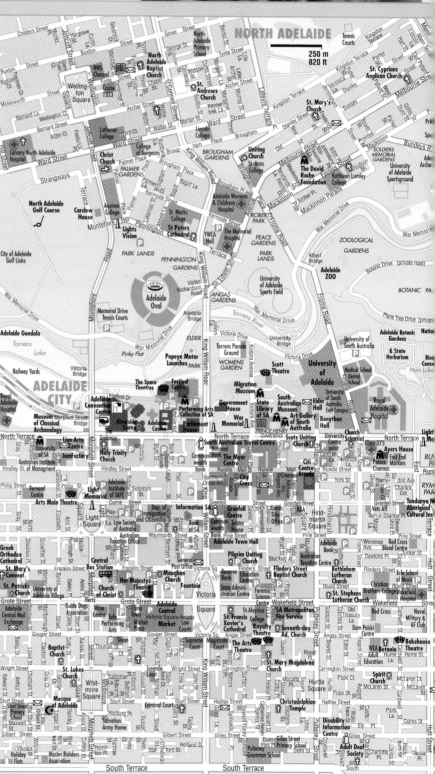

Thousands of Aboriginal rock paintings dot the spectacular landscape of Kings Canyon in Watarrka National Park.

Pillar, a 56-m-high (184-ft) sandstone monolith that early settlers used as a point of reference.

⑤ Ayers Rock (see page 248.) The Aborigines call this massive rock mountain Uluru (863 m/2,831 ft above sea level) and cherish it as a sacred place. Subsequently, since the path to the top is one of sacred significance, they 'kindly ask' that people do not climb it – but they do not forbid you to do so. Instead, they ask you to admire it from below as you stroll along the 9.4-km (5.8-mile) 'base walk'. The rock itself measures 3.5 km (2.2 miles) by 2.4 km (1.5 miles), and extends several kilometres down into the earth. It rises to 348 m (1,142 ft) above the steppe landscape like a whale stranded on a deserted beach. Due to its high iron content it changes colour with the movement of the sun – from crimson, rust, pink, brown and grey to a deep blue. After rainfall it even goes a silvery shade – a perpetually impressive show that will dazzle any visitor.

⑥ The Olgas (see page 248.) Known as Kata Tjuta by the Aborigines, the Olgas (1,066 m/3,497 ft above sea level) are a similarly spectacular sight. Kata Tjuta, meaning 'many heads', is 32 km (20 miles) to the north-

west of Uluru and comprises a group of thirty geologically similar, mainly dome-shaped monoliths that spread over an area of 35 sq km (13.5 sq mi), the highest point peaking at 546 m (1,791 ft). It would appear that the Olgas were once a single mountain that eroded over time into individual hills. The Valley of Winds traverses a stark mountain range through which either seasonal icy winds blow or burning hot air turns each step into a torturous affair.

⑦ Henbury Back on Stuart Highway the journey continues to the north. Approximately 2,000–3,000 years ago a meteor impacted not far from Henbury, leaving twelve distinct craters. The largest has a diameter of 180 m (560 ft) and the smallest just 6 m (20 ft). At Henbury, the Ernest Giles Highway splits off towards Watarrka National Park. It is a dirt track until it joins the Laritja Road where it becomes tarmac and eventually leads to the Kings Canyon Resort.

⑧ Watarrka National Park und Finke Gorge National Park (see page 249.) The centrepiece of the Watarrka National Park is Kings Canyon on the west end of the George Gill Range. With walls that rise to 200 m (656 ft), the canyon looks as if it were man-made. A number of Aboriginal rock paintings and carvings adorn the rugged canyon facades. The Aborigines aptly call the beehive-like eroded sandstone dome the 'Lost City'. Kings Canyon is best visited on foot by taking the Kings Creek Walk. From the resort, the Meerenie Loop (a dirt road) leads to the Aborigine town of Hermannsburg. On this slightly daunting stretch of road you'll cross low sand dunes that lead up to the base of the Macdonnell Range. East of the old Hermannsburger Mission, Larapinta Drive turns south and for the last 16 km

Large image: Ayers Rock, also called Uluru. Above: View over the impressive Olgas at sunset.

Roadtrains

The infamous Australian roadtrains are lorries that can measure up to 53 m (174 ft), have as many as fifteen axles and sixty-two tyres and supply the outback with basic necessities. Without them, life on an isolated farm or an inland mine would be impossible. These monsters of the road have 400–500 horsepower and barrel down highways, gravel roads and sand

'Roadtrains' ensure the supply of provisions in isolated areas.

tracks brushing aside any possible obstacles. The tractors are fitted with large grilles designed to protect the radiator from collisions with animals. Roadtrains run mostly across the sparsely populated outback. They can carry up to 80 tonnes of freight and regularly travel 4,000 km (2,484 miles).

One look at the little Agame makes it clear where the thorny devil got it's name from.

(10 miles) it runs through the dried-out Finke riverbed to Palm Valley. This last section is only really accessible with four-wheel drive vehicles. The main attraction of the Finke Gorge National Park is Palm Valley, home to more than 3,000 species of palm trees – all of them unique to this area – that line the picturesque watering holes. The route then leads via Hermannsburg and Larapinta Drive to the turn-off for Namatjira Drive, which will take you further to the north-west.

9 West MacDonnell National Park The Tropic of Capricorn runs straight across these mountains to the east of Alice Springs, which rise to heights of 1,524 m (5,000 ft). The principal attractions of the park are the numerous gorges that lie on a fault line alongside Larapinta Drive and Namatjira Drive. The most spectacular one is near Alice Springs and is called Simpsons Gap. The Standley Chasm, with depths of up to 100 m (328 ft), only gets sunshine for twenty minutes in the middle of the day.
Ellery Creek Big Hole, Serpentine

Gorge, Ormiston Gorge (giant blocks in Ormiston Pound) and Glen Helen Gorge are 133 km (83 miles) further down the road. The small lake there is sacred to the Aborigines because the mythical giant water snake is said to live there. The return route or continuing drive to Alice Springs follows the same road.

10 Alice Springs The geographical centre of Australia is about 1,700 km (1,055 miles) north of Adelaide and 1,500 km (931 miles) south of Darwin.
Alice Springs was founded in 1872 and its main attractions are the carefully restored Old Telegraph Station (1872) and the Flying Doctors centre from which medical assistance has been organized to serve the outback since 1939. You can enjoy a magnificent view of the nearby Macdonnell Range from Anzac Hill.
The famous Camel Cup takes place in July when up to fifteen dromedaries take part in a hard desert race. At the comical Henley-on-Todd regatta in springtime, 'oarsmen' race each other on foot in bottomless boats along the

usually dry Todd River.
North-east of the town is the Trephina Gorge National Park in the East Macdonnell Range. It can be reached via the paved Ross Highway. Eucalyptus trees grow alongside watering holes tucked between the steep walls of the gorge. A dirt track to the N'dhala Gorge Nature Park also branches off the Stuart Highway. Another track leads to Maryvale, the last outpost of civilization in the Simson Desert. From there it is about

58 km (36 miles) to Chambers Pillar. On the way to the Devils Marbles near Wauchope, the view to your right overlooks the Davenport Range, another national park. To the north of the West Macdonnell Range there are Aborigine reserves on both sides of Stuart Highway, for example the Pawu Aboriginal Land west of Borrow Creek. It was not until the end of the 20th century that the lands were returned to the indigenous people.

Numerous python species are native to Australia. Their bite is not poisonous, but can still be painful.

❶ Devils Marbles These eroded granite spheres look as if a mightier power had scattered them across the rocky plateau with mathematical precision. It seems as if the slightest breeze could blow them away. The Aborigines believe the marbles to be rainbow water snake eggs.

❶ Tennant Creek When the last gold rush began in Australia in 1932, Tennant Creek was known as 'Gold Town'. Within a few years, however, it became more of a ghost town until it was eventually reawakened by the discovery of nearby silver and copper mines. The Nobles Nob Mine and the Tennant Creek Stamp Battery Museum recall the bonanza. Some 11 km (7 miles) north-west are the Devils Pebbles, a scattering of granite boulders. A roadside memorial for John Flynn, the founder of the Flying Doctors, lies some 20 km (12 miles) in the same direction.

❶ Renner Springs Further along the route towards Katherine, north of Helen Springs, the road takes you to Renner Springs. This small town marks both the climatic and geographical border between the outback of the 'Red Centre' and the savannah of the northern coastal areas.
Newcastle Waters to the north was once an important telegraph station and crossing point for livestock herds.

❶ Daly Waters Still further north, it is definitely worth making a stop in Daly Waters, where the oldest pub in the Northern Territory has been wetting whistles since 1893. For decades, travellers have left various utensils here – from tickets for the legendary Ghan Express to autographed underwear. These are now all carefully arranged to decorate the walls of the pub.
In this hot, dry environment, a cold beer tastes even better than in other roadhouses along the highway. The next stop is Larrimah with its historic train station. From there it's on to Mataranka where you should not miss

out on a refreshing dip in Mataranka Pool in Elsey National Park, roughly 9 km (5.5 miles) away. The thermal hotsprings are surrounded by paperbark trees, from which hang long strips of bark. The Aborigines used this bark for thousands of years as wrapping for their food. From Mataranka it's now only 110 km (68 miles) to Katherine on the banks of the Katherine River, a river that never dries out.

❶ Katherine This town offers limited attractions, but there is a nostalgic train station dating from 1926 and the first biplane used by the Flying Doctors is on display here. Nature lovers in particular stop in Katherine because the Cutta Cutta Caves Nature Park is just 24 km (15 miles) away to the south-east. The stalactite and stalagmite formations in the caves are a refuge for rare bats and tree snakes.

Top left: View over Alice Springs. Top right: Devils Marbles. Above: Simpsons Gap, a beautiful spot on the West MacDonnell Ranges.

Lush green fauna can be found around the Wadi Falls.

Aborigines

When the European settlement of Australia began at the end of the 18th century, they saw the country as 'terra nullius' or unknowed land, but at least 350,000 Aborigines (from the Latin 'ab origine', meaning from the origin) had lived on the continent for more than 50,000 years. The Aborigines were organised in kinships, clans and tribes and roamed the continent as hunters and gatherers. The Aborigines' totemic and magical be-

Ritual body painting.

liefs have been around for thousands of years: mountains, rocks, rivers, lakes and trees all have souls. Their perception of the world is influenced by the 'Dreamtime' in which past, present and future are permanently interlinked. In the beginning, the world was a flat disk shrouded in darkness until the giants came with light, water, clouds and rain and created all forms of life. The giants then turned into mountains, rivers, lakes, trees and animals. Nature as a whole is therefore divine in Aboriginal 'Dreamtime'. All of these concepts feature in Aborigine rites, traditions and customs such as body painting, magical songs and rock paintings. The indigenous Australians have been fighting hard for the return of their lands and social recognition from European descendants for more than fifty years.

16 Nitmiluk National Park This impressive network of canyons formed over thousands of years by the Katherine River is one of the greatest natural wonders of Australia – Katherine Gorge. Red brown limestone canyon walls rise up to 100 m (328 ft) above the river. The best way to view them is from a sightseeing boat that embarks in Katherine, or you can explore the river by canoe when it is not the rainy season. During the rainy season the otherwise calm river turns into a raging torrent and is not really navigable. Biologists often marvel at Katherine Gorge for its unbelievable variety of wildlife – freshwater crocodiles live here, along with more than 160 species of birds and numerous butterfly species. All in all, nine of the thirteen gorges in the park are open to visitors. Edith Falls is a particularly spectacular natural phenomenon. You can reach the falls by either taking the rough 75-km (48-mile) track, or the more comfortabe Stuart Highway. Smaller pools and waterfalls invite sun-weary visitors to take a refreshing swim.

17 Pine Creek This town, 90 km (56 miles) north-west of Kath-

erine, was once a hot spot for gold diggers. Today it's a supply station for those on their way to Darwin, or the starting point for excursions to the Kakadu National Park to the east. If you would like to visit that world-famous national park, leave the Stuart Highway at Pine Creek and take the Kakadu High-

way towards Jabiru. You will find the park visitor centre there and can plan your trip.

18 Kakadu National Park (see pages 254-255.) Covering an

area of 20,000 sq km (7,800 sq mi), this national park in Arnhem Land is one of the largest and most attractive in Australia. The scenery shifts from the tidal zone at Van Diemen Gulf and the flood plains of the lowlands to the escarpment and the arid plateaus of Arnhem Land. The most impres-

sive attraction is the escarpment, a craggy 500-km-long (310-mile) outcrop with spectacular waterfalls such as the Jim Jim Falls, Tain Falls and Twin Falls, which are at their best towards the end of the

The area around the large natural Darwin harbour offers plenty of culture, dining and entertainment.

rainy season. The name of the park comes from 'Gagudju', which is the name of an Aboriginal language originating in this floodplain region.

Biologists have counted 1,300 plant, 10,000 insect, 240 bird and seventy reptile species, including the feared saltwater crocodile. The rare mountain kangaroos, wallabies and one-third of the country's bird species are also native to this area. Due to its diversity, this impressive park has been made into a UNESCO World Heritage Site.

There are over 5,000 Aborigine rock paintings here, the most famous of which are on Nourlinge Rock, Ubirr Rock and in Nangaluwur. The paintings, some of which date back as many as 18,000–23,000 years, not only demonstrate the area's climate change, but are also a striking portrayal of the culture of the Aborigines, who have allegedly lived on the continent here for 50,000 years. The best time of year to visit the park is in the dry season from May to November, as the roads are otherwise impassable.

The Arnhem Highway leads back through Cooinda and Jabiru to the Stuart Highway. From Noonaman

the road leads south before heading west through Batchelor into Litchfield National Park.

⑲ Litchfield National Park The main attractions of this park are immediately visible – the open eucalyptus forests, the thick rainforest around the escarpment, and the massive, skilfully crafted gravestone-like mounds of the magnetic termites can reach heights of 2 m (6.5 ft). Due to the extreme midday heat the termites have cleverly aligned the long side of their mounds with the north-south axis in order to warm their homes in the morning and evening sun while protecting them from the midday sun.

The Tabletop Range escarpment is a spectacular sight where waterfalls like Sandy Creek Falls, Florence Falls, Tower Falls and Wangi Falls cascade down the ridge even in the dry season. The unique environment around the falls has developed its own unique spectrum of monsoon rainforest wildlife.

⑳ Darwin Due to its proximity to the South-East Asian countries to the north of Australia, Darwin has developed into a culturally

very diverse city, which is reflected in its numerous markets and restaurants. One of the specialities here is the daily, slightly odd Aquascene Fish Feeding at Doctor's Gulley. At high tide various fish swim onto land to be fed by hand from humans. Wonderful white sand beaches can be found on both sides of the scenic harbour town of Beagle Gulf.

Since the destruction caused by Tornado Tracy during Christmas of 1974, the city of Darwin has changed dramatically. After the storm, almost nothing was left of the historic 19th-century buildings apart from the Old Navy Headquarters, Fanny Bay Jail, the Court House, Brown's Mart and the Government House with its seven gables. Your journey across the mighty outback ends here, on the coast at the doorstep to Asia.

Large image: The Kakadu National Park with its waterfalls is a natural spectacle. Left: Katherine Gorge in Nitmiluk National Park.

The wildlife of Kakadu National Park

This national park is renowned for its animal diversity. The park is made up of a tidal zone, flood plains, a steppe and the Arnhem Land Plateau.

One of the birds: Darter

Alone 240 bird species have been counted by ornithologists here, including the Jaribu. The crocodile is the best-known among seventy reptile species here. Daily almost fifty mammal species meet at the watering hole.

The extensive landscape areas of the National Park include the extensive Wetlands.

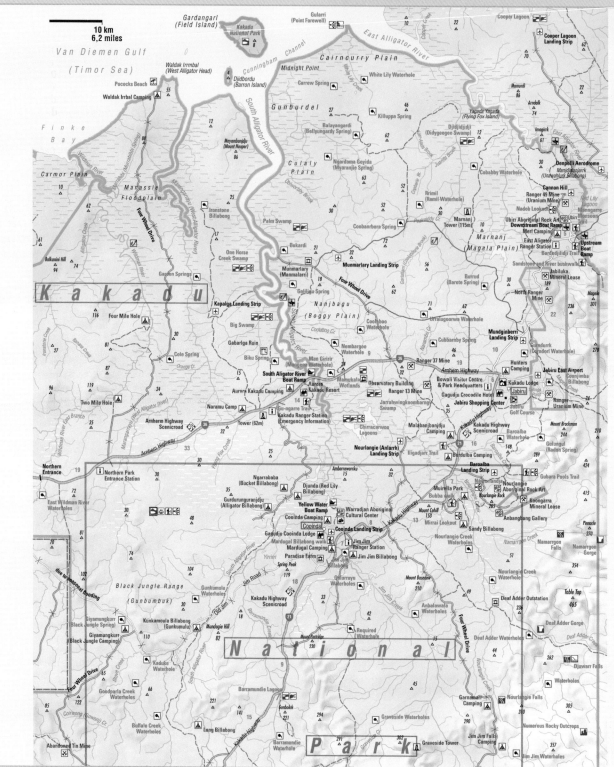

The rock paintings of the Aborigines were found on the massif of the impressive Nourlangie Rock.

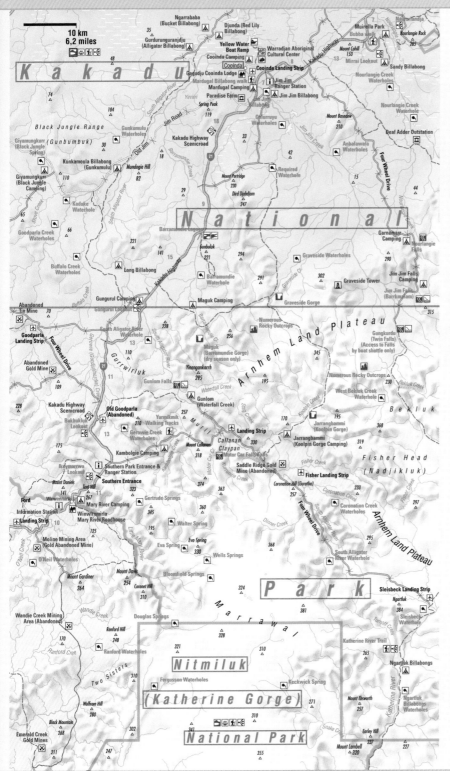

Kakadu National Park

Kakadu National Park, now expanded to its current area of 20,000 sq. km (7,700 sq. miles), lies 250 km (155 miles) east of Darwin and encloses five distinct kinds of landscape.

In the tidal river estuaries, mangroves have established root systems in the silt, protecting the hinterland from the destructive effects of wave action. In the rainy season, the coastal areas transform themselves into a bright carpet of lotus flowers, water lilies, and floating ferns. Rare waterfowl, such as the brolga, the Jesus bird, the white-faced heron, the great Indian stork, and the snake bird are native to here, as is the saltwater crocodile, the largest living reptile.

The adjoining hills, with their wide variety of open tropical forest, savannah, and grassy plains vegetation, form the greater part of the park and offer a refuge for endangered species, such as dingoes and wallabies. Several of the rarer kangaroo species live on the sandstone plateaus of Arnhem Land and on the Arnhem escarpment, a 500-km (310-mile) long cliff crossing the park from the south-west to the north-east.

The park, which is jointly managed by its traditional Aboriginal owners and the Australian Government, became internationally famous in the middle of the 20th century, when excavations uncovered Stone Age tools that were at least 3,000 years old. Numerous rock paintings reveal details of the hunting habits, myths, and customs of the Aboriginal tribes who lived here.

Kings Canyon Aboriginal rock paintings line the steep walls of this spectacular canyon.

Kata Tjuta The name means 'many heads' in the Aborigines language. This group of thirty-six rock monoliths in the middle of the steppe in central Australia is also known as The Olgas.

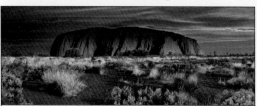

Uluru Like a beached whale, the 348-m-wide (1,142-ft) outcrop, named Ayers Rock by Europeans, emerges stoically from the red outback landscape. A mythical and sacred place for Aborigines, Uluru is an essential element in the divine acts of the ancestors who created life on earth.

Coober Pedy Opals have been mined at the foot of the Stuart Range since 1915. Nearly 70 % of the world's opals are mined here. Many people live in underground dwellings owing to temperatures above 50°C (122°F).

Dreamtrack For Aborigines, Australia's landscape is filled with traces of the creators. Songs and dances tell the complex stories of the creators and how the giants became the contours of the land.

Adelaide The capital of South Australia was founded in 1836 between the beaches of Gulf St Vincent and the Mount Lofty Range. It was named after Queen Adelaide.

Barossa This is the collective name for Barossa Valley and Eden Valley, the best wine-growing region in Australia, originally settled by Germans in the mid 19th century.

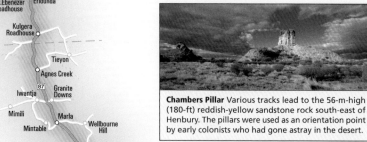

Finke Gorge National Park In this park, 12 km (7.5 miles) south of Hermannsburg, you will find the beautiful Palm Valley. Thanks to the tropical climate, many rare palm trees grow here.

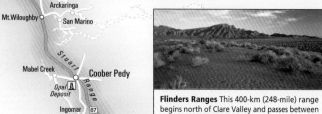

Chambers Pillar Various tracks lead to the 56-m-high (180-ft) reddish-yellow sandstone rock south-east of Henbury. The pillars were used as an orientation point by early colonists who had gone astray in the desert.

Flinders Ranges This 400-km (248-mile) range begins north of Clare Valley and passes between Lake Torrens and Lake Frome. The national park extends deep into the outback and includes the famous Wilpena Pound.

Map labels

Tennant Creek
MacDonnell Ranges
Mt.Zeil
Mt.Liebig 1524
Mt.Hay 1250
1511 West MacDonnell N.P.
Claraville
Sounds of Starlight Theatre
Trephina Gorge N.P.
N'dhala Gorge N.P.
Alice Springs
Hermannsburg
Santa Theresa
Watarrka N.P.
Finke Gorge N.P.
Orange Creek
Kings Canyon
Urrampinyu Jljiltjarri A.L.
Henbury
Maryvale
Wallara Ranch Roadhouse
Lake Amadeus
Northern Territory
Chambers Pillar
The Olgas (Kata Tjuta) 1066
Angas Downs
Yulara
4
Mt.Ebenezer Roadhouse
Erldunda
Uluru - Kata Tjuta N.P.
Curtin Springs
863 Ayers Rock (Uluru)
Kulgera Roadhouse
Tieyon
Agnes Creek
87
Granite Downs
Iwantja
Mimili
Marla
Mintable
Wellbourne Hill
Arckaringa
San Marino
Mt.Willoughby
Mabel Creek
Coober Pedy
Opal Deposit
Stuart Range
Ingomar
87
South
McDouall Peak
The Twins
Mount Eba
Bulgunnia
Bon Bon
Wymiet
Gosses
Wilgena
Kingoonya
Glendambo
Purple Downs
Bosworth
Australia
Woomera
Lake Torrens N.P.
Parachilna
Lake Gairdner N.P.
Pimba
Wonoka
Flinders Ranges N.P.
Bookaloo
Hawker
Cariewerloo
Quorn
Wilmington
Peterborough
Port Augusta
Mt.Remarkable N.P.
Kalgoorlie
Whyalla
Port Germein
Jamestown
Port Lincoln
Port Pirie
Crystal Brook
Port Broughton
Snowtown
Broken Hill
Auburn
32
Spencer Gulf
Kulpara
Port Wakefield
Mildura
Ardrossan
Virginia
1
Barossa V.
Yorke Peninsula
Gawler
Adelaide
Morphettville Racecourse
Port Noarlunga
Hahndorf
Melbourne
Cape Spencer
Fleuneu Peninsula

Darwin The port on the northern edge of the 'Top End' benefits from a subtropical climate. The few historic buildings include the Old Navy Headquarters, Fannie Bay and Brown's Mart.

Aboriginal rock art Rock carvings, rock and cave paintings, drawings of animals, sand designs, totem poles, carvings that feature and wickerwork are all part of Aborigine culture. The designs in their stone paintings were applied using ochre, charcoal and limestone and symbolize the relationship between humans and their environment, which are believed to mythically coexist in 'Dreamtime'.

Nourlangie Rock The Aborigine rock paintings at Nourlangie Rock in the Kakadu National Park are examples of the so-called 'X-ray style'.

Wangi Falls The waterfalls in Litchfield National Park crash spectacularly into the depths. It is safe to bathe in the bay.

Kakadu National Park Stone plateaus, waterfalls, flood plains and the South Alligator River characterize this park's landscape, one of Australia's best-known attractions in the 'Top End'.

Litchfield National Park This park is known for its magnetic termite mounds, which are designed to take advantage of the sunshine.

Cutta Cutta Caves Nature Park Rare bat species live alongside equally rare snakes in limestone caves 25 km (15 miles) south-east of Katherine, a jumping-off point for the park.

Nitmiluk National Park Some of the highlights of this park are the rivers and ravines of Katherine Gorge, which go down to depths of 100 m (328 ft).

Tennant Creek The town on the Stuart Highway was once a telegraph post on the Overland Telegraph Line. Gold was found here in 1932.

Devils Marbles The 170-million-year-old red granite blocks near Wauchope were formed by the constant temperature changes from glowing heat to icy cold.

Davenport Range National Park Waterful and giant red kangaroos have found refuge in the mountains and steppes of this park.

Pawu Aboriginal Land The 2,500 sq km (975 sq mi) around Mount Barkly, west of Barrow Creek and south of Willowra, was returned to the Aborigines in 1981, sixty-one years after they were driven off the land by European settlers.

West Macdonnell Ranges The highest peak in this craggy mountain range to the east and west of Alice Springs is Mount Liebig, at 1,524 m (5,000 ft).

Alice Springs At the heart of the 'Red Centre': 1,700 km (1,055 miles) from Adelaide and 1,500 km (931 miles) from Darwin.

Trephina Gorge Nature Park This park in the East Macdonnell Range is famous for its quartz cliffs and the eucalyptus stands that box in the Trephina Gorge watering holes.

257

Route 20: Australia

The Pacific Highway

As you travel along Australia's colorful Pacific coastline, you will soon appreciate why Australians call their homeland 'the lucky country'. The national parks transport visitors into a magical, largely unspoilt, subtropical wonderland. The stunning and romantic Blue Mountains, formed on a sandstone plateau, reach elevations of more than 1,000 m (3,281 ft) and feature magnificent primeval rainforests that are millions of years old. The coast is dotted with interesting towns and unfathomably long beaches.

Route profile:

Length: approx. 1,100 km (684 mi), excluding detours
Time required: at least 1 week
Traffic information: Be prepared for a high volume of traffic in the densely populated coastal areas at weekends and during holidays.

New South Wales, proudly named the 'Premier State', offers one of the most attractive sections of the Australia's Pacific coast. Not only is it the oldest state in the country, it is also has the largest and densest population, and the strongest economy.

Common theory says that navigator and explorer Captain Cook gave the state its name in 1770, as the coastline reminded him of his homeland of Wales. With its heavily populated areas and developed landscape, New South Wales now forms a stark contrast

to the vast empty expanses of the rest of the Australian continent. Indeed, it would be hard to beat the variety offered along the seaboard between Sydney and Brisbane. The steep slopes and deep wooded gorges of the Blue Mountains, cloaked in their signature bluish haze, are some of the most impressive sights in Australia. Combine that dramatic landscape of bizarre rock formations with the lush subtropical rainforests on the coastal plains nearby, with their huge variety of plant and animal life, and you could hardly ask for more. Lamington and Border Ranges National Parks on the border with Queensland have huge trees wrapped in vines, strangler figs and tree ferns. In fact, the entire string of national parks along the coast is a UNESCO World Natural Heritage Site, designated as East Coast Temperate and Subtropical Rainforest. The Eastern Highlands run parallel to the

coast, falling away dramatically to the east where the Great Dividing Range gives way to a fertile coastal plain. The plain begins to widen to the north, traversed by estuaries that have formed countless bays and inviting sandy

beaches. The major towns and cities are concentrated in this region. The Gold Coast, in the south of Queensland, has developed into a very popular holiday area for both locals and tourists. Favourable wind conditions and endless

Top: Sydney Harbour Bridge is a magnificent construction. The city's iconic building is the striking Opera House, opened in 1973, and declared a UNESCO World Heritage site in 2007.
Left: Australia competes with places like Hawaii and California as one of the world's surfing meccas.

beaches make it a paradise for surfers in particular, but sun worshippers will be more than satisfied as well.

Nestled in the romantic valleys at the edge of the highlands are Australia's oldest vineyards, including the Lower Hunter Valley west of Newcastle. Of the cities along the Pacific coast, Sydney holds the number one slot, with myriad examples of impressive modern engineering and architecture and a huge variety of cultural attractions. The south-east coast of Australia is best explored from the Pacific Highway. It connects the Bruce Highway, heading north from Brisbane, with the Princes Highway, which heads south from Sydney.

The scenic diversity of New South Wales is impressive: it has everything from sparkling stretches of coast to lush green-covered plateaus.

There is a wonderful view of Cawson Creek and the Hawkesbury River from Ku-ring-Gai Chase National Park.

Detour

Kanangra-Boyd National Park

Kanangra-Boyd National Park is connected to the southern section of Blue Mountains National Park, covers 700 sq km (271 sq mi) and forms part of that listed UNESCO site. The park is about 180 km (112 mi) west of Sydney and is easily reached on the Great Western Highway, via Katoomba and the famous Jenolan Caves. From here, a track leads into the park. The Jenolan Caves are among the largest and most magnificent limestone caverns on the continent. You can visit nine of the extraordi-

The overhanging cliffs of the Kanangra Walls.

nary caves, all of them featuring a spectacular light. They were discovered in 1867, but part of the network of caves remains uncharted and you can only explore a small section of the stalagmites and stalactites without a guide. Try to avoid visiting the popular caverns during the day, when they can be extremely busy. The landscape of the national park is full of variety, with deep valleys alternating with almost flat limestone plateaus that suddenly fall away to reveal spectacular views over the Blue Mountains. The tall overhanging cliffs of the Kanangra Walls are particularly impressive, and a paradise for rock climbers.

① **Sydney** (see pp. 262-263.) Sydney is in the center of Australia's south-eastern coast. The 2000 Olympic Games are now a thing of the past, but there is no shortage of interesting activities for everyone.

It is unlikely you'll be bored in Sydney, unless none of the following strikes your fancy: fabulous restaurants, huge shopping centers, a spectacular variety of cultural attractions and events, a fascinating history exhibited in various museums and buildings, stunning city beaches, and a range of national parks right at your doorstep.

② **Ku-Ring-Gai Chase National Park** This park is situated on a sandstone plateau traversed by rivers. Its northern border is formed by Broken Bay, an estuary of the Hawkesbury River. The park encompasses a classic Sydney landscape of beaches, bushland, eucalyptus forest and

heath land, and boasts a huge network of waterways to keep canoeists and anglers happy.

The well-preserved rock paintings and engravings by the Gurringai Aborigines, who once lived here and gave the park its name, are well worth seeing.

Follow the route inland via Sydney along the Great Western Highway (Hwy. 32) toward the Blue Mountains.

③ **Blue Mountains National Park** (see also pp. 264–265.) For many years the Blue Mountains, part of the Great Dividing Range, formed an insurmountable barrier for people living along the coast. The first successful crossing of the mountain range was not made until 1813, finally allowing access to much-needed pastures in the west. Sydneysiders flock to the Blue Mountains for their magnif-

The morning mist rests peacefully over the fern-covered lake in Wollemi National Park.

Wildlife in south-east Australia

South-east Australia is home to many of the country's best-known animals. At the top of the list are various kangaroo species, which are common to most parts of Australia. These marsupials of the macropod family have long, powerful hind legs that are responsible for their highly effective and energy-efficient means of locomotion – hopping. As they hop, the tendons in their hind legs act as springs, while the powerful tail helps them keep their balance. All kangaroos have an pouch on their belly. Eastern Australia's eucalyptus forests

The Tasmanian pygmy possum also lives here.

are the perfect place to look for koala bears lounging high up in the trees. The koala's diet has become extremely specialized and they feed on just a few species of Australian eucalyptus, of which there are more than five hundred. The nutrients in the leaves differ according to type, season and region, and koalas sometimes go in search of alternatives. Koalas have an built-in 'fermentation system' to help them digest their cellulose-rich diet: a koala's caecum (part of the intestines) is 2 m (6.5 ft) long (the animal themselves are a maximum of 80 cm/2.5 ft) and contains micro-organisms that help break down food.

icent cliffs, gorges and caverns. The Three Sisters rock formation and the Jenolan Caves are just two of the many attractions that lure city dwellers and travelers to theses mountains. Putty Road, between the small gold-rush towns of Windsor and Singleton, passes through the northern Blue Mountains and along the eastern boundary of Wollemi National Park.

④ Wollemi National Park This is the largest park of its kind in New South Wales, a huge wilderness area covering 5,000 sq km (1,930 sq mi) that is for the most part unspoilt and even very isolated in parts. The park features deep sandstone gorges and wonderful pristine landscapes along the Colo and Wollemi rivers. Basalt outcrops reach heights of over 1,200 m (3,937 ft), and rainforests

thrive on the mountains and in the valleys. Visitors can choose from a variety of activities including bushwalking through the wilderness, rock climbing or canoe-

Top: The magnificent 'Three Sisters' rock formation is a landmark in the World Heritage Blue Mountains park. Left: Jenolan Caves. Above: the port of Sydney at night.

Route 20: Australia

Sydney Harbour Bridge is the city's second great landmark. Opened to traffic in 1932, the bridge was built during the Great Depression. The distinctive arch has a span of 503 m (1,650 ft).

262

Top: The roofs of the Sydney Opera House look like upturned seashells or billowing sails, and are an iconic feature of the city's port.

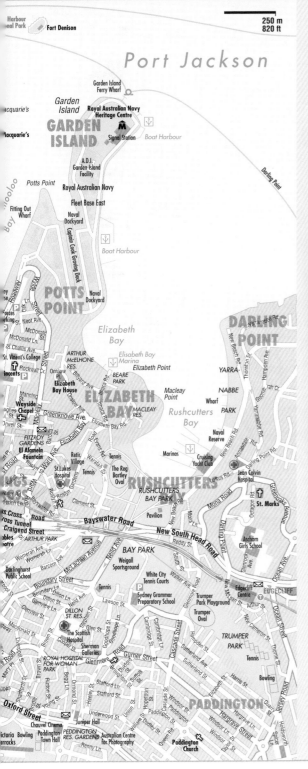

Sydney

The oldest and largest city on the Australian continent, Sydney, the capital of New South Wales, has a population of over four million and is Australia's leading commercial and financial center. Numerous universities, museums and galleries also make Sydney the cultural center of the south-east coast.

In 1788, when the first wave of settlers – mostly convicts and their guards – came ashore under the command of Captain Arthur Phillip, none of them could have imagined that Port Jackson would one day become one of the most beautiful cities in the world. Sydney's expansion first began with the arrival of European and then of Asian immigrants, a mixture that characterizes the city's present-day multicultural atmosphere. From 250 m (820 ft) up on the viewing platform of the 305-m (1,001 ft) Sydney Tower, you get a magnificent view of the skyline, the port, the smart residential suburbs, the Pacific coast and, further inland, the Blue Mountains – not to mention the city's second great landmark, the Harbour Bridge. This amazing construction forms a graceful arc across the bay at a height of 134 m (440 ft) and with a span of 503 m (1,650 ft). The best place to begin your tour of the city is the port, with the Harbour Bridge and the Opera House within striking distance. You could also start by people-watching from one of the many cafés, listening to the street musicians or taking a boat trip. The Rocks area is a must for shoppers and pub-goers. From the city center, an elevated railway takes you to Darling Harbour and its myriad attractions. On the somewhat quieter side, the Botanic Gardens feature a cross-section of Australian flora. Chinatown is on the south side of town, other districts worth visiting include Paddington and the nightclub district, Kings Cross.

Enjoy a walk along the largest natural port in the world.

Im Queen Victoria Building befinden sich exklusive Shops.

Tower rises between the roofs of the Sydney Opera House.

The 'Three Sisters' tower high above the valley of the Jamison River.

Blue Mountains National Park

The Blue Mountains are about 50 km (31 mi) west of Sydney on the western edge of the Cumberland Plain basin. It is an area of outstanding natural beauty and as such attracts no fewer than three million visitors every year.

The Blue Mountains range is actually a sandstone plateau that reaches elevations of over 1,000 m (3,281 ft) in places. Over millions of years, its rivers have eroded and dug their way into the rock to depths of hundreds of meters. The signs of these geological processes are unmistakable: gigantic gorges, precipitous cliffs, pounding waterfalls and a huge variety of flora and fauna including more than one hundred species of birds, eucalyptus trees, ferns and wild flowers. The Blue Mountains take their name from the bluish haze that often envelops them and is caused by the release of essential oils from eucalyptus trees. Blue Mountains National Park covers some 2,700 sq km (1,043 sq mi) and was established in 1959. The park has good facilities and is easy to get around. By car you can reach some spectacular vantage points along the Great Western Highway and Cliff Drive between Leura and Katoomba. Two tourist rail services, the Katoomba Scenic Railway and the Zig Zag Railway, also serve the park. But the best way to explore it is still on foot. Choose from one of the many hikes, among them the Federal Pass Walk, the Prince Henry Cliff Walk or the Grand Canyon Nature Track. The park's top attractions include the Wentworth Falls, some 300 m (984 ft) high, the Giant Stairway with over one thousand steps at Echo Point, and the Blue Gum Forest (blue gum is a type of eucalyptus) in Grose Valley. The ultimate, must-have photograph is of the 'Three Sisters': three giant rock formations towering high above Jamison Valley.

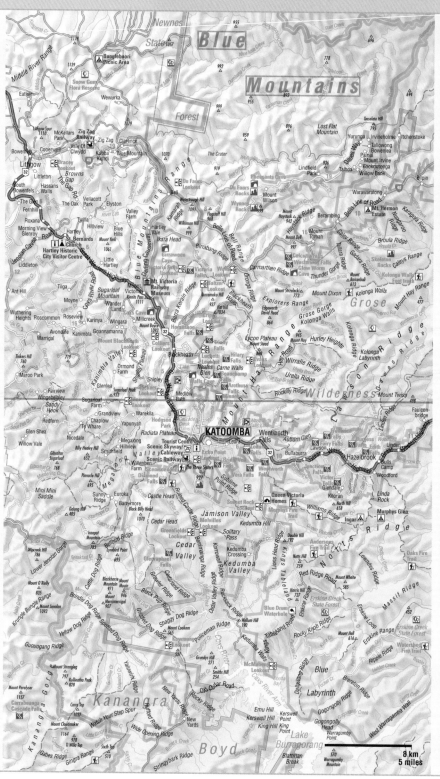

In addition to exciting structures made of sandstone, the National Park also features magical waterfalls.

Explore Dorrigo National Park on the Wonga Walk, which takes about 2.5 hours to walk.

Detour

Dorrigo National Park

Picturesque Dorrigo is situated on a plateau bordering a steep escarpment covered in pristine subtropical and cool-temperate rainforest. The entrance to Dorrigo National Park is 4 km (2.5 mi) south-east of the town of Dorrigo. The forest is connected to the New England National Park and, like its neighbour, belongs to the East Coast Temperate and Subtropical Rainforest parks. The wilderness of the subtropical rainforest and wet eucalypt woodland is an impressive sight, teeming with

A jungle of ferns in Dorrigo National Park.

an abundance of orchids, ferns and mosses. The animal world in this national park is equally colorful and diverse, allowing you the opportunity to see and hear a variety of brightly plumed birds with their shrill songs.

The steeply rising terrain attracts heavy rainfall in summer, making a visit to the waterfalls a memorable experience.

A number of good tracks lead through the middle of the park. Near the visitor center there is the Skywalk, a wooden walkway that runs 70 m (230 ft) above the treetops and provides some breathtaking views over the rainforest canopy.

ing along the rivers. At Singleton, north-east of the park, join Highway 15 and head east through the Upper Hunter Valley, a region famous for horse breeding and vineyards, to one of Australia's most famous wine regions, the Lower Hunter Valley.

5 Lower Hunter Valley Cessnock is the main town at the heart of the this wine-producing region. Farms and vineyards are nestled among gently rolling hills, and to the west you can just make out the foothills of the Great Dividing Range. Grapes have been cultivated in the fertile soil of this region since the 1830s, and there are around 140 wineries in the valley, most of them open to visitors. Among the most famous are Lindemans, Tyrrell's Wines and Wyndham Estate. In stark contrast, the main industries in nearby Newcastle, the second-largest city in New South Wales, are steel, coal and shipping.

Around 40 km (25 mi) north of Newcastle, it is worth making a stop in Port Stephens, the 'dolphin capital of Australia'.

6 Port Stephens Many tourists come to this port to enjoy a trip on a dolphin-watching boat

to see the 150–200 dolphins that make Nelson Bay their home. Between May and July, and September and November, pods of whales also swim past the coast here, among them killer whales, minkes and humpbacks.

Port Stephens is also famous for Stockton Beach, some 33 km (21

mi) long, where you can even take your four-wheel-drive for a spin in the sand.

Myall Lakes National Park is 60 km (37 mi) to the north and is the largest lake area in New South Wales.

7 Port Macquarie Founded in 1821 as a penal colony, Port Macquarie is one of the oldest towns

in Australia. The Port Macquarie Museum and Courthouse, St Thomas' Anglican Church and the Roto House, all built in the 19th century, are still standing today. Since the 1970s, tourism has boosted the town's fortunes remarkably, and it is also popular among retired Australians, who

enjoy the town's relaxed atmosphere. There are plenty of swimming and surfing beaches and a wide variety of other water sports in general on offer.

Heading north along the Pacific Highway, you enter increasingly humid and damp regions, home to dense rainforests. The route then leaves the coastal highway at Kempsey for another detour

Most Jacaranda trees display opulent flowers in violet tones, but some also bloom in white.

into the impressive Great Dividing Range. You travel via Bellingen and Dorrigo on the way to New England National Park.

⑧ New England National Park Covering an area of 300 sq km (116 sq mi), this park is situated on the escarpment of the New England Plateau at an elevation of 1,400 m (4,593 ft). It encompasses one of the largest rainforests in New South Wales and features snow gum trees in the upper regions, temperate rainforest vegetation at the middle elevations, and subtropical rainforest with tree-high ferns at the base of the plateau. Drive up to Point Lookout at 1,562 m (5,125 ft) for a wonderful view of the highland escarpment and the Bellinger Valley. On the return journey to the coast it is certainly worth making a detour to Dorrigo National Park (see sidebar left). From Dorrigo, the Waterfall Way takes you back to the coast.

Coffs Harbour boasts a series of attractive beaches and is one of the most popular holiday resorts in the state. Banana plantations have been the mainstay of the region's agriculture for more than one hundred years, and reflects the gradual change in cli-

mate from subtropical to tropical. Just a few miles north of Coffs Harbour, the Pacific Highway heads inland toward Grafton.

⑨ Grafton This country town, nestled on the banks of the Clarence River, is known as the 'Jacaranda capital of Australia', and

its wide, elegant streets are lined with these beautifully fragrant trees. The Jacaranda Festival takes place when the trees bloom in late October or early November.

Grafton was founded by lumberjacks around 1830, with cattle farmers following later. When gold was discovered in the upper reaches of the Clarence River, the town developed rapidly and a

busy river port flourished around 1880. Traces of the town's late 19th-century prosperity can be seen in a number of well-preserved buildings on the north side of the river.

A track from Grafton leads to Wooli, the gateway to Yuraygir National Park, about 50 km (31 mi) away.

⑩ Yuraygir National Park This national park encompasses the longest stretch of pristine coastline in New South Wales. It perfectly shows how the coast looked before it became so densely populated and boasts remote sandy beaches, heaths, swamps and lagoons.

The national park has some excellent walking trails and offers perfect conditions for both surfers and anglers.

⑪ Yamba This 19th-century fishing village is about 60 km (37 mi) further north, and has become an angler's paradise. The beautiful beaches offer myriad water sports options, and there are rewarding fishing spots on the Clarence River, in the nearby coastal lakes and along the coast. Angourie Point, just 5 km (3 mi) south of Yamba, is one of the best surfing beaches in the country.

The Pacific Highway now heads north along the seemingly endless string of white-sand beaches toward Byron Bay, about 120 km (75 mi) away.

⑫ Byron Bay This surfer, hippie enclave-cum-holiday resort gets its name not from the famous poet, but from his grandfather, John Byron, a renowned navigator in the 1760s. It has a mild and sunny climate, splendidly long beaches and perfect wind conditions, all of which have made this surfing paradise into one of the

Large image: Lighthouse in Byron Bay. Left side: The Yacaaba Head at Port Stephens. Above: You can often see pelicans in Yamba.

Detour

Lamington National Park and Border Ranges National Park

Lamington National Park is a well-developed park first listed as a conservation area in 1915. It is easy to reach from the Pacific Highway.

In the middle of the park is the Lamington plateau, which reaches 900 – 1,200 m (2,952–3,937 ft) and ends in steep cliffs and gorges in the south. The parkland contains more than five hundred waterfalls and a variety of woodlands, ranging from tropical and subtropical rainforest to southern beech for-

A waterfall in Lamington National Park.

est at higher elevations. The park also boasts a rich diversity of animal life, including almost two hundred different species of birds.

Border Ranges National Park, between New South Wales and Queensland, contains the remains of an extinct shield volcano. The park's rainforests are home to gigantic strangler figs, pade-melons (small kangaroos) and rare yellow-eared cockatoos.

At night, the buildings of Brisbane create a single sea of lights.

most popular seaside resorts on the north-east coast of New South Wales.

If you don't feel like exploring the beaches of the neighboring Gold Coast to the north, take a detour into the hinterland instead. Some 50 km (31 mi) north of Byron, in Murwillumbah, the Summerland Way turns off into the spectacular Border Ranges National Park (see sidebar, p.267).

13 Gold Coast There's nowhere else in Australia quite like it. The Gold Coast, with the city of the same name at its heart, is home to more luxury hotels, holiday complexes, motels, holiday apartments, guesthouses and youth hostels than anywhere else in the country. It offers an unrivaled variety of sporting and leisure activities, and more opportunities for entertainment and shopping than you are likely to find anywhere else. This section of coastline begins on the border with New South Wales and stretches to Coomera, south of Brisbane. The subtropical climate, with temperatures ranging from 22°C to 28°C (72°F to 83°F), and an annual quota of 300 days of sunshine, attracts over three million visitors per year.

14 Surfers Paradise The first holiday development in the Gold Coast's best-known resort opened in 1923. It was called 'Surfers Paradise Hotel' and just a few years later the entire area adopted the name. The town flourished in the 1950s, mostly because of the triple-S factor: sun, surf and sand. Buildings sprang up, and today the whole length of lovely, sandy beach is lined with a strip of hotel and apartment complexes. With all the leisure and sporting activities, entertainment and a lively nightlife on offer, Surfers Paradise just seems to get more and more popular.

15 Coomera The northern end of the Gold Coast is now home to a string of leisure and theme

parks. Dreamworld, right on the Pacific Highway, offers thrilling rides. Not far to the south is Movie World, a movie theme park. Wet'n'Wild offers aquatic fun, while Sea World, Australia's largest marine park, entertains visitors with a variety of shows featuring dolphins, sea lions, and aqua ballet.

Before reaching Brisbane, make a quick detour into the hinterland to the south-east of the city. From Coomera a minor road takes you 90 km (56 mi) to Highway 15. Main Range National Park is 15 km (9 mi) to the south.

16 Main Range National Park This national park covers an area of just under 200 sq km (77 sq mi) and features impressively high mountains, steep escarpments and plateaus. It forms the western border of the Scenic Rim, a spectacular semi-circle of mountains that runs from here to Lamington National Park, southwest of Brisbane. The range is protected by an almost uninterrupted chain of national parks. The park features a variety of vegetation, from rainforest in the humid, protected areas, and eucalyptus woodland at higher altitudes and on the dry slopes, to montane heath on the escarp-

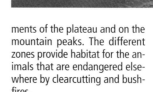

ments of the plateau and on the mountain peaks. The different zones provide habitat for the animals that are endangered elsewhere by clearcutting and bushfires.

Leaving Main Range National Park and its many hiking trails, it is only another 120 km (75 mi) on Highway 15 to Brisbane and the end of the Pacific Highway.

17 Brisbane The capital of Queensland is on the Brisbane River, a few kilometers west of the point where it flows into the Pacific. With a population of 1.5 million and a modern, expanding economy, Brisbane enjoyed a boom in the 1980s, triggered by EXPO 88, the World Fair, which was held on the Brisbane River. These days, Brisbane does not take part in national competitions

for Australia's best city. It is confident that it would win hands down anyway. Tourism and agriculture have meanwhile made Brisbane an affluent city, with a variety of cultural institutions including the Queensland Cultural Centre, several exhibition halls, concert and theater venues, and parks. The relatively small inner city area is easy to explore on foot, but for added charm and speed, try the old-style tram.

The Sunshine Coast to the north and the Gold Coast to the south both epitomize the Brisbane lifestyle – sun, sand, surf.

Large image: The Gold Coast is a symbiosis of nature and human creativity. Above: Not by accident a place here was named called Surfers Paradise.

Lamington National Park Five hundred waterfalls, subtropical rainforest and diverse birdlife make this the most popular park in Australia.

Border Ranges National Park This park contains the remnants of a former shield volcano. Its subtropical rainforests are a UNESCO World Heritage Site.

Dorrigo National Park Various trails and the Skywalk take visitors through subtropical rainforest and eucalyptus woodlands filled with orchids, ferns and birdlife.

Jenolan Caves/Blue Mountains The impressively lit Jenolan Caves in the Blue Mountains are among the largest limestone caverns on the continent.

East Coast Temperate and Subtropical Rainforest Park Wet eucalyptus forests typify the vegetation in the temperate and subtropical latitudes of Australia's Pacific coast. Mosses and ferns also grow in these zones.

Kanangra Walls Walks along the clifftops and ledges next to the vertical drops afford some breathtaking views – and might give you vertigo.

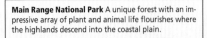

Main Range National Park A unique forest with an impressive array of plant and animal life flourishes where the highlands descend into the coastal plain.

(Map of Queensland and New South Wales showing locations including Rockhampton, Glasshouse Mts., Beerwah, Mundubbera, Bongaree, Moreton I. N.P., Woodford, Woodford, Esk, Miles, Toowoomba, Moree, Ipswich, BRISBANE, Queensland, Coomera, Sea World, Movie World, Dreamworld, Main Range N.P., Goondiwindi, Beaudeast, Surfers Paradise, Warwick, Lamington N.P., Gold Coast, Murwillumbah, Tweed Heads, Kingscliff, Woodenbong, Border Ranges N.P., Brunswick Heads, Byron Bay, Stanthorpe, Lismore, Broken Head, Sundown N.P., Girraween N.P., Mallanganee, Ballina, Tenterfield, Goondiwindi, Woodburn, Bundjalung N.P., Baryulgil, Angourie, Mt.Bajimba, Washpool N.P., Maclean, Yamba, Glen Innes, Nymboida N.P., Grafton, Yuraygir N.P., Tyringham, Dorrigo N.P., Wooli, Australian East Coast, Cathedral Rock N.P., Dorrigo, Woolgoolga, Coffs Harbour, Wollomombi, New England N.P., Urunga, Oxley Wild Rivers N.P., Macksville, Temperate and Subtropical, Bell Brook, Werrikimbe N.P., Kempsey, South West Rocks, Tamworth, Hat Head N.P., Yarrowitch, New South Telegraph Point, Port Macquarie, Wauchope, Wales, Bonnie Hills, Wingham, Rainforest Parks, Crowdy Bay N.P., Mt. Barrington, Gloucester, Taree, Tamworth, Harrington, Muswellbrook, Nabiac, Tuncurry, Denman, Bungwahl, Singleton, Bulahdelah, Myall Lakes N.P., Wollemi N.P., Maitland, Hawkes Nest, Cessnock, Karuah, Port Stephens, Blue Mountains N.P., Putty, Lower Hunter Valley, Yengo N.P., Newcastle, Dubbo, Lithgow, Wisemans Ferry, Budgewoi, Three Sisters, Windsor, The Entrance, Katoomba, North Avoca Back Reef, Jenolan Caves, Penrith, Ku-Ring-Gai Chase N.P., Kanangra-Boyd N.P., Liverpool, SYDNEY, Nattai N.P., Royal N.P., Canberra, Stanwell Park, Nowra, Wollongong)

Surfers Paradise The array of leisure activities, sports and entertainment leaves no time for boredom in what is probably Australia's best-known seaside holiday resort.

Byron Bay The lighthouse offers a magnificent panoramic view over land and sea.

Surfers' coast Australia's coasts offer surfers ideal conditions for their sport and some of the world's best surfers come from here. It's ususally possible to rent boards if you want to give it a go.

Port Stephens This port is famous for its dolphins. Take a boat out into the bay and in no time you'll be joined by a handful of these lively creatures. You can even swim with the dolphins in the safety of a drift net. It is a magical and unforgettable experience.

Hunter Valley The vineyards in Australia's oldest wine-growing region give visitors the chance to sample some of the excellent local varieties.

Sydney The oldest and largest city in Australia is one of the world's belvoed ports – even more so after the 2000 Olympic Games. In two hundred years, Sydney has grown from a penal camp into the most important economic center on the continent.

Route 21: New Zealand

Glaciers, fiords and rainforests

Visitors to New Zealand's South Island can expect some absolutely fabulous scenery. You will enjoy one spectacular view after another as you travel along the coast or to the highest peaks in the interior. Some of the more remote regions are difficult to reach, making for a great diversity of plant and wildlife. The island's mountains, lakes and rivers are ideal for those in search of outdoor adventures.

Route profile:

Length: approx. 1,500 miles
Time required: 2–3 weeks
When to go: Some higher altitude roads may become impassable during the winter (June to September). The best time to travel is from December to March.

Many consider that New Zealand's South Island embraces the whole range of the world's landscapes in perfect harmony. In the sun-drenched north, the Tasman Sea's large waves pound the shore, while you can relax on the sandy beaches in its sheltered bays. Further south, the agricultural flatlands of Canterbury Plain spread across the eastern side of the island.

Although the South Island is much larger than its northern counterpart, it is much less densely populated. Large areas of the interior are almost uninhabited. Only five percent of New Zealand's Maori population lives on the South Island, so there are far fewer Maori sacred sites than on the North Island. On the east coast, you will find two lively, cosmopolitan cities with a distinctly European flavour: Christchurch and Dunedin. Christchurch still boasts colonial buildings and extensive parks and is often described as the most English city outside England, with good reason. As you stroll through the port city of Dunedin with its many Victorian-Gothic buildings and its lovely parks, you will be reminded of its Scottish heritage: the very name of the city derives from the Gaelic name for the Scottish capital, while the names of some of its streets and quarters will transport you briefly to Edinburgh. Further to the south and west, the plains give way to more hilly

country, which rises to form the snow-covered peaks of the Southern Alps. This mountainous region, which forms the backbone of the South Island, is accessible by only a few roads. The highest mountain in the Southern Alps is Aoraki/Mount Cook, originally named after Captain Cook, the British explorer. Five power-

ful glaciers flow from its summit (3,764 m/12,350 ft) down into the valley. In the Maori language, the mountain is known by its more poetic name Aoraki (Cloud Piercer).

The south-west of the island is one of New Zealand's most attractive regions, and Queenstown, on the northern shore of

270

Top: Milford Sound, with its steep forest-clad rock faces, is one of the major attractions in New Zealand's South Island. Left: Because the rock formation in Tasman Bay is reminiscent of an apple divided in the middle, it was named Split Apple Rock.

Lake Wakatipu, makes a perfect starting point for exploring it. Several fiords, such as the famous Milford Sound, penetrate deep into the island. There are some dramatic waterfalls, Sutherland Falls among them, and a number of impressive dripstone caves. Fiordland National Park at 12,000 sq km (4,632 sq mi) is the country's largest protected area and a designated UNESCO World Heritage Site, a status it certainly deserves. It is home to a wide range of bird species.

This route takes you to a number of large mountain lakes, known collectively as the Southern Lakes Region, which includes Lakes Te Anau, Wakatipu and Wanaka. A little further north, in Westland National Park, fifty-eight glaciers flow down from the mountain tops almost to the west coast. The Franz Josef and Fox Glaciers are the most famous, but the South Island has around three hundred such ice-flows, some of which can be several kilometers long. Owing to the island's high levels of precipitation, the coastal areas are usually covered in jungle-like rainforests. Following our route northwards along the west coast, you will come across villages that look much the same as they did at the time of the New Zealand gold-rush, which lured many people to seek their fortunes in the area in the 1860s. When it came to an end, some communities, such as Greymouth, switched to coal-mining to sustain their economy. Agriculture continues to play an important role. Although the large majority of the population lives in the towns and cities, farming is vital to the economy of the South Island.

One face of the New Zealand countryside are snow-capped mountains like Mount Cook (both pictures) and Mount Tasman at Lake Matheson (above).

271

The view over Victoria Square onto the skyscrapers of Christchurch opens a magnificent panorama of the surrounding mountains of the Port Hills.

Nelson Lakes National Park

The northern tip of the South Island has some spectacular scenery in store for the traveller. Nelson Lakes National Park is one of the most impressive protected areas in the region, but Abel Tasman and Kahurangi National Parks are not far behind. On Highway 63, it is around 100 km (62 miles) from Blenheim to the St Arnaud visitor center on the shore of Lake Rotoiti, and the road comes to an end after a further 25 km (16 miles), when you rejoin Highway 6 at Kawatiri Junction. This park in the northern foothills of the Southern Alps covers almost 1,000 km² (386 square miles) and encapsulates all that is beautiful about the South Island: snow-capped mountains, lush, overgrown forests, roaring waterfalls and crystal-clear lakes. The park is at its most breathtaking around the two largest glacial lakes, Lake Rotoroa and Lake Rotoiti. When the ice retreated at the end of the last ice age, valleys and depressions carved

Lake Rotoiti.

out by the glaciers filled with water, creating the park's numerous lakes. Today, these lakes are popular for fishing, water sports and hiking. A network of hiking trails traverses Nelson Lakes National Park. The most demanding is the Travers Sabine Circuit Track.

The South Island is full of amazing scenic contrasts. It has every imaginable variety of landscape: from sandy beaches to jagged mountains, from rocky shores to impressive glaciers and from dense rainforests and expanses of southern beech to meadows and pastures. The island also has a good road network.

❶ Picton Our trip around the South Island starts from this pretty port in the far north of the island. It is here that the ferries arrive from Wellington. It usually takes around 3.5 hours to travel across the Cook Strait and through Queen Charlotte Sound to reach the former whaling station of Picton. Sailing ships anchor regularly in the picturesque bays of the fiord, and you can take boat trips to the most beautiful destinations along the magical coastline around Picton.

Picton itself is more than just a stopover on the way to the heart of the South Island. The Picton Community Museum, dedicated to the discoveries of Captain Cook and to the heyday of whaling, offers an excellent introduction to the history of the island. A number of museum ships are anchored permanently in the port, the main attraction being the Edwin Fox, the last survivor of a large fleet that brought thousands of immigrants from Europe to New Zealand. The Seahorse World Aquarium gives a wonderful overview of local marine life. There's an interesting excursion east to Robin

Hood Bay, although the route involves some very steep roads, and is a challenge for both cars and drivers. It takes twenty minutes to reach the Karaka Point peninsula where the fortifications of a former Maori settlement are worth visiting.

❷ Marlborough Sounds The fiords north of Picton are full of islands, bays, caves and a maze of waterways. Valleys in the area were flooded when the sea level rose after the last ice age. What were once hills are now mere islands jutting out of the sea. The coastline is 1,500 km (932 mi) long.

You will enjoy constantly changing views on the hiking trails, including the Queen Charlotte Track, which is 67 km (42 miles) long and can also be tackled by mountain bike.

A trip through the sounds by boat or kayak is a very special experience, and you will find several places where you can hire boats (and bikes).

The region's famed Queen Charlotte Drive is the most scenic road. Allowing for stops, you should complete the winding 35-km (22-mi) route in around three hours. It is a well-signposted road, ending up in Havelock, known for its green-shell mussels, from where you can continue to the next destination on our route, either back via Picton or via the vineyards in the Wairau Valley.

Christchurch City Council has built a modern art gallery as a showpiece in the tourist area around Worcester Boulevard.

③ Blenheim This town enjoys around 2,600 hours of sunshine per year, making it one of the country's most sun-drenched spots. Almost everything in Blenheim revolves around wine and the region's mild climate is perfect for growing vines.

West of Blenheim, New Renwick Road, Middle Renwick Road and Old Renwick Road take you to some of New Zealand's most famous vineyards, such as Highfield Estate, Allan Scott Wines and Estates and Stoneleigh Vineyards. Blenheim hosts a famous wine festival during the second week of February, featuring wine, food and entertainment.

New Zealand's only salt production plant is located 35 km (22 miles) south of Blenheim; its salt heaps are visible for miles. Highway I now hugs the water, running between the shore and the Seaward Kaikoura Range, parallel to the coastline.

④ Kaikoura In the 19th century, this town was a famous whaling station. Nowadays, only a few whalebones serve as a reminder of bygone days, such as those you can see in the Garden of Memories. Fyffe House has carvings made of whale teeth. Kaikoura Bay itself is spectacular, set against the backdrop of the coastal mountains reaching nearly 3,000 m (10,000 ft). It is a perfect spot for whale watching. Warm and cold ocean currents meet in the coastal waters, and you can enjoy spotting sperm whales, orcas and several species of dolphin, all of which come to feed on the plentiful supplies of fish. Remember to look up from time to time to spot great albatrosses with wingspans extending to more than 3 m (10 ft).

Only a few miles south of Kaikoura, you come to the Maori Leap Cave. Large numbers of bird and seal skeletons were discovered in this lovely dripstone cave. As you travel further south you will begin to notice more and more vineyards.

⑤ Waipara This town is now the center of a relatively new wine-growing area. Vines have only been cultivated here successfully since the 1980s. Many vineyards are located along the smaller roads leading off the main route. If you are coming from Kaikoura, the Main North Road takes you to Glenmark Wines and Torlesse Wines. Take Reeces Road to Daniel Schuster Wines and MacKenzies Road to Fiddler's Green Wines. Chardonnay, Pinot Noir and Sauvignon Blanc grapes are cultivated in the area, together with Gewürztraminers.

Many vineyards offer wine tastings. At Christchurch Information Centre, you can even book a trip in a horse-drawn carriage through the vineyards.

⑥ Christchurch The largest city on the South Island was founded as recently as 1850. Today, it is the political, economic and cultural hub of the island. Thanks to its lovely, sweeping parks and well-kept gardens, it is also known as the 'garden city'. Its clubs and cricket grounds and late 19th-century English-style architecture make Christchurch the 'most English town outside England'.

Try to park your car on the outskirts as, despite its size, the center of town is easily manageable on foot. Enjoy a sightseeing tour on one of the lovingly restored trams that make regular stops in the city center.

The city is laid out in a grid pattern, and as a result it is quite easy to find your way around. Cathedral Square is dominated by the massive cathedral (1864–1904), the city's landmark. Inside this monumental church, you'll find an exhibition on the history of the Anglican Church in New Zealand. You can climb halfway up the steeple (65 m/215 ft) to enjoy a beautiful view of the city. South of Cathedral Square is City Mall, the city's main shopping street.

Many visitors also take a boat trip on the River Avon which winds its way across the city in numerous loops, with lovely weeping willows growing along its banks.

In marked contrast to Christchurch itself is the mountainous Banks Peninsula just south of the city on the Canterbury Plains; the region is volcanic in origin.

The port town of Lyttleton and the summer resort of Akaroa with its quiet beaches are also worth visiting.

At the top: Lupines at Kaikoura. Left side: Ngakuta Bay at Picton. Above: Coast of Kaikoura and winery at Blenheim.

Lake Tekapo, east of the Aoraki/ Mount Cook range, is surrounded by forests and high mountains.

Southern Alps

New Zealand's longest and highest mountain range extends across most of the South Island, from the north-east to the south-west. In the Pleistocene or ice ago, glaciers flowed down from these snow-covered mountain peaks, carving out a truly striking landscape with numerous fiords, lakes and rivers.
This mountain range is known

The Southern Alps were formed as a result of tectonic forces. They are located at the point of contact between two mighty tectonic plates – the Pacific Plate and the Australian Plate, which slides beneath it. Many millions of years ago, the land began to be uplifted on a large scale, culminating in the creation of this mighty mountain range, the backbone of the South Island. The plate contin-

Hooker Valley overlooks the Southern Alps.

as the Southern Alps – and this is no mere accident as the mountains resemble the European Alps in many ways. At 3,764 m (12,350 ft), the range's highest peak, Aoraki/Mount Cook challenges the Alps in altitude and is also the highest in Australasia. The peaks are jagged and serrated, and at lower altitudes the slopes are covered with beech forests.

ues to rise to this day at a rate of 10 mm (0.4 in) per year. Similar forces shaped other 'younger' mountain ranges such as the Alps, the Himalayas, the Andes and the Rocky Mountains.
The Southern Alps divide the wetter western regions of the island from its drier eastern parts. They are the most-visited winter sports region in the country.

❼ Aoraki/Mount Cook National Park This National Park is one of the absolute highlights of a trip to the South Island of New Zealand, and not simply because of its altitude. The park was established in 1953 and covers an area of 700 sq km (270 sq miles). In addition to Aoraki/Mount Cook itself (3,764 m/12,350 ft), there are thirteen mountains, all at altitudes of more than 3,000 m (9,843 ft), including some very famous peaks such as Mount Tasman (3,498 m/11,477 ft). Forty percent of the park's surface area is covered in glaciers and high levels of precipitation around the mountain peaks provide a continuous supply of snow and ice. The Tasman Glacier flows directly from the summit of Aoraki/Mount Cook. It is some 27 km (17 miles) long and up to 3 km (2 miles) wide, making it the longest glacier in the country.
It will take you some time to get here from Christchurch, but you will find spectacular scenery along the way. Driving across the Canterbury Plains, you first reach Timaru, where you turn north-west onto Highway 8. From Twizel, take Aoraki/Mount Cook Road (Highway 80) to Aoraki/Mount Cook village. This access road is

sealed and generally in good condition. It climbs slowly, taking you along the western shore of Lake Pukaki in which, on a clear day, you can see the reflections of the park's giant mountains. The village sits at an altitude of 762 m (2,500 ft) amid the fabulous mountain scenery, and has all the amenities you are likely to need, including an information center. An alternative route takes you inland from Christchurch via Sheffield and Mount Hutt to Fairlie along Highway 8, and then follows the route already described. One of the highlights of the National Park is a visit to the lower part of the Tasman Glacier, which you can reach via the road to Blue Lake. After about 8 km (5 miles), park your vehicle and climb for around thirty minutes until you reach the Tasman Glacier viewpoint. From here, you can see the Aoraki/Mount Cook range in all its glory. At higher altitudes, skiers can enjoy a number of ski resorts that remain open throughout the year. The visitor center can provide you with detailed information on what to do in the National Park. Several hiking trails start here, too, and they are well signposted although very stony in places.

Even if the sky is not bright blue, Lake Pukaki is still glowing in intense blue.

8 Twizel This town at the junction of Aoraki/Mount Cook Road and Highway 8 started out as a builder's campsite erected to service the construction of a hydroelectric dam. As part of this project, several lakes were created, including Lake Pukaki and Lake

Tekapo in the north-east. The dam was highly controversial at the time, but one positive consequence was the development of the Mackenzie Hydro Lakes recreational area, which now provides ideal conditions for water sports. The lakes are full of fish,

and you can hire boats from various places. Another attraction in Twizel is the Kaki Visitor Hide where ornithologists can observe the wading kaki (black stilt), one of the country's rarest birds, undisturbed. Just 25 km (16 miles) south of Twizel you come to

Omarama, whose north-west thermals make it a perfect spot for gliders and paragliders. The 'Clay Cliffs' 10 km (6 miles) west of Omarama are a geological phenomenon but this jagged, rocky landscape with its many stone pinnacles is relatively difficult to

get to. Our route now follows Highway 8 south to Cromwell at the eastern flank of the Southern Alps.

9 Cromwell This town is located at the point where the Kawarau and Clutha rivers meet and started out as a settlement for gold-diggers. The gold-rush arrived in Cromwell in the 1860s but quickly moved on to the west coast. At the end of the 19th century, the last of the pioneers left town. Part of the settlement was flooded when the dam was built, but some buildings of historical significance were moved to higher ground and restored to create Old Cromwell Town.

At a few kilometers west of Cromwell is the Goldfields Mining Centre, which gives you a real flavour of just how labour-intensive the process of gold-mining can be. You can also enjoy a trip along the Kawarau River in a kayak or rubber dinghy. From Cromwell, Highway 8 follows the valley of the Clutha River for the most part. It rejoins Highway I in Milton. It is then worth taking a detour north to Dunedin along the south-east coast (see side panel, p. 468). Heading south, at Balclutha you will join Highway 92 to Invercargill, located on the southern tip of the island. The Cathedral Caves are worth a quick stop along the way, as are the Purakaunui Falls, where the river of the same name cascades from a height of over 20 m (66 ft).

10 Invercargill New Zealand's most southerly town boasts tree-lined avenues and sweeping parks, including Queen's Park, which has an area of 10 sq km (4 sq miles). The town's Scottish heritage is clearly visible today, and many roads are named after Scottish rivers. The Southland Museum and Art Gallery is renowned throughout the country and includes Maori works of art and a natural history exhibition that includes impressive fossils and petrified tree trunks. Next

stop is Bluff, around 30 km (18 miles) south of Invercargill. This small village at the southern tip of the island is home to a large fishing fleet and terminus for the ferries to Stewart Island. The Bluff Maritime Museum houses objects related to the history of whaling. Our next destination is the country's largest National Park, covering 12,000 sq km (4,632 sq miles) of the island's south-westerly tip.

11 Fiordland National Park (see pages 276-277). Its wide lakes, fourteen deep fiords and snow-capped mountains have made this National Park world famous. The park's protected area is traversed by around 500 km (311 miles) of hiking trails, among them the spectacular Milford Track. Our first point of call is Te Anau on the shore of Te Anau Lake. From here, a two-hour boat trip takes us to the fascinating underground world of the Te Anau Caves ('Glowworm Caves'). A drive along the Milford Road (120 km/75 miles) between Te Anau in the south and Milford Sound in the north, one of the scenic highlights of New Zealand, is an unforgettable experience. On both sides of the road, you can see the diverse landscapes of New Zealand's southern tip in all their glory and variety: luxuriant forests, jagged mountains, torrential mountain rivers, roaring waterfalls and tranquil lakes. The Milford Track passes Sutherland Falls which, at 580 m (1,900 ft), was once thought to be the world's tallest waterfall.

A trip to the south to see Doubtful Sound is well worth while, although the journey from Manapouri to Doubtful Sound involves two boat trips and a drive across Wilmot Pass. Several dolphin species live in the coastal waters.

Even if the sky is not bright blue, Lake Pukaki is still glowing in intense blue.

A wildly romantic picture shows off how the rock-strewn Cleddau River flows through the national park.

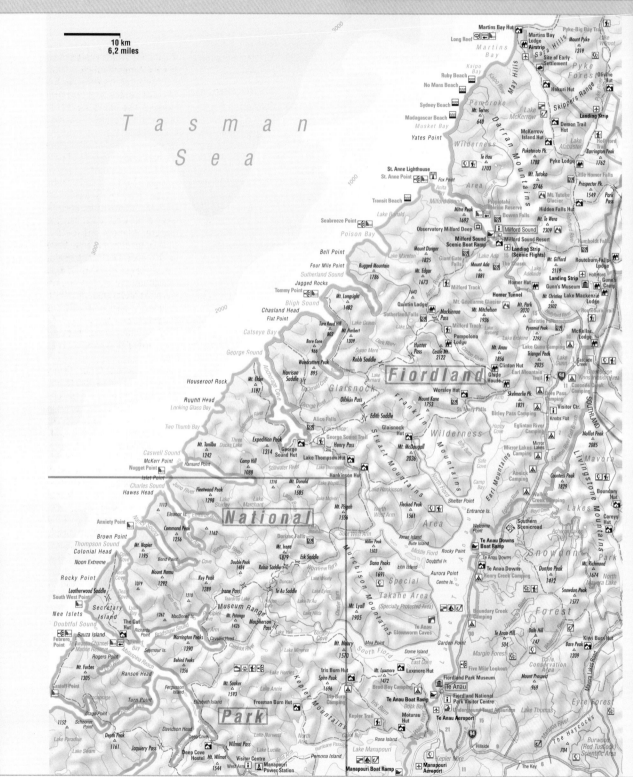

Even if you cannot get away with it, it's worth taking a kayak trip to the Bowen Falls on Milford Sound and the surrounding rainforests.

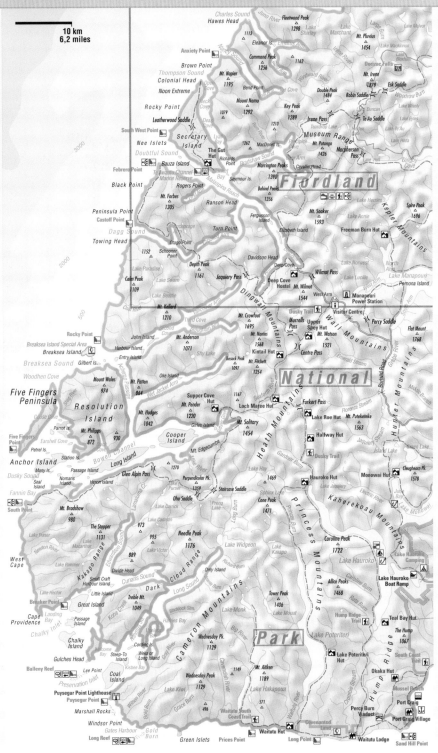

10 km
6,2 miles

Fiordland National Park

This park, which is New Zealand's largest National Park by far – at 12,000 sq km (4,632 sq miles) – is also considered the most beautiful National Park in the country.

Its snow-capped mountains are the backdrop to extensive beech forests with giant moss-covered 500-year-old trees, valleys with crystal-clear rivers and quiet lakes and, of course, the majestic fiords of the west coast. Only one of these, Milford Sound, is accessible by road. In this area, there are 700 endemic plant species as well as kakapos, a curious kind of flightless parrot. This masterpiece of natural creation (which includes the three National Parks of Aoraki/Mount Cook and Westland) definitely merits its status as a UNESCO World Heritage Site.

The sealed road to Milford Sound is spectacular. One hundred and 20 km (75 miles) long, it runs along the shore of Lake Te Anau and then across virtually untouched primeval landscapes, with magnificent views of Mount Christiana (2,502 m/8,209 ft). The route takes you through Hollyford Valley, past stunning natural features such as Mirror Lakes until you reach Homer Tunnel. At the western side of the tunnel, some steep hairpin bends take you down to Milford Sound. Mitre Peak (1,692 m/6,437 ft) rises up abruptly out of the sea. Lake Manapouri is located south of Te Anau; its islands and peaceful, bush-clad shores are best explored by kayak. At the lake's western arm, there is a hydroelectric power plant buried 200 m (650 ft) deep in the rocks. When this power plant was built, an access road also needed to be constructed. This road now connects the lake to Deep Cove on Doubtful Sound via Wilmot Pass – you can take it to reach the cruise boats on New Zealand's deepest fiord.

South Island wildlife

Thanks to the island's low population density, local fauna live in relative peace and there are many bird breeding-sites, giving the island its nickname of 'seabird par-

Dunedin

The city has close ties to the Scottish city of Edinburgh – and not simply because Dun Edin is the Gaelic name for Scotland's capital. New Zealand and Scottish elements mingle in the town's cultural life.

The Octagon is the city center, a circular thoroughfare area bisected by the city's main streets, with an

St. Paul's Cathedral.

Railway station.

inner pedestrian area surrounded by some of Dunedin's most important buildings, including the Anglican St Paul's Cathedral and Dunedin Public Art Gallery with its collection of European art. The Octagon itself is the venue for several festivals and markets. Dunedin's railway station is also architecturally interesting; the Flemish-style building with its 37-m (121-ft) tower is considered one of New Zealand's most beautiful stone buildings. Its magnificent mosaic floors were created from more than 700,000 pieces of porcelain.

Detour

The south-east coast

Milton is the ideal starting point for a trip north, taking you to some of the scenic and cultural highlights of the South Island's south-east. Via Clarendon, this route first goes to Dunedin and then to the Otago Peninsula, which is 25 km (16 miles) long. The most northerly point of this excursion is Oamaru, from which you retrace the route back to Milton on Highway I, also known as SH1.

Otago Peninsula

The 60 km (37 miles) of the Highcliff Road take you past the most important sights, with spectacular, ever-changing views of the sea. This thinly populated, hilly peninsula boasts a surprisingly varied range of fauna and flora. The northernmost tip (Taiaroa Head) is especially suited to wildlife watching. It is the only mainland breeding site of the royal albatross, and colonies of seals, sea lions and penguins make their home in the immediate vicinity. In the coastal waters, you can see orcas and other whales. Boat trips to these impassable cliffs can be booked in Dunedin. The small port village of Portobello is known for its aquarium, which gives visitors an interesting introduction to maritime life. Glenfallochs Woodland is a park with ancient trees, rhododendrons and azaleas.

Larnach Castle is an architectural highlight. This impressive mansion was built for a banker, William Larnach, between 1871 and 1885. When Larnach committed suicide, the surrounding land was sold and the building fell derelict until it was restored some forty years ago; it is now a hotel and conference center. The castle, with its

beautiful painted ceilings and its floating staircase, is open to visitors. It also has a 250-sq-m (2,690-sq-ft) ballroom.

Moeraki Boulders

When you continue your journey on Highway 1, it is well worth stopping at the Moeraki Boulders. These mighty stone spheres, measuring up to 3 m (10 ft) across, provided the Maori with the inspiration for many legends. For a long time, they were believed to be petrified food storage containers (Te Kai-hinaki), thrown ashore by their ancestors from their canoes. The scientific explanation, however, is much less colourful – the spheres were formed at the bottom of the sea from lime

deposits that built up around a hard core. When the land rose above the sea the stones were exposed and now lie on a fine stretch of sandy beach. Today, the nearby fishing village of Moeraki is populated mainly by Maori.

Oamaru

Our excursion to the southeast terminates in the small town of Oamaru. Most of the town's historic buildings were built from the pale limestone found in the surrounding area and some have been renovated several times. Particularly noticeable are the colonnaded porticoes framing many buildings such as the Courthouse and Forrester Gallery. South Hill Walkway above the port gives you a good view of the town. It is surrounded by impressive mountain ranges and if you arrive at sunset, you will enjoy some spectacular views.

Legend has it that the Moeraki Boulders are the ancestors stone baskets (top). Above: Larnach Castle.

adise'. As well as albatrosses, waders such as black-winged stilts find suitable habitats in this area. Along the coast, you can find several species of penguin, the coastal waters are home to many whales and dolphins. Wild boar, red deer, rabbits, martens and possums were introduced to the country by European settlers.

The fauna has a lot to offer for animals inhabiting the air and water.

⑫ **Milford Sound** This fiord is 16 km (10 miles) long and becomes wider as it makes its way inland. Tall mountains surround the coastline of the South West New Zealand World Heritage Site, known in Maori as Te Wahipounamu, and rise suddenly above the waterline, their slopes covered in rainforests. Mitre Peak

and saltwater fish can thrive. Milford Track (54 km/33 miles) is one of the most famous hiking trails in the country. It begins at Glade House at the northern tip of Lake Te Anau and runs through the Clinton Valley, past Sutherland Falls and up to the fiord. When booking, do bear in mind that the track is only walkable from No-

for an oasis of peace and tranquillity in what is a very busy town, you have come to the right place: the gardens' fir tree-lined lawns and rose beds are a quiet haven. The Mall is a popular meeting point for locals and visitors alike. Along this bustling shopping street, you will see some well-preserved colonial buildings, among

⑭ **Wanaka** This lakeside town lies around 55 km (34 miles) as the crow flies from Queenstown and sits at the southern tip of Lake Wanaka. Its proximity to Mount Aspiring National Park and to the lake itself makes this a very attractive spot. The Transport and Toy Museum located near the airport is definitely worth visiting –

(1,692 m/6,437 ft), with its remarkable conical shape, is one of the most-photographed spots in New Zealand. The mountain peaks are reflected in the clear, still waters of the fiord. From the town of Milford, located on the south-eastern shore of Milford Sound, you can arrange a boat trip on the fiord, or even book a cruise for a few days and really explore the area from the sea. From a zoological point of view, the diversity of fish species is very interesting. The heavy rains in the area mean that above the water that flows into the fiord from the sea there is a permanent layer of fresh water, several meters deep, providing an extraordinary environment in which both freshwater

vember to March. From Milford Sound, you return to Te Anau, where you pick up the eastbound Highway 94. The rivers near Lumsden are famous for their wealth of trout. From Lumsden, you follow Highway 6 to the north. In Kingston, at the southern shore of Lake Wakatipu, you can take a 75-minute ride on the Kingston Flyer, a vintage steam train.

⑬ **Queenstown** This town at the northern shore of Lake Wakatipu is one of the South Island's biggest tourist attractions. The town center is spread out around the Queenstown Bay. Queenstown Gardens are located on a peninsula that extends far into the lake. If you are looking

them Eichardt's Tavern (1871). At Underwater World, you can observe some of the local marine life. The Kiwi and Birdlife Park shelters several endangered bird species. The Skyline Gondola takes you up to Bob's Peak (450 m/1,475 ft), with its fantastic view of the town and the surrounding area.

its collection of vehicles and toys comprises more than 13,000 exhibits. And if you want to take a break from all this wonderful

Large image: Lake Wanaka.
Smaller images: Top left:
View over Queenstown.
Above right: Lake Wakatipu.
Below: Milford Sound.

A first impression of the beauty of Mount Aspiring National Park is provided by a short hike to the crystal-clear blue pools.

scenery, you can head for Stuart Landsborough's Puzzling World in Wanaka.

15 Mount Aspiring National Park Wanaka is the gateway to this National Park. Northwest of the town, a small road follows the Matukituki river right into the park which, at 3,555 sq km (1,372 sq miles) is New Zealand's third largest. At its heart is Mount Aspiring (3,027 m/9,932 ft), shaped like a pyramid, hence its nickname of 'New Zealand's Matterhorn'. The scenery consists of tall, snow-capped mountains. There are numerous densely forested valleys and picturesque river plains. Several hiking trails allow you to explore the beauty of the park on foot. The Dart Rees Track is well-known and makes an ideal trek lasting several days through mountainous terrain. However, do note that you have to be in very good physical shape if you plan to attempt it. Less demanding but still worth

doing is a hike on the Rob Roy Valley Trail along the Matukituki River. Keas, a species of mountain parrot, and timberline wrens are just two of the bird species you might spot in the park. You may be lucky enough to see keas at close range but the wrens tend to stick to higher altitudes. Many waterbirds live along the rivers and lakes.

16 Lake Hawea From Wanaka, on the next leg of our journey to the coast, Highway 6 runs between Lake Wanaka and Lake Hawea (140 sq km/54 sq miles). Surrounded as it is by impressive scenery, this lake, with its clear blue waters, is one of the most beautiful on the South Island. It is 410 m (1,345 ft) deep, which means it is actually below sea level. Its abundance of trout and salmon makes it one of New Zealand's most popular fishing grounds. You might want to stop en route for a rest and enjoy the view at the Cameron Creek Lookout. On the far side of the

Haast Pass (563 m/1,847 ft), you will pass Thunder Creek Falls, at a height of 30 m (98 ft). The road now runs along the Haast River, and once you get to Haast you'll have made it to the west coast.

17 Westland National Park This 1,176-sq-km (454-sq-mile) park stretches from the Okarito Lagoon on the island's west coast inland to Mount Tasman (3,498 m/11,475 ft), one of the highest mountains in the New Zealand Alps. Its variety of wet-

lands, lakes, rainforests, glaciers and rocky landscapes make this National Park particularly attractive. The west coast still bears witness in places to the 1860s gold-rush. Gillespies Beach on the coast is a former gold-min-

ers' settlement, and traces of the era are still visible today. A beautiful hike along a former mining track leads down to a beach with a seal colony.
Access roads such as Docherty Creek Road and Forks Okarito Road link Highway 6 to the west

The glacier field of the Franz Josef Glacier in the Westland National Park shines in a variety of tones: the bluer the ice, the older it is.

coast. The shore of Lake Mapourika is a popular spot for a picnic on the main road. Further south, you will find Lake Matheson, which is probably New Zealand's most photographed lake.

18 Franz Josef Glacier Like Fox Glacier to the south, this glacier stretches from its feeding point at more than 3,000 m (9,840 ft) to about 300 m (984 ft) above sea level, where the coastal rainforests grow right up to the edge of the glacier.

Named after the Austrian Emperor Franz Josef, it is around 13 km (8 miles) long and forms part of Westland National Park. There are some dangerous crevices, so hiking across the glacier is only permitted as part of a guided tour. During the last two centuries, the ice has advanced on a number of occasions, but then always receded to its current level. The melt waters form the Waiho River, on which Franz Josef Village is located. A road takes you to a car park, and from

there it is a one-hour tramp to the glacier gate at the lowest point of the ice flow.

19 Hokitika In this charming town, which you reach via Highway 6, the Hokitika Heritage Walk will take you to some interesting 19th-century buildings. An old ship is also open for visits. The West Coast Historical Museum is dedicated to the gold-rush era, as is the historical open-air museum at the recreated 1860s gold-mining town, known as Shantytown, located about 10 km (6 miles) south of Greymouth.

Mount Aspiring and Westland National Park offer an extraordinary variety of landscapes: this is where the mountains meet the rainforest.

The South Island rainforests

In the wettest parts of the South Island, annual precipitation levels reach 6,000–7,000 mm (232–270 in) ideal conditions for the development of species-rich rainforests. In particular, the wind-exposed western flanks of the New Zealand Alps, with their ascending rains, provide ideal growing conditions for this type of vegetation.

In places like the Fox and Franz Josef Glaciers, forests often grow right up to the glacier tongues — a surprising sight for Europeans. One of the trademarks of the South Island's evergreen rainforests is their jungle-like fern thickets in the undergrowth. These ferns thrive here even though only a tiny fraction of the sunlight filters through the dense roof canopy.

Lush greenery thrives in the Paparoa National Park above the karstic cliff landscape.

Arthur's Pass

An impressive mountain road (Highway 73) takes you across the Southern Alps between Springfield in the south-east and Kumara Junction on the north-west coast (Highway 6). The road's highest point is at Arthur's Pass (920 m/3,019 ft), na-

Avalanche Peak (top) and Temple Basin (bottom).

med after Arthur Dudley Dobson, who was the first European to scale it in 1864. Five km (3 miles) south of the pass, the village of the same name serves as a base camp for climbers and skiers and is also the administrative center for Arthur's Pass National Park, which was established here in 1929, making it the South Island's oldest National Park. Its main attraction is the kea, a type of parrot. The pass road is sometimes closed after heavy snow.

⓴ Greymouth This town had its heyday during the 19th-century gold-rush. When the region's deposits were exhausted, coal mining replaced gold digging as the town's principal source of revenue. However, Greymouth's development was severely restricted by recurrent heavy flooding. The History House Museum displays some interesting photographic documentation of the town's history and the Left Bank Art Gallery features Maori arts and crafts. If you are looking for something a bit more exciting, why not try floating through the network of the Taniwha Caves on inflated inner tubes.

㉑ Paparoa National Park This National Park covers 300 sq km (116 sq miles) and protects the karst formations of the Paparoa Range, which runs parallel to the coast. Its most popular attractions are the Pancake Rocks and the blowholes close to Punakaiki, a coastal village. The Pancake Rocks are huge limestone pillars, so-named because they look like pancakes piled one on top of the other. Heavy seas force water through the blowholes – funnels carved out by the surf – and it shoots up into the air in powerful jets. This karst area is entirely covered in subtropical rainforests that flourish thanks to the warm ocean cur-

rents in this part of the west coast. Dolomite Point Walk is a hiking trail that takes you right to the heart of this virgin forest and just fifteen minutes down Truman Track you come to a wild piece of coastline with a waterfall and several caves. Continuing to the north, you reach Westport, which serves as an ideal base for

a range of outdoor activities in the area. For thrill-seekers, the local underground rafting is particularly spectacular; accompanied by a guide, you can drift along underground waterways and visit hidden caves. A three-hour hike on Cape Foulwind Walkway takes you to a seal colony in Tauranga Bay.

㉒ Karamea In Westport, you leave Highway 6 and take Highway 67 to the north. The coastal town of Karamea is the starting point for several hikes into the Kahurangi National Park, of which the 15-km (9-mile) Heaphy Track is one of the most popular.

North of Karamea, you reach the Oparara Basin with its monumental limestone cliffs. There is also an extensive and intricate network of caves known as the Honeycomb Hill Caves. Inside the caves are the bones of nine species of the now extinct wingless – and therefore flightless – moa bird. It boasts the most varied collection of subfossil bird bones ever found in New Zealand.

From Karamea, take Highway 67 back to Westport and then follow Highway 6 to Matupiko and Nelson. From either place, you can pick up a road to Abel Tasman National Park and Cape Farewell. Eroded granite sculptures, sandy bays and estuaries all feature in this National Park. Return to Picton by following the shore of the Tasman Bay.

A country road leads through the dense rainforest of Paparoa National Park (top). Above: Kahurangi National Park.

Abel Tasman National Park Endless beaches and jungle-like rainforests – this National Park named after the Dutch explorer boasts some spectacular contrasts.

Marlborough Sounds Quiet bays and green hills are typical of the scenery at the South Island's northernmost tip. There are also some impressive dripstone caves on the coast.

Kaikoura Range In the north-east of the South Island the land gradually rises up from the coast to jagged mountains -- a hiker's paradise.

Paparoa National Park In the course of millennia, wind and waves have carved out the bizarre shapes of the Pancake Rocks – a breathtaking landscape.

Nelson Lakes National Park This National Park with an area of nearly 1,000 sq km (386 sq miles) is located at the northern end of the Southern Alps. It boasts two spectacular glacier lakes at its center .

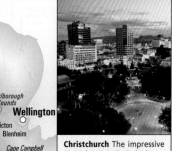

Christchurch The impressive Christchurch Cathedral is located in the center of this city with its many typical parks.

Westland National Park Massive glaciers – among them the famous Franz Josef and Fox Glaciers – extend down the slopes of the Southern Alps.

Puponga
Cape Farewell
Collingwood
Abel Tasman N.P.
Kahurangi N.P.
Nelson
Marlborough Sounds
Wellington
Karamea
Matupiko
Havelock
Picton
Blenheim
Westport
Cape Foulwind
St.Arnaud
Murchison
Cape Campbell
Paparoa N.P.
Reefton
Nelson Lakes N.P.
Punakaiki
Pancake Rocks and Blowholes
Springs Junction
Mangamaunu
Greymouth
Kumara Junction
Kaikoura
Maori Leap Cave
Hokitika
Culverden
Arthur's Pass N.P.
SOUTH ISLAND
Waipara
Okarito Lagoon
Springfield
Sheffield
Franz Josef Glacier
Gillespies Beach
Mount Hutt
Christchurch
Westland N.P.
Mt.Cook N.P.
Canterbury Plains
Akaroa
Mount Cook
Ashburton
Banks Peninsula
Haast
Geraldine
Lake Pukaki
Fairlie
Twizel
Timaru
Clay Cliffs
Canterbury Bight
Lake Wanaka
Omarama
Te Wahi-
Milford Sound
Mt. Aspiring N.P.
Wanaka
Lake Hawea
Lindis Valley
Queenstown
Sutherland Falls
Oamaru
Fiordland N.P.
Cromwell
Moeraki Boulders
Lake Wakatipu
pounamou
Palmerston
Te Anau
Doubtful Sound
Manapouri
Raes Junction
Dunedin
Otago Peninsula
Monowai
Lumsden
Larnach Castle
Gore
Milton
Puysegur Point
Owaka
Balclutha
Invercargill
Purakaunui Falls
Bluff
Waikawa
Cathedral Caves
Stewart Island

Aoraki/Mount Cook National Park Much of this park, named after New Zealand's highest mountain (3,764 m/12,350 ft), is covered by glaciers.

Keas Their home is the South Island's high country. These parrots were named after the hooting noise they make while flying.

Te Wahipounamu The coastal scenery of the South Island's south-west is incredibly varied and intricate. In places rainforests run all the way down to the shoreline; elsewhere, steep cliffs border fiords stretching far inland.

Dunedin A touch of Scotland in New Zealand: magnificent town houses, massive churches and lovely extensive parks make Dunedin so attractive. The railway station with its 37-m (121-ft) clock tower is one of the country's most impressive stone buildings.

Lake Wanaka This is one of several lakes at the eastern slopes of the Southern Alps. In summer, it is a popular water sports resort.

Milford Sound One of the landmarks of Fiordland National Park is the distinctive shape of Mitre Peak (1,692 m/6,437 ft), with its steep rock faces rising abruptly out of Milford Sound.

Queenstown Sloping down to Lake Wakatipu, in front of the 'Remarkables' – this is Queenstown. This former gold-diggers' settlement is now a popular holiday resort.

Purakaunui Falls The Purakaunui falls cascade down more than 20 m (66 ft) of rock faces and make a deafening roar.

283

The famous rock
monuments have served
as a backdrop in many
western films and
commercials. The
Monument Valley looks
even better when
you're actually there.

USA and Canada

In North America everything always seems to be a lot bigger. The streets are wider, the canyons deeper and higher and higher sky-scrapers are built. The continent is therefore predestined to travel by car. The distances offer landscape experiences in a dimension not known from Europe. Whoever drives through the Rockies on the Panamericana or explores the spectacular deserts and rocky landscapes of the Southwest, creates an idea of the feeling of the original freedom of being 'on the road'.

Route 22: Canada

On the Trans-Canada Highway from Vancouver to the Great Lakes

Built in 1962, the Trans-Canada Highway sweeps through Canada, the second-largest country on earth, for 7,821 km (4,860 miles). The western section, running from Vancouver Island to Lake Superior, passes through a variety of scenery, ranging from rainforest on the Pacific coast and magnificent national parks in the Rocky Mountains, through endless prairies to the 'shining waters', as the Iroquois called the Great Lakes.

Route profile:

Length: approx. 2,485 milies
Time required: at least 4 weeks

A journey from west to east through south-western Canada will take you through four different kinds of scenery, with the first, the 800-km (500-mile) expanse of the Rocky Mountains, being the most impressive. The greatest concentration of national parks is also to be found here, around the peaks of Jasper and Banff.

Fertile, sedimentary soil abounds where the Great Plains of East Alberta, Saskatchewan, and West Manitoba join the Rocky Mountains to the east; these plains are all that remain of the Ice Age lakes that once reached as far as the prairies of America. The Canadian Shield, a pre-Cambrian volcanic formation consist-

ing of some of the earth's oldest rocks, begins east of the Great Plains, near Winnepeg. Parts of it are 3.6 million years old. Its current form was shaped by Ice Age glaciers, which also gouged many lakes between the low granite peaks. The plain of the St Lawrence River, which begins near the Great Lakes in southern Ontario, exhibits similar glacial

features. Canada is famous for its endless forests, which cover more than half the country (4.5 million sq km/1.75 million sq mi). With the exception of a few areas in the south, this is all evergreen forest, made up of larch, Douglas fir, spruce, and pine. In the far west, there used to be expanses of rainforest with giant Douglas firs, Sitka spruce, and

Canadian hemlock. How things looked before the days of the chainsaw and deforestation by the logging companies is amply demonstrated in the Pacific Rim National Park on the west coast of Vancouver Island, the starting point of the Trans-Canada Highway. The montane forest of the Coastal Mountains and the Rocky Mountains, stretching out

Nestled in a beautiful setting, the mighty Rocky Mountains are reflected in the crystal-clear Elbow Lake (above). The Royal Canadian Mounted Police proudly displays their traditional scarlet jackets on horseback. The police unit has a long tradition, having been founded in 1874 (left).

further to the east, is home to many wild creatures, including moose, black and brown bear, red deer, Dall sheep, and mountain goats, all of which you might be able to spot from the car, if you are lucky.

As paradoxical as it might seem, the closest approximation to the ideal of Canada's wilderness is to be found in the national parks. There are as many as seven to be found along the border between British Columbia and Alberta, including the Mount Revelstoke, Glacier, Yoho, Banff, and Jasper National Parks. The last three, which make up the Canadian Rocky Mountains National Park, have been declared a UNESCO World Heritage Site. Despite preserving nature in the raw, Canadian national parks have an excellent infrastructure, including dedicated scenic routes as well as marked hiking paths and camping grounds in the most remote places.

Left side: Sunrise over Mount Assiniboine Provincial Park near Calgary. Top left: Downtown Vancouver against a fantastic mountain backdrop. Above: The colourful totem poles greet visitors at the Stanley.Park von Vancouver.

On the nine kilometer Garibaldi Lake Trek you can hike the fascinating natural landscape of the park.

Canada is a feast of high mountains, giant glaciers, virgin forests, endless wheatfields, and incomparable lakes; there are mountain villages and vibrant cities, too, and all of these are to be found along the 4,000-km (2,485-mile) stretch of the Trans-Canada Highway between Victoria and the Great Lakes.

Kilometer 0 of the Trans-Canada Highway (Highway 1) is located at the south-western end of Beacon Hill Park in Victoria on Vancouver Island. Ferries running between Swartz Bay, about 30 km (19 miles) north of Victoria, and Tsawwassen, south of Vancouver, provide a link to the mainland across Georgia Bay.

❶ Vancouver (see page 290.) From Vancouver, follow High-way 99 (also known as the 'Sea to Sky Highway') along Burrard Inlet. The route from the Pacific to the mountains of Garibaldi Provincial Park crosses five vegetation zones.

❷ Garibaldi Provincial Park About 80 km (50 miles) north of Vancouver, Garibaldi Provincial Park – whose highest point is Mount Garibaldi at 2,678 m (8,786 ft) – covers an area of 1,950 sq km (750 sq mi). The ski resort of Whistler has been spreading across Blackcomb Mountain on the northern edge of the park since the 1960s. Af-

ter 310 km (190 miles), the Sea to Sky Highway reaches its northern end at Lillouet; 75 km (46 miles) further on, Highway 99 meets Highway 97, which will take you past Kamloops Lake into Canada's 'Sunshine Capital'.

❸ Kamloops The Shuswap Indians once called the town Cumloops ('where the waters meet'), as it stands at the confluence of the North and South Thompsons. The Secwepmec Native Heritage Park, a reconstructed First Nations village, will tell you everything you need to know about the Shuswap tribe. Heading further eastwards on Highway 1, it is worth taking a detour to Monte Creek to visit the O'Keefe Historic Ranch of 1867, before entering the Rocky Mountains and the first of a series of national parks.

❹ Mount Revelstoke National Park The little town of Revel-stoke is the starting point for exploring the eponymous na-

tional park. There are two routes through the park: the 'Meadows in the Sky Parkway' is 26 km (16 miles) long and takes you to Mount Revelstoke (1,943 m /6,375 ft), although the last stretch must be covered by a

shuttle bus taking you to Balsam Lake. The alternative is the mountain road over Rogers Pass (1,327 m/4,354 ft), one of the world's most spectacular passes.

❺ Glacier National Park The park boasts any number of pristine high peaks, with wild and jagged glaciated summits reach-

ing heights of 3,390 m (11,120 ft). Up to 20 m (66 ft) of snowfall can be expected annually on the park's 422 glaciers, and 10% of the park is covered with snow and ice throughout the year. Until 1962, when the Trans-Canada Highway was built, the park was only accessible by rail. The scenic route crosses the park for 50 km (31 miles) and almost all of

Lying between the mountains and the lakes, Vancouver is one of the world's most beautiful cities. Above: Mount Sir Donald.

From May to October you have the best chance of spotting the passing orcas on a whale watching tour.

Detour

Vancouver Island und Victoria

At about 450 km (280 miles) in length and 100 km (62 miles) wide, Vancouver Island is the largest island on the North American Pacific coast. The island's interior is dominated by the development of dense temperate rainforest with an abundance of moss and ferns.

Victoria, the capital of British Columbia, lies at the south-eastern tip of the island, and is decidedly reminiscent of 'the mother country': the red double-decker buses, bright flower baskets hanging from blue lamp-posts, and well-tended parks all suggest Victorian elegance. Victoria was founded when the Hudson's Bay Company built a fort in the sheltered natural harbor in 1843; as was the practice, it was named after the ruling British sovereign. In 1868, Victoria became the capital of the Crown Colony of British Columbia, which was to join the Ca-

nadian Confederation in 1871. The Empress Hotel, built on the quayside by the Canadian Pacific Railway Company in 1908, has become a symbol of the town, and the picturesque Old Town to the north is filled with old buildings and traditional stores. Old warehouses have been transformed into attractive shopping malls and the Harbour Walkway is ideal for a stroll.

The town's main attraction, however, is the Royal British Columbia Museum, located between the parliament building and the Empress Hotel. It is considered West Canada's best museum of natural history and culture, employing the most modern technology to present the history of British Columbia. The Indian History Gallery, with its striking depictions of the history, culture, and art of the First Nations of the north-west coast, is of particular interest. Behind the museum, Thunderbird Park has the best totem poles by far, and in a Haida long house you can watch First Nation artists as they carve them.

The Scenic Marine Drive is reached from the southern end of Victoria. This 13-km (8-mile) route follows the coast to Cattle Point on Oak Bay. The famous Butchart Gardens are only 20 km (12 miles) north of Victoria, on Highway 17A. The first part of these magnificent gardens was built in an old quarry in 1904 by Jenny Butchart, the wife of a cement manufacturer. They have since blossomed into a large

park of some 20 ha (50 acres) with Canada's most beautiful floral collection. More than 5,000 species of flower are displayed in the most diversely themed gardens, enhanced by fountains, ponds, and water features.

Seventy km (44 miles) north of Victoria, Highway 1 reaches the little town of Chemainus on the east coast, famed for its many oversized house murals, which mostly depict events from the town's history. A number of the Victorian buildings show signs of tasteful restoration.

At Parksville, north of Nanaimo, Highway 4 forks westwards, towards the rainforests on the far side of the island. After 20 km (12 miles) the road reaches the blue pools, wild waterfalls, and romantic canyons of the Little Qualicum Falls Provincial Park, and 15 km (9 miles) beyond this is 'Cathedral Grove', a stand of 800-year-old Douglas firs in MacMillan Provincial Park. Highway 4 ends in the Pacific Rim National Park at Tofino on the west coast, where forests of Douglas firs, hundreds of islands, bays, and beautiful beaches such as Long Beach

thickly forested mountains with peaks rising to 2,200 m (7,260 ft). The peaks are less dramatic to the east and the abundant sunshine in the rain shadow area ensures a relatively dry climate. The west coast coincides with the orographic barrier of the mountains, however, and has a high rainfall, leading to

combine to form coastal scenery of a unique beauty.

Above: The small waterfalls fall directly into the sea at Mystic Beach. Top left: The picturesque inner harbour of Victoria. Above right: South Beach exudes maritime romance.

There are many restaurants along the False Creek promenade, and in good summer weather, guests can sit outside.

Vancouver

With a population of some 2 million, Vancouver is British Columbia's largest city. The core of the town lies on a peninsula, and a unique panorama is formed by the Pacific bays that reach deep inland on one side and the snowcapped peaks of the surrounding Coast Mountains on the other.

Its location is not the only reason Vancouver is considered one of the most beautiful cities in the world; modern shopping malls and skyscrapers offer a charming contrast to the more traditional districts of the city, and Gastown, the old quarter, has been a conservation area since 1971. The steam clock on the corner of Cambie and Water Street, which has become a symbol of the new Gastown, has weights which are raised up every five minutes by a steam engine. Canada Place on Burrard Inlet, a futuristic-looking convention complex with a luxury hotel and other amenities, is worth a visit and the art deco Cathedral Palace office tower, built in 1991, has become a new symbol of the city. However, the heart of the city is at Robson Square, where a man-made waterfall splashes through lush vegetation amid the concrete, a green island between modern office blocks and historic buildings. Granville Square and the Pacific Railroad station, where there is a revolving restaurant with a fantastic view of the city, are also worth a visit. North America's second-largest Chinatown has grown up east of the old quarter and the streets are a riot of neon signs with Chinese characters, jewelers, souvenir sellers, bookstores, laundries, fantastic dragons, and porches and telephone kiosks decorated with pagodas. A visible sign of the close relationship between the Canadians and the Chinese is the classical garden of Dr Sun Yat-Sen, laid out behind the Cultural Centre by Chinese artisans from Suzhou in Vancouver.

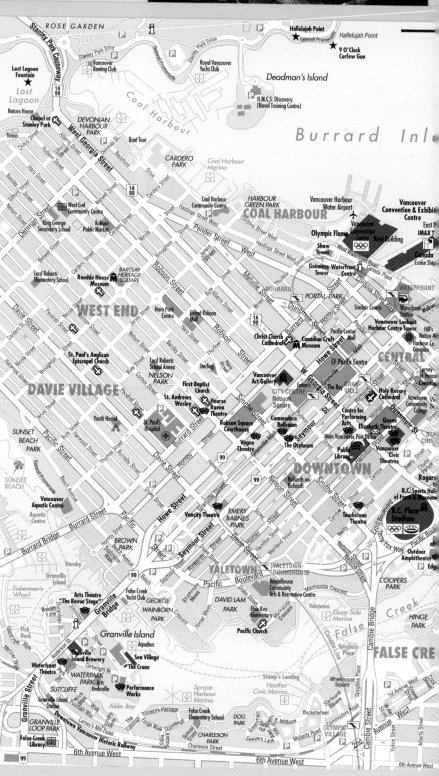

Animals in the Canadian Rocky Mountains

The montane forests of western Canada are home to bears, moose, wood bison, caribou, and red deer. There is also a great number of shy animals, much prized for their fur, such as beaver, marten, fox, and badger, and these are still hunted throughout the area. Water-

fowl flock to the lakes and anglers are drawn to the rich pickings, especially salmon, in the rivers.

Banff National Park is a habitat for wapitis.

the park's hiking routes begin from this road. Loop Brook Interpretive Trail (1.6 km/1 mile) includes some beautiful views.

6 Yoho National Park The little town of Golden is the gateway to this national park on the western slopes of the Rockies. From Highway 1, which crosses the park, there is a narrow side-road leading down into the Yoho Valley, which ends at the impressive 254-m (830-ft) Takakkaw Falls.

The end of the valley is surrounded by the impressive icefields of Mount Yoho, Mount Gordon, and Mount Daly, and above Mount Field there lies the Burgess Shale, where spectacular fossil finds have provided important insights into the flora and fauna of the Cambrian period; for all these reasons, Yoho National Park has been declared a UNESCO World Heritage Site. The observation terrace has a spectacular view of the Yoho Valley and the Spiral Tunnel. Highway 1 crosses Kicking Horse pass at a height of 1,627 m (5,330 ft) before descending into Banff National Park on the way to Lake Louise.

7 Lake Louise The Stoney Indians called Lake Louise the 'lake of little fishes' and its azure waters reflect Mount Victoria, whose glaciers stretch almost from the shores of the lake to a summit of 3,469 m (11,350 ft). The Grand Hotel Château Lake Louise, situated at the top of a terminal moraine, is no less impressive.

The top station of the cable car on Mount Whitehorn (2,034 m/6,675 ft) has a magnificent view of Lake Louise, Victoria Glacier, and the rows of peaks forming the Continental Divide. A 13-km (8-mile) mountain road

leads to the peace of Lake Moraine in the romantic Valley of the Ten Peaks; to reach Banff, 50 km (31 miles) away, visitors should take the Bow Valley Parkway (1A), which runs parallel to the Trans-Canada Highway and offers better chances to observe wildlife.

8 Banff National Park The magnificent mountain scenery of Canada's oldest national park boasts peaks rising to 3,500 m (11,500 ft), glaciers, Alpine meadows, and waterfalls. The main attractions are its lakes and caves, however, such as Castle-guard Caves. Banff, at the southern end of the park, is famed for its hot springs and historic hotels, such as the Banff Springs Hotel. The Banff Park Museum and the Whyte Museum of the Canadian Rockies are dedicated to the flora and fauna of the surrounding parks. The best views are from Mount Norquai (2,135 m/7,005 ft) and

The Yoho National Parks (both pictured above) and Banff (pictured above left) create a perfect combination of mountains and water.

Dinosaur Provincial Park

This 7,000 ha (17,300 acre) park to the east of Calgary (230 km/144 miles) is one of the most significant fossil sites in North America; any number of petrified dinosaur species have been excavated here and can be viewed in impressive scenic surroundings, where the Red Deer River has cut a 100-m (330-ft) gouge through the sedimentary rock, creating a

Sulphur Mountain (2,270 m/ 7,450 ft), both of which are accessible by cable car. The next whiff of city air is not for another 140 km (87 miles) to the east, at Calgary.

⑨ Calgary The 'Manhattan of the Prairies' grew up out of a market town for farmers and ranchers. Nowadays, the best view over this big, modern city is from the 191-m (625-ft) Calgary Tower. The high point of the year comes in July with the Stampede, the greatest cowboy show on earth, and all roads in the 24-ha (60-acre) Stampede Park, on a bend in the Elbow River, lead to the Saddledome, which seats almost 20,000 people. Fort Calgary Historic Park, situated at the confluence of the Elbow and Bow Rivers, commemorates the first post established by the North West Mounted Police (NWMP) in 1875. Still scarlet-clad, they are now called the Royal Canadian Mounted Police (RCMP), and during the summer they perform a daily presentation of their proud past as 'living history'. Calgary Zoo and Prehistoric Park on St George's Island in the river is worth visiting. The prehistoric theme park has models of dinosaurs that lived in south-western Canada.

⑩ Dinosaur Provincial Park About 200 km (125 miles) east of Calgary on Highway 1 you reach Brooks, which takes you on a detour to the Dinosaur Provincial Park. The park's scenic prairies and badlands are impressive, but the main attractions are the dinosaur fossils that have been found here.

⑪ Cypress Hills Interprovincial Park A winding 200-km (125-mile) detour through the Cypress Hills provides for an attractive change from the much bigger Highway 1. Fifty km (31 miles) east of Medicine Hat, Highway 41 turns south towards the spa town of Elkwater. The

Blackfoot tribe called this uniquely varied plateau and mountain landscape Ketewius Netumoo, meaning 'the hills that shouldn't be'. Fort Walsh National Historic Park, a reconstructed fort telling the story of the NWMP and the original native population, is not too far from Elkwater. Farewell's Trading Post is one of the infamous 'whisky forts' where unscrupulous whisky traders would barter alcohol with the First Nations people for skins and furs. The network of traders was broken only with the involvement of the Mounties.

Highway 21 leads back to Highway 1 via Maple Creek. Saskatchewan's prairie scenery takes on quite different shades, depending on the season: the

blue and yellow of the flax and rape fields predominate in the early summer, the wheat is golden in late summer. Huge red grain silos – the 'cathedrals of the prairie' – can be seen from a distance.

⑫ Regina Saskatchewan's capital is situated in the middle of endless wheatfields, and even today the Saskatchewan Wheat Pool, one of the world's largest wheat producers, has its headquarters here. Regina's expansion began in 1882 with the construction of the Canadian Pacific Railroad, and the RCMP, the successor to the NWMP, was also based here until 1920. The RCMP's national training academy, which has its own museum, is still on Dewdney Avenue.

The Sergeant Major's Parade (daily Monday–Friday) and the evening Sunset Retreat Ceremony (every Tuesday in July and August) always draw a crowd. Wascana Lake, a man-made lake in the middle of the city, and its 1,000 ha (2,400 acres) of grounds together form one of the largest municipal parks in the world. The Royal Saskatchewan Museum has geological and paleontological exhibits, as well as examples of dinosaurs and finds from First Nations culture. The Regina Plains Museum, telling the story of the Plains Indians, is the right place for historians and enthusiasts.

⑬ Brandon This wheat town, about 300 km (185 miles) further east on the Assiniboine Riv-

multi-hued rocky landscape. The Provincial Park is accessible via a circular path leading through typical badlands to excavation sites and dinosaur fossils. Visitors wishing to learn more about dinosaurs and their surroundings will find restored dinosaur skeletons and other fossilized prehistoric creatures in the adjacent Paleontological Museum.

Barren scenery in the Dinosaur Provincial Park.

found at the junction of Highways 1 and 26, where you can visit a schoolhouse, church, shops, and houses from the time of the settlers. The museum and the village commemorate the 18th century, when Portage La Prairie was an important French trading post; the original fort was built by the French explorer Pierre Gaultier de la Vérendrye in 1738. The museum's exhibits also has a comprehensive section devoted to the railroad, and exhibits include a private railway carriage from 1882 which once belonged to Sir William van Horne, the director of the Canadian Pacific Railway Company.

⓯ Winnipeg Situated to the south of Lake Manitoba and Lake Winnipeg, Manitoba's capital city represents the geographical halfway point of the Trans-Canada Highway between the Pacific and the Atlantic. Once called 'win nipi' ('muddy waters') by the local population, Canada's eighth-largest city is now home to more than three dozen ethnic groups, who all arrived at the beginning of the 20th century as the transcontinental railroad opened up the west of this gigantic country. Winnipeg's core stretches along the north bank of the Assiniboine River to its confluence with the Red River. The engine sheds and marshaling yards around Union Station, a beaux arts building from 1911, have been turned into a heritage park and some fortifications dating back to the Northwest Company and the Hudson's Bay Company have been preserved. The city's most prominent building is the Legislative Building (1919), whose mighty cupola is the seat of the

er, is Manitoba's second-largest city. The B.J. Hales Museum of Natural History has a display of more than 200 stuffed local bird species. Part of the museum is also dedicated to local First Nations culture.

It is worth making a detour to visit the steep rock formations and rolling prairies of the Riding Mountain National Park, about 100 km (62 miles) north of Brandon. There are another 200 km (124 miles) of endless wheatfields to be passed on Highway 1 before you reach Portage La Prairie, just before Winnepeg.

⓮ Portage La Prairie The Fort la Reine Museum and Pioneer Village, an open-air museum with 25 buildings, is to be

Large image: Dinosaur Provincial Park. Left side: Winnipeg. Right: Cypress Hills Interprovincial Park (top), bottom: Calgary, once a cattle ranchers' market town, now boasts an impressive skyline.

Detour

Woodland Caribou Provincial Park

This park, on the western edge of Ontario, is devoted to caribou, a North American sub-species of reindeer. Nature is still king here, and only visitors equipped with a canoe and a tent will be able to enter the habitat of one of the largest herds of woodland caribou south of Hudson Bay.

Getting anywhere near the park means joining Highway 105 west of Dryden and heading north to Red Lake, the last natural barrier before the park, and only a

The lakeland area in the Woodland Caribou Provincial Park remains undeveloped.

boat or a seaplane will get you any further. Those who make it across will soon discover that the woodland caribou live in smaller herds than their northern cousins, the Baffin and Peary caribou, and cover considerably smaller distances. They prefer to keep to the forests, avoiding the prairies. Both the males and the females grow mighty antlers.

In autumn, the rocky mountain larch tree turns bright yellow and almost merges with the ocher-coloured cliffs on Tumbling Pass when the sun is setting.

Mountains, glaciers, caves, and lakes – national and provincial parks in the Rockies

The Canadian section of the Rocky Mountains is one of North America's most striking mountainous areas and is covered by a string of National and Provincial Parks, which were declared World Heritage Sites in 1984 and 1990 respectively.

UNESCO's decision to include the National Parks of Jasper, Banff, Yoho, and Kootenay and the Provincial Parks of Mount Assiniboine, Mount Robson, and Hamber as World Heritage Sites rested on their geological significance, conservation of the local rare flora and fauna, and the extraordinary beauty of the scenery. The important fossil site at Burgess Shale in Yoho National Park was also a contributory factor.

Visitors to the parks are greeted by imposing mountain scenery, with peaks rising to 3,500 m (11,600 ft), glaciers, ice fields, waterfalls, canyons, caves, hot springs, and Alpine meadows. Three zones of vegetation have formed, according to their elevation: montane forest, sub-Al-

pine forest, and a zone of Alpine tundra. Influenced by its milder, Pacific climate, the south-western tip of Kootenay Park has some semi-arid features. Trees common here include hemlock pines, Douglas firs, cedars, pines, and spruce. Many different animals have been observed here, including marmots, beavers, deer, moose, mountain

goats, bighorn sheep, coyotes, wolves, lynx, pumas, black and grizzly bears, and many species of birds.

The infrastructure in this beautiful landscape is perfectly arranged: there are thousands of miles of winding but well-maintained scenic routes which cross spectacular passes and provide links to hiking trails and accom-

modation suited to every level of comfort.

Above left: In intense emerald green shimmers across the cold water in the swirl pot of Johnston Canyon. Above: The mountain scenery is reflected in the clear Bow Lake.

At 3,954 m (12,972 ft), Mount Robson, situated in the provincial park of the same name, is the highest point in the Canadian Rocky Mountains. Its massive form looms over the valleys at its feet.

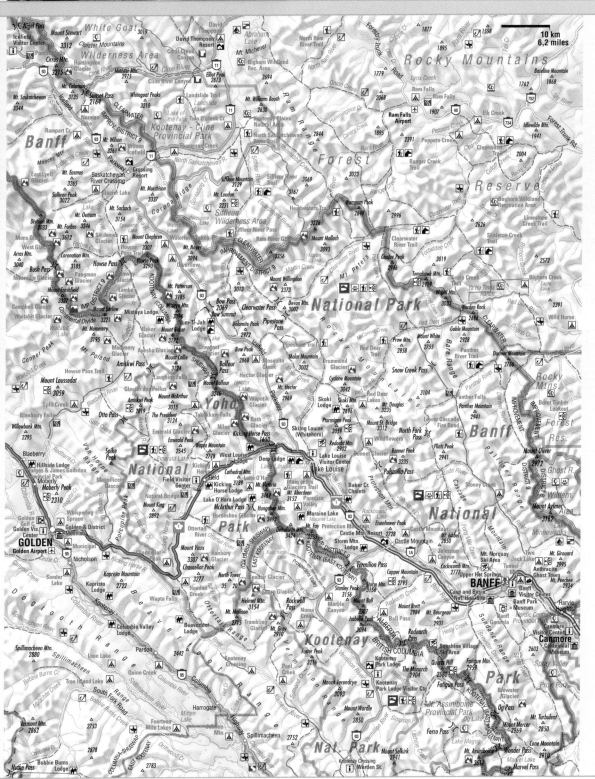

Old Fort William

In Thunder Bay you can take an interesting journey into the past at a Montreal North West Company fur trading post, reconstructed as it would have looked around 1803–1821. Fort William Historical Park, located on the Kaministiquia River at the south-western edge of the city, consists of 42 buildings surrounded by a high palisade. Trappers – the so-called voyageurs – and locals would meet here in summer to exchange primarily furs and pelts for household items. Today in summer, there are reenactments in original costumes of how this trading was carried out.

4-m (13-ft) 'Golden Boy'. Winnipeg Art Gallery has one of the best collections of Inuit art. The Manitoba Museum of Man and Nature, telling the story of the Hudson's Bay Company, is also worth a visit. Highway 1, now bearing the number 17, continues to Ontario, but not only the nomenclature is different – the Canadian Shield begins here and there is a significant change in the scenery. There are just a few small towns on the highway, which is now entering a large region of lakes.

At Vermilion Bay, the highway swings north into Pakwash Provincial Park and on to Red Lake and the Woodland Caribou Provincial Park. Further to the east you can take a detour to the heavenly lakes of Quetico National Park.

16 Thunder Bay The westernmost port on the Great Lakes and St Lawrence River that is still accessible for ocean-going boats lies here on the north-western shore of Lake Superior; much of the grain from the prairies passes through this

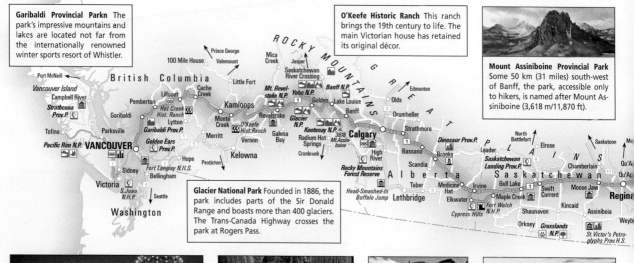

Garibaldi Provincial Parkn The park's impressive mountains and lakes are located not far from the internationally renowned winter sports resort of Whistler.

O'Keefe Historic Ranch This ranch brings the 19th century to life. The main Victorian house has retained its original décor.

Mount Assiniboine Provincial Park Some 50 km (31 miles) south-west of Banff, the park, accessible only to hikers, is named after Mount Assiniboine (3,618 m/11,870 ft).

Glacier National Park Founded in 1886, the park includes parts of the Sir Donald Range and boasts more than 400 glaciers. The Trans-Canada Highway crosses the park at Rogers Pass.

Vancouver Its spectacular location between ocean and mountains makes Vancouver one of the world's most beautiful cities. An array of skyscrapers welcomes new arrivals to the bay.

Mount Revelstoke National Park The alpine meadows around Mt Revelstoke (1,943 m/6,375 ft) are filled with the region's flora.

Yoho National Park A park in the Rocky Mountains with glaciated valleys and waterfalls; Emerald Lake is particularly idyllic.

Calgary Once Canada's 'Cowtown', now dominated by oil and skyscrapers. The Calgary Stampede, the world's largest rodeo, has survived, however.

Isle Royale National Park

Lying just off the north-western shores of Lake Superior, the whole of Isle Royal has been declared a National Park. The 2,000 sq km (772 sq mi) island is notorious for its inaccessibility and unpredictable weather, although its wolves and moose have also brought it fame. The park and island is accessible only by boat (from Grand Portage) or seaplane, and the island's interior is marked only by 250 km (155 miles) of hiking trails, some of which are little more than indistinct paths.

point. The most important tourist attraction is Old Fort William (see sidebar), and the best view to the south of the town is to be had from the 180-m (600-ft) Scenic Lookout at Mount McKay. The effort of reaching it is rewarded with a panoramic view of the whole of Thunder Bay.

17 Sleeping Giant Provincial Park East of Thunder Bay, a peninsula juts out far into lake Superior; the 'Sleeping Giant' is a series of ridges 11 km (7 miles) long and in places 335 m (1,100 ft) high at the tip of the peninsula. There is a gentle hiking path to the panoramic view at the summit. The canyons and forests of the park are home to black bears, deer, lynxes, foxes, and beavers. From here, Highway 17 passes Ouimet Canyon, rounding the northern tip of Lake Superior on the way to White River.

18 Pukaskwa National Park South of the village of White River on the north-eastern shore of Lake Superior, this national park is reached via Route 627. The Visitor's Center at the northern edge of the park will tell you about the flora and fauna in the virgin forest, which includes moose, bears, and wolves, and three nature paths also begin here. The 60-km (37-mile) Coastal Trail is suitable for hikers with outdoors equipment.

19 Sault Ste. Marie Highway 17 crosses Lake Superior Provincial Park on the wild eastern shore before reaching its destination at Sault Ste Marie (see eastern section of 'Trans-Canada Highway' Route).

Left side: The Pukaskwa National Park on the north bank of Lake Superior is set in extensive primeval forest landscape that remains undeveloped. **Above:** Black bears find a home in the Sleeping Giant Provincial Park. Looking at the young bear cubs you can hardly imagine what their future size will be. Fortunately, black bear attacks on humans are rare.

Dinosaur Provincial Park Dinosaur fossils dating back 60 million years have been found at this paleontological site, located on the Red Deer River.

Fort la Reine This museum village illustrates how farming was carried out on the prairie around 150 years ago.

Quetico Provincial Park This enormous, and still largely unexplored, park west of Thunder Bay has over 1,500 km (930 miles) of trails accessible by canoe, including some historic trappers' and settlers' trails.

Riding Mountain National Park The park is home to wolves, black bears, moose, bison, and hundreds of species of birds.

Lake Superior Provincial Park Located north of Sault Ste Marie, the park has numerous canoe and nature trails. The First Nations cave paintings at Agawa Rock near Highway 17 are particularly worth visiting.

Cypress Hills Interprovincial Park Reaching heights of 1,400 m (4,600 ft), the mountains here are covered in diverse Alpine vegetation.

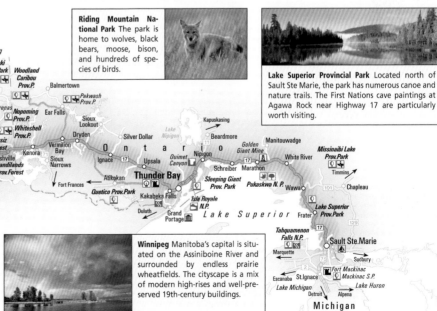

Winnipeg Manitoba's capital is situated on the Assiniboine River and surrounded by endless prairie wheatfields. The cityscape is a mix of modern high-rises and well-preserved 19th-century buildings.

Route 23: Canada and the USA
On the Pan-American Highway

A journey through the North American West is a journey of contrasts. The route passes through mountain landscapes and open plains, pine forests and vast deserts, mining villages and megacities, and illustrates the impressive diversity of this enormous continent.

Route profile:

Length: approx. 3,200 km
(1,988 miles), excluding detours
Time required: at least 3 weeks
When to go: The best time to go is
summer when it is mild in the north
and roads are open. Extreme heat
in the southern US can be
uncomfortable.

The full diversity of North America reveals itself in its entirety along the wide open stretches of the Pan-American Highway. From its begining on the Canadian Pacific coast to its end near the border between the USA and Mexico, this route initially travels in a south-easterly and then southerly direction. The roads on this long route are in exceptionally good condition but some of the side roads can be closed during the colder times of the year, especially in the north.

The northern section takes you through the Canadian provinces of British Columbia and Alberta as well as the US state of Montana. Larger towns are the exception here and the individual towns are often separated by large distances. Newer settlements originally developed from either trading posts or supply centres for the white fur hunters. There are also a number of old gold-digging locations along the Pan-American Highway, where visitors are taken back in time to the gold rush of the 19th century. In some places there are also remnants of Native American Indian cultures, such as the impressive totem poles, longhouses and pueblos.

The Canadian part of the route is loaded with absolutely breathtaking natural landscapes. Majestic, snowy mountains reflect in the shimmering turquoise hues of Rocky Mountain lakes.

To the east of the highway Mount Robson rises to 3,954 m (12,973 ft) above sea level, the highest peak in the Canadian Rocky Mountains. Glaciers and waterfalls drop powerfully to great depths from high cliffs. The Pan-American Highway is also lined with vast expanses of forest. In a number of areas such as Banff National Park, the oldest National Park in Canada, the

natural environment is protected from development.
Further south the scenery changes. In the distance you see the skyscrapers of Calgary, a modern metropolis built on wealth generated by oil and natural resources, and given a makeover for the 1988 Winter Olympics. Some three hours from Calgary are the spectacular lakes and mountains of Waterton-Glacier

Top: Banff National Park will show you everything that makes the Canadian Rocky Mountains such an attraction – rugged peaks, dense forests, vast open spaces and scenic lakes like Peyto Lake, shown here. Left: Old farmhouse in Grand Teton National Park in northwest Wyoming.

International Peace Park, a union of Glacier and Waterton National Parks.

The route continues through Idaho, Wyoming, Utah and Arizona. There are a number of remarkable contrasts here as well. Remnants of Native American cultures and the Spanish colonial era mix with modern cities and skyscrapers, and extensive forest areas stand in contrast to desert landscapes. A major highlight of this particular section of North America is Yellowstone National Park in Wyoming. Salt Lake City, the capital of Utah and the centre of Mormonism, is also an Olympic city, having hosted the 2002 winter games. In the vast desert expanses of Utah and Arizona the light and landscape change dramatically with the movement of the sun, producing impressive interplays of colours and shadows, and the rocky landscape of the Colorado Plateau is also impressive in places like Bryce Canyon National Park. The Grand Canyon, stretching over 350 km (217 miles) of magnificent desert, is one of the most visited sightseeing attractions in the USA – some 4 million people come here every year.

Sunset Crater, the youngest of Arizona's volcanoes, can be seen near Flagstaff and is today a training area for astronauts. In the adjoining 'Valley of the Sun' to the south the towns appear like oases in the desert. The exclusive golf courses and fields exist only due to artificial irrigation.

Phoenix, the capital of Arizona, still has a slight touch of the Wild West to it, but as a centre for the aircraft construction and high-tech industries, the city is part of the modern world. Tucson, the 'City of Sunshine', has 350 days of sunshine a year.

Mount Assiniboine after the first snow (left side). Spirit Island in Maligne Lake in Jasper National Park – postcard views par excellence (top).

Before the European colonisation, various tribes used the Athabasca River for fishing.

Whale-Watching

There are only a few other places on earth where they are better observed, these majestic giants of the ocean. Along the Canadian Pacific coast, in places like Prince Rupert Sound you can go on spectacular whale-watching

A humpback whale off the coast of Alaska in the so-called 'breaching'.

excursions that last several hours. Between March and July, grey whales are spotted frequently along the North American west coast, migrating to rich feeding grounds in the waters off British Columbia and Alaska. Killer whales and minke whales are also a regular sight in these frigid coastal waters.

The North American section of the Pan-American Highway leads from the Pacific coast via the Rocky Mountains to the arid regions of the American south-west. The route is lined with natural beauty that is protected in a series of spectacular national parks.

❶ Prince Rupert The Pan-American Highway comes up with important cultural and historic sights right from the start. The creative carved totem poles of a variety of Indian tribes can be found all over the harbour town, and the pristine wilderness in the province of British Columbia awaits you just outside the city limits.
Highway 16 initially takes you through the Skeena Valley. At Hazelton it is worth taking a detour to the Gitksan Indian villages. The Ksan Native Village is an open-air museum with several longhouses. In Kitwancool you can see what is alleged to be the largest standing totem pole. After 242 km (150 miles) a small road branches off at Vanderhoof towards Fort St James to the north (66 km/41 miles)

❷ Fort St. James National Historic Site On the eastern shore of the more than 100-km-long (62-mile) Stuart Lake is Fort St James, a town developed from what was originally a trading post founded in 1806. Actors

re-enact scenes from the lives of 19th-century fur hunters during the annual summer festival in the reconstructed fort. For fishing enthusiasts there are a number of isolated lakes nearby to drop a line.

❸ Prince George The Pan-American Highway crosses the Cariboo Highway (Highway 97) here. Once a satellite of Fort St James, Prince George grew into a lively town in the 19th century with the construction of a railway that brought new settlers and adventurers. The Railway Museum has an historic steam train on display.

❹ Bowron Lake Provincial Park A little detour leads you through Quesnel and Barkerville (the centre of a gold rush here in the 19th century) on your way to the wilderness around Bowron Lake. The drive over a gravel road at the end can be somewhat tedious but the effort is rewarded with fantastic landscape. The eleven lakes in the area are a major attraction for

fans of canoeing. You can paddle through the entire lake landscape in the course of eight days. Back on the Pan-American Highway, after driving 270 km (168 miles) through Fraser Valley, you reach Tête Jaune Cache, the gateway to the lovely Mount Robson Provincial Park.

❺ Mount Robson Provincial Park The highest mountain in the Canadian Rocky Mountains is Mount Robson at an impressive (3,954 m/12,973 ft). It is the king of this unique protected area (2,200 sq km/1,367 sq mi) and is beloved among hikers and mountaineers. High altitude glaciers, crystal-clear mountain lakes, tumbling waterfalls and exhilarating pine forests characterize this jewel of the Rockies.
After 100 km (62 miles) on Yellowhead Pass you reach Jasper in the Jasper National Park.

❻ Jasper National Park (see pages 302-303.) The huge mountains here tower majestically over what is the largest national park in the Canadian Rockies. It covers an area totalling 10,878 sq km (6,760 sq mi). You get closest to the natural beauty of the park either on foot or in a canoe, the latter of which

In July, it's hot in Calgary. This is in addition to the outside temperatures at the Calgary Stampede, which brings the atmosphere to a boil every year.

Detour

Glacier National Park

A detour from the main route onto the Trans-Canada Highway takes you along one of the loveliest mountain roads in the world. Beyond Rogers Pass at 1,327 m (4,354 ft) there are in breathtaking mountain landscapes. In the Columbia Mountains, a chain that runs parallel to the Rockies, is the Canadian portion of Glacier National Park, where the peaks are more jagged and cliffs even steeper than its neighbours on the US side. The scenery is dominated by

400 glaciers give the Glacier National Park its name.

is perfectly suited to the 22-km-long (14-mile) Maligne Lake. The Icefields Parkway (Highway 93) is the next portion of the route and is a highlight of the Pan-American Highway. It runs 230 km (143 miles) along the gorgeous panoramic route at the foot of the glacial ridge of the Rocky Mountains and past the Columbia Ice Field, the largest ice field in North America. The Athabasca Falls and the Sunwapta Falls are also worth seeing.

7 **Banff National Park** (please also see Route 24 'Wild West'). The road then takes you past the smaller Yoho National Park and on to the shimmering turquoise waters of Lake Louise. Nearby Moraine Lake is somewhat quieter. There are more than twenty-four 3,000-m (10,000-ft) peaks in this national

park. Highway 1 turns off westwards near Lake Louise and heads over the Rogers Pass towards Glacier National Park.

8 **Calgary** The largest city in the area is Calgary on the western edge of the vast prairie. The approach from the west is especially impressive on days when the Chinooks, warm, dry autumn winds, are blowing down from the Rocky Mountains. They ensure grand views of the peaks towering behind the city and create the bizarre illusion that you could reach out and touch the mountains.

The largest city in the province of Alberta can be seen from far away. The downtown high-rises, largely housing the offices of oil companies, banks and insurance companies, rise grandiosely against the backdrop of the mighty Rockies. The city has de-

veloped from an agricultural centre to a modern metropolis that attracts a great deal of foreign capital. A milestone in this development was the hosting of the 1988 Winter Olympics. Isolated though it may be in the middle of Alberta, Calgary is well on its way to becoming a million-strong metropolis and is an important inter-regional traffic hub.

Landmark, symbol and the most important orientation point in the city is the Calgary Tower, standing at a proud 191 m (627 ft). The Olympic Saddledome ice sport arena provides an architectural link between tradition and modernity, and is one of the most advanced of its kind in the world. The design of the arena in the shape of a saddle also reflects the spirit of the Wild West, which is really brought back to life in July every

Large image: The nocturnal skyline of Calgary has its charms. In the foreground, the sports arena Scotiabank Saddledome (formerly Pengrowth Saddle dome) can be seen. The Calgary skyline is an up-and-coming metroplis.
Above: Mount Robson Provincial Park and the so called peak.

ice fields and glaciers. More than 10 per cent of the area is under permanent ice, hence the park's name. In over 1,350 sq km (839 sq mi) of national park there are more than 400 glaciers. The low-lying areas are covered with rainforest as a result of the high rainfall and trees species include the hemlock fir and red cedar. Grizzlies are also at home in the Glacier National Park as are caribou and Rocky Mountain goats. Glacier National Park boasts a number of attractions from under the earth's surface as well – go spelunking in Nakimu Cave, one of the largest in Canada. The climate in the national park is as raw as the scenery is attractive. The weather changes constantly.

Beauvert Lake in Jasper National Park is a paradise for canoeists.

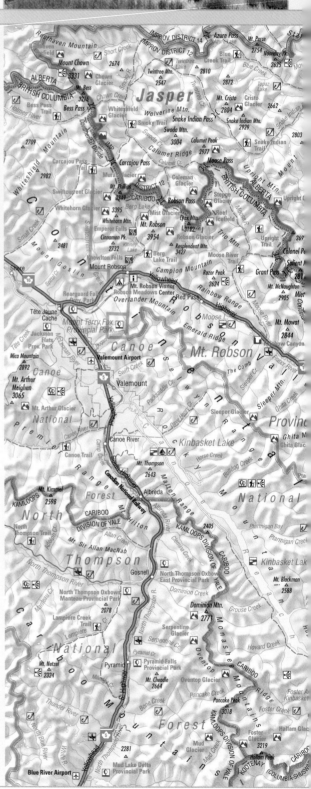

Jasper National Park

Jasper National Park, less overrun with tourists than Banff National Park and Lake Louise, boasts unspoilt Rocky Mountain scenery.

Jasper National Park lies on the state border with British Columbia and its area of 10,878 sq km (4,170 sq mi) makes it one of the biggest national parks in the Canadian Rocky Mountains. Mount Columbia is 3,747 m (12, 290 ft) high and the Columbia Icefield extends almost to the Icefields Parkway.

There are more than 800 lakes within the park boundaries, mostly fed from the surrounding glaciers; nearby Maligne Lake is considered the most picturesque and is one of the most photographed areas of the Rockies. Lac Beauvert, a jade green glacial lake, is very near the city, and Jasper Park Lodge, the old Grand Trunk Railroad's answer to the Banff Springs Hotel in the adjacent park, was built on its shores.

Jasper grew up out of a trading post for trappers, hunters, and prospectors and only became accessible to tourists when the Canadian Pacific Railway reached the town in 1911. The little town is less crowded than Banff – this is also true of the hotel – and the trails in the wilderness will allow you to explore the wonderful scenery of the Rockies in peace.

There is a funicular railway connection to Whistler Mountain, a popular tourist destination with breathtaking panoramic views. Jasper National Park has been a protected area since 1907.

Majestic mountain peaks dominate the scenery at Maligne. The Maligne River accumulates naturally at the end of the Medicine Lake and is drained by a large underground drain.

The Sunwapta River makes its way through the forests of Jasper National Park.

The grey autumn sky makes Sinopah Mountain at Two Medicine Lake seem dangerous.

Head-Smashed-In Buffalo Jump

The Pan-American Highway takes you from Calgary south towards Fort Macleod. At the end of the 19th century the town made a name for itself as a trading centre for both legal and illegal goods. Indians from the Blackfoot tribe traded bison skins for cheap whisky from white settlers. The Fort Macleod Museum has exhibitions covering the history of the Blackfoot Indians. At Head-Smashed-In Buffalo Jump, around 18 km (11 miles) north-west of Fort Macleod, you can see an example of one of the Blackfoot traditions and customs. For thousands of years these Indians used a spectacular cliff formation approximately 300 m (984 ft) long as a tool to hunt bison, an essential element of their livelihood. Bison herds were rounded up by hundreds of hunters on foot and sent run-

A UNESCO World Heritage Site – Head-Smashed-In Buffalo Jump.

ning in a panic towards the cliff edge. Their frenzy to escape combined with the blind herd instinct sent throngs of them falling to their deaths. This form of hunting was used until the 18th century. In 1981 UNESCO declared the Head-Smashed-In Buffalo Jump cliff a World Heritage Site as testimony to the way of life of the local Indians.

year during the hugely popular ten-day Stampede, when the ten-gallon cowboy hats, cowboy boots and blue jeans dictate the dress code throughout the city. Rodeos and covered wagon races bring back the 'good old days'.

Heading south again, after 170 km (106 miles) you reach Fort Macleod. About 18 km (11 miles) north-west of the Fort is the World Heritage Site of Head-Smashed-In Buffalo Jump (see sidebar left).

From here, take Highways 6 (via Pincher) or 5 (via Cardston) to reach Waterton, the entrance to another breathtaking Canadian national park.

❾ Waterton Lakes National Park There are two national parks near the border between Canada and the USA – Waterton Lakes National Park in the Canadian province of Alberta, and Glacier National Park in the US state of Montana. In 1932 the two were combined as the Waterton-Glacier International

Peace Park. For local Indians the entire area has always been known as the 'Land of the Shining Mountains'. Just after entering the park from the north-east (Highway 5 and 6) you reach Bison Paddocks.

A few kilometres further down, a narrow road branches off to the west towards Red Rock Canyon, named as such due to the red sedimentary rock in the area. The route continues to the 2,940-m-high (9,646-ft) Mount Blakiston, the highest peak in

the Waterton Lakes National Park. The Prince of Wales Hotel is one of the most striking buildings in the reserve, with stunning views of two lakes, Middle and Upper Waterton.

Access to Glacier National Park is via the Chief Mountain International Highway which travels along the eastern side of the park. The road was built in 1935 and is in good condition but is only passable between mid-May and mid-September.

Animals of Yellowstone National Park

For European visitors, bison in the wild are a special experience and even cause real traffic jams on the Grand Loop Road. Elks , mountain goats, pumas, coyotes and lynx are also at home here. Wolves have also been successfully reintegrated in recent years. Parts of the pine forests in Yellowstone are subject to recurring forest fires.

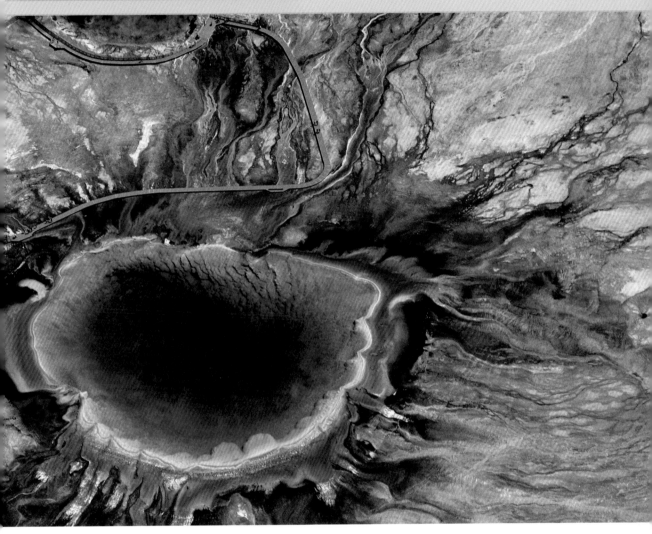

surprise that this is where the highest number of visitors will be found. You can even set your watch by some of the geysers and can plan your arrival accordingly. Old Faithful is one of the most 'punctual', displaying its skills almost every 80 minutes for a few minutes at a time, sending huge quantities of water about 50 m (164 ft) into the air. Other well-known geysers are Giant Geyser and Castle Geyser. And it's not just a visual experience. The accompanying noises as you approach are also fascinating. Make sure you stick to the marked pathways at all times as the unstable ground bubbles and hisses at many places in the park. Steam clouds sometimes even reach as far as the Grand Loop Road. All of this is evidence of volcanic activity within the park. Violent volcanic eruptions are not to be feared, however, as the last major eruption took place around 600,000 years ago. The waterfalls along the Yellowstone River in the south of the park are another

Top and right side: Like a being from another planet, the Grand Prismatic Spring - from a bird's-eye view – is the largest hot spring in the USA. It is named after its variety of colours, which comes from colourful unicellular organisms in up to 71 °C hot water. Left side: A meander of the Yellowstone River meandering through the National Park.

On Antelope Island, low water reveals a harmonious pattern in the sand of White Rock Bay. Algae brightly colour the puddles and the sun casts its light on the Elephant Head.

Detour

Great Salt Lake

About half an hour northwest of Salt Lake City is the Great Salt Lake at an altitude of almost 1,300 m (4,265 ft). Approximately 120 km (75 miles) long, and about 60 km (37 miles) at its widest point, it is the largest inland lake west of the Mississippi.

For its size, however, the lake is relatively shallow and only during the rainy season does it reach a depth of more than 10 m (33 ft). The lake is all that's left of a much larger body of water, Lake Bonneville, which had a surface area of 50,000 sq km (31,070 sq mi) in the last ice age more than 10,000 years ago. Since then both the surface area and the volume have constantly decreased as a result of rising temperatures and evaporation.

Salt in the water has also crystallized. Today the lake's salt content is several times higher than that of the ocean. With no outflow, there is nowhere for the saline water to escape. Nevertheless, some animals are still able to survive here. Saltwater prawns in particular have adapted to the prevailing conditions.

For many, however, the southern shore of Great Salt Lake State Park is simply good for its beaches.

striking attraction. At Upper Falls the river drops 33 m (108 ft) over the cliffs. At Lower Falls – only a few 100 m away – the drop is as much as 94 m (308 ft). The viewing points in the Lookout Point and Grandview Point parking areas offer especially dramatic views.

⑬ Grand Teton National Park From Yellowstone National Park, John D. Rockefeller Jr. Memorial Parkway takes you to a much smaller park, Grand Teton National Park (1,257 sq km/781 sq mi), which is often overshadowed by its famous neighbour. This is unjustified to say the least, however, as it also has a number of attractions on offer and is a more relaxed experience altogether.

The jagged peaks of the Teton Range, dominated by Grand Teton at 4,197 m (13,770 ft), are accompanied by glaciers that extend far into the steep valleys. The park's main axis is Jackson Hole, an 80-km (50-mile) valley through which the idyllic Snake River passes on part of its 1,670-km (1,038-mile) journey to the Columbia River, which eventually flows through Idaho, Oregon and Washington

into the Pacific. There are also a number of lakes in the valley. Teton Park Road takes you from Jackson Lake to the south-east, the panoramic road offering continuously lovely views of the mountain landscape.

Jackson Hole boasts one superlative in particular. In 1933 the lowest temperature ever recorded in Wyoming, -54°C, was measured here. Even though it can be very cold in winter, such temperatures are obviously not typical. This park is open all year and the best time to go is between June and September. Most of the tourist facilities are closed in the winter but winter sports are popular here.

⑭ Jackson Der Ort am südlichen Rand Situated on the southern rim of Jackson Hole, this is the ideal starting point for hikes in Grand Teton National

Park as well as for white-water rafting on the Snake River. And, with its Wild-West-style saloons and bars, Jackson is more than just a tourist staging post. The place retains an authentic Wild West atmosphere and can be a lot of fun. The Wildlife of the American West Art Museum has a worthwhile collection of paintings featuring the wild animals of the region. The cultural history of the local Indians is illustrated in the Teton County Historical Center.

A few kilometres south of Jackson a turn-off near Alpine heads west towards Idaho. Idaho Falls are a good distance beyond the state line. In addition to a Mormon temple that is worth seeing, the city is home to the Intermountain Science Experience Center, a first-class natural history museum. Back on Highway 89 you continue south from

The Fremont Indians left numerous petroglyphs on some of the walls of the fold mountains in Capitol Reef National Park.

Montpellier through the Wasatch Mountains, which emerge abruptly from the plains. The area, at more than 3,500 m (11,484 ft), is covered in snow all year and is a popular winter sport area for residents of Salt Lake City. One of the main attractions here is the salt lake to the west of the road, which you can reach by making a detour on Highway 80.

⓯ Salt Lake City The capital of Utah is one of the largest cities along the Pan-American Highway. Initially it seems an intimidating location for a city, with the Great Salt Lake to the west, the Wasatch Mountains forming a natural border to the east, and the Great Salt Lake Desert stretching west to the horizon. However, in the middle of the 19th century the Mormons were in search of just this type

of environment, remote and inhospitable. Yet the gold rush and the completion of the transcontinental railroad brought more and more people to the town, which had developed into a lively city by the start of the 20th century.

A century later the city received further impetus from the Winter Olympics in 2002.

The classical Capitol building (1915) is visible from afar and is the city's primary landmark, but Temple Square is really where things happen here. The 4-ha (10-acre) square is considered to be the Mormons' 'holy square' and the temple is accessible only to members of the Mormon church.

The city's highest building at 128 m (420 ft) is the Church Office Building, also a Mormon building, which houses the central administration of this reli-

gious community. The view from the platform on the 26th floor is especially popular with visitors to the city.

⓰ Timpanogos Cave National Monument On the northern slope of the 3,581-m (11,749-ft) Mount Timpanogo are three caves that have been formed over a long period of time due to the porosity of the limestone that is characteristic of the area. The bizarre stalactites are a real sight to behold. The three caves are connected by a man-made tunnel and can be viewed as part of a guided tour.

Due to its extraordinary nature the entire area has been declared a National Monument.

⓱ Capitol Reef National Park The Pan-American Highway is well-maintained in Utah.

After having covered more than half of this state you will reach some of the absolute highlights along this dream route. Leave Highway 15 at Scipio and turn off onto Highway 50 for around 30 km (19 miles). Highway 12 turns off at Salina to the next national park.

The Capitol Reef National Park is characterized by a colourful cliff face towering above the Fremont River. The Fremont River has cut its way deep into a geological shift known as the Waterpocket Fold. Parallel ridges rise out of the desert sands here in a wave formation over a distance of 160 km (99 miles). Water and wind have fashioned the unique shapes, which invite comparisons with chimneys, roofs and even fortresses. There are also rock paintings from the Fremont Indians, which frequently depict animals.

At the top: Salt Lake City, the capital of Utah, founded in 1915, lit up at night against the backdrop of the surrounding mountains. Left side: The mountains of the North Caineville Mesa are about 2000 metres high and are easy to climb. Above: Grand Teton National Park.

Like a work of art, the intricate bends of the Colorado River suggest the red sandstone of Glen Canyon is a fascinating contrast to the deep blue of the river.

The wonders of erosion

Bizarre rock formations display a wide array of colours depending on the angle of the sun and characterize the image of the south-western United States.

Nature presents a very mixed palette of colours here, but it is not only the colours, ranging from violet and all imaginable shades of red and orange to yellow and brown, that fascinate visitors but also the bizarre shapes. They are the work of erosion caused by water and wind that has modelled a magical rock landscape over millions of years.

Rivers like the Colorado have cut deep into the rock layers. The region also rose at the same time, but the cutting strength of the rivers was able to keep up with the rising earth. Over the course of time deep canyons were

Bizarre rock landscapes in Bryce Canyon National Park.

formed. The most spectacular of these is of course the Grand Canyon, but Bryce Canyon, Escalante Canyon or Glen Canyon are certainly not to be missed.

A further force has also played a key role in shaping the landscape – the wind. Smaller rocks are often exposed to the winds, particularly in drier areas with little vegetation.

Continuing along scenic Highway 12 you will reach Escalante where the road turns off to the south towards the Grand Staircase Escalante National Monument.

⑱ Grand Staircase Escalante National Monument Those in search of pristine nature will not be disappointed by this reserve between Bryce Canyon National Park to the south and west, the Capitol Reef National Park in the north, and the Glen Canyon National Recreation Area to the east. The National Monument was named after four towering layers of rock. The beauty of the landscape is characterized by gorges, rows of cliffs and plateaus and is best experienced from the dirt roads off the main highway.

The drive along the 200-km (124-mile) Burr Trail Loop weaves its way through the entire area. Initially a tarred road, it takes you along Deer Creek and then through the rocky labyrinth of Long Canyon.

It later becomes a bit more challenging but is easily done with an off-road vehicle.

Back on Highway 12 head towards Bryce Canyon Airport.

Shortly thereafter, Highway 63 turns off right to the Bryce Canyon Visitors Center.

⑲ Bryce Canyon National Park (please also see Route 24 'Wild West'). Unlike the rest of the landscape in the region, Bryce Canyon is not a canyon in the strict sense of the word. Rather, it is a series of crevices and smaller gullies. Some of the eroded gullies are more than 300 m (984 ft) deep.

A lovely panoramic route takes you 30 km (19 miles) through the park, which was founded in 1928, and leads to the southernmost point, Rainbow Point. The drive and its many vista points constantly provide splendid views over the dense pine forests.

Many of the orange, salmon-pink or red rock formations have characteristic names, such as Sunrise Point, Inspiration Point, Thor's Hammer or Chinese Wall. The landscape is other-worldly and is especially impressive at sunset or sunrise.

After Bryce Canyon it is worth making a detour some 100 km (62 miles) to the west to the Cedar Breaks National Monument. The turn-off to Cedar City is a few kilometres after the junction of Highway 12 and Highway 89.

⑳ Cedar Breaks National Monument Founded by the Mormons in 1851, Cedar City's Iron Mission State Park and Museum, with more than 300 old vehicles, documents the pioneering spirit of the Mormons.

The Marble Canyon is still considered an insider tip. The Navajo Bridge crosses the Colorado River and offers the best views of the river and cliffs.

The Shakespeare Festival also takes place here every summer in the Globe Theater. The National Monument's dimensions may be somewhat smaller than those of Bryce Canyon but the colours are just as enticing.
The next stop is Zion National Park, reached from the turn-off at Mount Carmel Junction (Highway 9).

㉑ Zion National Park (please also see Route 24 'Wild West'). This area was declared a national park in 1919 and has several entrances. The most important attractions are found in the southern part, and the Zion-Mount Carmel Highway (9) takes you via the plateau at the East Entrance 600 m (1,969 ft) downhill to the more deserty South Entrance. The Canyon Overlook provides one of the best views of the heart of the national park, Zion Canyon, created by the Virgin River, a tributary of the Colorado River.
A tunnel built 255 m (837 ft) above the valley floor makes the drive to the Zion Canyon Visitor Center all the more dramatic. From here the Zion Canyon Scenic Drive follows numerous serpentine bends of the winding

Virgin River for 12 km (7.5 miles). The most well-known hike in the park, the 2-km (1.2-mile) River Walk, starts at the end of the road and leads to the 600-m (1,969-ft) canyon walls. The waterfalls on the Emerald Pools Trail are also worth seeing, as are the Hanging Gardens, a cliff overgrown with vegetation.
If you have time, take the park's southern exit and return via the Pipe Spring National Monument and the Pan-American Highway where the A89 turns off from Highway 89 at Kanab heading south. At Jacob Lake a side road leads to the northern entrance of the Grand Canyon (North Rim), or you can continue along the A89 to the next stop, Marble Canyon.

㉒ Marble Canyon Close to the town of the same name in the far north of Arizona is Marble Canyon, a prime example of the state's diverse natural beauty. The canyon is traversed by the Colorado River and is spanned by a road bridge. Turn onto Highway 89 where it joins the A89 and drive a short distance north towards Page. From here you can either continue to

Glen Canyon Dam or make a detour to Antelope Canyon.

㉓ Lake Powell Since 1963 the Glen Canyon Dam has held back the Colorado River to create the 653-sq-km (405-sq-mi) Lake Powell, built to generate hydroelectric power.
The lake is now a haven for water-sports enthusiasts. There are also marvellous views of the sandstone formations whose perfectly flat plateaus look like they were measured with a ruler.
On the southern shore is the nearly 90-m-high (295-ft) Rainbow Bridge, considered the largest natural bridge in North America. The area around the lake was declared the Glen Canyon National Recreation Area in 1972.

Left side: The particularly distinctive Hoodoo rock formation (above left) in Bryce Canyon National Park is called 'Thor's Hammer'. The 'Devil's Garden' (below left is also striking. Above: The Colorado River runs through Glen Canyon.

Detour

Antelope Canyon

The two canyons of Antelope Creek are only a few metres wide, but the water has cut all the deeper into the rock here. During dry

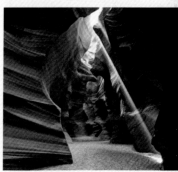

Midday sunshine in Antelope Canyon.

weather you can hike through the Lower Antelope Canyon, but after it has rained there is too much water in the river. It is particularly fascinating to visit the canyon at midday when the sun's rays shine directly into the depths of the canyon.

The North Rim has an even more spectacular view of the Grand Canyon than the southern part due to its higher position.

Phoenix

A metropolis in the midst of a dry desert landscape, Phoenix, Arizona attracts visitors with more than 300 days of sunshine a year. In the summer in particular, Phoenix and the surrounding area are characterized by the massive irrigation units that

Phoenix's business centre glistens in the evening light.

make decadent golf courses and the cultivation of vegetables possible.

There is also a bit of culture here. Heritage Square is lined with Victorian houses that are worth a look. The Heard Museum houses an extensive collection of Indian art with sculptures, weaving and paintings. The Arizona Science Center documents the world of science in all its many facets.

㉔ Grand Canyon National Park (see pp. 316-317.)
This world-famous national park can be reached from the north via the turn-off at Jacob Lake and from the south via Cameron (Highway 64) or Flagstaff (Highway 180), both of which lead to the South Rim. The northern side of the canyon, which is 30 km at its widest point, is about 360 m (1,181 ft) higher than the southern side and the canyon walls drop nearly 1,800 m (5,906 ft) down to the Colorado River here.

As the northern Kaibab Plateau is significantly higher than the southern Coconino Plateau, the

North Rim provides a completely different perspective of the canyon landscape than the South Rim. Bright Angel Point provides a marvellous backdrop near the Grand Canyon Lodge. Shortly before this viewing point there is a 35-km-long (22-mile) road that branches off to the north to Point Imperial which, at 2,683 m (8,803 ft), is the highest point in the national park. The southern part receives considerably more visitors. Grand Canyon Village is recommended as the starting point. From here a panoramic route provides access to West Rim Drive and East Rim Drive.

㉕ Flagstaff The drive from Cameron to Flagstaff passes the Wupatki National Monument with more than 2,000 historical sites once inhabited by Hopi Indians. Just outside Flagstaff is the 120-m-deep (394-ft) crater created in 1064 by a volcanic eruption. The volcanic cone is called Sunset Crater Volcano because of its colour.

The centre of Flagstaff is char-

acterized by red-brick buildings. It is worth paying a visit to the Lowell Observatory from which scientists discovered Pluto in 1930. The cultural highlight is the Museum of Northern Arizona with archaeological and ethnological displays.

㉖ Walnut Canyon South of town close to Interstate 40/Route 66, head west to Walnut Canyon with its famous Sinagua Indian dwellings. More than twenty of the dwellings open to visitors were built into the cliffs in the 12th and 13th centuries, and some of them are in especially adventurous locations.

㉗ Montezuma Castle National Monument This Indian site close to the town of Cottonwood was declared a National Monument in 1906 and comprises the remnants of a Sinagua Indian dwelling that was fitted into the recess of a rock face 30 m (98 ft) high. The Sinagua built twenty rooms in the dwelling more than 600 years ago and used ladders for access. An exhibition in the visitor centre beneath the cliffs documents the Sinagua culture.

From Cottonwood it is around 80 km (50 miles) to the junction of Highway 89 and Highway 60, which takes you to Phoenix.

Grand Teton National Park Elk roam the low-lying areas of the Teton Range, one of the most impressive mountain chains in the USA. The highest peak, Grand Teton, is 4,197 m (13,770 ft). Some of the mountains are covered with glaciers while former glaciers have formed lakes in the basins.

Salt Lake City The skyline of the Utah capital is dominated by the Capitol building (1915). Salt Lake City, venue for the 2002 Winter Olympics, is the centre of the growing global Mormon community.

Grand Canyon The canyon in north-west Arizona was formed by the Colorado River cutting into the Colorado Plateau. The 350-km-long (217-mile) and up to 1.8-km-deep (1-mile) canyon is one of the most impressive natural wonders in the USA.

Phoenix Once an Indian settlement, Phoenix is today an important high-tech centre. It boasts buildings from all eras, like this colonial-era mission church. The palms that grow throughout the city are characteristic of Phoenix.

Mission San Xavier del Bac This white mission church is an impressive example of Spanish mission architecture and one of the best-preserved churches in all of the United States.

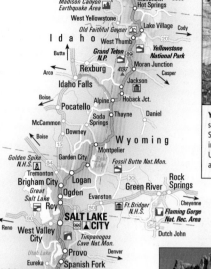

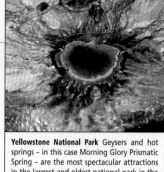

Yellowstone National Park Geysers and hot springs – in this case Morning Glory Prismatic Spring – are the most spectacular attractions in the largest and oldest national park in the USA, situated in the Rocky Mountains at an altitude of 2,400 m (7,874 ft).

Capitol Reef National Park Rock needles tower over a sandstone cliff 150 km (93 miles) long.

Wupatki National Monument The largest and best-preserved pueblo ruins, built by prehistoric Indians, are to be found north of Sunset Crater in the midst of a desert landscape. The most important pueblo building dates back to the 12th century and includes over 100 rooms

Tucson The centre of the second-largest city in Arizona, after Phoenix, is dominated by skyscrapers. A colonial-era neighbourhood with a number of adobe houses has been preserved in the shadows of the skyscrapers and makes a significant contribution to Tucson's charm.

Bozeman
Madison Canyon Earthquake Area
Mammoth Hot Springs
Mt. Wood 3859
West Yellowstone
Old Faithful Geyser
Lake Village
Cody
Idaho
West Thumb
Yellowstone National Park
Grand Teton N.P.
Butte
Moran Junction
Arco
Rexburg
4197
Jackson
Casper
Idaho Falls
Boise
Alpine
Hoback Jct.
Pocatello
Soda Springs
Thayne
Daniel
McCammon
Downey
Montpelier
Wyoming
Boise
Garden City
Fossil Butte Nat. Mon.
Golden Spike N.H.S.
Bear Lake
Green River
Rock Springs
Brigham City
Logan
Great Salt Lake
Ogden
Evanston
Cheyenne
Roy
Ft. Bridger N.H.S.
Flaming Gorge Nat. Rec. Area
SALT LAKE CITY
Reno
West Valley City
Timpanogos Cave Nat. Mon.
Dutch John
Provo
Denver
Little Sahara R.A.
Spanish Fork
Eureka
Nephi
Fairview
Delta
Utah
Ely
Scipio
Gunnison
Grand Junction
Salina
Cove Fort
Cathedral Valley
Loa
Capitol Reef N.P.
Cedar Breaks Nat. Mon.
Cedar City
Junction
Las Vegas
Cannonville
Escalante
Grand Staircase Escalante Nat. Mon.
Mt. Carmel Jct.
Hurricane
Bryce Canyon N.P.
Zion N.P.
Kanab
Glen Canyon Dam
Lake Powell
Pipe Spring Nat. Mon.
Marble Canyon
Page
Jacob Lake
Antelope Canyon
North Rim
White Mesa Natural Bridge
Grand Canyon N.P.
Cortez
Grand Canyon
Tuba City
Kingman
Cameron
Arizona
Flagstaff
Wupatki Nat. Mon.
Sunset Crater Nat. Mon.
Ash Fork
Walnut Canyon Nat. Mon.
Winslow
Tuzigoot Nat. Mon.
Meteor Crater
Prescott
Cottonwood
Montezuma Castle Nat. Mon.
Albuquerque
Kingman
Congress
Payson
Aguila
Wickenburg
Show Low
Arizona Pioneer Living Hist. Mus.
Tonto Nat. Mon.
Sun City
Mesa
Globe
Los Angeles
PHOENIX
Florence Junction
Florence
Lordsburg
San Diego
Casa Grande Ruins Nat. Mon.
Oracle Junction
Biosphere II
Arizona Sonora Desert Museum
Tucson
Pima Air and Space Museum
Mission San Xavier del Bac
El Paso
Nogales(MEX)

The 'Wild West': cowboys, canyons and cactus

'Go West, young man…' – It is no coincidence that tourists in America's South-West still follow the old call made to pioneers and settlers. Virtually nowhere else in the world will you find more bizarre rock formations, wilder mountains, more breathtaking canyons, more remote cactus deserts, more impressive caves, or hotter valleys. The remnants of ancient Native American pueblo culture are also unique, and their adobe buildings and handicrafts still fascinate visitors from all over the world.

Route profile:

Length: approx. 2,486 miles
Time required: 4 weeks
When to go: March to October is the best time. The desert blooms in spring, and in autumn the temperatures are a bit cooler than in late summer.

The American South-West stretches from the southern Rocky Mountains in the east to the Sierra Nevada in the west, and from the northern edge of the Colorado Plateau in Utah to the Mexican border in the south. Six states make up the region: Arizona, Nevada, Utah, Colorado, New Mexico and California. The north is dominated by the Colorado Plateau, which covers an area of roughly 110,000 sq km (2,460 sq mi) at elevations of 1,000 to 3,000 m (3,281 and 9,843 ft). The most impressive

and most beautiful national parks are found here, including the Grand Canyon, Bryce Canyon, Zion, Arches and Canyonlands. There are a total of eleven national parks in the South-West alone, as well as numerous monuments and state parks. The Organ Pipe Cactus National Monument near Why, Arizona, is even a UNESCO World Nature Heritage Site. Other national monuments are dedicated to ancient and historic Indian settlements. And if that isn't enough, there are also the national historic parks that are mostly dedicated to the pioneer days, such as the Hubbell Trading Post near Ganado, Arizona. In the south, the plateau stretches out to the Sonora Desert, which extends deep into Mexico. To the north is the Mojave Desert, home of Death Valley with the lowest point in North America. Temperatures of over 50°C

(122°F) in the shade are not uncommon here. But anyone driving into the valley before sunrise will experience an unforgettable interplay of colours on the bizarre rock in places like Zabriskie Point. The Colorado River is the dominant feature of the entire South-West and runs for over 2,300km (1,429 mi). It originates in the Rocky Mountains, flows through man-made Lake Powell in Utah, continues to

whittle away at the Grand Canyon as it has done for millions of years, and finally peters out before reaching the Gulf of California. The spectacular natural beauty of the American South-West was created over sixty-five million years ago when the pressure of the Pacific Plate formed the Rocky Mountains and the Colorado Plateau was pushed up. Giant fractures allowed stones more than a billion years

Top: Above: The 'left' and the 'right glove' greet one another in the Monument Valley across the plain, the Merrick Butte looks on silently. Left: The name says it all: Just like organ pipes, the organ pipe cactuses stand at the National Monument bearing the same name.

old to emerge, after which erosion from rivers and the elements created the fantastic worlds of pillars, towers, arches, craters and gorges.

The rugged, mostly arid land was originally exclusively Native American territory, and the oldest traces of their ancient desert culture are some eight thousand years old. About three thousand years ago, sedentary peoples built multi-storey settlements

called pueblos. The arrival of the Spaniards in the mid-16th century, however, marked the beginning of a drastic decline of their civilizations. In the 20th century, cities were built on former Native American lands.

The contrasts in the South-West are therefore remarkable: fascinating remnants of ancient cultures juxtaposed with raucous metropolises, puritan Mormon settlements near the glitz and

kitsch of Las Vegas. One journey is really not enough to take it all in, but anyone who follows the dream route laid out before you, starting in Los Angeles, following the Rio Grande northwards through New Mexico, exploring the wonders of Utah and then making a great arch back towards the City of Angels via Las Vegas and Death Valley will experience at least a handful of the highlights. And, at the end

of the trip, you will realize that the only option left is to come back and see more.

When the setting sun casts its light on the dunes, the sand in the White Sand National Monument (left side) begins to glow. Above: The sandstone buildings in Mesa Verde National Park were built in just 20 years.

Hollywood does not just symbolise glamor. Sunset Boulevards are also home to cosy sidewalk cafes.

Disneyland

Walt Disney wanted to create 'a place where people could find happiness and knowledge'. To make his dream come true, the first Disneyland was established in Anaheim, California, in 1955. Per-

Colourful shows are an attraction at Disneyland.

sonally greeted by Mickey Mouse, visitors enter the park on the 19th-century 'Main Street USA', where the main form of transportation is still horse-drawn streetcars.

In 'Tomorrowland', you can experience a rocket takeoff or dive to the seafloor in a submarine. In 'Fantasyland' visitors are transported to a land of fairytales. And in 'Frontierland' you are taken back to the Old West.

This journey from Los Angeles through Arizona, New Mexico, Colorado, Utah and Nevada back to the Pacific takes you through impressive rock landscapes, deserts and metropolises, and includes a look into the thousand-year-old history of the Native Americans.

❶ Los Angeles Your trip begins in the second-largest metropolis in the United States, Los Angeles. Approximately seventeen million people live in an area that stretches 71 km (44 mi) north to south and 47 km (29 mi) east to west. It is bordered in the West by the Pacific Ocean and in the north and east by high mountains. For some reason, however, the founders of the city, when they established the original Pueblo de Nuestra Señora La Reina de Los Angeles, chose a location 25 km (16 mi) from the coast.

Today, L.A., the most common abbreviation of the city's name, is the most important industrial and services metropolis in the western United States, a status to which the film industry has contributed immensely. The first American film was shot here in 1910, and the first film with sound was made in 1927, bringing world fame to Hollywood and Beverly Hills. Today, the Hollywood Freeway separates the city's two main centers. El Pueblo in the north-east is the

actual Old Town district, and the Civic Center in the south-west is the modern downtown. Chinatown borders the north of the Old Town, while Little Tokyo is located south of the Civic Center. The focal point of the historic center is the Plaza with the old mission church of Nuestra Señora La Reina, built by Spanish Franciscans in 1922. The picturesque Olvera Street unfolds as a Mexican street market and is also home to the city's oldest house, the Avila Adobe House, dating back to 1818. The focal point of the Civic Center district is the high-rise City Hall building, erected in 1928. The viewing platform on the 27th floor provides the best views of greater Los Angeles. The Museum of Contemporary Art on Grand Avenue was designed by renowned Japanese architect Arata Isozaki and is a striking. The section of Wilshire Boulevard between Highland and Fairfax avenues is known as the Miracle Mile and features interesting art deco buildings. Of course, you should not miss Hol-

lywood. Although very little of the former glitz and glamour of the neighborhood remains, Mann's Chinese Theater is still an eye-catcher designed in Chinese pagoda style. The cement blocks in the main courtyard have the footprints, handprints and signatures of more than two hundred Hollywood personalities. The theater also marks the start of the famous 'Walk of Fame' on Hollywood Boulevard, a collection of over two thousand pink marble stars with the names of Hollywood greats embossed on brass plaques.

Not far from the Chinese Theater are a few museums: the Hollywood Wax Museum with famous actors and politicians; the Guinness Book of World Records Museum, dedicated to the world's most bizarre records; and the CBS film and television studios near the Farmers Market. At Paramount Pictures you can get behind the scenes and even watch a live production if you are lucky. Sunset Boulevard begins at the Roosevelt Hotel, which hosted the first Oscars ceremony back in 1929. The point where it turns into Sunset Strip marks the start of Hollywood's nightclub district. The route then heads south-east along the Hollywood and Santa

The desert is alive – even flowering shrubs sometimes stand between the cacti in the organ Pipe Cactus National Monument.

Desert flora in Arizona

The only plants able to thrive in the often bone-dry deserts of Arizona are xerophytes, which are able to protect themselves from evaporation with their small nubs, thick outer skin

The flowers of the cacti shine in different colours.

Ana Freeways towards Anaheim, home of Disneyland.

2 **Anaheim** The Disneyland amusement park is by far the most significant attraction in Anaheim, a town founded by German immigrants in 1857. The most interesting building in the city is the Crystal Cathedral, a steel pipe edifice built in 1980 with a shell of mirrored glass. The route now follows Interstate 91 to San Bernardino, where you can make a detour to the surprisingly high San Bernardino Mountains north of the city. The Rim of the World Drive heads up to an altitude of 2,200 m (1,367 ft) and provides magnificent views.
You then follow Interstate 10 east before joining Highway 62 and heading north-east towards the town of Twentynine Palms

and the magnificent Joshua Tree National Park.

3 **Joshua Tree National Park** This park is living proof that the desert is alive. Apart from the striking Joshua trees, you will also find palm groves, cactus gardens and juniper bushes here. After exploring the park, you will come out on the south side where you will get back on Interstate 10 heading east towards Phoenix.

4 **Phoenix** (see page 324) After visiting Phoenix, Interstate 10 takes you quickly south to the region around Tucson, the second-largest city in Arizona. Anyone looking to spend a bit more time getting to Tucson, however, should travel west on the I10 back to Buckeye and from there head south on High-

way 85 to Why and the Organ Pipe Cactus National Monument. From there you can head east to Tucson on Highway 86 and take a detour through Saguaro National Park-West, just north-west of the city.

5 **Saguaro National Park** This park owes its name to the candelabra saguaro cactuses. These kings of the desert can live up to 150 years old, grow to a height of 15 m (49 ft) and weigh up to 8 tonnes (8.8 tons). The most beautiful specimens of this cactus can be found in both the East and West sections of

Large image: Joshua Tree National Park. Above: The snow on the Four Peaks in the Saguaro National Park is a delightful contrast to the desert landscape.

and very small stomata, or leaves that have basically become spines. Typical examples of these succulents, in other words water-storing plants, include species like the iconic Saguaro or the Organ Pipe Cactus. Southern Arizona is dominated by the candle bush and other types of Yucca cactus, the most beautiful – or at least the most famous – of which is the Joshua Tree. The seemingly infertile soil they thrive in is actually home to a multitude of seeds simply waiting for water; just a few weeks after a rainfall, the desert transforms itself into a sea of blossoms.

323

Phoenix reveals its busy center in the evening light with its impressive skyline. The Bank of America Tower is the heart of the Collier Center, an office and entertainment complex.

Phoenix

Phoenix, the capital of Arizona, is a mix of the Old West and unrelenting modernization represented by a series of museums, cultural and recreational facilities, and a booming high-tech industry.

At an altitude of 369 m (1,211 ft), this city in the Valley of the Sun typically has three hundred sunny days a year. Thanks to countless irrigation systems – which supply water for agriculture as well as golf courses –, however, and despite its desert location, Phoenix is actually quite green. The Camelback Mountains, which are the city's most famous icon, provide a good view over this urban sprawl in the Sonoran Desert. The suburb of Scottsdale is one of the city's best-known areas and is particularly popular for its pretty Old Town quarter. Alongside the modern high-rise buildings, you can still find traces of the past. The famous Heritage Square forms the center of the city and is lined with Victorian houses. The

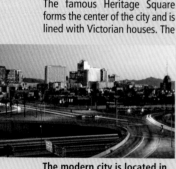

The modern city is located in the Sonoran Desert.

most famous of these is Rosson House, which dates back to the late 19th century. The square is part of Heritage and Science Park, which also includes the Arizona Science Center (with planetarium) and the Phoenix Museum of History. The Heard Museum has an extensive collection of prehistoric, traditional, and modern works; the Phoenix Art Museum has artwork by international artists. Phoenix Zoo is one of the most famous zoos in the world.

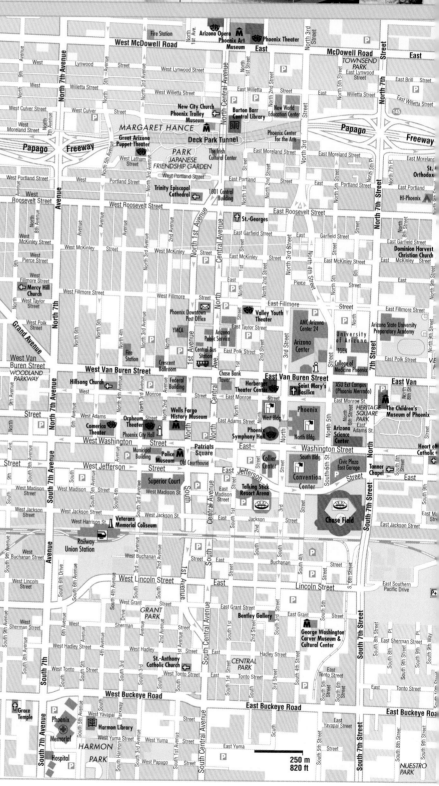

The modern buildings of Tucson will make you hardly believe it used to be the old city centre.

the 338-sq-km (130-sq-mi) Sonora Desert park. On the southern edge of the western section of the park, you should definitely not miss out on a visit to the Arizona Sonora Desert Museum.

6 Tucson The 'City of Sunshine', surrounded by the Santa Catalina Mountains, has an average of 350 sunny days a year. Spanish missionaries built a mission station in 1775, on the site of an old Native American settlement, and it quickly became a Spanish-Mexican colonial town. It is now the second-largest city in Arizona after Phoenix. It has a sizable university and, with military bases in the area, it has also become a high-tech center. However, there is also an Old Town district in modern Tucson where the Spanish colonial center was located, between Alameda and Washington streets. There are some meticulously restored adobe houses that are representative of the

old days. South of the historic Old Town is the Barrio Historico, originally the commercial quarter of the Spanish quarter. Today, many beautiful adobe buildings from the late 19th century are still in use here.

The Pima Air and Space Museum is an absolute must for aerospace enthusiasts. More than two hundred exhibits including airplanes, helicopters, ultra-light aircraft and all kinds of experimental devices are on display. Fans of westerns will get their money's worth in Tucscon as well. They only need to drive about 21 km (13 mi) west of the city to Old Tucson Studios, built in late 19th-century style as the set for some classic western films such as Gunfight at the O.K. Corral and Rio Bravo. Only a few miles further south is the San Xavier del Bac mission.

Leaving Tucson you head east on Interstate 10. In Willcox, you can make a detour on Highway 186 to the Chiricahua National

Monument, where innumerable rock pillars stand to attention like soldiers – eroded remains of a volcanic eruption several million years ago. The Apaches held their last stand against US Army troops in the remote gorges of this region.

Back on Interstate 10 heading east, Stein's Ghost Town will appear near the Highway 80 turnoff. It is a typical example of a stagecoach-era town that was eventually abandoned by its inhabitants.

Today, Stein is basically a tourist attraction. East of Las Cruces, you leave Interstate 10 and head north on Interstate 25, taking Highway 70 to Alamogordo after about 11 km (7 mi).

7 Alamogordo This city has undoubtedly made history. In the nearby San Andreas Mountains, US forces set up the White Sands Missile Range where the world's first atomic bomb, developed and built in Los Alamos, New Mexico, was detonated on July 16, 1945. Alamogordo now offers visitors both a technical and natural experience.

Technology enthusiasts will be drawn to the International Space Hall of Fame, which covers everything from the early Mercury capsule to the Apollo Program, and from the Russian space capsule to the Skylab. If it was important to the discovery of outer space, it's in this museum. Nature enthusiasts will enjoy an excursion to White Sands National Monument west of the city as it is home to a unique gypsum dune landscape with dunes as high as 18 m (59 ft). To get there take the 26-km (16-mi) Heart of Sands Drive.

At the top: Snow-white dunes characterise the White Sands National Monument. Above: The Mission San Xavier del Bac is a sample of baroque church architecture in a world colonised by the Spaniards.

Ghost Towns

There are quite a few ghost towns in the American South-West. Most of them are abandoned gold-mining settlements or pioneer villages that were not able to sustain a commercial foundation once the boom had busted. Some of them aren't even marked on maps anymore. The Old West sets built by the film industry are of course a completely different type of ghost town. Dodge City in Johnson Canyon is one of these many ghost towns to be captured on celluloid film. For twenty years it was used as the set for the Smoking Colts western series. Even Grafton, just a few miles to the north, was brought back to life for a bank robbery story with Paul Newman and Robert Redford – Butch Cassidy and the Sun-

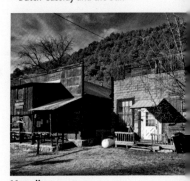

Mogollon was once a mining town.

dance Kid. Over thirty films were shot in the town of Moab in south-eastern Utah, and the Ponderosa Ranch is well known as the set for the TV series Bonanza. All of these towns have one thing in common: they contribute to the preservation of a disappearing culture, remind us of some of our favorite westerns, and have now become tourist destinations in their own right.

Down in front of the skyscrapers in downtown San Antonio, the 20 metre high Mexican-American friendship sculpture looks almost tiny.

Albuquerque

This city on the Rio Grande is the largest in the state of New Mexico. The intersection of Interstates 40 and 25 was apparently so attractive that around one-third of the state's population now lives in this area. Albuquerque was founded in 1716, when thirty families initially settled here. Around 1800, there were already well over 6,000 inhabitants. The railway came close in 1880, but one headstrong and rebellious landowner prevented it from coming directly into town, so tracks were laid 3 km (2 mi) outside, resulting in a new city forming around the train station. As a result, the Old Town center remained for the most part in its original condition.

Albuquerque's real draw is therefore its Old Town with the Plaza from 1780. Surrounding the square are some beautiful adobe buildings, in particular San Felipe de Neri

The San Felipe de Neri Church in Albuquerque.

Church (1706). Anyone interested in the city's historic development should visit the Albuquerque Museum. Opposite that is the New Mexico Museum of Natural History, with a history of the Southwest. North of Interstate 40, a visit to the Indian Pueblo Cultural Center is a must. No visitor to Albuquerque should miss the 4-km (2-mi) ride up the Aerial Tramway into the Sandia Mountains.

⑧ San Antonio After circling the rocket testing grounds of White Sands, the road reaches the Rio Grande near San Antonio. A vast wetland area straddles the river south of this small township. The Bosque del Apache National Wildlife Refuge is accessible to visitors through the Bosque del Apache Loop. There are viewing towers along the road for observing wild animals. Highways 60, 36 and 117 then take you through the Plains of St Augustin to Grants.

⑨ Grants South of this small town you will find the bizarre rock formations of El Malpais National Monument. Volcanic eruptions roughly four million years ago created the conditions for these fantastic rock structures. Lava covered the existing limestone, and erosion slowly shaped the canyons and uncovered the diverse stone layers. One of the highlights of a visit to the park is the Bandera Crater. It has several ice caves, the most impressive of which is the Candeleria Cave. The Big Tubes are the largest lava tunnels in the United States. About 48 km (30 mi) south-east of Grants is the most beautiful pueblo far and wide, Acoma, or 'Sky City'. The village has a picturesque location on a rock pla-

teau 110 m (361 ft) above the plain and has been there for about 1,200 years. Originally only accessible with ladders, the Spaniards called it 'the best fort in the world'. You can visit the pueblo as part of a guided tour. About 80 km (50 mi) east on Interstate 40 is Albuquerque.

⑩ Albuquerque (see sidebar left) After exploring this lovely town on the mighty Rio Grande, travel another 62 km (38 mi) or so north-east along Interstate 25 to Santa Fe.

⑪ Santa Fe (see sidebar right) Highway 68 takes you to the Native American and artisan town of Taos roughly 112 km (70 mi) away.

⑫ Taos Often referred to as the 'Soul of the Southwest', Taos

presents itself as an artists colony dedicated to Native American and Mexican styles with more than sixty galleries. The Artist Society was founded in 1912.

The Tiwa tribe had a permanent settlement on the Taos Plateau for some 1,100 years before the Spanish arrived. The city center's picturesque Plaza reflects the colonial style. South of the square on Ledoux Street are the town's oldest and most beautiful adobe buildings.

The Harwood Museum displays interesting works by Taos artists from the last 100 years. Just under 5 km (3 mi) north-east of town is Taos Pueblo where 1,500 members of the Tiwa tribe still live. The village has existed since the 12th century and was always exclusively inhabited by Native Americans.

Taos Pueblo is reminiscent of the culture of the Pueblo Indians with its traditional adobe buildings, some of them on several floors.

Santa Fe

The capital of New Mexico is the second-oldest city in the USA and, thanks to the mix of Indian and Spanish culture, also one of the most interesting. It is no coincidence that Santa Fe is one of the leading cities in the country when it comes to Indian handicrafts and contemporary art. The Spaniards officially ‚founded' the city in 1609, albeit on a Pueblo Indian settlement. Today, Santa Fe fascinates visitors with its charming adobe buildings made of yellowish-brown clay, wonderful Spanish colonial buildings, and modern adobe architecture. The bustling center is the Plaza, created in 1610, which once marked the end of the legendary Santa Fe Trail. On the north side is the Palace of the Governors, from 1614, one of the oldest government buildings in North America. The Saint

The route now heads west through the southern foothills of the San Juan Mountains towards Farmington.
At Bloomfield, a road heads south to the Chaco Culture National Historical Park in Nageezi.

⑬ Chaco Culture National Historical Park Chaco Canyon was the spiritual, political and commercial hub of the Anasazi as early as the 10th century. The most important sights in the valley can be reached on by the circular route.
The valley's main attraction is definitely Pueblo Bonito, which covered an area of 1,200 sq m (12,912 sq ft) and had 700 rooms for about 1,200 people spread over five levels. After returning to Bloomfield, head north on Highway 544 to Aztec.

⑭ Aztec Ruins National Monument This is another Anasazi ruin. It was inhabited by up to 1,300 people in 450 rooms arranged in a semi-circle around a kiva (ritual and meeting room). It has now been completely rebuilt, making it the only place in the United States to provide real insight into a major Native American settlement.
Take Highway 550 to Durango and then continue on Highway 160 until you reach the next spectacular national park.

⑮ Mesa Verde National Park The most beautiful and certainly the most impressive residential complex of the Anasazi is in this park. It is deservedly a UNESCO World Heritage site. Some of the pueblos, which cling impossibly to inaccessible rock overhangs, were built be-

tween the 10th and 13th centuries. They have over 100 rooms and many have several kivas. The entire area can be reached from Ruins Road Drive, which provides good views and insights but does not allow direct access. The best cave dwellings are in Cliff Palace, comprising over 200 rooms and twenty-three kivas. The Balcony House is similarly arranged and is only accessible via vertical ladders and a narrow tunnel pipe.
Highways 160 and 191 take you to the Canyon de Chelly National Monument.

⑯ Canyon de Chelly National Monument This canyon is roughly 300 m deep (984 ft) and is carved from red rock faces. From the canyon floor, freestanding formations such as Spi-

Top: The cliff settlement of the Anasazi Indians in Mesa Verde National Park was only accessible from above using vertical ladders that could be retracted in the event of danger. Left: Pueblo Bonito in Chaco Culture National Park. Above: Taos Pueblo: the adobe houses here were built onto each other like honeycomb squares.

Adobe buildings are often seen here.

Francis Cathedral dates back to 1884, and houses an extraordinarily beautiful statue of the Virgin Mary (1625). The city's oldest buildings are found on the south side of the Santa Fe River, in the Barrio de Analco, home to the oldest house in the USA – said to date back to the 13th century. Do not miss the Museum of Fine Arts, which displays numerous works by regional artists.

If water is available, even in the driest red rock landscape, a pretty green valley forms in the Canyon de Chelly National Monument.

If water is available, even in the driest red rock landscape, a pretty green valley forms in the Canyon de Chelly National Monument.

Animals of the South-West

Like the plants, animals in the South-West have also adapted to the arid climate here. Many of them are nocturnal and sleep away the heat of the day in the shade or in caves. Only the birds, in particularly the golden eagle, the prairie falcon and various species of vulture are diurnal. Many small birds build their nests in cactuses. New Mexico's 'state bird', the roadrunner, is itself a unique case, reaching speeds of 25 km/h (16 mph) while also starring as a sly comic figure.

There are some larger predators as well, but these are mostly limited to more mountainous regions. The best known among them are of course the mountain lion, which is fairly common but

A rare sight: A puma.

mostly invisible to humans, or the puma, which you hardly ever see either. You are more likely to hear and see coyotes or prairie wolves.

Limited enticcrely to the forests and equally hard to spot is the black bear. Cute but scavenging raccoons, on the other hand, are pretty much everywhere in suburban areas at night.

der Rock at 243 m (797 ft) in height will dazzle any visitor. Over 100 Native American settlements up to 1,500 years old were found in the canyon. As in Mesa Verde National Park, the pueblos here were built into the rock like birds' nests.

The main gorge can be accessed by two roads: North Rim Drive and South Rim Drive. Both offer spectacular views way down into the canyon. Highlights of the park include the White House Ruin, an Anasazi pueblo made from shiny white limestone; the Mummy Cave, which was once used as a cult and burial site; and Antelope House, which has a rock drawing with an antelope motif.

Highways 191 and 160 will take you to Kayenta and the entrance to Monument Valley.

17 Monument Valley Navajo Tribal Park In the middle of the Colorado Plateau, on the border between Arizona and Utah, Monument Valley is home to spectacular rock formations that have been used as the backdrop for countless Westerns. Anyone traveling through here in the early morning or late evening will experience an amazing flush of color as the rocks glow in all hues of red, pink and purple. This rugged land was a Native American hunting and settlement region for thousands of years and is now once again a Navajo reserve. The best view of the rock towers, which reach heights of 600 m (1,969 ft), is seen from the 27 km (17 mi) circle route. If you want to learn more about the lifestyle of the Navajo, take

a guided tour from the visitor center. Your journey continues now over Monument Pass to Bluff. From there you take Highway 191 to Moab. The 211 takes you to the southern part of Canyonlands National Park, and the 279 goes into the northern portion from Moab.

18 Canyonlands National Park (see p. 330.) The national park covers an area of 1,366-sq-km (527-sq-mi) and includes the confluence of the Green and Colorado rivers, which have carved their way into 600-m (1,969-ft) gorges whose walls gleam in red and beige hues. Bizarrely shaped rock towers with chimneys and needles inspire the imagination of visitors. The park is so vast that you have to approach it from two sides. The

The cliffs and canyons in Capitol Reef National Park are like a wildly romantic piece of art.

southern half (Needles) has enchanting rock sculptures and formations. Parts of the Needles district are accessible via two paved roads while other trails requiring four-wheel-drive vehicles lead down to the river.

The northern part of the park (Island in the Sky) comprises the headland between the rivers. The gorges reach depths of up to 600 m (1,969 ft) on both sides and the view is breathtaking in the truest sense of the word.

In the dry air, visibility usually reaches 150 km (93 mi). From the Grand View Point at the south end of the park road, you will experience a truly unforgettable canyon landscape. A bumpy but wide road for four-wheel-drives also runs below the White Rim in the northern part of the park.

⑲ Arches National Park (see p. 331.) Almost a thousand natural stone arches in all imaginable shapes, as well as giant mushroom rocks, rock towers, pinnacles and cones make this 313-sq-km (121-sq-mi) national park something really special. You can enter the park via Arches Scenic Drive, a 29-km (18-mi) panorama road. Back in Moab, you again follow Highway 191 as far as Interstate 70, which takes you west until the Highway 24 turns off going south at Green River. From there the road heads directly into Capitol Reef National Park.

⑳ Capitol Reef National Park This park covers an area of roughly 972 sq km (375 sq mi) around the Waterpocket Fold, whose ridges rise out of the desert floor like giant waves that extend over 160 km (99 mi) through the desert. Their exposed edges have been eroded away into a tangle of bulky domes formed from naked rock, steep cliffs and canyons. While the northern and southern parts of the park are less accessible and mainly prized by hikers, the easy-to-access middle section is home to the more rugged beauty of towering rock formations, among which the green Fruita oasis, created by the Mormons on the Fremont River, looks like an island in a vast ocean.

The most important part of the park is accessed on the 40-km (25 mile) Scenic Drive, which leads to the park's most impressive rock faces. The trip then follows Highways 24, 12 and 89 to Bryce Canyon National Park.

㉑ Bryce Canyon National Park This park extends over an area of 145 sq km (56 sq mi) on the fringe of the Paunsaugunt Plateau, whose cornices drop away 600 m (1,969 ft) over the d elicately divided escarpments. At the bottom is the Paria Valley with a natural amphitheater shaped like a horseshoe. Erosion has carved deep ditches and furrows into the soft sandstone slopes that have resulted in finely engraved heads, needles and arches. In the early morning, this magical world glows in a spec-

Large image: The rock formations in the Arches National Park are the result of the wind and weather. Left side: Capitol Reef National Park. Above: The Green River in Canyonlands National Park.

Large-scale table mountains are one of the hallmarks of the Canyonlands National Park: Flat as a table, in Spanish 'mesa', and steeply sloping at the edges.

Canyonlands National Park

The Colorado and Green Rivers have created the magnificent chasms of Canyonlands over the course of millions of years.

Canyonlands National Park in southern Utah boasts some of the most exciting and impressive scenery on earth. The area, accessible only to Native Americans and experienced riders until the second half of the 20th century, was declared a national park in 1964, and has since earned a reputation as a paradise for adventurous hikers. Numerous trails lead deep into canyons and hidden valleys, opening up a fairy-tale world of multi-hued rocks. It takes several days of hiking to really appreciate the park's treasures, and its true beauty only really unfolds many miles from the roads. Motorists are confined to two side roads. The park is divided into three zones. The 'Island in the Sky' lies between the Green and Colorado rivers, and here there are the striking depths of Shafer Canyon and the White Rim; Gooseneck Trail will take you down to Colorado. The 'Needles', a series of imposing rock towers and other formations.

Confluence Overlook affords a panoramic view of the meeting-point of the Colorado and Green Rivers, but the Maze District in the remote backwoods of the park is for experienced walkers only; it is easy to go astray in the rocky labyrinth. Horseshoe Canyon has the most beautiful rock formations and rewards those who dare to leave the road with exciting views of canyons up to 600 m (1,970 ft) deep.

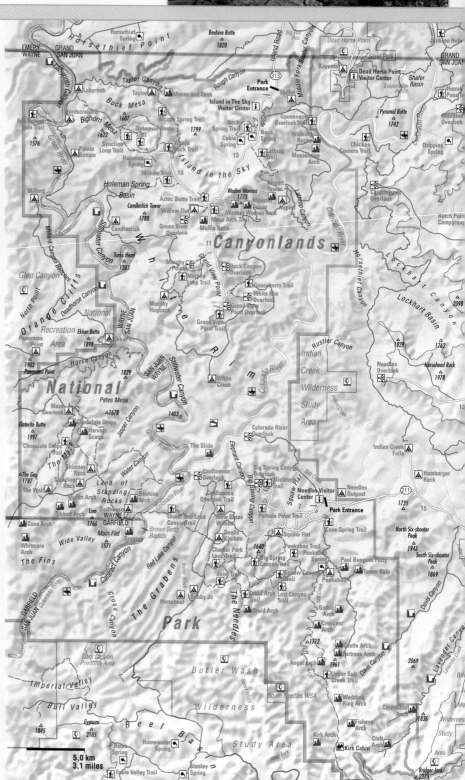

5,0 km
3,1 miles

With a brittle-looking side, the Delicate Arch seems close to collapsing – and has been around for about 100 years.

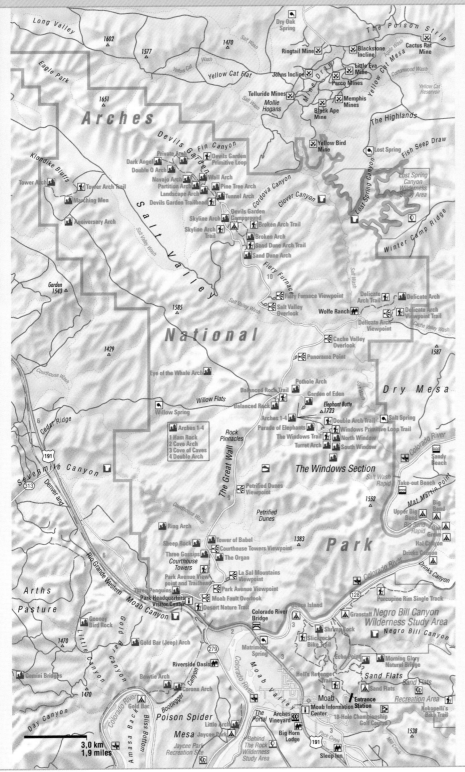

Arches National Park

Dozens of stone arches, domes, and pinnacles can be found in Arches National Park.

Eroded out of the rocks by wind and weather over a period of 150 million years, more than a hundred stone arches near Moab in Utah were placed under government protection in 1929, and since 1971 they have formed part of the Arches National Park. Arches Scenic Drive will take you past the mighty Courthouse Towers, a gleaming rock formation, and on to one of the most impressive vantage points in the park.

Several interesting and diverting paths will then take you through Park Avenue, a thoroughfare lined with steep stone walls and rock formations with evocative names like the Organ, the Tower of Babel, and Sheep Rock. The path continues to Balanced Rock, an enormous boulder weighing some 3,556 tonnes (3,500 tons), balanced on a narrow stone plinth. A rocky trail continues on to Eye of the Whale Arch and the jagged Klondike Bluffs.

The Windows section of the national park has several other natural wonders in stone, such as the Garden of Eden and the Double Arch, and other attractions include the Delicate Arch and Landscape Arch, whose 90-m (295-ft) span has earned it a place in the record books. The Devil's Garden boasts over 60 stone arches and there is a short trail that begins at the Double O Arch. The origins of this magical rocky landscape are to be found in a giant lake which covered the local canyons about 300 million years ago.

The edge of the Paunsagunt Plateau stretches over 30 km at Bryce Canyon, in the wind and weather have weathered away countless rock pillars - the hoodoos. The obliquely incident light emphasises the different sediment layers of the sandstone columns.

White Mesa Arch

Northern Arizona is home to a number of giant sandstone bridges that add considerably to the remarkable charm

The 25-m-high (82 ft) White Mesa Arch is made from white limestone.

of America's South-West. These natural stone arches were created by eons of erosion by the elements. Over time, relentless flows of water loosened the salts contained in the sediment stone and made the stone brittle. The interplay of extreme temperatures then caused the salty stone fragments to fall apart. Only the more resistant stones with a lower salt content remained.

trum of hues from pale yellow to dark orange. The rock amphitheatre can be accessed via the 27-km-long (17 mile) scenic drive around the upper rim.
East of Bryce Canyon, it's worth visiting the Kodachrome Basin State Park, which you can reach via Highway 12. It is home to splendid rock faces of red-and-white striped sandstone, towering rock chimneys and spindly rock needles that glow in all shades of red, especially at sunrise and sunset. A panorama trail takes you to the most beautiful formations whose rich colors can hardly be surpassed. Back on Highway 12 and Interstate 89 you will head to nearby Zion National Park.

㉒ Zion National Park The vertical walls of the Virgin River Canyon break away steeply here at heights of more than 1,000 m (3,281 ft), forming solid pillars and deep recesses. The Mormons saw this as a 'natural temple of God' back in the 19th century. Visitors feel like tiny ants but you can walk along the base of the canyon in areas where even the rays of the sun hardly ever shine. Only the southern

part of the park (593 sq km/229 sq ft) is open to vehicles along the 29-km-long (18-mi) Scenic Drive. The rest of the park is accessible on more than 160 km (99 mi) of hiking trails. An absolute must is the Gateway to the Narrows Trail. Along the Weeping Rock Trail, you will pass so-called 'Hanging Gardens', a rock overhang covered in ferns. The best panorama view over the entire canyon can be seen from Angels Landing, a cliff that drops away to a depth of 450 m (1,476 ft) on three sides. Your route follows Highway 89 past Marble Canyon to

Wupatki National Monument back in Cameron, Arizona.

㉓ Wupatki National Monument Roughly 40 km (25 mi) south of Cameron, you come across the ancient pueblo of Wupatki on Highway 89. More than 2,000 Sinagua dwellings dating back to between the 9th and 14th centuries can be found in this arid desert landscape on the western edge of the Painted Desert. A few miles further south of the pueblo ruins is Sunset Crater National Monument.
The focal point here is the 305-m-high (1,001-ft) cinder

The central part of Zion Canyon National Park is occupied by Kolob Terrace. It is accessible from spring to autumn on the same road from the village of Virgin. Rock formations with sharp ridges and pointed cones are what characterise the appearance.

cone of the Sunset Crater, the result of a massive eruption in 1065, followed by a second in 1250. The region can be accessed on the Scenic Drive with spectacular views over the volcanic landscape. Individual features are explained on the nature trail.

㉔ Grand Canyon National Park (please see also Route 23 'Panamericana'.) This park covers an area of 4,933 sq km (1,904 sq mi) and includes roughly 445 km (277 mi) of the mighty Colorado River, which has carved out a canyon that is up to 1,800 m (5,906 ft) deep with spectacular walls. At its farthest point, the canyon is 30 km (19 mi) wide, and the solid rock formations obviously make for unforgettable photographs. You can enter the Grand Canyon from both the northern and southern sides, but by far the most spectacular views can be seen from the southern side, which is also where the most important tourist facilities are located. Due to the crush of visitors, the entire South Rim has been closed off to individual vehicle traffic and instead there

are free shuttle buses which take you to all of the major vista points.
Back on Highway 64 and Interstate 40, you continue on to Kingman, where you take the turnoff to Highway 93 and head towards Hoover Dam.

㉕ Hoover Dam Just east of Las Vegas is the world's largest dam – until the Three Gorges project in China is completed. The Hoover Dam is 221 m (725 ft) high, 379 m (1,243 ft) wide, and roughly 200 m (659 ft) thick at the base. A feat of engineering in any era, the dam was completed in 1935. Lake Mead, which is 170 km (106 mi) long and up to 150 m (492 ft) deep, was the result of holding back the Colorado River here. The lake is a reservoir for Las Vegas and a major recreation area. After about 56 km (35 mi) on

The canyons in the North American National Parks offer a breathtaking view. Above Grand Canyon, left Bryce Canyon National Park. Right: The Narrows are the narrowest part of the Zion Canyon.

The largest living tree on Earth, the General Sherman Tree, grows steeply into the sky like an enormous pillar.

Rafting on the Colorado River

The Grand Canyon is the largest canyon in the world, cut out of the rock by the incessant flow of the Colorado River, which powers its way through the giant gorge.
Thus far, the river has carved the canyon down to depths of 1,800 m (5,906 ft). Experiencing this canyon as an active participant instead of as a silent observer, of course, is one of the highlights of any visit to the USA. The rafting trip down to the Grand Canyon is a mix of tranquil, contemplative

Adventure on the Colorado River.

stretches where the primary focus is appreciating the unbelievable landscapes that surround you, combined with more than 150 whitewater rapids where passengers feel more or less as if they are part of a rough rinse cycle in a washing machine.
Stops along the way include peaceful places near waterfalls, Indian ruins or tributary river valleys. It takes one to two weeks to cross the canyon completely, but some organizers also offer rides through sections of it.

Highway 93 you will arrive in Las Vegas.

26 Las Vegas (see p. 335). East of the city is the Valley of Fire State Park. Death Valley, which is 230 km (143 mi) long and 26 km (16 mi), begins just 80 m (50 mi) west of the gaming paradise.

27 Death Valley National Park (see pp. 336-337.) At 86 m (282 ft) below sea level, Badwater, in the middle of the park, is the lowest point in North America. It is the hottest and driest place in the United States. It recorded the hottest ever temperature in the Western Hemisphere, and the second-hottest in the world. In summer it can reach 57°C (135°F).
Highlights include: Dante's View, the marvelous Zabriskie Point, Artist's Drive, Mosaic Canyon, the vast sand dunes and the Rhyolite Ghost Town. By contrast, Sequoia National Park to the west of Death Valley, is a completely different world comprising granite peaks, redwood forests and Alpine rivers.

28 Sequoia National Park
Giant sequoias are the largest redwood trees by volume and only exist on the western slopes

of the Sierra Nevada. Some specimens have a circumference of up to 30 m (98 ft) and live to be over 3,000 years old.

29 Mojave Highway 14 runs along the western edge of the Mojave Desert back to Los Angeles. Dry lakebeds, dunes and precipices accompany you here before you finally reach the Pacific in Santa Monica.

Mojave National Preserve: Only seemingly dull and empty, because snakes and other reptiles are predominant out at night - and even some foxes (at the top).
Huge sand dunes tower in the Death Valley National Park in front of impressive mountain scenery (above).

Las Vegas is a city that never sleeps, and where you won't find a clock anywhere. At night it is almost brighter than during the day.

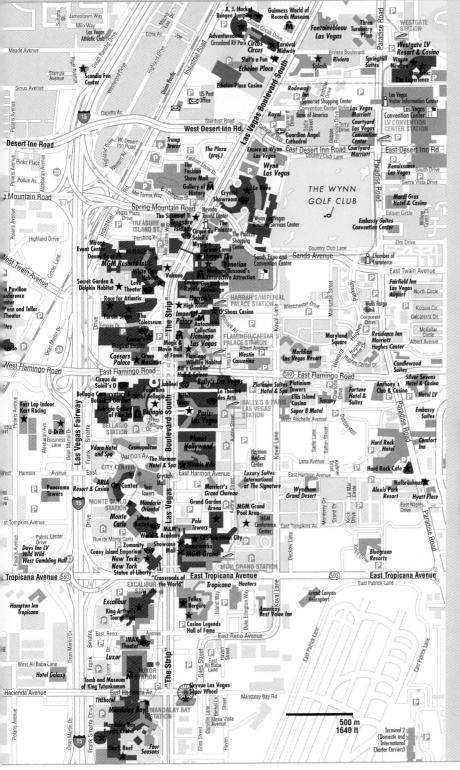

Las Vegas

This glitzy city in Nevada has an almost magic appeal. Bugsy Siegel, an underworld king from the east coast, opened the first casino palace here, the Flamingo Hotel, almost single-handedly making Las Vegas a gambling Mecca.

Gambling was legalized in Nevada as early as 1931, in order to create additional sources of income for the state. Special offers throughout the city now lure visitors inside as they stumble from one slot machine to the next. Life starts in the evening, when the neon lights begin flashing on the Strip and the gambling hordes in tour buses head for the tables.

Colorful billboards glint in front of the mega hotels while quarters, dimes, nickels and silver dollars jingle in the gaming halls.

Since the legendary appearances of Frank Sinatra and Elvis Presley, the stages of Las Vegas have become a make-or-break

City of illusions – in the game as well as in the architecture.

setting for many artists, at least in the USA. The extravagant shows feature lavish production and are aimed at a wide audience. On the Strip, hotels and casinos vie for visitors while the gaudy palaces flash one after another, showing off ideas borrowed from amusement parks like Disneyland.

An extra service in Tinseltown: You can be married in any of the numerous wedding chapels for cheap.

Lake Manly once stood where salt-crusts now spread across the landscape.

Death Valley

Death Valley, stretching out along the border between California and Nevada, is in many respects a place of extremes.

Death valley is considered one of the hottest places on earth – temperatures of over 50°C (122°F) have been recorded in this arid desert – and it is also one of the driest areas in North America, with less than 5 cm (2 in) of annual precipitation. Badwater is also home to the lowest point in the western hemisphere, 86 m (282 ft) below sea level.

Settlers attempting to reach the Golden West via a supposed short-cut during the 1849 California gold rush soon gave this valley its ominous name. Winding up in this isolated depression, they survived only thanks to the bravery of a few of their young men and are said to have cried 'good-bye, Death Valley!' after their rescue.

Borax was mined in Death Valley around 1880, with twenty-strong mule teams dragging the heavy wagons to Mojave. The valley has been protected since 1933 and was named a national park in 1994. Its austere beauty can be appreciated in the multi-hued badlands at Zabriskie Point, the sand dunes at Stovepipe Wells, and the bright wildflowers in the mountain meadows above Harmony Borax. Furnace Creek Ranch is a green oasis located in the middle of the magnificent, endless, unforgiving desert.

Iron and sulfur in the rock are what create the harmonious range of colours.

A special kind of lunar landscape: From Zabriskie Point in Death Valley you have a fantastic view of the barren and at the same time fascinating mountain ranges, which extend across the valley.

Las Vegas This has been the USA's gambling haven since 1931. The countless casinos give their all to outdo each other in an effort to lure more money from gamblers' pockets. Lavish hotel complexes, theaters and erotic shows provide entertainment and luxury around the clock.

Grand Canyon The Colorado River has carved a gorge through the Colorado Plateau up to 1,800 m deep (5906 ft), 30 km wide (19 mi) and 445 km long (277 mi). The view from the edge of the canyon sweeps over solid yellow-brown and milky white rock outcrops, pinnacles and towers. The layers in the canyon represent 1.7 billion years of the earth's history.

Death Valley This national park is a desert with impressive rocks, vast sand dunes and temperatures reaching 57°C (135°F). However, springs also allow for extensive flora and fauna. Rock drawings prove that the valley was already settled thousands of years ago.

Los Angeles Freeways are the lifeline of Los Angeles, which covers 1,200 sq km (463 sq mi) and comprises many individual towns that have grown together. Stretching from Malibu to Santa Ana, and from Pasadena to Long Beach, the city's highlights include a visit to the film studios in Hollywood.

Organ Pipe Cactus National Monument Many species of cactus bloom in April and May in the habitat of the rare 'organ pipe cactus'.

Joshua Tree National Park This park south of Twentynine Palms is part of the Mojave Desert and is home to dried-up salt lakes and sparse vegetation with cactuses, junipers and yucca palms.

Sonoran Desert This desert is full of surprises. The giant saguaro cactuses, for example are up to 150 years old and up to 15 m (49 ft) high. They flower in May. Everything else the desert has to offer is displayed in the Arizona Sonora Desert Museum in Saguaro National Park.

Phoenix The capital of Arizona is in the hottest and driest part of the Sonora Desert, and its warm winter climate has made it one of the most popular holiday destinations in the USA. Retirement communities such as Sun City have been established on its outskirts.

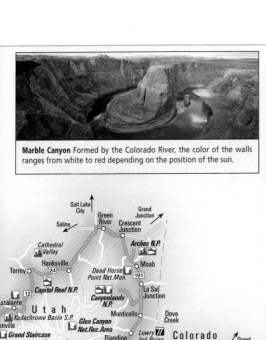

Marble Canyon Formed by the Colorado River, the color of the walls ranges from white to red depending on the position of the sun.

Arches National Park About one thousand freestanding stone arches are clustered here – more than anywhere else in the world – along with mushroom rocks, rock towers, pinnacles and domes of smooth sandstone. In the evening light, the red rocks look as if they are on fire.

Mesa Verde National Park These historic residential settlements of the Anasazi Indians are set into rock niches and caves. Though protected, many of the rock dwellings and pueblos can be visited.

Taos Pueblo The Pueblo Indians lived in these multi-storey flat-roofed houses more than one thousand years ago.

Mission San Xavier del Bac Founded by Spanish priests near Tucson, this church is located on the Tohono O'odham San Xavier Indian Reservation.

Chiricahua National Monument These charming rock landscapes near the Mexican border were once part of Apache hunting grounds.

White Sands National Monument This 600-sq-km (232 sq mi) dune landscape is made of white gypsum sand that glistens like newly fallen snow. Dunes rise to 18 m (59 ft) here. The US Army set off the world's first atomic bomb in the northern part of the desert on July 16, 1945.

From Maine to Maryland

A fairly narrow coastal plain stretches between the Atlantic Ocean in the East and the Appalachians in the West. Here on the East Coast the cities line up like pearls on a chain forming a massive conurbation that is also referred to as 'Boswash' (Boston to Washington). However, despite the high population densities there are still a number of remote natural landscapes to be found.

Route profile:

Length: approx. 1,056 miles
Time required: at least 2 weeks
When to go: Drive on the right in the USA. The typical speed limit (55–65 mph/90–105 km/h) can vary from state to state and breaches receive harsh penalties.

In 1620, when they disembarked from the Mayflower at Plymouth Rock in present-day Massachusetts, the Pilgrim Fathers could not have dreamt that they were playing 'midwife' to what is now the most powerful nation on earth, the United States of America. What they encountered was a largely untouched natural environment only sparsely populated by a number of Native North American tribes. Today the fascination of the US Atlantic coast derives not only from the bustling cities and the cen-

tres of political and economic power, but also from the peace and solitude of its idyllic natural setting. The mountain scenery of the Appalachians, which stretch from New England along the East Coast states to the south, can be demanding for hikers on parts of the famous Appalachian Trail. On the coast, beaches close to the metropolitan areas may be crowded, but further afield they are relatively untouched for miles and are a fantastic invitation to simply relax and unwind. Here you can also begin to imagine the courage the first settlers must have needed to set sail across the expansive ocean in their none-too-seaworthy sailing ships. The rich history can be seen at a number of places along the Atlantic Coast – from Plymouth Rock, where the Pilgrim Fathers landed, to Salem, where the witch hunts took

place (described so exactingly by the writers Nathaniel Hawthorne in The Scarlet Letter, and Arthur Miller in The Crucible), on through to Boston, the starting point of the rebellion against England.

The Declaration of Independence was proclaimed in Phila-

delphia, Pennsylvania, while Williamsburg presents itself as an historical picture book when actors in traditional costumes take to the streets to relive days of yore.

The eastern USA is also the political nerve centre of the USA as a superpower: Washington,

The Bass Harbor Lighthouse (above) guards the coast of Mount Desert Island in Acadia National Park. Lupins and leaves stand out in the Indian summer (left). Visitors flock to the protected area and enjoy the colourful splendour.

with the White House, Capitol Hill and the Pentagon, has formed the backdrop for the making and implementing of decisions with far-reaching historical impact. And then of course there is the city that, for many people, is the very embodiment of the 'American dream'. It's 'the city that never sleeps the 'Big Apple'. It's New York. Nestled between the Hudson and East rivers, New York is a melting pot of folks with an incredible diversity of languages, skin colours and religions, a shopping paradise with the most exclusive shops for the appropriate wallets, and a cultural centre with theatres and museums of international standing. In short, it's a truly cosmopolitan city that captivates nearly every one of its millions of visitors.

Left: The Statue of Liberty on Liberty Island welcomes those who reach New York by ship. Above: Some large luxury hotels have been built along the waterfront on Boston Harbor.

Lobster

Colourfully painted lobster pots decorate many of the fishermen's houses. For many gourmets, lobster, which loves cold, clear water, is one of the main reasons for

The dream route travels through the forests of New England via Boston and New York to Washington. It returns to the coast via Virginia. All twelve of the East Coast states have one thing in common – a view of the endless ocean.

1 Portland The route begins in the largest city in the state of Maine. Henry W Longfellow, a writer born here in 1807, often extolled Portland's attractive location on Casco Bay. Many parts of the city have been rebuilt after a series of disastrous fires. One of the few historical buildings left is the Wadsworth-Longfellow House, the oldest brick building in the city (1786). The Old Port, with its warehouses, new office buildings, and a variety of numerous shops and restaurants, is ideal for a relaxing stroll.

The route initially heads north via Rockland towards the Acadia National Park. Interstate 95 and Highway 1 run parallel to the coast and always offer wonderful views of the rocky cliffs and islands, scenic bays, and small harbour villages such as Bath, the 'City of Ships'.

2 Rockland This city at the south-west end of Penobscot Bay calls itself the 'Lobster Capital of the World' and attracts

visitors en masse at the beginning of August every year for its Maine Seafood Festival.

3 Acadia National Park Still outside of the National Park is

Two lighthouses ensure a safe approach to Penobscot Bay: Rockland Lighthouse and Owls Head Lighthouse. Information about the lighthouses can be found at the Shore Village Museum. Highway 1 continues via the harbour town of Camden, especially popular with sailors

and windsurfers, before passing through Belfast and Bucksport on the way to Ellsworth. Highway 3 takes you over a bridge to Mount Desert Island.

the fishing village of Bar Harbor, once a popular summer resort among American millionaires. Today, stately mansions reminiscent of this era still line the coast. The National Park, set up in 1916, encompasses half of Mount Desert Island and also includes the smaller islands of Isle

au Haut, Baker and Little Cranberry. When timber companies began felling timber on the islands at the end of the 19th century, Bar Harbor's 'high society' bought the endangered land and donated it to the nation on condition that it be declared a na-

tional park. The 500-m-high (1,640-ft) Cadillac Mountain is located within the park and attracts large numbers of visitors, especially during elusive Indian Summer days. The stark cliffs of Acadia National Park are constantly pounded by Atlantic surf. The park coincidentally lies on

visiting Maine. Lobster stocks have dropped dramatically in recent decades and strict fishing conditions are now in force. Having now become a rarity, Homarus americanus is now considered a particular delicacy. Yes, it's expensive, but in Maine it's still relatively affordable.

The animals are stored In the lobster baskets (far left). Alive, they are black (left), but turn red when cooked.

Indian Summer

Autumn stages a very spectacular display in the forests of New England – sometimes referred to as 'fall colours' or 'foliage' by Americans. Europeans tend to refer to it as Indian Summer. The Native North Americans believed it was the blood of the big bear that gave the leaves their magnificent colouring of wonderful red, and its fat the yellow tones. The botanists have a more prosaic explanation.

During the so-called Indian Summers, trees put on a symphony of yellow, orange and red tones.

a migratory bird route and can be explored on foot, by boat or by bicycle.

Back on the mainland, the return journey to Portland provides the opportunity to stop off at any of the quaint harbour towns on the coast road, stroll along one of

only 29 km (18 miles) to the next state, Massachusetts.

④ **Salem** This harbour town, founded in 1626 about 25 km (16 miles) north of Boston, achieved its tragic claim to fame when the devout Puritans of

House. The mansions, among the most attractive in the country, bear witness to the former wealth of this trading town. They also include the birthplace of author Nathaniel Hawthorne (1804–64), and the House of the Seven Gables.

There are significant differences in temperature during the autumn in New England, between the sunny, warm days and the very cold nights. During this time the trees produce a cork-like substance that blocks the exchange of liquid between the leaves and the branches. The level of chlorophyll in the trees drops while sugar and a variety of pigments remain. The red pigment anthocyan, which is especially prevalent in the American maple and oak species, is produced in greater quantities. 'Leaf-peepers' wanting to make their way to the autumn spectacle are best advised to consult the internet site www.foliagenetwork. com, which contains regular reports on where the autumn foliage is currently displaying the best of its red, orange, gold and yellow tones.

the piers, or take a sailing trip on a windjammer.

It is difficult to resist the fascination of the boats anchored so majestically in the harbours, or a graceful cruise along the coast at full sail.

From Portsmouth, the only harbour in New Hampshire, it is

Salem staged a crazed witch hunt in 1692 where twenty people were brought to 'trial' and executed.

The town has several museums dedicated to these woeful events – Salem Witch Museum, Salem Witch Village, Witch Dungeon Museum and the Witch

Large image: Night view of Portland. Left side: Sunrise over Mount Desert Island. Above: Camden in the colourful Indian summer.

One of the covered markets dating back to 1826 at the lively Quincy Market.

Boston

The capital of Massachusetts resembles a giant open-air museum, a European enclave with historic buildings and winding streets amid a modern inner city with glazed office towers, world-renowned universities and leading research establishments.

It was in 1776 that the Declaration of Independence was first read out from the balcony of the Old State House in Boston, a red-brown brick building erected in 1712 as the seat of the English colonial government. Today there is a modern subway station below the historic building, but there is still no avoiding history in Boston. There has been a settlement on the hills around Massachusetts

'the British are coming!'. The Paul Revere House, the oldest building in the city, has been converted into a museum.
The Freedom Trail begins at Boston Common, the first public park in the USA. Today it is the city's green belt and a popular leisure area for people working downtown. North of the park shines the golden dome of the new State House. The King's Chapel, built in

Numerous skyscrapers characterize the Boston skyline.

Bay from as far back as the 1720s. The settlement grew into an important harbour and, with its strategic position, became the economic and intellectual focus of the colony. The conflict with the colonial power exploded onto the public scene in 1770 when a number of citizens rebelled against the harsh tax policies of the British Crown and staged a boycott of all European goods. On 16 December 1773 the colonists met in the Faneuil Hall, moved on to the Old South Meeting House – both significant points on the present-day Freedom Trail – and gathered in the harbour where, dressed as Native North Americans, they boarded three British ships and threw the tea bales into the sea. Paul Revere was to become a hero in the war of independence that followed when on the evening of 18 April 1775 he rode from Boston to Lexington to warn citizens that

1754, was the first Anglican church in Boston. The Old Corner Bookstore, one of the best bookshops in the city, was already the literary centre of Boston in the 19th century. Other key points on the Freedom Trail are the Benjamin Franklin Statue, erected in honour of the scholars and signatories of the Declaration of Independence; the Old South Meeting House, a former church in which the 'Boston Tea Party' was plotted; the Faneuil Hall, another of the colonists' meeting places; and Bunker Hill, scene of an important battle in the American War of Independence.
Apart from the Freedom Trail, the historic area of Beacon Hill is reminiscent of the city's history and its rich tradition. Little has changed here since the 17th century. Romantic patrician houses still stand on both sides of the cobblestone streets.

The narrow Acorn Street in the romantic Beacon Hill area.

John F. Kennedy

In 1960 the American people elected the 42-year-old Democratic Senator from Massachusetts, John F. Kennedy, as the 35th President of the United States by a narrow majority over his opponent, Richard Nixon. He proclaimed his political vision and goals in his famous inaugural speech on 20 January 1961. With his charm and charisma he inspired countless, especially young, people throughout the world to confront the political and social problems in their countries. He rose to global political challenges such as the Cuban Missile Crisis with political skill and fortune.

ocean – were processed. The museum provides graphic displays of the history and methods of whale hunting. The numerous 'captains' cabins' in town are easily recognized by their Widow Walks. Siasconset was discovered by artists at the end of the 19th century and continues to attract countless bohemian types today. Many of the clapboard houses are framed by an attractive display of roses. Plants and nature in general are rated highly on Nantucket. About one third of the island is nature reserve, like the Nantucket Moors near Nantucket Town or the Nantucket State Forest. There

Detour

Martha´s Vineyard und Nantucket

These two islands off the coast of Cape Cod are among the most popular holiday destinations on the Atlantic coast. Martha's Vineyard is closer to the mainland, while the ferry crossing to Nantucket takes a good three hours.

Martha's Vineyard

The 32-km-long (20-mile) and 16-km-wide (10-mile) island was named by Bartholomew Gosnold after the grapes growing there and after his daughter, Martha. With its four harbours, Martha's Vineyard became a wealthy town in the heyday of the whaling industry. Today, expensive yachts are moored where the schooners used to anchor. The island is a popular location for the holiday homes of New York and Boston 'high society' types who, despite usually keeping to themselves, have unfortunately rendered large areas on the east of the island inaccessible to 'mere mortals'. Today the main harbour of Tisbury is usually referred to as Vineyard Haven, but when it comes to romantic flair it cannot compete with the other two larger locations on the island, Oak Bluffs and Edgartown. Oak Bluffs was originally founded by the Methodists

of Edgartown as a religious gathering place. Colourfully painted, picturesque wooden houses thus replaced the original tented camp and have now become popular as holiday homes. In Edgartown, numerous 'captains' cabins' are reminiscent of the town's heyday as a whaling harbour. The houses often have a roof terrace of sorts, the balustrades of which are known as the Widow Walk – it was from here that the wives used to keep a lookout for their seafaring husbands. Bicycles are available for hire in many places and you can take off on your own to explore the island and its beaches. Martha's Vineyard lies off Chappaquiddick, ideal for a lazy day on the beach or a walk through one of the nature reserves.

Nantucket Island

Nantucket Island, which was inhabited by the Native North Americans until the middle of the 17th century, experienced its heyday in the 18th century as an important whaling harbour. Today it is a popular holiday destination. Much of the main town and ferry harbour, Nantucket Town – one of the best maintained towns in New England – is reminiscent of days gone by. Main Street – paved with cobblestones like many of the streets in town – has an historic flair and attracts visitors with its inviting shops and good restaurants.

The Whaling Museum is housed in a former candle factory where the raw materials – spermaceti and blubber from the giants of the

are also countless gardens, lovingly tended, which bloom and blossom all summer long. The Daffodil Festival takes place in April when the daffodils bloom everywhere.

In October, cranberries are the main attraction. Like Martha's Vineyard, bicycles are also an important means of transport and can be hired everywhere.

Top: Since Nantucket was founded, the ocean has determined the way of life in fishing towns. Above: The popular holiday island of Martha's Vineyard is home to pristine nature, for example on the western tip at Gay Head Lighthouse.

His Berlin speech of 1963, when he proclaimed 'Ich bin ein Berliner' (I am a Berliner) will always be remembered by millions of Germans.

Only seldom are the darker sides of his policies mentioned today, such as increasing the military involvement in Vietnam.

His death on 22 November 1963 in Dallas from an assassin's bullet ensured that the dynamic President's legend lives on.

Kennedy spoke the famous words 'I am a Berliner' at Rudolph Wilde Square. This place was later renamed in his honor.

Newport and the coast of the wealthy

The Gilded Age, Newport's hey-day, began towards the end of the 19th century. Anybody who was anybody in New York built a 'summer house' in this harbour town with its picturesque alleyways, colonial-style houses and fantastic views of the bay and the ocean. These mansions often bore a striking resemblance to the European castles their owners had seen on trips to Europe. Some of these dream mansions are open to the pub-

The Breakers, Cornelius Vanderbilt's house, has 72 rooms.

... as well as Marble House.

5 Boston (see pp. 344-345.) Via Interstate 3 it is 65 km (40 miles) to Plymouth which, due to its long coastline and more than 300 lakes and sprawling forests, is a populated commuter area.

6 Plymouth The harbour town is itself a milestone in American history – it was here that the Mayflower landed on 21 December 1620 after a perilous crossing, and it was here that the Pilgrim Fathers first set foot on American soil. A replica of the ship, the Mayflower II, is anchored in the harbour. The museum village Plimoth Plantation provides an interesting insight into the world of the first settlers. Not only does it have 17th-century houses and tools on display, but actors also re-enact everyday life at the beginning of that century. The Pilgrim Hall Museum has artefacts from the Pilgrim Fathers on display, and Cole's Hill is the site of the graves of those who died in the first winter. From Cape Cod Bay the journey continues towards Hyannis on Cape Cod.

7 Hyannis The Steamship Authority ferries set off from Hyannis to Nantucket and Martha's Vineyard all year round.

8 Provincetown This little town at the northernmost end of the Cape Cod headland was founded by artists around 1900. Numerous writers and painters such as Edward Hopper and Jackson Pollock lived there for a time. Today the town still retains its artistic flair. Spectacular Whale-watching trips by boat are also on offer in Provincetown.

Cape Cod's elbow shape dates back to the ice age. The retreating glaciers left behind some 365 lakes that are ideal for swimming, fishing and boating. The beautiful Atlantic beaches are extremely popular today, particularly thanks to their warm waters. If you have time you really ought to take a detour to the nearby islands of Martha's Vineyard and Nantucket. From Falmouth to the south of the peninsula the route initially takes you along Buzzards Bay to Wareham. After crossing the Fall River, it then continues to Newport, Rhode Island (Highway 24).

9 Newport Founded in 1639, this town, which has 27,000 residents, is among the most beautiful places on the East Coast. Further along there are lovely views of the islands in the bay, with Providence lying at the northern end.

10 Providence The capital and economic centre of Rhode Island was founded in 1636 by Roger Williams, whom the Puritans had driven out of Salem because of his reputedly heretical, i.e. cosmopolitan, views. The most impressive building in the town is the State House, built entirely of white marble and with the second-largest self-supporting dome in the world.

Coastal Road 1 leads through a series of quaint villages and along the lovely beaches to Mystic Seaport.

11 Mystic Seaport This reconstruction of a harbour village from the 19th century in the south-east of Connecticut has now become an open-air museum. Since the end of the 1920s around sixty historic buildings have been reconstructed as replicas of the originals. There are up to 430 historic ships anchored in the large museum harbour. One of the yards specializes in the repair of historical ships. The modern neighbour-ing town of Mystic is a small coastal resort with an aquarium worth seeing. A few kilometres west of Mystic is the harbour of New London, where the ferries to Long Island set out.

Via Highway 25 along the coast of the Long Island Sound you can reach New York in around two hours.

Mystic Seaport is true to its name: Historic ships and buildings give it a special flair.

lic today, such as The Breakers, the property belonging to Cornelius Vanderbilt and built in the style of the Italian Renaissance; or Marble House, built by William K. Vanderbilt in the French style. The 5-km-long (3-mile) Cliff Walk from Easton's Beach to Bailey's Beach takes you past some of these grand mansions.

The skyline of Manhattan is simply overwhelming in the light of the sunset.

New York

New York City comprises Manhattan, Brooklyn, Queens, the Bronx and Staten Island. New York means the Statue of Liberty, the Empire State Building, the Chrysler Building, the Brooklyn Bridge, Broadway, Fifth Avenue, but also the ghettos of the now up-and-coming Bronx.

New York is sort of the 'capital of the Western world', a melting pot where immigrants from around the globe have gathered to become an intrinsic part of America's cultural fabric. Of course, many ethnic groups have retained their cultural identity by developing neighbourhoods such as Little Italy or Chinatown, just

Yonkers and Albany in Upstate New York. It is the city's lifeline – in the financial district in the south and especially in the theatre neighbourhood around Times Square. One of the most famous buildings in the world, the Empire State Building (1929–31), was built in art deco style and is 381 m (1,257 ft) high –

View from Brooklyn Heights to the southern tip of Manhattan.

The Brooklyn Bridge provides great views.

The statue is also affectionately called 'Lady Liberty'.

as they would in Palermo or Beijing. Indeed, New York gladly retreats into its 'villages', creating its own worlds in neighbourhoods such as Tribeca, Soho, Chelsea and Greenwich Village. Yet the chaos continues in Midtown and on the wide avenues: the wailing of police sirens, the honking horns of taxis and the pounding of jackhammers. The office towers rise up into the clouds. Be sure to check out Broadway, from the Battery in southern Manhattan as far as

with the aerial mast, 448 m (1,588 ft.). Central Park, the green oasis in the mega metropolis, stretches from 59th to 110th Street over an area of 340 ha (840 acres). People of all kinds, ball-playing teenagers, picnicking families and disabled variety artists make for interesting encounters. The Rockefeller Center (1930–40) is a giant complex with offices, television studios, restaurants and shops. Concerts and other events take place in the Radio City Music Hall (1930).

To illustrate the dimensions of the Central Park, they are best compared to 364 football fields.

In the 1970s TriBeCa was a derelict industrial district, but is now a trendy district.

Broadway is an elementary part of New York. With the huge selection of musicals and plays the choice is difficult.

The neo-Gothic St Patrick's Cathedral (1858–87) is a replica of the cathedral in Cologne. The main train station, opened in 1913 as Grand Central Station after several years under construction, was built in the beaux arts style and decorated with baroque and Renaissance elements. An artificial sky sprinkled with 2,500 stars stretches over the somewhat ostentatious main hall.

Once completed, the Chrysler Building (1930) was the highest building in the world for just one year. Specific aspects resemble the radiator grilles of the Chrysler

every immigrant was registered between 1892 and 1917. In the museum you trace the process from the luggage room to the Great Hall where checks were carried out.

With its winding, tree-lined streets, the famous artists' neighbourhood of Greenwich Village between 12th St, Houston St, Lafayette St and the Hudson River is reminiscent of the 'Old Europe' that early immigrants left behind. The Metropolitan Opera, or the 'Met', one of the most well-known opera houses in the world, is part of the Lincoln Center, a giant complex of thea-

The famous sea of lights on Times Square.

cars of that period. The United Nations building (1949–53) looks over the East River. A number of works of art are on display in the entrance hall.

The financial district, Wall Street, takes its name from a solid protective wall intended to protect the Dutch Nieuw Amsterdam from enemies such as the English and the Native North Americans. The Brooklyn Bridge is the most recognizable bridge in the Big Apple. Opened in May 1883 after sixteen years under construction, it is 1,052 m long (1,180 yds), excluding the access roads.

The Statue of Liberty stands out on Liber-ty Island (formerly Bedloe's Island), a small rock between Manhattan and Staten Island. In her right hand she holds a torch, in the left the Declaration of Independence. The statue became a symbol of freedom for immigrants on the approaching ships. The 'path to freedom' used to lead through Ellis Island where

The magnificent bronze 'Atlas with the globe' in the Rockefeller Center.

tres and concert halls. The Guggenheim Museum, built by architect Frank Lloyd Wright, was disparagingly referred to as the 'snail building' but there is no dispute over its art treasures. The new Museum of Modern Art (MoMa) complex was designed by the Japanese architect, Yoshio Taniguchi, and takes up an entire city block. Its galleries house the world's largest collection of valuable paintings from the late 19th century to the present.

Since the 1970s, residents of Baltimore have enjoyed the fine dining and shopping on Inner Harbor.

Detour

Atlantic City

Atlantic City, in the state of New Jersey, enjoyed its first heyday as a popular seaside resort in 1880. Some fourty years later its reputation for lively nightlife extended way beyond the city limits. Beauty contests and trial runs for Broadway Shows took place here before their New Yorker premiers want live. Alas, the demise of many a popular seaside resort began in earnest in the 1950s with the ad-

The boardwalk at night.

The casinos are pompous.

vent of long-haul travel. Atlantic City was no exception. However, in 1976 the citizens of New Jersey voted to have gambling legalized in Atlantic City, and with that law the East Coast counterpart to Las Vegas and Reno was born. Today, Atlantic City has an international draw with its attractions and theme hotels. A relaxing walk along the wooden boardwalk on the Atlantic is recommended as an alternative to the glitz, glamour and gambling.

⑫ New York (see pp. 348–351.) If you want to discover the rural charm of the state of New York, then you are best advised to go for an outing to the Hudson River Valley, which stretches north from New York City to Albany.

⑬ Hudson Valley Pine forests sprinkled with lakes, farms and small villages are what characterize the landscape along the Hudson River. Given the wonderful views, it is not surprising that many of the well-to-do from New York have built themselves stately homes here with well-tended parks. 100 km (62 miles) north of Yonkers is New Paltz, founded by the Huguenots in 1692.

The next section of the river is lined with historically significant properties. Springwood (Franklin D. Roosevelt Historic Site), the property where the later US President was born and grew up, is located there. Even more stately is the Vanderbilt National Historic Site, the palace built by the industrialist Frederick W. Vanderbilt in 1890 in the style of the Italian Renaissance. The trip along the Hudson Valley ends in Kingston, the gateway to the Catskills, an important recreational area for New Yorkers.

⑭ Philadelphia From the outskirts of New York the route continues towards Philadelphia, Pennsylvania. Up until the completion of the various government buildings in Washington, Congress was housed in the Congress Hall of this, the most historically significant city in the USA. The centre of the city is the Independence National Historical Park, with Independence Hall where the representatives of the thirteen colonies signed the Declaration of Independence on 4 July 1776. The Liberty Bell, which was rung to mark the occasion, is housed in the Liberty Bell Pavilion. Numerous significant museums line the Benjamin Franklin

Parkway, including the Philadelphia Museum of Art, the Rodin Museum and the Franklin Institute Science Museum.
From here it is around 100 km (62 miles) along Highway 30 to Atlantic City, the 'Las Vegas of the East'. Back on Interstate 95, Baltimore in the state of Maryland is the next stop.

⑮ Baltimore This small city only has a few historic buildings

left to show for itself after a large majority of them were destroyed by fire in 1904. Little Italy still gives some impression of how the city must have looked in the past. The renovated harbour area (Harbor Place) has become an attractive area again since the 1970s. Not to be missed are the National Aquarium, 19th-century Fort Henry and the Constellation in the docks, a triple-mast sailing ship built in

1854. The outskirts of Washington extend far into surrounding Maryland and Virginia, and it is therefore not long before you encounter the first suburbs of the capital city 50 km (31 miles) away.

⑯ Washington (see p. 353). In Washington you leave the coast for a short while and travel along the Manassas (Highway 29) and Warrenton (Highway

211) towards Washington, Virginia. Shortly before you enter town, Highway 522 branches off to Front Royal. The broad cave complex, Skyline Caverns, near Front Royal lies at the edge of the Shenandoah National Park.

At the top: View of the Philadelphia City Hall. Above: Plays of light project the American flag onto the Independence Hall.

The white marble tower in the form of an obelisk is the Washington Monument; It houses a monument to George Washington.

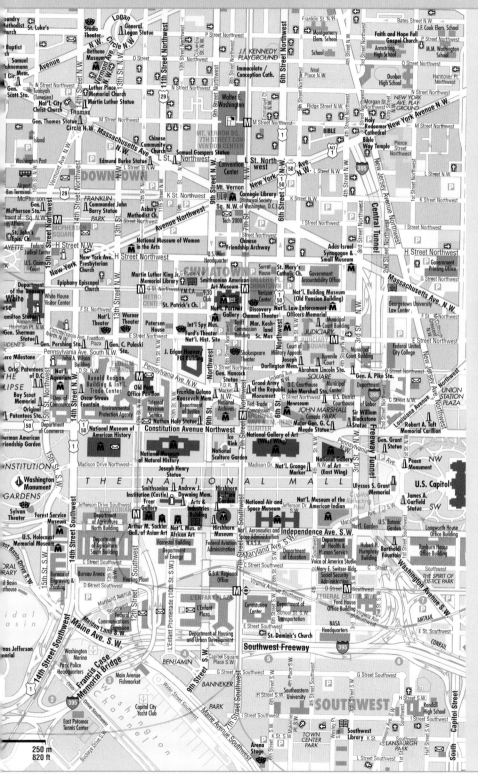

Washington

Washington, DC is the centre of Western democracy and the seat of the US President, a focal point of political power.

The capital of the United States derives its importance from its central geographic location between the northern and southern regions of the original Thirteen Colonies – and also its proximity to Mount Vernon, home of first US President George Washington. Today DC is one of the

The Capitol has been the seat of the Senate since 1800.

most attractive travel destinations in the USA. The Capitol sits on top of Capitol Hill opposite the Supreme Court and the Library of Congress. The National Mall is renowned for its cultural institutions. Numerous first-class museums such as the National Museum of Natural History and the National Air & Space Museum attract visitors all year round. The White House has been the office and residence of the US President since 1800.
The Washington Monument, a 170-m-high (560-ft) obelisk, commemorates the first president of the USA. The extermination of Jews in World War II is documented in the US Holocaust Memorial Museum. The Jefferson Memorial is a circular colonnade structure erected in 1943 in honour of Thomas Jefferson.

Williamsburg

Many of the countless colonial-era houses in Williamsburg were built in the 18th century, but when Richmond was declared the capital of the state of Virginia in 1780, the city gradually faded into insignificance. Today Williamsburg resembles an open-air museum. Employees in shops and restaurants often wear 18th-century costumes and on the Fourth of July a parade is staged in historic uniforms.

The most impressive buildings are the State House and the British Governor's official residence.

17 Shenandoah National Park You should plan five hours for the 170-km-long (106-mile) Skyline Drive through the national park because it is worth making multiple stops to take a look at the Shenandoah Valley. The park covers a particularly scenic part of the Appalachians with the panoramic route ending in Waynesboro. From there it is another 60 km (37 miles) to Monticello.

18 Monticello This property, is located to the east of Charlottesville. It once belonged to Thomas Jefferson (1743–1826) who designed the building for the Monticello plantation in Palladian style. Construction began in 1770. After 100 km (62 miles) on Interstate 64 you reach Richmond, the capital of Virginia.

19 Richmond The State Capitol on Capitol Square, designed by Thomas Jefferson, is considered to be the first neoclassical building in the USA. Here you will find the statue for which George Washington modelled in person. The Canal Walk on the northern bank of the James River is ideal for a leisurely stroll. With its Victorian houses the city has retained the flair of the Old South.

20 Williamsburg During the 18th century the town was the capital of Virginia. 'Colonial Williamsburg', as the town calls itself, is home to eighty-eight buildings restored as facsimiles of the originals. Parks in the style of the 18th century complete the scene. Highway 158 leads you to Point Harbor via Hampton, Nor-

folk and Chesapeake (Highway 64). The harbour town of Albermarle Sound is the gateway to the Cape Hatteras National Seashore. The Wright Brothers National Monument commemorates the Wright Brothers' attempted flights in 1903.

21 Cape Hatteras National Seashore The 210-km-long (130-mile) group of islands off the east coast of North Carolina is known as the Outer Banks. The only road that goes there is the 150-km-long (93-mile) Highway 12, which connects the islands of Hatteras to Roanoke.

The Outer Banks were once frequently targeted by pirates, and countless ships have been wrecked along the rocky coast. These days the often empty beachespicturesque lighthouses and other monuments attract nature lovers, recreational sports enthusiasts and even the odd surfer. The majority of the islands are protected areas with-

in the Cape Hatteras and Cape Lookout National Seashores.

On the return journey to Washington, DC take Highway 13 after leaving Chesapeake. At Salisbury turn off towards Ocean City (Highway 50) via Highway 611 and the bridge over Sinepuxent Bay. There you come to Assateague Island.

22 Assateague Island National Seashore Due to its exposure to wind and waves, this island is constantly changing shape. A diverse animal and plant world braves the raw climate here. From the only small road on the island you can see herds of wild horses roaming this narrow spit of windswept dunes and grass. The return to Washington takes you via Highway 50. A bridge links the eastern side of Chesapeake Bay with quaint Annapolis, Maryland. Picturesque fishing villages, quaint historic towns and scenic bathing spots line the shores of the bay. The founding of Annapolis, the capital of the state of Maryland, dates back to 1649. From Annapolis you are just a few kilometres away from Washington DC.

Large image: The Monticello property looks sublime. Small images: The Cape Hatteras Lighthouse and the Cape Lookout Lighthouse.

Nantucket Island Prosperity here came in the 18th and 19th centuries from whale hunting, as documented in the Whaling Museum.

Boston The colonial revolt against the English hegemony began with the 'Boston Tea Party'. You still encounter traces of history in many of Boston's neighbourhoods. It is also home to important research institutions and universities such as Harvard University and MIT.

Bath This town and its shipyards are rich in tradition. The Maine Maritime Museum and the Bath Iron Works document the history of shipping and shipbuilding in the area.

New York The heart of this megacity beats loudly in places like Times Square. Every year thousands of people gather here in the middle of downtown Manhattan on New Year's Eve to ring in the new year together.

Acadia National Park Mount Desert Island, with its impressive craggy coast, and Cadillac Mountain are part of this striking national park.

Philadelphia This is where the Declaration of Independence was signed and the constitution drawn up. Today the metropolis is an important commercial centre.

Martha's Vineyard The 'Vineyard' is a popular getaway among East Coast urbanites and plays host to the summer homes of the elite.

Atlantic City This East Coast counterpart to Las Vegas attracts visitors with the promise of big winnings and glamorous shows. The boardwalk along the Atlantic is especially scenic.

Washington The main American political nerve centres are in DC: the White House, the Capitol and the Pentagon, seat of the Dept of Defense.

Shenandoah National Park This beautiful park contains part of the Appalachian Trail, which stretches from Maine to Georgia.

Monticello This classic Palladian mansion was once the home of Thomas Jefferson, third President of the US.

Richmond This defiant granite building was constructed in 1894 and was for a long time the city hall in Virginia's capital.

Cape Lookout The 51-m-high (168-ft) lighthouse at Cape Lookout, built in 1859, rises above the shallows of Core Sound. It is characterized by its unusual decoration – black stripes on a white background.

Williamsburg The many old buildings in Williamsburg, such as the Governor's Palace (1706–22), bring the colonial history of this coastal town back to life.

Maine

Woodstock
Bangor
Ellsworth
St.John
Bucksport
Belfast
Bar Harbor
Acadia N.P.
Waterville
Camden
Mt.Desert I.
Augusta
Penobscot Bay
Wiscasset
Rockland
Brunswick
Bath
Portland
New Hampshire
North Windham
Cape Elizabeth
Sanford
Biddeford
Rochester
Sherbrooke
Portsmouth
Concord
Newburyport
Lebanon
Gloucester
Manchester
Salem
Lowell
BOSTON
Provincetown
Leominster
Cape Cod Nat.Seashore
Worcester
Plymouth
Massachusetts
Hyannis
Providence
Albany
Nantucket
New York
Fall River
Kingston
Newport
Hartford
Connecticut
Martha's Vineyard
Catskill Park
New London
Rhode Island
New Paltz
Mystic Seaport
Binghamton
Newburgh
Orient Point
New Haven
Scranton
Hudson Valley
Long Island
Yonkers
Fire Island Nat. Seashore
Akron
Jersey City
Newark
NEW YORK
Statue of Liberty
Scranton
Allentown
New Brunswick
Long Branch
Lakewood
Pennsylvania
Trenton
Island Beach S.P.
PHILADELPHIA
Lancaster
New Jersey
Hammonton
Harrisburg
York
Elkton
Atlantic City
Gettysburg
Wilmington
Ocean City
Hagerstown
Dover
BALTIMORE
Delaware Bay
Cape May
Frederick
Annapolis
Winchester
Arlington
Delaware
Front Royal
Manassas
WASHINGTON
Ocean City
Skyline Caverns
Washington
Salisbury
Assateague I. Nat.Seashore
Elkins
G.Washington Birthplace Nat.Mon.
Shenandoah N.P.
Fredericksburg
Modest Town
Harrisonburg
Ruckersville
Exmore
Waynesboro
Monticello
Richmond
Williamsburg
Charlottesville
Dixie
Cape Charles Lighthouse
Lewisburg
Pocahontas S.P.
Roanoke
Virginia
Petersburg
Norfolk
Virginia Beach
Lynchburg
Greensboro
Chesapeake
Currituck
Point Harbor
Elizabeth City
Wright Brothers Nat.Mem.
Whalebone
North Carolina
Columbia
Waves
Swanquarter
Cape Hatteras Nat.Seashore
Cape Hatteras Lighthouse
Kinston
Cedar Island
Ocracoke Lighthouse
Kinston
Morehead City
Cape Lookout Nat.Seashore
Jacksonville
Hubert
Cape Lookout Lighthouse
Folkstone

They can lighty climb with callus soles over rocks. You will not run out of steam in the hot deserts nor be gasping for air at heights of 5,000 metres when trecking through the Andes with a large backpack. Lamas are indispensable in South America.

Central and Southern America

Beige sandy deserts, sky-high volcanoes, lush green tropical forests and a turquoise-blue sea: The countries and island countries of Latin America offer fascinating colours and mysterious cult places of bygone civilizations. In the south, a continent of superlatives follows: the longest mountain range in the world, the largest jungle on the planet, the most beautiful of all glaciers – South America is a universe of extremes. The Andes almost touch the sky, while the lightless green of the Amazon forests is unimaginable. In addition, there are lively megacities that reflect the joie de vivre of their inhabitants in addition to the history.

Route 26: Mexico, Guatemala and Belize
Through the Kingdom of the Maya

Culture and beaches all in one – a journey through the Yucatán Peninsula. In the heartland of the Mayan region you can marvel at both ancient pyramids and Spanish-colonial-style baroque towns, while the white sand beaches of the Caribbean offer idyllic relaxation after your adventures.

Route profile:

Length: approx. 1,740 miles
Time required: at least 4 weeks

The name of the peninsula separating the Caribbean Sea from the Gulf of Mexico originally arose from a misunderstanding. When the Spanish conquistadors first set foot on the peninsula at the start of the 16th century they addressed the indigenous people in Spanish. The Maya answered in their language: 'Ma c'ubab than', meaning 'We do not understand your words'. This later became Yucatán.

Three countries lay claim to the Yucatán Peninsula: the north and west belong to Mexico, the south-east coast and Barrier Reef to Belize, and the mountainous south-east to Guatemala. Detours from the route also take you to the most significant

ruins in Honduras – Copán. When the conquistadors arrived in Mexico they discovered a uniquely advanced civilization. The Maya had both a precise calendar and their own alphabet. Their massive constructions – pyramids, palaces, places of worship – are all the more astounding given that the Maya had neither the wheel as a means of transport nor iron, metal implements, winches, pulleys, ploughs, or pack or draught

animals. Mayan ruins are often located in the midst of tropical rainforests, are often overgrown and have only been partly uncovered. Sites that are easily accessible for tourists along the route we suggest here are Chichén Itzá, Tulum, Tikal, Edzná and Uxmal. The city of San Cristóbal de las Casas and the surrounding Indian villages in the south-west of the peninsula, Chiapas (Mexico), provide wonderful insight into the pres-

ent-day life of the descendants of the Maya.

The Indian population of Mexico and Belize makes up around one-tenth of the overall population of each country. In Guatemala, however, half of all citizens are of Indian origin. In Mexico and Guatemala numerous Mayan languages are also still spoken. The Spanish who first landed on the Yucatán Peninsula in 1517 greatly underestimated the scale of Mayan civilization and unfortunately destroyed a large part of their physical culture and records. In their place rose a series of colonial cities from the ruins of older Mayan settlements. The Spanish legacy includes baroque monasteries, cathedrals, palaces and large town plazas. The oldest cathedral in the Americas is in Mérida (1560), Campeche was once the most important harbour on the Yucatán Penin-

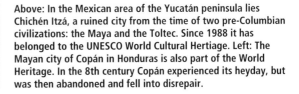

Above: In the Mexican area of the Yucatán peninsula lies Chichén Itzá, a ruined city from the time of two pre-Columbian civilizations: the Maya and the Toltec. Since 1988 it has belonged to the UNESCO World Cultural Hertiage. Left: The Mayan city of Copán in Honduras is also part of the World Heritage. In the 8th century Copán experienced its heyday, but was then abandoned and fell into disrepair.

sula for goods headed to Europe, and there are important monasteries dating back to the 17th and 18th centuries in Antigua, Guatemala.

The route we recommend includes some of the most scenic nature reserves in Central America. On the north-east coast is the Sian Ka'an biosphere reserve (a UNESCO World Heritage Site) covering 4,500 ha (11,120 acres) of jungle and swamp as well as a 100-km-long (62-mile) coral

reef. Belize is home to the Blue Hole National Park and the 300-km-long (186-mile) Belize Barrier Reef (also a UNESCO World Heritage Site). Guatemala is home to the Sierra de Las Minas biosphere reserve. Wild cocoa trees can still be found in the north-east of the peninsula and also in the mountainous regions of the south. Today the east coast, known as the 'Mayan Riviera', is a popular holiday destination – white sand beach-

es and the splendid reef between Cancún in the north and Tulum Playa in the south provide ideal conditions for both snorkelling and diving.

Yet swimming, diving, snorkelling and relaxing on the 'Mayan Riviera' are just some of the many options for an active holiday on the Yucatán Peninsula. If you go for a hike through the often still pristine tropical rainforests of the national parks and nature reserves in the interior of

the peninsula, you will discover an unparalleled wealth of flora and fauna.

Left: The buildings of San Miguel de Allende are outstanding examples of Mexican Baroque. Since 2008, the city has been a UNESCO World Heritage Site, previously it was honoured as a 'Magic Place'. Above: Bright red octopus and horn coral in the Belize Barrier Reef.

The Wizard's Pyramid is one of the most prominent buildings in Uxmal.

Cancún

The modern coastal resort of Cancún lies on the very north-east corner of the Yucatán Peninsula, in the small federal state of Quintana Roo. With its international airport, it is a handy gateway to the rest of the Yucatán Peninsula. Conditions in Cancún are ideal for modern tourism – it has clean, warm, turquoise water all year round, superb white-sand beaches, mild swimming weather and excellent diving along the various coral reefs. Archeologically significant Mayan sites – primarily Chichén Itzá, Uxmal and Tulum – are easy to reach within two or three hours.

Most holidaymakers spend their time on Isla Cancún with its 23-km-long (14-mile) 'zona hotelera'. Near the southern end of Cancún Island is the Mayan site of El Rey with two small pyramids. Two bridges connect the island with Cancún on the mainland with the Laguna Nichupté in between. The resort island of Isla Mujeres off the coast to the north of Cancún was once an idyllic Caribbean island with a romantic atmosphere. In recent years it has succumbed to the pressures of increased travel, but it is still a splendid alternative.

Ferries dock in Playa Linda in Cancún or in Puerto Juárez and Punta Sam north of the town. There are also ferry connections between Cancún and the island of Cozumel in the south where simpler, traditional accommodation can also be found. European explorers first landed on Cozumel in 1518. Within a few decades the island had been almost completely depopulated.

The Yucatán tour goes through Mexico, Guatemala and Belize, with a detour to the ruins of Copán in Honduras. From the idyllic Caribbean beaches you head to the mountainous regions of Guatemala before visiting the Petén rainforest and the magnificent coast of Belize then heading back to the start.

❶ Cancún The journey across the Yucatán Peninsula begins in Cancún on the north-east coast. The town's name derives from the name of the former Mayan settlement 'Can-Cune' ('End of the Rainbow'). Until the beginning of the 1960s Cancún was a tiny fishing village with barely 100 residents. The Mexican government then decided to create an international seaside resort, a project that met with massive success. Today more than 2.5 million tourists visit this town of 300,000 res-idents. South of the town the MEX 180 highway turns towards Mérida. The turn-off to the most architecturally significant Mayan site on the peninsula, Chichén Itzá, is well signposted, 40 km (25 miles) beyond Valladolid.

❷ Chichén Itzá The largest and best preserved pre-Columbian ruins on the Yucatán Peninsula represented an important economic, political and religious centre between the years 400 and 1260, with a population of about 35,000 people. The best-known building at the site is El Castillo, a 24-m-high (79-ft) pyramid. Other buildings worth seeing are the Templo de los Guerreros, the observatory (Caracol) and the Cenote de los Sacrificios, as well as the 168-m-long (180-yd) playing field, the largest of its kind in the whole of Mesoamerica. Four 45° angle steps lead up to the El Castillo platform from where you will have a breathtaking view of the entire site.

Four palace buildings that surround a courtyard form the so-called Nonnenviereck in Uxmal.

Mérida was built in 1542 on the site of the former Maya settlement, Tihó. The town was built in the early 16th century by Franciscan monks and has the appearance of a

The ruined site of Calakmul near Caleche was once a huge city.

town designed at a drafting table. A series of preserved buildings from the Spanish colonial era are worth seeing – the Casa de Montejo (governors' residence), the cathedral San Ildefonso (the oldestinthe Americas – construction began in 1560), the Jesuit church Templo de la Tercera Orden (17th century) and the Iglesia de Santa Lucia. The Palacio de Gobierno (1892), the city hall buildings on the Paseo de Montejo and the Museo de Antropologia e Historia date from the 19th century. Campeche, formerly a Mayan trading centre, also played an important role in the conquest of Yucatán. From the 1550s the Franciscans tried to resettle the Mayan population in 'congregaciones' or 'reducciones' in the region around Campeche. Two gates within the mighty city walls lead to the historic old city which, with its numerous renovated buildings, is a gem of colonial history. Among the loveliest 17th-century buildings is the Casa del Rey.

3 Mérida At the turn of the 19th century, the capital of the Federal state of Yucatán was a centre for the cultivation and production of sisal, a type of hemp. Magnificent town villas, spacious plazas and lovely parks are reminiscent of the town's heyday. Today it is an important industrial and commercial centre.

At Uman, 20 km (12 miles) south of the town, a road branches off from the MEX 180 to the Parque Natural Rio Celestún.

4 Parque Natural Río Celestún It is about 70 km (43 miles) to the small fishing village of Celestún on the Bahia de Campeche coast. In addition to

the white, sandy beaches, the waterfowl living here are the main attraction. Fishermen offer boat trips through the mangroves and to a petrified forest on the Isla de Pájaros.

The same route takes you back towards the MEX 180. In Uman the MEX 261 branches off towards Muna and Uxmal (60 km/37 miles).

5 Uxmal Archaeologists presume that the first stages of construction took place in the year AD 1. The majority of the buildings, however, date back to between the 7th and 10th centuries when parts of the peninsula were ruled from Uxmal.

Uxmal is the best-known example of the Puuc civilization, represented by elongated buildings with attractive courtyards, facades decorated with stone mosaics and the conspicuous lack of cenotes (natural limestone pools) typical of this style. Indeed, it was the ability to build artificial cisterns that enabled the Mayans to settle in this arid region.

Opposite the entrance to Uxmal stands the 35-m (115-ft) 'Fortune Teller's Pyramid', with its oval foundation, dating from the 6th–10th centuries. The steep, 60° staircase up the pyramid has a safety chain for visitors to hold when climbing.

From Muna it is then around 40 km (25 miles) to the MEX 180.

6 Campeche During the colonial era Campeche became an important harbour from which the Spanish shipped wood and other valuable raw materials back to Europe. The mighty city wall was reinforced with eight

The ruins of Chichén Itzá impress visitors with striking large buildings such as the famous Kukulcán pyramid (large picture), the 'church' (top) and warrior sculptures (left side).

Mayan writing

One of the features of an advanced civilization is a distinct system of writing, created once a people have reached a specific level of development. It entails the use of graphic symbols to record and communicate important information.

The Mayans did not invent their writing system themselves. Instead they took it from the original writing of the Olmeken (c. 30 BC). Within 1,000 years they had developed this further and become the only civilization in pre-Columbian America to have a complete writing system comprising of logograms and syllables.

bastions (baluartes) to protect it from constant pirate attacks. From this significant harbour town on the peninsula we then follow the MEX 180S to Champotón, where we turn onto the MEX 261 towards Francisco Escárcega.

7 Calakmul The detour to Calakmul in the Reserva de la Biósfera Calakmul is around 150 km (93 miles).

The reserve protects the largest continuous tropical rainforest area in Mexico and is also host to a number of important Mayan sites – Balamkú, Becán, Xpujil and Calakmul. After around 110 km (68 miles), at Conhuas, a road turns off the two-lane MEX 186 south towards Calakmul. During the rainy season the 60-km (37-mile) surfaced road, first built in 1993, is often passable only with four-wheel-drive vehicles.Although it has not been extensively researched to date, this sprawling settlement, which was continuously inhabited from 500 to 1521, is one of the most important examples of a classic Mayan town and was declared a UNESCO World Heritage Site in 2002.

Until the year 1000 Calakmul was the capital of a former kingdom. Thereafter it served merely as a ceremonial centre. The 50-m (164-ft) pyramid is the highest in Mexico and from the top is a breathtaking view of these overgrown rainforest ruins. There are around 100 pillars spread around the site, but more valuable archaeological treasures such as the priceless jade masks have been moved to the museum in Campeche.

Back in Francisco Escárcega take the MEX 186 to Palenque.

8 Palenque These ruins, covering an area of 6 sq km (4 sq mi), are about 12 km (7.5 miles) outside of town and surrounded by the last sicable area of rainforest on the peninsula. The town, which must have been an important trading centre in the region, experienced its heyday between 600 and 800. One important Mayan ruler is still known by name – Pacal the Great, whose reign coincided with one of the most splendid eras in Mayan history. Today only part of the site is accessible to visitors. Try to plan a whole day for it. Inside the most famous temple, the 20-m (66-ft) Templo de las Inscripciones (Temple of the Inscriptions), sixty steps lead 25 m (83 ft) down into the crypt. Similar to the Egyptian pyramids, the step pyramids of Palenque were also the tombs of rulers. The most valu-

able possessions are now on display in the Museo Nacional de Antropologica in Ciudad de Mexico.

Opposite the Temple of the Inscriptions is the El Palacio, where the royal family lived, while other accessible temples are located on the other side of the Otulum River.

One of the most important discoverers of ancient Mexican culture was the American John Lloyd Stephens, who visited the Yucatán between 1839 and 1841. According to his report, when Stephens first visited Palenque, 'a single Indian footpath' led to the archaeological site. He travelled all over the Yucatán with English draughtsman and architect Frederick Catherwood. Stephens recorded his impressions in travel journals while Catherwood captured his in drawings.

On the way from Palenque to San Cristóbal de las Casas it is worth making a stop at the Agua Azul National Park. The more than 500 waterfalls are especially worthy of their name, 'blue water', during the dry period between April and May. They vary in height from 3 m (10 ft) to an impressive 50 m (164 ft). Beyond Palenque the road climbs gradually into the moun-

The writing, which was very similar to other regional languages, was widespread throughout the entire Mayan lowlands. The oldest complete text was found on pillar 29 in Tikal (AD 292). The written texts, which are mainly preserved on wall panels, door frames, pillars, ceramic pieces and bark, tell of the lives of rulers – births, coronations, marriages, wars and burials. With only a few exceptions, the block-shape hieroglyphics are read in double columns from left to right and from top to bottom. First images were deciphered in 1820. The majority of the works, however, were decoded only after 1950.

tainous area of Montañas del Norte de Chiapas.

9 San Cristóbal de las Casas This lovely little town at an altitude of 2,100 m (6,890 ft) carries the name of the Spanish Bishop of Chiapas, who was especially committed to the interests of the indigenous peoples. Particularly noticeable are the low-slung buildings in the town, a result of constant fear of earthquakes.

San Cristóbal is the centre of one of Mexico's important cocoa-growing areas. The Mayans were already growing the wild plant as a monocrop before the arrival of the Europeans, and even used slave labour to work on their plantations. The striking terrace-like fields on these steep slopes (sometimes at an angle of 45°) date all the way back to the Mayans who built rows of stones running diagonally over the slope in order to fashion fields of up to 50 by 70 m (164 by 230 ft). The fields were enclosed by walls measuring over 1.5 m (5 ft) high.

Many visitors take trips from San Cristóbal into the outlying villages of the Chamula Indians, for example to San Júan Chamula (11 km/7 miles), or to Zinacantán, where the Tzotzil Indians live (8 km/5 miles). Another worthwhile excursion from San Cristóbal is to Cañon El Sumidero, with fantastic views of gloriously coloured craggy cliffs that tower to heights of 1,000 m (3,281 ft). With a bit of luck you might even see crocodiles during a boat trip on the river. From San Cristóbal to Ciudad de Guatemala the route follows the Pan-American Highway, known as the CA1 after the border.

Left: One of the many waterfalls in the Agua Azul National Park. At the top: Temple of Inscriptions in Palenque. Bottom left: Ruins of Palenque from a bird's eye view. Above: Campeche city centre.

San Cristóbal de las Casas

Founded in 1528, San Cristóbal has fortunately been able to retain much of its originality. The heart of the town is the Zócalo, a grand plaza surrounded by old mansions. The western side of the square is dominated by the Palacio de Municipio while the north side hosts the 16th-century Catedral Nuestra Señora de la Asunción with its baroque facade. The terraces of the Templo de Guadalupe and the Templo de San Cristóbal provide impressive views over the town.

Santo Domingo is one of the finest examples of Mexican baroque architecture and an arts and crafts market is held on its terrace. The San Jalobil monastery is involved in preserving the Indian weaving traditions of the surrounding villages.

The Stela K in Quiriguá is dated to the year 805 and display the important Mayan ruler K'ak ,Tiliw Chan Yopaat.

Guatemala's volcanoes

The Central American land bridge, between North and South America, has only existed for a few million years. The North American plate meets the Caribbean plate in Guatemala, where the tectonic fault line runs from west to east right across the country through Montaguatal.
Guatemala also lies directly over a subduction zone where the coconut plate is descending into the earth's mantle below Central America (the North American and

Tolimán volcano at the Atitlan lake.

the Caribbean plate) at a speed of around 6 cm per year. This causes molten magma to rise to the surface. When its gases reach a certain pressure they are discharged in the form of volcanic eruptions, which are often accompanied by earthquakes.
In this tectonically active region, thirty-seven volcanoes can be found in Guatemala The country's highest volcano (and the highest in Central America) is the extinct Tajumulco (4,220 m/13,546 ft) south-west of Huehuetenango. In addition to Acatenango, which last erupted in 1972, there are currently three other active volcanoes named Fuego, Pacaya and Santa Maria.

Around 85 km (53 miles) southeast of San Cristóbal is Comitán de Dominguez. From there you can take an excursion to the Mayan site of Chinkultic. You will reach the border at Paso Hondo after another 80 km (50 miles). On the Guatemalan side a mountain road leads via La Mesilla through the Sierra de los Cuchumatanes to Huehuetenango. The roads in the rugged mountainous regions of Guatemala are generally in bad condition and are often full of potholes. Turning off at Los Encuentros, Lago de Atitlan is one of the featured sights in these highlands.

⑩ Lago de Atitlán Three volcanoes – San Pedro (3,029 m/9,938 ft), Atitlan (3,535 m/11,598) and Toliman (3,158 m/10,361 ft) – are reflected in the water of this alpine lake, which lies at 1,560 m (5,118 ft). Alexander von Humboldt wrote of the beauty of this 130-sq-km (81-sq-mi) azure blue lake, describing it as 'the most beautiful lake in the world'.
There are fourteen Indian villages located around the lake, some of which already existed prior to the arrival of the Spanish conquistadors. Today the residents are farmers or make a liv-

ing from selling traditional handicrafts. The famous Friday market in Solólá, high above the lake on the northern shore, is even frequented by hordes of Indians from the surrounding areas. The largest settlement is Santiago Atitlan at the southern end of the lake. In 1955 the government declared the lake and surrounding mountains a national park. At Los Encuentros a narrow road turns off towards Chichicastenango, 20 km (12 miles) further north.

⑪ Chichicastenango This town, lying at an altitude of 1,965 m (6,447 ft) is characterized by its classic white colonial architecture.
In the pre-colonial era the town was an important Mayan trading centre. Markets are the main attraction and draw residents from the surrounding areas in their colourful traditional costumes, who come to sell their textiles and carvings. In 1540 a Spaniard erected the oldest building in the town on the ruins of a Mayan temple, the Santo-Tomás church.
Each of the eighteen roads leading to it represents a month in the Mayan calendar, which comprised 18 months each with 20 days.

⑫ Antigua This village in Panchoytal is situated in a tectonically active region at the foot of three live volcanoes – Agua (3,766 m/12,356 ft), Fuego (3,763 m/12,346 ft) and Acatenango (3,975 m/13,042 ft). In 1541, mud-slides from Agua destroyed the town of Ciudad de Santiago de los Caballeros founded by the Spanish in 1527, but it was rebuilt further north in 1543. Numerous religious orders settled in this Central American capital where monasteries, schools and churches were erected.
However, only parts of the Catedral de Santiago (1545) with its five naves have survived the earthquakes of the subsequent centuries. Nuestra Señora la Merced is one of the most attractive examples of the Churrigueresque style. Together with the Palacio de los Capitanes Generales and the Palacio del Ayuntamiento, the Capuchin monastery Las Capuchinas is an impressive example of Spanish colonial architecture. The town was destroyed by strong earthquakes in 1717 and 1773, but the Spanish rebuilt it as La Nueva Guatemala and it later became present-day Ciudad de Guatemala. The previous capital was then simply called Antigua. In 1979 the old city, which in the 18th

It is not known who is depicted on Stele C in Quiraguá; the face is worked as a high relief, the body as a low relief.

Detour

Copán

Copán, the southernmost of the Mayan towns close to the Honduran settlement of Copán Ruinas, lies on a promontory at 620 m (2,034 ft). Densely forested mountains surround the ruins on the Copán River, discovered by the Spaniard Diego Garcia de Palacio in the late 16th century. In 1576 he sent a report of his findings to the Spanish king, Philip II. By the time John Lloyd Stephens wanted to visit the Mayan town of Copán in 1839, none of the

'The Old Man' sculpture in the ruins of Copán.

residents in surrounding villages was able to answer his questions about the ruins. Copán appears to have been one of the oldest and most important Mayan religious sites. According to archaeologist estimates, the town had as many as 40,000 inhabitants. Copán's 'Acropolis', said to have been 600-m-long (1,969-ft) and 300-m-wide (1,086-ft) included pyramids, temples and plazas. The pillars, some of which were as high as 3 m (11 ft), are among the most impressive examples of Mayan sculpture. Copán had already been abandoned 500–600 years prior to the Spanish. Skeletons found in Copán indicate malnutrition and chronic illness.

century was one of the most beautiful baroque ensembles of the Spanish colonial era, and which still retains a great deal of flair today, was declared a UNESCO World Heritage Site.

⑬ Ciudad de Guatemala
The rebuilding of the residential town for the Spanish governor took place at a safer distance of 45 km (30 miles). Today, La Nueva Guatemala de la Asunción is still the economic and political centre of Guatemala. It lies at 1,480 m (4,856 ft) and is the seat of several universities. The main sightseeing attractions include the cathedral (1782–

1809), the National Palace (1939–43) and the Archaeological Museum. Another important Mayan site is located in Tazumal, not far from Santa Ana in El Salvador, roughly 200 km (124 miles) away.
From the capital it is about 150 km (93 miles) on the CA9 to Rio Hondo where the asphalt CA10 takes you via Zacapa, Chiguimula and Vado Hondo to the border post at El Florido. About 12 km (7.5 miles) beyond the Guatemala-Honduras border is Copán. On the return journey along the same road, about 70 km (43 miles) beyond Rio Hondo, you reach another UNESCO

World Heritage Site – the ruins of Quiriguá.

⑭ Quiriguá This Mayan town on the lower Rio Motagua saw its heyday between 500 and 800. Its layout is very similar to that of Copá, only 50 km (31 miles) away. Explorer John Lloyd Stephens discovered Quiriguá in 1840. Today the archaeological site at the edge of the Sierra del Espiritu Santo is still

Top: The three volcanoes form an impressive backdrop to Lago de Atitlan in the Guatemalan highlands.
Above: Archway in Antigua.

The ruined site in Altun Ha includes 300 discovered buildings, 13 of them temples and two main squares.

surrounded by thick jungle, and this is a major part of its attraction. The large mythical creatures carved in stone and the pillars measuring over 10 m (33 ft) in height, which constitute a high point of Mayan sculpture, are among the special attractions here. The highest pillar, E, is 10.5 m (34 ft) high and weighs 65 tonnes (71.5 tons). Approximately 45 km (28 miles) beyond Quiriguá you leave the CA9 and turn to the north-west towards Lago de Izabal. The lake, 590 sq km (367 sq mi) in size, is surrounded by dense rainforest. Between the largest lake in Guatemala and the Rio Dulce, lined by rainforest, is the Spanish Fort Castillo de San Felipe. The fortress was originally constructed in 1595 to defend the arsenals on the eastern shore of the lake from the repeated attacks of determined pirates plying the broad river.

The national road CA13 now crosses the foothills of the Sierra de Santa Cruz and continues via Semox into the lowlands of Petén. The small town of Flores on an island in Lago Petén Itzá is a good starting point for a visit to Tikal.

⑮ Tikal National Park This 576-sq-km (358-sq-mi) national park is surrounded by dense forest and includes one of the most important Mayan sites on the peninsula. Together, the park and rainforest, one of the largest continuous forests in Central America with over 2,000 plant varieties, has been declared a UNESCO World Heritage Site. Between 600 BC and AD 900 as many as 55,000 people lived in Tikal. Today, many of the 4,000 temples, palaces, houses and playing fields are buried under the encroaching forest.

A climb up one of the pyramids, the most important of which are on the Gran Plaza, gives visitors an impressive view of the 16-sq-km (10-sq-mi) Tikal National Park. The Jaguar Temple, some 45 m (148 ft) high, houses a burial chamber where the ruler Ah Cacao lies at rest. From Flores it is about 100 km (62 miles) to the border with Belize, and from there it is another 50 km (31 miles) to Belmopan, which has been the capital of Belize since 1970.

⑯ Guanacaste National Park 3 km (2 miles) north of Belmopan is the 20-ha (49-acre) national park named after the Guanacaste tree (Tubroos). It grows in the south of the park and is one of the largest tree types in Central America. The tree species in the park also include mahogany, the national tree of Belize. South of Belmopan is the Blue Hole National Park, on the road to Dangriga.

⑰ Blue Hole National Park This 2.3-ha (5.7-acre) national park is a popular leisure area for the residents of Belmopan. Large areas of the park contain cave formations and are covered by dense rainforest. Sightseeing attractions include the 33-m (108-ft) collapsed crater that feeds a tributary of the Sibun River. It flows briefly above ground before disappearing into an extensive underground cave system. The 7.5-m (25-ft) 'blue hole' takes its name from its sapphire blue colour. Also within the park is St Herman's Cave, also used by the Mayans as evidenced by the ceramics, spears and torches that have been found inside.

⑱ Belize City Until 1970, Belize City was the capital of the former British Honduras. Today it is still the largest city in the country as well as an important seaport. St John Cathedral, the oldest Anglican cathedral in Central America, was built in 1812 from bricks that sailing ships from Europe had used as ballast.

The British Governor lived at Government House starting in 1814 (today it is the House of Culture museum). The city is an ideal base for excursions to the Belize Barrier Reef, a renowned diving paradise.

⑲ Belize Barrier Reef System The 300-km (186-mile) Barrier Reef is one of the longest in the northern hemisphere.

The many islands and cays off the coast are covered with mangroves and palms. The cays that are within reach include Ambergris Cay some 58 km (36 miles) north of Belize City as well as the Turneffe Islands.

The reef's main attraction is its underwater world, with visibility of up to 30 m (98 ft), the bird reserve, Half Moon Cay and the Blue Hole, a massive collapsed cave.

⑳ Altun Ha The ruins of Altun Ha are close to the village of Rockstone Pond. It is postulated that this Mayan ceremonial centre was originally settled over 2,000 years ago.

The Mayans built up much of their trading around Altun Ha. The most valuable finds from Altun Ha include a jade head of

The Tomb of the Sun God is one of the many temples of Altun Ha.

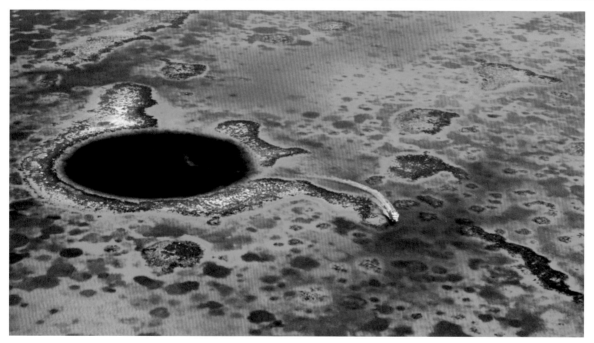

the Mayan Sun god that weighs 4.5 kg (9.9 lbs). Via Orange Walk the road continues through the lowlands of Belize to the Mexican harbour town of Chetumal and along the second largest lake in Mexico, Laguna de Bacalar (MEX 307), to Felipe Carrillo Puerto. Here an access road branches off to the Sian Ka'an biosphere reserve.

㉑ Tulum This ancient Mayan town is a popular destination on the peninsula, primarily due to its spectacular location on a cliff overlooking the sea.

The conquistadors were impressed by its imposing and protective walls. Five narrow gates opened the way into town. Outside the walls there were two ancient Mayan temple sites

north of town. Tulum has always had a safe harbour from which pilgrims in the pre-Columbian era once travelled to the island of Cozumel to honour the Moon god Ixchel with sacrifices.

After 1540 Tulum was engulfed by tropical vegetation and forgotten until 1840. From Tulum there is a road leading to the small fishing village of Punta Al-

The Blue Hole in Belize's Barrier Reef is 80 km (50 miles) east of Belize City. Charles Darwin had already provided a description of the reefs back in 1842. About 10,000 years ago a cave collapsed here as land sank into the sea. The hole has a diameter of 300 m (984 ft) and is 125 m (410 ft) deep.

The Gran Cenote at Tulum is one of the most popular dive sites with its stalactite formations.

Detour

Reserva de la Biósfera Sian Ka'an

This biosphere reserve on the east coast of the Yucatán Peninsula close to Tulum (declared a UNESCO World Heritage Site in 1987) covers around 100 km (62 miles) of beach as well as coral reefs, bays and lagoons.

In the Mayan language the name Sian Ka'an means 'the origin of the heavens'.

Tropical rainforest, mangroves and swamps are all close together here and there is a large reef off the coast. Beyond the underwater world, there are numerous bird and reptile species to be observed as well.

The biosphere reserve even provides an optimal habitat for crocodiles.

len in the Reserva de la Biósfera Sian Ka'an. In the forest 48 km (30 miles) north-west of Tulum you can visit another ruins complex – Cobá.

22 Cobá You can reach the site of the ruins on the well-made road in half an hour. US archaeologists began the first excavations of the complex (210 sq km/ 130 sq mi) in the 1920s, and further excavation projects that are still going on today began in the 1970s.

Cobá also has a pyramid. From the top you can see smaller pyramids, temples, a series of procession streets, a playing field, pillars with life-size images of kings and queens, and of course dense forest.

In Cobá you can see peccaris (wild pigs), iguanas, tortoises and the colourful toucan. The 130-km (81-mile) stretch of coast between Tulum and Cancún is also known as the 'Mayan Riviera'.

Small villages and bays such as Puerto Morelos provide swimming and diving opportunities for water enthusiasts. The famous seaside resort of Playa del Carmen is only a few kilometres south of the more upmarket Cancún, which is the start and end point of this round trip through the Yucatán Peninsula.

Top: Cobá with its temples, pyramids and palaces was built around the lagoon bearing the same name.
Above: Due to its idyllic positioning on a hill by the sea, the Mayan ruins near Tulum seem almost like a modern holiday resort.

Cancún With its magnificent beaches and tropical climate the former fishing village in the north-east of the Yucatán has become Mexico's most popular holiday destination. With 20,000 beds and all-night entertainment options, more than 2.5 million tourists visit the giant hotel town each year.

Uxmal The 'Fortune Teller's Pyramid' is a highlight of Mayan architecture. The name dates back to the Spanish era.

Mérida The 'white town' was founded in the 16th century. At its centre are the Montejo Palast and the cathedral.

Palenque This archaeological site in the middle of the rainforest is among the most attractive in Mexico. Many of the buildings date from the reign of King Pacal and his son, Chan Balum.

Lago de Atitlán This lake in the highlands of Guatemala (1,560 m/5,118 ft) is tucked between the San Pedro, Atitlan and Toliman volcanoes.

Antigua The Spanish Governor used to rule Central America from this Guatemalan town. A number of baroque churches and palaces from the Spanish colonial era survived the earthquakes of 1717 and 1773.

Tazumal Close to Santa Ana in El Salvador is the country's oldest Mayan settlement. The ruins of the 10-sq-km (6-sq-mi) complex with five temples were first cleared only 40 years ago.

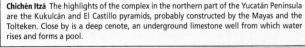

Chichén Itzá The highlights of the complex in the northern part of the Yucatán Peninsula are the Kukulcán and El Castillo pyramids, probably constructed by the Mayas and the Tolteken. Close by is a deep cenote, an underground limestone well from which water rises and forms a pool.

Tikal These ruins, buried in the jungle in the heart of the Mayan lowlands in present-day Guatemala, have inspired awe in many a visitor. Gustav Bernoulli discovered the ruins in 1877.

Route 27: Peru and Bolivia

The Inca Trail

The Inca Trail connects the capitals of Peru and Bolivia and passes through culturally and historically significant sites in the highlands of the Andes Mountains. Travellers will be amazed by magnificent monuments dating back to early Inca civilization and Spanish colonial times.

Route profile:

Length: approx. 2,000 km (1,243 miles), excluding detours
Time required: 3 weeks
When to go: The best time for travelling to the Andes is during the southern hemisphere winter (May to September), as the southern summer (December to March) is the rainy season.

The Inca Trail begins in the Peruvian capital of Lima, extends through the western cordilleras (range) of the Andes and runs right across Peru to Lake Titicaca. From there, one of the most spectacular routes in the whole of South America travels over Bolivian territory through the basin scenery of the Altiplano to the south-east and finally terminates in the eastern cordilleras of the Andes, in Sucre, the country's constitutional capital.

A fascinating natural environment, protected in a number of national parks such as the Parque Nacional Manú, provides a stunning backdrop for the region's cultural treasures.
At the beginning of the 16th century, before the arrival of the Spanish, the Inca Empire covered almost the entire Andes region, including parts of the An-

dean foreland. A large number of the architectural treasures of this advanced civilization have been preserved along the Inca Trail. The architectural highlights include spectacular temples and palaces as well as a series of fortresses built at impressively shrewd locations. Most of these huge buildings, such as the large sun temple at

Cuzco, were also built without significant technological assistance. A prime example of the strategic locations selected for Inca settlements is Machu Picchu, an extraordinary terraced site and one of the Inca's last places of refuge from advancing colonial troops. Ironically, the Spanish never actually discovered this well-hidden settle-

Top: A view of the ruins of Machu Picchu, a glorious terraced Inca city in the high Andes. Left: Llamas, which can have many different colours, are very common in the South American Andes.

ment, which lies at around 2,800 m (9,187 ft). It was an American explorer who first discovered it in 1911. However, the discovery brought with it more riddles than answers regarding Inca culture. Lake Titicaca, which still has a healthy fish population, straddles the Peru-Bolivia border. It lies 3,812 m (12,507 ft) above sea level and is not only

the largest lake in South America, it is also the highest navigable lake in the world. Close to its southern shores is the town of Tiahuanaco (also known as Tiwanaku) which, up until the 10th century, was the religious and administrative centre of an important pre-Columbian civilization. The natural environment in the region around Lake Titi-

caca is also spectacular. Some of the highest mountains in the Andes are here, including the 6,880-m (22,573-ft) Nevado del Illimani south-east of Bolivia's largest city and administrative capital, La Paz. Numerous remnants of the Spanish colonial era can also be seen here, in particular in the area around Lago de Poopó. The Europeans were especially interested in the mineral wealth of the 'New World', and many Indians were forced to work as slaves in Spanish mines, many of them losing their lives in the process. At the beginning of the 17th century Potosí was the world's most important centre for silver mining. As a result of its historical significance the town has been declared a World Heritage Site, together with Cuzco, Machu Picchu and the Old Town in Lima. The distinction is intended for both the time-honoured Inca

sites and for some of the architectural achievements of the Spanish colonial rulers.
In addition to these cultural and historical features, the diverse natural environment in this South American region has also been given its share of attention – the Manú National Park, in the transition zone between the Amazon lowlands and the middle Andes, has also been declared a UNESCO World Heritage Site. With its dramatic differences in altitude, the Inca Trail provides a wonderful cross-section not only of Peru and the northern reaches of Bolivia, but also of the history and natural environment of an entire continent.

Left side: Lake Titicaca is one of the examples of Bolivia's wonderful nature. Right side: Men at Inca celebrations at the winter solstice.

Pachacámac

Pachacámac was a popular pilgrimage destination as far back as the 9th century – long before the advance of the Inca. The sites are around 30 km (19 miles) south-east of Lima and are still shrouded in legend. Pilgrims covered great distances on difficult routes to come and consult the oracle. Interestingly, Pachacámac lost none of its mystery following the Inca invasion in the

The Inca Trail runs from Lima on the Peruvian Pacific coast through countless Andean passes, majestic mountains and high plateaus on its way to Sucre in Bolivia. The route features both desert landscapes and tropical rainforests as well as high mountain lakes. The well-preserved Inca ruins make the journey an unforgettable experience.

1 Lima Our journey begins in the largest city on the Inca Trail, where traffic is characterized by the expected noise and chaos of a large urban centre. Lima was founded by the Spanish in 1535 and they quickly established it as the focal point of their colonial empire in South America. In 1826 Lima replaced Cuzco as the capital and grew into a wealthy metropolis.

Some of the most magnificent buildings from this era – both palaces and churches – have since been beautifully restored to their original glory. The main cathedral (1535–1625) is located on Plaza San Martín in the historic Old Town, which itself has been declared a World Heritage Site in its entirety. The tomb of the conqueror Francisco Pizarro, the founder of Lima, is also said to be somewhere in the city. Lima is a junction for important transcontinental routes such as the Pan-American Highway. When you leave Lima heading east you will unfortunately encounter few inviting locations. Due to significant migration from the countryside, sprawling slums have developed on the outskirts of the city. Road conditions in the outer areas can

15th century. On the contrary, not only did the new rulers take over the existing temples, they also extended the site to include the 80-m-high (262-ft) sun pyramid. Pachacámac subsequently became one of the most important administrative centres in the Inca Empire. The excellent condition of the ruins is particularly remarkable.

Remains of a pyramid in Pachacámac.

be very bad at times. The multi-lane Pan-American Highway runs past these outskirts before heading south towards Pachacámac. You will soon leave the coastal flats as the road climbs quickly into the Andean foothills toward the market town of La Oroya. There are some steep, winding sections here. From there a detour (64 km/40 miles) heads north to Junín. Several memorials here commemorate the battle of Junín in 1824 between Simon Bolívar's troops and Spanish soldiers, one of many South American battles for independence.

The journey then continues through the narrow Mantaro valley towards Huáncayo.

2 Huáncayo The Mantaro Valley is renowned for its numerous pre-Columbian ruins. It ends in Huáncayo, the largest town in the region. Maize, potatoes and vegetables are grown outside the town using irrigation and in some places the allotments seem to stretch beyond the horizon.

Huáncayo, at an altitude of roughly 3,350 m (10,991 ft), is an important regional trading centre. Today there is little left as a reminder that the town was once a centre of the Inca Empire. It is now characterized by Spanish colonial architecture.

The route now heads along a valley towards the south and the climate becomes milder with the decreasing altitude. Prickly pears grow right up to the roadside, their fruit highly prized by the Peruvians.

3 Ayacucho This city, at an elevation of 2,760 m (9,056 ft), is an interesting combination of past and present. Ayacucho was at one time the capital of the Huari Empire, one of the first advanced civilizations in the Andes and, as such, a predecessor to the Incas.

The city was discovered and refounded in 1539 by Francisco Pizarro. It is known as the 'City of 33 churches' and religious ceremonies play an important role here. The Holy Week processions (Semana Santa) are among the most important of their kind in South America, drawing visitors from all parts of the country.

4 Huari Approximately 22 km (14 miles) north-east of Ayacucho is Huari, once the centre of the culture of the same name (6th–12th centuries). Nearly 100,000 people lived here during the heyday of the Huari Empire in the 9th century. The city was carefully planned and the grid-like layout of the streets can still be seen today. The well-organized Huari armies had a history of subordinating enemy peoples, but the city was ultimately abandoned in the 10th century.

Back on the main route we now head east past more Andean peaks towards Cuzco, the red

Left top: The Plaza de Armas in the popular tourist destination Cuzco. Bottom left: Cathedral in Lima. Above: Inside the Cathedral Santo Domingo in Cuzco.

Detour

Inca architecture

Where they came from is uncertain, but it is beyond dispute that the Inca's architectural legacy is the most magnificent on the South American continent. Their monumental buildings are considered the most important cultural achievements of the Inca, despite the fact that the craftsmen of this advanced Indian civilization had no significant technological aids at their disposal. Today it still seems barely conceivable that huge blocks of stone could be worked so smoothly without the use of metal tools, much less assembled without the use

ed to remote, nearly inaccessible locations at high altitudes, such as Machu Picchu. The remains of Inca architecture can also be found in the beautiful city of Cuzco and a number of other places. All the sites have in common a high degree of functionality (even the religious buildings) and a simplicity of decoration. One essential function of the monumental buildings was to intimidate enemies. To this end, the Inca secured their settlements with mighty walls. Despite, or perhaps because of the aura of magic that still pervades their architecture today, Inca architecture is among the best researched architecture of the pre-Columbian era.

of joints. And yet it was not just individual houses, temples, palaces and tombs that were built. Whole cities were constructed without even the use of the wheel. Furthermore, the materials often had to be transported

Top: Fort Sacsayhuaman, built from boulders near Cuzco, was the site of the biggest battle between the Spaniards and Incas. Above: Ruin site in Cuzco.

Valle Sagrado de los Incas

One of the most revered destinations on a journey through Peru is the Sacred Valley of the Incas, best reached via Pisac. The Span-ish name for the central section of the Urubamba Valley, Valle Sagrado de los Incas, refers to its fertile soils – and it's no surprise. The mild climate and the protect-ed location made it possible for the Inca to make incredibly pro-ductive use of the land. It was here, between Pisac and Ollanta, that the foundation for this ad-vanced Indian civilization was formed. It was here that the staple crops were cultivated and the seeds sold for distribution throughout the country. And it is here that evidence still indicates the sophisticated methods used by the Incas to work the land. The steep slopes were laboriously ter-raced in order to grow staple crops like potatoes, maize and

tiled roofs of which can be seen from miles away.

5 Cuzco For many travellers, Cuzco is one of the most impor-tant destinations in Peru. With its scenic location in the Andes, relaxed atmosphere, easy access to its attractions, and especially as a base for tours to the Urubamba Valley and Machu Picchu, the city is indeed a high-light along the Inca Trail.

For the Incas, Cuzco was the fo-cal point of their empire and therefore the centre of the world as they knew it. They estab-lished the city as a political, re-ligious and cultural hub. Upon their arrival the Spanish knew of the city's importance but were dazzled by its wealth and grandeur. Unlike other Inca strongholds, the Spanish de-stroyed only a few of the build-ings when they invaded Cuzco, and only the most significant structures with political or reli-gious functions were razed. On those foundations the colonial rulers then erected a series of their own buildings, some state-ly in scale, others of religious importance.

The Plaza de Armas, for exam-ple, was constructed on the site of the former main square, Hua-caypata, at the time 600 m (1,969 ft) long. Santo Domingo monastery was built from the ru-ins of the Coricancha sun tem-ple. The Jesuit church La Com-pañía (1571) was constructed on the foundations of the grand Inca palace, Huayna Capac.

In 1950, parts of the city were destroyed by a strong earth-quake. Fortuitously, however, the quake actually unearthed a number of Inca remains that had been previously hidden from view.

Cuzco's importance remains un-changed for the descendants of the Inca. The Quechua-speaking Indians hold colourful ceremo-nies in the city, in which the cus-toms and traditions of their fore-bearers are relived, and yet Christian festivals are also cele-

quinoa. Land in this region was thus made available for agriculture.These fields are still worked by family groups to this day. The villages, which seem to have remained untouched by the passing of time, are further testimony to the Sacred Valley's cultural legacy – dusty roads between simple adobe houses, wobbly wooden stands at the markets and people in traditional costumes retain the valley's authenticity. But it was not always so tranquil here. This valley was the scene of bloody battles between the Inca and Spanish invaders.

Salt mining has been carried out in the Sacred Valley of the Incas for centuries.

attraction in the Cuzco area. Today it is assumed that the fortress was built to control the most vulnerable entrance to the city. The complex includes a number of store rooms for food and an armory for weapons. During the Spanish invasion, hundreds of Inca warriors barricaded themselves within the walls of Sacsayhuamán, right up until the bitter end. In addition to the heavy fighting, strong earthquakes have also caused significant damage to the structure. Today only about one-third of the fortress remains.

7 Pisac On a 32-km-long (20-mile) detour to the north you are led along a scenic road via the cult site Kenko, the 'Red Fortress' (Puca Pucara), and the sacred spring of Tambo Machay in the idyllic village of Pisac, which can be reached by a metal bridge. Inca influences clash here with colonial era flair. Market days in Pisac are full of activity. Souvenirs such as flutes, jewellery, and clothing made from llama wool are traded on the central plaza. Just as attractive, however, are the ruins of an Inca ceremonial site located 600 m (1,969 ft) above the village.

8 Ollantaytambo At the end of the Sacred Valley, 19 km (12 miles) beyond the main town of Urubamba, is the village of Ollanta (2,800 m/9,187 ft), named after Ollantay, an Inca military leader. The fortress, with its spectacular stone terraces, stands on a bluff above the village. The Inca began construction on the well-fortified complex in 1460, but the project took much longer than planned. Ollantaytambo was not yet complete when the Spanish attacked

brated with enthusiasm. The annual Corpus Christi processions in particular attract much attention.
In 1983 the Old Town was declared a UNESCO World Heritage Site.

6 Sacsayhuamán Situated above Cuzco – about 3 km (2 miles) north of the city – are the remains of a mighty fortress. Between 1440 and 1532 the Inca built an imposing citadel here encircled by three concentric walls.
Sacsayhuamán can be reached on foot from Cuzco in just under half an hour. The path leads from the Plaza de Armas via the Calle Suecia, past San Cristobal church and via the old Inca path up to the fortress.
In their time the stone blocks, which are up to 5 m (16 ft) high and weigh 200 tonnes (220 tons), intimidated many a would-be attacker and thus fulfilled their purpose as a demonstration of the power of their owners. The fortress is a main

Above: Terraced hills near Pisac. Left side: Woman in traditional costume with lama and ruins of Ollantaytambo.

Detour

Manú National Park

Some 100 km (62 miles) north of Cuzco is the Manú National Park (15,300 sq km/9,507 sq mi) in the area between the Amazon lowlands and the Andes. Due to the changes in altitude here, from 400–4,000 m (1,312–13,124 ft), the range of habitats extends from tropical lowland rainforest to mountain and cloud forest to highland steppe. The fauna is equally diverse. In addition to some 800 bird, 200 mammal and 120 fish species, there are also countless insect species. As a result, the area was declared a National Park in 1973 and a UNESCO World Heritage Site in 1987.
To protect its flora and fauna, the national park has only minimal road infrastructure, but it is not empty of people. There are about thirty villages here. Approach the park via Paucartambo and the Acjanacu Pass to the mountain village of Atalaya on the Río Alto Madre de Dios. From here, boats bring visitors to Boca Manú, at the edge of the area open to tourists.

Biodiversity in the Parque Nacional Manú: Squirrel monkeys, ocelot and green winged macaws.

On the terraces in Tipón, the Incas tested which plants thrived best and at what altitude.

in 1523. Despite that, residents of Ollanta are still enjoying the benefits of the irrigation system developed back then by the Inca. Even during the dry season there was, and is, enough water available for agriculture.

Costumes worn by local residents are especially eye-catching and have hardly changed from those worn by their forefathers 500 years ago. The last few metres to the fortress have to be covered on foot. While the landscape in the Cuzco hinterland is characterized by sparse vegetation, the scenery changes drastically as you head towards Machu Picchu. It becomes more tropical and the monotone flora of the highlands gives way to dense rainforest. The road starts to wind pretty heavily now, with tight curves and an occasionally hair-raising climb up to the 'City of Clouds'.

⑨ Machu Picchu The 'City of Clouds', as Machu Picchu is also known, is about 80 km (50 miles) north-west of Cuzco. Surrounded by imposing mountains and set in the midst of a dense forest is the most significant and fascinating archaeological site in South America. It is spectacularly located on a high mountain ridge nearly 600 m (1,969 ft) above the Urubamba River. There is hardly any other site where the technical and mechanical skills of the Inca are demonstrated more tangibly than Machu Picchu, and it is therefore no surprise that the site was declared a UNESCO World Heritage Site in 1983. It is also no surprise that myths and legends still surround this magical place today.

In fact, its very origins remain unknown. It is assumed that Machu Picchu was built in the 15th century. One theory holds that Machu Picchu served as a place of refuge during the Spanish invasion. Another theory supposes that the Inca relocated their political centre to this barely vis-

ible and even more inaccessible site. One thing remains certain, however – the colonial Spanish were fully unaware of the existence of this city. The site was first discovered in 1911.

The city's structure is still easily recognizable. Stone houses comprise one room only and are arranged around small courtyards. What might appear simple at first is in fact the result of considerable technical and mechanical skill on the part of the builders. The structures are grouped around a central, more or less quadratic formation. The most striking buildings include the temple tower, or Torreon, and the Sintihuatana sun temple, with seventy-eight stone steps leading up to it.

From Machu Picchu you first need to return to Pisac via the same road, where another road then branches off toward Huambutiyo. On a narrow, gravel road you will then come to Paucartambo and Atalaya, jumping-off point for a visit to the Manú National Park. From Pisac back on the Inca Trail you soon branch off onto a sign-posted side road heading north to Tipón. The gravel road here is typically in good condition. After about 4 km (2.5 miles) you will reach the ruins of the old city of Tipón at an altitude of about 3,500 m (11,454 ft).

⑩ Tipón Especially noteworthy here are the well-preserved terraces, where a sophisticated system of irrigation still enables productive cultivation of the land. It is now surmised that the Inca used the site as an experimental area for acclimatizing plants that otherwise only grew in lower-lying areas.

On the onward journey from Tipón towards the south-east you pass the little village of Andahuaylillas where the 17th-century baroque church is worth a brief visit. The peak of Nudo Ausandate towers 6,400 m (20,998 ft) above you on the left.

⑪ Raqchi Located at the base of the Quinsachata volcano, this town hosts an important traditional festival every year on the 3rd Sunday of June. From a distance, the temple, which is dedicated to Viracocha, the most important Inca god, resembles a viaduct because of its 15-m-high (49-ft) walls. It provides an impressive backdrop for the festivities.

⑫ Sillustani The well-built road from Raqchi now leads south-east towards Lake Titicaca. Near the northern shore of the lake a road branches off to the right towards one of the archi-

tectural attractions on this section of the route – the burial mounds of Sillustani, a peninsula on Lake Umayo.

The mounds, known as chullpas, were constructed out of clay in the pre-Inca era and are up to 12 m (39 ft) high.

They served as the burial sites of regional rulers. Some chullpas seem to defy gravity, with base diameters smaller than those of their tops.

Above: You can hike the Inca Trail along the slopes. Right: The ruins of the famous Machu Picchu.

In some places, the Inca Trail through the greenery is paved with stones.

The condor

A lonely figure circling high above the peaks of the Andes – zologically one of the New World vultures, in the old world the condor was considered the symbol of South America. It is one of the largest volant birds in the world and its wing-span can reach more than 3 m (10 ft). Its black plumage and fluffy white ruff are especially striking. Condors do not build an eyrie. Instead they lay their only egg in a rock crevice. The carcasses of larger mammals are their main source of food.

Hardly any animal is as symbolic of South America as the Andean condor nesting on rocks.

Reed construction on Lake Titicaca

In addition to the 'stationary' islands in Lake Titicaca there are also a number of 'floating' islands. They were constructed by the Uros people, fishermen who lived on them out on the lake. The Uros built these islands, which are named after them, out of reeds, a raw material that is readily available on the shores of the lake.

Initially they simply built the foundations of their houses on land using rushes mixed with soil. With the lake's rising water level, however, they had to keep raising the level of the foundations until some houses began to float on the lake during times of flooding.

Since this had advantages for fishing, the Uros decided to make a virtue out of necessity since this way of life also provided protection against attacks by the Inca.

It is known that the material for the burial mounds comes from quarries near the lake. Particularly noticeable here, too, is the precise working of the stone blocks, which were put together without the use of joints.

It is possible to drive around Lake Titicaca to the north and the south, and both roads run close to the shores almost all the way. You will reach Puno after about 32 km (20 miles) on the southern route of the Inca Trail.

🔞 **Puno** The location of this town, directly on Lake Titicaca, is striking enough in itself, giving you the impression that you are at the coast. Puno is considered to be a cradle of Inca civilization. One legend has it that the first Inca rose from the lake here to create the empire. The surrounding area used to be ruled from Tiahuanaco.

Puno, at an elevation of 3,830 m (12,566 ft), was founded by the Spanish in 1668 and quickly equipped with a number of Christian churches intended to evangelize the Indians living here. Part of this religious centre remains today. Many Peruvians associate Puno with colourful folklore. Every year in February, residents stage one of the most well-known festivals in the country, named after the Virgen de la Candelaria. Lively markets are held on the Plaza Mayor, which is flanked by the cathedral completed in 1757. Boats depart from Puno's harbour to some of the islands on the lake. The region around the city is used intensively for agriculture, and pastures for the llama and alpaca herds extend almost to the edge of the road. After a short drive you will reach Chucuito, a village with two colonial churches and an Inca fertility temple.

🔞 **Lake Titicaca** This is a lake in a class of its own. With a sur-

When invasion threatened, the Uros retreated to their floating islands on Lake Titicaca. However, the reeds served the Uros not only as 'foundations', they also used them to make their boats. The descendants of the Uros now live on the lake shores and the floating islands have become popular tourist destinations.

Even today, on Lake Titicaca 'Tunupas', boats made of reeds, are being built.

Inti Raymi

The Spanish invaders may have destroyed the Inca Empire but the descendents of this advanced Indian civilization maintain many of the customs and traditions of their forebearers. The result of this is that many of the festivities and rituals have survived to this day.

The most well-known event is the solstice festival, Inti Raymi, which the Indian residents of Peru celebrate in Cuzco every year on 24 June. This date marks the winter solstice in the southern hemisphere. On this, the shortest day of the year, people traditionally brought the sun back to earth with symbolic bonfires. They also celebrated the harvest and the start of the new solar year. Wearing colourful costumes and headdresses, they made sacrifices to the Sun god, Inti. The present-day ceremony is still reminiscent of the sun worship of the early Inca Empire. Celebrations begin at the sun temple and then continue on the main square. The main ceremony takes place in the Sacsayhuamán fortress near Cuzco.

Admittedly, sacrifices are now less spectacular than in the days of the Incas. Today only one white and one black llama are sacrificed. During colonial rule the festival was forbidden. Spanish rulers suppressed the Inca's cultural traditions for fear of an outbreak of resistance.

Times have changed, however, and the festival has become a modern event. The once religious ceremony is now a grand spectacle where music groups come from all over to play the old folk songs. Yet despite the commercialization, Inti Raymi reflects the great importance of sun worship among the Inca. The ceremonies are also all held in Quechua, the Inca language, a fact that reinforces the immense importance of these traditions for the identity of Peru's Indian residents.

face area of 8,300 sq km (5,158 sq mi), Lake Titicaca is the largest lake in South America and the border of Peru and Bolivia runs right through it. The water level lies at 3,812 m (12,507 ft). But it is not only these record features that characterize this unique body of water. The scenery and the remains of Inca civilization in the area around the crystal-clear 'Andean Sea' constitute the real attraction of the lake, which belongs to both Peru and Bolivia. Ruins and ritual sites exist on the Isla del Sol (Island of the Sun) as well, which rises nearly 200 m (656 ft) out of the lake. The Incas created a variety of myths that proclaimed the island as their place of origin. The Templo del Sol (sun temple) in particular, situated on the highest point of the island, is still shrouded in mystery.

Isla de la Luna (Island of the Moon) is also worth a brief visit. In addition to the 'stationary' islands there is also a series of 'floating' islands, designed by the Uros people in the pre-Inca era and still surviving today (see sidebar on the right).

⑮ **Copacabana** Turn off the southern coastal road to the border town of Yunguyo. On the Bolivian side, between the Cerro Calvarío and Cerro Sancollani mountains, is the fishing village of Copacabana, on the peninsula of the same name extending far out into Lake Titicaca. Excursion boats to the islands of the sun and moon depart from here. The climate is rough and the water temperature is usually quite cool. Copacabana is an important pilgrimage destination for Bolivians. On August 4th every year a large procession of pilgrims arrives for the Fiesta de la Virgen de Copacabana. The

Ganz oben: Many of the massive stone tombs in Sillustani, which are visible from great distances, have been partially destroyed by grave robbers or lightning. Left side: The lake can be explored on small boats.

Colourful costumes are worn for the solemnity of the winter solstice.

Tiahuanaco, the sacred site and capital of an Andean culture of the same name that experienced its heyday between the 3rd and 9th centuries.

Detour

Cordillera Real

A lofty name that certainly delivers on its promises as these mountains are indeed majestic. In Bolivia the Cordillera Real (the King's Range) extends east of Lake Titicaca and on sunny days the glittering high-altitude glaciers are visible from miles away.

In addition to the highest peak in the group, the 6,880-m (22,573-ft) Nevado del Illimani, there are quite a few other 'six-thousand-footers' rising up into the cobalt blue

The Cordillera Real forms a dramatic background to Lake Titicaca.

skies of the Andes. They are so spectacular that many passionate European climbers and hikers travel to South America exclusively for trekking tours in the Cordillera Real. From La Paz it is a fairly short journey here. The capital city lies just below 4,000 m (13,124 ft) above sea level so it does not take long to acclimatize. Yet the altitude is not without its problems.

The air becomes very thin and climbers therefore should proceed slowly, their luggage being carried by llamas. When they finally reach the peak, however, the view over the Andes, Altiplano and Lake Titicaca is simply spectacular.

Virgin is also sanctified in the Moorish-style basilica (1820). From Copacabana you can either return to the southern route via Yunguyo (crossing the border for the second time), or continue your journey without the border crossing by taking the northern route around the lake towards La Paz.

16 Tiahuanaco The ruins of this city (also called Tiwanaku) lie about 20 km (12 miles) from the southern end of Lake Titicaca. The site used to be directly on the lake shore but the lake has become smaller over the centuries. Very close to the former ceremonial site is present-day Tiahuanaco, just a short drive from the ruins. The first traces of settlement here have been dated back to approximately 1500 BC. Tiahuanaco was probably founded in around AD 300. It subsequently developed into the centre of an empire that covered most of the region and whose cultural and religious influences extended far beyond Peru, even as far as northern Chile and Argentina. The civilization experienced its heyday between 300 and 900. It is meant to have been the most advanced civilization in the central Andes. Around 20,000 residents lived together on only a few square kilometres. Agriculture was the most important economic activity in Tiahuanaco, with nearby Lake Titicaca providing water for effective cultivation. Using an advanced system of canals, farmers here channelled lake water to their fields, which extended over an area of about 80 sq km (50 sq mi). Most of the temples, pillars and monoliths were built between 700 and 1200. An important place of worship, in this case a step pyramid about 15 m (49 ft) high, is situated in the middle of the city.

The most famous construction, however, was the sun gate, sculpted out of one stone that

weighs almost 44 t (48 tons). Many buildings were removed by the Spanish who needed ready-made stone blocks for the construction of their own showcase buildings. Blocks from Tiahuanaco were used to build a number of churches in La Paz, for example. Only a few remains of the site survived the centuries of destruction and overall disregard for their cultural significance. It was only at the beginning of the 20th century that extensive excavations began. The site was reconstructed as precisely as possible to the original once archaeologists were able to clear sufficient remains of the buildings.

Ultimately, the site was declared a UNESCO World Heritage Site in the year 2000. However, there are still many unanswered questions. Why was the city abandoned? Was it due to climate change, or had the population become too large? Without any doubt, the stonemasonry in Tiahuanaco is among the most skilled in South America. Shortly before La Paz the road following the eastern shore of Lake Titicaca joins National Road 1.

17 La Paz The largest city in Bolivia, and the highest city in the world, is nestled impressive-

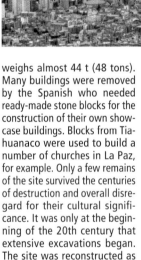

ly among the slopes of a steep valley.

The metropolis is not the constitutional capital but it is the seat of the Bolivian government – and the heartbeat of the country. The city's neighbourhoods seem to cling to the mountain slopes and are striking even from afar.

La Paz is situated at an elevation of between 3,650 and 4,000 m (11,976 and 13,124 ft). Those who can afford it choose to live in the low-lying suburbs as the climate is somewhat milder in the 'lower city' and the residents are more protected from the Altiplano winds.

If you arrive from the west, the road passes the international airport of El Alto. Temperatures in this now independent suburb are often up to 10°C (50°F) cooler than in the city centre. From El Alto the road crosses a basin where many stop to enjoy the view of the city. On the onward journey the colourful markets of the famous 'Indio neighbourhood' pop up on the right. Behind that is the Old Town, which has been able to retain its colonial era character. A wide boulevard passes straight through the entire inner city and while the various sections of it have different names, the locals simply

Reliefs of human heads are embedded in the walls of Tiahuanaco.

call the road the 'Prado'. From here it is not far to the sightseeing attractions such as the cathedral, which was completed in 1933 and has capacity for 12,000 people.

The Bolivian metropolis is a good base for tours to the Nevado del Illimani, the highest mountain in the country, to the east of the city.

18 Nevado del Illimani The journey to this 6,880-m-high (22,573-ft) mountain in the Cordillera Real can be tedious as the road leading directly to the base of Illimani is occasionally closed. The road to the small Indian village of Comunidad Uno is recommended as an alternate route. Climbers can start the ascent of the mountain from here too, and base camp is reached in about five hours of hiking. For locals the mountain is not only a symbol, it also represents an image of their country. With a little imagination you can recognize the outline of an Indian with wife, child and llama in the three peaks of the Nevado del Illimani.

The southernmost of the three peaks is the highest and easily the most accessible, but it takes several days to complete the challenging hike.

Another awe-inspiring peak, the Mount Sajama volcano, lies to the west of the Inca Trail.

From La Paz travel south-east to Patacamaya. From there a well-paved road branches off to the south-west. After 150 km (93 miles) on this road you reach the Sajama National Park in the centre of which is the majestic 6,520-m (21,392-ft) volcano of the same name. Back in Patacamaya, follow National Road 1, which has oil and gas pipelines running parallel to it. After 90 km (56 miles) turn off to the south-east at Caracollo, taking National Road 4 towards Cochabamba. The road passes a vast expanse of fertile farmland where grain, fruit and vegetables are grown.

19 Cochabamba In contrast to the raw climate of the highlands, the weather is much milder in Cochabamba, which is situated at 'only' 2,570 m (1,597 ft) above sea level. This city on the eastern slopes of the Andes has appropriately earned the name 'The city of eternal springtime'. The name Cochabamba, however, actually derives from

View over La Paz with snowcapped volcano.

Detour

Altiplano and Sajama National Park

The whole of western Bolivia is covered by high mountains. The landscape is characterized by high ranges with extensive basins between them. These contrasts are especially typical of the area near the border with Chile.

The Altiplano Basin extends between the Cordillera Occidental (western Cordillera) and the Cordillera Oriental (eastern Cordillera) of the Andes at an altitude of between 3,600 and 4,200 m (11,812 and 13,780

ft). The region is relatively arid as the mountains keep rain clouds away, and vegetation is largely limited to grassland and dwarf shrubs, with minimal tree growth. Agriculture in the raw Altiplano climate is laborious, but a number of local grain types yield satisfactory harvests. Livestock farming also plays an important role for residents. To the west of the Altiplano the road diver-

ging to Patacamaya passes the village of Curahuara, site of a thatched-roof church dating from the 16th century, which is the main sightseeing attraction here. The scenery left and right of the road is impressively dramatic. The next highlight is the Cañon de Sajama with its fantastic cliff formations. As you make your way down the road, Mount Sajama (6,520-m/ 21,392-ft) and its neighbours, the Parinacota (6,342 m/20,808 ft) and Pomerape volcanoes (6,282 m/ 20,611 ft), will continue to draw your attention. At an elevation of more than 5,300 m (17,389 ft), this extinct volca-

no is permanently covered in snow. Mount Sajama itself is inactive but the tectonic activity in the entire region is so substantial that volcanic eruptions and earthquakes are frequent occurrences.

There are stretches of water in the region such as Hedionda Lagoon (top) and Lake Chiarkhota (top).

The Quechua

The term Quechua refers both to a group of Indian peoples and to their language. The Quechua live in the Andes, mainly in Peru but also in parts of neighbouring Bolivia and Ecuador. Most of them have retreated to the high-altitude regions above 4,000 m (13,124 ft).

Agriculture is hardly possible at these altitudes and most Quechua make a living from raising llama and alpaca. Lamas serve principally as pack animals and sources of meat while the closely related alpacas are kept for their high-quality wool.

The Quechua Indian culture had already achieved a high degree of sophistication before the arrival of European colonialists, especially in the areas of social organization and architecture. Even during the colonial era the Quechua language remained the predominant language in the

the Quechua language and basically means 'swampy flatland'. It is home to a renowned university and, with about 600,000 residents, is one of the largest cities in Bolivia. Unlike most of the cities along the Inca Trail it has no pre-colonial history, having been first founded by the Spanish in 1574. Many Spanish immigrants settled here due to the comfortable climate.

In the centre of the city there are a number of houses and churches dating back to the city's early history. A poor-quality road leads from Cochabamba to the Tunari National Park, which extends to the mountain of the same name.

20 Oruro Back in Caracollo, continue for a few kilometres through some pretty bleak scenery until you reach the city of Oruro, elevation 3,710 m (12,173 ft). At the height of the tin-mining era, from the early 19th century to the middle of the 20th century, Oruro was one of the most important economic locations in Bolivia. That has changed since the mines were closed. The locals' zest for life, however, remains the same and Oruro continues to be the centre of the Bolivian carnival, which is celebrated here with sophisticated revelry. The dancers adorn themselves with colourful, ornately carved devil and ghost masks.

21 Lago de Poopó Only a short distance beyond Oruro is Lake Poopó. With a surface area of 2,800 sq km (1,740 sq mi), it is the second-largest lake in Bolivia after Lake Titicaca. Lake Poopó receives some of its water from the outflow of Lake Titicaca from the Río Desaguadero. The lake is very shallow in comparison to the up to 280-m-deep (919-ft) Lake Titicaca, with a depth of just a few meters. High levels of evaporation over the decades have caused a slow but consistent drop in the water lev-

el and surface area of the lake. Its swampy shores are only sparsely populated.

22 Laguna Tarapaya The road now heads south-east to another scenic highlight of the region, an almost perfectly circular lake with a diameter of some 100 m (328 ft) in the crater of an extinct volcano, Laguna Tarapaya. This thermal pool has a temperature of about 35°C (95°F). The Balnearío de Tarapaya, at 3,400 m (11,155 ft), is a perfect place to relax, especially after long hikes at this altitude.

The onward journey is a steep climb towards Potosí, about 25 km (15 miles) away.

23 Potosí At just below 4,000 m (13,124 ft), Potosí was one of the wealthiest cities in all of South America between the 16th and 18th centuries. The wealth came from a mountain with relatively unspectacular looks, but

of spectacular intrinsic value – the conical, 4,830-m-high (815,847-ft) Cerro Rico ('Rich Mountain').

The Spanish colonial rulers were fortunate enough to discover extensive silver reserves within this mountain, which they then proceeded to mine mercilessly. Tens of thousands of tonnes of silver were extracted but the lucrative mining activities had another side to them, namely Indian slave labour that led to countless deaths.

The silver mines have since been abandoned but tin-mining has become increasingly important in recent decades. Unfortunately for the people of Potosí, tin mining is not nearly as lucrative as silver.

Traces of the former wealth can be found in the city centre – stately homes and churches from the Spanish colonial era, some of which have striking facades. The city and the neighbouring silver mines were de-

clared a UNESCO World Heritage Site in 1987 and a bumpy road leads to the visitors' mine, located at an altitude of 4,300 m (14,108 ft).

Beyond Potosí the road (No 5) winds its way north. En route to the much lower-lying city of Sucre you descend some 1,400 m (4,593 ft) in altitude over a relatively short distance, with very steep gradients in places.

24 Sucre On the approach to the capital, at an altitude of about 2,600 m (8,531 ft), the glittering buildings of the 'White City' are visible even from a distance. Ivory-coloured baroque churches and religious buildings, whitewashed houses and regal palaces define Sucre, which was founded in 1538.

There are only a few Spanish colonial cities that are as well-preserved as this one. Buildings with stylish balconies and lovely arcades characterize the Old Town, which was declared a UNESCO World Heritage Site in 1990. Even though Sucre has been the capital of Bolivia since 1828, there are only a few civil authorities here. The government and its ministries are based in La Paz.

The university here, founded in 1624, is one of the oldest in South America. Celebrated as the jewel of Bolivian colonial architecture, Sucre makes a fitting conclusion to the Inca Trail, running through two countries and two worlds.

At the top: In the past, coins were minted in the Casa de la Moneda in Potosí, today it houses a museum. Above: The San Francisco church in the colonial town of Sucre was built in 1581 by the first settlers and is under protection.

middle Andes region. The European missionaries first achieved greater success when they addressed the Indians, as would-be converts, in the Quechua language. The language is still maintained today, and in Peru and Bolivia Quechua is even an official language, along with Spanish. It is one of the few Indian languages to have been granted this status.

According to estimates the language is spoken by approximately 8 million people and is therefore more widespread than any other Indian language in South America.

Lima With its two towers, the 16th-century cathedral here is one of the Peruvian capital's featured architectural treasures.

Machu Picchu These ruins represent the zenith of Inca architecture. Built in the 15th century, the city was situated on sophisticated terraces and its construction is evidence of highly accomplished technical know-how. This complex is a UNESCO World Heritage Site.

Huari In its heyday (6th–10th century), the Huari Empire extended over almost the whole of Peru. Theories postulate that up to 100,000 people lived in this centre of Huari power. The giant stone sculptures are testimony to their high degree of artistic ability.

Cuzco This city, at 3,500 m (11,484 ft), is characterized not only by buildings from the Inca era but also by those from the Spanish colonial period. The Renaissance-style cathedral (17th century) is an example.

Manú National Park This national park extends from the central Andes to the rainforest in the Amazon lowlands.

Tipón Inca settlements such as Tipón arose around Cuzco. The remains of the now uncovered village are open to visitors.

Lake Titicaca The lake belongs to both Peru and Bolivia. Descendants of the Uros people living here are renowned for their 'floating' islands built from reeds.

Tiahuanaco So-called 'nail heads' portray priests on a temple wall of the former centre of an Andean culture, Tiahuanaco. The town was founded in around AD 300.

Potosí Following the discovery of a silver mine in Cerro Rico in 1545, this town became one of the largest cities in the world. It then went into decline once the silver reserves were depleted around 1800.

Sucre Bolivia's official capital (La Paz is the seat of government) is home to one of the oldest universities in South America (1624).

Route 28: Argentina and Chile

Through the Pampas and Patagonia

Argentina is characterized by three major geographical regions that could scarcely be more different from one another – the endless Pampas, the high peaks of the Andes, and the plains of Patagonia with their steep isolated mountains and glaciers. Part of the Andes and some of the southern foothills of Patagonia near the Tierra del Fuego belong to Chile.

Route profile:

Length: approx. 3,315 miles
Time required: at least 4 weeks

Covering an area of more than 2.8 million sq km (1 million sq mi), Argentina is the second-largest country in South America after its signficantly larger neighbour Brazil. The Pampas, which make up the heartland of Argentina, are a vast green expanse on which isolated mountain ranges emerge like islands in an ocean, from Buenos Aires all the way to the western border with Chile. One such 'island' is the Sierra de Córdoba, a range that rises west of Córdoba in the Cerro Champaqui to a height of 2,884 m (9,614 ft), indeed a considerable height, but that is nothing compared to the peaks west of Mendoza. There, the Cerro Aconcagua, or 'Stone Sentinel', towers

to 6,963 m (23,000 ft) and is both the highest peak in the Andes and the highest mountain in the Americas.

The Andes Mountains mark the natural border between Argentina and neighbouring Chile. National parks have been established on both sides of the border in magnificent mountain landscapes containing virgin forests interspersed with shimmering blue and green lakes and rivers of cloudy glacier water. The areas are a paradise for hikers and include the Lanín National Park,

where dense forests of araucaria and Antarctic beech engulf the mighty Lanín volcano. At the base of this 3,747-m (12,290-ft) volcano is a deep blue lake, Lago Huechulafquén.

While northern Patagonia occasionally offers gentle landscapes

The Paine massif (above and left) in the Torres del Paine National Park is made of granite – typical of southern Patagonia. The river bearing the same name flows past it.

It was not until the last ice age that the Strait of Magellan, once just a cleft in the Andes, split off from the mainland and created the island of Tierra del Fuego. This main island in the archipelago is 47,000 sq km (20,000 sq mi) with a landscape that clearly resembles that of Patagonia. In the north is a broad plateau while in the south the last foothills of the Cordilleras reach heights of 2,500 m (9,000 ft), finally sinking spectacularly into the sea at the notorious Cape Horn, whose perpetually stormy seas have been the bane of so many a brave sailor.

such as that of the Nahuel Huapi National Park, in the south the landscape becomes progressively more windswept and barren. The constant Westerlies bring humidity from the Pacific, falling as rain on the Chilean side of the Andes. They then sweep over the

icy inland regions, glaciers and ice fields of Patagonia, which chill them before they whip over the eastern plains.
The Andes open up here and there, revealing gaps between the peaks like the ones at Lago Buenos Aires – known as the

Lago General Carrera on the Chilean side – and at the Los Glaciares National Park. Also typical of southern Patagonia are the isolated granite peaks that dominate the plains: the FitzRoy Massif and the Torres del Paine, for example.

Left side: The Cerro Torre – a granite mountain – with its steep, smooth walls is considered a great challenge for mountaineers. Above: Clouds over the pampa in the Los Glaciares National Park.

Nahuel Huapi National Park owes its name to the lake around which it extends.

Detour

Aconcagua

The 'Stone Sentinel' – translated from the Quechua term Ackon-Cauak, from which the name Aconcagua is derived – is not only the highest mountain in Argentina at 6,963 m (23,000 ft), but also the highest in the Andes, the Americas, and in the entire southern hemisphere. Aconcagua, in the centre of the Provincial Park Aconcagua, is a favourite destination for thousands of moun-

The landscape around the Aconcagua.

taineers from all over the world, for it is considered a relatively easy climb. First, mountaineers need to acclimatize themselves by scaling the Puente del Inca, a mere 2,720 m (9,000 ft) above sea level, then move to the base camp at about 4,000 m (13,333 ft). From there, the ascent begins on the glacial northern route.

The Swiss climber Matthias Zurbriggen was the first in modern times to get to the top, on 18 January 1897, but the peak was almost certainly conquered much earlier by the native inhabitants. After all, in 1982 a 500-year-old Inca mummy was found at an elevation of 5,200 m (17,333 ft). It was the body of a boy aged about seven who had been given a ritual burial.

From the Pampas through the mountains, past the granite massifs and glaciers of Patagonia, through the Strait of Magellan to Ushuaia, this dream route leads you all the way down through Argentina along the Pan-American Highway to the southern tip of Tierra del Fuego on Lapataia Bay.

❶ Córdoba Argentina's second-largest city, with 1.5 million inhabitants, is known as 'La Docta', 'the Erudite', and it bears the nickname with pride. For it was here in 1614 that the country's first university was founded, and Córdoba still possesses excellent university faculties. The city, founded in 1573, is surprisingly tranquil in its centre. The plaza contains the arcaded Cabildo, the colonial-style government building, and the cathedral, built in 1574 in a mixed baroque and neoclassical style. A few steps further, through the pedestrian zone, you come to the so-called Manzana Jesuítica, the Jesuit quarter, with a Jesuit church and the first university buildings. Passing through some dull suburbs, we leave Córdoba on Ruta 20 in the direction of Carlos Paz and reach the Sierra de Córdoba, which rises impressively from the Pampas to a height of 2,884 m (9,614 ft) in the Cerro Champaqui. At Villa Dolores, some 170 km (105 miles) south-west of Córdoba, you will leave the mountains behind and enter a flatter landscape that remains as such for the next 500 km (310 miles) until Mendoza.

❷ Mendoza The green countryside around Mendoza is deceptive, as this city of 600,000 is located in a desert known as the Cuyo, meaning 'sandy earth'. Plentiful water from the near-by mountains has allowed the desert to bloom, and it is here that the finest Argentinian wines are produced. Although Mendoza was founded as early as 1561, the city centre is mostly modern because older portions have been repeatedly razed by earthquakes, most severely in 1861. All that remains is the Church of San Francisco, dating from 1638. The pedestrian area of the Calle Sarmiento, with its cafés and restaurants, and the suburb of Maipú, with bodegas that offer wine tastings, are worth a visit.

From Mendoza, take a detour to the stunning Puente del Inca.

❸ Puente del Inca The 'Inca Bridge', at a height of 2,720 m (9,000 ft), is a natural arch over the Río Mendoza that was formed by mineral deposits. Following the road westwards, you soon come to the best view of

The 3,500-year-old trees in Los Alerces National Park can reach 70 m (235 ft) in height.

town with the best approach to Lanín National Park.

④ Lanín National Park This park surrounds the extinct volcano for which the park is named. The 3,747-m (12,490-ft) volcano, which has a perfectly formed cone peak, is mirrored in glorious Lago Huechulafquén. It is the ideal backdrop for extended hikes. Back on Ruta 40, San Carlos de Bariloche is not far away.

⑤ San Carlos de Bariloche Bariloche was founded by Swiss immigrants, and is the 'Swiss side' of Argentina. The Centro Civico, the community centre, is built to resemble a Swiss chalet. Best of all, the main shopping street features one chocolate factory after another, and all the restaurants have cheese fondue on the menu. The first settlers sought and found a rural idyll here. Bariloche lies on one of Argentina's most beautiful lakes, Lago Nahuel Huapi, at the heart of the national park of the same name. The road leads further south through a magnificent mountain landscape until you reach Los Alerces National Park near the town of Esquel.

⑥ Los Alerces National Park This national park covers an area of 260,000 ha (650,000 acres) and is dedicated to the preservation of the alerces, gigantic evergreen trees that can reach heights of 70 m (235 ft) and have diameters of 4 m (14 ft). Some of them are estimated to be 3,500 years old. In the centre of the park is the 78-sq-km (30-sq-mi) Lake Futalaufquén. From the national park, Ruta 40 continues on to the south. It is 381 km (237 miles) from Esquel to Río Mayo, but shortly before

Above: Cerro Catedral and Lake Toncek in Nahuel Huapi National Park. Left: The Compania de Jesús church in Córdoba.

The Pampas

The word 'pampa' is taken from the language of the Quechua Indians. It means 'treeless plain', which aptly describes this vast region. The Pampas extend from the Atlantic to the Andes, and are bordered to the north by the Chaco, to the north-east by the Río Paraná and to the south by Patagonia.
The Pampas make up the heartland of Argentina. Two-thirds of the country's cattle breeding and about ninety per cent of its agriculture are

The Pampa is the epitome of the Argentine countryside.

based here. It is a natural grassland as the compact and firm soil encourages the growth of grasses, but it is so hostile to trees that they are unable to take root here of their own accord.
Yet despite all its natural appearance, the Pampas are the landscape in Argentina where flora and fauna have undergone the greatest changes as the result of human intervention. Many new grasses were introduced, and the Pampas became a cultivated steppe. In addition, cattle-breeders planted trees to give their cattle shelter from the temperature extremes on the vast open plains. In some places, grassland and cattle-breeding have been abandouned in favor of more lucrative soybean cultivation.

Aconcagua (see sidebar left). A dirt road then leads up to the old border zone on the Bermejo Pass at 3,750 m (12,500 ft). From there your climb will be rewarded by a wonderful view over the High Andes.
From Mendoza, Ruta 40 leads south. After about 300 km (190 miles) through the Cuyo, a road branches at El Sosneada to the west towards Las Leñas, Argen-

tina's greatest skiing area. You will then head another 490 km (310 miles) south, parallel to the Andes, to Zapala.
This city has a museum displaying beautiful local minerals and fossils. The distances are great in Argentina, but after another 156 km (100 miles) on Ruta 40 there is a road turning off to the west, leading to San Martín de los Andes, a little mountain

Cuevas de las Manos

The cave paintings discovered in the Río Pinturas Canyon are among the oldest human artifacts in South America. The local inhabitants, who lived here

José Ormachea Petrified Forest

If you turn west at the Río Mayo, after about 100 km (62 miles) you will come to the town of Sarmiento on Lake Muster. South of Sarmiento, in the José Ormachea Petrified Forest, one of several petrified forests in Patagonia, it becomes clear that this region was not always an empty, stark plain, overgrown with short, coarse grass. Approximately 150 million years ago, dense forests grew here, with giant trees (including araucaria) that were up to 100 m (330 ft) in height and more than

Remains of the primeval forest in the Bosque Petrificado José Ormachea.

1,000 years old. Movements in the earth's crust then created the Andes, which resulted in numerous volcanic eruptions. A layer of ash covered Patagonia up to 20 m (65 ft) deep. Plants and animals suffocated, died and were buried under the thick layer of ash. Over the course of hundreds of thousands of years, water permeated through the ash layers and dissolved some of the minerals and silicates in the ash. The water then flowed into the dead tree trunks and, as it dried out, minerals gradually replaced the cell walls of the organic matter, turning them into stone.

this, Ruta 26 branches off to the east towards Sarmiento via the petrified forests (see sidebar left). To the west, Ruta 26 winds through the Andes to the Chilean city of Coyhaique. From this crossroads it is another 129 km (80 miles) south to Perito Moreno.

7 Perito Moreno This small town does not offer anything special, but it is the starting point for excursions to the milky, teal-coloured Lake Buenos Aires, the second-largest lake in South America after Lake Titicaca. The Argentinean side of the lake lies in the middle of the Patagonian plains; the Chilean side is sur-

rounded by snow-covered peaks. You can cross the Chilean border at Los Antiguos, on the southern edge of the lake. Some 56 km (35 miles) south of Perito Moreno, the road forks, one branch leading to Cueva de las Manos (see sidebar right). It is another 239 km (148 miles) from Perito Moreno through the desolate Patagonian plains to the next settlement, Hotel las Horquetas, just a handful of houses in the Río Chico Valley.

At an intersection here, a gravel road branches off to the west in the direction of Estancia la Oriental and Lake Belgrano. This is the route to the Perito Moreno National Park.

8 Perito Moreno National Park This is one of Argentina's most isolated and spectacular national parks. There are glaciers and shimmering mountain lakes with floating blocks of ice, and the park is teeming with wildlife such as pumas, foxes, wildcats, guanacos and waterfowl.

The second-highest mountain in Patagonia, Monte San Lorenzo (3,706 m/12,159 ft), is the home of the condor. The park can only be explored on foot or on horseback. There are hardly any roads or facilities – only campsites. Tres Lagos is the name of the next crossroads on Ruta 40, about 235 km (146 miles) fur-

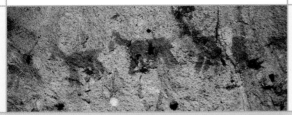

between 9500 BC and 1000 BC, left behind depictions of animals, often hunting scenes, as well as palm prints in various colours. The various drawings date mainly from between 5000 BC and 1500 BC. The cave has been designated a UNESCO World Heritage Site.

Left side: Handprints in the Cueva de las Manos; left: representations of animals.

ther on. At this point, Ruta 288 goes east towards the Atlantic. After another 45 km (28 miles) heading south is Lake Viedma. The road on this lake's northern bank leads westward and, on clear days, there is a fantastic view of the FitzRoy Massif.

9 El Chaltén This small town is the northern access point for Los Glaciares National Park, a dream destination for mountaineers from all over the world as it is home to the 3,375-m (11,072-ft) Mount FitzRoy. But it is not just for climbers. Hikers will also find a plethora of activities. You can organize one-day or multi-day excursions from

El Chaltén. Back on Ruta 40, you pass through the Leona Valley and along the eastern bank of Lake Argentino to the junction to El Calafate.

10 Los Glaciares National Park There is considerably more activity at the southern end of this park, near El Calafate, than in the northern part. This is due to the spectacular glaciers that can be much more easily accessed from here than from anywhere else. Large slabs of ice break off from the 70-m (230-ft) glacial walls, landing in the lake with an immense crash. The biggest of these giants is the Upsala Glacier, with a surface area

of 595 sq km (230 sq mi). The most popular spot, however, is the Perito Moreno Glacier about 80 km (50 miles) from El Calafate, whose glacial tongue pushes out into Lake Argentino to such an extent that every few years it seals off the Brazo Rico, one of the lake's offshoots.

11 Puerto Natales The town, situated on the Ultima Esperanza Estuary, was the last hope of sailors who had got lost in the countless channels of southern Patagonia in their search for an east-west passage. Puerto Natales is the best starting point for a visit to nearby Torres del Paine National Park, and also a

worthwhile stop for arranging various excursions. For example, you could take a boat ride on Seno de la Ultima Esperanza (Last Hope Sound) up to the border of the Bernardo O'Higgins National Park to Cerro Balmaceda (2,035 m/6,676 ft) with its impressive glaciers. Bird lovers should visit the town's old pier

Large picture and left side: The drastic edge of the Perito Moreno Glacier in Los Glaciares is up to 70 m (230 ft) high. With a great roar, ice chunks the size of houses continually break off from its walls. Above right: Waterfall in front of Fitz-Roy.

Detour

Patagonia's animals

Most visitors to Patagonia will first encouter guanacos and rheas. The guanaco, a dark-brown

in the late afternoon. It's a meeting place for hundreds of cormorants.

12 Cueva del Milodón En route to the Torres del Paine National Park, it is well worth taking time to pay a short visit to Cueva del Milodón. To get there, go 8 km (5 miles) north out of Puerto Natales and head west. After 5 km (3 miles) you reach the cave where German immigrant Hermann Eberhard found remains of a huge dinosaur, a 4-m (13-ft) megatherium, in 1896. A replica of the creature by the entrance to the cave shows how it may have looked.

13 Torres del Paine National Park The peaks of the Torres del Paine Massif rise dramatically from the windswept plain. These steep, seemingly impregnable mountains have granite peaks, the highest of which is Cerro Torre Grande at 3,050 m (10,007 ft), surrounded by the peaks of Paine Chico, Torres del Paine and Cuernos del Paine. This is Chile's adventure paradise. Visitors can choose between embarking on long hiking trails in the park, day-long tours, or a hiking trail around the entire massif. All these trails pass by bluish-white, opaque, glacial lakes with floating icebergs.

They include Grey Glacier and the amazing Río Paine, which plummets into Lake Pehoe as a cascading waterfall. The stunted trees brace themselves against the wind here, but in early summer the plains form a sea of flowers. In addition to guanacos, you will likely spot condors and sundry waterfowl. Remember to take warm clothing.
To the south of Puerto Natales, the route continues straight through the plains. Stubby grass grows on both sides of the road. You'll often see guanacos, rheas and sheep.
This is Ruta 9 to Punta Arenas. Some 34 km (21 miles) before

the city, a road branches westwards. After 23 km (14 miles) you reach Otway Sound, home to a large penguin colony.

14 Monumento Natural Los Pinguinos There is another large penguin colony to the north-east of Punta Arenas, right on the Strait of Magellan. In the summer months, some 2,500 Magellan penguins, the smallest of the species, live in this colony. They only grow to between 50 and 70 cm (20 and 28 in) and weigh a mere 5 kg (11 lbs). They can be easily recognized by their black-and-white heads and the black stripe

type of camel and a relative of the llama, live in herds of five to twenty-five animals in the national parks of the south. The steppes of Argentina are also home to the ostrich-like common rhea or nandu. At the beginning of incubation, the males of the species carve out their territories while the females gad about in groups. Rarer sights are the Pampas hare (maras), the pudu, and the Patagonian huemul, a species of deer about 1.5 m (5 ft) in height. The red fox and the puma are the only predators in this part of the world.

Guanacos, in a flowery meadow in the Torres del Paine National Park.

running across the upper part of their torsos.

⑮ Punta Arenas This city, founded in the mid 19th century as a penal colony, grew quickly and was an important port for ships plying the west coast of America until the construction of the Panama Canal in 1914. Patagonia's profitable sheep-farming also made its contribution to the city's success, allowing wealthy inhabitants to build large sheep estancias (ranches) around the city centre. The Palacio Braun-Menéndez, today a museum, shows how the upper class lived in those days: walls covered in fabric imported from France, billiard tables from England, gold-plated fireguards from Flanders and Carrara marble decorations from Italy. Burials were no less regal here. The Punta Arenas cemetery contains the enormous mausoleums of the city's wealthier families. The Museo Regional Mayorino Borgatallo is also worth a visit.

From Punta Arenas you can drive 50 km (31 miles) back to the intersection of Ruta 9 and Ruta 255. Then follow Ruta 255 in a north-east direction until you reach Punta Delgada. From there, Ruta 3, which starts in Argentina, leads south and soon reaches the Strait, where a ferry transports travellers to Puerto Espora in Tierra del Fuego.

⑯ Strait of Magellan / Tierra del Fuego In 1520, Fernando de Magellan was the first to sail through the Strait later named after him. As he skirted the mainland and the islands, he saw fire and smoke, hence the archipelago's name. The island group covers an area of 73,500 sq km (28,378 sq mi). Its main island, the western part of which belongs to Chile, covers an area of about 47,000 sq km (18,147 sq mi). It is some 280 km (174 miles) from Puerto Espora to the Río Grande through vast, open countryside. At San Sebastián Bay, you can cross the border into Argentina.

South of the Río Grande, the landscape changes – the valleys become narrower, the hills higher, and dense forests come into view. After about 250 km (155 miles), you reach Ushuaia and the adjacent Tierra del Fuego National Park.

Large image: Waterfalls at Río Paine. At the top: Última Esperanza inlet. Above: Laguna Figueroa in Torres del Paine National Park.

The Tierra del Fuego National Park entices adventuresome travellers with its expansive steppe, mountainous landscape and impenetrable jungles and rainforests.

Detour

The Patagonia coast and its marine life

The Patagonian coastal areas are rich in species variety, but the true animal paradise is located far to the east of the route on the Váldes Peninsula, where every year from July through to mid December you can see black-and-white killer whales (orcas) and loads of southern right whales. In many coastal waters, you can catch sight of sea lions – especial-

A sea lion colony, including Golden-faced penguins.

ly in Tierra del Fuego's Beagle Channel – as well as dolphins, which are crossing the Strait of Magellan. The largest colony of the 70-cm-tall (28-in) Magellan penguins along your route lives at Seno Otway near Punta Arenas.

⑰ Tierra del Fuego National Park Hikers will enjoy Tierra del Fuego National Park, which begins 18 km (11 miles) west of Ushuaia. It is easily accessible in its southern part but inaccessible in the north, and stretches along the Chilean border offering marshes, rocky cliffs and temperate rainforests.
Ruta 3, the Argentinean part of the southern Pan-American Highway, leads directly into the park and ends picturesquely at the Bahía Lapataía.

⑱ Ushuaia The southernmost city in the world is set between the icy waters of the deep Beagle Channel and the peaks of the Cordillera which, despite being only 1,500 m (4,921 feet) high, are always covered in snow. Originally founded as a penal colony, the city lives mostly from tourism these days.
The Museo Fin del Mundo has a collection depicting the early and colonial history of the region.
If the weather is good, take a boat trip to the glorious 'End of the World', Cape Horn.

Both images above: Lonely landscape in the Tierra del Fuego National Park. Below: View of Ushuaia harbour, the southernmost city in the world. The foothills of the Darwin Cordillera rise up in the background.

Aconcagua The highest mountain in the Americas at 6,963 m (23,000 ft), Aconcagua is near Mendoza on the Chilean border. It was first 'officially' climbed in 1897. Today, 2,000 to 4,000 mountaineers enjoy it every year.

Los Glaciares National Park This park consists mainly of two formations, the high mountain landscape in the north, with the FitzRoy Massif, and the inland glaciers in the south, with the Upsala and Perito-Moreno Glaciers.

Mendoza This modern city of 600,000 also has a colonial past, though it has largely been destroyed by earthquakes. Mendoza has now become the hub of Argentina's flourishing grape growing and wine industry. It has many wineries and bodegas where visitors can get a taste of the local wine amid some stunning landscape.

Los Alerces National Park Massive alerces trees, some are believed to be over 3,500 years old, grow to a massive height and girth.

The Torres del Paine National Park The highest peak in the park is the 3,050-m-high (10,007-ft) Cerro Torre Grande, surrounded by Paine Chico, Torres del Paine and Cuernas del Paine.

Ushuaia This city, the southernmost in Argentina, lies on the Beagle Channel. The Museo del Fin del Mundo (End of the World Museum) displays exhibits from the prehistoric and colonial history of Tierra del Fuego.

The Los Pinguinos and Seno Otway Penguin Colonies Thousands of Magellan penguins live here near Punta Arenas in the summer. They are the smallest species of penguin in South America.

Córdoba Argentina's second-largest city (1.5 million inhabitants) is home to the country's oldest university. The picture shows the cathedral and Cabildo in the central plaza of town.

Nahuel Huapi National Park This park near Bariloche has several different landscape zones including the High Andes, rainforest, transitional forest and steppe.

Cueva de las Manos In a sizeable cave in the Río Pinturas Canyon, the original inhabitants of this area left behind the oldest indications of human settlement in South America.

Punta Arenas Until the Panama Canal was built in 1914, this port town was of great importance at the tip of South America. Some of the typical houses from that period still remain.

Perito Moreno National Park The national park surrounding Lake Belgrano (the picture shows the broad Belgrano Peninsula) showcases wild and pristine Patagonian nature. Numerous indigenous animals live here, including pumas, guanacos, nandus, flamingos and condors.

Tierra del Fuego National Park This national park, close to Ushuaia in Terra del Fuego, runs to the Chilean border with its lakes, glaciers and rainforests.

A

Aalst 69
Aberdeen 18
Aborigines 252
Abu Mena 162
Abu Simbel 173
Abydos 168
Acadia National Park 342
Aconcagua 386
Addo Elephant
    National Park 182
Adelaide 244, 246
Agadir 156
Agra 216
Aït-Ben-Haddou 152
Ajmer 220
Akhmîm 168
Alamogordo 325
Albufeira 105
Albuquerque 326
Alcobaça 100
Alexandria 162
Algarve, west coast 106
Alice Springs 250
Alkmaar 64
Almería 93
Alor Setar 234
Altiplano 381
Altun Ha 366
Alwar 217
Amboise 82
Amsterdam 66-67
Anaheim 323
Ancona 126
Andermatt 56
Annapurna Massif 206
Antelope Canyon 313
Antigua 364
Antwerp 68
Aoraki 274
Aquileia 120
Ar-Rachidia 149
Arches National Park 331
Arcos de la Frontera 95
Arezzo 116
Arizona, Desert flora 323
Arthur's Pass 282
Ashmunein/Hermopolis 167
Assateague Island
    National Seashore 354
Assisi 116
Assiût 167
Athens 134-135
Atitlán Lake 369
Atlantic City 352
Ayacucho 373
Ayers Rock 247, 248
Ayutthaya 230
Azay-le-Rideau 83
Aztec Ruins
    National Monument 327

B

Balmoral Castle 18
Baltimore 352
Banff National Park 291, 300

Bangkok 232-233
Bari 125
Barossa 256
Barra 20
Batalha 100
Bath 34
Batu Caves 234
Bayonne 86
Beachy Head 27
Beja 105
Bejin 194-195
Belize Barrier Reef System 366
Belize City 366
Ben Nevis 21
Beni Hassan 167
Berchtesgaden Region 61
Berlin 40-41
Bern 55
Beveland 68
Bhaktapur 204
Bikaner 224
Blair Castle 16
Blenheim 273
Blenheim Palace 35
Blois 77
Blue Hole National Park 366
Blue Mountains
    National Park 260, 264-265
Bodiam Castle 35
Bologna 110
Bolzano 59
Bordeaux 85
Border Ranges
    National Park 267
Boston 344-345
Boumalne Dadès 151
Bowron Lake
    Provincial Park 300
Braga 103
Bragança 103
Brandon 292
Bratislava 48
Breda 68
Brig 55
Brighton 26
Brisbane 268
Bruges 72
Brussels 70-71
Bryce Canyon
    National Park 312, 329
Buckingham Palace 28
Budapest 50
Budva 124
Burano 120
Byron Bay 267

C

Cádiz 95
Cairo 163
Calakmul 362
Calgary 291, 301
Camel ride 154
Campeche 361
Cancún 360
Canyon de Chelly National
    Monument 327

Canyonlands
    National Park 328, 330
Cape Agulhas 181
Cape Hatteras
    National
    Seashore 354
Cape Peninsula 176
Cape Sounion 132
Cape St. Francis 182
Cape Town 178-179
Capitol Reef
    National Park 311, 331
Carnuntum 47
Carrara 113
Casa Grande Ruins
    National Monument 315
Casablanca 158
Cascais 100
Castel del Monte 125
Castelo Branco 104
Cattolica 127
Cedar Breaks
    National Monument 312
České Budějovice 44
Český Krumlov 44
Chaco Culture
    National Historic Park 327
Chae Son
    National Park 228
Chambers Pillar 256
Chambord 77
Chapman's Peak Drive 176
Chartres 76
Château Mouton-Rothschild 85
Châtellerault 84
Chefchaouen 146
Chengde 193
Chengdu 196
Chenonceau 82
Cheverny 82
Chiang Mai 228
Chichén Itzá 360
Chichicastenango 364
Chinon 84
Chioggia 128
Chiricahua National
Monument 339
Chittaurgarh 221
Chongqing 196
Christchurch 273
Chur 57
Cinque Terre 112
Ciudad de Guatemala 365
Cobá 368
Cochabamba 381
Cognac 85
Coimbra 102
Colorado River, Rafting 334
Coober Pedy 245
Coomera 268
Copacabana 379
Copán 365
Copts 162
Cordillera Real 380
Córdoba, Argentina 386
Córdoba, Spain 90

Corfe Castle 27
Corinth 138
Corinth Canal 140
Cortina d'Ampezzo 59
Cortona 116
Costa del Sol 94
Côte d'Argent 86
Côte des Basques 86
Coto de Doñana 96
Cotswolds 34
Cres 122
Crikvenica 123
Cromwell 275
Cueva del Milodón 390
Cuevas de las Manos 388
Cutta Cutta Caves
    Nature Park 257
Cuzco 374
Cypress Hills
    Interprovincial Park 292

D

Dahshûr 167
Dali, China 199
Daly Waters 251
Dartmoor National Park 32
Darwin 253
Datong 192
Davenport Range
    National Park 257
Dax 86
Death Valley
    National Park 334, 336-337
Děčín 39
Delft 65
Delhi 218-219
Delphi 133
Delphi, Oracle 132
Dendera 168
Devils Marbles 251
Diakoftó 140
Dinosaur Provincial Park 292
Disneyland 322
Doge's Palace 121
Dolalghat 207
Dorrigo National Park 266
Dreamtrack 256
Drepung 212
Dresden 39
Dubrovnik 125
Dufftown 23
Dujiangyan 198
Dunedin 278
Dunnottar Castle 18
Dynastic towers 115

E

Eastbourne 26
East Coast Temperate and
    Subtropical Rainforest Park 269
Eden Project 32
Edinburgh 16-17
Edfu 173
Eilean Donan Castle 21
El Chaltén 389
El-Jadida 156

El-Kelaâ M'Gouna 151
El-Minia 167
Elba 114
Elbe Sandstone Mountains 39
Elvas 104
Emei Shan 196
Enns 45
Epidauros 138
Erfoud 149
Erg Chebbi 148
Essaouira 156
Estremoz 104
Eswan 173
Euboea 132
Évora 104
Exeter, Cathedral 26

F
Faro 105
Fatehpur Sikri 216
Fátima 102
Fez 147
Fiesole 111
Fife Peninsula 16
Finke Gorge National Park 247
Fiordland National Park
  275, 276-277
Flagstaff 314
Flamenco 90
Flims 57
Flinders Ranges
  National Park 245
Florence 111
Fontevraud-l`Abbaye 83
Fort La Reine 297
Fort St James
  National Historic Site 300
Fort William 23
Franschhoek 186
Franz Josef Glacier 281
Freistadt 44
Furka-Oberalp Railway 56

G
Gajner Wildlife Sanctuary 223
Ganden Monastery 212
Gargano Peninsula 126
Garibaldi Provincial Park 288
Geneva 54
Gent 69
George 181
Ghost Towns 325
Gibraltar 95
Giza 163
Glacier National Park
  288, 301, 305, 306
Glasgow 22
Glastonbury 33
Glencoe 21
Gold Coast 268
Gonggar Monastery 211
Gorges du Dadès 150
Gorges du Todra 150
Gorkha 206
Gouda 68
Grafton 267

Granada 92
Grand Canyon National Park 313,
  316-317, 333
Grand Staircase Escalante
  National Monument 312
Grand Teton
  National Park 310
Grants 326
Great Salt Lake 310
Great Wall 193
Great White Sharks 180
Greymouth 282
Grindelwald 56
Großglockner
  High Alpine Road 60
Guadix 93
Guanacaste
  National Park 366
Guarda 104
Guatemala, vulcanoes 364
Guimarães 103
Gwalior 216
Gyangzê 210
Győr 48

H
Haarlem 64
Hallein 60
Hassan II Mosque 158
Hastings 26
Hat Yai 234
Head-Smashed-In Buffalo Jump 304
Heiligenblut 59
Henbury 247
Hermanus 177
Hokitika 281
Hoover Dam 333
Huancayo 373
Huari 373
Hudson Valley 352
Hunter Valley 269
Hyannis 347

I
Ifrane 148
Île de Ré 84
Indian Summer 343
Inca ,architecture 373
Interlaken 56
Inti Raymi 379
Inveraray 22
Invercargill 275
Inverewe Gardens 21
Inverness 18
Ipoh 234
Isle of Lewis and Harris 20
Isle of Mull 22
Isle of Skye 21
Isle Royale
  National Park 297
Isles of Scilly 33

J
Jackson 310
Jains 220
Jaipur 217

Jaisalmer 223
Jasper National Park 300, 302
Jeanne d'Arc 82
Jerez de la Frontera 96
Jodhpur 222
John o'Groats 19
José Ormachea
  Petrified Forest 388
Johor Bahru 238
Joshua Tree National Park 323
Jurassic Coast 27
Jüterbog 38

K
Kaeng Krachan National Park 230
Kaikoura 273
Kakadu National Park
  252, 253, 254-255
Kata Tjuta 256
Kamloops 288
Kamphaeng Phet 229
Kanangra-Boyd
  National Park 260
Karamea 282
Karlovy Vary 42
Karlštejn 42
Katherine 251
Kathmandu 205
Kellie's Castle 238
Kennedy, John F. 346
Keoladeo Ghana
  National Park 216
Keukenhof 64
Khao Sok National Park 231
Kilchurn Castle 22
Kinderdijk 68
Kings Canyon 249
Klosterneuburg 47
Knokke 72
Knysna 181
Komárno/Komárom 48
Koper 120
Korčula 124
Kotor 124
Krabi 231
Krems 46
Ku-Ring-Gai Chase
  National Park 260
Kuala Kangsar 234
Kuala Lumpur 238
Kunming 198
Kwai Bridge 230

L
La Paz 380
La Rochelle 84
La Spezia 112
Labin 122
Lago de Atitlán 364
Lago de Poopó 382
Lagos 106
Laguna Tarapaya 382
Lake Geneva 54
Lake Hawea 280
Lake IJssel 85
Lake Louise 291

Lake Neusiedl 48
Lake Powell 313
Lamington
  National Park 267
Lampang 229
Land's End 32
Langtang
  National Park 204
Lanín National Park 387
Larache 158
Las Vegas 335
Lausanne 54
Leiden 64
Leiria 102
Les Landes 86
Leshan 196
Lhasa 212
Lhaze 207
Libourne 85
Lienz 59
Lijiang 199
Lima 372
Linz 45
Lisbon 101
Litchfield
  National Park 253
Litoměříce 42
Little Bighorn 305
Livorno 114
Loch Lomond 22
Loch Rannoch 21
Longmen Shiku 201
London 28-31
Los Alerces
  National Park 387
Los Angeles 322
Los Glaciares National Park 389
Los Pinguinos,
  Monumento Natural 390
Louis XIV 77
Lower Hunter Valley 266
Lucca 113
Luckenwalde 38
Lumbini 207
Luoyang 196
Luther 38
Luxor 168

M
Machu Picchu 376
Mae Ping National Park 228
Mafra 100
Main Range National Park 268
Makarska-Riviera 124
Málaga 94
Mandawa 224
Máni Peninsula 138
Marais Poitevin 84
Marble Canyon 313
Mariánské Lázn 42
Marlborough Sounds 272
Marrakech 155
Martha's Vineyard 346
Marvão 104
Massa Marittima 115
Mateus, Wine estate, Vila Real 105

Mathura 216
Matterhorn 55
Moorish art 92
Maya, writing 362
Mechelen 69
Medici 110
Medina Azahara 90
Meidum 167
Meißen 38
Meknès 147
Melaka 238
Melk Abbey 46
Melk 46
Mělník 42
Memphis 166
Mendoza 386
Merano 58
Mérida 361
Mértola 105
Mesa Verde
    National Park 327
Metéora Monasteries 136
Mevagissey 32
Milford Sound 279
Ming Tombs 193
Mistrás 138
Modena 110
Moeraki Boulders 278
Mojave 334
Monemvassía 139
Monsaraz 104
Montefrío 92
Montepulciano 116
Montezuma Castle
    National Monument 314
Monticello 354
Montreux 54
Montrose 18
Monument Valley
    Navajo Tribal Park 328
Mossel Bay 180
Moulay-Idriss 146
Mount Abu 222
Mount Aspiring
    National Park 280
Mount Cook
    National Park 274
Mount Everest 213
Mount Revelstoke
    National Park 288
Mount Robson
    Provincial Park 300
Moura 105
Mourão 104
Mozart 61
Murano 120
Mycenae 138
Mystic Seaport 347

N
Nagarzê 211
Nahuel Huapi
    National Park 393
Nakhon Pathom 230
Nantucket 346
Nauplia 138

Neemrana 224
Nelson Lakes
    National Park 272
Nepal, Royal cities 204
Nevado del Illimani 381
New England National Park 267
New York City 348-351
New Zealand, Rainforests 281
New Zealand,
    South Island Wildlife 434
Newport 347
Nitmiluk National Park 252
Noordwijk aan Zee 64
North Uist 20
Northwest Highlands 18
Nourlangie Rock 257
Nyalam 207

O
Oamaru 278
Óbidos 100
Old Fort William 296
Olgas 248
Ollantaytambo 375
Olympia 139
Opatija 123
Orkney Islands 23
Orléans 76
Oruro 382
Ósios Loukás 132
Otago Peninsula 278
Oudtshoorn 184
Outer Hebrides 20
Oxford 35

P
Paarl 185
Padaung 228
Padua 128
Palenque 362
Palma del Río 90
Pampas 387
Paparoa National Park 282
Paris 87-81
Parma 112
Patagonia,
    coast and marine life 392
Patan 204
Patras 140
Pawu Aboriginal Land 257
Peloponnes, west coast 139
Penang Island 234
Penzance 32
Perito Moreno 388
Perito Moreno,
    National Park 388
Pesaro 126
Pescara 126
Phang-Nga-Bucht 231
Philadelphia 352
Philae 173
Phi Phi Islands 239
Phoenix 314, 323, 324-325
Phuket 239
Picton 272
Pimba 245

Pine Creek 252
Pingyao 192
Piombino 115
Piran 120
Pisa 113
Pisac 375
Písek 42
Pistoia 110
Plettenberg Bay 182
Plitvice Lakes 123
Plymouth 347
Poitiers 82, 84
Pokaran 223
Pokhara 206
Poreč 122
Port Augusta 244
Port Elizabeth 184
Port Macquarie 266
Port Stephens 266
Portage La Prairie 293
Portimão 106
Portland 342
Porto 103
Portofino 112
Potosí 382
Potsdam 38
Prague 43
Prato 110
Příbram 42
Prince George 300
Prince Rupert 300
Providence 347
Provincetown 347
Puente del Inca 386
Puerto Natales 389
Pukaskwa
    National Park 297
Pula 122
Puno 378
Punta Arenas 391
Pushkar 220
Puszta 50

Q
Quechua 382
Queenstown 279
Quetico Provincial Park 297
Quiriguá 365
Quxu 211

R
Rab 122
Rabat 157
Rambouillet 76
Ranakpur 220
Raqchi 376
Ravenna 127
Ravenna, Early Christian
    Byzantine Churches 128
Red Basin 196
Reggio nell'Emilia 112
Regina 292
Renner Springs 251
Rice Cultivation 228
Richmond 354
Rijeka 123

Rimini 127
Rio Celestún, Parque Natural 361
Rissani 149
Roadtrains 247
Robertson 184
Rockland 342
Rocky Mountains, Canada 294
Ronda 95
Rongbuk Monastery 210
Rotterdam 65
Rovinj 122
Royal Chitwan
    National Park 207

S
S. Benedetto del Tronto 126
Sa'gya 210
Sacsayhuamán 375
Safi 156
Sagarmatha National Park 208
Sagres 106
Saguaro National Park 323
Saint-Denis 76
Saint-Émilion 85
Saint-Jean d'Angély 84
Saint-Jean-Pied-de-Port 86
Saintes 84
Sajama National Park 381
Sakkara 166
Salem 343
Salisbury, Cathedral 28
Salt Lake City 311
Salzburg 60
Samye Monastery 211
San Antonio 326
San Carlos de Bariloche 387
San Cristóbal de las Casas 363
San Gimignano 114
San Marino 127
San Xavier del Bac 315
Sanlúcar de Barrameda 96
Sanmenxia 196
Sanssouci 51
Santa Fe 327
Sariska National Park 217
Sault Ste. Marie 297
Saumur 83
Saxon Switzerland 51
Schelde Estuary 68
Scheveningen 65
Sequoia National Park 334
Sera Monastery 212
Setúbal 106
Seven Sisters 26
Seville 91
Shaftesbury 27
Shekhawati 224
Shenandoah National Park 354
Sherry 96
Sian Ka'an,
    Biosphere Reserve 368
Šibenik 124
Sidney 260, 262-263
Siena 115
Sillustani 376
Similan Islands 231

Singapore 236-237
Sintra 100
Sleeping Giant
   Provincial Park 297
Sohâg 168
Souks 152
South Island, rainforests 281
South Island, wildlife 278
South Uist 20
Southern Alps, New Zealand 274
Sparta 138
Split 124
St Andrews 16
St Austell 32
St Ives 33
St Moritz 58
Stellenbosch 186
Stilbaai 180
Stirling 16
Stonehenge 26-27
Stratford-upon-Avon 34
Sucre 382
Suez Canal 162
Sukhothai 229
Surfers Paradise 268
Sveti Stefan 124
Swellendam 180
Sydney 262-263

T
Taddert 153
Tafraoute 154
Taiyuan 192
Taj Mahal 225
Tangiers 146
Taos 326
Taroudannt 154
Tata 50
Tazumal 369
Tell el-Amârna 167
Telouèt 153
Tennant Creek 251
Tétouan 146
Thar Desert 222
The Hague 65
The Olgas 247
Thebes 132
Thunder Bay 296
Tiahuanaco 380
Tierra del Fuego
   National Park 392
Tikal National Park 366
Timpanogos Cave
   National Monument 311
Tinerhir 150
Tintagel 33
Tioman Island 238
Tipón 376
Tiryns 138
Titicaca Lake 378, 379
Tizi-n'Test 153
Tiznit 154
Tomar 102
Torquay 32
Torres del Paine
   National Park 390

Tours 82
Trephina Gorge
   Nature Park 257
Triest 120
Trogir 124
Tsitsikamma National Park 182
Tucson 315, 325
Tulbagh 185
Tulln 47
Tulum 367
Tuna el-Gebel 167
Twizel 275

U
Udaipur 221
Udine 120
Ullapool 19-20
Uluru-Kata Tjuta
   National Park 248
Umag 122
Urbino 126
Ushuaia 392
Ussé 83
Uxmal 361

V
Valle Sagrado
   de los Incas 374
Vancouver 288, 290
Vancouver Island 289
Vega del Guadalquivir 90
Venedig 121
Versailles 76
Vevey 54
Via Mala 57
Viareggio 113
Vienna 47, 49
Victoria 289
Vieste 126
Vila Real 104
Villandry 83
Viseu 104
Volterra 114
Volubilis 146

W
Wadi el-Natrun 163
Waipara 273
Walcheren 68
Walnut Canyon 314
Wanaka 279
Wangi Falls 257
Wartburg 51
Washington 353
Watarrka National Park 249
Waterton Lakes
   National Park 304
Weimar 39
Wells 33
Werfen 60
West MacDonnell
   National Park 250
Westland National Park 280
Whale Watching 300
White Mesa Arch 332
Whiskey Trail 19

Wilderness National Park 181
Williamsburg 354
Winchester, Cathedral 28
Windsor und Ascot 35
Winnipeg 293
Wittenberg 38
Wollemi National Park 261
Woodland Caribou
   Provincial Park 293
Wupatki National Monument 332

X
Xi'an 196
Xigazê 210

Y
Yamba 267
Ybbs 45
Yellowstone National Park 308
Yellowstone National Park,
   animals 309
Yellowstone National Park,
   Geysers 308
Yellow River 196
Yichang 196
Yoho National Park 288
Yuraygir National Park 267

Z
Zaandam 64
Zadar 124
Zákinthos 140
Zermatt 55
Zion National Park 313, 332

Picture Credits

C = Corbis
G = Getty
M = Mauritius Images

Cover: G/Jon Hicks

P. 002-003 M/Hartmut Roeder; P. 004-005 G/Oktay Ortakcioglu; P. 006-007 G/Jeffrey Murray; P. 008-009 C/Ian F. Gibb; P. 012-013 C/Guy Edwardes; P. 014 C/Gavin Hellier; P. 014 Look/age; P. 014-015 G/Scott Robertson; P. 015 G/David Chadwick; P. 015 G/British Modern ; P. 016 G/Anik Messier; P. 016 C/Guido Cozzi; P. 016 G/Anik Messier; P. 016 G/Andrea Pistolesi; P. 017 M/Alamy; P. 018 C/Massimo Borchi; P. 018-019 M/Rainer Mirau; P. 018 M/Alamy; P. 018 G/VWB photos; P. 019 C/Peter Giovannini; P. 019 M/Alamy; P. 019 M/Alamy; P. 019 G/Allan Baxter; P. 020 G/Luca Quadrio; P. 020 C/Jim Richardson; P. 020 C/Patrick Dieudonne; P. 021 G/Mathew Roberts; P. 021 C/Jim Richardson; P. 022 G/Brian Lawrence; P. 022 G/Simon Butterworth; P. 022 M/Alamy; P. 023 G/Angus Clyne; P. 023 M/Alamy; P. 023 G/David Baker; P. 023 C/Guido Cozzi; P. 023 G/Derek Croucher; P. 023 G/Peter Burnett; P. 024-025 G/Rob Funffinger; P. 024 M/Alamy; P. 025 M/Alamy; P. 025 C/Franz-Marc Frei; P. 026 G/Sebastian Wasek; P. 026 G/John Freeman; P. 026 Look/The Travel Library; P. 026 G/Alex Robinson; P. 027 G/Paul Mansfield; P. 027 G/Nick Cable; P. 027 C/Matt Gibson ; P. 027 M/Alamy; P. 028 C/Alan Copson; P. 029 G/Pawel Libera; P. 029 H. & D. Zielske; P. 030 C/Alan Copson; P. 031 C/Rudy Sulgan; P. 031 C/Massimo Borchi; P. 032 M/Alamy; P. 033 G/Heritage Images; P. 033 C/Adam Burton; P. 033 G/Tony Howell; P. 033 G/Joe Daniel Price; P. 034 M/Paul Williams; P. 034 G/Ron Sutherland; P. 034 C/Richard T. Nowitz; P. 035 G/Banana Pancake; P. 035 C/Franz-Marc Frei; P. 035 C/John Doornkamp; P. 036 H. & D. Zielske; P. 036-037 G/Mauricio Abreu; P. 037 M/Rainer Mirau; P. 037 G/Domingo Leiva; P. 038 M/Andreas Vitting; P. 039 H. & D. Zielske; P. 039 H. & D. Zielske; P. 039 G/Hiroshi Higuchi; P. 039 H. & D. Zielske; P. 038-039 G/Michele Falzone; P. 039 M/Hwo; P. 040 G/Spreephoto.de; P. 041 G/Siegfried Layda; P. 042 C/Michele Falzone; P. 042 C/Guido Cozzi; P. 042 G/Ricardo Liberato; P. 043 G/Miroslav Petrasko; P. 044 C/Michele Falzone; P. 044-045 M/Bahnmueller; P. 044 C/Richard Nebesky; P. 045 Look/Franz Marc Frei; P. 045 G/Allan Baxter; P. 046 Look/Rainer Mirau; P. 046 G/Krzysztof Dydynski; P. 046 Look/Andreas Strauß; P. 046-047 M/Martin Siepmann; P. 047 M/Werner Lang; P. 047 M/Stefan Obermeier; P. 047 G/Inti St. Clair; P. 048 M/Gerhard Wild; P. 048 M/Rudolf Pigneter; P. 048 G/Miroslav Petrasko; P. 049 M/Egmont Strigl; P. 049 G/Guy Vanderelst; P. 050 C/Rob Tilley; P. 050 M/age; P. 050 G/Domingo Leiva; P. 051 H. & D. Zielske; P. 051 M/Westend61; P. 051 C/Pure Passion; P. 051 C/Rob Tilley; P. 051 M/Jürgen Henkelmann; P. 051 C/Pietro Canali ; P. 051 C/Rudy Sulgan; P. 051 M/David Ryan; P. 051 G/Michele Falzone; P. 051 H. & D. Zielske; P. 052 Look/Martin Kreuzer; P. 052-053 G/Stefano Rossi; P. 053 C/Douglas Pearson; P. 053 G/Thomas Winz; P. 054 M/John Warburton-Lee; P. 054-055 Look/Tobias Richter; P. 055 C/Werner Dieterich; P. 055 M/Alamy; P. 055 C/Werner Dieterich; P. 056 M/Alamy; P. 056-057 C/Frank Lukasseck; P. 057 M/Prisma; P. 057 M/Radius Images; P. 058 M/Christian Handl; P. 058 G/Simeone Huber; P. 058 G/EyesWideOpen; P. 059 G/Anita Stizzoli; P. 058-059 C/Luca Benini; P. 060 C/Werner Dieterich; P. 060 Look/age; P. 060 Look/Tobias Richter; P. 060 Look/Thomas Stankiewicz; P. 060 G/Dan Tucker; P. 061 M/Karl F. Schöfmann; P. 061 Look/Andreas Strauß; P. 061 C/Riccardo Spila; P. 061 M/Jose Fuste Raga; P. 061 G/Sergio Parisi; P. 62-063 G/Jeroen P; P. 62 M/Alamy; P. 63 G/Visions Of Our Land; P. 63 M/age; P. 64 G/Michel Porro; P. 64 G/David Hanson; P. 64 C/Henryk Sadura; P. 64 G/Peter Zelei; P. 65 M/Jochen Tack; P. 65 Look/Hans Georg Eiben; P. 65 M/Alamy; P. 66 C/Hafiz Ismail; P. 67 C/Russ Rohde; P. 68 M/Alamy; P. 68 M/Alamy; P. 69 C/Dave Bartruff; P. 69 M/Jochen Tack; P. 68-069 M/ANP Photo; P. 70 C/Jean-Pierre Lescourret; P. 71 C/Ian Cumming; P. 71 M/Rainer Mirau; P. 72 G/Hiroshi Higuchi; P. 72 G/Elodie Drouard; P. 72 C/Miles Ertman; P. 72 M/Alamy; P. 73 G/Hiroshi Higuchi; P. 73 M/Alamy; P. 73 Look/Rainer Mirau; P. 73 C/Marcos Semola; P. 73 C/Frans Lemmens; P. 73 M/Wilfried Wirth; P. 73 G/Miles Ertman; P. 074-075 G/Raimund Linke; P. 074 C/Ken Kaminesky; P. 074 C/Leemage; P. 075 G/Adrien Chanut; P. 075 Look/age; P. 076 G/Julian Elliott Ethereal Light; P. 076 M/Alamy; P. 077 C/Jason Langley; P. 077 M/Alamy; P. 077 G/Imagno; P. 076-077 C/Marc Dozier; P. 078 G/Jeroen P; P. 079 M/Alamy; P. 079 C/Sylvain Sonnet; P. 080 C/Peet Simard; P. 081 C/Ken Kaminesky; P. 081 C/Scott Stulberg; P. 082-083 C/Luca da Ros; P. 083 M/age; P. 083 C/Peet Simard; P. 083 C/Julian Elliott; P. 084-085 G/Simon Greenwood; P. 084 M/GTW; P. 084 M/Alamy; P. 085 G/Jean-Pierre Muller; P. 085 G/Gonzalo Azumendi; P. 085 C/Sylvain Sonnet; P. 085 G/Luis Davilla; P. 085 M/Alamy; P. 086 Look/Brigitte Merz; P. 086 G/Juergen Richter; P. 086 Look/Photononstop; P. 087 G/Eric Bouloumie; P. 087 M/Alamy; P. 087 M/Photononstop; P. 087 G/Julian Elliott; P. 087 M/Jason Langley; P. 087 M/Alamy; P. 087 L/Romain Cintract; P. 087 M/Photononstop; P. 087 G/Linda Mckie; P. 088-089 G/Slow Images; P. 088 G/Slow Images; P. 089 G/Panoramic Images; P. 089 M/Jean-Pierre Lescourret; P. 090 M/Alamy; P. 090 M/Alamy; P. 090 C/Peter Adams; P. 091 M/Alamy; P. 092 G/Gonzalo Ortuño; P. 092 G/Shaun Egan; P. 092 G/David Sutherland; P. 092-093 G/Jeremy Woodhouse; P. 093 Look/age; P. 093 C/Jean-Pierre Lescourret; P. 093 G/Thomas Dressler; P. 094 C/Mel Stuart; P. 094 Look/Domingo Leiva Nicolás; P. 094 G/Altrendo Panoramic; P. 095 C/Destinations; P. 095 G/Will Selarep; P. 095 G/Charles Bowman; P. 096 C/Ben Welsh; P. 096 C/Ramon Navarro ; P. 096 M/Alamy; P. 096 C/Neil Farrin; P. 097 G/Domingo Leiva; P. 097 C/Hendrik Holler ; P. 097 C/Alan Copson; P. 097 C/Paul Panayiotou; P. 097 C/Michele Falzone; P. 097 Look/Rainer Martini; P. 097 Look/Juergen Richter; P. 097 C/Michele Falzone; P. 098-099 C/Paolo Giocoso; P. 098 Look/Juergen Richter; P. 099 G/Elena; P. 099 G/Guy Vanderelst; P. 100 C/Gran Tour Collection; P. 100 C/Frank Krahmer; P. 100 C/Ocean; P. 101 C/Demetrio Carrasco; P. 101 C/Paolo Giocoso; P. 102 Look/age; P. 102 G/Sven Hagolani; P. 102 G/Panoramic Images; P. 103 G/Shaun Egan; P. 103 M/Alamy; P. 102-103 C/Sven Hagolani; P. 103 C/Mauricio Abreu; P. 104 C/Mauricio Abreu; P. 104 M/Alamy; P. 105 Look/SagaPhoto; P. 105 G/Csantos; P. 105 Look/age; P. 105 M/Michael Howard; P. 106 Look/Travelstock44; P. 106 Look/Juergen Richter; P. 107 C/Mauricio Abreu; P. 107 Look/Photononstop; P. 107 Look/age; P. 107 C/Hans Georg Roth; P. 107 G/Zu Sanchez; P. 107 G/Iñigo Fdz de Pinedo; P. 107 C/Peter M. Wilson; P. 107 G/Davis McCardle; P. 108 C/Stefano Amantini; P. 108-109 C/Guido Cozzi; P. 109 G/Jason Arney; P. 109 M/Alamy ; P. 109 G/Slow Images; P. 110 C/Leemage; P. 110 G/David Noton; P. 110 M/imagebroker; P. 111 C/Massimo Borchi; P. 111 Look/Juergen Richter; P. 112 M/age; P. 112 M/Alamy; P. 112-113 G/Hiroshi Higuchi; P. 112 C/Peter Adams; P. 113 G/Bruno Morandi; P. 113 C/Guido Cozzi; P. 114 C/Massimo Borchi; P. 114 C/Dennis Marsico; P. 114-115 C/Guido Cozzi; P. 115 G/Marius Roman; P. 115 G/Jorg Greuel; P. 115 C/Guido Cozzi; P. 116 G/Antonio Busiello; P. 116 G/Funkystock; P. 116 C/Maurizio Rellini ; P. 117 C/Reed Kaestner; P. 117 Look/age; P. 117 Look/Juergen Richter; P. 117 G/Allan Baxter; P. 117 C/Dennis Marsico; P. 117 C/Doug Pearson; P. 117 C/Guido Baviera; P. 117 G/Maremagnum; P. 117 C/Da Ros Luca; P. 118-119 C/Angelo Cavalli; P. 118 Look/Rainer Mirau; P. 119 M/Pixtal; P. 119 G/Alan Copson; P. 119 G/Jose Maria Cuellar; P. 120 G/Philip Lee Harvey; P. 120 C/Matteo Colombo; P. 120 G/A. De Gregorio; P. 120 G/Rilind Hoxha ; P. 121 C/Angelo Cavalli; P. 122 M/Rainer Mirau; P. 122 Look/Rainer Mirau; P. 122 M/age; P. 122 M/Lumi Images; P. 123 G/Gonzalo Azumendi; P. 123 C/Alan Copson; P. 123 C/Jose Fuste Raga; P. 124 C/Domingo Leiva; P. 124 C/Doug Pearson; P. 125 C/Funkystock; P. 124-125 G/SaimirKumi; P. 125 G/Arnaud Spani; P. 126 G/De Agostini; P. 126 G/Manolo Raggi; P. 126-127 C/Guido Cozzi; P. 126 G/Valentino Grassi ; P. 127 G/Ken Scicluna; P. 127 M/Alamy; P. 127 C/Francesco Iacobelli; P. 128 Look/Katharina Jaeger; P. 128 M/United Archives; P. 129 C/Douglas Pearson; P. 129 C/Funkystock; P. 129 C/Matthew Williams-Ellis; P. 129 C/Jose Fuste Raga; P. 129 M/Paul Williams; P. 129 M/Cultura; P. 129 C/Guido Cozzi; P. 129 G/Lysvik Photos; P. 130-131 G/Ed Freeman; P. 130 C/Marc Dozier; P. 131 M/Paul Williams; P. 131 M/Alamy; P. 132 M/Alamy; P. 132 M/Alamy; P. 132-133 C/Sandra Raccanello ; P. 133 M/Alamy; P. 133 G/Walter Bibikow; P. 133 M/Paul Williams; P. 134 G/George Papapostolou; P. 135 G/Jean-Pierre Lescourret; P. 135 C/Sandra Raccanello; P. 136-137 M/Alamy; P. 137 C/Marc Dozier; P. 138 M/Paul Williams; P. 138 G/Nassos Triantafyllou; P. 138 G/Jean-Pierre Lescourret; P. 139 M/Alamy; P. 139 G/Dimitrios Tilis; P. 139 M/Alamy; P. 140 M/Alamy; P. 140 M/Alamy; P. 140 G/Paul Boyden ; P. 141 G/Jean-Pierre Lescourret; P. 141 G/Evgeni Dinev; P. 141 M/Alamy; P. 141 M/Alamy; P. 141 M/Paul Williams; P. 141 M/Alamy; P. 141 M/Alamy; P. 142-143 C/Martin Harvey; P. 144 C/Marco Cristofori; P. 144-145 G/Mark Hannaford; P. 145 C/Neil Farrin; P. 145 Look/age; P. 145 M/Jose Fuste Raga; P. 146 C/Massimo Borchi; P. 146 M/Alamy; P. 146 C/Mauricio Abreu; P. 146 M/Alamy; P. 148-149 C/Peter Adams; P. 148 C/Paul Williams ; P. 149 G/Artur Debat; P. 149 M/Alamy; P. 149 C/Marco Cristofori; P. 150 C/Walter G. Allgöwer; P. 150 C/Wigbert Röth; P. 150-151 G/Adrian J Warren; P. 151 Look/age; P. 152 M/Alamy; P. 153 M/Robert Harding; P. 152-153 G/David Deveson; P. 153 C/Mauricio Abreu; P. 153 C/Guido Cozzi; P. 154 C/Mauricio Abreu; P. 154 G/Doug Pearson; P. 154 C/Walter Bibikow; P. 155 C/Neil Farrin; P. 155 M/Fabian von Poser; P. 156 C/Massimo Borchi; P. 156 Look/Photononstop; P. 156 C/Massimo Borchi; P. 156 G/Nikki Bidgood; P. 157 M/Alamy; P. 158 C/Bruno Morandi; P. 158 Look/The Travel Library; P. 158 G/Gavin Hellier; P. 158 C/Michele Falzone; P. 159 Look/Axiom; P. 159 G/Bernardo Ricci Armani; P. 159 C/Ben Pipe; P. 159 M/Alamy; P. 159 Look/age; P. 159 M/Jose Fuste Raga; P. 159 C/Frank Fell; P. 159 M/Alamy; P. 160 Look/TerraVista; P. 160-161 M/Josef Niedermeier; P. 161 C/Sandro Vannini; P. 161 Look/age; P. 161 G/Pablo Charlón; P. 162-163 Look/Reinhard Dirscherl ; P. 162 Look/TerraVista; P. 163 Look/Robin Laurance; P. 163 C/Peter Langer; P. 163 G/Robertharding; P. 164 C/Stuart Westmorland; P. 165 Look/age; P. 165 C/Ivan Vdovin; P. 165 Look/age; P. 166 C/Jon Arnold; P. 166-167 Look/TerraVista; P. 166 C/Lizzie Shepherd; P. 166 C/Jose Fuste Raga; P. 167 C/Jose Fuste Raga; P. 168 M/Tuul & Bruno Morandi; P. 168 G/Bernard Grua; P. 168-169 C/Jon Arnold; P. 169 G/Radius Images; P. 169 C/Tuul & Bruno Morandi; P. 170 Look/age; P. 170-171 G/Michele Falzone; P. 171 G/Hisham Ibrahim; P. 171 G/Paule Seux; P. 171 C/Darrell Gulin; P. 172 M/Alamy; P. 172 G/A. Vergani; P. 173 M/Alamy; P. 173 C/Jon Arnold; P. 173 C/Paul Panayiotou; P. 173 C/Jon Arnold; P. 173 Look/Reinhard Dirscherl; P. 173 G/Simon Podgorsek; P. 173 G/G. Sioen; P. 173 C/Blaine Harrington III; P. 173 C/Jose Fuste Raga; P. 173 G/G.Sioen; P. 173 M/Alamy; P. 173 C/Richard T. Nowitz; P. 173 M/Ikonica; P. 173 G/Wolfgang Kaehler; P. 173 Look/Reinhard Dirscherl; P. 174 G/Gallo Images; P. 174-175 G/Kathrin Ziegler; P. 175 M/Africa Media Online; P. 175 Look/age; P. 176-177 G/Johan Sjolander; P. 176 M/Alamy; P. 176 G/Hoberman Collection; P. 176 Look/Jan Greune; P. 176 C/Sohns; P. 177 G/Tim Jackson; P. 177 M/Reinhard Dirscherl; P. 177 G/Hougaard Malan; P. 177 G/Michael & Patricia Fogden; P. 177 G/Art Wolfe; P. 178 M/Alamy; P. 179 G/Sabine Lubenow; P. 179 G/Chad Henning; P. 179 M/Dirk Bleyer; P. 179 G/John Snelling; P. 180 M/Prisma; P. 180 C/Jon Hicks; P. 180-181 M/Michael Müller; P. 181 G/M-Net Local Productions; P. 181 G/Steve Corner; P. 181 C/Image Source; P. 182 M/Africa Media Online; P. 182 C/Franziska Ritter; P. 182 G/Peter Chadwick; P. 183 G/Nigel J Dennis; P. 183 Look/age; P. 183 C/Ann & Steve Toon; P. 184 G/Andy Nixon; P. 184 G/Jon Arnold Images; P. 184 G/Allan Baxter; P. 185 M/Africa Media Online; P. 185 G/Panoramic Images; P. 186 G/Jan Greune; P. 186 Look/Photononstop; P. 186 G/Panoramic Images; P. 186 Look/Hendrik Holler; P. 187 G/Panoramic Images; P. 187 G/Andy Nixon; P. 187 C/Jon Hicks; P. 187 G/Kim Walker; P. 187 M/Africa Media Online; P. 187 Look/Photononstop; P. 187 G/Christian Heinrich; P. 187 G/Ariadne Van Zandbergen; P. 187 M/Alamy; P. 187 C/Ann & Steve Toon; P. 187 Look/Jan Greune; P. 187 C/Chris Clor; P. 187 G/Allan Baxter; P. 188-189 C/Nicolas Marino; P. 190 G/Sino Images; P. 190-191 G/ViewStock; P. 191 M/Alamy; P. 191 M/Alamy; P. 191 Look/age; P. 191 G/Luis Castaneda ; P. 192 C/He Wei Bj; P. 192 M/SuperStock; P. 192 G/Li Jingwang; P. 192 G/View Stock; P. 192 Look/Karl Johaentges; P. 193 G/Franck Guiziou; P. 193 G/Urs Blickenstorfer; P. 193 G/Quan Long; P. 194 G/Best View Stock; P. 195 G/Andre Distel; P. 195 G/Ispyfriend; P. 196 G/Philippe Lejeanvre; P. 196 G/Peng Wu; P. 197 C/Keren Su; P. 197 C/Gavin Hellier; P. 197 G/View Stock; P. 197 G/View Stock; P. 197 C/Stefan Huwiler; P. 198 M/SuperStock; P. 198 C/Jose Fuste Raga; P. 198-199 G/Seng Chye Teo; P. 199 C/Simon Montgomery; P. 199 G/John W Banagan; P. 199 G/Christian Kober; P. 199 G/Andreas Brandl; P. 200 C/Frank Krahmer; P. 200 G/Dan Eggleton; P. 201 Look/age; P. 201 M/Danita Delimont; P. 201 C/Roland Gerth; P. 201 Look/age; P. 201 C/Astock; P. 201 G/Sino Images; P. 201 G/Keren Su; P. 201 G/View Stock; P. 201 C/Stringer; P. 201 G/Yongyuan Dai; P. 201 G/Krzysztof Dydynski; P. 202 G/Reinhard Goldmann; P. 202-203 G/Coolbiere photograph; P. 203 C/Charles Lenars; P. 203 G/Premium; P. 203 G/Niels Busch; P. 204 G/Mitsuo Ambe; P. 204 M/Alamy; P. 204 M/Robert Harding; P. 204 M/Pablo Galan Cela; P. 204 G/Paul Biris; P. 205 C/Yustinus; P. 206 G/Jonas Gratzer; P. 206 G/Punnawit Suwuttananun; P. 207 G/James Warwick; P. 207 G/Coolbiere photograph; P. 207 G/Stockbyte; P. 207 C/Wolfgang Kaehler; P. 207 Look/age; P. 208-209 G/Tibet; P. 208 G/Benjamin Straker; P. 208 G/M Koleosho; P. 209 G/

MONACO BOOKS is an imprint of Kunth Verlag GmbH & Co KG
© Kunth Verlag GmbH & Co KG, Munich, 2018
Concept: Wolfgang Kunth
Editing and design: Kunth Verlag GmbH & Co KG

Text: Gerhard Beer, Dr. Ambros Brucker, Gerhard Bruschke, Hanna Egghardt, Christiane Gsänger, Waltraud Hor-
bas, Rudolf Ites, Thomas Jeier, Dr. Sebastian Kinder, Barbara Kreißl, Carlo Lauer, Dr. Dieter Maier, Raphaela
Moczynski, Michael Neumann, Daniela Schetar-Köthe, Manuela Schomann, Peter Schröder, Dr. Manfred Vasold,
Dr. Heinz Vestner, Walter M. Weiss, Günther Wessel
Translation: Sylvia Goulding, Emily Plank, Katherine Taylor

For distribution please contact:
Monaco Books
c/o Kunth Verlag GmbH & Co KG
St.-Cajetan-Straße 41
81669 München
Tel. +49.89.45 80 20-0
Fax +49.89.45 80 20-21
www.kunth-verlag.de
info@kunth-verlag.de

Printed in the EU

All facts have been researched with the greatest possible care to the best of our knowledge and belief. However,
the editors and publishers can accept no responsibility for any inaccuracies or incompleteness of the details
provided. The publishers are pleased to receive any information or suggestions for improvement.